THE GARUDA PURANAM

THE GARUDA PURANAM

EDITED AND PUBLISHED BY

MANMATHA NATH DUTT (SHASTRI), M.A.,

Rector, Keshub Academy,
Author of the English Translations of the Ramayanam, Mahi-
Bharatam, Srimadbhdgavatam, Mahanirvana-Tantram,
Harivams'a, Agni Puranam, Markandeya Puranam, &c. &c.

GYAN

Published by

GYAN

Gyan Publishing House
5, Ansari Road
Daryaganj, New Delhi-110002
Phone: 011-47034999, 9811692060
E-mail: books@gyanbooks.com

Distribution Network
gyanbooks.com
India, USA, Canada, UK, Australia, France

ISBN : 978-81-212-2450-5 (HB)
First Published, 1908

2nd Impression 2021

Printed at: Gyan Press, Delhi.

The Garuda Puranam
Edited by: Manmatha Nath Dutt

THE GARUDA PURANAM.

EDITED AND PUBLISHED BY

MANMATHA NATH DUTT (Shastri), M.A.,

Rector, Keshub Academy,

Author of the English Translations of the Rámáyanam, Mahá-Bhárātam, Srimadbhágavatam, Mahánirvána-Tantram, Harivams'a, Agni Puránam, Márkandéya Puránam, &c., &c.

CALCUTTA

SOCIETY FOR THE RESUSCITATION OF INDIAN LITERATURE.

3, FURRIAPUKUR STREET, P. O., SHAMBAZAR.

1908.

CONTENTS.

SUBJECT.	PAGE.
CHAPTER I.—Discourse between Suta and Shaunaka and other Rishis in the forest of Naimisha—Suta promises to narrate the Garuda Puranam	1—4
CHAPTER II.—Sources of the Garuda Puranam—Vishnu charges Garuda to compose the Garuda Puranam	4—8
CHAPTER III.—Suta describes the subjects dealt with in the Garuda Puranam	9—10
CHAPTER IV.—Order of Universal creation described by Narayana to Rudra	10—13
CHAPTER V.—Creation of the Prajapatis. The progeny of Daksha described	14—16
CHAPTER VI.—Re-incarnation of Daksha in the form of Prachetas—Origin of the different races of men, the progeny of Kashyapa described	16—21
CHAPTER VII.—Description of the sun-worship, etc. as performed by the Self-origined Manu	21—23
CHAPTER VIII.—Description of the mode of worshipping Vishnu	23—24
CHAPTER IX.—The mode of spiritual initiation	24—25
CHAPTER X.—The mode of worshipping the goddess Lakshmi	26
CHAPTER XI.—Description of the Nava-Vyuha form of worship	26—30
CHAPTER XII.—Description of the order to be observed in the course of worship	30—33
CHAPTER XIII.—The prayer of Vishnu Panjaram	33—34
CHAPTER XIV.—A brief discourse on Yoga	34—36
CHAPTER XV.—Enumeration of one thousand epithets of Vishnu	36—47
CHAPTER XVI.—Description of the mode of meditating on Vishnu as well as of the rite of sun-worship	47—49
CHAPTER XVII.—Description of another form of sun-worship	49—50
CHAPTER XVIII.—Mode of worshipping the death-conquering deity (Mrityunjaya)	51—52

SUBJECT.	PAGE.
CHAPTER XIX.—The Garudi Vidya which is the cure for all kinds of snake-bite	53—56
CHAPTER XX.—Mantra-cures (curative formulas) of snake-bite as narrated by S'iva	56—58
CHAPTER XXI.—Mode of worshipping the Panchavaktra (five-faced) manifestation of S'iva	58—59
CHAPTER XXII.—The mode of worshipping S'iva ...	59—60
CHAPTER XXIII.—Description of another form of S'iva worship	60—63
CHAPTER XXIV.—The worship of Ganapati	63—64
CHAPTER XXV.—Sandal-worship (Paduka puja) described ...	64—65
CHAPTER XXVI.—The mode of performing the rites of Karanyasa (location of the energies of different divinities in the different limbs by a votary by dint of occult and psychic force)	65—66
CHAPTER XXVII.—Rites for neutralising the effects of snake venoms	66—67
CHAPTER XXVIII.—The mode of worshipping the Gopala Manifestation of Vishnu	67—68
CHAPTER XXIX.—Mantras to be used in connection with the worship of S'ridhara manifestation of Vishnu	68—69
CHAPTER XXX.—Elaborate description of the mode of worshipping the S'ridhara manifestation of Vishnu	69—72
CHAPTER XXXI.—Description of another form of Vishnu worship	72—76
CHAPTER XXXII.—Adoration of the five fundamental principles of the universe	77—81
CHAPTER XXXIII.—Worship of the divine discus (Sudars'anam)	81—82
CHAPTER XXXIV.—Hayagriva worship	82—86
CHAPTER XXXV.—The mode of worshipping the Hayagriva manifestation of Vishnu	87
CHAPTER XXXVI.—Mode of performing the rite of Gayatri Nyasa	87—89
CHAPTER XXXVII.—Description of the glories of Gayatri ...	89—90
CHAPTER XXXVIII.—The mode of worshipping the deities, Durga, etc.	90—93
CHAPTER XXXIX.—Description of another form of Sun-worship	93—95

SUBJECT.	PAGE.
CHAPTER XL.—Maheshvara worship	95—98
CHAPTER XLI.—Enumeration of diverse incantations, Mantras (Nana Vidya)	98—99
CHAPTER XLII.—Description of investing a phallic emblem with sacred thread (S'iva-pavitrarohanam)	99—101
CHAPTER XLIII.—Description of the rite of investing an image of Vishnu with the holy thread (Vishnu-pavitrarohanam)	102—105
CHAPTER XLIV.—Contemplation of embodied and dis-embodied God	105—107
CHAPTER XLV.—Characteristic marks of S'alagrama Stones ...	107—110
CHAPTER XLVI.—Adoration of the deity presiding over homesteads (Vastu)	110—112
CHAPTER XLVII.—Essential features of a divine temple or of a palace	113—117
CHAPTER XLVIII.—Installations of divine images... ...	117—126
CHAPTER XLIX.—Discourse on Yoga and acts of piety ...	126—130
CHAPTER L.—Discourses on charities and gift-makings, etc. ...	130—137
CHAPTER LII.—Regulations of Prayaschittas (penitential rites)	137—142
CHAPTER LIII.—Traits of conduct of men marked by the several kinds of Nidhis	142—143
CHAPTER LIV.—Progeny of Priya Vrata and incidental description of the Seven Islands of the Earth	144—145
CHAPTER LV.—Description of the Geographical situations of the different countries of the earth, as well as of India with its physical features	145—146
CHAPTER LVI.—Enumeration of the names of princes of the continent of Plaksha, etc.	147—148
CHAPTER LVII.—Cosmogeny of Hell and the nether regions ...	148—149
CHAPTER LVIII.—Positions and dimensions of the sun and other planets	149—151
CHAPTER LIX.—Discourses on Astrology, presiding deities of the different planets and constellations of stars, situations of Yoginis on the different days of the fortnight, etc. ...	152—156
CHAPTER LX.—Discourses on the period of influences of the different planets with that of the sun	157—158
CHAPTER LXI.—Influences of the moon in her different mansions	159—160
CHAPTER LXII.—Discourses on Langnamana and determination of what one ought or ought not to do from the stable or mobile character of the Lagna	160—162

SUBJECT.	PAGE.
CHAPTER LXIII.—A brief discourse on the auspicious and inauspicious marks on the persons of males ...	... 162—164
CHAPTER LXIV.—A brief discourse on the auspicious or inauspicious marks on the person of females ...	... 164—165
CHAPTER LXV.—Auspicious marks on men and women as disclosed by the science of Samudrikam ...	... 165—175
CHAPTER LXVI.—Description of the specific marks of S'alagrama, description of Tirthas, and of sixty countries such as Prabhasa	... 175—176
CHAPTER LXVII.—The science of Pavana Vijaya (conquest of breath) and auguring bad or evil from the direction of the breath-wind	... 177—180
CHAPTER LXVIII.—(Agastya Samhita). Description of the origin of gems in the treatise on Ratna Pariksha (test of gems) by the holy Agastya	... 180—186
CHAPTER LXIX.—Tests of Pearls	... 186—191
CHAPTER LXX.—Tests of Ruby	... 191—195
CHAPTER LXXI.—Tests of Emerald	... 195—198
CHAPTER LXXII.—Tests of Sapphires ...	... 198—200
CHAPTER LXXIII.—Tests of Lapis Lazuli (Vaidurya) ...	200
CHAPTER LXXIV.—Tests of topas (Pushpa-raga)...	... 202—203
CHAPTER LXXV.—Tests of Karketana ...	... 203—204
CHAPTER LXXVI.—Tests of Bhishma-stone ...	... 204—205
CHAPTER LXXVII.—Tests of Pulaka stones	206
CHAPTER LXXVIII.—Tests of blood-stone	207
CHAPTER LXXIX.—Tests of crystals	... 207—208
CHAPTER LXXX.—Tests of Corals	208
CHAPTER LXXXI.—A brief description of holy pools and sanctuaries	... 209—212
CHAPTER LXXXII.—Description of the sanctity of Gaya, and its early history	... 212—215
CHAPTER LXXXIII.—Description of different rites to be performed at different places at Gaya and of their merits	... 215—224
CHAPTER LXXXIV.—Ablutions in the river Phalgu, merit of making offerings of funeral cakes at Rudra. History of king Vishala	... 225—230
CHAPTER LXXXV.—Merit of offering funeral cakes at Preta-s'ila in Gaya	... 230—233
CHAPTER LXXXVI.—Merit of performing S'raddhas at Preta-Shila	... 233—237

SUBJECT. PAGE.

CHAPTER LXXXVII.—Enumeration of the names of fourteen Manus and of the Devas and Saptarshis who flourished in the times of their sons ... ... 237—243

CHAPTER LXXXVIII.—Annals of Ruchi incidentally narrated in the discourse between Markandeya and Kraushtika ... 243—246

CHAPTER LXXXIX.—Ruchi hymnises the Pitris, who in their turn grant him a boon ... ... 246—255

CHAPTER XC.—Marriage of Ruchi and birth of Rauchya Manu 255

CHAPTER XCI.—Contemplation of Hari ... ... 256—257

CHAPTER XCII.—Contemplation of Hari and its process ... 258—260

CHAPTER XCIII.—Laws of virtue as promulgated by the holy Yajnavalkya ... ... 260—262

CHAPTER XCIV.—Initiation with the holy thread and study of the Vedas . ... 262—266

CHAPTER XCV.—Duties of house-holders ... ... 266—271

CHAPTER XCVI.—Origin of mixed castes—the five great Yajnas, Sandhya-rites, duties of house-holders aud members of different castes ... ... 271—280

CHAPTER XCVII.—Purifications of defiled articles ... 280—281

CHAPTER XCVIII.—Gift-making and Charity ... ... 281—281

CHAPTER XCIX.—Mode of performing S'raddhas ... ... 281—289

CHAPTER C.—Exorcism of Vinayakas ... ... 290—291

CHAPTER CI.—Propitiation of malignant Planets ... ... 292—293

CHAPTER CII.—Duties of the order of forest-dwelling hermits 294

CHAPTER CIII.—Duties of Yatis 295

CHAPTER CIV.—Signs of sinful souls ... ... 295—296

CHAPTER CV.—Rites of atonement ... ... 296—305

CHAPTER CVI.—Impurities ... ... 305—309

CHAPTER CVII.—A synopsis of the Dharma-Shastra by Parashara ... ... 309—315

THE VRIHASPATI SAMHITA.

CHAPTER CVIII.—Synopsis of rules of conduct ... ... 315—318

CHAPTER CIX.—Advice on thrift and economy in the Nitisara 318—324

CHAPTER CX.—Advice as to the non-rejectment of a certain good, etc. ... ... 324—328

CHAPTER CXI.—Commendable traits in kings, etc, (in the Nitisara) ... ... 328—330

CONTENTS.

SUBJECT.	PAGE.
CHAPTER CXII.—Commendable traits in servants (in the Nitisara)	331—333
CHAPTER CXIII.—Injunctions as to the appointments of the honest and the erudite in the King's service, etc. ...	333—339
CHAPTER CXIV.—Injunctions as to the distinction of friends and enemies (in the Nitisara)	339—346
CHAPTER CXV.—Counsels on forswearing bad wives, etc., (End of the Vrihaspati Samhita)	346—354
CHAPTER CXVI.—Enumeration of the names of Vratas (vows and penances) commenced	354—355
CHAPTER CXVII.—The Ananga Trayodashi Vratam ...	355—357
CHAPTER CXVIII.—The Akhandya Dvadashi Vratam ...	357—358
CHAPTER CXIX.—Agastyargha Vratam	358—359
CHAPTER CXX.—The Rambha Tritiya Vratam	359—360
CHAPTER CXXI.—The Chaturmasyam Vratam	361—362
CHAPTER CXXII.—The Mashopavasha Vratam	362—363
CHAPTER CXXIII.—Kartika Vratas	363—365
CHAPTER CXXIV.—The Shiva Ratra Vratam	365—367
CHAPTER CXXV.—The Ekadashi Vratam	367—368
CHAPTER CXXVI.—Vishvaksena Puja	368—369
CHAPTER CXXVII.—Bhaimi Ekadashi and Dvadashi ...	370—372
CHAPTER CXXVIII.—Various Vratas described	372—374
CHAPTER CXXIX.—The Pratipad Vratas	375—378
CHAPTER CXXX.—The Shashti Vratas, Maricha Saptami Vratas	378—380
CHAPTER CXXXI.—Rohini Ashtami Vratas etc.	380—382
CHAPTER CXXXII.—The Sadgati Vratam, etc.	383—385
CHAPTER CXXXIII.—Ashokastami Vratas etc.	385—387
CHAPTER CXXXIV.—Maha-Kausika Mantra	387—388
CHAPTER CXXXV.—The Viranavami Vratas, etc.	388—389
CHAPTER CXXXVI.—The S'ravana Dvadashi Vratam ...	389—390
CHAPTER CXXXVII.—The Damanaka Trayodashi, etc., Vratas	390—392
CHAPTER CXXXVIII.—Geneology of royal princes (solar race)	392—397
CHAPTER CXXXIX.—Geneology of the princes of the lunar race	397—402
CHAPTER CXL.—Description of the race of Puru ...	403—406
CHAPTER CXLI.—Descriptions of kings who came after Janamejaya	406—408

SUBJECT. PAGE.

CHAPTER CXLII.—Incarnations of Vishnu and the glory of nuptial fidelity described ... ... 408—411
CHAPTER CXLIII.—The Ramayanam ... ... 411—416
CHAPTER CXLIV.—Description of the Harivamsha ... 416—418
CHAPTER CXLV.—The Mahabharatam ... ... 418—422

THE DHANVANTARI SAMHITA.

CHAPTER CXLVI.—Description of the Nidanam of all the diseases ... ... 422—425
CHAPTER CXLVII.—The Nidanam of Fever ... ... 426—437
CHAPTER CXLVIII.—The Nidanam of Raktapittam (Hæmorrhage) ... ... 437—439
CHAPTER CXLIX.—The Nidanam of Cough ... ... 439—442
CHAPTER CL.—The Nidanam dyspnœa ... ... 442—444
CHAPTER CLI.—The Nidanam of Hic-cough ... ... 444—445
CHAPTER CLII.—The Nidanam of pulmonary consumption ... 445—449
CHAPTER CLIII.—The Nidanam of Aversion to food ... 449—450
CHAPTER CLIV.—The Nidanam of heart-disease ... ... 451—454
CHAPTER CLV.—The Nidanam of diseases resulting from the excess or abuse of wine ... ... 454—458
CHAPTER CLVI.—The Nidanam of Hæmorrhoids ... 458—464
CHAPTER CLVII.—The Nidanam of Dysentery ... ... 464—467
CHAPTER CLVIII.—The Nidanam of Stangury, etc. ... 468—472
CHAPTER CLIX.—The Nidanam of diseases of the Urinary organs (Pramehas) ... ... 472—477
CHAPTER CLX.—The Nidanam of abscesses, etc. ... ... 477—485
CHAPTER CLXI.—The Nidanam of Ascites, etc. ... ... 485—491
CHAPTER CLXII.—The Nidanam of Chlorosis ... ... 491—495
CHAPTER CLXIII.—The Nidanam of Erysipelas ... ... 496—499
CHAPTER CLXIV.—The Nidanam of cutaneous affections (Kusthas) ... ... 499—504
CHAPTER CLXV.—The Nidanam of bodily parasites ... 504—506
CHAPTER CLXVI.—The Nidanam of diseases of the nervous system ... ... 506—512
CHAPTER CLXVII.—The Nidanam of Vata-Raktam ... 512—515
CHAPTER CLXVIII.—The Nidanam of Mukho-roga ... 515—522
CHAPTER CLXIX.—The Nidanam of diseases of the ears ... 522—525
CHAPTER CLXX.—The Nidanam of diseases of the nose ... 525—528
CHAPTER CLXXI.—The Nidanam of diseases of the eyes ... 529—538

SUBJECT.	PAGE.
CHAPTER CLXXII.—The Nidanam of diseases of the head ...	538—540
CHAPTER CLXXIII.—The Nidanam of diseases of the female reproductive organs	540—544
CHAPTER CLXXIV.—The Nidanam of difficult labour ...	544—546
CHAPTER CLXXV.—The Nidanam of diseases peculiar to parturient women	546—547
CHAPTER CLXXVI.—The Nidanam of diseases peculiar to infant-life	547—550
CHAPTER CLXXVII.—The Nidanam of Syphilis	550—554
CHAPTER CLXXVIII.—The Nidanam of Variola	554—557
CHAPTER CLXXIX.—The Nidanam of minor affections ...	557—561
CHAPTER CLXXX.—The Nidanam of Fistula in Ano, etc. ...	561—562
CHAPTER CLXXXI.—The Nidanam of poisons	563—572
CHAPTER CLXXXII.—The Nidanam of Goitre, scrofula and glandular swellings	572—575
CHAPTER CLXXXIII.—The Nidanam of vomiting ...	575—578
CHAPTER CLXXXIV.—The Nidanam of Urticaria ...	579—581
CHAPTER CLXXXV.—The Nidanam of S'ula, neuralgic pain, etc.	581—585
CHAPTER CLXXXVI.—The Nidanam of aphonia ...	585—586
CHAPTER CXXXVII.—The Nidanam of Udavarta ...	586—588
CHAPTER CLXXXVIII.—The Nidanam of traumatic ulcers etc.	588—592
CHAPTER CLXXXIX.—The Nidanam of S'arira Vranas (Idiopathic ulcers)	592—593
CHAPTER CXC.—The Nidanam of fractures	594—595
CHAPTER CXCI.—Medicinal recipes of inffalible efficacies ...	595—606
CHAPTER CXCII.—Medical treatment of fever, etc. ...	606—613
CHAPTER CXCIII.—Medical treatment of Sinus, etc. ...	613—619
CHAPTER CXCIV.—Medical treatment of female complaints	619—623
CHAPTER CXCV.—Therapeutic properties of drugs ...	623—627
CHAPTER CXCVI.—Preparations of medicinal oils and Ghritas	627—629
CHAPTER CXCVII.—Various medicinal compounds disclosed by Hari to Hara	629—630
CHAPTER CXCVIII.—Various other medicinal Recipes ...	630—632
CHAPTER CXCIX.—The same continued	632—639
CHAPTER CC.—The same continued	639—642

SUBJECT.	PAGE.
CHAPTER CCI.—The same continued	... 639—642
CHAPTER CCII.—The same continued	... 642—644
CHAPTER CCIII.—The same continued... ...	... 644—645
CHAPTER CCIV.—The same continued ...	... 645—646
CHAPTER CCV.—Various other Recipes ...	... 646—648
CHAPTER CCVI.—The same continued ...	... 648—651
CHAPTER CCVII.—The same continued ...	... 651—654
CHAPTER CCVIII.—Aphrodisiacs, Love, charms, etc.	... 654—658
CHAPTER CCIX.—Various other Recipes ...	... 658—659
CHAPTER CCX.—The same continued ...	... 659—660
CHAPTER CCXI.—Medical treatment of cuts, wounds, scalds, burns, etc.	... 661—662
CHAPTER CCXII.—Other Medicinal Recipes ...	... 662—663
CHAPTER CCXIII.—The same continued ...	... 664—666
CHAPTER CCXIV.—Medical treatment of snake-bite, etc.	... 666—668
CHAPTER CCXV.—Various Recipes	... 668—670
CHAPTER CCXVI.—Medical treatment of the diseases of cows, etc.	671
CHAPTER CCXVII.—Various Recipes for the cure of sterility, virile impotency, etc.	... 671—675
CHAPTER CCXVIII.—Various Recipes of fumigation-compounds, etc.	... 675—676
CHAPTER CCXIX.—The prophylactic charm of Vaishnava Kavacham	... 677—679
CHAPTER CCXX.—The Sarvarthada Mantra	680
CHAPTER CCXXI.—The Vishnu-Dharma Vidya ...	... 681—682
CHAPTER CCXXII.—The Garuda Vidya ...	... 682—687
CHAPTER CCXXIII.—The Tripura Vidya ...	... 687—689
CHAPTER CCXXIV.—The Chudamani ...	... 689—692
CHAPTER CCXXV.—The Pavana Vijaya ...	... 692—693
CHAPTER CCXXVI.—Medical treatment of the diseases of horses	... 693—697
CHAPTER CCXXVII.—Different names of the Ayurvedic Drugs	... 698—705
CHAPTER CCXXVIII.—Rules of Grammar ...	... 706—711
CHAPTER CCXXIX.—Duties of Brahmanas, etc. ...	... 712—727
CHAPTER CCXXX.—A Synopsis of practical pieties	... 727—729
CHAPTER CCXXXI.—Expiatory Penances ...	... 730—738
CHAPTER CCXXXII.—Dissolution of the Universe	... 738—742
CHAPTER CCXXXIII.—Naimittika Pralaya, etc. ...	... 742—743

SUBJECT. PAGE.

CHAPTER CCXXXIV.—The Wheel of Existence (Samsara Chakra) ... ... 743—746
CHAPTER CCXXXV.—The mode of Practising the Great Yoga 746—751
CHAPTER CCXXXVI.—Vishnu Bhakti ... ... 751—755
CHAPTER CCXXXVII.—The same continued ... ... 755—756
CHAPTER CCXXXVIII.—The contemplation of Vishnu ... 757
CHAPTER CCXXXIX.—The excellence of Faith ... ... 758—761
CHAPTER CCXL.—Traits of a true Vaishnava ... ... 761—763
CHAPTER CCXLI.—The hymn to Nri-Sinha ... ... 763—765
CHAPTER CCXLII.—The Jnanamritam Stotram ... ... 765—769
CHAPTER CCXLIII.—The hymn to Vishnu composed by the holy Markandeya ... ... 769—770
CHAPTER CCXLIV.—The hymn to Achyuta ... ... 770—775
CHAPTER CCXLV.—The knowledge of Brahma ... ... 775—780
CHAPTER CCXLVI.—The knowledge of Self ... ... 780—782
CHAPTER CCXLVII.—Synopsis of the Gita ... ... 782—783
CHAPTER CCLVIII.—The eight essentials of Yoga, etc. the merit that may be acquired by hearing the narration of the Garuda Puranam etc. ... ... 783—784

PREFACE.

A few preliminary remarks on the history, scope and contents of the Garuda Puranam may be necessary. The Garuda Puranam may be safely described as a sister work to the Agni Puranam. Each of them treats of Pará Vidyâ and Apará Vidyâ, secular knowledge and metaphysical truths, and partakes more of the nature of a catechism of the then prevailing Brahmanism, or of what a Bráhmana was required to know at the time, than of the Puranm proper, at least if we may be admitted to look upon the Rámáyana or the Mahábháratam as the model of that class of literature. Superficially conforming to the Rules of Pancha Sandhis, etc., the Garuda Puranam, like its sister work, reflects but the knowledge of the Bráhmanical world at the time, and had its uses then as it has even now.

Without doing violence to the antiquarian instinct, we must say that it is quite futile to attempt to lay down the precise date of the composition of the Garuda Puranam. Its name occurs in the Haláyudha's *Bráhmana Sarvasvam*. Chakrpani Dutta has quoted many a recipe from it, and the *Vishnu Dharmottaram*, according to several eminent authorities, orginally formed a portion of the Garuda Puranam. All these factors emphatically demonstrate the fact that, the Garuda Puranam was in existence even before the tenth century of the Christian Era. On the contrary, we have reasons to believe that, hosts of Puranas and Upapuranas were composed in the age of Brahmanic renascence, which immediately followed the overthrow of Buddhism in India. The Garuda Puranm, like the Agni, Shiva, Padma, and the like Puranas, were the exponents of the victorious Brahmanism, which, being inevitably divided into schisms, tried to invest the tutelary deity of each sect with the attributes of supreme divinity or Brahma, and to equip its members with a complete code of rituals, law and other necessary informations regarding the incidents of every day life, subservient to, and in conformity with, the Vedas and the Vedic literature. Thus each schism or faction, or more correctly, each Puranam, the scripture of each sect of special, tutelary divinities, became a new school of law, medicine and metaphysics, etc., re-instating the old errors of the Vedic literature, as if to ignore the many advanced truths and principles of the later day Buddhistic science, and to confirm the victory of Brahmanism even in error and fallacy.

The description of the incidents of the life of Buddha, however meagre and incidental it might be, and the occurrence of the name of Sushruta in the medical portion of the Garuda Puranam leaves not the slightest doubt that its author was intimately acquainted with the Buddhistic literature of the age, both medical and metaphysical. It is a settled fact of history that the Sushruta Samhita, at least the recension of the Sashruta Samhita by the Buddhist Nagarjuna, was written in the second century before the birth of Christ. Now, the Sushruta Samhita says that, the number of bones in the human body is three hundred. The Vishnu Smriti (Institutes of Vishnu) following the orthodox (Vedic) non-medical opinion on the subject gives it as three hundred and sixty-six.

We know that Nagarjuna, the Buddhist redacter of the Sushruta Samhita, mentioned in his recension of the work that there are "three hundred bones in the human organism, but the followers of the Vedas say that their number is three hundred and sixty" which tallies with the number given in the Yajnavalkya Samhita. The Garuda Puranam gives the number as the three hundred and sixty two (*Asthnâm Dvyodhikam Proktam Sashthyadhika S'atatrayam)* —a sort of compromise between the Vedic and the Buddhistic osteology, or between the dictates of conscience, imperatively urging the man to state the whole truth, and the pride of conquest impelling him to set up a schism against truth. The author of the Garuda Puranam, whoever he might be, must have been sufficiently familiar with the works of Nagarjuna and other Buddhistic Medical Acharyas so as to be fully convinced of the truth of their statement, and attempted to make the Vedic number of skeletal bones as near to the truth as possible. This fact serves to throw a new light upon the date of the composition of the Garuda Puranam. It unmistakably points to a period of history when the victorious Brahmanism once more attempted to restore the teachings of the Vedas in their pristine glory, and the truths of the Buddhistic science or metaphysics were still too potent a factor to be ignored or lightly dismissed—a fact which supports our contention and lends a plausible colour to the view we have adopted as regards the probable date of the composition of the Garuda.

The second question, that confronts us, is the purity of the text, *i.e.*, whether the Garuda Puranam, as we now possess it, is what it was originally written by its author; or whether its bulk has been considerably increased by subsequent additions? In the first Chapter we learn that, the Puranam consists of eight thousand and eight hundred verses, and the subjects dealt with therein are creation of the universe, Pujas, Holy pools and shrines, Cosmogony and Geography, Ages of Manus, Duties of different social orders, Gift-making, Duties of kings, etc., Laws, Vratas, Royal dynasties, Therapeutics with Ætiology, Vedangas, Pralaya, Laws of Virtue, desire, and money, and Knowledge (of Brahma and external things). These then were the main themes that were originally dealt with in the Garuda Puranam, and we may say that this was so in the light of the principle of *Adhyâya Sampravibhâga* (classification of chapters) which forms one of the cardinal rules in forming the plan of a Sanskrit work. We regret to say that, many things, having no legitimate connection with the main themes of this Puranam, nor having a direct bearing thereon, have been added to it, and a large mass of original matter has been expunged from it so as to bring it within the compass of the eight thousand and eight hundred Slokas, as laid down in the introductory chapter. Thus we see that the Pretakhanda or Vishnu-dharmottara was added to it by way of an appendix, and the reason of these successive accretions to the text can be easily understood if we consider that, the Garuda Puranam, like the Agni, etc., although originally a compendium of the available Brahminical knowledge, and rituals, pursued and followed by the Vaishnava section of the community, came to gather in many tributaries from the other branches of Brahmanic thought and religion, as the distinction between the sect of Vishnu and other sects of S'iva and Sakti etc., came to be less marked and pronounced, and the points of difference or antagonism between them were more rounded off. Thus we see many Tantrik rites and Mantras such as, the *Tripurâ Vidyâ*, *Nityaklinnâ Vidyâ* were introduced into the Garuda Puranam, one of the Scriptural Puranas of Vaishnavism; and the *Preta-khanda*, which we find invariably appended to the Puranam in many of the manuscripts, does but reflect the necessity of subsequently adding to it a treatise on funeral rites, or on punishment and reward after death according to one's deserts, only to enhance the utility of the work as a book of reference in every day life, as the members of the sect began to be more bigoted and averse to reading religious works, or Puranas dedicated to the tutelary gods of other sects. It requires nothing more than an average intellect to detect that the part under reference (Preta-Khanda) is manifestly an interpolation, inasmuch as the subject has been already dealt with in chapters on *S'raddha-vidhi*, *Papa-Chinha Lakshanam* and *Prayaschittâ*, etc., and the insertion of a more detailed and elaborate dissertation on the subject under the style of *Preta-Khanda* is an unnecessary repetition and re-opening of a finished discourse (*Samápta Punarâttatâ*) which is bad both in reason and rhetoric. We have attempted to expunge all spurious portions, or passages of questionable authenticity from the text in the light of the reasons stated above, and tried to restore it to its original form as far as possible after the progress of so many centuries since it first saw the light.

We may be asked the rationale of our conduct in undertaking the English translation of the Garuda Puranam. The question is natural enough, if the work is nothing but a compendium of Brahmanic rituals and mysteries, what is the profit of disinterring it from beneath the oblivion which it so unqualifiedly deserves. Our answer is that, in addition to the many mystic rites and practices, which legitimately fall within the range of studies in spiritualism, the Garuda Puranam contains three Samhitas, *viz.*, the Agastya Samhita, the Brihaspati Samhita (Nitisara), and the Dhanvantari Samhita; any one of which would give it a permanent value, and accord to it an undying fame among the works of practical Ethics or applied medicine. The Agastya Samhita deals with the formation, crystallisation and distinctive traits of the different precious jems, and enumerates the names of the countries from which our forefathers used to collect those minerals. The cutting, polishing, setting, and appraising, etc., of the several kinds of jems and diamond, as they were practised in ancient India, can not but be interesting to artists and lay men alike, and the scientific truths, imbedded in the highly poetic accounts of their origin and formation, shall, we doubt not, be welcomed even by the present day mineralogists, if they only care to look through the veil and to see them in their pure and native nuditity. In these days of Oriental research, it is quite within the possibilities of every ardent enquirer to make himself acquainted with the terms and technicalities of the science of our Rishis, and we are confident that any labour he may bestow on the subject in connection with the Agastya Samhita will be remunerated a hundred-fold.

The next Samhita in the Garuda Puranam is the Brihaspati

Samhita, commonly known as the Nitisara, in which we find observations on practical conduct and a knowledge of human nature, which strongly remind one of Bacon's essays and in comparision with which the Samhita gains one or two points more, not to speak of its excellent poetry and harmony. In the Ætiological portion of the Dhanvantari Samhita, one is astonished to find that in "certain types of fever the blood undergoes a sort of chemical change which produces the morbific factors of the disease, that in hæmoptisis the blood comes from the spleen, liver or the blood-vessels (facts unknown to the Nidanist, Madhava), that there is a kind of parasites that produces leprosy, and cutaneous affections in general," facts which, it was but yesterday, that the science of the west have gained access to. The therapeutical portion of the Samhita contains many excellent remedies which can not but benefit man in the art of living a long, healthy life. It is almost impossible for us to give within such a small compass even the faintest glimpse of the splendid truths that lie scattered through the pages of this noble Puranam ; enough if we conclude our remark with the saying that, it broadens the vision of a man into regions where systems and worlds are but bubbles and atoms, and enables him to consolidate his amity with those profound realities, which encompass "being and becoming" in every plane of existence, or at least helps him to lift up the veil of the Nature's workshop and to catch a view, however slight and momentary, of the nature and essence of things.

CALCUTTA,
The 12th June, 1908.

M. N. DUTT.

THE GARUDA PURANAM.

CHAPTER I.

I SALUTE the One Supreme, without birth, decay or end, identical with knowledge, great, auspicious free from impurities, without beginning, devoid of elemental body and actions, stationed in all creatures, Hari, freed from impurity and illusion and present everywhere. With mind, speech and actions I do always salute Hari, Rudra, Brahma, the lord of Ganas and the goddess Saraswati. Having adored and lauded the poet Suta, well-versed in Puranas, of a quiet nature, the master of all scriptures, devoted to Vishnu and high-souled when he came to the forest of Naimisha while making a pilgrimage to sacred shrines and seated on a holy seat was meditating on the sinless Vishnu, the great Rishis, Sounaka and others, dwelling in the forest of Naimishi, having asceticism for their wealth, of quiescent souls, effulgent like the sun and ever engaged in the celebration of sacrifices, said.

The Rishis said :—O Suta, thou art informed of every thing and therefore we ask you :— Amongst the celestials who is Iswara and who is worthy of adorations? Who should be meditated on? Who is the creator of the universe? Who protects it and who destroys it? From whom proceeds religion? Who suppresses the wicked? With what vowed observances is he pleased? By what yoga can he be obtained? What are his incarnations and what is his family? Who has instituted the various castes and orders and who protects them? O Suta, O thou of great intellect, do thou describe unto us, all this and every thing else, the most excellent themes about Narayana.

SUTA said:—I will describe the Garuda Purana, the essence of all accounts relating to Vishnu. Formerly Garuda described it to Kashyapa and I myself had heard it from Vyasa. The Lord Narayana alone is the lord of all the lords of the deities, the great soul and the great Brahma; from him proceeds birth &c. For the protection of the universe Vāsudeva, without birth and death, assumes various incarnations by his body, namely that of Koumara and others. Having undertaken the incarnation of Koumara and lived in the celestial region the first deity Hari, O Brahman, practised the most difficult vow of celebacy without any break. Secondly having assumed the Boar-form the lord of sacrifices, for the general well-being, released and held up the earth sunk deep under the nether region. Thirdly for the creation of the Rishis, he, assuming the form of a Brahma Rishi, performed Sattwik (pervaded by the quality of goodness) actions from which alone proceed desireless actions. Then for protecting righteousness, Hari, assuming the form of Nara Narayana, practised hard penances. He was then adored by the celestials and Asuras. His fifth incarnation was Kapila, the lord of Siddhas* who expounded unto

---

* Inspired seers. A *Siddha* is a semi-divine being supposed to be of great purity and holiness characterised by *Siddhis* or eight supernatural faculties or perfections.

the celestials the Sankhya,* which ascertains the Tattwas or elementary particles which had been lost in time. In his sixth incarnation he was born as the son of Atri and communicated to Alarka, Pralhada and others, the knowledge of Anwikshiki (metaphaysics) obtained by him from Anasuā. His seventh incarnation, in the Sayambhuva Manwantara, was Yajna, the will-begotten child of Akuti, who performed sacrifices in the company of the celestials. In his eighth incarnation he was born as the powerful son of Nabhi from Merudevyā. Adored of all the orders he pointed out to men the real road. Solicited by Rishis he assumed the body of Prithu as his ninth incarnation and the Brahmanas and other creatures were revived by him with the milk of herbs. When the Earth was submerged under water in the end of the Chākshusa Manwantara he assumed the form of a Fish and saved the Manu Vaivaswata by placing him on a boat. In his eleventh incarnation the Lord, in the shape of a tortoise, held on his back the mount Mandara with which the celestials and Asuras churned the ocean. In his twelfth incarnation as well as in the thirteenth in the form of a woman he stupified the Asuras and pleased the celestials. Assuming the form of a man-lion in his fourteenth incarnation he subdued the Daitya chief by cutting his entrails with his fierce claws. Assuming the form of a dwarf in his fifteenth incarnation he went to the Sacrifice of Bali and praying for room for his three feet obtained it. Beholding the kings aggrandise the Brahmanas in his sixteenth incarnation, he, filled with anger, divested the earth of the Kshatriyas for twenty one times. In his seventeenth incarnation he was begotton on Satyavati by Parasara (as Veda-Vyasa); and seeing the feeble intellect of the people he divided the Vedas. Then for accomplishing

---

* It is a system of philosophy ascribed to Kapila. It is called Sankhya because it enumerates twenty-five *Tattwas* or principles. According to this system final liberation is obtained by a true knowledge of these principles.

the work of the celestials he was born as a king (Rama), built a bridge over the ocean and performed other feats. in his nineteenth and twentieth incarnations the Lord was born as Rama and Krishna and relieved the earth of her burden. Then at the junction of the Kali yuga, for stupefying the enemies of the celestials he was born as Buddha, the son of Jina. In the period of the eighth junction (change of cycles), when all the kings will be on the verge of destruction, he will be born as Vishnujasa's son Kalki, the lord of the world. Innumerable are the incarnations of Hari, the mine of Sattwa, O twice-born ones. The prime Manus, the knowers of the Vedas, are all said to have originated from Vishnu. From them proceeded the work of creation. And they should be adored with vowed observances and other rites. This Garuda Purana consisting of eight thousand and eight hundred verses Vyasa formerly narrated to me.

——:o:——

CHAPTER II.

THE RISHIS said:—Why did Vyasa describe to you the Garuda Purana? Do thou describe thus the most excellent theme relating to Vishnu.

THE SUTA said:—In the company of the ascetics I had gone to the hermitage of Vadarika. There I saw Vyasa meditating on the great Ishwara. Having bowed unto him I took my seat and accosted that foremost of ascetics saying:—

"O Vyasa, relate unto me the form of Hari from which has emanated the creation of the universe. Methinks, while thou dost meditate on the Lord, thou must be knowing it."

Hear, O Vipras, what he did relate on being thus accosted by me.

VYASA said :—Hear, O Suta, I will recount the Purana Guruda which Brahmā described to me in the company of Nārada, Daksha and others.

THE SUTA said :—How did Brahmā relate the sacred Purana Garuda, describing the true essence, unto thee when united with Daksha, Nārada and others.

VYASA said :—Having saluted Brahmā who was residing in the Brahmaloka, myself, Daksha, Nārada, Bhrigu and others said to him. "Describe unto us the quintessence (of the sacred lore)."

BRAHMA said :—O VYASA, I will recount to you, the Garuda Purada, the cream of sacred learning which Vishnu described to me and Rudra formerly while in the company of other celestials.

VYASA said :—O Brahman, describe to me the Garuda Purana, pregnant with great significance, the essence of all, which Hari formerly described to Rudra while in the company of other celestials,

BRAHMA said :—With Indra and other celestials I had gone to the mount Kailasha. There I saw Rudra engaged in the meditation of the great station. Having saluted him I addressed him, saying :—"O Shankara, on what art thou meditating? Save thee, I do not know of a greater deity. Do thou therefore describe unto me [the subject of thy meditation] the quintessence [of the sacred learning] who, along with the celestials, am anxious to listen to it."

RUDRA said :—I meditate on Vishnu, the great soul, the Demiurgus, who gives all, who is present everywhere and who resides in the hearts of all creatures. O grand-father, my body is besmeared with ashes and my hairs have been clotted. All my vowed observances are intended for the adoration of Vishnu. I will describe him unto you, the essence of all, on whom I meditate. I meditate on the deity

Hari, Vishnu, Jishnu, who is lotus-navelled and shorn of a body; who is purity, the source of purity; who is the impersonal self and the individual soul; who is the great Ishwara and unites all souls with himself. In him exist all the worlds and elements and into him they enter. All the *gunas* (qualities) and elements exist in that lord of elements as pearls are strung by a thread. He has a thousand eyes, a thousand heads, a thousand thighs and a most beautiful face. He is the minutest of the minute, the firmest of the firm, the heaviest of the heavy and the best of all that is good. In the words, letters, principal and minor sacred lores and in the true Saman he is lauded as truth and the author of true deeds. He is called the ancient Purusha and Brahmā amongst the twice-born. He is called Sankarshana in destruction. I therefore adore him in whom all these worlds shine us the Shakula fishes in the water. He is the divine law, the word (Om), Brahma, the that, the existent and non-existent and the supreme. The celestials, the Yakshas, the Rakshasas and the Pannagas adore him. Fire is his mouth, the heaven is his head, the sky is his navel and the earth is his feet and the sun and moon are his two eyes. I meditate on him. I meditate on that deity whose breaths are the wind, in whose belly the three worlds exist and whose arms are the divisions of the time. I meditate on that deity in whose hairs are the clouds, and in the joints of whose body are the four oceans. I meditate on that deity who is above time, who is above sacrifices, who is above the existent and non-existent and who is the beginning and end of the universe. I meditate on that deity from whose mind emanates the moon, from whose eyes the sun and from whose mouth the fire. I meditate on that deity from whose feet the earth is produced, from whose ears the directions and from whose head the *Div* (celestial region). I meditate on that deity from whom have proceeded the works of principal and minor creations, the various races, Manwantaras, and histories of the families.

We will proceed to him, to witness the true essence, on whom I do meditate.।

BRAHMA said:—I was thus formerly addressed by Rudra. Having lauded and saluted Vishnu, the dweller of the white island (Shweta-dwipa) we sat calmly desirous of listening to (the subject). From amongst us Rudra said to Vishnu, the great Iswara:—"Describe to us the most essential of all essence; we salute thee." What, O Vyasa, you have asked me the Lord Bhava asked Vishnu in the hearing of myself and other celestials.

RUDRA said:—O Hari, O king of gods, tell us who is the god of gods; who is Iswara; who should be meditated on; who should be adored; with what vowed observances, the great is propitiated? With what religious observances, with what process of self-restraint, with what form of adoration and with what sort of conduct is He pleased? What is his form? From what deity the universe has emanated and who protects it? What are his incarnations? In whom the world is dissolved? From what deity proceed the works of principal and minor creations, the various families and Manwantaras? In whom do all these exist? Do thou describe all this and every thing else, O Hari.।

Then Hari described to Rudra the glories of the great Iswara, the Yoga and eighteen sorts of learning.

HARI said:—Hear, O Rudra, I will describe it, along with Brahmā and other celestials.

I am the god of gods, the lord of all the worlds. I am the object of meditation and adoration and am lauded by the celestials with panegyric verses. When I am worshipped by men with self-restraint, vowed observances and good conduct O Rudra, I grant them the most excellent stage.

I am the seed of the preservation of the world and I am also the destroyer of the universe, O Shiva. O Hara, I am also the suppressor of the wicked and the protector of religion. With fish and other incarnations I do protect the earth. I am the import of the mystic formula and am engaged in adoration and meditation. I am the creator of heaven and I am myself the heaven, &c. I am the knower, the hearer, the speaker and the object of speech. I am all and the deity identical with all. I am the source of worldly enjoyments and emancipation. I am the presents of meditation and adoration; I am the Mandalas, the Itihasas, O Rudra. O Shiva, I am all the deities. O Shambhu, I am all the forms of knowledge. I am at one with Brahma, O Shiva. I am Brahma, all the regions, and identical with all the deities. I am the personification of righteous conduct and the religion of Vishnu. I am the Varnas (castes) and Ashramas (orders) and I am the ancient religion. I am the process of regulation, that of self-restraint and the various vowed observances, O Rudra. I am the sun, the moon, and all the auspicious things. Formerly with asceticism the bird Garuda had worshipped me on earth. Pleased with him I asked him to pray for a boon; and he too prayed for a boon.

GARUDA said:—O Hari, my mother Vinatā had been made a slave by the Nagas. Do thou so order, that I may bring ambrosia after vanquishing the celestials, that I may release her from slavery and that I may be thy carrier. Do thou so order that I may be highly powerful, greatly strong, omniscient, the afflicter of the Nagas, and the author of Puranas and Samhitas.

VISHNU said:—What you have said, O Garuda, will all be accomplished. You will release your mother Vinatā from the Nagas. Having vanquished all the deities and others you will bring ambrosia. You will be the highly powerful carrier. By my favour you will be the author of the Purana, describing my glories and forms. By your name it will be celebrated on earth as Garuda. O son of Vinatā, as I am the God of gods and Shree is celebrated so the Garuda Purana will be celebrated amongst all the Puranas. As I am worthy of being lauded so thou shalt be. Meditating on me by your mind do you describe this Garuda Purana by your bird mouth." Thus accosted, O Rudra, Garuda described it to Kashyapa. Hearing the Garuda Purana Kashyapa revived the burnt tree. Hearing yourself with fixed attention do you revive others with your learning. "The bird, Om, Um, Swaha"—This is the great learning of Garuda. Hear, O Rudra, the great Garuda Purana narrated by Garuda.

——:o:——

CHAPTER III.

SUTA said:—Thus did Rudra hear it from Vishnu; Brahmā from Rudra; from Brahmā the ascetic Vyasa; and myself from Vyasa. And I relate it to you, O Shounaka, in the forest of Naimisha. In the assemblage of the ascetics have been described by me, the creation and the adoration of the deities, the various sacred shrines, the wealth of the world and the Manwantaras; the duties of the various Varnas (castes) and Ashramas (orders); the gifts, the regal duties, the laws, vowed observances, families and the medical science with a diagnosis of diseases; the various auxilliary sciences, the universal dissolution; religious profit, desire, worldly profit and the most excellent knowledge. The illusory deeds, and those beyond the range of illusion, of Vishnu have all been narrated in Garuda Purana. This Garuda is *Bhagavan*.* By the favour of Vāsudeva he has been endued with great strength. Having become the

* It is an epithet applied to a god or demi-god or a great ascetic. Literally the word means one endued with six qualities,—prosperity, might, glory, splendour, wisdom and dispassion.

carrier of Hari he is the instrument of creation &c. Having vanquished the celestials Garuda brought ambrosia, by which the appetite of the universe, lying in the belly of Hari, was appeased. His very sight or recollection destroys the serpents. Through Garuda Kashyapa revived all the burnt trees. Garuda is Hari. He related it unto Kashyapa. The auspicious Garuda Purana, when read, gives piety and all objects. Hear, O Shounaka, how Hari describe it unto Rudra.

——:o:——

CHAPTER IV.

RUDRA said:—O Janārddana, do thou described the primary and scondary creations, the families, Manwantaras as well as the histories of the families.

HARI said:—Hear, O Rudra, I will describe the old sport of Vishnu, consisting of creation, preservation and destruction, which destroys all sins.

The Lord Vāsudeva, void of passion, Nara-Nārāyana, is the great Soul, Para Brahma, the creator and the destroyer of the universe. All this exists in Him as both manifest and unmanifest. He exists in the form of Purusha (male-being) and Kāla (Time). Vishnu is both manifest and unmanifest. He is Purusha and Kāla. Understand, his actions are like those of a sportive child. He is without beginning, the Creator; He is without end and Purusottama (the most exalted of male beings). From him originate the unmanifest as well as the soul. From him emanate the intellect, mind, the Tattwas (principles) ether, air, fire, water and earth. O Rudra, He is the golden egg and is himself his own end.

The Lord assumes a body for the purposes of creation. Having assumed the body of Brahmā with four mouths, parvaded by the quality of *Rajas* (darkness) he creates the entire world, moveable and stationery. This entire universe consisting of the celestials, Asuras and human beings lies inside the egg. As Creator he creates the universe; as Vishnu he protects it; and he destroys it in the end. Hari himself is the destroyer. Having assumed the body of Brahmā Hari creates the universe and as Vishnu he protects it. And assuming the form of Rudra the Lord destroys the universe at the end of a Kalpa. When Brahmā was engaged in the work of creation, He, assuming the form of a boar, held up with his tusks the earth sunk under water. Hear, O Shankara, I will describe all in short beginning with the first creation of the deity.

The first creation is *Mahat* or intellectual principle; it is simply a metamorphosis of Brahma. The second creation is that of *Tanmatras* or the subtle elementary particles. This is known as the creation of elements. The third is called *Vaikârika* or the creation of organs. This is the (Prākrita) material or elementary creation originating from intellect. The fourth is the primary creation—and all the stationery bodies are known as primary creations. The next is *Tiryyaksrotas** who are otherwise called *Tiryyakjonya i.e.* beasts &c. The sixth is the *Urdhasrotasa*† which is called the creation of the celestials. The seventh is the creation of *Arvakasrotas*‡ or human beings. The eighth is the creation of *Anugrahas*§ pervaded by the qualities of *Sattwa* (goodness) and *Tamas* (ignorance).

---

* *Lit* the stream of beings living according to nature.

† *Lit* the stream of beings tending upwards.

‡ Cf. And as these eat by swallowing down they are called *Arvaraskotasas.*

§ A class of deities.

These are the five orders of the *Vaikarika* (organic) creation. There are three orders of the elementary and organic creation. Koumāra makes the ninth. O Rudra, there are four orders of creation beginning with the celestials and ending with the stationery creation.

While engaged in the work of creation Brahmā first procreated his mind-born sons. Then desirous of creating the four classes of beings, viz the celestials, Asuras, Pitris and human beings, all, going under the name of *Amva* he adored his own self.* As the lord of beings, although himself of unfettered soul, concentrated his soul, being desirous of creating, passion overspread him and first from forth his hips came out the Asuras. And then he renounced his person surcharged with *Tama* or darkness; and his darkness, on being renounced by him, O Shankara, was converted into Night. Having assumed another body he became desirous of creating and felt delight. Then O Hara, came out from the mouth of Brahmā, the celestials surcharged with the quality of *Sattwa* (goodness). On being renounced by him his body, surcharged with the quality of *Sattwa*, was converted into Day. Therefore it is that the Asuras are powerful in the night and the celestials during the day. He then assumed a person fraught with the quality of goodness and then sprang from him the ancestors. And that body, on being renounced by him, became Twilight remaining between day and night. Then having assumed a body fraught with the quality of *Rajas* (darkness) he created human beings. And on being renouned by him that form became moon-light which is termed *Praksandhya*.† Moonlight, Night, Day and Twilight are his bodies. And then he assumed another body fraught with the quality of darkness and thereat sprung hunger

* The passage is not clear. Perhaps by the expression "adored his own self" the author means that Brahma was engaged in the process of mental retrospection.

† Meaning *going before twilight.*

from him and from hunger wrath. Brahmā then created Rakshasas exercised with hunger. [Those that said 'Save him'] are called Rakshas and those [that said 'We shall eat him up] are called Yakshas from *Yakshana* eating. And from the movement (*Sarpana*) of his hairs sprang the serpents. Waxing wroth he generated some beings of wrathful temper. O sinless, then the Gandharvas came out singing. All these beings were created by him.

He created goats from his mouth, the kine from his belly and sides; the horses, elephants, asses and camels from his feet, and medicinal herbs furnished with fruts and roots from the hairs of his body. Fair complexloned male sheep, horses, mules and asses are called *grâmya* or household animals. Hear, I will describe the wild ones. [They are] the beasts of prey, the cloven-hoofed, elephants, monkeys, and fifthly, birds and sixthly, acquatic animals and seventhly, reptiles. From his eastern and other mouths he created the Rik and other Vedas. The Brahmanas originated from his mouth, the Kshatryas from his arms, the Vaishyas from his thighs and the Shudras from his feet. The region of Brahma is for the Brahmahas, that of Shakra for the Kshatryas, that of Marut (wind-god) for the Vaishyas and that Gandharvas for the Shudras. Those practising the Brahmacharya injunctions attain the region of Brahma. The householders, performing duly their duties, repair to the region of the Creator. Those, living in the forest, acquire the region of the seven Rishis. The sphere of the *Yatis*, going at will, is the eternal region.

——:o:——

CHAPTER V.

HARI said :—Having created the world and all orders of beings the Lord created his mind-begotten sons for multiplying his creation ; namely Dharma, Rudra, Manu, Sanaka, Sanātana, Bhrigu, Sanatkumāra, Ruchi, Shuddha, Marichi, Atri, Angira, Pulastya, Pulaha, Kratu, Nārada and the Patris Varhisadas.

The Lotus-sprung deity, from his right thumb, created Daksha endued with four forms and his wife from his left thigh. Daksha begat on her beautiful daughters. He gave them away unto the sons of Brahmā and conferred Sati on Rudra. Numberless, highly powerful sons were born unto Rudra. He conferred the auspicious Khyāti, matchless in beauty, on Bhrigu. Bhrigu begat on her Dhātā and Vidhātā. He also begat Shree who was Nārāyana's wife. Hari begat on her himself Bala and Ukshmadi. Ayati and Niyati were the two daughters of the high-souled Manu. They were the wives of Dhātā and Vidhātā. They gave birth to two sons, Prāna and Mrikandu. Mārkandeya was the son Mrikandu. Marichi's wife Sambuti gave birth to Pournamāsa. Viraja and Sarvaga were the two sons of that high-souled one. Angiras begat on Smriti sons and daughters namely Sinivalee, Kuhu, Rākā and Anumati. Atri begat on Anasuyā sinless sons, Soma, Durvāsā and the yogin Dattātreya. Pulastya begat on Priti Dottoli. Three sons, Karman, Arthavira and Sahishnu were begotten by the patriarch Pulaha on his wife Kshamā. Krati begat on his wife Sumati the sixty thousand Rishis of controlled passions by name Vālakhilyas. They were all of the height of a thumb and effulgent like the burning sun. Vashistha begat on Urjjā seven sons, viz, Rajo, Gatra, Urdhavāhu, Sharana, Anagha, Sutapa, Sukra. These are the seven Rishis.

Daksha conferred Swāhā on the fire-god who had assumed a body. O Hara, from him Swāhā obtained three highly effulgent sons viz Pāvaka, Pavamāna and Shuchi, all eaters of water. Swadhā gave birth to Menā and Vaitarani. They were both *Brahmavadinis.** Menā was married to Himachala (mount Himalaya).

O Hara! the Lord appointed Manu Swayambhu (self-create) formerly sprung from Brahma's self and resembling himself to rule creatures. Swayanbhuva Manu accepted as his wife Shatarupāa who had destroyed all her sins by ascetic penances. And to that person Satarupā bore Pryavrata and Uttānapada; and daughters named Prasuti, Akuti and Devahuti; of them Manu conferred Akuti on Ruchi, Prasuti on Daksha and Devahuti on Kardama. To Ruchi were born Yajnc2 and Dakshinā3. Again Yajna begat on Dakshinā twelve highly powerful sons by name Yamas.

The most excellent Daksha begat twenty four daughters. They were Sraddhā,4 Lakshmi,5 Dhriti,6 Tushti,7 Pushti,8 Medhā,9 Kriyā,10 Buddhi,11 Lajjā,12 Vapu,13 Sānti,14 Riddhi,15 Kriti16. These thirteen daughters of Daksha were wedded by Dharma for procreating sons. Khyāti,17 Sāti,18 Sambhuti,19 Smriti,20 Priti,21 Kshamā,22 Saunati,23 Anasuya,24 Urjjā,25 Swāhā and Swadhā26 [were the remaining ones]. The foremost of asceties Bhrigu, Bhava, Marichi, Angira, Pulastya, Pulaha, Kratu, Atri, Vasistha and the Pitris duly married all these daughters beginning with Khyāti. And

---

* Female interpreters of the divine Science.

1 Having an hundred forms. 2 Sacrifice. 3 Gifts in sacrifice 4 Veneration. 5 The goddess of wealth. 6 Patience. 7 Satisfaction. 8 Nourishment. 9 Intelligence. 10 Act. 11 Intellect. 12 Bashfulness. 13 Body. 14 Suceess. 15 Fame. 16 Righteousness. 17 Renown. 18 Chastity. 19 Birth. 20 Memory. 21 Gratification. 22 Forgiveness. 23 Reverence. 24 Good-natured. 25 Energy. 26 This and the last words are uttered while offering oblations to fire.

then Sraddhā brought forth Kāma,[1] Chala,[2] Darpa,[3] Niyama[4] and Dhriti[5] as her sons, and Tushti Santosha[6] and Pushti Lobha.[7] Medhā[8] brought forth Shruta[9] and Kriyā,[10] Dandam[11], Laya[12] and Vinaya[13] and Buddhi,[14] Bodh[15] and Lajjā, Vinaya Vapu[16] and Vyavasaya[17] as her sons. And Shanti brought forth Kshemā and Riddhi, Sukham[18] and Kirti Yaças.[19] These are the offspring of Dharma.

Kāma's wife was Rati whose son was Harsha.[21] Daksha once undertook the celebration of a horse sacrifice at which all his sons-in-law were invited. They all went there accompanied with their wives except Rudra and Sati. But Sati went there uninvited and was insulted by Daksha. Having renounced her body she was again begotten on Menā by Himavan. Gouri became Shambhu's wife whose sons were Vināyaka and Kumāra. Rudra, the powerful master of Bhringi, was by nature wrathful. He destroyed Daksha's sacrifice and imprecated a curse on him, saying "You will be born as a man, in the family of Dhruva."

—:o:—

CHAER VI.

HARI said:—Uttanāpada begat a son on Suruchi by name Uttama and another on Suniti by name Dhruva who attained to the most exalted station, having adored Janārddana, the god of gods, by the favour of the ascetic. Dhruva's son Shnisthi was greatly strong and highly powerful. And his son was the greatly intelligent Prachinavarhi.

1 Sexual desire. 2 Lakshmi. 3 Pride. 4 Restraint. 5 Nourishment. 6 Contentment. 7 Avarice. 8 Intellect. 9 Knowledge or what is heard. 10 Action. 11 Punishment. 12 Justice. 13 Humilation. 14 Intellect. 15 Apprehension. 16 Body. 17 Exertion. 18 Felicity. 19 Fame.

His son was Divanjaya whose son was Ripu. His son was known as the beautiful Manu Chākshusha. His son was Ruru whose son was the beautiful Anga. Anga's son was Vena who was an atheist and an irreligious person. Vena, the perpetrator of iniquities, was killed by the Rishis with Kuçā. They then churned his thigh for a son and thereat sprang a son, greatly dwarfish and black. They then said "sit down, sit down" and he was called Nishāda dwelling on the mount Vindhyā. Then the twice-born ones suddenly churned his right thigh. From there sprang a son assuming the mental form of Vishnu, by name Prithu. By that son Vena repaired to the celestial region. The king milched the earth, for giving life to his subjects.

Prithu's son was Antarddhāna whose son again was Havirdhāna. His son Prāchinavarhi became the Lord Paramount of the world. He espoused the daughter of the ocean of salt water and begat on her ten Prachinavarhis who were called Prāchetas and were masters of the science of archery. They all practised the same religious austerities and remained immersed in the bed of the deep for ten thousand years. They attained to the dignity of the Patriarchs; and their wife was Marishā. Of her was born Daksha by the imprecation of Bhava.

As before Daksha again created four classes of beings from his mind. Obstructed by Hara they did not multiply. The Patriarch then desired to carry on the work of creation by sexual intercourse. He then espoused Asikni, the daughter of the Patrirch Varuna. He begat on the daughter of Varuna a thousand sons. The end of the earth being described by Narada they went there to learn it and did not return. On their being lost Daksha created another thousand, named Savalakha, who also followed the foot-steps of their brothers, O Hara. Worked up with anger Daksha cursed Nārada saying "You will obtain a birth" and he was again born as the son of the ascetic Kashyapa. On his sacrifice being destroyed Daksha imprecated the terrific Maheshwara, saying "Having worshipped thee with necessary articles the twice born will leave them aside. Even in another birth, your hostilities will not terminate, O Shankara."

Daksha begat on Asikni sixty beautiful daughters. He gave away two of them unto Angiras. He conferred two on Krishāshwa, ten on Dharma, thirteen on Kashyapa and twenty seven on Indu. He conferred Suprabhā and Bhāmini on Vahuputra. And O Mahadeva, he gave unto Aristhanemi, his four daughters viz Manoramā, Bhānumati, Vishālā and Vahudā. He conferred on Krishāshwa Supraja and Jayā.

Arundhati, Vasu, Yâmi, Lamvâ, Bhānu, Marutvati, Sangkalpa, Muhurta, Sādhyā, Vishwā, these ten are known as the wives of Dharma. I will now describe the names of the wives of Kashyapa. They were Aditi, Diti, Danu, Kālā, Anāyu, Sinhikā, Muni, Kadru, Prādhā, Ira, Krodhā, Vinātā, Surabhi and Khagā. Vishwâ gave birth to Vishwadevas and Sadhya to Sadhyas; Murutvati to Marudyant and Vasu to Vasus. From Bhanu were born the Bhānus and from Muhurtta the Muhurttas. Ghosa was born of Lamva and Nagavithi (milkway) was born of Yami (night). All the objects of the world were born of Arundhati and Sankalpa (pious determination) was the son of Sankalpa. Apa, Dhruva, Soma, Dhava, Anila, Anala, Pratyusha and Prabhasa are the names of the Vasus.

Apa's son were Vaitundya, Srama (weariness), Sranta (fatigue) and Dhani. And the son of Dhruva was the great Kala (Time) the cherisher of the world. The son of Soma was Varchas (light) by whom was generated Varchaswi (radiance). Dhava begat on his wife Manoharâ Ruhina, Hutahavya, Shishira, Prana and Ramana. Anila's wife was Shiva. Her son was Pulomya and Avijnatagati (unknowable motion). These were the two sons of Anila. The son of Agni, Kumara, was born in a clump of Sara reeds whose sons were Shâkha, Vishâkha, Naigameya and Prishtata. The son of Kirtikas was known as Kartikeya. Pratyusha's son was the ascetic Davala. Vishwakarmâ, the celebrated architect of the celestials, was the son of Prabhâsa. His sons were Ajaikapada, Ahirvadhna, Twastri and Rudra, all very energetic. And the own begotten son of Twastri was the great ascetic Vishwarupa. There are eleven Rudras, the lords of the three worlds. They are Hara, Vahurupa, Tryamvaka, Aparajita, Vrishâkapi, Shambhu, Kapardi, Raivata, Mrigavyadha, Sarva, and Kapali, O great ascetic. Soma's wives were twenty seven in number known as stars. Kashyapa begat on Aditi twelve suns. Vishnu, Shakra, Aryama, Dhâtâ, Twastha, Pushâ, Vivashwan, Savita, Mitra, Varuna, Angshuman and Bhaga—these were the twelve Adityas.

Hiranyakashipu and Hiranyaksha were born of Diti. A daughter, by name Sinhika, was also born who was married to Viprachitti. Hiranyakashipu had four very powerful sons viz., Anuhlāda, Hlāda, the powerful Pralhada and Sanghlada. Of them Pralhada was devoted to Vishnu. The sons of Sanghlāda were Sivi, Ayushman and Vashkala. Pralhada's son was Virochana who begat Bali, who again had a hundred sons of whom Vāna was the oldest, O bull-emblemed deity.

All the sons of Hiranyākasha were also gifted with great prowess—Utkara, Shakoni, Bhutasantapana, Mahānābha, Mahâvāhu and Kālanābha.

Danu's sons were Dwimurdhā, Shankara, Ayomukha, Shankusira, Kapila, Samvara, Ekachakra, Mahāvāhu, the highly powerful Taraka, Swarbhānu, Vrishaparva, the great Asura Puloma and the mighty Viprachitti.

Swarbhānu had a daughter by name Suprabha and Sarmistha was the daughter of Vrishaparvan who had two other celebrated daughters, namely Upadānavi and Hayasira. Vaishwānara had two daughters named Pulomā and Kālakā who were both married to Māricha. They gave birth to sixty thousand sons, the leading Danavas. Poulamas and Kala Kānjas are known as the sons of Māricha.

Viprachitti begat on Sinhikā Vyansha, Shalya the strong, Nabha the powerful, Vatapi, Namuchi, Itwala, Khasrimā, Anjaka, Naraka, and Kālanābha.

In the family of the Daitya Pralhāda the Nivatakavachas were born. Six daughters, gifted with great energy, were born to Tāmrā, named Shuki, Syeni, Bhāsi, Sugrivi, Suchi and Gridhrika. Shuki gave birth to parrots, owls and crows; Syeni to hawks; Bhāsi to kites; Gridhrika to vultures; Suchi to water-fowl; Sugrivi to horses, camels and asses. These are known as the offspring of Tāmrā.

Vinatā gave birth to two sons celebrated as Garuda and Aruna. The offspring of Surasā were a thousand powerful serpents. Kadru had also a thousand sons—many-hooded serpents of unmitigated prowess. The most celebrated amongst them were Shesha, Vāsuki, Takshaka, Shanka, Sweta, Mahāpadma, Kumvala, Ashwatara, Elapatra, Nāga, Karkota, Dhananjaya and many other deadly and poisonous serpents.

Krodhā gave birth to highly powerful Pishachas. Surabhi gave birth to kine and buffaloes. Irā gave birth to trees, creepers, grass &c. Khagā gave birth to Yakshas and Rakahas and Muni to Apsaras. Aristha gave birth to highly powerful Gandharvas.

Then were born the deities Maruts, forty nine in number, viz., Ekajyoti, Duryyoti, Trijyoti, Chaturjyoti, Ekashukra, Dwishukra, the highly powerful Trishukra, Idrik, Anyadrik, Sadrik, Pratisadrik, Mita, Samita, the highly powerful Sumita, Ritajit, Satyajit, Sushena, Senajit, Atimitra, Amitra, Duramitra, Ajila, Rita, Ritadharmā, Viharta, Varuna, Dhruva, Vidhārana, Grihamekagana, Idriksha, Sadriksha, Etadriksha, Mita, Shana, Etana, Prasadnksha, Sutra, the great ascetic Tadngugra, Dhvannibhasa, Vimukta, Vikshipa, Dyuti, Vasu, Valādrishya, Lābha, Kama, Jayi, Virat, Udveshana and Guna.

They all ride the wind. These all are the forms of Hari, All the kings, Dānavas and the celestials adore Hari with mystic formulas along with the sun and other members of the family.

——:o:——

CHAPTER VII.

RUDRA SAID:—I will describe in brief the adoration of Suryya (the sun) as instituted by Shywambhuva, which is essential and gives enjoyment and emancipation. Listen to it, O Vyása.

RUDRA SAID:—I will describe the adoration of the sun yeilding religion, desire &c.

Om, salutation unto the seat of the sun. Om salutation unto the form of the sun. Om, Hrám, Hrim, salutation unto the sun. Om saluation unto the moon. Om salutation unto Mars. Om salutation unto Mercury. Om salutation unto Jupiter. Om salutation unto Venus. Om salutation unto Saturn. Om salutation unto Ráhu. Om salutation unto Ketu. Om salutation unto the bundle of effulgence.

O bull-emblemed deity, one should adore the sun and other planets by offering them seats, conveyances, water for washing feet, Arghya, water for rinsing mouth, water for bathing, raiments, sacrificial threads, scents, flowers, incense, lamps, and salutation, by circumambulating them and performing the ceremony of Visarjjana (the withdrawal of life).

Om, Hám, salutation unto the seat of Shiva. Om, Hām, salutation unto the form of Shiva. Om, Hám salutation unto his heart. Om, Him, unto the head, Swáhá. Om, hum, unto the tuft of hair, Vashat. Om, Haim, unto the amulet, Hum. Om hum unto the three eyes Voushat. Om, Ham, salutation unto the weapons. Om, Ham, salutation unto the immediate born. Om, Him, salutation unto Vámadeva. Om, Haim, salutation, unto Tatpurusha. Om, Houm, salutation unto Ishāna. Om, Hām, salutation unto Gouri. Om, Hum, salutation unto the preceptors. Om, Ham, salutation unto Indra. Om, Ham, salutation unto Adhora.

Om, salutation unto the seat of Vāsudeva. Om, salutation unto the form of Vàsudeva. Om, Am, Om, salutation unto the Lord Vàsudeva, Namas. Om, Am, Om, salutation unto the Lord Sangkarshana, Namas. Om, Am, Om, salutation unto the Lord Pradyumna Namas. Om, Am, Om, salutation unto the Lord Aniruddha Namas. Om salutation unto Nàràyana. Om salutation unto the Eternal, existent Brahma. Om, Hum, salutation unto Vishnu. Om, Kshoum, salutation unto the Lord Narasimha (man-lion). Om, Bhus, Om, salutation unto the Lord Baràha (Boar). Om, Kan, Tan, Pan, Sham, salutation unto the son of Vinata. Om, Jam, Khan, Vam, salutation unto Sudarshana. Om, Khan, tan, Pham, Sham, salutation unto the club. Om, Van, Lan, Man, Koham salutation unto the conch-shell Panchajanya. Om, Gham, Dham, Bham, Ham salutation unto Shree. Om, Gan, Dan, Van, San, salutation unto Pushti (nourishment). Om, Dham, Sham, Vam, San salutation unto the garland of forest flowers. Om, Sam, Dam, Lam, salutation unto the mystic mark Srivatsa. Om, Tam, Cham, Bham, Yam, salutation unto the (jem) Koustava. Om salutation unto the preceptors. Om Salutation unto Indra and other deities. Om Salutation unto Vishwaksena.

O bull-emblemed deity, with these mantrams, seats and other offerings should be dedicated to Hari. Hear now of the adoration of the female energy of Vishnu, Saraswati.

Om, Hrim, salutation unto Saraswati. Om, Ham, salutation unto her heart. Om, Hrim, salutation unto her head. Om, Hum, salutation unto her hairs. Om, Ham, salutation unto her amulet. Om, Hrum, salutation unto her three eyes. Om, Hus, salutation unto the weapons.

Shradhà, Hriddhi, Kalà, Medhà, Tushti, Prabhà, Mati, these energies of Saraswati, should be adored wlth mantrams beginning with Om and ending with Namas.

Om salutation unto the Kshetrapalas. Om salutation unto the preceptors. Om salutation unto the great Guru.

He should then dedicate seats and other offerings to Saraswati standing on a lotus. The sacred *Arohana* [installation of the image] of Suryya (sun) and other deities should be performed with their respective *mantrams*.

—:o:—

CHAPTER VIII.

HARI said :—Having bathed in the Mandapa (temple) built on earth one should adore Vishnu in Mandala (circular figure).

With powders of five colours, this circular figure, Vajranabha, should be drawn. O Rudra, sixteen rooms should be drawn there. In the fourth and fifth corners strings should be placed. The strings in the corner should be extended to both the other corners. A man, well versed in all these rites, should thus place strings in all the corners. Similarly he should deal with interior corners. The first should be placed in the centre and then at the junction of the lines in the middle. In all the interior parts there are eight centres. The centres of the eastern and central figures should be connected with a string. O Hara, the foremost of the twice-born should draw the base in the interior parts. O Shiva, connected with it the pericarps of the central string should be drawn. On two sides of the pericarps an expert should draw the filaments. A learned man should draw petals on their heads. O thou of firm vows, a worshipper, conversant with the knowledge of the true object, should draw figures of lotuses in all the centres.

With the division of the first string one should draw the doors. With the half he should make decorations for the same. The pericarp should be drawn with yellow colour, the filaments with dark blue, the inside with violet and the petals with crimson. The four parts should be filled up with black powder, the doors with white powder and the five lines of the Mandala in order with crimson, yellow and dark-blue. Having performed *Nyasa* (assignment of the limbs he should adore Hari in the five mandalas. He should assign his heart to Vishnu, the middle part to Sankarshana, the head to Pradyumna and the tuft of hair on the head to Aniruddha. His entire body should be assigned to Brahma and the fingers to Shridhara. Meditating "I am Vishnu" he should perform the Nyasa of Hari in the pericarps. He should perform the Nyasa of Shangkarshana in the east, that of Pradyumna in the south, that of Aniruddha in the west, that of Brahma in the north that of Shridhara, Indra and other deities in Rudra and other corners. Having adored them with scents and other articles a worshipper attains to the great station.*

—:o:—

CHAPTER IX.

HARI said :—Being initiated in proper time and having his eyes covered with a cloth a disciple should offer one hundred and eight oblations with the principal mantram.

* In this chapter occurs the drawing of a figure with various colours. Such a figure is necessary for the celebration of a religious rite. Even in a Hindu marriage such figures are drawn for the solemnization of religious rites.

O Rudra, twice the number should be offered in a Putraka Homa,* thrice the number in Sadhaka† and four times the number in Nirvànadeshika.‡ A destroyer of a preceptor, Vishnu's image, Brahmana and a woman deserves death at the hands of those who are not initiated. I will describe his *Dikshá* or initiation destructive of virtue and sin.

Having caused his disciples to sit outside he should make them concentrate their minds. O Rudra, he should consider them purified by the wind, burnt by the fire and again sprinkled with water. Uniting the sentiency with fire he should consign it to fire. He should meditate on Pranava, the instrument of all, in the sky and in the body. He should next unite it with *Kshetrajna*§ for its being the cause of the body. Then imagining all the *Saktis* or female energies of of the deity in the various Mandalas he should adore Hari. There should be four doors in order of *Brahma Tirtha* (shrine) and others. The head is the lotus; the fingers are the petals; the palm is the pericarp and the nails are the filaments. Then meditating there on Hari, the sun and fire, he, with a controlled mind, should place it on the head of the disciple, for in the hand is stationed Vishnu, his own hand being that of Vishnu, and with its touch the entire collection of sins is dissipated.

Having adored the disciple, covered his eyes with a piece of cloth, and placed him in front of the deity the preceptor should throw flowers there. He should throw flowers where the head of the deity, the holder of Shrānga bow, is. He should mention his name as well as those of his wives. In the case of a Shudra, an expert preceptor should mention the name of his master.

* A Homa or offerings to fire for the acquisition of a son.

† One intended for becoming a worshipper.

‡ One intended for attaining emancipation.

§ The lord or the divine emanation residing in the body.

CHAPTER X.

HARI said :—I will describe the adoration of Shree and other deities in *Sthandilas** for the attainment of *Siddhis*†

Om, Shrim, salutation unto the great Lakshmi.

Shrām, Shrim, Shrum, Shroum, Shras. He should gradually worship the heart, head, the tuft of hair, amulet, the eyes, the seat and the image. One who wishes to attain his desired-for objects should offer oblations to the *Mandala*, the sun, moon, Lakshmi and her limbs in one corner, Durgâ, Gana, preceptor and Kashtrāpala (Vishnu) in the Mandal a having the figure of a lotus drawn inside it, four doors painted with dust and sixty four corners.

With the mantram, "Om, Gham, tam, dham, Ham, salutation unto the great Lakshmi" he should adore Lakshmi together with all the members of the family as narrated before.

Om, Soum, salutation unto Saraswati. Om, Hrim, Soun, salutation unto Saraswati. Om, Hrim, say, say. O goddess of speech, Swāhā. Om, Hrim, salutation unto Saraswati.

—:o:—

CHAPTER XI.

I WILL now describe the mode of adorning the nine *Vyuhas* as narrated unto Kashyapa. Having drawn up the

* A level square piece of ground prepared for a sacrifice.

† Supernatural powers acquired by Yoga. The word *Siddhi* may also mean "the accomplishment of the object for which a religious rite is undertaken."

vital breath through the head one should place it in the sky through the navel. Then with the mantram *Ram* he should consume the body identical with the up-going vital air. And he should destroy all with the mantram *Yam*. With the mantram *Lam* he should overflood the entire world mobile and immobile. Then with the mantram *Vam* he should meditate on ambrosia. Thereupon by *dhyana* (meditation) he should think of the four-armed deity, clad in a yellow raiment, in the middle of the bubble, as well as of his bathing. He should next perform the three-fold *mantra-nyasa** ceremony of the fingers and body.

After the recitation of this mantram, with one composed of twelve letters, he should make assignment of six limbs so that Hari himself might appear there. Beginning with the thumb of the right hand he should assign the middle finger to the petal. Having assigned the two *Vijas* in the middle he should assign them to the other limbs viz, heart, head, the crown of the head where lies the tuft of hair, mouth, eyes, belly, back, arms, hands, thighs and feet. Having converted the hand into the shape of a lotus he should place the thumb in the middle. And there he should meditate on the Lord of all, the great undecaying Principle. Then in order he should assign all the other mantrams to fore and other fingers. He should then in order make assignment of the head, eyes, mouth, throat, heart, navel, buttock, thighs and feet. Having assigned the mantrams of six limbs or parts to the palms he should assign others to the body. He should assign the five mantrams to the five fingers beginning with the thumb and ending with the youngest.

He should assign the mantram of the eye to the hand and then make assignment of other limbs. Having assigned heart to the heart he should assign head to the head, Sikhā (tuft of hair) to the Sikhá and amulet to the entire body.

* The assignment of mystic syllables to various deities.

Eyes should be assigned to the eyes and the weapon to the two hands. Having bound all the quarters with the weapon he should commence the rite of adoration. First of all with a controlled mind he should meditate on *Yogapitha* (the seat of yoga) in his heart, and in due order on religion, knowledge, disassociation from the world, and prosperity. He should assign iniquity &c. to the north-east and east. The body, free of all these sins, should be then converted into *Pitha* (seat). He should afterwards assign Ananta. Having meditated first, by means of the Vedas &c. on learning, the eight quarters like unto eight petals of a lotus born in a tank, a white lotus of a hundred petals covered with filaments he should meditate on Mandalas identical with the sun, moon and fire and then think of the deity on one above the other. He should then perform the assignment of eight energies of Keshava stationed in the east and of the ninth in the pericarp.

Having thus meditated on and adored the *Yogapitha*, he should invoke the lord thereof, Hari, the holder of Shrānga bow and assign him there. He should assign heart &c to the lotuses of the four quarters, east &c., the eye in the middle and the weapon in the corners. He should assign the mantrams of Sangkarshana &c. to the east and other quarters and Vinatā's son to the eastern and western doors and the discus Sudarshana of a thousand rays to the southern gate. He should assign Shree to the south, Lakshmi to the north, the club to the northern gate and the conch-shell to the corners.

An intelligent worshipper should place the Shrānga bow either on the right or on the left of the deity. Similarly conch-shell and discus should be placed on both the sides. According to the distinction of their respective quarters all the guardian deities thereof should be assigned. In the same way the various weapons, such as thunder-bolt &c., should be assigned. He should meditate on Brahma upwards and

Ananta downwards. Having meditated on and adored them all he should display *Mudra*.*

Anjali (the folding of palms) is the first *Mudra* which speedily secures the favour of the deity. *Vandani* is the next when it is placed on the breast with the right hand raised half-way up. *Urdhangustha* (thumb raised up) is formed by the clasping of the fist of the left hand with the thumb of the right hand. In this the thumb of the left hand should be raised up. These are the three ordinary forms arranged according to the difference of the forms of the idols.

With the intertwining of the youngest finger eight *Mudras* are formed in order. These should be formed with the recitation of the first eight mantrams. With the thumb the three sucessive fingers ending with the youngest should be bent. Then the two hands should be bent. This is the *Mudra* of *Narasimha* (man-lion). Having raised up the left hand he should whirl it. This is the *Mudra* approved of Varâha (the boar-form). Having raised up the two fists he should straighten the fingers of the one and then bend all of them. This *Mudra* is called *Anga*. Having intertwined in order the two fists the *Mudras* for the ten guardian deities of the quarters should be formed. The first vowel, the second, the last but one and the last should be in order assigned to Vâsudeva, Bala, Kâma and Aniruddha. "Om, *Tatsat*, Hum, Kshroum, Bhus" are the mantrams for Narayana, Brahma, Vishnu, the man-lion and Boar forms. White, red, green, violet, blue, dark-blue, crimson, cloud-colour, fire-colour, honey-colour and twany colour are the nine names.

Kan, tan, jam, pam, Sham, Garutman.

Jam, Kham, ban, Sudarshana. Kham, cham, pham, Sham, the club.

Vam, lam, man, Ksham, conch-shell. Gham, dham Vam, bham, Ham, Shree. Gam, jam, dam, vam, Sham, nourishment.

---

* A mode of intertwining of the fingers during religious worship.

Dham, Vam, the garland of the forest flowers. Dam, Sam, is for the mystic mark Srivatsa.

Chham, dam, pam, Yam is for the jewel Koustava.

He should then say "I am Ananta" These are the ten limbs of the Lord of gods.

Garuda is smoke-coloured. The club is white. Pushti (nourishment) is of the colour of a Sirish flower. Lakshmi is gold-hued. The conch-shell is effulgent like the full-moon. Srivatsa is of the colour of a Kunda flower. The garland is of five colours. Ananta is of the colour of a cloud. All the weapons described before are of the hue of lightnings.

According to the light of the science of the lotus-eyed deity one should offer Arghya, Pâdhya (water for washing feet) &c.

—:o:—

CHAPTER XII.

HARI said:—I will describe the order of adoration for achieving the success thereof.

The recollection of the great soul should be made with the mantrams, "Om, Salutation, &c."

With the mantram "Yam, Vam, Lam, Ram" the purification of the body should be performed.

With the mantram "Om, salutation" the image of the four-armed deity should be made.

Then the three sorts of the making of idols should be made. Then follows the adoration of *Yoga-pitha* stationed in the heart.

Om, salutation unto Ananta. Om, salutation unto religion. Om, salutation unto disassociation. Om salutation unto knowledge. Om salutation unto prosperity. Om salutation unto sin,

Om salutation unto ignorance. Om salutation unto worldliness. Om salutation unto proverty. Om salutation unto the lotus. Om salutation unto the solar disc. Om salutation unto the lunar disc. Om salutation unto the disc of the fire. Om salutation unto Vimala. Om salutation unto Utkarshina. Om salutation unto knowledge. Om salutation unto action. Om salutation unto ignorance. Om salutation unto inaction. Om salutation unto yoga. Om salutation unto Prarhâ. Om, salutation unto Satya. Om salutation unto Ishana. Om salutation unto Sarvatomukh. Om salutation unto Hari's seat with all its accompaniments, principal and minor. Om salutation unto Vāsudeva. Om salutation unto the heart. Im, salutation unto the head. Um salutuation unto Shikha (tuft of hair on the head). Em, salutation unto the amulet. Oum salutation unto the three eyes. As, phat, salutation unto the weapon. Am, salutation unto Sangkarshana. Am salutation unto Pradyumna. As salutation unto Aniruddha. Om, As salutation unto Narayana. Om, *Tatsat* salutation unto Brahma. Om, Hum, salutation unto Vishnu. Kshroum, salutation unto his man-lion and boar forms. Kam, Tam, Jam, Sham, salutation unto Vinata's son. Jam Khem, Vam, salutation unto Sudarshana. Kham, Cham, Pham, Sham, salutation unto the club. Vam, Lam, Mam, Ksham, salutation unto the conch-shell Panchajanya.

Gham, Dham, Bham, Ham, salutation unto Shree. Gam, Dam, Vam, Sham, salutation unto Pushti. Dham, Vam, salutation unto the garland of white flowers. Dam, Sham, salutation unto Shrivatsa. Chham, Dam, Yam, salutation unto Koustava. Sham salutation unto Shrānga bow. Im, salutation unto the arrows. Cham, salutation unto the leathern fence. Kham, salutation unto the sword, and the lord of the Suras. Dhām, salutation unto the giver of riches and the lord thereof. Ham salutation unto Ishana, the lord of learning. Om, salutation unto the thunder-bolt. Om unto dart. Om unto rod. Om unto sword. Om unto noose, standard, club, and trident.

Lam, salutation unto Ananta the lord of the nether region. Kham salutation unto Brahma, the lord of all the worlds. Om salutation unto the Lord Vāsudeva.

Om, Om, Namas; Om, Nam, Namas; Om, Mom, Namas; Om, Bham, Namas; Om, Gam, Namas; Om, Vam, Namas; Om Tem, Namas; Om Vam Namas; Om Sum, Namas; Om, Dem, Namas; Om, Vam, Namas; Om, Yam, Namas.

Om, Om Namas; Om, Nam, Namas; Om, Mom, Namas; Om, Nam, Namas; Om, Ram, Namas; Om, Yam, Namas; Om, Nam, Namas; Om, Yam, Namas; Om salutation unto Narayana. Om, salutation unto Purusottama.

Salutation unto thee, O thou having lotus eyes; salutation unto thee O creator of the universe, O Subramanya; salutation unto thee, O great Purusha, O thou the first-born.

In Homa rites this mantram ending with the word *Swaha* should be recited. Having duly recited this mantram one hundred and eight times the worshipper should offer *Arghya* and bow unto the Deity again and again. Afterwards having worshipped the fire he should duly adore with his own mantram Achyuta the god of gods.

Having first lighted fire, fed it and whirled it one, conversant with mantrams, should adore it in the Kunda with auspicious results. Having first meditated on all he should assign his mind to the Mandala. Then with the Tattwa called Vāsudeva he should offer one hundred and eight oblations. Then with Sangkarshana and other mantrams he should offer six adorations, three each time to his limbs as well as to the guardian deities of the quarters. Then in the end he should offer *Purnāhuti*. Then he should immerse his own self in the great principle which is beyond the range of speech. Then taking his seat, making again Mudras he should again bow. This is the daily Homa rite; the occasional one requires double the rituals. [He should then say] "Go, go to that great region where dwells the deity who is devoid of passions. May all the deities repair to their respective quarters."

Sudarshana, Shri, Hari, Achyuta, Trivikrama (three foot-steps), Chaturbhuja (four-arms), Vāsudeva, the sixth Pradyumma, Sangkarshana, Purusha are the nine *Vyuhas*. Then comes Aniruddha and Ananta. With all these *Chakras* the gods are known and marked. And they are worshipped in a house along with the Rakshsas and Danavas.

Om Chakrāya Swaha, Om Vichakrāya Swaha, Om Suchakráya Swaha, Om Mahachakraya Swaha, Om, the remover of the Asuras, Hum, phat, Om, Him of thousand flames, Hum, Phat.

This adoration of the discus at the door of the house is auspicious. It gives also protection.

——:o:——

CHAPTER XIII.

HARI said :—I will now describe the most auspicious mantram of Vishnu called *Panjara*.*

Salutation unto thee, O Govinda. Take up thy discus, Sudarshana and protect me in the west, O Vishnu. I have taken refuge with thee. Take up thy club Koumodaki, O lotus-navelled deity, salutation unto thee. Protect me in the south, O Vishnu, I have taken refuge with thee. Salutation unto thee, O Purusottama. Taking up thy plough-share Sunanda, protect me in the east, O Vishnu, I have taken refuge with thee. Taking up thy mace Shatana, O thou having lotus eyes, protect me in the north, O lord of the universe, I have taken refuge with thee. O Hari, taking up

* A mantram of invoking the various weapons and embellishments of Vishnu to one's help.

thy sword, leathern fence, and other weapons, protect me, O destroyer of Rakshasas. I bow unto thee, I am under thy protection. Taking up thy great conch-shell Panchajanya and thy lotus Anudbodha, protect me, O Vishnu, O Boar, in the south-east. Taking up the sun, and moon as well as the sword Chandramasu do thou protect me in the south-west, O thou of a celestial form, O man-lion. Taking up Vaijayanti* and Srivatsa, the ornament of thy throat do thou protect me in the north-west, O god, O Hayagriva. I bow unto thee.

O Janârddana, having ridden Vinata's son do thou protect me in the sky, O thou unvanquished by the Rakshas. I bow unto thee, O thou never defeated. Having ridden Vishālaksha† do thou protect me in the nether region, O tortoise,‡ salutation unto thee. Salutation unto thee, O great fish. O truth, making thy *Vahupanjaram* in the hand, and fingers, do thou protect me, O Vishnu. Salutation unto thee, O Purusottama.

This great *Vishnu Panjara* was thus described unto Shankara, who again described it unto Katyayani. By this she killed the immortal Asura Mahisha, the Dânava Raktavija and other thorns of the celestials. By reciting it with reverential faith a man always destroys his enemies.

—:o:—

CHAPTER XIV.

HARI said :—I will now describe the great Yoga which gives emancipation and enjoyment. The Dhyāyins (yogins)

* Flag or banner of Indra that was given by him to Vishnu.

† Garuda, Literally it means having large eyes.

‡ These are the various forms assumed by Vishnu in his various incarnations.

hold that the Lord Hari is alone to be meditated on. Therefore, listen to it, O great Ishâna.

Vishnu, the lord of all, is the destroyer of sins, without end and devoid of feet and body. He is Vâsudeva, the lord of the universe and identical with Brahman. Although he daily assumes various bodies he is [in sooth] devoid of them all. He is shorn of the natural functions of the body and is devoid of death and decay. Stationed in the six fold objects he is the seer, hearer and smeller and is (at the same time) above the reach of organs. He is devoid of the functions of senses, the creator and has no name or family. The deity is in the mind but does not himself possess it. He is devoid of mental faculties, discriminative knowledge and knowledge. He perceives all by intellect, is stationed in it, the witness of all and omniscient; (and at the same time) he is devoid of intellect. He is devoid of the functions of intellect, is all, present every where, and is in the mind of all. He is freed from vital airs and is devoid of their actions. But he is the vital principle of all creatures, of a quiescent soul and divorced from fear. He is shorn of *Ahankara* (egoism) and other principles and devoid of their natural actions. But, he is their witness, the ordainer thereof and of the form of great felicity. He is the witness of the various states of of waking, dreamless sleep and dreaming sleep and himself is above them all. But he is *Turiya*,* the great ordainer, of the form of the quarter and devoid of gunas (qualities). He is emancipated, enlightened, undecaying, all-pervading, all-auspicious and always present in self.

Understanding this the men, who meditate on this great Isha (God), attain to his form. There is no need of ascertaining actions in this matter. O Shankara, O thou of good vows,

---

* The fourth state of the soul in which it becomes one with Brahman or the Supreme spirit.

I have thus described the Dhyâna. He, who always reads it attains to the region of Vishnu.

—:o:—

CHAPTER XV.

RUDRA said:—O Lord, O Janārddana, do thou describe unto me the Great Being by reciting whose name a man may cross the dreadful ocean of Samsara.*

HARI said:—Reciting the thousand names of Vishnu, the Demiurgus, the great Brahman, the Absolute, Undecaying Self, a man attains to emancipation. O bull-emblemed deity, hear with fixed attention, I will describe this sacred and great object of recitation (*Japa*) which destroys all sins.

He is Vāsudeva, the great Vishnu, Vâmana (Dwarf),† Vasava, Vasu, effulgent like the newly risen sun, and the highly powerful Balabhadra. He fettered (the Asura) Bali, is the all-knower, the worshipful knower of the Vedas and the poet. He is the creator of the Vedas, of the form of the Vedas, worthy of being known and filled with the Vedas. He is the knower of the Vedangas,‡ the lord of the Vedas, the mine of strength and the aggrandiser of the strong. He is without changes, the lord of boons, the giver of boons, and

* Commonly worldliness—but really it is the transmigatory series.

† An incarnation of Vishnu in which he put down the great Asura Bali, who had grown excessively powerful by his rigid austerities.

‡ Certain classes of works regarded as auxilliary to the Vedas, and designated to aid in the correct pronounciation and interpretation of the text and the right employment of the Mantras in ceremonials. They are six in number, *viz.*, (1) *Siksha*, the science of proper articulation and pronounciation; (2) *Chhandas*, the science of prosody; (3) *Vyakarana* grammar; (4) *Nirukta*, elymological explanation of difficult Vedic words (5) *Jyotish*, Astronomy; (6) *Kalpa*, ritual or ceremonial.

the master of Varuna. He is the slayer of heroes, the great hero and the great Ishwara adored of all. He is the soul, the great soul, the inward self and above the sky. He is lotus-navelled, the Padmaniddhi,* the lotus-handed and the holder of club. He is the Great, above the elements, the foremost Purusha and the Demiurgus. He is lotus-waisted, Pundarika wears a garland of lotuses and is beloved of all. He is lotus-eyed, Padmagarbha,† Parjanya (rain-god) and seated on a lotus. He is beyond the range of all, the great object, the greatest of the great lord. He is most learned of all learned men, holy and destroyer of sins. He is pure, manifests all, holy and the protector. He is devoid of thirst, Padya,‡ the Purusha and Prakriti (Nature). He is Pradhāna (intellectual principle), the lotus, the earth, the lotus-navelled and the giver of desirable objects. He is the lord of all, present every where, the All, Omniscient, the giver of all and the great. He is identical with all and the entire universe, the witness and up-holder of all. He is the Deity who shows favour unto all and is stationed in the hearts of all creatures. He is the protector of all, is adored of all and is saluted by all the deities. He is at the root of the entire universe, is the destroyer of all and the fire. He is the protector of all, pervades all and the cause of all causes. He is meditated on by all, the friend of all and the holder of the various forms of the deities. He is the object of the study of all, the commander of the celestials and is adored of the gods and Asuras. He is

* One of the nine treasures of Kuvera, *viz.*, Padma, Mahapadma. Sankha, Makara, Kachhapa, Mukunda, Nanda, Nila and Kharva; their nature is not exactly defined though some of them appear to be precious jems; according to the Tantrik system, they are personified and worshipped as demi-gods attendant either upon Kuvera or Lakshmi. Here the term is an epithet of Vishnu.

† Name of Brahma, meaning from born of a lotus. Here it is an epithet of Vishnu showing that he is identical with Brahma.

‡ Water for cleaning feet. This shows that Vishnu permeates every object in the world.

always the destroyer of the wicked and Asuras. He is the protector of truth, the centre of good people, the lord of Siddhas, is adored by them, is obtained by the Siddhas and the Sadhyas and the lord of their hearts.

He is the refuge of the world, the auspiciousness, the doer of good, beautiful, humble, truthful and having truth for prowess. He is stationed in truth, of a true determination, the knower and giver of truth. He is religion, the observer of religious rites and a Karmin (one who practises religious rites) but he is devoid of all actions. He is the ordainer of actions, the action itself and the practice of religious rites. He is the lord of Shree and of men, beautiful, the lord of all, but himself having no master. He is the lord of the celestials, the master of Vrishnis, of Hiranyagarbha and of the destroyer of Tripura. He is the lord of the beasts, Vasus, Indra, Varuna, trees, wind, fire, Yama, Kuvera, stars, medicinal herbs and trees. He is the master of the Nagas, of the sun, of Daksha, of friends and of kings. He is the master of the Gandharvas, the most excellent lord of the Asuras, of the mountains and rivers. He is the most powerful lord of the celestials, of Kapila, of creepers and of Veerudhas (spreading creepers). He is the master of the ascetics, the most excellent lord of the sun, moon, and of Shukra. He is the lord of planets, Rakshasas, the Kinnaras and the most excellent master of the twice-born ones. He is the lord of the rivers, oceans, lakes and goblins. He is the master of the Vetalas, Kushmandas, birds and beasts.

He is the high-sould Mangala, Mandara, the lord of Mandara. He is creator of Meru and Mädhava and devoid of mind. The great deity wears a garland and is adored by Mahâdeva. He is of a quiescent soul, and is the illustrious slayer of Madhu. He is highly powerful, the great vital air and is lauded by Mārkandeya. He is identical with Màyā (illusion), fettered by it and devoid of it. He is lauded by the ascetics and is their friend. He has a nose, big cheeks, big arms, big teeth and is freed from death. He has a huge mouth, a great soul, a great body, a great belly, big feet and a high neck. He is greatly respected, is high-minded, of great intellect, of great fame, of great form and the great Asura. He is Madhu, he is Mādhava, he is Mahàdeva, and he is Maheshwara. He is adored in sacrifices, of the form of a sacrifice and is the worshipped lord of the sacrifices. He is the great wind, the great luck and the superhuman Mahesha. He is man, Manu and does good unto men. He is deer, is adored by them and is their lord. He is the master of Mercury, Venus, Saturn, Ràhu and Ketu. He is the good mark and is endued with it; he has long lips and is handsome to look at. He is bedecked with various ornaments and besmeared with sandal of different kinds. His face is painted effulgent with various colours and adorned with diverse flowers. He is Râmà, the great Iswara with his consort. He gives jewels and takes them away. He is with and without any boon. He is of a great, terrific and calm appearance. He is like unto a blue cloud, is pure and resembles a cloud at the end of a cycle. He is smoky cloud, of yellow hue, of various forms and without any colour. He is of a distorted figure, the giver of forms and is white-hued. He is of all colours, the great yogin, the sacrificer. He is gold-hued and is called gold. His body is made of gold and he puts on a golden girdle. He is the giver of gold or parts of it. He is fond of gold and houses made of gold. He is beautiful and of huge wings and the creator of Suparna. He is Vinatā's son, the sun, the beginning, the the creator of beginning and auspiciousness. He is the cause of the intellectual principle, of the Puranas, of intellect and mind. He is the efficient cause of consciousness, egoism, elements of fire, ether, earth, egg and Prakriti (Nature). He is the cause of the body, eyes, ears, skin, tongue, vital breath, hand, foot, speech and the organ of generation. He is the efficient cause of Indra, Kuvera, Yama, Ishàna and the most excellent creator of Yakshas and Rakshasas. He is the most excellent cause of ornaments, virtue, creatures, Vasus (gods of riches), of Manus and of birds. He is the foremost cause of the ascetics, the Yogins, the Siddhas, the Yakshas, the Kinnaras and Gandharvas.

He is the cause of the river, male and female, the oceans and trees. He is the cause of Veerudhas, the worlds, the nether region and celestials. He is the cause of serpents, the auspiciousness, the beasts and of all.

He is identical with the body, the organs of sense, the soul, the intellect, the mind, egoism, consciousness, the condition of waking, that of dreaming sleep, the intellectual principle and the great soul.

He is identical with ether, water, and the great soul of earth and air. He is the great soul of the smell, colour, sound, speech and touch. He permeates, as the great soul, the ears, skin, tongue, nostrils, hand, foot, organ of generation. He permeates Indra, Brahmā, Rudra, Manu, and the Patriarch Daksha. The great is identical with truth. He is identical with Isha, the great soul, the Rudra and the Yati conversant with the knowledge of emancipation. He is energetic and is the very energy itself. He is the holder of the leathern fence and sword and the destroyer of the Asuras. He is modest by nature and engaged in the well-being of the ascetics. Hari is of the form of a Yatin, a Yogin and is meditated on by the Yogins. He is Shiti.* He is perfect knowledge, genius, time, summer, rainy season, determination, year, the ordainer of emancipation and destroyer of Moha (stupifaction). He stupefies the wicked, is Mandavya and mare-mouthed. He is Sangvartaka (fire), the creator of time, Goutama, Bhrigu, Angira, Atri, Vashistha, Pulaha Pulastya, Kutsa, Yajnavalka, Devala, Vyasa, Parāshara, Sharmada, Gāngeya, Hrishikesha, Vrihatshrava and Keshava. He is the destroyer of miseries, has beautiful ears and is without them. The great Narayana is the lord of Prana, of

* Literally "white or black." It is an epithet of Shiva.

vital air the Apāna, of Vyāna, of Udana and of Samana. He is the best master of sound, touch and colour. He is the master of the destruction of the world, the first-born, has a sword in his hand, the plough-share for his weapon, the discus in his hand, the Kundalas [on his ears] and the mystic mark Srivatsa on his breast. He is Prakriti, has the Koustava gem on his neck and is clad in a yellow raiment. He has a beautiful face, an ugly face and is without any. He is without end, of endless forms, has beautiful nails and is the handsomest of all the celestials. The lord Vishnu has a beautiful quiver and most resplendent arrows. He is the destroyer of Hiranyakashipu, the grinder of Hiranyaksha, the killer of Putanā and Bhàskaranta. He is the grinder of Keshin, and Mushtika. He is the killer of the demon Kansa, of Chānura and Aristha. He is fond of Akrura. He is without wickedness, is wily and is adored by those who are fond of simplicity. He is the destroyer of the lordly powers, is himself endued with them, the sun and the Lord himself. He is Uddhava, Uddhava's lord, and is being meditated on by Uddhava. He is the holder of discus, is fickle and is devoid of the moveable and immoveable properties. He is egoism, determination, mental faculties, the sky, earth, water, air, eye, ear, tongue, nose, palate, hand, foot, waist and the organ of generation. He is Shankara, the giver of auspiciousness, the giver of endurance; and he forgives men. He is fond of his votaries and is their protector. He is endued with reverential faith and himself increases it. He is lauded by his votaries, devoted to them and gives fame; and he multiplies it.

He is fame, resplendence, forgiveness, patience, reverential faith, compassion, the great, the gift, the giver, the agent of action, is fond of the celestials, is purity, is pure, the giver of felicity, emancipation and the object of desire. He has a thousand feet. He is the thousand-headed physician who opens the gate of emancipation. He is the door of subjects, has a thousand ends and a thousand hands. He is Shukra, has a beautiful head-gear, and a beautiful neck. He is Keshava, Pradyumna, Aniruddha, Hayagriva, Shukara (boar), Matysa (fish), Parashurâma, Pralhāda and Bali. He is daily sought by people for help, enlightened, emancipated and the holder of forms. He is the destroyer of Khara and Dushana and the grinder of Rāvana. He is the husband of Sita and the prosperous Bharata. He is the killer of the victor of Kumbhendra, the grinder of Kumbhakarna, the destroyer of the killers of men and celestials. He is the destroyer of the wicked Asuras and the enemy of Shamvara. He is the destroyer of (the demon) Naraka as well as of the three-headed demon. He broke down [the trees] Yamala and Arjuna and always helps asceticism. He plays on the musical instrument and is himself the instrument. He is enlightened and the giver of boons. He is the substance and is fond of substances. He is Soura and the destroyer of time and is incapable of being cut. He is Agastya, Devala, Nàrada, and fond of Nārada. He is Prana, Apäna, Vyana (vital airs), the qualities of Rajas (darkness), Sattwa (goodness) and Tamas (ignorance). He is beyond Tamas (ignorance). He is Udana, and Samana (vital airs). He is medicine and the medical man.

He is perpetually and universally the same. His form is transparent and he is devoid of any form. He is devoid of the organs of vision and speech, of hands, fat, the organs of generation and excretion. He is devoid of great asceticism. He is devoid of perception, intellect, consciousness and vital airs, Prana, Apana, Vyana, Udana and Samana.

He is devoid of the ether and fire, water and earth. He is devoid of sound, touch and all colours. He is devoid of carnal passion and other inferior appetites. He is shorn of grief and the power of speech. He is devoid of the quality of *Rajas* (darkness) and six-fold deviations from the natural state. He is devoid of sexual passion, anger, avarice, and pride. He is the subtlest of the subtle and the grossest of the gross. He is clever, leader of the strong and the agitator of all. He agitates Prakriti (nature), Mahat (intellectual principle), the elements, intellect, the organs of sense and of the objects thereof. He is the agitator of Brahma and Rudra. He is beyond the range of vision and hearing. Skin cannot touch him. He is tortoise. Tongue cannot perceive him. He is beyond the range of smelling and speech. The hands and feet cannot reach him. Hari is beyond the range of mental and intellectual perception and understanding. He is within the comprehension of the sense of ego and mental faculties.

He holds the conch-shell in his hand, is undecaying and holds also the club and Shrānga bow in his hands. He is dark-blue, the image of knowledge and the scorcher of the enemies. He is within the range of the knowledge of the ascetics; he is endued with knowledge and knows all by his knowledge. He is comprehended by knowledge and manifests the consciousness of the objects of knowledge. He is the soul, object of mental perception, the creator of the world and the destroyer of it. He is Govinda, the lord of kine and the giver of felicity unto the cow-herds. He is the protector of kine, the master of kine, Gomati and Godhara. He is Upendra, Nrisimha, Shouri, Janārddana, Araneya, Vrihatbhanu and highly effulgent. He is Dámodara, the three-fold time, cognizant of time and devoid of time. He is the three-fold Sandhya (periods of conjuction), is Dwapara, Treta, the creator of subjects and of the foot steps. He is powerful and holds a rod in his hand. He holds one and three rods in his hand. He is the division of the Samaveda, its means, of the form of Saman and the chanter of Saman. He is conversant with Atharvan Veda and is the preceptor thereof. He is the Rik of the Rik Veda and is stationed there. He is the reader of the Yayush, the Yayurveda itself and is conversant with the rituals thereof. He has one foot, many feet, beautiful foot, a thousand feet, four feet, two feet.

The powerful lord is like unto Smriti and Nyaya. He is a Sanyasin (disassociated from the world, and is the four orders of hermit &c viz, a Brahmacharin (student), Grihasta (householder), Vānaprasta (retired into forest) and Bhikshsu (a hermit living on alms). He is the four Varnas (castes) viz the Brahmanas, the Kshatryas, the Vaishyas and the Shudras. He gives good character, is endued with the same and devoid of a bad character. He is emancipation, is engaged in spiritual communion, is the encomiastic verse, the encomiast and the worshipper. He is worshipful, the speech, the object of speech and the speaker. He is the knower, the grammar, the word and is conversant with words.

He is within the reach of words, lives in sacred shrines, is the sacred shrine and is conversant with the knowledge of all the shrines. He is resident in all the sacred shrines, is Sankhya, Nirukta and the presiding deity thereof. He is *Pranava*,* the lord of *Pranava* and is adored with *Pranava*. He is *Gayatri*† and the holder of club. He lives in Shalagrama and is Shālagrama itself. He resides in water, lies in Yoga, on Sesha and Kushâ. He is the earth, is the action, the cause and the holder of the earth. He is the Patriarch, and the eternal. He is the object of desire and the universal creator of desire. He is the Lord Paramount, the sun, the heaven, is stationed on a car and the strength of the charioteer. He is rich, the giver of riches, blessed and engaged in the well-being of the Yadavas. He is the favourite of Arjuna and he is both Arjuna and Bhima. Unbearable is his prowess and he is a master of all the

---

* The sacred syllable *Om*, an abbreviation of the Hindu triad, *viz*, Brahma, the creative force, Vishnu, the protecting force and Shiva, the destructive force. These three forces or the deities presiding over them are represented by *Om*. The abbreviation is intended for the purpose of recitation. The prayers and sacred hymns and mantrams of the Hindus are all presented by *Om*.

† The sacred verse which the Brahmanas recite. It is one of the verses of the Rik veda, embodying the worship of the sun-god.

scriptures. He is Saraswati, the great Bhishma and the captor of Parijata flowers. He is the giver of ambrosia, the ocean of milk and the milk itself. He is the protector of Indra's son and the upholder of the mount Govardhana. He is the destroyer of Kansa, the master of his elephant and the killer of the same. He is Shipidisthe* (pervaded by rays), cheerfulness and the destroyer of the calamities of all people. He is Mudra, the maker of Mudras and is devoid of all Mudras. He is endued with a body, is stationed in a body and the organizer of the body. He is the hearer, the creator of the ears, the object of hearing and the power of hearing. He is stationed in skin, is one who touches, the object and power of touching. He resides in the eye, is the seer of forms and the creator of the eye and is the object of vision. He resides in the tongue, has a strong taste and is the organiser of taste. He resides in smell, creates smell, himself smells and is the creator of the organ of smelling. He resides in speech, is the speaker, the object of speaking, the power of speech and the creator of the same. He resides in vital airs. He is the creator of fine arts, is the fine art itself and the creator of hands. He is the foot, the agent of going, the place of going and the power of going. He is the ordainer of gifts, is stationed in the organ of generation and is the pleasure. He is the slayer of enemies, Kārtavirya, Dattātreya, is engaged in the well-being of Alarka and is the destroyer of Kartavirya. He is Kàlanemi, Mahānemi, the cloud and the lord of clouds. He is the giver of food, of the form of food, the eater of food and the ordainer of food. He creates smoke and is of a smoky form. He is the most excellent son of Devaki. He is the delight of Devaki, Nanda and Rohini. He is a favourite of Vasudeva and his son. His smiles are both like Dundhuvi (trumpets) and flowers. He is fond of laughing aloud. He is the lord of

* An epithet of Vishnu.

all, decaying and undecaying. He is Achyuta (undecaying), the lord of truth and is fond of truth. He is the most beloved husband of Rukshmini. He is the favourite of milk women and his piety has been sung in well known verses. He is Vrishàkapi, Yama, Guhya, Mangala, Budha, Ràhu, Ketu, the crocodile and the union of the mouths of the elephants. He is the destroyer of crocodiles and the protector of the headmen of villages. He is the Kinnara, Siddha, the Prosody and easiness. He is of the universal form, of large eyes and the slayer of the Daityas. He is of endless forms, is stationed in elements, in the celestials and Danavas. He exists in dreamless sleep, is dreamless sleep itself and is the place for it. He exists in an awakened state, is the agent and the place thereof. He exists in the state of dreamless sleep, is conversant with it and is the dream itself. He also exists in the fourth state devoid of these three states of dreamless sleep, dreaming sleep and awakening. He is the discriminating knowledge, is Chaitra, the sentiency and the creator of sentiencies. He is the lord of the worlds and the ordainer of the worlds. He resides in the nether region, the nether region itself and the destroyer of all sorts of feverish complaints. He is of the form of great felicity and the propounder of various forms of faith. He is easily accessible, and accessible with difficulty. He is engaged in Prānāyāma (suppression of vital. air). He is Pratyahara,* Dhārака† and the maker of Pratyahara. He is effulgence, personal grace, rays, pure and like unto crystal. He is above

* It is the Yogic process of restraining the organs of senses from suscipitibility to outward impressions, and directing them entirely to mental perceptions. This is one of the means for effecting the entire subjugation of the senses.

† Steady thought; retention or holding of the image or idea formed in the mind by contemplation.

perception, white coloured, the all and pure. He is Vashatkar,* Vashat, Voushat, Swadhâ, Swâhā and inclination thereto. He is the agent of cooking, giving delight, eating, understanding and thinking. He is identical with knowledge and understanding. He is the Great and the Creator of all Creators. He is the river, Nandi,† the lord of Nandi and the destroyer of the trees of India. He is the holder of discus, the husband of Shree and the king of the Lords Paramount. He is the master of all the celestials and is the leisure. He is Pushkara,‡ the lord of Pushkara and the Pushkara island. He is Bharata, Janaka, Janya§ and is devoid of all forms. He is without any form, without any cause, without any fear and without any help. O bull-emblemed deity, I have thus described to you the thousand names of the Lord Vishnu destructive of all sins. By reading them a Brahmana attains to Vishnu-hood, a Kshatriya acquires victory, a Vaishya acquires riches and a Shudra is endued with reverential faith in Vishnu.

—:o:—

CHAPTER XVI.

RUDRA said :—O holder of conch-shell, discus and club, do thou again describe the Dhyana (meditation) of the Deity, the Lord Vishnu, the pure, impersonal self.

HARI said :—Hear, O Rudra, Hari's *dkyana*, destructive of the tree of transmigatory series, never seen before, extending all over and eternal. It is undecaying, present always

---

* An exclamation used in making an oblation to a deity with the dative form of the deity.

† The attendant of Shiva. It may also mean the character in a drama who introduces the prelude.

‡ Literally it means a "lotus." It is an epithet of Krishna.

§ Father.

and every where and consists only in the thought "I am Brahma." [Meditate on him as] the root of the entire world, the lord of all, the Great Demiurgus, as stationed in the hearts of all creatures, as the great lord of all creatures. He is the container of all, having none to contain him and is the cause of all causes. He does not come in contact, is emancipated and is being meditated on by emancipated Yogins. He is without the gross body, the eyes, organs of vitality, the action of vital airs, the organs of generation and execretion, the organs of sense, the mind, the action of mind, intellect, mental faculties, egoism, the action of intellect, the vital airs, Prāna, Apāna and their actions.

HARI said:—I will describe again the adoration of the sun which had been related formerly unto Bhrigu.

Om salutation unto Khakholka.

This is the principal mantram of the sun affording emancipation and objects of enjoyment.

Om salutation unto God Khakholka. Om unto rays ta, ta, salutation unto the head. Om unto knowledge, salutation unto the tuft of hair on the head. Om unto him of thousand, ta, ta, salutation unto the amulet.

Om salutation unto the master of all light. Ta, Ta, salutation unto the weapon. Om, burn, burn, burn burn, ta, ta, salutation.

This is the fiery mantram of the sun destructive of the sin.

Om Adityāya, Vidmahe, Vishwabhavaya dhimahi, Tanna Suryye Prachodayat.

The worshipper should perform the *Sakalikarana* rite with this Gayatri of the sun. He should worship Dharma in the east, Yama in the south, Dandanāyaka and Vaivarna in the north, dark-blue, twany and other colours in north-east and north-west, the holder of thunder-bolt in the south-west and the earth and sky in the north-west.

Om salutation unto the moon the lord of stars. Om salutation unto egoism the son of the earth. Om, salutation unto Budha, the son of Soma. Om salutation unto the lord of speech, the master of all forms of learning. Om salutation unto Bhrigu's son, the great saint Shukra. Om salutatation unto Shani (Saturn) the son of the sun. Om salutation unto Rāhu. Om salutation unto Ketu.

In all the quarters beginning with the east and ending with the north-east all these should be adored, O bull-emblemed deity.

Om salutation unto Anuruka. Om salutation unto the lord of Pramathas.* Om salutation unto Budha. O lord! O thou endued with immeasurable rays! O lord of the entire world! O thou carried by seven horses! O thou having four arms! O thou, the giver of great supernatural powers! O thou twanty-coloured with scintillations! O auspicious deity, take this *arghya*. Salutation unto thee. Take this dreadful fire. Burn, burn, ta, ta, salutation.

Having invoked the sun-god with this mantram he should make the *Visarjana* (life-destroying rite) with the following mantram.

Om salutation unto the sun endued with six lordly powers, of a thousand rays. Go happily to return again.

——:o:——

CHAPTER XVII.

HARI said:—I will describe the adoration of the sun formerly related unto the god of riches.†

---

* Shiva. † Kuvera.

In a purified place a worshipper should draw the figure of a lotus with eight petals and pericarps. Then making *Avahani* mudra* he should invoke Hari there.

He should place in the middle the diagram form of the sun and sprinkle it with water. He should place the heart of the deity in the quarter presided over by the fire-god. He should place the head in the north-east and the tuft of hair in the south-west. He, having his mind fixed in concentration, should assign Dharma to this quarter presided over by Purandara. He should place his eyes in the north-west and his weapon in the corner presided over by Varuna. He should place Soma in the north-east and *Lohita* in the quarter belonging to Purandara. He should place Soma's son in the east and Vrihaspati in the south. He should place the preceptor of the Danavas† in the south-west and Shani (Saturn) in the corner presided over by Varuna. He should place Ketu in the north-west and Rahu in the quarter presided over by Kuvera.

In the second apartment, he should adore the twelve suns viz Bhaga, Suryya, Aryamā, Mitra, Varuna, Savita, Dhātā, the highly powerful Vivashwan, Twasta, Pusha, and Indra. The twelfth is Vishnu. In the quarters beginning with the east, a man, filled with reverence, should adore Indra and other deities, Jayā, Vijayā, Jayanti, Aparajita, Sesha, Vāsuki and other Nagas.

——:o:——

* A particular kind of the arrangement of fingers made before invoking a particular deity.

† Shukra.

CHAPTER XVIII.

SUTA said :—I will describe the Archnā (adoration) of Mritunjaya (the victor of death) narrated unto Kashyapa by Garuda, which gives redemption, is holy and identical with all the deities.

First Om should be placed, then jumkara and thirdly *Virsarga*. This mantram destroys death and poverty. This great mantram of three letters is the lord of ambrosia. By reciting it people become freed from death and all sorts of sins. By reciting it a hundred times one reaps the fruit of Vedic recitations and of the celebration of sacrifices at sacred places. By reciting it one hundred and eight times at three periods of junction one defeats the Death and his enemies. He should meditate on the lord of ambrosia, seated on a white lotus, the giver of boons, with the promise of protection in one hand and jars full of nectar in two other hands. He should think of the goddess of ambrosia as stationed on his limb, sweet-speeched like ambrosia, holding the pitcher in her right hand and lotus in the left. He, who recites it eight thousand times at the three periods of junction for one full month, becomes freed from decrepitude, death and leprosy, defeats his enemies and gives peace unto all creatures. He is the [real] worshipper who knows the site [of a temple], the placing [of an idol], the suppression of vital airs, the appearance, the temple, water for washing feet, the water for rinsing mouth, the water for bathing, Arghya, Aguru, pastes, lamps, raiments, ornaments, edibles, drinks, drinking water, Matra, Mudra, recitation, meditation, gifts, oblation, the chanting of glories, playing on musical instruments, singing, dancing, Nyāsa (assignment of limbs), yoga, circumambulation, bowing, mantrams, clarified butter, eulogy, (the life-destroying rite) Visarjana, the adoration with six ingredients emanating in order from the mouth of the great Deity.

The Arghya, Padya, &c., should be fanned with a piece of cloth, and then purified with *Kavacha* mantrams and then the rite of Amriti-Karana (conversion into nectar) should be performed. Then *Adhara Saktis** should be adored and Prāṇāyāma (suppression of vital airs) should be practised in the seat. Then the purificatory rite of *Pinda*† should be performed. Then with Agni and other mantrams he should meditate on the self as being identical with the deity. He should then make assignment of hands and other limbs and afterwards adore the self in the form of light stationed in the lotus of the heart. He should then throw shining flowers on the idol or the altar. For the adoration of the door of the self the Adhāra Saktis should be worshipped. And bringing one's self near the deity he worships his family. For the adoration of six Angas (limbs) the quarters should be divided. Dharma and other gods, Shakra and other celestials, the various members of their families and their weapons, the cycles, and the Muhurttas (divisions of time) should be adored. This worship yields enjoyment and emancipation. He should first adore the Matrikas, Ganas, Nandiganga, Mahakāla, Yamuna and Dehalya.

Om salutation unto Bhairava, the lord of ambrosia. Evam, Om, Jum, Sas, salutation unto the sun. In this way adorations should be offered to Shiva, Kṛishna, Brahma, Gana, Chandikā, Saraswati, Mahalakshmi and others.

—:o:—

* Female deities presiding over various articles.

† Balls of food offered to the departed manes.

CHAPTER XIX.

SUTA said :—I will now describe the Praneshwara* rite of Garuda narrated by Shiva.

I shall first describe the places where a person, bitten by a serpent, does not survive, *viz.*, funeral pyre, ant-hill, well, and the cavity of a tree. The person, three lines on whose limbs, are hidden, does not live. [A man dies if he is bitten] in the sixth day of the fort-night, when the sun is in the constellation Cancer, when it is in the Aries, when it is with the asterism Mula or when it is in the Magha† or Ashlesha‡ [A man dies when he is bitten] on the sides, on the loins, on the throat, on the joints or the temple, ears or belly. The *Dandin* (hermit), a person holding weapons, a mendicant and a naked person are the emissaries of Death.§ If a person is bitten on the mouth, arms, neck, and on the back, he does not survive.

Every day the sun, first of all, lords, for half a Yama,|| over all the serpents. Then with six revolutions the six planets lord over them. In the night with five revolutions the five planets lord over them. The sun is the presiding star of Sesha, the moon of Phani, Mars of Takshaka, Jupiter of Karkotyna, Venus of Padma and Mahapadma, Saturn of Shankha, and Rahu of Kuluka and Ahi. Jupiter is the Death itself in both days and nights.¶ Saturn is Death in the day and

---

* It perhaps refers to the rite for counteracting the evil effects of the poison.

† The ninth Nakshatra or lunar mansion containing five stars.

‡ The tenth lunar mansion containing five stars.

§ The meaning is that if these persons are sent for calling a physician the patient dies.

|| Eighth part of a day. A watch of three hours.

¶ If a person is bitten on Thursdays he never survives under any circumstances.

the period when Rahu presides over Kuluka at the hours of the conjunction of two-half Yamas, it is hostile to life.

A day, consisting of sixty *dandas*,* should be distributed over a human body divided into three sections. Five *dandas* should be assigned to the toe, twelve to the feet, five to the calf, two to the knee and one to the organ of generation. Six *dandas* should be assigned to the navel, four to the breast and eight to the throat. Fifteen *dandas* should be allotted to the tip of the nose and one each to the eye, ear, eye-brow, and temple. Then all the days, beginning with *Pratipat*, the first day of a fort night, should be allotted to all the limbs beginning with the head. If the moon lords over the right part of a man's body he does not survive. If it lords over the left part of a woman's body she dies. The benumbed part should be rubbed over with a hand till unconsciousness is not removed.

The great mantram of self, pure like crystal, called Hansa, is to be known as one which counteracts the evil effect of poisoning. Its *Veeja* is of four sorts.

Om, Kuru, Kunde Swāhā.

Formerly this learning was kept by Garuda for protecting the three worlds. Desirous of killing the serpents he assigned *Pranava* to his mouth. An intelligent worshipper should assign *Kuru* to his throat, *Kunda* to the calves, and *Swaha* to the two feet. This *Nyasa* is called *Yugaha*. The serpents leave the house in which this mantram is written. Having recited it a thousand times one should place a thread on his ear. The serpents leave the house in which sugar, after reciting this mantram, is thrown. By reciting it seven lacs of times the celestials and Asuras obtain *Siddhi*.

Om, Swaha unto golden lines, unto him having the form of a fowl.

In this way two letters should written on each petal of a

* One sixtieth part of day and night. Twenty four minutes.

lotus of eighteen petals. When a person, bitten by a snake, is sprinkled with water with this mantram the poison goes out.

Om, pakshi (bird) Swāhā. Then the assignment of all fingers, beginning with the thumb and ending with the youngest finger, should be made in the body. Garuda should be assigned to the mind, mouth, heart, organ of generation and feet. Even in a dream the venomous serpents do not transgress his shadow. He, who recites this mantram for a lac of times, destroys the poison even by his very sight. Om, Hrom, Hroum, Hrim, Bhirundāyai Swāhā.

Having recited this mantram by placing his finger on the ear one should destroy the poison of the person bitten. He should then assign *a*, *ā* to the tips of the feet, *e.i.* to the calves and knees, *u*, *ú*, *a aú* to the waist, or to the navel, and *on* to the heart. He should assign *am* to the mouth and *as* to the head. *Hansa*, when recited, meditated on and adored, destroys all sorts of poison. Having meditated "I am Garuda" he should perform the rite destructive of poison. Having assigned the mantram *Ham* to the body he should say "Destroy poison, &c." Having assigned *Hansa* to the left hand, he should close up his mouth and nostrils. This mantram destroys the poison affecting the skin and flesh. Having attracted it by the air he should remove the poison of the person bitten. He should next assign it to the body of the person bitten and meditate on the blue-throated deity (Shiva). When the juice of the root of *Pratyangira* is drunk with rice it destroys poison. The root of the new *Phalin* is equally effective. When clarified butter is pasted on the head it also destroys poison. If a person drinks up hot *ghee* (clarified butter) the poison is not increased. If the root of *Sirisha* compounded in five parts with one part of red garlic (Grinjana) is pasted all over the body or is drunk it destroys poison.

Hrim destroys the poison of Gonasha (a large kind of

snake *Boa*). When the mantram Hrim ending with *Visarga* is meditated on it brings all under control; when it is assigned to the female organ it brings a maiden under control and clears up the muddy water. Having recited "Garuda is every where" fifty-six thousand times a person becomes a poet, well read in Sruti and obtains a submissive wife. The theme of the Muni Vyasa forsooth destroys poison.

—:o:—

CHAPTER XX.

SUTA said:—I will now now describe the highly secret mantrams narrated by Shiva. His weapons are the noose, the bow, the discus, the club, the dart and Pattisha. Having used these weapons inspired with mantrams in a battle a king conquers his enemies. The mantram for purifying the mantrans should be first written on a lotus petal. Om is the Brahma *Vijam*. Hrim is the Vishnu *Vijam*. These three Vijams should be assigned to the head of Shiva thrice in order.

Om, Hrim, Hrim.

Having taken up the dart in his hand he should whirl it in the sky. By seeing it all the evil stars and serpents are destroyed. Having held the smoky coloured bow by the hand a man should meditate on it in the sky. By it the wicked serpents, the evil stars, clouds and Rakshasas are destroyed. This mantram protects the three worlds, what to speak of the land of mortals?

Om, jum, Sam, Hum, Phat. Eight sticks of Catechu wood, inspired with mantrams, should be placed on the ground. That will prevent the falling of thunder-bolt. The eight sticks should be inspired with great mantram described by Garuda. The ground should be dug twenty one times in the night. This will ward off the dangers proceeding from lightning, mouse, and thunder-bolt.

The mantram is :—Hara, Kshara, amala, Vashat, added with Vindu Sadasiva.

Om, Hram, salutation unto Sadashiva.

He should then assign *pinda* (balls of rice) effulgent like Darimi flowers with the fore-finger. By seeing it the evil clouds, lightning and other enemies viz. the Rakshasas, goblins and female ghosts fly away into the ten quarters.

Om, Hrim, salutation unto Ganesha. Om, Hrim, salutation unto the chakra of Sthambhana.

Om, em, salutation unto the Damaras of the three worlds.

This *pinda* is called Bhairava which counteracts the effect of poison and the evil effects of the hostile planets. It protects the field and grinds the goblins and Rakshasas.

Om, Namas. Having meditated on the thunder-bolt of his hand he should ward off the evil influence of wicked clouds and with Vajra Mudra all the ghosts, the enemies with poison. Om, Kshum, Namas. He should meditate on his left hand. It destroys all venomous creatures.

Om, Hram, Namas. The very recitation of this mantram destroys the evil clouds and stars. Having meditated on death he should consume the universe with the destroying weapon.

Om, Kshma, Namas.

Meditating on Bhairava one should remove the evil influences of stars, goblins and poison.

Om lasat, jhvaksha Swāhā. This mantram destroys the enemies of the field *viz*, the evil stars, goblins, poison and birds.

Om Ksham Namas. The figure of a cistern should be drawn with blood and then the names of planets should be written there.

Om, Mara, Mara, Maraya, Maraya Swāhā. Om, Hum, Phat, Swāhā.

The dart should be inspired mentally with eight hundred mantrams. it destroys all the enemies.

With higher energies the lower ones should be suppressed. Then the mantrams should be practised in *Puraka** and should be again well inspired in *Kumbhaka.*† They should then be received with Pranava. When the mantrams are thus properly received and used they yield fruts like servants.

CHAPTER XXI.

SUTA said:—I will now describes separately the adoration of *Panchavaktra* (five mouths) which yeilds enjoyment and emancipation.

Om bhur [salutation unto] Vishnu, the first bhuta, the stay of all, unto him having a form, Swāhā.

First of all with this mantram invocation of *Sadyajata* (Shiva) should be made.

Om, Ham salutation unto Sadyajata. His *kalas* (parts) are eight in number *viz.* Siddhi, Riddhi, Dhriti, Lakshmi, Medhā, Kānti, Swadhā, Sthiti.

Om, Ham, salutation unto Vāmadeva. His *kalas* are thirteen in number, *viz,* Rājā, Rakshā, Rati, Pālyā, Kanti, Trishnā, Mati, Kriyā, Kāmā, Buddhi, Rati, Trāsani, and Mohini.

---

* A Yogie posture in which the thumb is placed on the right nostril and the fingers raised from the left through which the breath is inhaled.

† The posture in which both nostrils are closed and breathing suspended.

Manonmani, Aghorā, Mohā, Kshudhā, Kala, Nidrā, Mrityu, Maya—these are the eight dreadful Kalas.

Om, Hraim, salutation unto Tatpurusha. His *Kalas* are Nivrithi, Pratishtha, Vidyā, Shanti and Kevalā.

Om, Hroum, salutation unto Ishāna. His *kalas* are Nishchata, Niranjanā, Shashini, Anganā, Marichi and Jvalini.

CHAPTER XXII.

SUTA said :—I will now describe the great adoration of Shiva which yeilds enjoyment and emancipation. He is of a quiescent soul, present every where, void and stationed in a room of twelve parts. His five mouths are represented by five short vowels and his limbs by long vowels added with Vindu. His weapon is represented by Visarga. Then the word Shiva should be written upwards. With the sixth the great mantram Houm impregnated with various meanings should be written. With hands the after parts of the feet should be held and then the ends thereof should be placed on the head. This is the great Mudrā. Then the assignment of hands should be made. With the *astra* mantram the back should be purified. Then beginning with the youngest finger and ending with the fore all the fingers should be assigned.

I will now describe the adoration in the pericarp of the lotus of the heart. One should adore religion, knowledge, disassociation from the world and prosperity in the heart. The invocation and the installation [rites of the Deity], the water for washing feet and Arghya should be dedicated to the heart. And similarly the rinsing of the mouth, sprinkling of water and adoration should be made.

I will now describe the rites of fire worship. They should be written with the *astra* mantram. Then the coat of mail should be sprinkled with water. And *Sakti* should be assigned to the heart. Then he should place fire either in the heart or in the pit for *Sakti*. Having performed the Garbhādhāna he should celebrate the other rites. Afterwards having assigned to the heart the freedom from all those rites as well as all other rites he should perform Homa for Shiva and all the members of his family. Then in a diagram having the figure of a lotus drawn inside it he should worship the bull-emblemed deity Shambhu.

CHAPTER XXIII.

SUTA said:—I will describe the adoration of Shiva by which religious profit, desire &c. are secured. With three mantrams beginning with Om and ending with Swāhā the mouth should be rinsed with water.

Om, Ham, salutation into the principle of self. Hirm, salutation unto the principle of learning. Om, Hum, salutation unto the principle of Shiva Śwaha. The ears should be closed with the heart.

Om, ham, yam, Swaha, are the mantrams for bathing with ashes and offering oblations of water. All the gods and all the Munis should be adored with the mantram "Salutation bhoushat."

All the Pitris and all the Pitamahas (patriarchs) should be adored with mantrams ending with the word Swadhā.

Om, Ham, salutation unto the great grand-fathers. The same is for the maternal grand-fathers. [The next is] Hang, salutation unto all the Matris. Then the vital airs should be suppressed. Then he should rinse his mouth with water, rub his body and recite the Gayatri [which is as follows].

Om, Ham, Tan Maheshaya Vidmahe, Vāgvíshudhaya dhimahi Tanno Rudra Prachodayat.

Then having placed near the sun he should adore him with *Surya* (sun) mantrams. [It is] Om, ham, Him, Hum, Haim, Houm, Has salutation unto Shiva Suryya. Om, Ham salutation unto Kakolka, the form of the sun. Om, Hram, Hrim, Sas, salutation unto the sun. In the same way [the attendants of the sun] Dandina and Pingala should be remembered. Then in the south-east and other corners of the mystic diagram Vinata, Ishā and other powers of the sun should be adored with great felicity. Then he should adore Padmā with the mantram *Ram*, Dipta with the *Sreem*, Sukshma with *rum*, Jayā with *rem*, Bhadrā with *raim*, Bibhuti with *rom* and Vimalā with *Roum*. He should adore lightnings with *Ram*, in the east and other quarters, *rom* in the middle and *ran* on all sides. He should adore the seat of the sun, the form of the sun and the sun itself with the mantram "Hrām, Hrum, Sas."

Om and am are the mantrams for the heart of the sun and his head and tuft of hair. Roum is for heaven, sky and earth. The burning mantram Hum is for the coat of mail; astram is for the initiated queen. The worshipper should adore all in the heart of the sun.

Som is the mantran for Soma, Man for Mangala, Vam for Budha, Vrim for Vrihaspati, bham for Bhargava, Jum for Shani and ram for Rāhu. With Ram one should adore Ketu and with Om the solar disc.

Having adored the sun and rinsed his mouth with water he should assign all the fingers beginning with the youngest.

Ham, Him is the mantram for the head, Hum for Sikhā (tuft of hair), Haim for coat of mail, Houm for eyes and Hos for the weapon. Having thus placed the Sakti he should perform again the nyāsa of *bhuta-suddhi* (purification of elements).

Then making a vessel of arghya, he should sprinkle it with water and then adore the self as being stationed in the lotus, in the exterior with the mantram "Salutation unto Shiva," then Nandi and Mahākāla at the gate, then Ganga, Yamuna, the goddess of speech, (the mystic mark) Srivatsa, the presiding goddess of the land, Brahmā, Gana, the preceptor, Sakti and Ananta in the middle pericarp, Dharma (the god of virtues and others, in the east and other sides, the god of sin (Adharma) and others in the south-east pericarp, Yama and Jejeshtha in the middle pericarp, Roudri, Kāli and Shivāsita in the eastern pericarp of the lotus of the heart. Then the Valavikarini should be adored with the mantram "Om, Houm, salutation unto Valavikarini". The goddess of strength, which subdues all creatures, should be next adored. Then in the pitha before Shiva Manonmani should be adored. He should then make a seat for Shiva and his great image. He should invoke the spirit of Shiva within the image. He should then perform the rites of Sthapanam (installation of the image), Sannidhana, Nirodha, Sakalikarana, Mudra, Arghya, Padya, Achama, Abhyanga, Udvarta, Snāna (bathing) and Nirmanchana (rubbing). Next he should offer raiments, unguents, flowers, incense, lamps, charu (a kind of food) water for rinsing mouth, delightful habitation, betel, umbralla, chowries, and sacred thread. He should then imagine the form of one God, recite his name and dedicate it to him. With eulogy, bowing and [meditation in the] heart this adoration of Nāmānga (Name and limbs) should be finished. Agnisha should be placed in the north-west. He should then adore Indra and other deities and Chanda and dedicate to them offerings, saying "Thou art the mysterious of the mysterious and the protector. Do thou accept this my recitation. O god, may I, by thy favour and on thy being present here, attain success. O god! O thou the giver of fame! do thou destroy all my actions, good or bad whatever I have done who am of the dignity of Shiva. Shiva is the giver, Shiva is enjoyer and Shiva is the entire universe. Shiva is victorious everywhere. I am myself Shiva. O Shiva! thou art the saviour and the leader of the universe. Save thee I have no other lord."

I shall now describe another method of the adoration of Shiva. Gana, Saraswati, Nandi, Mahākāla, Gangā, Yamuna, and the presiding deity of the house—all these should be assigned to the eastern gate. Then should be adored Indra and other deities, earth, water, fire, air, sky, smell, taste, form, sound, touch, speech, hand, feet, the organ of generation, ear, skin, tongue, nose, mind, egoism, nature, man, anger, malice, learning, proper time, improper time, fate, illusion, pure learning, Ishwara (creator) and Sadasiva.

Having known all these as the powers of Shiva an emancipated person, having the true knowledge of the deity, becomes himself Shiva. [He should also meditate] "He who is Shiva is Hari and Brahmā.

—:o:—

CHAPTER XXIV.

SUTA said:—I will now describe the most excellent adoration of Ganas* which gives all and even heaven. The worshipper should adore the seats of Ganas, the images of Ganas and the lord of Ganas. Heart and other limbs should be assigned to Durgā. The sandals of the preceptor, the seat of Durgā and her image should be adored with the

* Troops of inferior deities considered as Shiva's attendants and under the special superintendence of Ganesha.

mantram :—"Hrim, O Durgā, protect." Then assignm ent should be made to the eight Saktis, called Chandikas, viz Rudrachanda, Prachanda, Chandogra, Chandanayika, Chanda, Chandavati and Chandarupa with the mantram "O Durgā, O Durgā, O protectress" Then Vajra, Khanga and other Mudras of Shiva should be adored in the south-east. Then Sadasivā, the lord of goblins and the lotus seat [should be adored.]

Em, Klim, salutation unto Sonstripura. Om, Hram, Hṛim, Kshem, Kshaim, Strim, Skom, Rom, Sphem, Sphom, the lotus seat and the heart &c of Tripura.

Then in the lotus pitha (altar) should be adored Brahmani, Maheshwari, Koumâri, Vaishnavi, Vàrâhi, Indradevatā, Chamundā and Chandika. Then the Bhairavas should be adored. Asitānga, Ruru, Chanda, Krodha, Unmattabhairava, Kapāli, Bhishana, and Samhara, are the eight Bharavas[a]. He should meditate in his heart, in a mandala (diagram) with a lotus inside it and having three corners, on Rati, Priti, Kāmadeva, the five arrows, Yogini, Valuka, Durga, Vighnarāja, Guru (preceptor) and Kshatrapa.

By reciting this mantram for a lac of times and by offering oblations to the fire Tripura gives Siddhi.

CHAPTER XXV.

SUTA said :—Em, Krim, Shrim, Sphem Kshoum, I adore the paduka (shoe), of Ananta-Sakti.

Em, Hrim, Phroum, Kshoum, I adore the *paduka* of Adhārā-Sakti, salutation.

---

[a] These are the personifications of the terrific power of Shiva.

Om, Hum, I dore the *paduka* of Katagni Rudra, salutation. Om, Hrim, Hum, I adore the *paduka* of Hatakeshwara, salutation.

Om, Hrim, Shrim, I adore the seat called Ananta, having the earth, insular continents and the oceans on all sides, salutation.

Hrim, Srim, Nrivritti and other Kalas. Earth and other elements. Ananta and other worlds. Omkar and other letters. The nine syllables Hakar etc. Sadyajāta and other Mantrams.

Ham, the heart and other limbs. This is the mantram of Maheswara. It is identical with the most consummate learning and is the ocean of great ambrosia.

—:o:—

CHAPTER XXVI.

SUTA said :—Thereupon Karanyasa (assignment of hands) and the purificatory rite should be performed. Having formed Padmamudra he should make the assignment of mantrams.

Koum, salutation unto the youngest finger. Noum, salutation unto the nameless (ring) finger. Moum, salutation unto the middle finger. Toum, salutation unto Tarjani. Am, salutation unto Augustha. Lām salutation unto the soles of the hands. Vam, salutation unto the back of hands.

Then Deha (body) Nyāsa. Kam, salutation unto Manivandha. Em, Hrim, Shrim, salutation unto Kāraskara. He should consecrate the hands with Hum Hum, effulgent like the great fire.

Em, Hrim, Hrim, Shrim, Hraim, Saphaim, salutation unto Bhagavate. Sphaim salutation unto Kuvjikâyai.* Hrum,

* An unmarried girl of 8 years.

Hrim, Kroum Anganame of dreadful mouth. Ham, Him, Kilikili, Hrim, Hrim, Shrim, Em, salutation unto Bhagavate of the upper mouth. Sphoum, salutation unto Kuvijakayai of the left mouth. Hrim, Shrim, Hrim, salutation unto Anganame of the southern mouth. Om, Hrim, Shrim, salutation unto Kilikili right mouth. Om, salutation unto Aghoramukhi (dreadful mouthed) of the northern mouth. Om, Namas salutation unto the heart of Bhagavate. Kshem, Em, Kuvjikayai, Sirase (head) Swāhā. Hrim, Krim, Hrim, Pram, Ang, A Na Name, Shikhayai (tuft of hair), Aghoramukhi, Kavachāya, (coat of mail) Hum. Haim; Im, unto three eyes Voushat. Kiliki unto weapons phat.

Em, Hrim, Shrim, salutation unto the mystic diagram of the great dart of a connected circular form. Em, Hrim, Shrim, salutation unto the circular orb of the air. Em, Hrim, Shrim salutation unto the disc of the moon. Em, Hrim, Shrim, salutation unto the mystic diagram of Mahakulavodhāvali. Em, Hrim, Shrim, salutation unto the mystic diagram of Koula. Em, Hrim, Shrim, salutation unto the mystic diagram for the preceptor. Em, Hrim, Hrim, salutation unto the mystic diagram of the Saman. Em, Hrim, Shrim, salutation unto the diagrams of the principal and minor pithas of all Siddha yoginis, of all the principal fields and minor ones and of all their offspring.

These twelve mystic diagrams should be adored in order of succession.

CHAPTER XXVII.

SUTA said:—Om, O thou the skeleton of Kāla and Vikāla! O Chandini! O thou the destroyer of creatures! O thou the venom of serpents! O Virathanarayani! O Uma! O thou of burning hand! O Chandā! O Roudri! O Māheswari, O thou of a huge mouth, O thou of a burning mouth! O thou having dart-like ears! O Sukamundha! O thou the destroyer of all, destroy the enemies. Khakha, thou dost look at all with thy entire body covered with blood. O goddess Manasā! Stupify all, stupify all. O goddess! thou art born in the heart of Rudra, thou art stationed there and thou dost appear in a terrific form. Protect, Protect Mam, Hum, Mam, Phapha, Tata, O thou wearing a girdle of beads. O thou destroyer of the poison of plants and enemies. O O Shālā! O Mālā! Hara, Hara, Vishoka, Ham, Ham! Shavari, Hum, Shavari, Prakonavishare! Sarve! Vinchamegha Mile! It is destructive of the poison of all serpents.

CHAPTER XXVIII.

SUTA said:—I will now describe the adoration of Gopāla which yeilds emancipation and enjoyment. In the door Dhātā, Vidhātā, Gangā with Yamunā, the Nidhis Sangka and Padma, Sharanga, Sharabha and Shree should be adored. In the east should be adored Bhadra and Subhadra, in the south Chanda and Prachanda, in the west Vala, and Pravala and Jaya and Vijaya in the north. In the four doors Shree, Gana, Durgā and Saraswati should be adored.

In the south-east and other corners of the field Nārada, Siddhas, the preceptor, Nalakuvara should be adored. In the east the worshipper should adore Vishnu, his asceticism and power. Then in the middle he should adore the family of

Vishnu, the Saktis, the tortoise, Ananta, earth, religion, knowledge and disassociation from the world. He should adore prosperity in the south-east and the manifest self in the north. He should then adore the Sattwa guna identical with Prakriti (nature), and Rajas identical with Moha (stupefaction) and Tamas, the lotus and the principle of egoism, learning, the great principle and the solar and lunar discs. Then in the east he should adore Vimala and other seats with the mantrams Shrim, Hrim, salutation unto the dearest lord of milk-men, Swāhā. This is the mantram.

In the eastern corners of the diagram of the heart he should adore his weapons viz Achakra, Suchakra, Vichakra, the discus Sudarshana, which protects the three worlds and destroys the Asuras. Then in the east he should adore the Saktis namely Rukshmini, Satyabhāma, Sunanda, Nāgnajiti, Lakshmanā, Mitravrindā, Jamvavati and Sushita. Then in the east he should also adore his conch-shell, discus, club, lotus, mace, the Shranga bow, sword, noose, goad, the mystic mark Srivatsa, and the jewel Koustava. He should then adore his crown, garland of wild flowers, his Indra and other flags, Kumudas, Vishwaksena and Krishna along with Shree. By reciting his name and adoring him one attains all desired-for objects.

CHAPTER XXIX.

HARI said:—I will now describe the Trailokyamohini rite (fascinating the three worlds) of the foremost of male beings, its adoration and the mantram called Shridhara which yeilds religious profit, desire and wives.

Om, Hrim, Shrim, Klim, Hum, Om, Namas: O foremost of male-beings! O thou of an incomparable form! O thou the abode of the goddess of prosperity! O thou the agitator of the entire universe! O thou who rivest the hearts of all women! O thou who maddenst the three worlds! Distress the hearts of all beautiful women amongst the celestials and Asuras; dry them up, strike them, check them, melt them and attract them. O thou of great auspiciousness! O thou of good luck! O thou the giver of all desired-for objects! destroy such and such person with thy discus, club or sword. Cut him with all thy weapons, strike him with thy goad, inflict him. Why dost thou wait.? Save me, save me, so long my Siddhi is not perfected. Hum, phat, salutation. Shrim, salutation unto the holder of Shree and the enchanter of the three worlds. Klim, salutation unto the foremost of male beings, the enchanter of the three worlds.

Hum, salutation unto Vishnu, the enchanter of the three worlds. Om, Shrim, Hrim, Klim, salutation unto Vishnu, the enchanter of the three worlds.

All the Trailokyamohana mantrams are capable of securing the accomplishment of all objects. They may be meditated upon again separately and in brief.

Having adored with mantrams the seat, the image, the six limbs, discus, club, sword, mace, conch-shell, the Shrānga, arrow, noose, goad, Lakshmi, Garuda and Vishwaksena one attains to all.

———:o:———

CHAPTER XXX.

SUTA said:—I will describe in full the auspicious adoration of Shridhara. The family of all should be looked at impartially by the learned.

Om, Shrām, salutation unto the heart. Om, Shrim, unto the head Swāhā. Om Shram, unto the tuft of hair on the head, Vashat. Om, Shraim unto the coat of mail, Hum. Om, Shroum, unto the three eyes, Voushat. Om, Shras unto the weapon, Phat.

Having thus shown unto self the various Mudras as Sangka, Chakra, Gadā etc. and meditated on self known as Shridhara, the holder of conch-shell, discus and club a worshipper should adore the deity in the mystic diagram Sastika and others. He should first of all adore the seat of the god of gods, the holder of Shrānga with the following mantram, O Mahādeva. Hear them, O Shankara.

Om, O presiding deity of the seat of Sridhara, come here. Om, salutation unto the entire family of the presiding deity of the seat of Achyuta.

Om salutation unto Dhātri, Om salutation unto Vidhātri. Om salutation unto Gangā. Om salutation unto Yamunā. Om salutation unto the Adhāra Saktis. Om salutation unto the tortoise. Om salutation unto Ananta. Om salutation unto the earth. Om salutation unto religion. Om salutation unto knowledge. Om salutation unto Vairagya (the spirit of disassociation from the world). Om salutation unto prosperity. Om salutation unto irreligion. Om salutation unto ignorance. Om salutation unto worldliness. Om salutation unto poverty. Om salutation unto Skanda. Om salutation unto Neela. Om salutation unto the lotus. Om salutation unto Vimalā. Om salutation unto Utkarshini. Om salutation unto Jnānā. Om salutation unto Kriyā. Om salutation unto Yogin. Om salutation unto Putrā. Om salutation unto Prarhá. Om salutation unto Satyā. Om salutation unto Ishānā. Om salutation unto Anugraha. Having worshipped them, O Rudra and invoked Hari a greatly wise worshipper should adore him with these mantrams destructive of all sins.

They are :—Om, Hrim, salutation unto Shridhara, Trailokyamohana and Vishnu.

Om, salutation unto Shree. Om, shrām, salutation unto the heart. Om, Shrim, salutation unto the head. Om, Shrum, salutation unto Sikhā (the tuft of hair on the head). Om, Shraim, salutation unto the coat of mail. Om, Shroum, salutation unto the three eyes. Om, Shras, salutation unto the weapon. Om, salutation unto the conch-shell. Om, salutation unto the lotus. Om salutation unto the discus. Om, salutation unto the club. Om, salutation unto the mystic mark Srivatsa. Om salutation unto the jem Koustava. Om salutation unto the garland of forest flowers. Om, salutation unto the yellow raiment. Om, salutation unto Brahmā. Om, salutation unto Nārada. Om, salutation unto the preceptors. Om, salutation unto Indra. Om, salutation unto Agni. Om, salutation unto Yama. Om, salutation unto Nirhita. Om, salutation unto Varuna. Om, salutation unto Vāyu. Om, salutation unto Soma. Om, salutation unto Ishāna. Om, salutation unto Ananta. Om, salutation unto Brahman. Om, salutation unto Sattwa. Om, salutation unto Rajas. Om, salutation unto Viswaksena.

Then he should dedicate raiments, sacred thread, scents, flowers, incense, lamps and food and then circumambulate the deity. Having dedicated them with great Mantrams he should recite the mantram.* Having recited it one hundred and eight times he should dedicate it. Then for a moment he should meditate on the deity stationed in his heart, pure like crystal, effulgent like a koti of suns, of a delightful countenance, gentle, adorned with shining ear-rings, crown, beautiful limbs and a garland of forest flowers. A learned worshipper should think of Shridhara in his own form as identical with Para Brahma. With the following hymn he should chant the glories of the great Ishwara.

Salutation unto the deity the abode of Shree. Salutation unto the lord of Shree. Salutation unto Shridhara with the

Shrānga bow, unto the giver of prosperity. Salutation again and again unto the dearest lord of Shree of a quiescent soul, unto Shriman. Salutation unto the abode of Shri mountain, unto him who does us good. Salutation again and again unto the mass of spiritual well-being. Salutation again and again unto Shrikara. Salutation again and again unto him who is worthy of adoration and being taken refuge with.

Having thus chanted the hymn, bowed unto him the worshipper should perform the Visarjana (the life-destroying rite) of the god of gods.

O Rudra, I have thus described the adoration of the great Vishnu. He, who does it with great reverential faith, attains to the great station. He, who reads this chapter describing the adoration of Vishnu, has all his sins washed off, and attains to the exalted station of Vishnu.

CHAPTER XXXI.

RUDRA said:—O lord, do thou again describe unto me the adoration of the lord of the universe by which I may cross over the most difficult ocean of Samsara (transmigatory series.)

HARI said:—O bull-emblemed deity, hear, O great one, I will describe the adoration of the Lord Vishnu which yeilds the most auspicious emancipation and enjoyment.

Having bathed and performed the rite of Sandhyā a worshipper should enter the sacrificial room. Having washed hands and feet and rinsed his mouth particularly he should assign the words of the principal mantram to his hand. Hear, hear, O Rudra, I will describe the principal mantram of the deity.

Om, Shrim, Hrim, salutation unto Shridhara Vishnu.

This is the mantram of the Lord Vishnu, the king of the celestials. It destroys all diseases, counteracts the evil influence of the planets, dissipates all sins and gives enjoyment and emancipation. A learned worshipper should then make the assignment of the limbs.

Om, Ham, salutation unto the heart. Om, Him, salutation unto the head, Swāhā. Om, Hum, salutation unto the tuft of hair, Vashat. Om, Haim, salutation unto the coat of mail, Hum. Om, Houm, salutation unto the three eyes, Voushat. Om, has, salutation unto the weapon, phat.

I have thus described unto thee the mantram of the powerful Vishnu. Having performed Nyāsa (assignment of mantrams) a self-controlled worshipper should make Mudras. He should then meditate on the great Vishnu—Hari, white as the moon or a Kunda flower, holding conch-shell and discus, bearing the mystic mark of Srivatsa and the Koustava jem and adorned with the garland of forest flowers—the great Ishwara bedecked with a jewelled necklace and a crown. Having meditated "I am Vishnu" he should perform the purificatory rite. With the mantrams yam, Ksham and Ram he should [mentally] harden and form an egg and then cut it with Pranava. Then, O bull-emblemed deity, thinking of the form as described before he should make the worship of self with sacred sweet-scented flowers. Then invoking spirit unto all the deities seated there he should worship them with mantrams. Hear them, O Mahādeva! O Shankara.

O ye deities! come to the seat of Vishnu. Om, salutatation unto the entire family of Achyuta. Om, salutation unto Dhatra. Om, salutation unto Vidhatra. Om, salutation unto the Ganges. Om, salutation unto Yamunā. Om, salutation unto Sankha Nidhi. Om, salutation unto the Nidhi, lotus. Om, salutation unto Chanda. Om, salutation unto Prachanda. Om, salutation unto the presiding goddess of the gate. 'Om, salutation unto the Adhāra Sakti. Om, salutation unto the tortoise. Om, salutation unto Ananta. Om, salutation unto Shree. Om, salutation unto Dharma. Om, salutation unto knowledge. Om, salutation unto the spirit of disassociation from the world. Om, salutation unto religion. Om, salutation unto worldliness. Om salutation unto poverty. Om, salutation unto Sattwa. Om, salutation unto Rajas. Om, salutation unto Tamas. Om, salutation unto Skanda. Om, salutation unto Neela. Om, salutation unto the lotus. Om, salutation unto the solar disc. Om, salutation unto the lunar disc. Om, salutation unto the orb of fire. Om, salutation unto Vinata. Om, salutation unto Utkarshini. Om, salutation unto knowledge. Om, salutation unto action. Om, salutation unto disease. Om, salutation unto Prarhā. Om, salutation unto Satya. Om, salutation unto Ishāna. Om, salutation unto Anugraha.

With these mantrams and scented flowers these deities should be adored. Thereupon having worshipped Vishnu, the author of creation and destruction and invoked his spirit in the mystic diagram, O Rudra, the worshipper should worship the great Ishwara. O Rudra, this religions rite of Vishnu destroys all sins. He should first of all make assignment of mantrams in self and the deity. He should then show Mudra and afterwards offer Arghya. Then he should bathe the deity and next offer raiments and water for rinsing the mouth. Next he should present scented flowers, incense, lights and charu. Then circumambulating the idol and reciting the name he should dedicate it to him. A worshipper should also adore his limbs with other mantrams. Know this to be the principal mantram of the deity. Hear, O three-eyed deity, I will now describe the other mantrams.

Om, Ham, salutation unto the heart. Om, Him, salutation unto the head. Om, Hum, salutation unto the tuft of hair. Om, Haim, salutation unto the coat of mail. Om, Houm, salutation unto the three eyes. Om, Has, salutation unto the weapon. Om, salutation unto Shree. Om, salutation unto the conch-shell. Om, salutation unto the lotus. Om, salutation unto the discus. Om, salutation unto the club. Om, salutation unto the mystic mark Srivatsa. Om, salutation unto the jewel Koustava. Om, salutation unto the garland of forest flowers. Om, salutation unto the yellow raiment. Om, salutation unto the sword. Om, salutation unto the mace. Om, salutation unto the noose. Om salutation unto the hook. Om, salutation unto the Shrānga bow. Om, salutation unto the arrow. Om, salutation unto Brahmā. Om, salutation unto Nārada. Om, salutation unto all the Siddhas. Om salutation unto Bhagavan. Om, salutation unto the preceptor. Om, salutation unto the great preceptor. Om, salutation unto Indra, the king of the celestials, his carrier and entire family. Om, salutation unto Agni, the king of fire, his carrier and the entire family. Om, salutation unto Yama, the king of the dead, his carrier and the entire family. Om, salutation unto Nirhiti, the king of Rakshas, his carrier and the entire family. Om, salutation unto Varuna, the king of waters, his carrier and the entire family. Om, salutation unto Vayu, the king of vital airs, his carrier and the entire family. Om, salutation unto Ishāna, the king of learning, his carrier and the entire family. Om, salutation unto Ananta, the king of serpents, his carrier and the entire family. Om, salutation unto Brahmā, the lord of creation, his carrier and the entire family. Om, unto thunder-bolt, Hum, phat, salutation. Om, unto Sakti, hum, phat, salutation. Om, unto rod, hum, phat, salutation. Om unto the sword, hum, phat, salutation. Om, unto the noose, hum, phat, salutation. Om unto the standard, hum, phat, salutation. Om, unto the club, hum, phat, salutation. Om unto the trident, hum, phat, salutation. Om, unto the discus, hum, phat, salutation. Om, Voum, salutation unto Vishwaksena.

With these mantrams, O Mahādeva, his attendants and

paraphernalia should be adored by men. Having adored the great Vishnu, identical with Brahman he should chant the glories of the great undecaying Atman, with the following hymn.

Salutation unto the powerful lord Vishnu, the god of gods. Salutation unto Vishnu, unto Vāsudeva, the author of creation. Salutation unto Grasishnu who lies at the time of universal dissolution. Salutation unto the lord of celestials and sacrifice. Salutation unto Vishnu, the lord of Munis and Yakshas. Salutation unto the great Jishnu, the lord of all gods and present every where. Salutation again and again unto the lord of all adored of Brahmā, Rudra and Indra. Salutation unto the lord of the world who encompasses the well-being of all creatures, who protects all, who creates all, who destroys the wicked, who gives boons, who is of a quiescent soul, who' is worthy of adoration, who is worthy of taking refuge with, who is manifest in his own form and who gives religious profit, worldly profit and desire.

Having thus chanted his glories the worshipper should meditate on the undecaying Brahman in his heart and should thus adore Vishnu, O Shankara, with the principal mantram. The man, who recites this principal mantram, goes to Hari. O Rudra, I have thus described unto thee, the most excellent theme of Vishnu, mysterious, highly secret and yeilding emancipation and enjoyment. The learned person, devoted to Vishnu, who reads this, listens to it or makes others listen to it, goes to the region of Vishnu.

—:0:—

CHAPTER XXXII.

MAHESHWARA said :—O holder of conch-shell, discus and club, do thou describe the adoration of five Tattwas* by knowing which discriminately a man attains to the most exalted station.

Hari said :—O Shankara! O thou of good vows! I will describe the adoration of five Tattwas, which yeilds auspiciousness and is itself auspicious, heavenly, secret, great and yeilds all desired-for objects. Do thou listen to this most sacred subject, O Mahādeva, which destroys Kali.

Vāsudeva is one, undecaying, peaceful, the great soul, eternal, unstained. O god, by his Māyā (illusive power) Hari exists in five forms, viz. as Vishnu who favours the creation and destroys the wicked, as Vāsudeva, Sangkarshana, Pradyumna and Aniruddha. In his own form Nārāyana exists as five. O bull-emblemed deity, listen to the mantrams expressive of these five forms.

Om, am, salutation unto Vāsudeva. Om, ām, salutation unto Sankarshana. Om, am, salutation unto Pradyumna. Om, salutation unto Aniruddha. Om, salutation unto Nārāyana.

I have thus related the five mantrams expressive of the five deities. They are destructive of all sins and diseases and are holy. I will now describe the most auspicious adoration of the five Tattwas—the religious prescription and the mantras involved therein, O Shankara.

A worshipper should first of all bathe and then perform the Sandhya rite. Then entering the temple of worship he should wash his head, rinse his mouth and then sit in a *baddha* posture. Then with the mantram "Am, Kshroum, Ram"

---

* Five Tantrik ingredients worship.

the purificatory rite of all the articles should be performed. Then hardening the ordinary article he should make an egg. And then dividing it he should meditate on the great Ishwara in it—Vāsudeva, the lord of the universe clad in a silk raiment, effulgent like a thousand suns and wearing shining Kundalas. Then in the lotus of the heart he should meditate on the great Ishwara. Then he should meditate on the lordly deity Sangkarshana, his own self, Pradyumna, Aniruddha, Narāyana and all the celestials headed by Indra, all originating from the god of gods. Then he should make assignment of two hands. Then with the mantrams for limbs he should perform the Anganyāsa called Vyāpaka, O Mahādeva. Listen to these mantrams, O thou of firm vows. Om, ām, salutation unto the heart. Om, Im, salutation unto the head. Om, um, salutation unto the tuft of hair. Om, Em, salutation unto the coat of mail. Om, Oum, salutation unto the three eyes. Om, as, salutation unto the weapon, phat.

Om, salutation unto the entire family of Achyuta. Om, salutation unto Dhātri. Om salutation unto Vidhātri. Om, salutation unto the Adhāra Sakti. Om, salutation unto the tortoise. Om, salutation unto Ananta. Om, salutation unto the earth. Om, salutation unto knowledge. Om, salutation unto the spirit of disassociation from the world. Om, salutation unto prosperity. Om, salutation unto irreligion. Om, salutation unto ignorance. Om, salutation unto poverty. Om, salutation unto the solar disc. Om, salutation unto the lunar disc. Om, salutation unto the orb of fire. Om, salutation unto Vāsudeva, the great Brahman, Shiva in the form of fire, extending all over, the presiding lord of all the celestials. Om, salutation unto Panchajanya. Om, salutation unto Sudarshana. Om, salutation unto the club. Om, salutation unto the lotus. Om, salutation unto Shree. Om, salutation unto Kriyā (action). Om, salutation unto Pushti (nourishment). Om, salutation unto Sakti (energy). Om, salutation unto Priti (affection). Om, salutation unto Indra. Om, salutation unto Agni. Om, salutation unto Yama. Om, salutation unto Nairita. Om, salutation unto Varuna. Om, salutation unto Vāyu. Om, salutation unto Ishāna. Om, salutation unto Ananta. Om, salutation unto Brahmā. Om, salutation unto Vishwaksena. Om, salutation unto the lotus.

O Rudra! I have thus described to thee all the mantrams. The adoration should be offered in the mystic diagram of Sastika and others. Having made the assignment of limbs the worshipper should show all the Mudras. Having meditated as the self, Vásudeva and the Great Ishwara a man should first worship the seat and then invoke the spirit. O bull-emblemed deity, Dhātri and Vidhātri should be adored in the door. O Shankara, before the image of Vāsudeva a person should adore that of Garuda. He should adore in the middle of the diagram [all his parapharnalia] beginning with the conch-shell and ending with the lotus. In the east [the presiding gods of] religion, knowledge, the spirit of disassociation from the world and prosperity [should be adored.] In the south-east pitha corners he should adore the four deities of irreligion &c. In the petals of the eastern side Sangkarshana and other deities should be adored. A person should adore the Lord Vāsudeva in the pericarp. In the north-east and other corners Panchajànya and other weapons should be adored. O Shankara, on the eastern side of the god of gods all his Saktis should be adored. In the eastern and other sides Indra and other guardian deities of the world should be adored. A good worshipper should adore the serpent downwards and Brahman upwards. O Shankara, thou shouldst thus learn of the positions in the mystic diagram. O Shankara, having invoked the spirit of the deity in the mystic diagram, performed Nyāsa and displayed Mudras a worshipper should dedicate, with the principal mantram, water for washing feet and other ingredients. He should then, O Shankara, bathe him, offer raiment, water for rinsing mouth, salutation, and circumambulation. Then he should recite the name with the principal mantram and dedicate it. Then recollecting Vāsudeva he should recite afterwards the following hymn.

Om, salutation unto Vāsudeva. Salutation unto Sangkarshana. Salutation unto the first deity Pradyumna. Salutation unto Aniruddha. Salutation unto Nārāyana. Salutation unto the lord of men. Salutation unto him who is adored by men, whose glories are described and sung by them, and who gives boons. Salutation unto the ancient who is without beginning and destruction. Salutation unto the lord of Brahma who is the agent of creation and destruction. Salutation unto him who is known in the Vedas and who is the holder of conch-shell and discus. Salutation unto the lord of celestials who saves all from the sins of Kali. Salutation unto him who cuts the tree of Samsāra (transmigatory series) and snaps Māyā (illusion). Salutation unto him of manifold forms, who is identical with all the sacred shrines and the three gunas (qualities). Salutation unto him of the form of Brahmā and Vishnu, who is the giver of salvation. Salutation unto the road of emancipation, unto religion and renunciation. Salutation unto him identical with Para Brahman and who gives all desired-for objects. Do thou save me who am immersed in the dreadful deep of Samsāra. O lord of celestials! O lord of the universe! save thee there is no other saviour. I seek refuge with thee, O Vishnu! O thou omnipresent! By giving me the lamp of knowledge, do thou make me freed of ignorance.

This is the hymn of the king of gods destructive of all sorts of afflictions. Having chanted his glories with other Vedic hymns, O blue-throated deity! a man should meditate in his heart on Vishnu with the five Tattwas. Afterwards he should throw away the image of the deity. Thus, O Shankara, the most excellent adoration of Vāsudeva is described which yields all desired-for objects. By offering this adoration a man becomes successful in all his objects. The man, who reads this adoration of the five Tattwas, who listens to it or makes others listen to it, repairs to the region of Vishnu.

CHAPTER XXXIII.

RUDRA said :—O holder of conch-shell and mace, do thou describe unto me the adoration Sudarshana.

Hari said :—O bull-emblemed deity, listen to the adoration of the discus Sudarshana. A man should first of all bathe and then adore Hari. And afterwards he should perform the rite of Nyāsa with the principal mantram. Listen to the principal mantram.

Om, Sahasram, Hum, Phat, Namas. This mantram destroys all wicked beings. A man should meditate on the deity Sudarshana in the pure and auspicious lotus of the heart. O Hara, then invoking, according to the mantram described before, the deity of gentle form, adorned with a crown and holding conch-shell, discus, club and lotus, in the mystic diagram he should worship him, O Meheshawara, with scents, flowers and other ingredients. Having adored him a man should recite the mantram one hundred and eight times. O Rudra ! he, who makes this most excellent adoration of the discus, attains, freed of all diseases, the region of Vishnu. Afterwards he should recite the following hymn destructive of all ailments.

Salutation unto Sudarshana, effulgent like a thousand suns, lighted up with a garland of flames, having a thousand blades for eyes, the destroyer of all wicked beings, the grinder of all sins. Salutation unto Suchakra, Vichakra, the river of all mantras, the originator of all, the protector of the universe and the destroyer of the same, the protector of the worlds and the slayer of the wicked Asuras. Salutation unto him of a terrific form, unto him of a gentle form, unto Chanda, unto him of the form of an eye, unto him who dissipates the fear of Samsara. Salutation unto Shiva, the breaker of the bone of Māyā. Salutation unto him of the form of a planet and the lord of planets. Salutation unto Kāla, death and Bhima. Salutation unto him who shows favour unto his votaries and protects them. Salutation, again and again unto the form of Vishnu, unto him of a dispassionate mind, unto the holder of weapons, unto the weapon of Vishnu and unto discus. Thus the highly sacred hymn of Vishnu is described. He, who reads it with great reverential faith, goes to the region of Vishnu. O Rudra! the self-controlled man, who reads this prescription of the adoration of the discus, reduces his sins to ashes and reaches the region of Vishnu.

——:o:——

CHAPTER XXXIV.

RUDRA said:—O Hrishikesha! O holder of club! describe again unto me the adoration of the deity. I am not satiated with listening to thy account of adoration.

Hari said:—I will describe unto thee the adoration of the deity Hayagriva. Listen to it, O lord of the universe, by which Vishnu is pleased. O Mahādeva! O Shankara! listen, I will describe first the highly sacred principal mantram of Hayagriva.

Om, Houm, Kshroum, salutation unto the head (Shirase Namas) Om.

This mantram, consisting of nine letters, gives all sorts of learning. O Mahādeva, O bull-emblemed deity, listen to its limbs.

Om, Kshrām, salutation unto the heart. Om, Hrim, salutation unto the head, Swāhā. Shiras, Proktam, Kshrum, Vashat. O bull-emblemed deity, the deity's tuft of hair should be known as being added with Om.

Om, Kshrim, unto the coat of mail, Hum. This is described as the mantram for the coat of mail. Om Kshroum, unto the three eyes, Voushat. This is the mantram described for the eye. Om, Has, unto the weapon, phat. This is the mantram for the weapon of the deity.

Hear, I will describe the prescription of the adoration. Having bathed first of all and then rinsed his mouth a worshipper should enter into the room of adoration. Entering there he should duly perform the rite of Soshana.

With the mantram Yam, Kshroum, Ram, Lam, he should harden and create an egg, and then cut it open with Om. In the egg he should meditate on the self as Hayagriva, white-hued like a conch-shell, Kunda flower or the moon, effulgent like silver, four-armed, holding conch-shell, discus, club and lotus, bedecked with a garland of forest flowers, of a beautiful mouth and cheeks and clad in a yellow raiment.

Having meditated on this Great Deity along with other gods with the mantram for limbs he should perform the rite of Nyāsa with the principal mantram. He should then make Sangka, Padma and other Mudras. Then, O Shankara, with the principal mantram, he should meditate on and adore Vishnu. O Rudra, he should then invoke the presiding gods, of the seat of the Deity.

Om, O ye gods, come to the seat of Hayagriva. Having invoked them in the mystic diagram of Sastika and others he should adore them. O bull-emblemed deity, the adoration of Dhātā and Vidhāta should be offered in the door, [with the mantram] "Salutation unto Achyuta with his entire family." This worship should be offered in the middle of the diagram. He should adore Gangā in the door. In the fore part, Yamunā, Mahadevi, Sangka and Padma Nidhis and the Adhāra Saktis should be adored. O Mahādeva, he should next worship the tortoise and then Ananta, Earth, religion and knowledge. In the south-east corner he should adore the spirit of disassociation from the world and prosperity. In the east he should adore irreligion, ignorance, worldliness and poverty. He should adore the qualities Sattwa, Rajas and Tamas in the middle of the diagram. He should also adore there Nanda, Nāla and the lotus. The orbs of the sun, the moon and fire, O Rudra, should also be adored in the centre of the diagram. O bull-emblemed deity, Vimolotkarshini, Jnāna, Kriyā, Yoga, Prarhi, Satya, Ishāna, Anugrahā—these Saktis should be adored in the eastern petals and Vimalā and others in the pericarp. Anugrahas should be adored by men seeking well-being. With the mantrams formed of their names in the dative form beginning with Pranava and ending with Namas the worshipper, O Mahādeva, should adore the seat. The most auspicious adoration of the seat should be made with the offerings of bathing water, scents, flowers, incense, lamps and edibles.

I have thus described the prescription, O Hara. He should next invoke the deity, Hayagriva, the king of the celestials. He should think of his arrival through the left nostril. The invocation rite of the god of gods, the holder of conch-shell, should be performed, O Shankara, with the principal mantram. Having invoked his spirit in the mystic diagram a careful worshipper should perform the rite of Nyāsa. Having performed the Nyāsa he should meditate on the Great Ishwara as being stationed there——the great deity Hayagriva, adored of the celestials and Asuras. Having meditated on the undecaying Vishnu accompanied by Indra and other guardian deities of the quarters he should make the Mudra Sangka, Chakra and others. He should next offer unto

Vishnu water for washing feet, Arghya and water for rinsing mouth. Then he should bathe the changeless, lotus-navelled deity. Having duly placed the image of the deity, he should first dedicate to him, raiment, O bull-emblemed deity, then water for rinsing mouth and sacred thread. Thereupon in the mystic diagram, O Rudra, he should meditate on the Great Ishwara. Having meditated on him, O Shankara, he should again offer unto him water for washing feet and other articles. He should offer these with the principal mantram, O Shankara.

With mantram "Om, Ksham, salutation unto the heart" he should adore the heart. With the mantram "Om, Kshim, salutation unto the head," he should adore the head. With the mantram "Om, Kshum, salutation unto the tuft of hair," he should adore Shikhā. With the mantram "Om, Ksham, salutation unto the coat of mail," he should adore the coat of mail. With the mantam "Om, Kshoum, salutation unto the eye" he should adore the eye. With the mantram "Om, Kshas, salutation unto the weapon" he should adore the weapon.

In the eastern and other sides he should adore the heart, the head, the tuft of hair and the coat of mail. O Rudra, in the corner of the diagram he should adore the weapon and the eye in the centre. In the eastern side he should adore the conch-shell, the lotus, the discus and the club. O Rudra, again in the eastern side with those mantrams describing their names, he should adore the sword, mace, noose, and the bow with the arrows. O Rudra, he should next adore in the east, the mystic mark Srivatsa, Koustava, garland, the sacred yellow raiment as well as the holder of conch-shell, discus and club. He should next adore Brahmā, Nārada, Siddhas, the great preceptor, the shoes of the preceptor, those of the great preceptor, Indra, his carrier and the entire family, Agni, Yama, Nirhiti, Varuna, Vāyu, Soma, Ishana, and Nagas, from the east upwards, O bull emblemed deity. He should next adore thunderbolt,

Sakti, rod, sword, noose, standard, club, trident, discus, lotus and other weapons. In the north-east corner he should worship Vishwaksena, with these mantrams beginning with Om and ending with Namas (salutation) O bull-emblemed deity. O Mahādeva, O bull-emblemed deity, adoration of the deity Ananta should be made with the principal mantram. He should next offer scents, flowers, incense, lamps, and edibles. He should circumambulate the deity, bow unto him and recite his name. With the following hymn beginning with om he should chant his glories, O bull-emblemed deity.

Om, Namas, salutation unto Hayasira, the master of learning. Salutation again and again unto him of the form of learning, and the giver of the same. Salutation unto the deity of a quiescent soul, identical with three gunas, the destroyer of the celestials and Asuras and of all wicked beings. Salutation unto him of the form of Brahman, the lord of all the worlds. Salutation unto him adored of Ishwara, the holder of conch-shell and discus. Salutation unto the first cause, who is self-controlled, devoted to the well-being of all creatures, invested with three gunas, devoid of them, identical with Brahmā and Vishnu, the creator, destroyer, the king of the celestials and present everywhere.

Having recited this hymn, O Rudra, a worshipper should meditate in his pure lotus of the heart, on the god of gods, the holder of conch-shell, discus and club, effulgent like a Koti suns, perfectly beautiful—Hayagriva, the undecaying impersonal self. O Shankara, I have thus described unto thee the adoration of Hyagriva. He, who reads it with great reverence, attains to the most exalted station.

CHAPTER XXXV.

HARI said :—I will now describe the nyāsa and the metre of Gāyatri. Vishwamitra is the Rishi thereof and Savita (the Sun) is the god. She has Brahman for her head, Rudra for the flame and is stationed in the heart of Vishnu. She has application for her one eye and is born in the race of Kátyāna. She is known as having the three worlds for her feet and is placed in the belly of the earth. It consists of three words and eight letters and again of four words and six letters. The one of three words should be used for the purposes of recitation and that of four words for the purposes of adoration. In the rites of Nyāsa, recitation, meditation, adoration and fire a worshipper should daily use Gayatri destructive of all sins. One should assign it to the toes of the feet, insteps, knee-joints, organ of excretion, scrotum, tubes, navel, belly, breast, heart, throat, mouth, palate, eyes, eye-brows, fore-head, in the east, south, north, west and head. The color of sappire, the color of fire, yellow, dark-blue, twany-colour, that of white, that of lightning, dark, crimson, that of conch-shell, grey, that of wine, and sun [constitute it]. All articles which he touches with his hands or sees with his eyes become purified. There is nothing superior to Gayatri.

CHAPTER XXXVI.

HARI said :—Hear, O Rudra, I will now describe the rites of Sandhyā which destroy all sins. Having practised Prānāyāma, (suppression of vital airs), thrice the worshipper should bathe at the period of conjunction. That process of Yoga is called Prāṇāyāma in which a man, having controlled his vital breath, reads thrice the Gayatri with Pranava and Vyarhriti.* By the yogic process of Prāṇāyama a twice-born one destroys the impurities of the mind, speech and body and therefore practises it during all hours of the day. Then reciting the mantram "Sayam Agni (fire in the evening" as well as "Prāta Surya (the sun in the morning" he should drink water. Then duly touching water in the noon and by reciting the Rik "Apohista" he should rub his body with the water of Kuça blades. Then adding to this mantram Pranava he should sprinkle water at every step. With nine he should destroy the nine-fold impurities originating from Rajas (darkness), Tamas (ignorance), Moha (stupefaction), from waking state, dreaming state and that of dreamless sleep, those originating from speech, mind and action. Taking up water in his two palms and reciting [the Gayatri) he should throw it quickly thrice, six, eight or twelve times. It destroys all sins. He should stand facing the sun and recite it. It destroys immediately all sins which a man commits day and night. Sitting in the west he should recite the first Sandhya—the Gayatri, consisting of the great Vyarhriti and Pranava. Gayatri destroys sins committed before in ten or a hundred births, and in three or a thousand yugas (cycles). Gayatri is crimson-coloured and Savitri is white-hued and Saraswati is dark-blue. These are called the three Sandhyas. Having assigned the letters *Om, bhur* to the heart he should assign *Om, bhuvas* to the head and *Om, Shwar* to the tuft of hair on the head. A learned man should assign the first word of the Gayatri to the coat of mail, the second to the eyes, the third to the limbs and the fourth to every where. Having made this assignment at the

---

* A mystical word or sound as *Om*, *Swer*, *Bhuvas*, etc., which commence the daily prayers of the Brahmin.

period of junction he should recite the mother of the Vedas. This Gayatri consists of three padas and is identical with Brahma, Vishnu and Maheshwara. Having learnt its application, saintly author and verse one should begin its recitation. Being shorn of all forms of sins he repairs to the region of Brahma.

—:o:—

CHAPTER XXXVII.

HARI said:—The great goddess Gāyatri gives enjoyment and emancipation. He who recites it has even mighty iniquities dissipated. I will now describe the Gayatri Kalpa which yeilds enjoyment and emancipation. Having recited it one thousand and eight times or one hundred and eight times at three periods of junction one repairs to the region of Brahma. Then after reciting it a hundred times he should drink water. Having invoked the spirit of the goddess having twelve names who destroys all sins at the period of conjunction he should adore her, with her own mantram "Bhur, Bhuvas, Swas.

Om, salutation unto Gayatri. Om, salutation unto Savitri. Om, salutation unto Saraswati, unto the mother of the Vedas, Sangkriti, Brahmani and Koushiki. He should assign the mantram "Bhur, Bhuvas" to Sādhyā, having a thousand eyes, who accomplishes all objects. With the mantram "Swar" he should offer unto fire, one thousand and eight or one hundred and eight times, sacrificial twigs, butter and Havi. He should make all these oblations for attaining success in religious rites, personal undertakings and all other works. Having adored an image, made of sandal wood or gold, recited the name a lac of times, lived on water, roots and fruits and performed two Ayutas of Homas a person attains to all desired-for objects. O goddess, ordered by Brahma, do thou, at thy pleasure, repair to the land situated on the northern summit.

CHAPTER XXXVIII.

HARI said:—A worshipper should adore Durgā in a Navami and other days with the mantram:—"Hrim, O Durga! Protect me, O mother, O foremost of mothers, O thou who dost grant all desired for objects. Being gratified with this offering do thou give me all desired-for objects. Gouri, Kāli, Umā, Durga, Bhadra, Kanti, Saraswati, Mangala Vijaya, Lakshmi, Shiva, Nārāyani—he who adores all these in order beginning with the third day of the dark or light fornight, does not suffer from separation. He should then meditate, with mantrams, on her having eighteen arms, on Khetapa, hell, mirror, the fore-finger, bow, standard, axe damaru (a small drum), noose, Shakti, mace, dart, skull, goad made of adamant, arrow, a discus and probe. I will now describe the recitation of the names of the auspicious goddess.

Om, salutation unto the auspicious goddess Chāmundā, living in the cremation ground, having a skull in her hand, seated on the back of a huge goblin, having a garland of huge conveyances, the night of death, encircled by a number of Ganas, having a huge mouth and many arms, armed with a bell, a small drum and Kinkini and laughing aloud with the sound of *Kilikili*, Hum. [Salutation unto her], making enough of loud sound, having her body covered all over with the skin of an elephant, as well as blood and flesh, having a tongue hanging down, a great Rakshasi, having hideous teeth, laughing aloud, effulgent like lightning, having terrific eyes. Hili, Hili, do thou put thy tongue into thy mouth. Hum, salutation unto thy tongue Trini, O thou having a face covered with frowns, O thou having an auspicious seat, wearing a garland of skulls, (around the neck), braided locks, crown and the moon (on the head) and laughing aloud *Kili Kili*. Hum, Hum, O thou having terrific teeth, O thou who dost dissipate all obstacles, do thou make me accomplish this work, Do it! Do it! Kaha! Kaha! do thou make me enter with the goad. Vanga! Vanga! make me tremble! make me tremble. Go! Go! guide me! guide me! O thou fond of blood, flesh and wine, kill, kill, grind, cut, cut, strike, strike, make my body strong as an adamant. Destroy all the wicked beings of the three worlds. Make me possess every thing that is taken or not taken. Make me walk! Make me walk. Dance! Dance! Bind! Bind! Jump! O thou having eyes entered into sockets! O thou having hairs tied up! O thou having the face of an Uluka! O thou wearing a garland of hands! burn, burn, rot, rot, take, take, make me enter this mystic diagram. Make me possessed by the energies of Brahma, Vishnu, Rishi and Rudra. Kili, Kili, Khili, Khili, Mili, Mili, Chili, Chili, O thou having a good appearance! O thou having thy body encircled by a black serpent! O thou having all the planets in thee! O thou having elongated lips! O thou having a nose sunk between the two eye-brows! O thou having a grim face! O thou, having twany coloured braids! O Brāhmi! break, break, burn, burn. O thou having a death-like face! Khala, Khala, strike down, strike down. O thou having red shot eyes, roll them, strike, strike the ground. Take, take, open up your eyes, open. Break, break feet, take, take. Display, display, the Mudras. Hum, Ham, phat, rive, rive, cut asunder with the trident. Kill, kill with the trident, strike, strike with the rod. Cut,

cut, with the Sakti; 'wound, woud with discus. Bit, bit, with the teeth. Strke with a stick. Strike, strike with the goad. Take, take the head suffering from fever coming every day, every second day, every third day and every fourth day. Release me, release me from the she goblins, Skandas and evil stars. Lana, Lana, raise up, raise up the earth. Strike down, strike down. Take, take Brahman. Come come, Māheswhari. Come, come, Koumāri. Come, come, Vārāhi, come, come, Aindri. Come, Come, Chamundā. Come, come, Vaishnavi. Come, Come, Nārasimhi. Come, come, Shivaduti. Come, come, Kapālini. Come, come, Revati. Come, come, Sushkarevati. Come, come, Akāsha Revati. Come come, O thou ranging on the mount Himalaya. Come, Come O thou ranging on the mount Kailāsha. Come, come, cut open this great mantram. Kili, Kili, O thou having Vimva-like lips, O thou of a dreadful form, O Chamundā, O thou originating from the anger of Rudra, O thou who dost destroy the Asuras and range in the sky, bind, bind the time with thy noose. Enter, enter into this mystic diagram. Strike, strike, take, take, bind, bind the mouth. Bind the eyes, bind the feet, bind the hands and feet, bind, bind all the evil stars. Bind, bind all the directions. Bind, bind, all the opposite directions. Bind, bind the up and down. Bind, bind with the ashes, drinks, earth and sessamum seeds. Possess, possess, strike, O Chamundā. Kili, Kili, Vichhe, Hum, Phat, Swāhā.

This is the recitation of the Mula mantram consisting of one thousand and eight letters. Each word should be recited eight thousand times. With sessamum seeds mixed with sugar, honey and clarified butter eight thousand Homas should be performed. With human flesh, sugar, honey and clarified butter one should recite a word one thousand and eight times. With sessamum seeds, sugar, honey and clarified butter he should perform one thousand and eight Homas. Or with human flesh, honey, sugar and clarified butter he should perform all the rites. By throwing water, sessamum seeds and ashes one achieves victory in battle &c.

The goddess should be meditated on as having twenty-eight arms, eighteen arms, twelve arms or four arms. Her two hands are adorned with sword and Kheta, the other two with club and rod, the other two with arrow and bow, the other two with dagger and mace, the other two with conch-shell and bell, the other two with standard and rod, the other two with axe and discus, the other two with a small drum and mirror. The other hands are endued with Sakti, mace, noose, Tomara, drum and Panava. With the other hand she is striking a drum and a making a sound. She gives protection, kills the buffaloe-faced demon, and rides a lion. Victory unto thee, O queen of ghosts and others encircled by goblins. Save me from thy goblins and accept my sacrifice. Salutation unto thee.

RUDRA said :—O Janarddana, do thou describe, again in brief, the adoration of the deity, the sun, another form of Vishnu, which yeilds emancipation and enjoyment.

Vāsudeva said :—Hear, O Rudra, I will describe again the adoration of the sun.

Om, salutation unto Ucchaishravas. Om, salutation unto Aruna. Om, salutation unto Dandin. Om, salutation unto Pingalā. O bull-emblemed deity, these should be adored at the door with the following mantrams.

Om, A, salutation unto the Bhutas. These should be adored inside the mystic diagram—these known as Prabhutāmala.

Om, am, salutation unto Vimalā. Om, am, salutation unto Sārā. Om, am, salutation unto Adhāra. Om, am, salutation unto Paramamukha. These Vimalā and others should be adored in the south-east and other corners.

Om, salutation unto the lotus. Om, salutation unto the pericarp. O Rudra, a worshipper should adore them inside the diagram and in the east and other directions. He should then adore Dipti and others as well as Sarvatomukhin inside the diagram.

Om, Vam, salutation unto Dipta. Om, Vini, salutation unto Bhadrà. Om, Vaim, salutation unto Jayā. Om, Voum, salutation unto Bibhuti. Om, Vam, salutation Aghorā. Om, Vam, salutation unto Vidyajuta. Om, Vas, salutation unto Vijayā. Om, salutation unto Sarvatomukhi.

Om, salutation unto the seat of the sun. Om, Hram, salutation unto the form of the sun. Om, Ham, Sam, Kham unto Khakhola, Kram, Krim, Sas, Swāhā. Salutation unto the form of the sun.

With this mantram a worshipper should invoke life in the image of the sun, install it, and perform the rite of Sannidhānakan (bringing near). Then with the Sannirodhana mantram he should perform the rite of Sakalikaranam. O Rudra, then he should adore the mudras. He should meditate on the sun, as being of the form of light, of crimson hue, seated on a white lotus, riding a car with one wheel, having two arms and holding a lotus. Listen to the principal mantram.

Om, Hram, Hrim, Sas, salutation unto the sun.

He should next form Padma and Viniva Mudra thrice. Om, am, salutation unto the heart. Om, unto the sun, unto the head, swāhā. Om, As, a, Bhur, Bhuvas, Swas, Jvalini, Shikhai, Vashat. Om, Hum unto the coat of mail. Hum, Om, bhām unto the eyes, Voushat. Om, Vas, unto the weapon, phat. O Hara, a worshipper should adore heart &c. in the south-east, north-east and south-west and the eyes in the north-west corner. In these directions he should adore the white-hued Soma. In the eastern petal, O Rudra, he should adore Sudha. He should adore the yellow-hued preceptor in the southern petal. In the west he should adore the lord of goblins and the white-hued Bhārgava in the north. He should adore the black Shani (Saturn) in the south-west, Rāhu in the north-west, the smoky-coloured

Ketu in the north-east. They should be adored with the following mantrams, O Mahādeva. Hear them, O Shankara.

Om, Som, salutation unto Soma. Om, bum, salutation unto Budha. Om, Vrin, salutation unto Vrihaspati. Om, bham, salutation unto Bhārgava. Om, am, salutation unto Angaraka. Om, sham, salutation unto Shani. Om, Ram, salutation unto Rāhu. Om, Kam, salutation unto Ketu.

Having, with the help of the principal mantram, dedicated unto the Sun, the water for washing feet and then offered edibles, the best of worshippers should display the Dhenu mudra. Having recited the mantram eight thousand times he should dedicate them unto him. In the north-east and other corners, O lord of goblins, he should adore Tejaschanda (the power of the Sun) [with the mantram] "Om, Tejaschandāya, Hum, phat Swadhā, Voushat." O Hara he should next dedicate unto him flowers and Arghya, consisting of sessasum seed, rice, red sandal, scented water, flower and incense. Having placed that vessel on his head and supported it by his knees, he should offer it, with the mantram *Ham* unto the sun, O bull-emblemed deity. Having adored the Ganas and the preceptors he should worship all the deities.

Om, gam, salutation unto the lord of Ganas. Om, am, salutation unto the preceptors. I have thus described the adoration of the sun. Having offered it one attains to the region of Vishnu.

——:o:——

CHAPTER LX.

SANKARA said:—O Shankara, describe unto me the adoration of Māheshwari, by knowing which, O great God, men attain to Siddhi.

Hari said :—Hear, O bull-emblemed deity, I will describe the adoration of Maheshwari.

Having bathed first, then rinsed his mouth, taken his seat and performed Nyasa a worshipper should adore Maheshwara in the mystic diagram together with her family, with the following mantrams, O great Ishāna.

With the mantram, "O Ye presiding deities of Shiva's seat, come here" he should, O Rudra, invoke the presiding deities of the seat.

Om, Hām salutation unto the lord of Ganas. Om, Ham, salutation unto Saraswati. Om, Ham, salutation unto Nandi. Om, Ham, salutation Mahākāla. Om, Hām, salutation unto Gangā. Om, Ham, salutation unto Lakshmi. Om, am, salutation unto the weapon.

O Hari, with water for bathing and scents these should be adored at the door.

Om, Hām, salutation unto Brahmā, the presiding deity of the habitation. Om, ham, sulutation unto the preceptors. Om, ham, salutation unto the Adhāra Sakti. Om, ham, salutation unto Ananta. Om, ham salutation unto knowledge. Om, Hām salutation unto the spirit of disassociation from the worid. Om, ham, salutation unto wealth. Om, ham, salutation unto irreligion. Om, ham, salutation unto ignorance. Om, ham, salutation unto worldliness. Om, ham, salutation unto poverty. Om, ham, salutation unto Urdhachhandas. Om, ham, salutation unto Adhaschandas. Om, ham, salutation unto the lotus. Om Ham, salutation unto the pericarp. Om, ham, salutation unto Vāmā. Om, ham, salutation unto Jyestha. Om, ham, salutation unto Roudra. Om, Ham, salutation unto Kali. Ham, salutation unto Kalavikarini. Om, Ham, salutation unto Balapramathini. Om Ham, salutation unto her who suppresses all beings. Om, Ham, salutation unto Manonmanā. Om, Ham, salutation unto Mandaltritaya. Om, Ham, salutation unto the form of Shiva. Om, Ham, salutation unto the President of learning,

Om, Ham, Him, Houm, salutation unto Shiva. Om, Ham, salutation unto the heart. Om, Him, salutation unto the head. Om, Hum, salutation unto the tuft of hair on the head. Om, Haim, salutation unto the coat of mail. Om, Houma, salutation unto the two eyes. Om, Has, salutation unto the weapon. Om, salutation unto Sadyajāta.

Om, Hum, salutation unto Siddhi. Om, Ham, salutation unto Riddhi. Om, Hum, salutation unto Dyuti. Om, Ham, salutation unto Lakshmi. Om, Ham, salutation unto Bodha. Om, Ham, salutation unto Kali. Om, Ham, salutation unto Swadhā. Om, Ham, salutation unto Prabhā.

These are known as the eight Kalas or parts of Satya. They should be placed in the east and other sides.

Om, Ham, salutation unto Vamadeva. Om, Ham, salutation unto Rajas. Om, Ham, salutation unto Raksha. Om, Ham, salutation unto Rati. Om, Ham, salutation unto Kanyā. Om, Ham, salutation unto Kama. Om, Ham, salutation unto Sajani. Om, Ham, salutation unto Kriyā. Om, Ham, salutation unto Vriddhi. Om, Ham, salutation unto Kārjā. Om, Ham, salutation unto Ratri. Om, Ham, salutation unto Brahmi. Om, Ham, salutation unto Mohini. Om, Ham, salutation unto Twarā.

O bull-emblemed deity, these thirteen are known as the Kalas or parts of Vamadeva.

Om, Ham, salutation unto Tatpurusha. Om, Ham, salutation unto Vritti. Om, Ham, salutation unto Pratisthā. Om, Ham, salutation unto Vidyā. Om, Ham, salutation unto Shanti.

O bull-emblemed deity, these four are known as the Kalas or parts of Tatpurusha.

Om, Ham, salutation unto Aghora. Om, Ham, salutation unto Umā. Om, Ham, salutation unto Kshmā, (forgiveness). Om, Ham, salutation unto Nidrā (sleep). Om, Ham, salutation unto Vyādhi (disease). Om, Ham, salutation unto Kshudhā (hunger). Om, Ham, salutation unto Trishna (thirst). O Hara, these are the eight terrific parts of Aghora.

Om, Ham, salutation unto Ishāna. Om, Ham, salutation unto Samiti. Om, Ham, salutation unto Angadā. Om, Ham, salutation unto Krishnā. Om, Ham, salutation unto Marichi. Om, Ham, salutation unto Jvāta. O bull-emblemed deity, know these to be the *Kalas* of Ishana.

Om, Ham, salutation unto the family of Shiva. Om, Ham, salutation unto Indra, the king of celestials. Om, Ham, salutation unto Agni, the lord of fire. Om, Ham, salutation unto Yama, the lord of departed spirits. Om, Ham, salutation unto Nairita, the lord of Rakshas. Om, Ham, salutation unto Varuna, the lord of waters. Om, Ham, salutation unto Vāyu, the lord of vital airs. Om, Ham, salutation unto Soma, the lord of eyes. Om, Ham, salutation unto Ishāna, the lord of all forms of learning. Om, Ham, salutation unto Ananta, the king of serpents. Om, Ham, salutation unto Brahmā, the lord of all the worlds.

Om, Ham, salutation unto Dhulichandeshwara.

O Shankara, a worshipper should thus perform the rites of invocation, installation, making near, concentration and Sakalikarana, and next the assignment of Tattwas, the displaying of Mudras and meditation. He should next dedicate water for washing feet, that for rinsing mouth, Arghya, flowers, water for bathing, scents, unguents, raiments, ornaments, objects of enjoyment, incense, lamps, food. [He should also propitiate the deity] with water for washing feet, water for rinsing mouth, scents, betel, umbrella and Mudras. He should meditate on the form and recite the name and dedicate the adoration and recitation with the principal mantram. O Rudra, I have thus described the adoration of Māheshi which destroys all sins.

—:0:—

CHAPTER XLI.

VASUDEVA said :—Om, there is a Gandharva, by name Vishwāvasu, the master of maidens. I will secure him for you. "Having begotten maidens. Unto Vishwavasu, Swāha." This is the recitation of the mantram for obtaining wives. I will describe the night of death.

Om, salutation unto the auspicious goddess, having ears like those of a bear and four arms. O thou having hairs, tied up! O thou, having three eyes! This is the night of death for men in the matter of feeding upon marrow and blood. May death approach such and such person who has come to the proper time. Ham, phat, kitt, kitt, burn, burn, flesh and blood, pacha, pacha, Rikshapatni (wife of the bear) Swahā. There is no restriction for the observance of lunar days, stars, or fasting.

A worshipper should rub his hands with blood and then take up all articles with them. Early in the morning he should recite the name of the phallic emblem and strike it with a mangoe leaf. Om, salutation unto all the weapons, so that, O Jambhani, O thou who charmest all, O thou who dost destroy all the enemies, protect me, such and such a person, from all fears and calamities, Swahā. On the destruction of Shukra, O Mahadeva, I described it which saves all the twice-born.

—:o:—

CHAPTER XLII.

HARI said :—I will now describe the eternal rite of Shiva called Pavitrārohana* which, O Hara, a priest, a worshipper or his son or a person, observant of a vow, should perform.

* The rite of putting sacred thread around the neck of the image of a particular deity.

Having performed the adoration extending over full one year one should perform this rite in the month of Ashāda, Shrāvana, Māgha or Bhādrapada. He should first of all procure a thread made of gold, silver, copper or of cotton spun by a maiden. Having made nine folds of this thread he should perform the rite of Pavitrakam. With the Vāma-deva mantram he should make the Granthis (knots). With the Satya mantram, O Shiva, he should wash the thread, with the Aghora mantram he should purify it, with the Tatpurusha mantram he should tie it and with Isha mantram he should place incense. The following are known as *Tantudevas* or deities of the thread viz., Omkāra, Chandramā, Vanhi, Brahmā, Nāga, Shikhidwaja, Ravi, Vishnu and Shiva. The length of [the sacrificial thread, O Rudra, should be either one hundred and eight fingers in length, or fifty or twenty five. There are ten Granthis or knots. And the interstice between one Granthi and the other should be four fingers ; or it may be two fingers or one. [The names of the ten Granthis are :—] Prakriti, Pourushi, Veerā, Aparājita, Jayā, Vijayā, Rudrā, Ajata, Manonmani and Sarvatamukhi. On the seventh or the thirteenth day of the light fortnight one should dye it with saffron and perform the Pavitraka rite with scents. Having sprinkled the phallic emblem with thickened milk he should rub it with scents and dedicate the sacred perfumeries to the self—the Brahman.

He should place scented flowers at the foot of the image of Ishanā, sticks for cleansing teeth in the east and fruits of emblic myrobalam in the north. He should place earth in the west and ashes in the south. One, conversant with mantrams, should place, with Sikha mantram, Aguru in the south-east corner and sessamum seeds with the Kavacha mantram, O bull-emblemed deity.

Having encircled the house with a thread he should offer sacred scents. Then after offering oblations to fire he should place offerings for pernicious spirits.

O king of gods. O Maheshwara, thou hast been invited with thy ganas (goblins). Do thou come near, I will adore thee in the morning.

Having thus invited the deity he should spend the night in singing and place, by the side of the image, sacred articles inspired with mantrams. Having sprinkled the sun with water on the fourteenth day of the dark fortnight he should adore Rudra. He should first meditate on self, in the form of the universe, as being stationed on the fore-head and then adore it. He should sprinkle it with water with the astra mantram and adore it with the Hridaya mantram. He should next dedicate incense inspired with mantrams. He should first of all adore Shiva Tattwa, then Vidyā Tattwa and next Atma Tattwa.

Om, Houm, salutation unto Shiva Tattwa (essence of Shiva). Om, Him, salutation unto the essential spirit of learning. Om, Ham, salutation unto the essence of self.

Om, Ham, Him, Hain, Kshoum salutation unto the essence of all. O God! O Shambhu! what-ever, thou, identical with time, hast seen in me, whatever I have done, have offered as oblations to fire, whatever I have created, have all been done by me, by thy will, for the rite of Pavitrakam. Om, fulfill my vow of sacrifice. Om, Ham, Him, Hum, Haim, Houm, salutation unto Shiva, the lord of observances, identical with all essences and the cause of all.

With this mantram the four offerings of a Pavitraka rite should be made. Having offered Pavitrakam to the fire one should make presents unto the preceptor, offer food, feed the Brahmanas, worship Chanda and then perform the Visarjana (life-destroying) rite.

CHAPTER XLIII.

HARI said :—I will now describe the Pavitrarohana rite of Hari which yeilds emancipation and enjoyment. Formerly in the war between the gods and Danavas, the celestials, headed by Brahmā, sought refuge with Vishnu who conferred on them the standard *Graiveyaka*. Seeing them Hari said that they would overcome the Danavas. On Vishnu saying so, the Nāga, Vāsuki's younger brother, said :—" O bull-emblemed deity, I pray from thee this boon, called Pavitraka, so that the Graiveya, conferred by Hari, may pass by my name". On his thus addressing the Devas they conferred on him the same boon.

The mortals, who worship me with the Pavitraka rite during the rainy season, have their adoration extending over full one year rendered useless. The Pavitrārohana rite of all the deities should be celebrated in order on the lunar days respectively reserved for them, beginning with the first day after the full moon. On the twelfth day of the dark or light fortnight the one for Vishnu should be performed. It is always necessary to perform the Pavitra rite during the rainy season, preference being always given to a *Vyatipata** day, to a solar or lunar ecclipse, to a day when the Vriddhi rite of Vishnu is performed or when the precepter comes. The sacred thread should be made of either red silk, silk fibres, cotton or linen. The twice-born should offer a thread made of Kuça reeds, the kings that made of silk, the Vaishyas that of wool and the Sudras that made of new barks. O Ishwara! one, made of cotton or of fibres of a lotus, is preferable unto all castes.

* The seventeenth of the astrological Yogas. Day of new moon when it falls on a Sunday and the moon is in certain mansions, Sravana.

Three knots of three folds each should be made of a thread spun by a Brahmana. A worshipper should next recite the names of the presiding gods of the thread beginning with Om. They are Shiva, Soma, Agni, Brahmā, Phani, Ravi, Ganesha and Vishnu. Brahmā, Vishnu and Rudra are the three presiding gods of the three threads. One should keep the thread in a golden vessel, or in one made of silver, or of copper, or of bamboo or of earth. The size of the best vessel should be sixty four fingers in circumference, that of the middling one its half, and that of the youngest one its half again. The best thread must be one hundred and eight fingers in length, the middling one its half, and the youngest its half again. The best knot should be of the size of a knot of the thumb; the middling one of that of the middle finger and the smallest one of that of the youngest finger. The measurement of the sacrificial altar must be guided by these general characteristics. The sacrificial thread must be placed on the idol (of Vishnu) which should be of the size of that of Shiva. It must pass through breast, navel, thigh and hang up to the knee-joints. With a thread measuring one thousand and eight fingers in length should be formed four, thirty-six, twenty four and twelve knots severally, each being of the size of a finger knot. It should be then dyed with saffron, turmeric or sandal. After fasting a worsipper should place the sacred thread on a vessel and perform the initiatory rite of consecration. Then in vessels made of fig leaves it should be placed in the eight quarters. Twigs and Kuça blades should be dedicated to Sangkarshana in the east. Rochanā (yellow figment) and saffron should be dedicated to Pradyumna in the south. A person, who is about to undertake a war and seeks for victory, should dedicate to Aniruddha in the west, sandal, blue colour, sessamum seeds, ashes and Akshata. In the south-east and other corners he should make assignment of Shree and other goddesses.

Having then inspired the sacred thread with Vāsudeva mantrams, looked at it again and worshipped it he should cover it with a piece of cloth. He should then place it before the image of the deity or the mystic diagram. Having placed duly as before Brahmanas in the west, south and north he should worship the pitchers. Then having drawn the mystic diagram with a weapon he should place the offerings.

Having thus performed the Adhivāsa rite of the sacred thread he should encircle the altar with three or nine threads and then connect his own body and the pitchers with it. Connecting the well of sacred fire, the pedastal, the awning and the temple with one thread he should place it on the head of the deity. Having thus offered the thread and worshipped the great god the worshipper should recite the following mantram.

"O King of gods! O Great Ishwara! I have invoked thy presence here for adoring thee. I will adore thee in the morning. Do thou come near these articles." Having performed the Adhivāsa rite of the sacred thread for one or three nights a worshipper should keep up the night and adore Keshava in the morning. He should next place (on the image) the biggest, middling and the smallest threads. Then having incensed the sacred thread he should inspire it with mantrams. Having recited the names of the knots he should adore them with flowers and other articles. Then having recited the Gayatri he should adore the deity with the following mantram.

May my sons and wife hold this thread. O god, I hold before thee this purified and beautiful knot destrutive of the greatest iniquity and of all sorts of sins.

Having thus worshipped the sacred thread with incense and other articles he should dedicate the middling and other ones. [He should next say] " For achieving sucess in religious rites and worldly undertakings I hold on my neck this sacred energy of Vishnu." Then having worshipped the garland of forest flowers with its own mantram he should offer it. Next he should place various offerings, flowers and edibles. Then having offered oblations to the sacred fire deposited in an well measuring twelve fingers he should offer one sacred thread, one hundred and eight fingers in length.

Having first offered Arghya unto the Sun-God he should dedicate to him a sacred thread. O Hara, he should next adore Vishwaksena and his preceptor with Arghya. Clasping his hands he should recite before the deity the following mantram.

O lord of celestials, may all adorations, whatever I have offered knowingly or unknowingly, be crowned with success by thy favour. O Garuda-emblemed deity, I offer this thy adoration extending over a year with garlands of jems and sapphires and of Mandāra flowers. O god, hold this sacred thread on thy breast as thou dost always carry the garland of forest flowers and the mystic mark of Srivatsa.

Having thus adored the deity, fed the twice-born and distributed presents amongst them a worshiper should perform the life-destroying ceremony of the deity in the evening. Having thus duly performed the adoration extending over a year as well as the offering of sacred thread one repairs to the region of Vishnu.

CHAPTER LXIV.

HARI said :—Having adored Brahman with Pavitra and other rites and meditated on him one becomes Hari. I will now describe the meditation of Brahman which destroys the weapon of Māyā (illusion). The learned man, who recites the name of Brahman by words and mind, acquires the knowledge of self. He, who desires to acquire this knowledge, gains great knowledge.

Brahman is shorn of body, organs of sense, mind, intellect, vital principle and egoism. It is shorn of elements, Tanmatras (subtle particles), the gunas (qualities), birth and decay. It is manifest of itself, devoid of a form, eternally blissful, without any beginning, eternal, purified, intelligent, undecaying, existent, blissful, without second and eternal. [The state of mental realization). "I am Brahman, I exist in Brahman" is known as Samādhi (mental concentration). The soul is known as the charioteer, the body as the chariot and the organs of sense are known as the horses. The objects of sense are known by the latter. The soul is endued with mind and the organs of sense. Therefore the learned designate it as the enjoyer. He, who is endued with the discriminative knowledge of the external objects and mental perception, attains to the station of Brahman and is not born again. The man, whose charioteer is the discriminative knowledge, goes to the other side of the world by the help of mental abstraction and attains to the most exalted station of Vishnu. Not to hurt animals &c. is called Yama (restraint). Purification and other rites are called Niyama (religious observances). Padma and other postures are called Asana and the suppression of vital airs is called Prānāyāma. The withdrawal of organs from the objects of sense is called Jaya; the meditation on the Lord is called dhyāna; the restraint of mental faculties is called Dhāranā. Although Brahman is without any forms still a worshipper should meditate on a form in the pericarp of his heart's lotus as holding conch-shell, discus and club, bearing the mystic mark of Srivatsa and the Koustava jem, adorned with a garland of forest flowers, as being eternal, pure, intelligent, ever existent, blissful and supreme, thinking "I am self, the impersonal and Absolute self, the Great Light." Hari, having twenty four forms, situate on the Shālagrāma stone and on the height of Dwārakā, is worthy of being adored and meditated on.

Having meditated on this form, lauded it and recited its name, a person, acquiring all the objects of his desire, becomes an etherial god, and shorn of desire, obtains emancipation.

CHAPTER XLV.

HARI said :—As a side issue of this discourse I shall describe the characteristic marks of Shālagrāma, by touching which stone, one has the sins, accumulated in a Koti of births, dissipated.

The holder of conch-shell, discus, club and lotus, known as Keshava, is [also called] Gadādhara (the holder of club]. The Lord Nārāyana is also the holder of lotus, the bow Koumodaki, discus and conch-shell. He is the holder of discus, conch-shell, lotus and club and is also named Mādhava and Shree Gadādhara. Govinda, Gadādhara, the holder of club, lotus, conch-shell and discus is adorable.

Salutation unto thee of the form of Vishnu, the holder of lotus and the conch-shell, unto thee of the form of Madhusudana, the holder of conch-shell, lotus, club and discus. Salutation unto that form of thine which holds the club, conch-shell and lotus, unto that form, which is of three foot steps, unto that form which holds the bow Koumodaki, lotus and conch-shell and unto thy dwarfish form. Salutation unto thee the holder of conch-shell, lotus, discus and club. Salutation unto that form which bears the mystic mark of Srivatsa, unto Hrishikesha, and the weilder of lotus, club, conch-shell and discus. Salutation unto the holder of lotus, discus, club, conch-shell, unto Padmānabha (lotus-navelled), unto Dāmodara, unto the weilder of conch-shell, discus, club and lotus. Salutation unto Vāsudeva, unto the holder of conch-shell, club and lotus. Salutation unto Sangkarshana. Salutation unto the form of Pradyumna, the holder of a beautiful conch-shell, a beautiful club and a beautiful lotus. Salutation unto Aniruddha and the weilder of club, conch-shell and lotus. Salutation unto the Purusottama form with lotus, conch-shell, club and discus. Salutation unto the form of Adhokshaja, the holder of club, conch-shell, and lotus. Salutation unto Man-lion form, the holder of lotus, club and conch-shell. Salutation unto the form, Achyuta, the weilder of lotus, conch-shell and club. I will bring here Janārddana with his conch-shell, discus, lotus and club and Upendra with his wheel, club, lotus and conch-shell. Salutation.

Salutation unto this form of Hari, holding a beautiful discus, lotus, club and conch-shell. Salutation unto the form Srikrishna weilding club, lotus, wheel and conch-shell.

The Shālagrāma stone, known as Vāsudeva, is of a white colour and possesses two ring-like marks around its mouth. The one, known as Sankarshana, is of a red colour, has two ring like marks around its mouth or lateral aperture and has the mark of a lotus on its eastern side. The one, known as Pradyumna, is of a yellow colour, has a small ring-like mark, is of an elongated shape and bears on its surface a large number of impressions like pin-holes. The one, known as Aniruddha, is of a circular shape and blue colour and is marked with three lines around its mouth. The one known as Nārāyana is of a black colour, contains the mark of a club-like line in its cavity and has the circular mark at the navel or a little raised up. The Nrisimha alone is elevated on the breast, is of a twany colour, and is dotted with fine spots; while a Varāha resembles a Sakti in shape and has two rugged and uneven circular marks. A Sthula stone is of blue colour, has three lines, is of the form of a tortoise and is dotted with marks. The stone, known as Krishna, is round and depressed at the back. Sridhara has the marks of five lines, that of a garland of forest flowers and that of a club. The Vāmana stone is of a round and puny size and Sureshwara has a circular mark on its left side. The one, known as Anantaka, has various forms and bears an impression like the hood of a serpent. The Damodara stone is thick, of blue colour, and contains a circular mark of blue colour in the central part of the cavity. Brahma stone has a small mouth and is of thick blue colour. Sushira stone has marks of long lines, while Amvuja stone has the mark of one circular figure and is thick. A Sthulachakra stone has deep holes and is dotted with dark marks. A Hayagriva stone is of the shape of a goad; while a Kaustava stone possesses marks of five lines. A Vaikuntha stone is of the hue of a jem on the hood of a serpent, of dark colour and bears one circular mark. A Matsya stone is of the shape of a long lotus and has marks of lines at the mouth. A Trivikrama stone bears the mark of a circle on the left side, that of a line on the right side and is of a dark-blue colour.

Salutation unto the holder of club who is situate in Shālagrāma as well as in Dwārākā.

A Lakshmi Narayana stone is of the shape of a Kadamva flower, bears marks of four circles at one mouth, is adorned with the figure of a garland of forest flowers, is marked with golden lines and cow's hoofs.

The Sudarshana class has got only a single circular mark, while the existence of two characterises the class Lakshmi Narayana. The Tivikrama class has got three circular marks, the Chaturvyuha class has got four, the Vasudeva class has got five, the Pradyumna class has got six, the Sangkarshana class has got seven, the Purusottama class has got eight, the Navavyuha class has got nine, the Dashàvatara class has got ten, the Aniruddha class eleven, and the Dwādashātmā class has twelve circular marks. The Ananta class bears more marks than twelve. He, who reads this poem, describing the forms of Vishnu, repairs to the celestial region.

The image of Brahmā has four mouths and is endued with a staff and Kamandalu (water-pot). That of Maheswara has five mouths, ten arms, is seated on a bull with weapons as well as Matrika goddesses, such as Gouri, Chandrikā, Saraswati and Mahālakshmi. The image of the sun holds a lotus in the hand. Gana has the head of an elephant. Skanda has six mouths.

Adored these images should be placed in the edifice worshipped of Vastu deities. By adoring them a man obtains religious profit, worldly objects and emancipat ion.

CHAPTER XLVI.

HARI said:—I will now describe in brief the adoration of the Vastu deity presiding over the house which destroys all impediments. Beginning with the north-east corner a worshipper should adore him in a diagram of eighty one rooms. He should adore the head in the north-east corner, feet in the south-west and two hands in the south-east and north-west corners. In a temporary dwelling house, in one's own house, in a city, in a village, in a merchantile thorough-fare, in palaces, pleasure-houses, forts, temples and Mathas a person should adore the twenty-two deities outside the diagram and thirteen in the end of the same. [The deities are] Isha, Parjanya, Jayanta, the weilder of thunder-bolt (Indra), Surya (sun), Satya (the god of truth), Bhrigu, Akasa (the god of sky), the wind-god, Pushā, Vitatha (the god of untruthfulness), Graha, Kshetra, the two Yamas, Gandharva, Bhrigu-raja, Mriga, the Pitris, Dwouvarika, Sugriva, Pushpadanta, Ganesha, Asura, the two Seshapadas, Roga (god of disease), Ahimukhaja, Bhattata, the two Somasarpas, Aditi and Diti. These are the thirty-two deities who should be adored outside. Hear of the four deities who should be worshipped in the end. A learned man should adore the four deities stationed in the four corners, north-east etc, viz. Apa, Savitri, Jaya and Rudra,

In the ninth room of the central part of the diagram he should adore Brahmā and his eight attendant deities beginning with the east. Hear their names. Aryamā, Savita, Vivaswān, Vivudhādhipa, Mitra, Raja-Yakshmā, Prithvidhara, and Apavatra are the deities known as encircling Brahmā. The group beginning from the north-east is called Durga; while the one beginning from the south-east is called Durdhara. Having worshipped the three deities Aditi, Himavanta and Jayanta, as well as Nāyikā, Kalika, Sakra, Gandharvas—all those Vāstu gods, a worshipper should undertake the construction of a divine palace.

First of all the image of the teacher of gods should be erected in front. Then the great seat should be constructed in the south-east corner. The altar of sacrifices should be constructed in the east. The house of scents and flowers should be constructed in the north-east corner. The store-room should be erected in the north and the cow-shed in the north-west. The room, for keeping water, should be constructed with windows in the west; while that for keeping sacrificial twigs, grass, fuels and weapons should be constructed in the south-west. The guest-house, beautiful and containing beds, shoes, water, fire, lamps and good servants, should be constructed in the south. Other minor houses should be constructed containing water, plantain trees and be adorned with flowers of five colours. A wall should be erected around the divine edifice, five cubits in height. Thus the divine edifice of Vishnu should be erected containing forests and gardens.

The edifice of Vastu, containing sixty four rooms, should, first of all, be adored. In the central part one of four rooms should be dedicated to Brahma and one of two rooms should be dedicated each to Arjama and other deities. All other celestials have houses of two rooms dedicated to each of them severally. These are the deities known as presiding over sixty four rooms.

Charaki, Vidari and the sinful Rākshasi Putanā should be adored in the north-east and other corners. The Hetuka and other deities should be worshipped[1] outside. They are Hetuka, Tripurāntā, Agni, Vetalaka, Yama, Agnijihva, Kālaka, Kalara, Ekapādaka, Bhimarupa (terrific-visaged deity) should be adored in the north-east corner, the regent of the spirits in the nether region, Gandhamāli and Kshetrapala in the sky.

A worshipper should next undertake the extension, multiplication, lengthening and the numbering of the Vāstu. A person should build his dwelling house before the Vishnu temple and not behind it. And he should sleep on the left side. There is nothing to be questioned in this matter. It is better for those persons whose births are respectively governed by Leo, Libra, and Scorpi, to have the door of the house opening out in the north and for others whose births are governed by Scorpi and the succeeding signs of the Zodiac to have them in the east, south and west. The breadth of the door should be half of its length. And there must be eight doors.

CHAPTER XLVII.

SUTA said :—O Sounaka, hear me describe the essential features of a divine temple or palace. A plot of ground should be divided into sixty-four equal rectangular divisions occupying all the points of the compass. The Chatuskon or the inner court of the adytum should be comprised of four such rectangular divisions, and the doors of the temple should be made to number twelve in all. The walls of the edifice should be raised upon such forty-eight quadrilateral divisions. In height the plinth should be made commensurate with the length of the platform at the top of the ground elevation and twice that measure above that. The inner cavity of the vault should be made co-extensive with the entire length of the adytum. The indents on both sides should measure a third or a fifth part of the chord of the inner vault, which should be so arched as to rise up to the half of the entire height of the pinnacle. The height of the terrace or the pinnacle part of the divine edifice should be divided into four equal parts over the third part, from the bottom of which the *Vedi* or the top of the platform should be constructed; and on the top of the fourth part the ornamental figure should be placed which is generally made to edge the entire height of the temple from the bottom.

In the alternative, the homestead land should be divided into sixteen equal parts over the four central parts of which the adytum of the temple should be raised. The walls of the edifice should be raised upon twelve such rectangular divisions or chambers, and the height of the walls should be made commensurate with the length of four such parts as are compatible with the laws of proportion. The height of the terrace or the pinnacle should be made to measure twice the height of the wall, and the open verandah or the platform all around the temple should be made of a quarter part of the height of the terrace in breadth. The indents on both sides of the temple should be of a fifth part of the length of the adytum in breadth. Again an indent should be left out which would measure such a fifth part. The essentials described above are what should be complied with in building divine edifices in general.

Now I shall deal with another class of divine structures which are usually constructed in proportion to the lengths of the images of their inmate deities. The *Peetha* or the pedestal of the image should be made commensurate with the length of the latter and the adytum should be made, O Sounaka, of twice that length. The walls should be of equal length with the latter, while the plinth should be made half as much broad as the adytum. O Sounaka, the pinnacle should have twice the height of the plinth and the vault of the temple should be made so as to cover the entire space occupied by the pedestal and the adytum combined, the indents having been left aside to the measure previously directed.

O Sounaka, I have described the characteristic measures of temples which are built in proportion to the dimensions of images of their inmate deities. I shall presently deal with a class of divine edifices which are constructed in measures proportionate to those of their door-frames. A measure of four forearms should be divided into eight equal parts which would be the measure for the breadth of the door, or the same might be made of twice that breadth. The upper part of the door, like the upper part of the pedestal, should be perforated with holes, as the upper part of the door would be taken in by the wall to the length of a pada measure. The plinth should be made twice as much broad as the door and the terrace or the pinnacle part of the temple should be made of twice that measure. The vault should be arched from the spring line as before laid down on the regions of indents at the top of the walls of the temple.

I have already described the essential traits of a divine temple built proportionate to its *mandap*; now I shall describe one of a different structure. The ground, on which the image of the deity would be installed, should be tripled in measure, which would thus give the dimensions of the exterior; the area of the temple must be less than that of the ground on which the same should be erected by a pada in all directions, and the area of the adytum should be made half of that of the latter. The walls should be made equal in height to the length of the adytum or the space enclosed within them, and the pinnacle should be twice as much high as the height of the wall.

Now I shall describe the different classes of temples according to their respective measure and origin. The different forms of divine edifices are mainly grouped under five heads such as the Bairaja, the Puspakāksa, the Kailasa, the Malikahvaya and the Tripistapam, which should be looked upon as the abode of all deities and in which their images might be safely installed. The first of the above classes of temple is characterised by a rectangular shape; the second class is marked in a quadrilateral shape; the third class has a circular shape, the fourth class of temples has a shape which appertains to the different segments of spheres; while the fifth class of temple is octagonal. These five classes of temples, which are the proper abodes for all forms of divine manifestations, admit of being divided into various sub-divisions as it were, thus giving rise to forty-five different shapes of temples which are the Meru, the Mandara, the Vimana, the Vadraka the Sarvatovadra, the Ruchaka, the the Nandana, the Nandivardana and the Shrivatsa, these nine arising out of the class of the rectangular Vairaja form of the temple. The nine temples which owe their origin to the genus Puspaka are known as the (1) Badavi, (2) the Griharaja,

(3) the Shalagriha, (4) the Mandira, (5) the Vimana, (6) the Bramhamindara, (7) the Vavana, (8) Uttamva, and (9) the Shivikāveshma. The names of the nine circle temples which appertain to, and proceed out of, the genus Kailasa are the 1 Valaya, 2 Dundubhi, 3 Padma, 4 Malāpadma, 5 Mukuli, 6 Ushnishi, 7 Shankha, 8 Kalasa, 9 Guvābriksa. The class Malakahvaya has fathered the nine spheriodical temples which are called the 1 Gaja, 2 Vrisava, 3 Garuda, 4 Sinha, 5 Bhumukha, 6 Bhudhara, 7 Shrijaya and 8 the Prithividhara and 9 the Hansa. The nine octagon-shaped temples, which fall under the genus Tripistapa, are named as 1 Vajra, 2 Chakra, 3 Mustika, 4 Vabhru, 5 Vakra, 6 Svastika, 7 Gada, 8 Shrivriksa, and 9 Vijaya which is also known as Vijaya Sveta.

Now I shall describe the situations of the triangular, lotus-shaped, crescent-shaped, rectangular and the octagonal divine edifices, and narrate the purposes for which they should be built in those shapes. A temple, built in the shape of a triangle, imparts wealth and sovereignity, increases the duration of life and gives wives and male offsprings to the consecrator. The consecrator should plant a banner on the top of the temple, and build the Garbha Griha or the entrance chamber just in front of the door; and the *mandap* or the sanctuary of the temple should be built with an equal number of lines with the latter, one full window and a half having been opened therein. The *mandap* should be commensurate with the measure of a wall and a half should be made to measure twice the thickness of the walls in length. The ornamental cornices should be laid down so as to include spaces of unequal measure between them, the intervening spaces having been filled in with horizontal lines of unequal thickness. A divine edifice, of the *Meru* class, should be provided with doors and furnished with four sheds or top chambers over them, while the terrace should be decorated with a hundred turrets. The *mandapas* or the top chambers of the above edifice should be so constructed as to have three arches differing from each other, both as regards their shape and dimension. In some of the temples the bullocks are carved out in relief while in others they are carved into the body of the top chambers. Thus the temples differ from each other in appearance, shape and size which vary in construction according as the character of the image residing therein varies. No hard and fast rule can be laid down for constructing temples for the gods who are self-originated, and accordingly they should be built according to the measures stated before, of rectangular shape and possessing courts and turrets and top-chambers over their terraces; and the hall for musical entertainments should be built contaguous to the door of the temple. The celestial warders of the gods should be sculptured on the various angular quarters of the divine mansion, and a little remote therefrom the houses for monks should be built. The ground should be washed with water containing fruits and flowers. The consecrator should previously worship the gods about to be installed in the temple. Vasudeva is the god of gods, and a person, who consecrates a temple to him, attains all merit.

——:o:——

CHAPTER XLVIII.

SUTA said :—I will now describe in brief the installation of the images of all the deities. Under an auspicious planet and in a beautiful building a preceptor should perform the rite of installation. He should, in the company of sacrificial priests, elect a Brahmana of the Central Provinces as the presiding priest. According to the religious prescription of his own branch or with the recitation of Pranava he should, with five or more Mudrikas, offer Pādya and Arghya as well raiments, scented garlands and unguents. Then having made the assignment of mantrams the preceptor should begin the rite of installation. Before the temple should be erected a sacrificial shed of ten or twelve cubits supported by sixteen pillars. In its centre an altar of four cubits should be constructed and bedecked with standards. Then sand, procured from the confluence of rivers, should be scattered thereon. Beginning with the east five fire receptacles should be constructed of the shape severally of a square, of a bow, of a circle and of a lotus. Or all the five should be of the shape of a square. After performing the peace-giving rite, the presiding priest, for attaining success in all works, should perform the Homa ceremony near the head of the image. Some say that Homa ceremony should be first performed in the north-east after pasting the sacred spot (with the solution of cow-dung). Near the gate-way of the sacrificial shed four doors should be constructed. The branches of Nyagrodha, Oudumvara, Plaksha and Khavira should be planted at the different doors of the shed. The gates should be five cubits in height and bedecked with clothes and flowers. Four pits, each of one cubit in depth, should be made on four sides. He should place the figure of a lion in the eastern gate, that of the king of horses (Ucchaisrava) in the southern, that of a bull in the western, and that of a celestial tiger in the northern door. With the mantram Agnimiti [tho preceptor] should place the first in the east, with the Ishetwa mantram he should place the second in the south, with the Agnaāyahi mantram he should place the third in the west, and with the Shaunodavi mantram he should place the fourth in the north. The flag, in the east, should be of the colour of a cloud, that in the south-east should be smoky-coloured, that in the north should be black, that in the south-west should be dark-blue, that in the west should be greyish, that in the north-west should be yellowish, that in the north should be crimson-coloured, and that in the north-east should be white. Vahurupā (one of various forms) should be placed in the middle. Indravidya should be placed in the east and with the Samsapti mantram Yamanāga should be placed in the south. Rakshahanā should be adored both in the north and west. Then two pitchers should be placed at each door, covered with two pieces of cloth, pasted with sandal, bedecked with profuse flowers and creepers and inspired with mantrams.

Thereupon the guardian deities of the quarters should be adored there according to the rites sanctioned by the Scripture. With mantram "*Trataram Indra*" Agni (the fire-god) should be worshipped upwards. The next mantram is *Asmin Vriksha Itanchaiva Prachari*. The other mantrams are *Kinchedhatu Achatya Vinnâdevi* and *Imakudra*. Having thus adored the guardian deities of the quarters a learned worshipper should place articles and necessary implements for Homa in the north-west. The preceptor should, with the eyes, make the assignment of white conch-shells as sanctioned by the Scriptures. Forsooth, all articles are purified by looks. A person, who longs for all objects of desire, should make the assignment of heart and various limbs with Vyahriti and Pranava and that of other articles with the Astra mantram. Fried grains and handfuls of Kuça or sacred grass should be consecrated with *Astra* mantrams. The preceptor should touch all articles, collected in the sacrificial shed, with the blade of Kuça. Next he should scatter on all sides fried grains consecrated with the *Astra* mantram. Beginning with the quarter (east) presided over by Indra he should scatter fried grains so long as they do not come within the perception of Ishana and then rub the ground of the sacrificial shed with cow-dung. The preceptor should next perform the assignment of the entire mass of mantrams in the vessel of *Arghya* with scents and other articles. Then with the water of the Arghya vessel he should wash the sacrificial shed. He should next make the assignment of a pitcher named after the deity whose image is to be installed. He should adore the pitcher in the north-east and the Vardhani (broom) in the north with the *Astra* mantram. He should place the pitcher, the Vardhani, the planets and the Vastu god in their respective seats with the recitation of Pranava. The preceptor should adore the pitcher, having a thread round its neck, containing jems, covered with a piece of beautiful cloth and scented with all the medicinal herbs. The deity should be adored in the pitcher together with the Vardhani and the most excellent cloth. He should afterwards roll the pitcher together with Vardhani (broom); then sprinkling the ground with drops of water pouring from the broom he should place it before. Then having worshipped the broom and the pitcher he should adore the deity in the sacrificial altar. Having invoked the pitcher in the north-west quarter as well as the Gana deities a learned worshipper should recite the name of the Vastu deity in the north-east quarter. For making good the imperfections of the ground he should with the Vastospati mantram dedicate offerings of animals to the evil spirits and their leader on the eastern side of the pitcher. Afterwards a learned worshipper should perform the rite of slaughtering those animals. With the mantram "Yoga, Yoga" he should next spread sacrificial fuels and Kuça blades. Then the presiding priest should place the images along with the Ritwikas (sacrificial priests) on the altar of bathing. Then having recited many holy and auspicious verses through the Brahma ghosas* the twice-born should place the image of the deity in the Brahma-car. Then having brought the altar to the north-east corner the preceptor should place it in the sacrificial shed. With the mantram "Bhadra Karne" he should

* The reciters of Vedic hymns.

bathe the image and then put on the sacrificial thread. Having sprinkled the image he should make the door after saluting it from a distance. He should next put collyrium for the eyes in a bell-metal or a copper vessel containing honey and Sarpi.* Then with the "Agni-Jyoti" mantram he should open up its eyes with a golden probe. Then with due rites he should give the name. Then with the Ganga mantram "Imamme" he should perform the rite of cooling the eyes. With the mantram "Agni-Murdheti" he should place the dust of an ant-hill. With the mantram "Yajnayajna" he should place the branches of astringent trees, *viz.*, Bel, Oodumvara, Ashwatha, Vata and Palasha. He should then sprinkle the image with five products of cow together with the goddesses, *viz.*, Sahadevi, Balā, Shatamuli, Shatāvari, Kumari, Guduchi, Sinhi and Vyagrihi.

The image of the animal, the god rides upon, should be built in the front of his temple, and gems, cereals, paddy and the Cotapuppika should be buried in the four corners of the edifice, the eight oceans such as the Ksherodi, Dadhi, etc., having been located by imagination in all the corners thereof by reading aloud the mantras which respectively begin as Apyasva, Dadhikratro, and Ya Ousadhi (those cereals) etc. The sacrificial pitchers should be invoked by uttering the mantra which runs as Tejosi, (thou art the light) etc., and bathed with water by repeating four times the mantra, known as the Samudraksa mantra. The preceptor, having bathed and dressed well, should offer the incense sticks together with the perfumed gum resin known as the Guggula, and invoke the particular sacred pools for bathing the sacrificial pitchers therein. The pitchers should be invoked with the mantra which runs as Ya Ousadhi; and they should be bathed in the sacred pools previously invoked by reading aloud the following

* A small medicinal shrub.

mantra. "A man, who bathes in that water, is purged off all sins etc." Having performed the rite of oblation unto the sacrificial pitchers and by uttering the mantra of the ocean (Samudra mantra), the Argha offering should be presented to them. The perfumed sandal paste should be presented repeating the mantra which begins as Gandhadvara, etc., and the Nyasa (rite of locating the fiery images of mantra or god in the different parts of the body) should be performed by uttering the mantras of the Veda. The cloth should be offered with the mantra which reads as this obtained with the means approved of the Shastras. The god should be taken into the sacrificial shed by reciting the mantra known as the Kavivaha, and laid down in the bed with the mantra which runs as Shambhavaya, etc. All the articles should be purified with the mantra known as the Devatacchakan. Then having merged himself in the supreme principle of the universe, the preceptor should perform the Nyasa rite known as the mantra Nyasa. Then the mantra should be worshipped under a covering.

Then as directed by the Scripture he should place offerings at the foot of the image. He should place the pitcher with gold, covered with pieces of cloth and inspired with Pranava mantra, where the head of the idol lies. Having placed it near the receptacle the preceptor should perform the rite of placing the sacred fire either according to the religious prescription of his own sacrificial code or according to the Vedic mantrams. One should recite Srisukta,* along with fire, its dwelling place, servants and deer-skin, Vrishākapi and Mitra in the west. A successful Adhyaryu† should recite in the south Rudra, Purushasukta,‡ Slokādhyaya§

* A hymn describing the glories of the goddess of prosperity.

† A Bramhan well-versed in the Atharva Veda.

‡ A hymn of the Rig-Veda.

§ A Chapter of verses of praise.

Bramha, the Pitris and Maitra. A person, versed in Chhandas (prosody), should recite, in the west, the Vedic observance Vāmadevya, Jyesthasama,* Bherundas† and Samans.‡ A Bramhan, well-versed in the Atharvan Veda, should recite in the north the principal portion of the Artharva, the (Kumbha Sukta verse) of the Atharva Veda, Neela Rudras§ and Maitra.

Touching the receptacle with the astra mantram, the Acharya (preceptor) should bring the fire, either in a copper vessel or an earthen one, according to his means, and place it before. A worshipper should light the fire with the astra mantram, should encircle it with the Kavacha mantram and afterwards perform the rite of Amritikarana with all the mantrams. He should take up the vessel with his two hands and roll it over the receptacle; and then with the Vishnu mantra he should throw the most excellent fire there. Either with the general mantrams or with those of his own sect he should place Brahma in the south and the sacrificial vessels in the north. Then with Kuça grasses he should place Paridhis|| in all the quarters. Brahmā, Vishnu and Hara should be adored with the general mantrams. He should place fire in the sacrificial grass and should encircle it with the same. That which is touched with a sacrificial grass is purified even in the absence of the mantrams. Encircled by uncut sacrificial grasses, with their blades directed in the east, west and north, the fire, of its own accord, comes near. One, well versed in mantrams, should do what has been said for the protection of the fire. Some preceptors hold that

---

* A portion of the Sama Veda. A religious rite of which its perusal is a part.

† One of Yakshinis or female attendants of Durga.

‡ Verses of the Sama Veda.

§ Mantrams of the Artharva Veda.

|| A wooden frame round the hole in which the a sacrificial fire is lighted.

the rite, consequent on the birth of a child, should be performed after the installation of the sacred fire. Thereupon performing the rite of Pavitra one should purify his kingdom. The preceptor should next see that the rite of prostration is performed with mantrams. He should pour clarified butter in drops into the fire for making the former sucessful. He should next offer ten oblations of clarified butter unto fire. As long as the rite of giving away kine continues so long Garbhādhāna and other rites should be solemnized. Either with the mantrams of his own Scriptural code or with Pranava a preceptor should perform the rite of Homa. Thereupon he should offer Purnāhuti (consummated oblation) from which one's desires are all fulfilled. A fire, thus generated, yeilds success in all works.

Thereupon having worshipped the fire he should place it in the receptacle. Then with his own mantrams he should offer a hundred oblations in honor of Indra and other gods. Then unifying his own self with all the gods, mantrams and fire he should offer the Purnàhuti. Then coming out the Acharya should offer sacrificial beasts to the guardian deities of the quarters, the evil spirits, gods and Nagas. Sessamum seeds and sacrificial fuels are the two necessary articles of Homa. Clarified butter is an auxilliary to them.

He should next assign Purushasukta to the east, Rudra to the south, and Jyesthasama and Bherunda to the west. Neelarudra is a great mantram of the Kurma Sukta (hymn) belonging to the Atharva-Veda. He should offer a thousand oblations to each of the gods—to their head, body and foot, and then offer Purnāhuti. In due order and without any distinction he should offer oblations to the spot where the head of the image is placed. The twice-born should offer oblations in honor of the gods either with the principal mantram, the mantrams of his own Scriptural code or with the Gayatri, or with only Gayatri, Vyarhriti and Pranava. Having thus duly performed the Homa rite a worshipper should make assignment of the mantrams. He should assign Agnimili to the feet, Ishitwa to the ankles, Agniayāhi to the hips, Saunodevi to the knee-joints, Vrihadantara to the thighs, Shwatira to the belly, Dirghāyustra to the heart, Shree to the neck, Trataramindra to the breast, Triyugmaka to the eyes, and Murdhābhava to the head.

Thereupon a preceptor should raise up the image saying "Rise up, O lord of the Brahmanas." Then with the Vedic and other sacred recitations he should circumambulate the divine edifice.

A person, well versed in mantrams, should next make the foot-stool of the deity. With jems he should place the image, of the deities of the quarters, metals and medicinal herbs and Louha Vijani behind the image. The image should not be placed in the centre of the adytum nor it should be absolutely abandoned. It should be placed a little distant from the centre and all imperfections should be removed thereby. Then sessamum seeds should be placed in the north. Afterwards reciting the mantram "Om, remain here permanently and do good unto the creatures, salutation unto thee" the preceptor should make assignment of mantras to the deity, the Sun and the six other gods. Having made the six-fold assignments for accomplishing success he should inspire them with mantrams.

He should next sprinkle the well-fixed image with the water of the Sampāta pitcher and adore it with lamps, incense, scents and edibles. Having offered Arghya and bowed unto the deity he should pray for forgiveness. Then according to his means, vessels, two pieces of raiment, umbrella and good rings should be presented as Dakshina (fee) to the officiating priests. Afterwards, with a controlled mind, the sacrificer should offer a hundred oblations and then the Purnāhuti. And then coming out of the temple the preceptor should dedicate offerings to the guardian deities of the quarters. With flowers in his hands and saying "Forgive" he should dedicate them. After the termination of the sacrifice the sacrificer should present unto the preceptor a Kapila cow, chowri, head-gear, ear-rings, umbrella, bracelet, an ornament for the waist, fans, villages, and raiments &c. He should then give a grand dinner party. Being liberated by the favour of the divine edifice a sacrificer becomes successful.

—:o:—

CHAPTER XLIX.

BRAMHA said:—Hari, the author of creation, &c., should be adored by the Self-create Bramha and other gods, and Bramhana and other castes, according to the rites of their respective orders. Hear their respective duties, O Vyasa.

Celebrating sacrifices for themselves and others, making gifts and accepting them, study and teaching constitute the six-fold duties of the Brahmanas. Making gifts, studying and celebrating sacrifices are the duties of the Kshatryas and the Vaishyas. To govern is also the duty of a Kshatrya whereas cultivation constitutes that of a Vaishya. To serve the twice-born is the duty of the Sudras. Handicraft and menial service are also their duties. Begging, attending the preceptor, Vedic study, abandonment of worldly affections and possessions and the preservation of the sacred fire constitute the duties of a Bramhacharin.

All the four Ashramas (orders) have two-fold conditions. They are called Bramhacharin (religious student) Upakurvana (house-holder), Vaishthika* and Bramhatatpara.† He

* The Bramhan who continues with his spiritual preceptor and always remains in the condition of the religious student.

† He, who giving up every other work, is solely engaged in the meditation of Para-Bramha.

who having duly studied the Vedas enters into the order of the house-holder, is called Upakarvānaka. He, who continues the life of the religious student till his death, is called Vaishthika. O foremost of the twice-born, the preservation of sacred fire, the entertainment of the guests, the celebration of sacrifices, making gifts and the adoration of the deities constitute the duties of a house-holder. A Udāsina (one disassociated from the world) and a Sādhaka (one devoted exclusively to religious practices), becomes a house-holder in two ways. A Sadhaka, while he is busy with maintaining his relations, becomes a house-holder. He, who having neglected the payment of three-fold debts* and renounced wife and earthly possessions, &c. roves about alone, is a nominal Udāsina.

The duty, of a dweller of the forest (hermit), consists in duly sleeping on earth, living on roots and fruits and studying the Vedas. He is the best of ascetics living in the forest who practises austerities in the forest, worships the gods, offers oblations to fire and studies the Vedas. Being emaciated greatly by practising hardest austerities, he, who is engaged solely in the meditation of the Deity, is known as a Sanyasin stationed in the Vanaprastha order. The Bhikshu or the mendicant, who daily practises Yoga, is self-controlled and follows the light of Jnāna (knowledge), is called Pārameshthika. The great ascetic, who delights in self and is ever gratified and besmeared with sandal, is called Bhikshu. Begging alms, Vedic studies, vow of silence, asceticism, meditation, perfect knowledge and disassociation from the world constitute the duties a Bhikshu. Pārameshthikas are divided into three classes—*viz.*, Jnāna Sanyasins†

* Every one, that is born, has got three debts to pay off:—to sages, gods and the Manes.

† The Sanyasins who follow the road of Knowledge.

Veda Sanyasins* and Karma Sanyasins.† Yoga is also three-fold—Bhoutika,‡ Kshatrā; and the third is Antashrami. Abstract meditation of the Deity is also three-fold—Prathamā, Duskara, Antimā. Religious rites beget emancipation and pursuance of worldly objects creates desire. Vedic rites are two-fold—Pravritti and Nivritti.§ Nrivritti or extinction of desire is preceded by Jnāna or knowledge and Pravritti is worked out by the worship of sacred fire.

Forgiveness, self-restraint, compassion, charity, want of avarice, simplicity, want of jealousy, visiting sacred shrines, truthfulness, contenment, faith in the existence of God, the subjugation of senses, the adoration of the deities, the worship of the Brahmanas, abstinence from doing injury, speaking sweet words, not to slander and amiability,—these are the duties of the various orders of the four castes. The region of Brahmā is reserved for those Brahmanas who perform sacrificial rites. That of Indra is intended for those Kshatryas who never fly away from the battle-field. That of the Gandharva is reserved for the Sudras who steadfastfy serve [the three higher castes].

The region, of the eighty-eight-thousand Rishis who have controlled their vital powers, is also reserved for those who live for ever with their preceptors. The region, which is reserved for the seven Rishis, is also intended for the ascetics who live in the forest. The blissful region of Brahma is reserved for the Yatis who have controlled their mental and intellectul faculties, for those who practise Nyasa and those who uphold the discharge of vital fluid. No ascetic returns from this region. The immortal, eternal, undecaying, ever

---

* Those who read the Vedas.

† Those who follow the road of action—*i.e.* who always engage in disinterested works.

‡ Elemental.

§ Pravritti is what destroys desire and *Nivritti* withdraws the mind from worldly objects.

blissful region of Ishwara, called Vyom, from which an emancipated person never returns, is reserved for the Yogins. Hear, I will describe in brief the eight sorts of Mukti or emancipation.

Yama* is of five sorts, *viz.*, abstaining from harming others, abstaining from killing animals, truthfulness, doing good to all creatures, restraint of speech, belief in God, abstaining from knowing a woman, Brahmacharya (life of a religious student), renunciation of all and accepting no gifts. Niyamas† are five, beginning with truthfulness and divided into two classes, external and internal. They are purification, truthfulness, contentment, penance and subjugation of senses. Sādhyaya is the recitation of Vedic Mantrams. And with the concentration of mind one should adore Hari. Asāna (yoga posture) consists of Padma and others, and Prānāyāma is the suppression of vital airs. Inhaling the breath and sending it with Mantrams and meditation, either twice or thrice, is called Puraka. Absolute suspension of breath is called Kumbhaka. Expiration by one nostril is called Rechaka. The withdrawal of the organs of senses from external objects is called Pratyahāra. Dhyāna is the meditation on self and Brahma. The steadying of the mind is called Dhāranā. The state of mind in which one's soul is absolutely immersed in Brahma and when he thinks "I am Brahma" is called Samādhi.

I am Self, the Para-Brahma, ever existent, full of knowledge and without end. The bliss of knowing Brahma

---

* Self-control;—a great moral or religious duty or observance. And here though it is mentioned five, but ten sorts of Yama are enumerated. The names are given differently by different writers.

† Religious rites or austerities which are not so obligatory as Yama. (In Yoga philosophy) Restraint of the mind, the second of the eight principal steps of meditation in Yoga.

is realized when one understands *Tattwamasi.** I am Brahma, am without body and organs of senses. I am devoid of mind, intellect and egoism. I am the light in three states of wakefulness, dreaming sleep, and dream-less sleep. I am eternal, pure, enlightened, existent, blissful and without second. I am that Prime Purusha. I am that undivided, portionless Purusha.

A Brahmana, thus meditating, is freed from the fetters of the world.

—:o:—

CHAPTER L.

BRAHMA said:—He who performs religious rites daily attains to Jnāna (knowledge). Having got up from bed at the Brahma-muhurta† he should meditate on religious profit and worldly profit. He should also meditate, in the lotus of his heart, on blissful and undecaying Hari. When the dawn approaches a learned man, having performed the necessary rites, should repair to a river of pure water for bathing, and perform there duly the purificatory rite. Even sinful wights are sanctified by morning ablutions. Therefore with every possible care a person should bathe early in the morning. Wise men speak highly of morning ablutions [in consequence of their yielding fruits] seen and unseen. When a person sleeps at ease saliva and other impurities come out. Therefore without bathing first no one should perform a religious rite. Poverty, misfortune, bad

* It is a transcendental Vedic phrase occurring in the Chhandogya Upanishad, meaning "That art Thou."

† Early part of the day.

dreams, and anxious thoughts—all these sins are forsooth destroyed by morning ablutions. It is not proper for persons to perform religious rites without bathing. Particularly in Homa and Japa one must bathe. He should sprinkle his head with water and rub his body with a piece of wet cloth. He should perform the six forms of bathing, viz., Brāhma, Agneya, Vāyavya, Divya, Vāruna and Yougika. The Brāhma form of bathing consists in rubbing the body with drops of water poured through Kuça reeds and accompanied with Mantrams. Agneya form consists is besmearing the body, from head to foot, with ashes. The most excellent form of bathing, namely, Vāyavya, consists in rubbing on the body the powder of cow-dung. Bathing in the sun-shine is called Divya. Varuna consists in plunging into water and knowing the self in mind. Meditation on Hari by means of Yoga is called Yougika form of bathing. It is the shrine of self resorted to by Brahmavadins.

With his face directed towards either the north or the east a person should cleanse his teeth with the twigs either of Kshira, Malati, Vilwa or Karavira trees. Standing on a purified spot he should wash his teeth and mouth and then throw the stick away. Afterwards having bathed he should offer libations of water to the celestials, Rishis and the departed manes. Having rinsed his mouth he should do it again observing silence. Having sprinked his body with drops of water through Kuça reeds and with Mantrams, Apohistha, Vyarhriti and the auspicious Vāruni and having recited the Gayatri, consisting of Om and Vyarhriti, the mother of the Vedas, he should offer libations of water to the sun with his mind fixed in him.

Thereupon sitting on Kuça grass in the morning, controlling his mind and suppressing his vital air he should meditate on Sandhyā Mantrams. She, who is Sandhyā, is the mother of the universe, beyond illusion, sinless, divine and sprung from three-fold energies. Having thus meditated a learned man should recite crimson-coloured, white and dark-blue Gayatri. With his face directed towards the earth a Brahmana should always perform his Sandhya rites. He, who does not make Sandhya worship, is impure and is not competent to perform any action. And he does not reap the fruit of any thing else he does. Having duly adored Sandhya, the pure and self-controlled Brahmanas, the masters of the Vedas, attain to the most excellent region. That best of the twice-born, who, neglecting the Sandhya rites, tries to perform any other religious ceremony, goes to a million of hells. Therefore with every possible care one should perform the Sandhya rites. By doing so one gets the most excellent celestial and Yoga body.

A learned man, controlling his senses, purifying his own body and mind, and sitting with his face towards the east, should recite the Gayatri, a thousand, hundred or ten times. Having controlled his mind, he should sit facing the rising sun. With many potent Mantrams, belonging to the Rik, Yayush and Sama Veda, he should adore and salute the Sun, the god of gods, touching the ground with his head, saying "Om, salutation, I dedicate my self unto Khasholka, the cause of the three-fold causes, unto him of the form of knowledge. Thou art Brahma, the great water, fire and juice. Thou art earth, heaven and sky, Om and the eternal Rudra." Having recited mentally this most excellent hymn in the morning and noon one should bow unto the Sun.

Then returning to his house and rinsing his mouth duly with water a Brahmana should light up (himself) the sacred fire and offer oblations unto it. With the permission of the sacrificer, his priest, son, wife, pupil or brother may also offer oblations. Any religious rite, that is performed without Mantrams, yields no fruit in this world. He should bow unto the deities and dedicate unto them offerings. He should adore his preceptor and do what is conducive to his well-being. A twice-born should afterwards, according to his power, study the

Vedas with proper care; he should recite the Mantrams, teach his pupils, conceive the meaning and discuss the same. That best of the twice-born should also read the Dharma Shastras (Religious Codes), the Vedic texts and the Vedangas.* For making his Yoga successful the twice-born should approach the Deity and afterwards do various works, for his relatives. Thereupon in the noon he should collect,—for the purpose of bathing, earth, flowers, dried paddy, sessamum seeds, sacrificial grass, and the pure cow-dung. He should bathe in a river, in a tank dedicated to a deity, in a pool or in a pond (of his own) but he should never bathe (in a well or tank) belonging to another person. If he does not offer five pindas every day his bathing becomes impure. The head should be washed once with earth, the navel twice, the part beneath it thrice, and the feet six times. Earth should be of the quantity of a ripe Myrobalam; cow-dung should also be of the same quantity. He should then besmear his body with it. Having washed his body and rinsed his mouth, he should bathe with a controlled mind. Then coming on the shore, he should besmear his body with earth, reciting the Linga Mantrams. He should then inspire the water with the auspicious Varuna Mantrams. At the time of bathing he should think of the Nārāyana form of Vishnu in the water. Having looked at the sun with Om, he should thrice plunge himself into the water and again rinse his mouth with the following mantram.

"Thou rangest in the mind of creatures and art the

---

* Certain classes of works regarded as auxiliary to the Vedas and designed to aid in the correct pronounciation and interpretation of the text and the right employment of Mantrams in the ceremonials. They are six in number:—(1) Siksha, Ortheopy, or the science of proper articulation and pronounciation; (2) Chhandas, Prosody; (3) Vyakarana, Grammar; (4) Nirukta, Etymology, or derivative explanations of Vedic words and phrases; (5) Jyotish, Astronomy; (6) Kalpa, Ritual.

mouth of the universe. Thou art Yama, Vashatkara, water, fire, juice and ambrosia."

He should repeat thrice the Drupada Mantram consisting of Vyahriti and Pranava. The learned worshipper should next recite the Savitri Mantram destructive of sins. Thereupon he should cleanse the earth with the Apohistha Mantram, with the Mantram "flow pure water" and with Vyahriti. He should next inspire water with Apohistha Mantram. He should next repeat thrice the Mantram "Antarjalamavagagnon" destructive of all sins, or Drupadā or Savitri, the most excellent region of Vishnu. He should next recite Pranava and meditate on Hari the god of gods. Taking up water in his hands and reciting the Mantram, he should sprinkle the head therewith, and would thus be freed off all sins.

Having made the Sandhyā adorations and rinsed his mouth, he should daily meditate on the God, and sit facing the sun, placing his palms full of flowers on the crown of his head. Throwing them he should look at the god stationed on the rising mountain (*i.e.* the rising sun) with the Mantram "Thou art the eye, ever pure, supreme soul and existent," or particularly with the Savitri or other Vedic Mantrams. He should next repeat Gāyatri and various other mantrams. Sitting on a seat of Kuça grass with his face towards the east he should look at the sun and repeat prayers with a controlled mind. The garland of beads should either be made of crystal, lotus, Rudraksha or Putrānjiva. If his cloth be tattered he should stand in the water and perform his adorations. Else he should sit, with a controlled mind, on Kuça grass spread on a sanctified spot. Then going round, he should bow touching the ground with his head. Then rinsing his mouth as sanctioned by the Shastras, he should read the Vedas according to his power. Afterwards he should offer libations of water for the gods, Rishis and the departed manes with the prayer "Om, salutation unto you all, I offer these libations of water." He should dedicate libations of water and fried paddy unto the celestials and Brahma Rishis. He should dedicate offerings reverentially unto the departed manes, gods and ascetics according to the prescription of his own Religious Code. He should gratify the celestial saints and the departed manes with palmfuls of water. Sacrificial threads are also offered to the gods along with water, Niveeta (the Brahminical thread suspended round the neck) to the Rishis and Prācheenavitins (the sacrificial thread worn over the right arm and passing under the left) to the departed manes.

Pressing the water out of the cloth after bathing, rinsing his mouth and observing silence, he should adore the deities with flowers, leaves and water, and Swa Mantrams. O wrathful Hara, [he should adore] Brahmā, Shankara, the sun-god, the slayer of Madhu (Vishnu) and various other approved deities. With the Purusha Sukta Mantram he should dedicate flowers and other offerings; or he should adore all the deities with water only. Controlling his mind he should meditate on the deity repeating Om. Then saluting him he should keep flowers and other offerings in separate places. Without adoration no Vedic rite becomes consecrated. Therefore in the beginning, middle and end of every rite, one should mentally meditate on Hari. With the Mantram "Thou art Vishnu" and the hymn of the Purusha-Sukta, one should dedicate his self unto Vishnu of pure effulgence. Having all his mental faculties tranquilized and his mind fixed on the deity, he should, with the Mantram, "thou art Vishnu," perform the five sacrifices, namely that for the deities, that for the evil spirits, that for the departed manes, that for men and that for Bramha. Without the offering of libations of water Brahma Yajna is not finished. After celebrating the sacrifice for men (Mānushayajna) one should read the Vedas. In a sacrifice for the gods offerings should be made to that class of gods called Vishwadevas. In a

Bhutayajna animals should be sacrified for the evil spirits. The foremost of the twice-born should next offer food to the dogs, the degraded caste people, outcastes and birds, on the ground outside the house.

In honor of the departed manes the best of sacrificers should feed at least one Brahmana. He should perform the daily Srāddha in their honor. Such a Pitriyajna yields blessed regions. Then with a controlled mind he should, commensurate with his means, take up a portion of food and offer it to a Brahmana well-read in the Vedas. He should daily treat his guests hospitably and welcome a Brahmana who comes to his house and adore him with mind, words and deeds.

A mouthful of food is called Bhikshā (alms) and enough is given when four times as much is distributed. A guest should wait for the period that is necessary for milching a cow. One should, as much as lies in his power, treat uncalled-for guests hospitably. One should daily offer alms to a mendicant, and food to a Brahmacharin (religious student) and to beggars what they want proportionate to his means, and being himself freed from avarice. He should next take food in the company of his friends. The foolish Brahmana, who takes his food without celebrating these five sacrifices, is born in a degraded caste. Those, who are competent to celebrate a great sacrifice, should study the Vedas. The adoration of a god dissipates speedily all sins. He, who, either out of ignorance or laziness, takes his food without worshipping the deity, goes to hell and is born as a hog.

I will now describe what is impurity. An impure man is visited by sins. Impurity is generated either by associating with impure persons or avoiding the company of pious men. The learned Brahmanas speak of ten sorts of impurity. The Brahmanas are impure if any person dies in their family or any child is born. When a child dies before teething the period of impurity is immediately over; it lasts for a day before the solemnization of the rite of tonsure. It lasts for three days before the rite of wearing sacred thread is not performed. After that it lasts for ten nights. For the Kshatryas the period consists of twelve days, and for the Vaishyas fifteen days. A Shudra is cleansed from impurity after a month. For a Yati there is no impurity. For abhortion it lasts either for a night or for a month.

—:o:—

CHAPTER LI.

BRAHMA said:—I will now describe the most excellent rules of making charities. Wealth should be respectfully given to a worthy person. Charity yields enjoyment and emancipation. Riches, acquired by fair means, when given away in charities, yeild the fruits of enjoyment. Teaching, officiating as priests and accepting presents are the duties of the Brahmanas. Usury, agriculture and trade are the duties of the Vaishyas. When charity is made to a worthy person it is called Svattwik (*v.* one pervaded by the quality of goodness). Besides there are various other forms of charity, *viz.*, Nitya (daily), Naimittika (occasional), Kamya (made with the desire of fruits) and Vimala (pure, or disinterested). Whatever is daily given to persons who have done us no good or to the Brahmanas without any expectation for fruits it is called Nitya. Whatever is given to a learned person, for the expiation of sins or for averting evils, is called Naimittika. Such charities are made by pious men. Whatever is given for having children, achieving victory, or attaining heaven, is called by the Rishis, well read in the

Religious Code, Kāmya. With a mind pervaded by the quality of Svattwa (goodness) when a man makes presents to persons conversant with the knowledge of Brahma, only with the object of pleasing God such a gift is called Vimala.

If a man gives lands abounding in barley and corns and outskirted on all sides with sugar-cane plants, he is never born again. There never had been nor there will be any charity superior to the giving away of lands. By giving education unto the Brahmanas one becomes glorified in the region of Brahma. By giving reverentially food unto the Brahmacharins one, freed off of all sins, attains to the region of Brahma. If a person, after fasting on the full-moon day in the month of Vaishakha (March-April), adores twelve Brahmanas with honey and cakes of sessamum seeds or with scents or with sweet and moral words, all the sins, committed by him all through his life, are immediately dissipated. Having placed sessamum seeds, gold, honey and sarpi on skin of a black antelope he, who makes them over to a Brahmana, crosses over all his iniquities. He, who specially in the month of Vaishaka treats the Brahmanas with clarified butter, boiled rice and water in honor of Dharmaraja, becomes freed from all fear. If on the twelfth day of a fortnight a person adores Vishnu who destroys all sins he forsooth becomes freed from all sins. Whatever deity a man wishes to adore he must beforehand worship the Brahmanas and feed the women and celestials. He, who wishes to recover from a disease, must worship the Sun; while one, wishing for riches, should worship the fire-God. One, wishing for success in all his undertakings, should worship Vināyaka and one, wishing for enjoyments, should worship the moon. One, wishing for strength, should adore the Wind-god. And he, who wishes for emancipation from worldly fetters, should with every care adore Hari. He, who does not desire for any thing or he, who desires for everything, should adore Gadādhara. The giver of water attains to gratification. The giver of boiled rice enjoys happiness. The giver of sessamum seeds obtains good offspring and the giver of lamps most excellent eyes. One, who gives away lands, attains to all while the giver of gold acquires longevity. The giver of houses attains to the most exalted station in the world and the giver of silver a most handsome appearance. The giver of dwelling houses attains to the region of the moon and the giver of horses to that of Ashwins. The giver of bulls attains prosperity while the giver of kine attains to the region of Brahmā. He, who gives conveyances and beddings, obtains a wife, and the giver of protection attains wealth. The giver of corns enjoys eternal happiness; while the giver of Brahma (knowledge of) attains to the neighbourhood of Brahma. Imparting knowledge on the knowers of the Vedas one becomes glorified in the celestial region. By giving grass to the kine one becomes freed from all sins. By giving sacrificial fuels a man becomes effulgent like fire. By giving to the diseased, for the removal of his ailments, medicines, attendance and food one becomes freed from diseases, enjoys happiness and lives long. By giving away umbrellas one passes unscathed through a road of Asipatra leaves, sharp as razor and does not suffer from the fierce rays of the sun. He, who wishes things never to end, must give away unto qualified persons the various desired-for objects of the world and whatever is most favourite unto him in the house. If any thing is given away in charity during the equinox, the solar and lunar ecclipses and on the last day of a month it becomes never exhausted. There is no religious rite for a man to perform in this world superior to the making of charities in Prayaga (Allahabad) and various other sacred places and especially in Gayā where charities are made for attaining heaven and averting evils. The sinful person, who prevents a Brahmana from worshipping sacred fire and celebrating sacrifices, goes to hell. He, who does not give food during a famine, becomes the hateful destroyer of the Brahmanas on account of their meeting with death (for his negligence).

—:o:—

CHAPTER LII.

BRAMHA said :—I will describe the regulations of Prāyaṣchitta or penances. The principal sinners are those who kill Brahmanas, those who drink spirituous liquors, those who commit thefts and those who violate the beds of their preceptors. And the fifth class of sinners are those who associate with all those people. The minor sins, as described by the celestials, are the slaughtering of kine, etc. One, committing the sin of Brahmanicide, should make a cottage in a forest and live there for twelve years; or he should fast or level the summit of a mountain; or he should himself either enter into fire or water. For the Brahmanas or the kine, one should entirely give up his life. By giving food to the learned one may expatiate the sin of Brahmanicide. By performing a horse-sacrifice or bathing in a sacred shrine, one is freed from the sin. Or he should make over his all to a Brahmana, well read in the Vedas. A twice-born one should bathe thrice a day at the sacred and celebrated confluence of all the streams of the river Saraswati and fast for three nights. By bathing at the Setuvandha,* at Kapalmochana and Benares, one is freed from the sin of Brahmanicide. The twice-born, who has drunk spirituous

* Near Rameshwaram in the District of Madura in the Madras Presidency where Rama, the hero of Ramayana, constructed a bridge over the ocean for going to Lanka (Ceylon).—The Adam's Peak of Modern Geography.

liquor, is freed from the sin by drinking, hot as fire, wine, milk, clarified butter and cow's urine. By being killed by a king with a mace the stealer of gold is freed from the sin. For expiating the sin of Brahmanicide, a twice-born one should, clad in bark, live in the forest. A Brahmana, who possessed by lust, knows his preceptor's wife, is to embrace the heated figure of a woman made of black iron. Or he may observe the penance of Brahmanicide or perform the Chāndrāyana* vow. A Brahmana, who keeps company with degraded people, should perform the following penance for cleansing himself of the sin. He should undergo hardships without any sleep for one full year and duly give away his every thing. This will destroy all sins. Due celebration of Chandrayana accompanied with all possible hardships and the visiting of sacred places, such as Gaya, also leads to the destruction of the sin. He, who on an Amāvashyā day adores Bhava and feeds the Brahmanas, is also freed off of all sins. If one, bathing in a river in the forenoon and fasting on the fourteenth day of the dark fortnight, offers seven handfuls of water with sessamum seeds to Yama, Dharmaraja, Mrityu, Anantaka, Vaivaswata, Kala and SarvabhutaKshaya (the destroyer of all creatures) he becomes freed from all sins. Having controlled his intellectual and mental faculties he should observe the vow of celibacy, sleep on earth, fast and adore the twice-born. On the sixth day from the full moon he should, with a controlled mind, adore the deity (Vishnu), and on the seventh day, the sun-god. He would thus be freed off of all sins. Having fasted and adored Janārddana on the eleventh and the twelfth days

* A religious observance or expiatory penance regulated by the moon's age (the period of its waxing and waning); in it the daily quantity of food, which consists of fifteen mouthfuls at the full-moon, is diminished by one mouthful every day during the dark fortnight till it is reduced to zero at the new moon and is increased in like manner during the light fortnight.

of the light fort-night, one becomes freed from all great sins. Recitation, visiting the sacred shrines and the worship of the deities and Brahmanas during an eclipse also destroys sins. Even if visited by all sorts of sins, a man duly renounces his life at a sacred shrine he becomes freed from them all. If a woman enters into fire with her husband, she reclaims him, even if he be guilty of Brahmanicide, ingratitude or of other vile iniquities. The chaste woman, who is always anxious to serve her husband, is visited by no sin either in this world or in the next. As it is said that the lucky wife of Rama, the son of Dasharatha, Sita, celebrated in the world, defeated the king of Rakshasas. By bathing in the sacred Phalgu river one reaps the fruit of all the religious rites. Formerly thus did the divine Vishnu speak to me, O ye of controlled actions.

CHAPTER LIII.

SUTA said :—Thus did Brahma describe the eight Nidhis* as he had heard from Vishnu. They are Pâdma, Maha-Padma, Makara, Kachchapa, Mukunda, Nanda, and Neela. And the other Nidhi is Sangkha. I will now describe their characteristic marks. A person, bearing the mark of Padma, becomes Svattwika (pervaded by the quality of goddess).

* Divine treasures of Kuvera nine of which are enumerated *viz.*, the Padma, Mahapadma, Sankha, Makara, Kachchapa, Mukunda, Nanda, Nila and Kharba: their nature is not exactly defined though some of them appears to be precious gems. According to the Tantrik system, they are personified and worshipped as demi-gods attendant either upon Kuvera or upon Lakshmi.

He is compassionate by nature, collects gold, silver, etc., and dedicates them to Yatis, celestials and ascetics. A person, bearing the mark Mahāpadma, gives away wealth unto the pious. Persons, bearing the marks of Padma and Maha-Padma Nidhis, are called Svattwika. A person, bearing the mark of Makara, becomes the collector of swords, arrows and lances. He gives away wealth unto persons, well-read in Shrutis and contracts friendship with kings. He also destroys his enemies in battle. Makara and Kachchapa are the two Tamasik (pervaded by the quality of ignorance) Nidhis. One, bearing the mark of Kachchapa, does not confide in any one and does not eat; nor does he give anything to any one. That singular person, bearing the mark of this Niddhi, fills the earth with treasures.

A person, bearing the mark of the Rajasik (pervaded by the quality of darkness) Nidhi Mukunda, becomes the collector of kingdoms. He enjoys freely and liberally and makes presents to the songsters and prostitutes. A person, bearing the mark of Nanda pervaded by the qualities of darkness and ignorance, becomes the support of his family, always pleased with eulogy and the husband of many wives. He loses affection for his former friends and finds delight in new ones. One, bearing the mark of Neela, is endued with the virtues of Svattwa guna. He collects clothes and corns and digs tanks, etc. The Niddhi Sangka is selfish and himself squanders away his money. His relatives live on a very wretched fare and do not put on beautiful raiments. One, bearing the mark of Sangka, is always busy with seeking his own pleasure and does not give his money to any one else. The characters of these Nidhis were thus described by Hari unto Hara and others. I describe the treasures of the world as recounted by Hari.

CHAPTER LIV.

Hari said:—Agnidhra, Agnivahu, Vapushman, Dyutiman, Medhatithi, Bhavya, Shavala, Putra, and the tenth Jyotisman—these were the sons of Priyavrata. Medha and Agnivahu had three sons each, who were given to Yoga, were great, had the recollection of their pristine births and fixed their minds on the kingdom. Having divided the earth into seven insular continents the king conferred them on his seven sons. The earth is situated on the water like unto a boat and is five hundred koti yojanas in dimension. O Hara, the two insular continents are Jamvu and Plaksha. The next is Shalmala. The others are Kusha, Krouncha and Shaka. The seventh is Pushkara. All these islands are each girt by seven oceans. They are Lavana, Ikshu, Sura, Sarpi, Dadhi, Dugdha, and water. Each ocean is double in dimension than the island it encircles, O bull-emblemed deity. In the insular continent of Jamvu is situate the mount Meru extending over a lak of Yojanas. Its summit is eighty four thousand Yoyanas in height. Its base is sixteen thousand Yojanas and is of the shape of a pericarp of a lotus. The boundary mountains Himavan, Hemakuta and Nishadha are situate on its south, while Neela, Shveta and Sringi mountains are situate in the north. O Rudra, the persons, who live in the insular continent of Plaksha, are immortal. O Shankara, there is no division of Yugas (cycles) in all these islands. Agnidhra, the king of the insular continent Jamvu, had nine sons, *viz.*, Nabhi, Kimpurusha, Harivarsha, Ilavrita, Ramya, Hiranwān, Shastha, Kurubhadrāshwa and Ketumāla. The king divided his kingdom into nine parts and conferred them on all his sons. Nabhi begat on Merudevya a son by name Rishabha. His son, the ascetic Bharata lived in Shālagrāma.

Bharata's son was Sumati whose son was Tejasa. His son was Indradyumna, whose son was known as Paramesthi. The latter's son was Prateehāra whose son was Pratiharta. He begat a son by name Prastara whose son was the powerful Prithu. His son was Nakta whose son was Gaya. Gaya's son was Nara whose son was Buddhirat. His son was the intelligent and highly powerful Bhouvana. He had four sons, viz., Twastha, Twasthu, Virajā and Rajas. Raja's son was Shatajit whose son was Vishwakjyot.

—:o:—

CHAPTER LV.

HARI said :—In the centre is situate the kingdom of Ilāvrita ; while that of Bhadrāshwa is situate in the east. In the south-east is situate Hiranwānvarsha, O bull-emblemed deity, Kimpurusha Varsha is situate in the south of the mount Meru. Bharata Varsha is situate in the south, while Hari, in the south-west. Ketumāla is situate in the west, while Ramyaka, in the north-west. In the north is situate Kuruvarsha covered with Kalpa trees. O. Rudra, except Bharata Varsha, Siddhi is naturally obtainable every-where. Indradwipa, Kasherumana, Tamravarna, Gabhasti-man, Nāgadwipa, Kataha, Simhala and Varuna—these are the nine islands each encircled by an ocean. The Kiratas live in the east, the Yavanas in the west, the Andhras in the south, and the Turashkas in the north. The Brahmanas, Kshatryas, Vaishyas and Sudras live in the central group of the islands.

Mahendra, Malaya, Sahya, Shuktiman, Riksha, Vindhya, Paribhadra,—all these are the seven boundary mountains.

Vedasmriti, Narmadā, Varadā, Surasā, Shiva, Tapi, Payoshni, Sarayu, Kaveri, Gomati, Godāveri, Bhimarathi, Krishnavarnā, Mahānadi, Ketumāla, Tamraparni, Chandrabhagā, Saraswati, Rishikutyā, Mritagangā, Payashwini, Vidarbha and Satadru—these are the sacred rivers destructive of all sins. The inhabitants of the central countries drink the water of all these rivers.

Panchalas, Kurus, Matsyas, Youdheyas, Sapatacharas, Kuntis and Surasenas, are the the clans who inhabit the central countries. O bull-emblemed deity, the Padmas, Sutas, Magadhas, Chedis, Kāshāyas, Videhas live in the eastern countries. Koshalas, Kalingas, Vangas, Pundrangas, Mulakas as well as those living around the Vindhya ranges are said to inhabit south-eastern countries. The inhabitants of Pulinda, Ashmaka and Jinutanaya as well as Kambojas, Karnatas and Ghatas are called Southerners. The people of Amvastha, Dravidā, Latta, Kamboja, Strimukhā, Sakā, and Anartha are said to inhabit south-western, countries. Strairājyas, Saindhavas, Mlechchhas and the godless Yavanas together with Naishadas and the people of Mathura are known as inhabiting the western countries. Māndavya, Tushāra, Mulika, Musha, Kosha, Mahākesha, Mahānāda are the countries lying in the north-west. Lamvakas, Tananāgas, Madragandharavahyikas are the Mlechchhas living in the north beyond the Himālaya. Trigarta, Neelakolabha, Brahmaputra, Satangkanā, Ablushāha and Kashmira are all situated in the north.

——:o:——

CHAPTER LVI.

HARI said :—Medatithi, the king of the insular continent of Plaksha, had seven sons, viz., the eldest Shāntabhava, Shishira, Sukhovaya, Nanda, Shiva, Kshemaka and Dhruva. These seven were the kings of the insular continent Plaksha.

Gomeda, Chandra, Nārada, Dundubhi, Somaka, Sumanā, and Shaila were the seven sons of Vibhraja. Anutaptā, Sikhi, Vipāsha, Tridivā, Krama, Amritā and Sukritā were the seven rivers. Vapushmān was the king of the insular continent Shalmala. His sons were called Varshas. They were Sweta, Harita, Jimuta, Rohita, Vaidyuta, Mānasa and Saprabha. Kumudary, Unnata, Drona, Mahisha, Valāhaka, Krouncha and Kakudman, these seven were the mountains. The rivers were Yoni, Toā, Vitrishna, Chandra, Shuklā and Vimochani; the seventh was Vidhrit; and they all afforded release from sins.

Jyotishmān, the king of the insular continent Kusha, had seven sons. Hear their names. They were Udvida, Venumān, Dwairatha, Lamvana, Dhriti, Prabhākara and Kapila. The mountains were Vidrumā, Hemashaila, Dyutimān, Pushpamān, Kusheshaya, Hari and the mount Mandara. The rivers were Dhutapāpā, Shivā, Pavitra, Sammati Vidyudambhā, Mahikāsha. They were all destructive of all sins.

Dyutimān had seven high-souled sons in the insular continent of Krouncha. Kushala, Mandaga, Ushna, Pivara, Andhakāraka, Muni and Dundubhi; these seven were his sons, O Hara. The seven mountains were Krouncha, Vamana, the third Andhakāraka, Devavrit, Mahashaila, Dundubhi and Pandarikavan, Gouri, Kumudvati, Sandhya,

Ratri, Manojavā, Kyati and Pundariva—these seven were the boundary rivers.

The king of the insular continent of Shāka begat seven sons, viz., Jalava, Kumara, Sukumāra, Mashivaka, Kusumoda, Samodārki and the seventh Mahādruma. Sukumari, Kumāri, Nalinī, Dhenukā, Ikshu, Venukā and Gabhasti were the seven rivers.

Shavala, the king of Pushkara, begat the great hero Dhātaki. The two Varshas were situate on the mount Mānosottara. It was a thousand Yojanas in height. Its summit was five hundred yojanas high and its extent an all sides was the same. The insular continent of Pushakara is encircled on all sides by the ocean of sweet water. Before the sweet water is seen the country inhabited by people; the gold fields, shorn of all animals, constitute the half of the continent. The mountain is Lokāloka, one Ayuta of yojanas in extent. One part of this mountain is enshrouded with darkness and the other part is free from it.

CHAPTER LVII.

Hari said:—Twenty seven thousand yojanas is the extent of the earth and ten thousand and one is that of the nether region. O bull-emblemed deity, Atala, Vitala, Nitala, Gabhastiman, Mahakshya, Sutala and Agra are the seven Pātālas. Krishna (dark-blue), Suktaruna (white as sun), Pita (yellow), Sarkara and Shailakanchana are the lands there where the Daityas and serpents reside. In the terrific insular continent of Pushkara are situate the hells. Hear their names.

They are Rourava, Sukara, Vodha, Tāla, Vishasana, Mahajvāla, Taptakumbha, Lavana, Vimdhita, Rudhira, Vaitarani, Krimisha, Krimibhojana, Asipatravana, Krishna, the terrific hell Nānabhaksha, Pujavaha, Papa, Vanhijvāla, Sadangsha, Krishnasutra, Tama, Avichi, Swabhojana, Apratishtba, Ushnavichi. The sinners who administer poison, use weapons and set fire, are wasted there. O Rudra, the various lokas or regions are situate one over another. The various elements are also situate in this order. O Rudra, the egg is encircled by the principle of greatness and that again by water, fire and ether covering the space ten times that occupied by the egg.

——:o:——

CHAPTER LVIII.

HARI said :—Hear, I will now describe the position and the dimension of the sun and other planets. The sun has nine cars, each a thousand yojanas in dimension. Twice this number is the dimension of its plough, O bull-emblemed deity. Half a Koti and seven Niyuta of yojanas is the dimension of its Aksha (part of wheel), where the wheel is placed. It has three naves and six Nemis (circumference). This wheel goes one round within one full year. The second Aksha of the car of Vivashwan is forty thousand yojanas in dimension. The five others have each half the same dimension, O bull-emblemed deity. The extent of each of the two Akshas is half a yuga (cycle) ; the smaller Aksha, of the car, with half the cycle is stationed in the polar star. And the second wheel is stationed in the mount Mānasa.

Gayatri, Samvrihati, Ushnic, Jagati, Tristuv, Anustup, and Pankti—these metres are the the horses of the sun.

Dhātā, Kratusthala, Pulastya, Vasuki, Rathakrit, Agramanī, Heti and Tamvaru reside in the solar disc in the month of Chaitra, Aryamā, Pulahā, Rathonjas, Punjikasthala, Praheti, Kachcha, Nira and Narada in the month of Vaishaka. Mitra, Atri, Takshaka, Raksa, Pourusheya, Menaka, Haha, Rathaswana reside on the car of the sun in the month of Jaistha. Varuna, Vasistha, Rambhā, Sajanya, Kuhu, Budha, Rathachitra and Sukra live in the month of Ashāda. Indra, Vîshwavasu, Srota, Elāpatra, Angira, Plamocha and Nabha—these serpents live in the month of Srāvana. Vivaswān, Ugrasena, Bhrigu, Apurana, Anumlochā, Shangkapāla and Vyagra live in the month of Bhādrapāda. Pushā, Suruchi, Dhātā, Goutama, Dhananjaya, Sushena, Ghritachi live in the sun in the month of Ashwin. Vishwāvasu, Bharadwāja, Parjanya, Airavata, Vishwāchi, Senajit, and Apā—these are entitled to live in the month of Kartika. Angsu, Kāshyapa, Tarkshya, Mahāpadma, Urvashi, Chitrasena, and Midyut live in the month of Agrahayana. Kratu, Bharga, Urnāyu, Sphurja, Bharga, Urnāyu, Karkot, Aristhanemi, Purvachitti, and the most excellent Apsaras live in the solar disc in the month of Poush. Twastha, Jamadagni, Kamvala, Tilottamā, Brahmāpeta, Ritajit and Dhritarastra live in the solar disc in the month of Māgha. Vishnu, Ashwatara, Rambhā, Suryavarchcha, Satyajit, Vishwāmitra, Raksha and Yajnapela live in the month of Phalguna.*

* The following is the list of English months corresponding with Hindu ones :—

Hindu.			*English.*
Vaishak	...	...	... March, April.
Jaista	...	...	... April, May.
Ashara	...	...	... May, June.
Shravan	...	...	... June, July.
Bhadra	...	...	... July, August.
Ashvin	...	...	... August, September.
Kartik	...	...	... September, October.
Agrahayan	...	...	... October, November.

O Brahman, the solar disc is pervaded by the energies of Vishnu. The ascetics laud the sun and the Gandharvas sing before. The Apsaras dance and the night-rangers follow the sun. The Pannagas carry (the vehicle) and the Yakshas collect the bridles. The Valikhilya Rishis sit encircling him.

The car of the moon has three wheels and the horses are white as Kunda flowers. It runs, drawn by ten horses, on the right and left. The car of the son of the moon (Budha) is made of [the essence of] air and fire. It is drawn by eight yellow-coloured steeds fleet as the wind. The great chariot of Shukra has a Varutha,* Anukarsha,† is drawn by horses born of earth and adorned with flags. The huge chariot of Bhumi's (earth) son (Mars) is of the colour of molten gold and is drawn by eight steeds, of the colour of the filaments of a lotus and born of fire. Jupiter resides for one year at every sign of a Zodiac sitting on his golden car drawn by eight yellowish-white horses. Riding a car drawn by horses of variegated colour and born of ether Saturn moves slowly on; Swarbhanu‡ has eight horses of the colour of the earth and his car is grey-hued. O lord of goblins, yoked to his car they carry him, day and night. Rāhu's car has eight horses, fleet as the wind and smoky-coloured and which have their tongues coated with saliva. On it he roams over the earth consisting of islands, rivers and mountains.

Poush	...	...	... November, December.
Magh	...	...	... December, January.
Phalgoon	...	...	... January, February.
Chaitra	...	...	... February, March.

* A sort of wooden frame or fender with which a chariot is provided as a defence against collision.

† The axle-tree or bottom of a carriage.

‡ Rahu; the personified ascending node.

——:0:——

CHAPTER LIX.

SUTA said:—Having learnt the solar system and the dimension of the earth Keshava communicated, unto Rudra, the essence of astronomy having four characteristic marks.

HARI said:—Krittikā (Gemini)* is the planet of the fire-god and Rohini (Cancer) is of Brahma. Illwalā (stars in the Orion's head) belonging to Soma and Ardra (Virgo) to Rudra Aditya (the sun) and Punarvasu (Libra) are the planets of the preceptor. Ashlesha (Sagita) is the planet of the serpents while Maghā (Capri) is that of the departed manes. Purva-Phalguni (Aquari) is the planet of good luck as well as the sun, Uttara-Phalguna (Pisces), Savitrā (sun) Hasta,† Chitra‡ and Twastā (sun).

Shyati is known as the star of the wind-god and Vishakha, O bull-emblemed deity, is that of Indra and Fire-god. Maitram, Iksham, Anurudha and Jyestha are the stars of Shakra. Mulas is the star of Nirhriti. Ashada Purva is that of water-god and Uttarā is that of Vishwadevatās. Abhijit is the star of Brahma, and Shravana is that of Vishnu. Riksham is the star of Vasava, and Dhanistha is that of Budha; while the star Shatabhisha is that of Varuna. Bhadrapada appears in the east, Ahivradhana in the north as well as Poushya, Revati, Riksham, Ashwajuk. Bharani appears in the north. These are called Riksha-devatas.

On the first and ninth day of the fortnight Brahmani is stationed in the east, on the second and tenth day

* The third of the lunar mansions or constellation in the moon's path, consisting of six stars and corresponding to Pleiades.

† The thirteenth lunar asterism designated by a hand and containing five stars.

‡ A star in the virgin's spike.

of the fortnight, Maheshwari is stationed in the north, on the fifth, and the thirteenth days, Varâhi appears in the south, on the sixth, and the fourteenth days, Indrâni is stationed in the west on the seventh day and on the full-moon day, Chamundâ appears in the north-west, on the eighth, and Amarvashya day, Mahalakshmi is stationed in the north-east, on the eleventh, and third days of the fortnight, Vaishnavi appears in the south-east, on the twelfth, and on the fourth day Koumari appears in the south-east.

One should not leave his house for another place while Yogini* is in front. Ashvini, Revati, Mrigamula, Punarvasu, Pushya, Hasta and Jyesta are the most auspicious stars under whose auspices one should leave his house. The five Rikshas, Hasta,† the three Uttaras, Ashvini, Rohini, Pushya,

---

* A female fiend or spirit attendant on and created by Durga. Here it refers to the star presiding over evil spirits.

† These groups of fixed stars or "constellations" can be identified on clear star-light nights by the following marks :—

1.	Ashvini	...	3 stars resembling a horse's face.
2.	Bharani	...	3 stars in the shape of deep-laid triangle.
3.	Kirttika	...	6 stars resembling a barber's razor.
4.	Rohini	...	5 stars resembling a cart,
5.	Mrigasira	...	3 stars in the shape of a man's head.
6.	Adra	...	1 star bright as coral bead.
7.	Punarvashu	...	5 stars in the form of a potter's wheel.
8.	Pushya	...	3 stars resembling a blood-sucker.
9.	Ashlesha	...	6 stars like a serpent.
10.	Magha	...	5 stars like a planquin.
11.	Purva Phalgooni	...	2 stars resembling eyes.
12.	Uttara Phalgooni	...	2 stars resembling eyes,
13.	Hasta	...	5 stars like human fingers.
14.	Chitra	...	1 star shining like a pearl.
15.	Svati	...	1 star like a sapphire.
16.	Vishakha	...	5 stars like a potter's wheel.
17.	Anuradha	...	3 stars resembling an umbrella.
18.	Jaista	...	ditto ditto.

Dhanistha, Punarvasu are the stars most favourable for putting on new raiments. Kirttikā, Bharani, Ashleshā, Maghā, which are known to have their faces directed downwards, are favourable for digging tanks, wells and reservoirs of water and for cultivating lands and laying foundations of temples and dwelling houses. When these stars and others, O bull-emblemed deity, go down it is the best time to begin the study of Mathematics, Astronomy and enter into mines, ditches, etc. When Revati, Ashvini, Chitra, Shyati, Hasta, Punarvasu, Anurudha, Mriga, Jyestha, all these lie sideways it is the the best time for taming elephants, camels, bulls and buffaloes. for sowing seeds and for paying visits. The cows should also be tamed under the influence of these stars. The wheels and machineries of cars should be constructed and boats should be floated. When Rohini, Ardra, Pushya, Dhanishtha, the three Uttaras, Vāruna, Shravana,—these nine have their faces upwards it is the best time for installing a king in the kingdom, and putting on silk raiments. The most inauspicious days are the fourth, sixth, eigth, ninth and Amāvashyā. The full-moon, the twelfth, the fourteenth, and the first day of the dark fort-night, are most auspicious days as also the second day when presided over by the Moon's son (Mercury), the third, by the Earth's son (Mars), and the fourth, by Saturn. The fifth day of a fortnight is auspicious when it is presided over by Jupiter, the sixth day, when by Mars and Venus, the seventh day, when by Mercury,

---

19.	Moola	...	5 stars like a crouching lion.
20.	Purbashara	...	2 stars each resembling the points of a square.
21.	Uttarasara	...	2 ditto ditto.
22.	Shravana	...	3 stars like an arrow.
23.	Dhanista	...	3 stars like a man's head.
24.	Shathabhisha	...	A hundred stars in the shape of a flower.
25.	Purbabhadrapada	...	2 stars each forming the sides of a cot.
26.	Uttarbhadrapada	...	2 ditto ditto.
27.	Revati	...	3 stars in the shape of a fish.

the eighth when, by Mars, the ninth day, when by the Moon, and the tenth, when by Jupiter. The Jupiter is auspicious and pure on the eleventh day of a fort-night, the Mercury, on the twelfth day, the Venus, on the thirteenth day, the Saturn on the fourteenth day, and Jupiter is the most auspicious both on the Amāvashyā and the full-moon day.

The Sun burns the twelfth day of a fort-night, the Moon, the eleventh day, the Mars, the tenth day, the Mercury, the ninth day, the Jeeva,* the eighth day, Bhargava (Venus), the seventh day, and the Sun's son, the sixth. One should not leave his house on such a day. On the first, ninth, fourteenth, and eighth day of a fortnight, and on Wednesday one should postpone his departure for a distant country. The sixth day under the influence of Aries† and Cancer, the eighth day of Virgo and Gemini, the fourth day of Taurus and Aquaris, the twelfth day of Capricornus and Libra, the tenth day of Libra and Scorpio and the fourteenth day of Sigattarius and Pisces are all inauspicious, and no man should leave his house on any these of days. When the three stars of Dhanistha are in conjunction with Mars, when the three

---

* The constellation Pushya—the eighth lunar mansion (Scorpi) consisting of three stars.

† The following are the English equivalents of the Rashis or signs of the Zodiac under the influence of which men are born.

Mesha	... Aries	... 1st sign.
Karkata	... Cancer	... 4th ,,
Kanya	... Virgo	... 6th ,,
Mithuna	... Gemini	... 3rd ,,
Vrisha	... Taurus	... 2nd ,,
Kumbha	... Aquaris	... 11th ,,
Makara	... Capricornus	... 10th ,,
Tula	... Libra	... 7th ,,
Vrishchika	... Scorpio	... 8th ,,
Sihha	... Leo	... 5th ,,
Dhanu	... Sagittarius	... 9th ,,
Meena	... Pisces	... 12th ,,

stars of Revati are with Mercury, when the three stars of Vishaka are with the sun, when the moon is in the three stars of Purvashāda, when the three stars of Rohini are in Pushyā and when the three stars of Pushya are with Venus—[they always fore-bode evil.] One should avoid the three stars of Uttara Phalguna on Saturday. These conjunctions forebode calamities either ending in death or a fatal disease.

When the Sun is in conjunction with Mula, when the moon is with Shravana, when Mars is with Purva and Uttara Bhadrapada, when Mercury is with Kirttika, when Jupiter is with Punarvasu, when Venus is with Purva Phalguna, when Saturn is with Shyati—these conjunctions are called *Amrita-yoga* which yields success in all undertakings. Vishkumbha-yoga lasts for five hours. Shula-yoga lasts for seven hours. Ganda-, and Atiganda-, yogas, last for six hours, and Vyāghātavajra, for nine hours. And Vyatipat-, and Pareegha-, yogas, last for one whole day. These combinations may even bring on death and therefore a man should avoid then every work. The combination between Hasta and the Sun, Jupiter and Pushya, Mercury and Anuradha, 'Rohini and Saturn, Moon and Souma, Venus and Revati and Mars and Ashivini is always auspicious. These combinations are called Siddhi-yogas and they avert every form of calamity. The combinations between the Sun and Bharani, the Moon and Chitra, Mars, Uttara-Ashada, Mercury and Dhanistha, Saturn and Revati are called, O Shambhu, Visha-yogas (poisonous combinations.)

When the combination takes place between Pushya, Punarvasu, Revati, Chitra, Shravana, Dhanistha, Hastā, Ashivini, Mriga, and Shatabhisa, a man should perform rites consequent upon the birth of a child. O Rudra, if a man leaves home for another place under the combination of any three planets of Vishakhā, Uttara, Maghā, Ardrā, Bharani Ashleshā and Kirttikā, he meets with death.

CHAPTER LX.

HARI said :—The Dashā, or the maximum influence of the Sun lasts for six years, that of the Moon, for fifteen years, that of Mars, for eight years, that of Mercury, for seventeen years, that of Saturn, for ten years, that of Jupiter, for nineteen years, that of Rāhu, for twelve years, and that of Venus, for twenty one years. The influence of the Sun produces misery and anxiety and brings on the destruction of a king. The influence of the Moon yields wealth, happiness and savoury edibles. The influence of Mercury gives heavenly bride and kingdom and increases wealth. The influence of Saturn brings on the destruction of kingdoms and the misery of friends. The influence of Jupiter gives kingdom, happiness and virtue. The influence of Rāhu brings on the destruction of kingdoms, misery and diseases. The influence of Venus gives elephants, horses, kingdom and women.

The constellation of Aries is the house of Mars; Tauras, is of Jupiter; Gemini, is of Mercury; Cancer, is of the Moon; Leo, of the sun; Virgo is of Mercury; Libra, is of Venus; Scorpio, is of Mars; Sagittarius, is of Jupiter; Capricornus and Aquaris are the houses of Saturn; Pisces, is of Jupiter.

When there are two full-moon nights in one month, two Purva Ashadas and two Ashadas Vishnu sleeps in Cancer.

The stars Ashvini, Revati, Chitrā, and Dhanisthā are the most auspicious stars for starting for a new place. Deer, monkey, cat, dog, parrot, mungoose and mouse, when seen on the right side, are auspicious at the time of departure. The daughter of a Brahmana, a dead body, conch-shell, bugle, earth, bamboo, a woman, a pitcher full of water are auspicious when seen at the time of departure. A jackal, camel, and ass are auspicious when seen on the left hand side at the time of departure. Cotton, oil of a medicinal plant, burning embers, snakes, a woman with dishevelled hairs, a garland of red flowers and a naked person are always inauspicious when seen.

I will now describe the characteristic marks of hiccough. When a man stands facing the east hiccough produces great fruits. When he faces the south-east it produces sorrow and anxiety. When he faces the south it does injury. When he faces the south-west it produces sorrow and anxiety. When he faces the west it gives sweet food. When he faces the north-west he obtains wealth. When he faces the north he enters on a quarrell. When he faces the north-east he is doomed to die. These are the good and evil fruits of hiccough.

Having drawn the solar circle one should imagine it to be the figure of a man. He should next calculate in what stars the Sun resides. He should then attribute three stars to the head; another three, to the face; one, to each shoulder; one, to each arm; one, to each hand; five stars to the heart; one, to the navel; one, to the buttock; and one, to each knee-joint. The remaining stars should be assigned to the feet of the Sun.

When one's presiding star is at the foot, the man becomes short-lived. When it is on the knee-joints, he goes to live in foreign countries. When it is on the buttock, he knows other people's wives. When it is on the navel, he becomes contented with little. When it is on the heart, he becomes Maheshwara. When it is on the hands, he becomes a heroe. When it is on the arms, he loses his position. When it is on the mouth, he obtains dainty dishes. When it is on the head he obtains silk raiments.

——:o:——

CHAPTER LXI.

HARI said :—When the Moon is on the increase from its seventh digit it is always and everywhere favourable. It should be adored by people and the Moon is seen like Jupiter.

There are twelve Dashas or stages of the Moon. Hear them. I will describe his station in every three stars beginning with Ashvini. The twelve stages are Pravāsas (living in a foreing country), Punarnastha (lost again), Mrita (dead), Jaya (success), Hāsya (smiling), Krida (sporting), Pramoda (enjoying), Vishāda (sorrowing), Bhoga (enjoying), Jvarā (decrepitude), Kampa (trembling) and Svastha (sound health). The Moon, in his condition of Pravasa, brings on injury and death, and in that of Jaya, merriment, sexual pleasure, and happiness. The other stages, viz., Shoka, Bhoga, Jvara, Kampa and Sukha respectively produce their destined fruits.

When the Moon resides in the first house of constellation at the time of birth he always gives satisfaction; when in the second, the person does not feel satiation; when in the third, the person enjoys royal honours; when in the fourth, he quarrels with other people; when the moon is in the fifth house the person obtains a good wife; when in the sixth, the person acquires wealth and corns; when in the seventh, he enjoys sexual pleasures and becomes the adored of all; when in the eighth there is danger to his life; when in the ninth, his wealth is accumulated; when in the tenth, he brings his work to a successful close; when in the eleventh, he meets with success; when the Moon is in the twelfth house there is, forsooth, death for the man.

Under the influence of the seven stars forming the constellation of Kirttika it is better to start for the east. Under the influence of Maghā it is better to start for the south; under the influence of Anurādhā it is better to start for the west. Under the influence of Dhanistha it is better to start for the north. Ashvini, Revati, Chitra, Dhanistha, Mrigashiras, Pushya, Mula and Hasta are [always favourable in marriage, for giving away a daughter in marriage, for going out on business, for consecrating temples and for other religious and social ceremonies.

If the Moon and Jupiter reside in the second house at the time of birth they are auspicious. The Moon, Jupiter and Pushya are auspicious when they live in the third house with Gemini. Mars, Saturn, Moon, Sun and Mercury are most auspicious when they live in the fourth house. Saturn, Sun and Mars are auspicious in the sixth house, while Jupiter and Moon in the seventh. Venus is most auspicious in the eighth house, while Jupiter in the ninth. The Sun and Moon are auspicious in the tenth house, while all the planets are auspicious in the eleventh house. Venus and Mercury are favourable in the twelfth house.

The combinations, between Leo and Capricornus, between Virgo and Aries, between Libra and Pisces, between Aquarius and Cancer, between Sagittaries and Taurus and between Gemini and Scorpio are most auspicious. These fourteen combinations always conduce to well-being.

CHAPTER LXII.

HARI said:—Beginning from the time of its rising the sun lives in the various Rashis (signs of the Zodiac), O Hara. He lives for six days and six nights in his own Rashi. He lives for five hours in Pisces and Aris, four hours in Taurus and Aquaris, three hours in Capricornus and Gemini, five hours in Sagittarius and Cancer, six hours in Leo and Scorpio and seven hours in Virgo and Libra. This is described as the extent of Lagna.* If a woman is born when the Sun is in Aries she becomes barren; when he is in Taurus she becomes handsome in person ; when, in Gemini, she becomes lucky ; when, in Cancer, she becomes dissolute ; when, in Leo, she becomes the mother of few children ; when, in Virgo, she becomes supremely beautiful ; when, in Libra, she is endowed with both beauty and fortune ; when, in ocorpio, she becomes foul-mouthed ; when, in Sagittarius, she becomes fortunate ; when, in Capricornus, she becomes mean ; when, in Aquaris, she becomes the mother of few children ; when, in Pisces, she is endued with the spirit of disassociation from the world. The Rashis Libra, Cancer, Aries, Capricornus are both moveable and fixed. Leo, Taurus, Aquaris, and Scorpio are all fixed groups of stars. Virgo, Sagittarius, Pisces, and Gemini, are endued with two-fold characters. It is better to leave any place under the infiuence of moving stars and enter the house under that of fixed ones. The installation of an image of the deity should be made under the influence of that group of stars which are both moveable and fixed.

The first, sixth, or the eleventh, day of a fortnight is called Nandā. O bull-emblemed deity, the second, seventh, or the twelfth day is called Bhadrā. The eigth, third, or the thirteenth, day is called Jayā, O Rudra. The fourth, or the ninth, day is call Riktā. The fourteenth day is called Varjya. The fifth, or the tenth, day is called Purnā. And the full-moon day is called Shubhā.

Mercury is always on circuit, Jupiter is always quick in motion, Venus is slow, the Sun is certain, Saturn is terrific, Mars is fierce, and the Moon is calm. Under the influence of Mercury and Jupiter one should leave his house ; under

* The Sun's entrance into a Zodiacal sign.

the influence of Venus and Sun one should enter a house; under the influence of Saturn and Mars the Kshatryas, who desire for success, should be engaged in battle.

The installation of a king and sacred fire should be done on a Monday. Under the influence of the Moon one should lay the foundation of a dwelling house. Under the influence of Mars one should accept the command of an army, undertake a war and practise arms. Under the influence of Mercury any work, deliberation, or journey, is crowned with success. Under the influence of Jupiter one should study, adore the gods, and put on new habiliments 'and ornaments. Under the influence of Venus it is better to give away a daughter in marriage, ride an elephant, enter into contracts, or espouse a wife. Under the influence of Saturn it is auspicious to enter a house for the first time, or entrap an elephant.

CHAPTER LXIII.

HARI said:—Hear, O Shankara, I will now describe in brief the characteristic marks of men and women.

Tender palms like lotus petals and not perspiring, fingers adjoining each other, copper-coloured nails, beautiful ankles, well-formed head and feet, plump like a tortoise, mark out a man to be a king. Yellow nails, rough face, high head, feet like winnowing baskets, and withered fingers of the feet, are the marks for sorrow and poverty. There is no doubt about it. Thighs like the trunks of elephants containing few hairs, and one hair in the navel are the marks for great kings. The learned men and persons conversant with Srutis have two hairs each on their thighs. Those, who are poor, have three hairs and diseased men have their knee-joints devoid of flesh. One, who has got a small genital organ, becomes a rich man with no issue. One, who has got a big genital organ, becomes poor. One, who has got one scrotum, becomes poor. One, who has got unequal testes, gets a fickle wife. One, who has got equal testes, becomes a king. One, with hanging testes, becomes short-lived. One, having a bad wrist, becomes poor. With pale-coloured wrists a person becomes happy.

An idigent person passes urine with great sound. Those, who pass urine without any sound, become kings. Those, who have even bellies, enjoy various pleasures of life. Those, who have bellies like pots, become indigent. Those, who have serpentine bellies become poor. Linear marks indicate longevity. He, who has three lines on the fore-head, becomes happy, gets sons, and lives for sixty years. One having two lines lives for forty years. One, who has a line on the fore-head extending to the ears, lives for twenty years. If one has three lines on the fore-head extending up to ears he lives for a hundred years. One, having two lines, lives for seventy years. One, having three lines, lives for sixty years. The person, having two lines one clear and another indistinct, lives for twenty years. One, who has short lines, lives for forty years. The person, who has broken lines, meets with an accidental death. The person, on whose head are seen the marks of a trident or Pattiça, is favoured with riches and children, and lives for a hundred years. The person, whose line of life passes through the middle and fore-fingers, lives for a hundred years, O Rudra. The person,—on whose palm the line of knowledge extends up to the thumb, and the line of life extends up to the foot of the middle fingers from the youngest in an unbroken and undivided condition,—lives for a hundred years. The person, on whose palm the line of life appears in a distinct form, lives for a hundred years and becomes the happy recipient of all earthly blessings. The person, on whose palm the line of life extends also from the youngest to the middle finger, lives for eighty years.

—:o:—

CHAPTER LXIV.

HARI said :—The maiden, who has got curling locks, a round face and a deep navel, increases her family. A woman, whose colour is like that of gold, and whose hands are red, is called Padmini. Such a woman, born one in a thousand, is personification of chastity. The woman, who has uneven hairs and round eyes, becomes widowed, and is always unfortunate in her surroundings. The maiden, who has a face like the full-moon, is effulgent like the rising Sun, has expensive eyes and Vimva-like lips, enjoys happiness. Many lines indicate misery and dearth of the same signifies poverty. One, having crimson-coloured lines, enjoys happiness, and one, having dark-blue lines, becomes unchaste. A wife is like a minister to her husband in works, a friend in enjoyments, a mother in affection, and a public woman while on bed.

The woman, who has the marks of a goad, circle and discus on her palm, gives birth to a son and obtains a king as her husband. The woman, whose two sides and breasts are covered with hairs and whose lips are high, soon destroys her husband. The woman, who has the marks of a wall or gateway on her palms, becomes a queen even if she is born as a maid servant. One, who has rows of reddish and high hairs on her person, becomes a maid servant even if she is born in a royal family. One, who has got her thumb and ring-finger of an unusually high stature, soon kills her husband and leads a loose life. Oily eyes indicate good luck, oily teeth indicate good eating, oily skin indicates a good bed, and oily feet indicate conveyances. The auspicious signs of women are cool and high breasts, copper-coloured nails, beautiful feet, marks of fish, goad, lotus, discus and plough-share on the soles and palms which do not perspire, a beautiful hip without hairs, thighs like the trunk of an elephant, most excellent and capacious buttock like a fig leaf, spacious and deep navel and chest and breast shorn of hairs.

——:o:——

CHAPTER LXV.

HARI said :—I will now describe the auspicious marks of men and women as described by Samudra (Palmistry). by knowing which one may without any labour calculate the past and future.

Unperspiring palms, lotus-like belly, fingers adjoining one another, copper-coloured nails, warm feet like tortoise, strong ankles and beautiful sides are the marks of a king. Rough, uneven feet like winnowing baskets, dry locks, twany coloured nails, and distantly placed fingers are the marks of poverty. Well-formed and red feet, equal shanks without hairs, thighs like the trunks of elephants and equal knee-joints are the characteristic marks of a king. The indigent have shankles like those of a jackal and have hairs in the navel. The kings, the Srotiyas and the intelligent have two hairs each. Persons, having three hairs, become poor, miserable and are always objects of censure.

A person, having curling hairs, dies in a foreign country. A knee-joint without sufficient flesh indicates good luck (in a man). With a knee-joint of insufficient flesh one knows degraded women. One, having deformed knee-joints, becomes poor and one having plump ones obtains a kingdom.

A person, having a short genital organ, lives long and becomes rich and has few offspring. One, having a huge genital organ, becomes proud of his wealth. When the left testes is swollen the person does not get sons. When the testes are uneven the person obtains sons; and when they are bent down it indicates poverty. When the genital organ is small a person obtains sons; when the head of the genital organ is plump the person becomes happy; when there are thick chords in the organ the person becomes happy. When the testes are thick-set the person becomes a king; and when they are long and rugged the person becomes poor. One, who has a small testicle, becomes a strong and powerful warrior. One, who has got one teste, becomes weak; and one, who has got uneven testes, gets a fickle wife. One, who has got even testes, becomes a king; and one, who has got a long testicle, lives for a hundred years.

One, who has got high wrists, lives for many years; one, who has got rugged wrists, becomes a master. With yellow-coloured wrists people become poor, and with dark wrists they enjoy happiness.

Persons, who pass urine either with or without any sound, become poor. When urine comes out in one, two, three, four, five, or six lines and passes towards the right, it indicates the signs of kinghood. Those, who pass urine in a scattered way, become indigent, those, who pass urine in a strong flow, become happy and obtain good wives. When urine remains on an equal level a man obtains wife, gems and riches, and when it goes down he obtains maidens.

When the semen is dry a person becomes indigent and when there is scent of flower in the semen he becomes king. When there is smell of honey in it he acquires immense riches. When there is the smell of fish in the semen he gets a son. When semen is scanty he obtains maidens. When there is the smell of meat he enjoys various luxuries of life; when there is the smell of wine he becomes a priest. When there is smell of ashes he becomes poor.

One, who finishes soon his sexual intercourse, lives long. He, whose sexual intercourse lasts long, is short-lived.

One, having big buttocks, becomes proud of his wealth. One having fleshy buttocks becomes happy; and one having leonine buttocks becomes a king. One, having a monkey-like waist, becomes indigent. Persons, having serpentine bellies, become poor. Those, having pan-or pot-like bellies, become rich.

People, having spacious arm-pits, become indigent; those, having equal arm-pits, enjoy various objects of life; those, who have hollowed arm-pits, become proud of wealth; those, who have elevated arm-pits, those, who have uneven arm-pits, and those, who have crooked arm-pits, become kings. Those, who have got fish-like bellies and navels, become happy. Those, who have got capacious or low navels, are doomed to suffer miseries. If there is wrinkle inside a navel it brings on death at the stake for the person. If there is wrinkle on one side the man lives for ever. If it is in an equinoctial position he becomes the possessor of riches. If it is downwards he becomes the possessor of kine. It it is of the shape of a pericarp of a lotus he becomes a king. If there is one wrinkle the person lives for a hundred years. If there are two he enjoys prosperity. If there are three wrinkles he becomes a preceptor.

If the wrinkles are straight the person becomes happy. If the wrinkle is awry he knows women unworthy of being known. If the arm-pits are fleshy, tender, even and covered with rows of hairs on the right side, the person becomes a king. If the rows of hairs tend towards the opposite direction the person becomes devoid of all objects and happiness.

If the nipples of the breasts are not high the persons become very lucky. But if they are uneven, high and of yellow colour they become poor.

The kings have high and fleshy chests which do not tremble, are sinewy and covered with strong hairs going downwards. A rich man has an even chest. One, having plump chest, becomes very powerful. Persons, having uneven chests, become indigent and are killed by weapons.

Persons, having rugged collar-bones, become indigent. Those, having elevated collar-bones, enjoy various objects of life; those, having depressed ones, become indigent; and those, having plump ones, become rich. One, who has a flat neck becomes indigent. He, who has got the arteries of his neck, not very prominent, becomes happy. He, who his buffalo-necked, becomes a hero. He, who has a neck like that of a deer, masters the Holy Scriptures. One, who has a neck like a conch-shell, becomes a king; whereas one, who has a long neck, becomes a voracious eater.

A back, not covered with hairs and even in shape, always indicates auspiciousness, while of any other kind it is the forerunner of inauspiciousness.

The most auspicious arm-pit is that of the shape of a fig-leaf, which is covered with brown hairs and from which good smell comes out. Any other description is the mark of poverty.

Fleshy, well-formed and well-joined arms are the most auspicious. Well-rounded and fleshy arms, extending up to the knees, indicate the signs of royalty. Short arms, covered with hairs, indicate signs of poverty. Arms, like the trunks of elephants, are the best. Fingers of the hands, when straight, are most auspicious. Those of the intelligent are short and those of the servants are flat. The indigent have either fat, crooked or bent and lean fingers. Those, who have hands like those of a monkey, become indigent. That like a tiger indicates strength. The depressed palm of a person indicates the destruction of his paternal property. The kings have well-formed, thick-set and sweet-scented wrists. Those, whose fingers make a sound when handled, become degraded and poor. Persons, who have uneven fingers, always pay taxes. Those, who have red hands and palms, become very rich. Those, who have yellow-coloured and rough ones, become indigent and addicted to other people's wives.

Those, who have nails like husks, become eunuchs. Those, who have rugged and broken nails, become indigent. Those, who have discoloured and disfigured nails, always pry into other's business. Those, who have copper-coloured nails, become kings. Those, who have the mark of a barley on their thumbs, become rich. When there is such a mark at the foot of the thumb a person gets sons. If a person has long knots in the fingers he lives a long life and becomes lucky. He, who has disjoined fingers, becomes poor. He, who has got close fingers, becomes a rich man.

The person, on which palms three lines appear from the wrist, becomes a king. When the figures of two fishes appear on the palm the person becomes a great sacrificer. The sign of a thunder-bolt appearing on the palm indicates the possession of riches. The sign of the tail of a fish indicates intellect. The signs of conch-shell, umbrella, vehicle, elephant and lotus indicate royalty. The marks of a pitcher, goad, flag and lotus-stalk indicate the possession of jems. The mark of a chord indicates the possession of kine; that of Swasthika indicates royalty. The marks of discus, sword, Tomara, bow and teeth appear on the hands of a king. The mark of a mortar appears on the palms of a person who celebrates sacrifices and that of a sacrificial altar appears on the palm of an Agnihotri. The marks of a tank and triangle indicate righteousness.

22

Lines, originating from the root of the thumb, indicate the possession of sons and happiness. A line, extending from the tip of the thumb to that of the fore-finger and originating from the root of the youngest finger, makes one live for a hundred years. When it is broken it indicates danger from a tree. Many lines indicate poverty.

A spare chin indicates want; while a fleshy one indicates riches. Red lips indicate royalty. Smiling and tender lips, resembling Vimva fruits, indicate the same. Those who have rugged lips become poor. Thick-set and cool teeth are the best. Sharp but even teeth are also most auspicious. Red tongue is also most auspicious. Blue and tall tongue is also the best and a white palate indicates the destruction of wealth. There are two kinds of faces—dark and rough; tender and gentle. Clean and tender face indicates royalty and its opposite indicates poverty. A son, possessing the face of his mother, suffers great miseries. A rich person has a round face and a poor man a tall one. The vicious have cowardly faces and the wicked cunning ones. Those who have depressed faces get no sons. The misers have short faces. The happiest of men, who enjoys all the luxuries of life, has tender, thin and beautiful beards. A thief has got thick, short and crimson-coloured beards. The sinful persons have red and rugged beards.

The misers have short ears. Those who have got spear-like ears become kings. Those, who have got hairs on their ears, die soon. Persons, having big ears, become kings and rich men. Persons, endued with hanging and fleshy ears, also become kings. One, having depressed cheeks, enjoys all the luxuries of life. One, having well-formed cheeks, becomes a minister. One, having a nose like that of a parrot, becomes happy. One, who has got a thin nose, lives long. One, who has got a well-like nose with its tip broken, knows women unworthy of being known. One, who has got a long nose, enjoys good luck. A thief has got a flat nose. A flat nose also indicates death and misfortune. A straight nose, with beautiful tip and small nostrils, indicates the signs of royalty. A little curve on the right side indicates crookedness. Continual sneezing indicates strength. A flat nose indicates the possession of delight and that with sound indicates the possessor as being the supporter of all creatures.

Persons, having eyes like lotus-petals with a little curve at the corners, enjoy all the luxuries of life. Sinful persons have eyes like those of a cat and wicked wights have twany-coloured eyes. The crooked are squint-eyed and the sinful persons have yellow-coloured eyes. The heroes have oblique eyes and the warriors have eyes like those of an elephant. The kings have got grave eyes and the ministers fleshy ones. The learned have eyes like the petals of a red lotus; while the fortunate men have dark-blue eyes. Dark-blue pupils and the absence of eye-lids indicate the destruction of the possessor. The sinful wights have round eyes and the indigent have poorly-looking eyes.

Those, who have got cool skin, enjoy the various objects of life. Those, who have got elevated navels, live for a short time. Those, who have got capacious and elevated navels, become happy. Those, who have got uneven eye-brows, become poor. Long but unconnected eye-brows indicate riches. He, who has got crescent-shaped eye-brows, becomes rich. One, who has got a cut between the two eye-brows, becomes indigent. Those, who have got bent down eye-brows, know women unworthy of being known.

A high, capacious, conch-shell-like and rugged fore-head indicates poverty. Persons, having crescent-shaped fore-heads, become rich. Persons, having spacious fore-heads, become preceptors. Persons, having sinewy fore-heads, become sinners. Persons, having high and triangular fore-heads, become the possessors of wealth. Persons, having depressed fore-heads, are addicted to wicked deeds and worthy of being slain. A round fore-head indicates miserliness. An elevated fore-head indicates royalty. A dry unperspiring fore-head is not auspicious for men. A sufficiently perspiring and rough fore-head indicates happiness. Untrembling and expensive fore-head is the best and expressive of happiness. A laughing and wicked fore-head indicates madness.

Three lines on the fore-head indicate longevity for a hundred years. Four lines indicate royalty and longevity for ninety-five years. Absence of any line indicates longevity for ninety years. When the lines on the fore-head are broken a man becomes licentious. If the lines extend up to hairs a person lives for eighty years. If there are five, seven or six lines, a person lives fifty years or more. If they are dark-blue in colour a man lives forty years; and if they extend up to the eye-brows the person lives thirty years. When there are twenty lines bending towards the left it indicates longevity and when there are short lines it indicates short life.

An umbrella-like head indicates royalty, auspiciousness and riches. A bland head indicates the death of one's father while a circular head indicates riches. A pitcher-like head indicates vile desire and poverty.

Black, straight, thin and not too much hairs indicate royalty. Hairs, having many roots, uneven, with gross tips, twany-coloured, bent down, thick and dark-blue also indicate signs of royalty. Highly rough, sinwey body, devoid of flesh, is most inauspicious. Any other description is auspicious. For kings there are three deep, spacious and long marks, five very fine, six elevated, four short and seven crimson-coloured. Navel, voice and understanding—these three should be deep. Fore-head, face and chest should be broad. Eye, side, tooth, nose, mouth and back of the neck should be high. Shank, neck, genital organ and back—these four should be short. Palms, corners of the mouth, nails, corners of the eyes, feet, tongue and lips should be red. Teeth, knots of fingers, nails, hairs and skin—these five should be very fine. The distance between breasts, arms, teeth, eyes and nose should be long. I have thus described the characteristic marks of men. I will now describe those of women.

She, who has got cool and equal feet and palms, coppery nails, joining fingers with elevated tips, becomes a queen. One, obtaining her [as a wife] becomes a king. Well-formed ankle, lotus-like, tender and unperspiring palms containing the marks fish, goad and flag single out a woman for a queen. The feet of a queen bear the marks of a thunder-bolt, lotus and plough-share. Well-rounded hips, devoid of hairs and arteries, are most auspicious. Well-formed joints and even knee-joints are most auspicious. Thighs, like the trunk of an elephant, even and without hairs, are most auspicious. A capacious buttock, like unto a fig-leaf, is most auspicious. Loins, fire-head and chest, when they are of the form of a tortoise, are most auspicious. Fleshy wrists and hips are most auspicious for women. A navel, capacious, deep and fleshy with three wrinkles inside, is most auspicious. Even and pointed breasts without hairs are most auspicious. Red lips are most auspicious and round and fleshy mouth is the best. Teeth must be like Kunda flowers and speech must be sweet like the notes of a coel. Mercy, simplicity and even nose are the most beautiful marks for women. Eyes like blue lotuses well attached to the nose, eye-brows not very plump and like unto the rising moon, fore-head not very elevated and without hairs, not very fleshy and tender ears of equal size, and tender, curling and dark hairs are the most auspicious marks. Well-formed head and soles or palms, bearing the marks of horse, elephant, tree, sacrificial stake, wheat, Tomara, flag, chowri, garland, hill, well, altar, conch-shell, umbrella, lotus, fish, Swastika, car and goad are the signs of royalty in women. The auspicious marks in women are well-formed wrists and hands like lotuses and palms not depressed nor very elevated. Linear marks on the palms are the signs which show that a woman will not be widowed and enjoy her life. If a line rising from the wrist goes to the middle finger it indicates the possession of kingdom and happiness in women. A line originating from the root of the youngest finger indicates life for a hundred years. If a line passes from the tip of the thumb to that of the fore-finger it indicates the shortness of life. If a line originates from the foot of the thumb and is long it indicates the possession of sons; and if it is short it indicates the possession of women. If that line is broken at many places it indicates the shortness of life; and if it is broken at a long interval it indicates longevity. These are the auspicious marks for women and others are inauspicious.

The woman, whose youngest or ring finger does not touch the ground or whose thumb is bigger than the fore-finger, becomes unchaste. Elevated calves, sinewy, hairy or fleshy hips, pitcher-like belly, depressed and small buttock are the signs of misery. Short neck is the sign of poverty and a long one is the sign of the extinction of the family. Fat women are forsooth terrific. Squint and twany-coloured eyes, dark-blue smiling looks, and smiling and depressed cheeks are the signs of unchastity. If a woman has a tall fore-head she kills the younger brother of her husband. If the belly is long she kills her father-in-law and if the hips are high she kills her husband. Hairy lips are most inauspicious for husbands. Hairy breasts, rugged ears, sharp and uneven teeth conduce to their miseries. If the flesh is dark-blue it shows she will be a thief and if it is tough it indicates the death of her husband. A sinewy, uneven and dry body indicates poverty. If the upper lip is high it shows she will be quarrelsome and harsh-speeched. Want of accomplishments and an ugly feature are both short-comings in women.

I have thus described the characteristic marks of men and women which confer wisdom on men.

—:o:—

CHAPTER LXVI.

HARI said :—It is better to adore a stone which has no characteristic marks than the one which has a circular mark on it.

The first image is Sudarshana. The second is Lakshmi-Narayana. The third is Tree-Chakra (three discus), the fourth is Achyuta, the fifth is Chaturchakra and the sixth is Chaturbhuja (four-armed). The next is Vasudeva, then Pradyumna, then Sangkarshana and the eighth is Purusottama. Navavyuha is the tenth. Aniruddha is the eleventh, then Ekadasa and then Dwadashatmā. Ananta is on the top of all the lines.

Where there is Shalagrāma stone there lives the lord of Dwāravati (Vishnu). Where is the meeting between these two there is forsooth emancipation. Shālagrāma, Dwāraka, Naimisha, Pushkara, Gya, Baranashi, Prayaga, Kurukshetra, Gangā, Narmudā, Chandrābhaga, Saraswati, Purusottama, and Mahakāla—these are the sacred shrines, O Shankara, which dissipate all sins and yield enjoyment and emancipation.

Prabhava, Vibhava, Shukra, Pramoda, Prajapati, Angira, Shrimukha, Bhāva, Pushā, Dhāta, Ishwara, Vahudhanya, Pramāthi, Vikrama, Vidhu, Chitrabhānu, Swarbhānu, Dāruna, Prarthiva, Vyaya, Sarvajit, Sarvadhāri, Virodhhi, Vikrita, Khara, Nandana, Vijaya, Jaya, Manmatha, Darmukha, Hemalamva, Vilamva, Vikāra, Sharvari, Plavā, Shubhakrit, Shobhana, Krodha, Vishwāvasu, Parābhava, Plavanga, Keelaka,

Soumya, Sādhārana, Virodhakrit, Paridhāra, Pramādi; Ananda, Rakshasa, Nala, Pingala, Kālasiddharta, Durmati, Sumati, Dundubhi, Rudhirodgāri, Raktāksha, Krodhana, Akshaya—are the names which indicate years to be either auspicious or inauspicious.

O Rudra, I will now describe time leading to success according to the system of Panchasara* (five vowels.) They are Rājā, Sājā, Sāja, Udāsā, Peedā and Mrityu. In the figure of five fires one should write the vowels A, I, U, E, OU. Six fires should come from the lines drawn upwards or askance. In the house of one fire the times Raja, Sāja, Udasā, Peedā and Mritiyu are in order presided over by Mars, Mercury, Jupiter, Venus, Saturn, the sun and the moon. The first division of the time is presided over by the stars beginning with Revati and ending with Mrigasira. Beginning with the month of Chaitra each group of five stars appears. From the first letters of the names of the stars twelve days and two months are derived. In the fifth house of the figure the characteristic marks of the various divisions of Time are found. From the first letter of the name of any article pronounced by a party divisions of Time, the various Tithis, various days, stars and months are calculated.

The mantram is "Om, Kshoum, Sivāya Namas." It is called Trailokyamohana. It counteracts the influence of evil stars on mental faculties and yeilds success, when written on a Bhurja leaf with Gorochana and along with the names of Siva, Gana and Lakshmi, it is placed on the neck or arms.

---

* *Panchasura* is one of the divisions of Hindu Jyotish (astrology). It refers to the five elements viz, earth, air, fire, water and ether which compose the human body. Auspiciousness and inauspiciousness of time is calculated, according to the Panchasara, by the increase or decrease of all these elements severally.

CHAPTER LXVII.

SUTA said :—Now I shall narrate to you the science of divination which the god Hara learned from Hari and disclosed to his consort Gouri, and the data of which can be gathered from one's own internal system or organism. The Mars, the Fire-God, the Sun, the Earth, the Saturn, the Water-God and the Nodes (Rahu), should be deemed as seated in, or permeating with their respective influences, the air or the vital wind that blows through the right nostril of a man ; whereas the Jupiter, the Venus, the Mercury and the Moon should be regarded as the presiding planets of the wind that escapes through his left nostril. Rites or incantations undertaken or practised for the acquisition of territories or a place in the king's service, as well as acts such as the first starting of a trade or the first interview of a king, and auspicious works in general, should be performed when the breath-wind would blow through one's left nostril. The Saturn, the Nodes, the Mars, the Sun, and the Planet of Water, should be deemed as ascendant when the process of respiration would be performed through the right nostril, and all baneful principles should be likewise regarded as dominant with them.

The good or evil fate of a man can be divined from the escapage of the breath-wind through the different nostrils as well as from the predominance of the concomitant principles (Svarodaya) in the diviner. Net works of nerves of varied shape and immense extensions run through the body in all directions. From the nerve-bulb or nerve ganglion alone, situated below the umbilicus, there branch out no less than seventy-two thousand nerves, rolled up in the form of a coil or wheel, each carrying away the stream of life in their course. Three out of these innumerable nerves, pre-eminently rank as the most important. These three (occult) nerves run below the spinal column of a man, the left one being called the Ida, and the right one, the Pingala. The central one of this nerve system is called the Sushumna. The Moon is the presiding deity of the Ida or the left nerve, the Pingala or the right nerve is effulgent with the light of the sun, while the Sushumna or the central one owns the Fire-God as its tutelary divinity, and is the destroyer of all phenomenal life. The Ida or the left nerve flows with the stream of divine ambrosia and laves the shores of the organic world with a perpetual flow of life. The Pingala or the right nerve is permeated with the essence of the god of destruction (Rudra) and carries within it the principle of universal dissolution. The concerted work of these two nerves (the left and the right) leads to death and ushers in an absolute breakdown of all undertakings.

Inspiration or taking in of the breath wind is performed by means of the Ida, while respiration or the process of letting it out, is done with the help of the Pingala.

All blissful or auspicious acts, should be undertaken when the vital energy of the doer would remain confined to the Ida, while all fatal, or harmful incantations should be practised when the same would be lodged in the Pingala. Sojourn to a distant land and all processes for the elimination of poison from the human system, should be started under the auspices of the flowing of the vital stream through the Ida, while a predominance of the Pingala (flowing of the life stream through Pingala) in a man, should be deemed as the most auspicious occasion for taking his dinner, or visiting his wife, or fighting his antagonist. Similarly a predominance of the Pingala should be made use of, in practising incantations which are fatal in their effect or can send one's adversary crazy from his household. A dinner, or a battle, or a sexual intercourse, partaken of, entered into, or commenced during the assendency of the Pingala, is sure to be crowned with success.

Kings and crowned heads, should take advantage of such a state of the Ida, in undertaking all acts which tend to make men happy, as well as in commencing a sojourn to a distant country, or in practising venomous charms or those which bring about the fruition (realisation) of one's own speech. A simultaneous flowing of the life current through both of these occult nerves (Ida and Pingala) should be interpreted to indicate an occasion when charms of both blissful and fatal virtues, should not be practised, and such a state should be deemed as the equator of life. A predominance of the left occult nerve is the most auspicious occasion for the purposes of a journey and for practising all lucky incantations, as well as for undertaking all works of profit and victory and those that contribute to the preservation of health and life. Similarly an ascendency of the right occult nerve, Pingala, should be deemed as the signal moment for starting on a military expedition, or for visiting the bed of a woman and for undertaking all minor acts in general.

A battle should be commenced, when the general or the warrior leading the attack, would feel his vital wind blowing through the occult nerves of the Sun and the Moon, and a person with such a state of vital air, enquiring about the probable result of the battle, should be assured of the success of the party on whose behalf he had consulted the diviner. Such a party is sure to conquer the whole country lying at the angle of the compass which the vital wind blows to, even if the lord of the celestials confronts his army as an opposing rival. The ten occult nerves, such as the Aries, etc., and which are arranged in both sides of a human frame, represent the Lagnas such as the Chara (mobile) the Sthira (fixed), etc.

The diviner or prophet should hold up his face, in the shape of a bell after the enquirer had finished putting his query, and he would take in or let out his breath wind simultaneously with the inspiration or respiration of the enquirer. O Shiva, the five fundamental material principles of the universe, are situated in the right and left sides of a human organism. The predominance of the principles of fire in a human system, should be inferred from the escaping of the vital wind along the upper part of the nostril, while the ascendency of the water principle, should be judged from its outflow, touching the bottom line of the nostril. In the same manner the escaping of the breath-wind in a slanting direction, would indicate the predominance of the principle of wind. The predominence of the earth principle would be indicated by the breath-wind keeping a middle path inside the nostril, while the predominance of the principle of sky should be inferred from the outflow of the breath as stuffing the nostril and running in all directions.

Incantations, endued with the mystic virtues of destroying life, should be practised during the ascendency of the principle of fire, rites of pacification during the predominance of the water-principle, charms for distracting human mind during the predominance of the wind, spells for benumbing the faculties of one's adversary during the ascendency of the earth principle, while penances for the emancipation of one's own self, should be practised during the predominance of the principle of the sky or ether.

——:o:——

CHAPTER LXVIII.

SUTA said:—Now I shall discourse on the method of testing the genuineness of gems and precious stones. There lived in ancient time a demon, named Vala. Vala conquered the god Indra and his celestials, and reigned supreme and invincible in the universe. The gods, on the occasion of a religious sacrifice, jocularly asked him to play the part of the animal of the sacrifice. This Vala consented to do and pledged his word for the performance of the part and suffered himself to be bound at the sacrificial stake. Whereupon the gods turned the jest into earnest and killed the invincible Vala in that mockery of a religious sacrifice. Thus Vala yielded up his ghost for the good of the universe and the welfare of the gods, and, behold, the severed limbs and members of his sanctified body, were converted into the seeds of gems.

Then the gods and the Yakshas and the Siddhas and the Nagas eagerly rushed to collect those seeds of gems and there were mighty flutterings of celestial pinions and rustlings of celestial garments in heaven. The gods came riding in their aerial cars, and carried away the seeds of gems for their own use, some of which dropped down on earth, through the violent concussion of the air. Wherever they dropped, whether in oceans, rivers, mountains or wildernesses there origined mines of those gems through the celestial potency of their respective seeds.

Of the gems and precious stones, some are endued with the virtues of expiating all sins or of acting as a prophylactic against the effects of poison, snake bites, and diseases, while there are others which are possessed of contrary virtues. Gems, such as the Padmaraga, the Emerald, the Indranila, the Vaidurya the Pushparaga, the diamond, the pearl, the Karketana, the Pulaka, Rudhirakhya (blood stone) the crystal, and the coral, should be carefully collected, subject to the advice of experts on the subject. First the shape, colour, defects or excellences of a gem should be carefully tested and then its price should be ascertained in consultation with a gem expert who has studied all the books dealing with the precious stones.

A king or a ruling chief with a view to acquire a greater prosperity, shall collect and wear a gem that has been found pure after a satisfactory test. Men, dealing in gems and experienced in the art of detecting its defects and well versed in the knowledge relating to the appraising of precious stones, should be deemed as the only persons capable of fixing the price and ascertaining the water of a gem. Since the learned hold diamond to be the most effulgent of all precious stones, we shall first describe the mode of testing the diamond.

The least particle of bone of the conquerer of Indra, falling or dropping down from the sky in a country, germinates diamond-crystals of varied shapes. The eight regions or divisions of the country in which diamond is found, are the Himalayas, the Matangas, the provinces of Anga, Saurastra, Poundra, Kalinga, Koshala, the basin of the river Venva, and the country of the Souveras. Diamonds found in the region of the Himalays, are tinged with a little copper-colour, while those found in the basin of the Venva are coloured like the disc of the full moon. Diamonds found in the country of the Souvera, are possessed of a lustre similar to the deep shade of a black rain cloud; while those found in the country of Sourashtra, shine with a copper-coloured effulgence. Diamonds found in the country of Kalinga, are coloured like the molten gold, while those found in Koshala are yellow. Diamonds found in the country of Poundra, are coloured blue, while those found in the regions of the Matangas, are yellowish in their hue.

Gods are supposed to dwell in a particle of diamond, wherever found, which is possessed of a clear, light shade and the usual commendable features, is smooth and even at the sides, and is divested of all threatening traits such as scratches, dot like impressions, marks of crow's feet, or clouding impurities in its interior. Coloured diamonds, should be be regarded as presided over by different divinities according to ther riespective hues. Green, white, yellow, brown, blue and copper-coloured diamonds are ascribed to the direct tutelage of the Sun, Varuna, Indra, the Fire-God, the Lord of the Pitris and the Maruts, respectively.

A Brahmana is enjoined to wear a diamond which is coloured like a conch shell, or a Kumuda flower or a white crystal, whereas a Kshatriya should wear one that is coloured brownish yellow like the eyes of a hare. A diamond possessed of a soft greenish colour like the tender leaves of a plantain tree, prove beneficial to a man of the Vaishya class, while a Shudra would do well to wear a diamond that has a lustre like that of a newly washed sword. Diamonds which are coloured yellow or possessed of a hue like that of a coral or a Java flower, (China Rose) should be held as fit only for the use of a king and would prove positively harmful to any man occupying a lower position in life. A king in his capacity of the lord of all the castes, is privileged to wear diamonds of any colour he pleases, provided they are not vitiated by the prohibited features, whereas such a conduct on the part of an ordinary man, is sure to be attended with evil consequences.

A diamond possessed of a double or dubious shade or colour, should be looked upon as portending dire calamities like the birth of an illegimate or half caste child in the family, etc. A diamond should not be used only with a look to the caste or class it specifically belongs to, inasmuch as a diamond possessed of all the commendable features proves as a source of boundless prosperity to its wearer, whereas a diamond vitiated by any of the condemnable traits, turns out to be a spring of unmitigated evil.

A diamond with one of its angles or horns broken or mutilated, or looking as if scratched, withered or trampled down, should not be retained in the household, though otherwise possessed of all commendable features, as it would certainly bring hosts of unsuspected evils in its train. The goddess of wealth is sure to part company with a person who is impudent enough to wear a diamond which emits a red glare through one of its mutilated horns or angles and looks cloudy and impure at the centre. A diamond scratched in any part of its body and which appears to be painted with stripes of red in the inside, robs the decent competence of its wearer, and subsequently brings on his death and ruin. A diamond found in its natural state in the bed of a mine, is either hexagonal or octagonal in shape or appears like a polygon of twelve sides with all its exterior angles or points prominently marked and equally sharpened.

A diamond, cut into the shape of a regular hexagon with well-smoothed sides and well-marked points or angles, and shedding a clear prismatic lustre from the inside and divested of all the harmful traits described in the books on gems and precious stones, is to be rarely found even amidst the treasures of crowned heads. Prosperity, long life, increase of wives and progeny and domestic animals, and the bringing home of a teeming harvest, attend on the use of a diamond, keen and well marked in its points, clear in lustre and divested of the characteristic baneful traits. Serpents, tigers, and thieves fly from the presence of a person wearing such a diamond. Fatal and dreadful poisons, secretly administered, prove inoperative in his system and all his possessions enjoy a sort of immunity from acts of incendiarism or erosions by water. The complexion of such a person improves in its healthful glow and all his undertakings become prosperous and thriving.

A diamond, devoid of all the characteristic blemishes and weighing twenty tandulam in weight, and worn by a man, should be regarded as double in value of the standard of appraising used in respect of ascertaining the water, lustre price and the commendable traits of diamond. Fractions such as $\frac{1}{3}$, $\frac{1}{8}$, $\frac{1}{10}$, $\frac{1}{16}$, $\frac{1}{25}$ or $\frac{1}{100}$ should respectively used in computing the price of a diamond, wherever it would be found necessary to appraise a diamond by the standard of another diamond of greater weight and brilliancy. An infinitesimally small fraction in such an instance, should be computed as equal to a thousandth part of the latter in price. Eight seeds of white sesamum equal a Tandulam in weight, and the use of a diamond weighing less than even the latter standard-measure, is not prohibited. A diamond possessed of all the commendable traits and found to float on the water in test, should be worn by a man in exclusion of all the other gems happening to be in his possession.

A diamond found to be affected with small defects whether visible or invisible to the naked eyes, should be appraised at a price equal to a tenth part of that of a diamond of similar water and weight, but devoid of all such blemishes. A diamond marked with many a patent defect, whether great, or small should not be appraised at a price even equal to a hundredth part of that of a similar stainless diamond. A diamond otherwise defective, but set in a prepared article of ornament, should be valued at a very low price. A diamond of the first water, but found to be otherwise possessed of any of the condemnable traits, should not be set in a royal ornament even for the purpose of decoration. Diamonds are prohibited as articles of female wear, as they are possessed of the mystic virtues of making them sterile and unhappy. A diamond which has a stunted, elongated or a flattened look like that of a thrashed paddy, should be looked upon as devoid of all commendable features.

Imitation diamonds are made by skilful artisans with such substances as the iron, the Pushparaga (topaz) the Gomeda, the Vaiduryyam (lapis-lazuli), the crystal and the glass, and hence their genuineness should be made to be tested by experts, well-versed in the art of recognising and appraising precious stones. A diamond offered for sale, should be put to such tests, as scratching, shana (emery wheel) and immersion in alkaline solutions. A diamond would scratch all other metals or gems, such as the iron, etc., without being scratched by any of them in return. Weight goes a long way towards the determination of a higher price of a gem or a metal, whereas the contrary should be regarded as the cr i-terion of judgment in the case of a diamond, as laid down by the immortal gods. A Kuruvinda of inferior water can be scratched or written upon by a Kuruvinda of a higher water, while a diamond is alone capable of cutting a diamond. The lustre of all genuine gems, pearls or diamond, cut or set in an ornament, never shoot upwards, while those that are obliquely or laterally cut, emit a ray of slanting or lateral light.

A diamond scintillating with flashes of rainbow coloured hue at the centre, though otherwise stained and marked with dots and lines, or narrow at the sides, blesses its wearer with a prosperous family and well-filled granaries. A king wearing a diamond dazzling with lightning flashes, is sure to subdue the prowess of his neighbouring monarchs and to exercise an unbounded control upon his vassals and liege subjects.

——:o:——

CHAPTER LXIX.

SUTA said :—Pearls are found in the temples of elephants and wild boars, in conch-shells, in oysters, in the hoods of cobras and in the hollow stems of bamboos. The origin of a species of pearls is abscribed to the effect of thunder. Pearls found in Oyster shells, abound in numbers and are usually included within the category of gems. An oyster pearl is capable of being pierced with a hole in the middle (running through its entire length) while the remaining species do not admit of being similarly bored. Pearls found in the stems of bamboos or in the temples of elephants and wild boars or in the mouths of whales or in the entrails of conch-shells, are devoid of lustre, though possessed of other auspicious virtues.

Of the eight species of pearls described by the connoisseurs of gems, those obtained from conch-shells and the temples of elephants should be deemed as standing in the bottom of the list as regards colour and brilliancy. A conch-shell pearl is usually as big as a large Kona (point of a rapier) and assumes a colour similar to that of the mollusc it is found in.

A pearl found in the temple of an elephant, is marked by the absence of any definite colour and is lustreless like a pearl found in the stem of a bamboo. A pearl found in the mouth of a fish, is a perfect sphere in shape and is marked by a yellowish hue, like the back of a pathenam fish as is occasionally found inside the mouth of a whale that frequents the unfathomable depths of ocean beds. A boar-pearl resembles the tip of its tusk in colour, and is obtained in certain quarters of the globe and is blissful like the boar incarnation of the divine Vishnu. A pearl obtained from inside the hollow stem of a bamboo, resembles a hailstone in colour, and is found only in a bamboo that grows in the land of the honest and the pious, and not in every tope of that grass.

A pearl found in the hood of a cobra is round in shape like the one obtained from the mouth of a fish and emits a dazzling effulgence from its own natural seat. After copious washing such a pearl assumes the lustre of a well-polished sword. The possessor of a cobra or serpent-pearl, meets with a rare good fortune, and becomes a pious and illustrious king in time, with a treasury full of other species of precious gems.

Dark clouds, hung down and heavily charged with rain, and roaring with the voice of the eternal trumpets blown upon at the time of universal dissolution and spangled with flashes of lightning, closely envelop the sky,. at the time, when the Bramhana, well versed in the religious and ceremonial proceedings, after enquiring about the acquisition of such a pearl, and having done the necessary rite of protection unto it, formally takes it into the interior of the house of its possessor. Neither the serpents, nor the Rakshas, nor diseases, nor disturbances of any kind would assail the man amidst whose treasure such a snake-pearl would lie.

A cloud-grown pearl rarely reaches this mortal globe, and usually falls to the lot of the celestials. By illumining the four quarters of the sky with its native lustre, a cloud-begotten pearl, like the sun, dispels the gloom of a cloudy day. Outshining the combined effulgence of the fire, the moon, and the myriads of scintillating stars, such a pearl, like the dawn of day, can dispel the gloom of even the darkest night on earth. The whole earth, girdled by the four oceans containing innumberable gems in their fathomless depths, can not be deemed as the adequate price of such a pearl, even if she be covered over with layers of pure gold. A man, born in indigence and of humble parents, but happening to be the possessor of such a pearl, only through the transformation of a good deed done in a previous existence, is sure to be the paramount sovereign of the entire surface of the Earth. Not to the good deeds of the king alone, but to the better fortune of the whole humanity, should be ascribed the advent of such a man on earth, and no evil would ever strike the land to the extent of a thousand Yojanas round the place of his birth.

The teeth of that great Vala lay scattered and perched up over the wide expanse of heaven like the gallaxy of stars, and dropped down one by one into the wonderfully coloured waters of the oceans, and originated the seeds of gems vieing with the beams of the full moon, and the rainbow tint of a peacock's feathers in colour. Some of these seeds entered into the inner organisms of oysters that lay in the deep beds of oceans and gave rise to pearls.

Pearls are divided into eight different species according to the places of their origin, such as the Sainhalika (off the coast of Ceylon), the Paraloukika (heavenly) the Sourashtrika (born in the country of Shourashtra), the Tamraparna (off the coast of modern Tamluk), the Parashava (Persian), the Kouvera, the Pandyahataka and the Hemaka. Pearls obtained from oysters fished off the coast of Ceylon, Vardhana and Persia or the coast of any other foreign or southern islands (Patala) do not lose much in comparison with the other species as regards shape, size, colour and other properties.

The place of origin, should not be taken into account in determining the price of a pearl. A learned gem-expert shall only notice its shape and size. Nor can it be said that defects or excellencies are restricted to any particular species, since pearls of all shape and size can be obtained from oysters of the several fisheries described above.

An oyster-pearl, grounded into a well round shape, should be appraised at a price of thirteen hundred and five silver coins. A pearl, weighing half a mashaka less in weight than the former, should be valued at a sum of mony equal to a two-fifth part of that of the former. A pearl weighing three Mashakas, should be valued at two thousand silver coins. According to a similar computation, the price of a pearl weighing two Mashakas and a half, should be fixed at two thousand and three hundred silver coins. A pearl, weighing two Mashakas only, but otherwise belonging to the commendable type, should be valued at eight hundred silver coins. A pearl weighing a Mashaka and a half, should be valued at three hundred and twenty-five silver coins. The price of a pearl weighing six Gunjas, should be laid at two hundred silver coins, while a pearl, weighing half as much as the former, should be valued at a hundred silver coins only. A pearl, weighing less than the preceding one by sixteen Dharanas, is called a Darvikam as regards its weight, and can fetch a price of hundred and ten silver coins only from the hands of the ignorant. A pearl, weighing less than the foregoing one by twenty Dharanas, is called a Bhavakam by the experts and should not be valued at a higher sum than seventy-nine silver coins.

A string of thirty pearls, each weighing a Dharanam, should be valued at forty-four coins. A string of forty-four pearls of Shiktha class, should be valued at thirty silver coins. A string of sixty pearls, each weighing a Nikara, should be valued at fourteen silver coins. A string of eighty or ninty pearls of the Kupya class, should be respectively valued at eleven and nine silver coins.

The process of cleansing and perforating the pearl seeds, is as follows :—First, all the pearls should be collected and kept in a bowl of boiled rice, previously saturated with the expressed juice of the Jamvera fruits (lime). Then the whole contents of the bowl, should be kept simmering for a while, after which the pearls should be taken out and rubbed with the liquid extract of boiled rice. Thus softened they, should be pierced through as desired. The process of cleansing consists in gently heating the pearl seeds placed in a covered crucible, known as the Matsaputa and covered over with a plaster of clay, after which they should be boiled in milk, water or wine, according to the process known as the Vitanapatti. Then the pearls should be gently rubbed with a piece of clean linen, until they would begin to shine with their characteristic lustre, which would indicate the completion of the process of cleansing. This is what the mighty Vyadhi laid down as regards the cleansing of pearls out of his compassion towards the good and the erudite.

Pearls used for the personal decorations of kings and noblemen, should be kept immersed in mercury contained in a glass receptacle saturated with a solution of gold. This is what is done by experts in the island of Ceylon. A pearl of suspected genuineness, should be kept immersed, for a night, in warm oil saturated with a quantity of common salt. Its genuineness should be pronounced in the event of its successfully stood the preceding test. In the alternative, a pearl of questionable appearance, should be covered with a piece of dry linen and rubbed with a seed of Vrihi grass, and its genuineness should be presumed from the fact of its colour having not been any way affected by the friction.

A pearl which is white, of good size, heavy, transparent, round and possessed of cool and effulgent lustre, should be regarded as the best of its kind. A pearl, which is possessed of a pretty large size, is white, and round, emits rays of effulgent lustre, is pierced with a hole of uniform girth throughout its length and evokes even the pleasure of a person not disposed to purchase the same, should be looked upon as a pearl of rare virtues. Not even a single evil can befall the possesor of a pearl which is possessed of all the commendable features and qualities enumerated in the present chapter.

—:o:—

CHAPTER LXX.

SUTA said:—The sun-god, having collected the gem-begetting blood of that great demon (Vala) who was high in dignity and mighty in prowess, attempted to stealthily fly away by scaling the expanse of ether, blue like the colour of a newly polished sword blade, when Rávana, the king of Lanka, the conqueror of the celestials in a thousand battles, intoxicated with his prowess, strength and victory, obstructed his path in heaven like a second Ráhu (Nodes). The sun-god, afraid of his dreadful presence, dropped that blood in dismay into the unfathomable depth of the pool of Lanka, tossing with myriads of sun-lit waves and girdled with a belt of Arecanut trees. From that day, the pool has acquired the celebrity of the Ravana Ganges and ranks equally with the sacred Ganges in respect of religious merit and sanctity.

From that day, the foreshores of that sanctified pool are found to be strewn over with innumerable precious gems, and shine with wonderful effulgence in the night as if pierced with hundreds of golden shafts (Narachas). On its banks are originated the bright and the beautiful-coloured Padmaragas (Ruby) and crystals and Kuruvindas of untold virtues are begotten of the perfume wafted from its fragrant foreshores. Several of the Kuruvindajas (which belong to the family of the crystals, as are found in the country of Sougandhika) resemble the flowers of the Vandhuka, the Gunja and the Kinshuka trees in colours, some are coloured like the human blood, while several of them resemble the colour obtained from the insects known as the Indragopas or that of the seeds of a pomegranate. Several of them are coloured like vermilion or the Utpala flowers or saffron or like the dye obtained from the solution of shellac, which though coloured uniformly deep throughout their body, shine with a special intrinsic light at their centre. These members of the family of crystals, illuminated by the light of the sun, shoot forth rays of wonderful colour and brilliancy from their sides which lighten up the surrounding space and are refracted in all directions.

Some of these gems are coloured like the water dyed with indigo and the expressed juice of the Kusumbha flowers. Some of them vie with the extremely deep red of the Utpala flowers. Some of them are tinged with a hue similar to that of the flowers of a Kantakari plant, while several species bear the colour of asafœtida. Some of them shine with an effulgence which resembles the eyes of a chakora or a male cuckoo in colour, while the rest of the group are tinged deep red like the flower of a Kokonada plant (red lotus). Gems, born of Sougandhika, which are coloured like the red Utpala flowers, or are possessed of a bluish hue, are nearly equal to those of the crystal family, as regards bright ness, hardness, heaviness, etc. The colour of the gems belonging to the Kuruvinda family, is not so deep as that which characterises the species of crystals, the former being somewhat dull-hued and devoid of brilliancy, though there are several shining Kuruvindas which are decidedly inferior to the crystals in point of lustre and brilliancy.

Kuruvindas, found in the bed of the river Ravana Ganga, are possessed of a deep red hue like the gems known as the Padmaragas, and can be favourably compared with the members of the crystal family, as regards lustre and brilliancy. A species of gems, resembling the Kuruvindas in colour, is not usually found in the country of the Andhras and fetches an inferior price, if accidentally obtained in that division of Bharatavarsha. Similarly, gems, possessed of properties kindred to those of the crystal family, are found in the country of Tamvaru and are valued at a lower price. Brilliancy of colour, heaviness, coldness, equal transparency throughout its body, effulgence and dimension are the good features of a gem.

A gem, though genuine and otherwise possessed of the characteristic features of the family it belongs to, should not be commended to use or wearing, if found to be stained, or sandy or cracked in the inside, or rough, dull and lustreless. Grief, care, disease, death, ruin and loss of fortune overtake the man who wears such a gem of the condemnable sort, even out of ignorance or lack of sufficient knowledge about the properties of precious stones. The five genuine species of beautiful gems are usually substituted with the inferior or the alien one's, which the wise and the intelligent would carefully mark at the time of purchase or selection. The gems, found in the countries of Kalasapura, Sinhala, Tamvaru, Muktapaniya and Shreeparnakas, which go by the name of the Padmaragas, are allied to one another, and should be regarded as alien to a Padmaraga of the genuine species.

The first of the above named species (kalasa) is marked by a frosty or husky aspect. The alien species, found in the country of the Tamvaru, is characterised by a redish or copper-coloured hue, that found in the island of Sinhala, looks thin and perched up, the Muktapaniyam is marked by a shade of sky blue tint, while the Shreeparnakam is devoid of lustre and brilliancy. These, in conjunction with the following, form the distinctive traits of the several alien species of the Padmaraga, *viz.*, that they are either marked by a copper-tint, or look frosty at the centre, or seem to be clouded with an oily coating, or shine with a faded or discoloured light after rubbing, or cast a dark shade at the sides, if pressed on the head with the fingers. In testing a Padmaraga, which excels in lustre and brilliancy all other members of its own family, but which bears a weight unequal to the specific weight of a gem of its own class and size, the wise should give their verdict, as regards genuineness, to the one of greater weight of the two gems compared. In a case of doubtful and bewildering testimonies, the gem should be subjected to the test of a testing stone, or examined by scratching it with a gem of the same species. Excepting diamond and Kuruvinda, no other gem can cut or scratch a bit of Padmaraga or Indranila.

A gem, belonging to an alien or an incompatible group, should not be worn with one of the genuine species and possessed of great virtues. Even the wearing of such a gem is forbidden, if strung together with the Koustabha of divine potency. As a Chandala in the company of a host of mighty Brahmanas, can defile them without the least effort, so a gem of the incompatible type, can nullify the potencies of all other precious stones, if worn or strung together. No evil can befall the wearer of a genuine Padmaraga, even if he lives in the midst of his deadly enemies, or walks in the path of illusion and unrighteousness. Diseases, incidental to the derangement of the vital humours, or disturbances of any kind, can never assail the man who wears a Padmaraga, burning with the effulgence of its own stirring and sterling properties.

The price fixed for a tandulam weight of cut and polished diamond, should be understood as equal to that of a Mashaka weight of cleansed and polished Padmaraga. A gem is valued for its hue and brilliancy, and hence any deterioration of these two qualities will correspondingly deteriorate its price or value.

——:o:——

CHAPTER LXXI.

SUTA SAID:—Vasuki, the lord of the serpents, carried away the bile of that chief of the demons (Vala) and rent in twain the vast expanse of heaven with the sweep of his mighty tail. The body of that primordial Hydra, illumined with the effulgence of gems glowing on his thousand hoods, lay like a bridge of shining silver across the infinite deep of dark blue ether; whereupon behold, the mighty Gurada, whirling round with the strokes of his mighty pinions, darted down upon that lord of the nether worlds and obstructed his way. Vasuki in his turn, terrified at that dreadful presence, dropped that bile, in dismay, down in that vale of the mount of Manikya, shaded with the luscious boughs of resinous Turaksha trees, and perfumed with the scents of the forests of Nalika.

Simultaneously with the fall described above, a portion of the bile dropped down in the country, situated beyond the Himalayas (Varalaya) and graced with the presence of the goddess of fortune; and the coast of the land-locked sea of that country] was transformed into one bed of Emerald The mighty Garuda, the lord of the celestial birds, picked up a few of the emeralds with his beaks, even from the coast of that inland sea, but he soon dropped down in a fit of fainting and all the emeralds were cast forth through the apertures of his nostrils.

An emerald, possessed of a colour resembling the tint of the neck of a parrot, or that of a Shirisha flower, or tinged like the blade of a green grass or a new grown moss, or glowing with a hue that marks the feathers of a peacock or the back of a fire-fly, should be deemed as possessed of the virtue of bringing good luck to its possessor. The country in which the bile of the lord of the demons dropped down from the beaks of that dreadful destroyer of the serpents (Garuda), thus originating the veins of emerald therein, is very difficult to get at, though Nature has bestowed her bounties upon it with the most lavish hand.

An Emerald found in that emerald bed, is endued with the virtue of neutralising the effects of poisons. Poison, secreted from the fangs of a Maha-Sarpa (*lit*: the great serpent, black cobra) or incidental to the bite by such a snake, which baffles the virtues of all medicinal herbs and incantations, is neutralised by its simple touch. An emerald, not found in the abovesaid bed, but mined from any other place in the same country, is the holiest of the holies.

The gem experts accord the highest praise to an emerald, which is possessed of a dark green colour, and sheds a soft glow, and looks as if stuffed with powders of gold in the inside, in company with the one which is coloured with an uniform shade of green all through its body, is heavy in weight, is devoid of the condemnable traits and shoots forth rays of effulgence with the reflection of the sunlight. An emerald whose inside changes its natural green hue and shines with a dazzling light like that of a flash of lightning modified with a greenish shade, as well as the one which pleases the mind of the onlooker at the first sight, should be deemed as possessed of the most excellent qualities. An emerald, possessed of a transparent hue at the centre, though coloured like the tender blade of a kusha grass in its body, ranks very high as regards value and quality. An emerald, simply glowing with its native dark green hue, should be deemed inferior to one of the preceding type.

An emerald, blackish (dark blue), lustreless, looking sand-grained, dry and hard, and encrusted with Shilajatu (bitumen) should be deemed as of a very inferior sort. A person seeking his own good and prosperity, shall never wear, nor purchase a gem which has been made to look like an emerald by means of dying or any other chemical process. Similarly, the use of an emerald, possessed of a double shade of colour, is prohibited by the injunctions of the Shastras. An emerald coloured like a Putrika or a Bhallataka, should be deemed as not belonging to the genuine type (vijati). The colour or the glow of a Putrika-coloured emerald, is perceptibly affected by rubbing it with a piece of linen, which is often suspected to be a bit of glass for its lightness of weight. The colour of an emerald possessed of a variety of shades and attributes, is affected by the contact of a wind, saturated with the essence of the Bhallataka.

Diamonds, pearls, or any other gems belonging to the alien species, fail to shoot up rays in the upward direction when not set in an ornament. In certain cases the upward rays are perceptible, if the gems are cut straightwise or held longitudinally, which disappear as soon as they are held in a slanting position.

The wise and the intelligent, should wear an emerald set in gold, at the time of religious ablution, or of rinsing the mouth with water on the occasion of a religious sacrifice, or during the performance of protective incantions, or at the time of making gifts of cows and gold, or during the performance of obsequious rites done unto the gods and one's departed manes, or for the cure of diseases, brought about by the deranged condition of the vital winds, or incidental to the effects of poison. Similarly an emerald devoid of all blemishes and set in gold, is possessed of the mystic virtue of bringing victory to its wearer, if engaged in a battle with his adversary.

A pure emerald fetches a higher price than a ruby (Padmaraga) of equal weight, while a defective one should be valued at a lower price than a similarly defective Padmaraga of the same weight.

——:o:——

CHAPTER LXXII.

SUTA SAID :—The eyes of the lord of the demons (Vala) which resembled the full blown blue lilies in hue and shape, were severed from his dismembered organism and cast into a country, where the beautiful damsels of Sinhala cull the fragrant flowers from the stems of suppliant and inviting creepers, in testimony whereof the expanding foreshores of the ocean that washes the coasts of that favoured isle, edged with a slender border of the Ketaka plants, glow as paved with one continuous bed of sapphire (Indra-Nila). These gems are coloured like the black (dark blue) flowers of the mountain Karnika which grow on those banks and around which swarms of black bees hum day and night, and which flowers are endued with a sour taste through the contact of the throat-serum of the Chakravakas (birds) that greedily suck their luscious sap and flap about their gladsome wings. Several of these gems are coloured like the clear and transparent water of that tranquil sea, others are tinged like the breast-feathers of a peacock, others are possessed of a hue which resembles the colour of the bubles that burst out on the surface of that dark blue sea, while the rest are coloured like the hue that comes upon the breast of a male cuckoo in spring.

An Indra-Nila gem possessed of an uniform shade of colour throughout its body, and clear and effulgent in its lustre, should be deemed as a gem of a very high value. An Indra-Nila possessed of a colour like that of an impregnated rain-cloud or any way scratched or splintered, or found encrusted with bits of stone, earth, or other ores or impurities, or looking sandy in its grain, should be regarded as possessed of dreadful features. Learned men, wise in the wisdom of the Shastras, are loud in the praise of those excellent gems which are largely found in the foreshores of the sea of Sinhala.

Men acquire the same merit in and derive the same benefit from, using an Indra-Nila which they derive from wearing a gem of the Padmaraga species, and in the case of doubt, an Indra-Nila should be subjected to the same tests as are laid down in the case of a Padmaraga. The features which characterise the three alien species of the Padmaraga, apply mutatis mutandis to the case of an Indra-Nila, which should be carefully noticed at the time of purchase.—An Indra-Nila would stand a greater amount of heat or fire than a Padmaraga of equal size and weight. But under no circumstance, a gem should be subjected to an ordeal of fire, inasmuch as a gem burnt for the purpose of being purged off of all impurities, or for a greater brilliancy, brings ill luck to the person who burns it, as well as to him on whose behalf such burning is performed.

Glass, marble, Vaiduryaya (lapis-lazuli) and crystals, though made to be possessed of a colour like the Indra-Nila, should be regarded as alien to the latter in species. The weight and hardness of these gems which are found to grow in an increasing ratio from the glass upward, should be always tested. An Indra-Nila which shoots forth dark or faint rays of copper-coloured light from its inside, as well as the one shining with the blended colours of a Karavira and a blue lotus, should be carefully preserved as a precious treasure. An Indra-Nila which scintillates with the blended colours of a solar spectrum, should be looked upon as a rare find on earth.

An Indra-Nila, immersed in a quantity of milk weighing hundred times its own weight and tinging the latter with its native hue, is called the Maha-Nila. The price of a Masha weight of Padmaraga is same as that of the four Masha weights of Indra-Nila.

—:o:—

CHAPTER LXXIII.

SUTA SAID :—O thou twice-born one, the mode of testing such gems as the Vaiduryaya, the Padmaraga, the Karketana and the Bhisma-stone, were first described by the god Brahma to the holy sage Vyasa, who subsequently disclosed them to the world for the good of the human race.

The bosom of that primordial ocean was violently agitated by the thundering war-cry of that lord of the demons, whose swollen and frenzied waters began to madly lash the jagged faces of its rock-bound coasts; and behold, Vaiduryayas of varied colours and matchless brilliance, were showered down through the clefts of those water-riven shores, turning them into beds of shining light. Accordingly the brow of the contiguous hill of Vidura was transformed into a mine of Vaiduryaga, which was originated by the war-cry of the demon Vala and is named after the rock in which it was first found to be imbeded.

The thunder like roar of the demon, gave rise to the formation of packs of sable clouds, and Vaiduryyas of varied colours were formed under their influence, as so many effulgent shootings off from that primordial sky. Colours which mark the several classes of the Padmaraga, as well form the distinctive features of the several species of the Vaiduryya, of which those that are tinged like the breast-feathers of a peacock, or coloured pale green like the leaves of a bamboo, are the best as regards price and quality. A Vaiduryya, possessed of a blended hue like that of the primary or the exterior feathers of the wings of a Chasa (bird) occupies the lowest place in the list as regards value and intrinsic virtues, and accordingly its use is forbidden by the gem experts.

A Vaiduryya, belonging to the commendable type, brings good luck to its wearer, whereas the use of one of the condemnable species, is attended with dreadful consequences. Hence a Vaiduryya should be carefully observed and tested before wearing. Stones, known as the Girikacha, Shaishopala, or glass crystals, appearing as clouded smoke, may be easily mistaken for a Vaiduryya, though they are alien to it in species. They should be pronounced as bits of glass in the event of their proving incapable of cutting or scratching a Vaiduryya of tested genuineness, whereas a Shaishopalakam stone, simulating the properties of a Vaiduryya, should be detected by its lightness. A crystal, mistaken for a gem of the species under discussion, should detected by its greater brilliance.

The price of two pala weights of Vaiduryya, should be laid at the amount fixed for the value of a Suvarna weight of Indra-Nilam. Gems apparently resembling a Vaiduryya in colour, but virtually belonging to the alien species, should be compared in respect of gloss, softness, lighter weight, etc., with a Vaiduryya of tested genuineness. The price of a Vaiduryaya, in common with the rest of the gems, varies according to its setting and purification and depends upon the fact of its being possessed of auspicious or inauspicious features. A gem losing nothing of its excellence in course of ages, and carefully set by a jeweller in a suitable metal, or found in a mine of Samateta or in a country near the sea coast, should be valued at a price six times greater than that of an ordinary gem belonging to the same species. The price enumerated above, should be deemed as obtaining in markets near the sea coast and in vicinity of the gem mines.

Sixteen Mashakas are equivalent to a weight, technically known as the Suvarnam in the parlance of the gem dealers, a seventh part whereof is called a Sana. Four Krishnalas make a Masha or a Mashaka. A tenth part of a Pala makes a Dharana.

——:o:——

CHAPTER LXXIV.

SUTA said :—Gems known as the Pushparagas (topaz) origined out of the perched skin of that dismembered body of Vala, which fell on the summits of the Himalays and were thus naturally endued with high qualities. A topaz possessed of pale yellow colour, usually passes under the denomination of the Padmaraga, while the one tinged with the blending of a reddish and yellow hue, is called the Kourunda. A topaz which is transparent and possessed of a reddish colour, is designated as the Kashayaka, while the one, tinged with a cold shade of bluish white, is known by the denomination of Samanaka. A topaz coloured deep red or dark blue is known by the epithet of Padmaraga or Indra-Nila. The price of a topaz should be appraised at a rate as previously laid down by the gem experts in the case of a lapis lazuli. The virtue of a topaz consists in removing the sterility of a woman, and in crowning her with the glory of maternity.

—:o:—

CHAPTER LXXV.

SUTA said:—The nails of the deceased Vala, the paramount king of the demons, scattered by the wind in the lovely tufts of the lotus plants, were transformed into the seeds of the gems known as the Karketanam, the most prized of all gems in the world.

A Karketanam is usually found to be possessed of a hue like the colours of honey, blood, and the moon beam blended together, and shines with a peculiar dazzling effulgence of a yellowish copper-tinged shade. A Karketanam which is blue or white or lustreless, should be looked upon as of inferior quality, or affected with the inauspicious traits, or with any disease, peculiar to minerals.

Karketanas which are naturally coloured with an uniform shade of light yellow throughout their bodies, and are heavy, cool, glossy and devoid of all dreadful or inauspicious features as dullness of hue, cracks, fissures, etc., due to a deranged or defective (*lit.*, diseased) process of crystalization in the course of its growth, should be looked upon as extremely rare and the holiest of the holies.

A Karketanam, set in an article or an ornament of gold, and appearing as if glowing with the blaze of a living fire, acts as the greatest known panacea and should be regarded as endued with the mystic virtue of increasing the progeny and the duration of life of its wearer, and of bringing happiness to his household by destroying the evil propensities of his mind, which are the inseparable companions of the miscreant Kali (the lord or creator of all moral evils).

Men who use such a Karketanam gem of high and wonderful virtues, whether for the purposes of decoration, or otherwise, are sure to be the masters of untold wealth, and are glorified in the world, and enjoy universal fame and perpetual felicity amidst the unsolicited affections of many a true, tested and devoted friends.

Stones of inferior light, shade, lustre, weight and origin, may be found to simulate a Karketam of the genuine species, which may be detected, at the first sight, by its high and inimitable excellence in respect of the foregoing points or attributes.

A Karketanam, clear and effulgent like the rays of the midday sun, should be valued by a connoisseur at a proper and adequate price, and according to its weight and native excellence.

—:o:—

CHAPTER LXXVI.

SUTA SAID :—The (seeds) semen of the lord of the demons which was contained in its natural receptacle at the time of his dissolution, was cast in a country situate to the north of the Himalayas, and was transformed into the mines of that excellent gem which is known as the stone of Bhishma.

A Bhishma stone is usually found to be of a white colour like that of a conchshell and resplendent like a ray of the unclouded sun, while the one of a comparatively later origin, is sometimes mistaken for a diamond.

The man who devoutly wears a pure Bhishma stone, set in gold, about his neck, perpetually meets with the good in life.The wild and fierce beasts of the forest, such as wolves, leopards, Sharabhas (fabulous eight-feeted beasts of the rhinoceros tribe) elephants, tigers and lions, shun the presence of a man who wears a Bhishma stone about his neck, and hurriedly fly away even if happened to be near his person. Such a man can easily satisfy any number of wives, and usually gets the upper hand in matters of sexual enjoyment. Libations of water or obsequious oblations offered to one's departed manes with a hand, adorned with a ring set with a Bhishma stone, give them a satisfaction which lasts for years to come, and poisons of such venomous creatures, as serpents, moles, scorpions or of any other oviparous animals, however strong and active, readily yield to its mystic potency. The wearer of such a stone enjoys a sort of immunity from the dangers of a watery grave and acts of incendiarism, and thieves and robbers dare not intrude upon the precincts of his house.

A wise man shall shun, from a distance, a Bhishma stone which is possessed of a blended colour (greenish blue) like the hues which respectively mark a rain cloud and the zoophytes (water plants,) or tinged with a dull, lifeless yellow, or faded and discoloured. The intelligent shall fix the price of a Bhishma stone with an eye to the nature of the season of the year and the place of its origin, one obtained in a remote country fetching a higher price than its kindred of local origin, or obtained in a country which is not distant from the place of its sale.

——:O:——

CHAPTER LXXVII.

SUTA said :—The serpents, having worshipped the nails of the deceased lord of the demons, carried them away in their mouths and deposited them on the summits of the holy mountains (Himalayas) and in the beds of rivers which flow through the hallowed confines of the countries beyond (situate to the north of) those mountains.

Pulakas (a kind of gem) found in the beds of rivers flowing through such countries as Dasharna (the eastern part of modern Malwa), Agadha, Makala (Modern Amarakantaka, the source of the Narmada) and in the provinces of Gandhara (modern Afghanisthan) and Valhika (Bactria or modern Balkh), and coloured like the seeds of the Gunja (a kind of shrubs bearing red-black berries) honey and the stems of the lotus plants or earth-coloured, should be regarded as belonging to the most commendable type.

Pulakas possessed of variegated colours like those of conchshells, lotus flowers, black bees, and Arka flowers and chequered with lines, should be deemed as the most auspicious and holiest of their species, and as granting increase of wealth and progeny to their wearers.

Pulakas possessed of a hue like the colour of a crow or of an ass or of a jackal or of a wolf or carried away and deposited in a place by vultures in their blood-stained beaks, bring death to the person who collects or keeps them in his possession. Hence the intelligent should avoid a Pulaka of any of the aforesaid characters.

A Pulaka of the commendable type, weighing a Pala in weight, should be valued at five hundred silver coins.

—:o:—

CHAPTER LXXVIII.

SUTA said :—The Fire God, having picked up the complexion of the lord of the demons, cast it into the waters of the Narmada, a portion of which fell into the low-lying lands of the vicinity, occupied by the communities of vile caste. From the complexion so cast about, originated the gem, known as the blood-stone, coloured like the hue of the Indragopa insect blended with that of the mouth of a parrot, and characterised by an uniform elevation and brightness of all its parts.

Blood-stones of various colours have been obtained on different occasions, some of which are extremely clear and coloured pale red like the disc of the half moon. A blood stone should be subjected to the same test as a sapphire, and looked upon as possessing the mystic virtue of increasing the wealth and the number of servants of its wearer. A blood-stone fully matured, assumes the colour of a flash of lightning.

—:o:—

CHAPTER LXXIX.

SUTA said :—The god Langali took up the fat of the deceased demon king, scattered it with his plough-share over the countries traversed by the river Kaveri and the Vindhya mountain, as well as over the countries of Nepal and China and the tracts of land inhabited by the Yavanas. The scattered bits of fat were transformed into crystals which assume a white colour like that of conch shell or of the fibres found inside the stems of a lotus plant. No other gem can vie with the present one in respect of absolving the sin of a man. A crystal cut and polished by a skilful artizan, should fetch a higher price than one in its uncut or natural state.

——:o:——

CHAPTER LXXX.

SUTA said :—The primordial hydra (Vasuki) carried away the entrails of the lord of the demons and cast them into the countries of Kerala, etc., out of which the corals of high and excellent virtues were originated. Of these, those that are coloured like the blood of a hare or that of a Gunja berry or of a China rose, should be deemed as the best of their kind, the countries of Romaka, Devaka and Sunilaka, being the places of their origin. Corals obtained from any other source are not so good as the aforesaid ones. The price of a coral depends upon its cutting. A coral which is coloured dark red and possessed of a cool, pleasant and soft shade, should be deemed as belonging to the best species and as endued with the virtue of augmenting the riches and filling in the granaries of its wearer, as well as the best eliminator of poison and a safeguard against all dreaded evils. O Sounaka, the corals and the crystals should be included within the category of gems and used in testing their genuineness.

——:o:——

CHAPTER LXXXI.

SUTA said:—Now I shall describe the holy pools and sanctuaries of which the river Ganges pre-eminently stands as the most sacred, and which is easily accessible everywhere throughout its course, except in three places, such as Haridvara, Prayaga and Sagara (the Gangetic estuary) Prayaga is the best of all sanctuaries, inasmuch as a man quitting this life within the precincts of that sacred city, becomes a liberated soul after death, and oblations offered therein for the absolution of the departed souls, fully serve their initiative purpose, and moreover because, men resorting to its blessed sanctum for the fruition of any definite desire, are sure to witness its realisation.

The city of Benares is the foremost of all the sacred places in which the god Keshava is transformed into the shape of the god Vishvesha. The field of Kurukshetra is a great sanctuary where men by making gifts and doling out charities, become entitled to the privileges of an emancipated soul or to the enjoyment of creature comforts, as the case may be, in the life to come. The sacred pool at Prabhasa, is a great place of pilgrimage where the divine image of the god Somnath is installed. The fair city of Dvaraka is the holiest of the holy spots on earth and grants enjoyment of earthly cheers or salvation to those who resort to its sanctum. The eastern bank of the river Sarasvati is holy and likewise is the country of the Sapta Sarasvatam. The sanctuary at Kedara has the merit of absolving a pilgrim from all sins, whereas the village of Shambhala is a good place of pilgrimage. The sanctuary of Narayanam is a great shrine, whereas a pilgrimage to the holy forest of Vadarika, leads to the emancipation of self.

27

Similarly, places or pools or hills like Shvetadvipa, Mayapuri, Naimisha, Pushkara, Ayodhya, the Aryatirtham, the Chitrakutam, the Gomati, the Vainayaka, the hermitage of Ramagiri, Kanchipuri, the Tunga-Bhadra, the Shreeshailam, Setubandham, Rameshvaram, the Kartikeyam, the Bhrigutungam, the Kamatirtham, Kamaram and Katak, should be regarded as important sacred pools, places or hills.

The god Mahakala is the presiding deity of the sanctuary at the city of Ujjayani, while the god Hari, installed in the shape of the imaged Shri-dhara, is the guardian deity of Kuvjaka. Likewise Kuvjabhrakam is a great place of pilgrimage, whereas a resort to Kalasarpi fulfills the desires of a pilgrim.

The other renowned places of pilgrimage are the rivers Maha-keshi, the Kaveri, the Chandrabhaga, the Vipasha, the sacred forest of Ekamram, the Brahma-tirtham, the Devakotakam, the beautiful city of Mathura, the rivers Shona, Mahanada and the Jamvusara. Sacred is the spot where stands an image of the god Hara or of Hari or of Gana or of the Sun-god.

Rites of religious ablutions, acts of worship, and charity, Shraddha ceremonies, repetitions of Mantras, or offerings of oblations to one's departed manes, performed or done within the sanctum of any of the abovesaid pools or places, tend to bear immortal fruits.

A pilgrimage to the sacred village of Shalagrama, is rewarded with the fruition of all desires, while the sanctuary sacred to the god Pashupati, should be deemed as the holiest of all holy places, like those known as the Kokamukha, the Varaha, the Bhandiram and the Svamitirtham.

The Maha (supreme) Vishnu manifestation of the god Hari, is the presiding deity of the sanctuary at Mohadanda, while the Madhusudana manifestation of the same deity is the tutelary god at the sanctuary at Mandara. The sanctuary of Kamarupam where resides the goddess Kamakshya, should be deemed as one of the most sacred spots on the globe, and likewise is the sanctuary at Pundravardhanam where resides the god Kartikeya. Extremely holy are the sanctuaries at Viraja and Purushottam and sacred are the hills and rivers which go by the denominations of the Mahendra, the Kaveri the Godavari, the Payoshni, and the sin absolving Vindhya.

Similarly sacred are the hills and cities and pools which are known by the names of the Gokarna, the city of Mahishmati-pura, Kalanjara and the sanctuary of the Shukra-Tirtham, where acts of charity and obsequious offerings performed and made in the presence of the bow-wielding (Sharnga-Dhara) manifestation of Vishnu, lead to the emancipation of one's self, and grants a religious merit equal to that of resorting to a million of other sancturies. The sacred shrines at Nandi-Tirtham, Nasika, the Govardhana, the Krishna, the Veni, the Bhimaratha, the Gandaki, the Tviravati, the Vindu-Sara, as well as the washings of the feet of an image of Vishnu, should be deemed, as the sancto sanctum of all sanctuaries.

A meditation upon the infinite self of Bramha, is the holiest of all sanctuaries. A control or subjugation of the senses is a great sanctuary. Holy is the sanctuary of one's curbing the evil propensities of one's own mind, and holy is the sanctuary of the purity of thought. The man who makes an ablution in the waters of divine meditation of the pool of pure knowledge, undefiled by the sediments of passion and envy, attains to the highest station of spiritual existence.

Men who make any nice discrimination as regards the sacred or non-sacred character of a particular sanctuary, alone acquire the merit of making any pilgrimage. The man who beholds the universe as but the manifestation of the one and the secondless Bramha, stands above the necessity of resorting to any so-called sacred place in the world. To him all places are alike, as being equally sanctified by the presence of that supreme entity.

All pools and rivers, all hills and mountains which are the

favourite haunts of the gods, are hallowed shrines, and acts of religious ablutions and charities and the offerings of obsequious cakes to one's departed manes on the occasions of Shraddha ceremonies, done and performed at any of these sacred places, bear immortal fruits.

The sanctuary at Shriranga, sacred to the god Hari, the holy river Tapi, the seven sanctuaries along the banks of the Godavari, the sacred hill of Kona, the sanctuary of Maha-Lakshmi with the close flowing sacred streamlet of the Pranita, situate in the brow of the Sajhyadri (the western Ghauts) and the shrines sacred to the deities Ekavira and Sureshvari, are renowned places of pilgrimage. A man by bathing in any of the sacred pools at the Ganga-Dvara, Kushavarta, Kankhala, the Vindhyaka and the Nil-Parvarta, never reverts to the miseries of human life.

Suta said :—The god Bramha first heared of all these all-giving sanctuaries from the god Hari, and subsequently described their sacred characters to Vyasa, Daksha and to the rest of the brotherhood of the sages. O Bramhan, a description of the origin and sanctity of the holy shrines at Gaya, a pilgrimage whereto ensures a perpetual residence in the region of Bramha, formed the sequel to that sacred topic.

—:o:—

CHAPTER LXXXII.

Said THE GOD BRAHMA :—Hear me, O Vyasa, briefly discourse on the sanctity of the holy city of Gaya, which is the holiest of the holies, and a patient hearing whereof entitles the listener to all the good things in this life and to salvation in the next. Once on a time, there lived a mighty demon named Gaya, who agitated the whole universe with the energy of his own well-practised and austere penances. The gods scorched, as it were, with the fiery emanations of his austerities, deliberated his death in a synod duly convened, and resolved to seek the umbrage of the protecting arms of Vishnu to that end.

The latter promised them protection and the impending fall of the mighty Gayasura, and the Gods, encouraged by the words of that supreme divinity, repaired to their respective abodes.

Once upon a time, the mighty Gayasura culled several lotus flowers which decked the waters of the ocean of cream, the favourite haunt of Vishnu, with the object of offering them to the god Shiva in the course of a worship, and carried them away to the country of Keekata. Misguided by the illusive energy of Vishnu, the demon turned them to a sacrilegious purpose, by making a bed of them for his own use, and fell under the fatal stroke of the celestial mace of that divinity and departed his life in peace.

Since then, the mace-wielding Vishnu has been staying within the precincts of that sacred city (Gaya) and on the ossified remains of that mighty demon, with the single object of granting salvation to those who might come there on pilgrimage, and likewise the gods Bramha and Kalesha have been living ever since within their imaged embodiments, installed on the sanctified remains of that illustrious Gaya.

"Now then," said the mace-bearning god—"Behold, I shall make a sanctuary of this blessed city. The man who bathes in the holy pools which flow within its sacred confines, or makes any gift or performs the Shradha ceremonies in honour of his departed manes therein, shall ascend to the region of Bramha, and shall never be doomed to the sufferings of hell."

Then the god Bramha, the grandfather of the celestials, having been informed of the sacredness of the city (Gaya) celebrated a religious sacrifice therein. The Bramhanas who were invited on the occasion, were honoured with substancial tokens of devotion, and the priests, who officiated at the sacrifice, were rewarded with as much gold as they could carry. Streams of milk, curd, cream and thickened milk, were made to flow through the city, and reservoirs of cordials and luscious drinks were opened free to the public, not to speak of other sweet and costly viands were served to all who were present there. The god Bramha, by way of sacrificial remuneration, transferred to the Bramhanas the proprietary right of the whole city to the circuit of about ten miles, but cursed them for their greed of gold which they did not take the trouble of hiding on the occasion. Thus addressed them the offended god :—" Cursed be ye all. Futile will be the knowledge acquired by yourselves and your fathers, and the studies of your progenies in the Vedic lore will fail to bear any fruit. The wealth acquired by you and your fathers shall be miserably squandered, and penury shall fall to the portion of your children. Cursed be the soil of your city, cursed be the hills which defend its borders, cursed be the clouds which bring rain to your country, and cursed be the rivers which irrigate your fields."

The Brahmanas, on their turn, fell on their knees and propitiated the enraged divinity, who, in a relenting mood, assured them that men coming on a pilgrimage to their sacred city, would purchase their satisfaction for good value, and that they would live on the bounties contributed by persons performing Shraddha ceremonies in honour of their departed manes at Gaya.

The fourfold means of salvation consists of a knowledge of the Supreme Brahma, performance of Shraddha ceremonies in honour of one's departed forefathers at Gaya, death in a cowshed, and residence within the confines of the holy field of Kurukshetra.

O Vyasa, all the holy oceans and pools and rivers and wells attend upon the man who makes a religious ablution in any of the sacred pools at Gaya. Sins incidental to the murder of a Brahmana, or to the drinking of wine, or due to one's defiling the bed of a superior person, or incidental to the company of a person guilty of any of the aforesaid crimes, is absolved by performing a Shraddha ceremony in honour of his soul at Gaya. Persons who have departed this life without the rites of purification done unto their souls, or killed by thieves and ferocious wild beasts, as well as the souls of persons died of snake bites, enter the region of paradise through the merit of a Shraddha ceremony done unto them at Gaya. I cannot exhaust the merits and benefits which a man acquires and derives by offering an obsequious oblation at Gaya, if I go on relating them even for millions and millions of years.

——:o:——

CHAPTER LXXXIII.

Said THE GOD BRAHMA:—The city of Gaya is a sacred sanctuary in the country of Keekata and likewise is the forest of Rajagriha (modern Rajgir) in that part of the continent of India. Sacred is the place called the Vishaya Charana, and the rivers which drain the aforesaid tracts are the holiest of the holies. The part of Gaya known Munda-Prishtha covers an area of a crosha and a half (three English miles) measured from north to south and from east to west, the entire site of the sanctuary (Gaya) enclosing an area of ten square miles. The part of the sanctuary known as the Gaya-Shirah (*lit.*, the head of Gaya) measures a crosha (two English miles) in length, and oblations offered to one's departed manes within its limit, secure them an elevated status in the next world. A man, by simply making a pilgrimage to Gaya, stands absolved from all debts due by him to his forefathers. The God Janarddana stands as the embodied image of the Pitris at Gaya, and a simple glance at that lotus-eyed deity, is enough to discharge the threefold obligation which he has incurred in the capacity of a son, a created being, and a disciple to a particular sage or Rishi.

Similarly, by witnessing the images of the gods Rudra, Kaleshvara and Kedara at Gaya, a man is supposed to pay off the debts he owes to his fathers. By seeing the image of the celestial grandfather at Gaya, a man is absolved from all sins, whereas by repairing to the presence of the divine image of the great grandfather at Gaya, a man is sure to enter the sinless region after death.

The man who approaches in a humble and contrite spirit the divine image of the mace-bearing deity and devoutly lays himself prostrate before that best of all male subjects in the universe, is freed from the cycles of necessary existence and never reverts to the pangs of mortality after death.

O thou sage among the twice-born ones, the man who visits the shrines of the god Mounaditya and Kanakarka in a spirit of devotion, is purged of all sins and is discharged from all obligations to his fathers. By worshipping the god Brahma at Gaya, the worshipper is sure to ascend, after death, to the region presided over by that divinity. The man, who having performed his daily right of Sandha (recitation of certain Vedic hymns and verses by a Brahmana at the three divisions of a day) repairs to the divine presence of the imaged Gayatri at Gaya, acquires the merit of reciting the entire Vedas through the grace of that benign goddess. Similarly by resorting, in the noon, to the shrine of the goddess Savitri, a pilgrim acquires the merit of celebrating a religious sacrifice. A visit to the shrine of the goddess Sarasvati in the evening, adds to the credit of the votary the merit of making an unsolicited gift.

A visit to the image of the divine sage Augusta, or to the forest of Dharma graced by the presence of that imaged god of virtue, and situate within the holy confines of that sacred city, absolves a man from all debts to his fathers. Where is the man, where is that degraded, abject, and hardened sinner who does not feel himself emancipated from the trammels of life in the presence of the divine image of Gridhreshvara? The man who sees the cow-goddess in the sylvan abode of that divinity, is sure to lead his departed manes to the region of Brahma. The man who pays a visit to the shrine of the god Prabhashesha at Gaya, acquires an elevated status in after life. By viewing the image of god Kotishvara, or by resorting to the sanctuary of Ashvamedha, a man is freed from all indebtedness to his forefathers. By seeing the divine image of the god who commands the gates of heaven, a man is liberated from the trammels of existence. The man who visits the shrine of Rameshvara or that of the mace-playing God at Gaya, ascends to the region of the immortal gods. Similarly by paying a visit to the shrine of Bramhesha, a man is absolved from the sin which he had committed by killing a Bramhana.

By resorting to the shrine of the goddess Mahachandi at Munda-Prishtha, a man is enabled to witness the realisation of all his heart-felt desires. By paying a visit to the shrine of the god Phalgvisha (the god of the river Phalgu) or by seeing the images of the goddesses Phalgu Chandi and Gouri or of such gods as Gomaka and Gopati, a man is supposed to fully discharge his debts to his fathers. A similar benefit is derived from paying a visit to the shrines of Angaresha, Siddhesha, Gayaditya, Gaja and Markandeya-shvara. Does not an ablution in the holy pool of the Phalgu and a visit to the shrine of the god Gadadhara, signify the acme of one's good fortune? What more can the pious and the devout expect for the recompense of their good deeds in life? The merit of these acts leads the souls of one's departed ancestors, removed even up to the twenty-first degree in the ascending line, to the region of Brahman.

All the holy streams, lakes and mountains which sanctify our mortal globe, resort to the waters of the river Phalgu, once a day. Gaya is the most sacred spot in the world. The quarter known as the Gayashiras, is the sancto sanctum of that hallowed sanctuary, and the river Phalgu is the holiest of the holies as well, since it forms the mouth of the immortal gods.

The holy pool known as the Nabhi-tirtham lies to the north of the river Kanaka, and occupies a middle place between that river and the holy well of Brahma-Sada an ablution wherein leads the bather to the region of Brahma after death. The man who offers oblations or obsequious cakes to his departed manes on the rim of that sacred well and casts them in its holy waters, is freed from all moral indebtedness to his forefathers. Similarly a Shraddha ceremony performed by a man at the shrine of the immortal Vata tree, leads the souls of his departed forefathers to the region of Brahma. The man who bathes in the holy pool, known as the Hansa-tirtham, is absolved from all sins. A Shraddha ceremony performed by a man at any of the following sacred spots or shrines, such as the Koti-Tirtham, the Gayaloka, the Vaitarini, and the Gomaka, leads the souls of his ancestors, removed even to the twenty-first degree in the ascending line to the region of Brahma.

The man who performs a Shraddha ceremony of his deceased ancestors at the Brahma-tirtham, or Rama-tirtham, or Agni-tirtham, or Soma-tirtham or at the banks of the Rama-hrada, ensures the residence of his departed manes in the region of Brahma. By performing a Shraddha ceremony at the banks of the Northern Manasa, a man is liberated from the trammels of re-birth, while a similar ceremony performed at the banks of its name sake in the south, leads his departed manes to the region of Brahma. A ceremony of Bhishma-Tarpanam, performed at the sanctuary known as the Kuta, brings salvation to the performer, while a man can fully discharge his debts to his fathers by performing a similar ceremony at the shrine of Gridhreshvara (the lord of cormorants).

The man who pays a visit to the goddess Dhenuka (cow-goddess) in the forest named after her, and performs a Shraddha ceremony in honour of his departed manes after having made a gift of the type, technically known as the Tila Dhenu (cow of sesamum) ensures their residence in the region of Brahma. A similar ceremony performed at any of the following sacred places such as the Aindra-Tirtham, the Nara-Tirtham, the Vasava-Tirtham, the Vaishnava-Tirtham, or on the banks of the river Mahanadi, is attended with the same result.

The man who bathes, or performs the rites of his daily Sandhya worship and offers libations of water to the gods and his departed manes, and performs a Shraddha ceremony for the welfare of their soul, in or about any of the following sacred shrines such as the Savitri, the Gayatri, the Sarasvati, etc., succours the souls of a hundred and one generations of his fathers and cognates, and ensures their residence in the region of Brahma.

By passing through the hill crevice or the natural tunnel known as the Brahma-Yoni, with his mind absorbed in the contemplation of his forefathers, a man is exempted for good from the trouble of passing through the uterine canal of any woman in the shape of a child. Libations of water, offered by a man to his departed manes at the shrine of Kakajangha, give them infinite and perpetual satisfaction. The man who performs a Shraddha ceremony at the well of Matanga in the holy forest of Dharmaranya, ascends to heaven after death. A similar ceremony performed at the well of virtue or at the shrine of the stake of virtue (Dharma Yupa) absolves a man from all obligations to the souls of his forefathers. The gods should be invoked to bear testimony to the fact as follows:—"Witness, O ye gods, and the guardian angels of the different regions or abodes, that I have come to the well of Matanga in this holy forest and have brought about the liberation of my departed manes."

The man who performs his ablution in the holy pool of Rama-Sara and celebrates a Shraddha ceremony in honour of his departed manes, at the sacred shrine of Prabhasaka, witnesses their liberation from astral existence on the summits of the hills of the ghosts (Preta Shila) if they had been doomed to the tortures of such a life through the effects of their misdeeds in this mortal globe. The man who performs a Shraddha ceremony at the sacred shrine of Svapushta or at the sacred hill of Mundapristha, leads his departed manes to the region of Brahma.

There is not a single spot within the boundaries of the city of Gaya which is not a sanctuary in itself. An oblation offered any where within the precincts of that sacred city, bears immortal fruit and carries the departed manes of the person making the offering to the eternal region of Brahma. The man who offers an obsequious cake for the benefit of his own soul into the hands of the god Janarddana, by reciting the prayer which runs as.—"I have offered this obsequious oblation, O Janarddana, in thy eternal hands. May this oblation last me for eternal time and make me an emancipated self in the world to come," is sure to ascend to the region of Brahma in the company of all his departed manes.

An oblation offered to the soul of one's ancestors either at the sanctuaries of Dharma Prishtha, Akshayavata or Gaya Shiras or on the banks of the sacred pool of Brahma (Brahma-Saras) bears immortal fruit. The man who performs a Shraddha ceremony of his forefathers after having visited the holy forests of Dharmaranyam, Dhenukaranyam and the sacred hill of Dharmapristham, is sure to succour the souls of his cognates to the twentieth decree of consanguinity.

That quarter of the sacred city which lies to the west of the river Maya, is called the forest of Brahma, the hermitage of Bharata, while the hill of Nagadri and Brahma Sada occupy the eastern portion thereof. A Shraddha ceremony should be performed at the foot of the god Matanga in the hermitage of Bharata. The hill known as the Pandushila is situated in the forest known as the Champaka Vanam, lying to the south of the Gaya Shiras and to the west of the river Mahanadi. A Shraddha ceremony performed under the auspicies of the third phase of the moon and within the boundaries of the sacred pools of Nischira or the great lake or the Koushiki, bears immortal fruit.

The hill known as the Krounchapada lies close to the lake of Tritiya which is situated to the north of the river Vaitarini, and there, by performing a Shraddha ceremony of his departed manes, a man is sure to carry them up to the eternal heaven. The lake called the Nischira lies to the north of the hill known as the Krounchapada.

The man who contemplates that a visit to Gaya is not a matter of every day probability, and that it does not fall to the lot of every one to offer obsequious cakes at Gaya to one's departed manes more than once in life, shall do well to touch the holy waters of the river Mahanadi and to offer libations of the same to his departed manes, whereby they would be enabled to ascend to the regions of eternity, accompanied by the souls of all the departed cognates of the offerer. The man, who recites at the shrine of the goddess Gayatri, the Vedic hymns and verses composing the rite of his daily Sandhya, is sure to acquire the merit of such continuous recitation for the period of twelve consecutive years.

The man who resides for two fortnights, both light and dark, within the sacred walls of Gaya, sanctifies the seven generations of his own family and children. By visiting the sacred hills of Mundaprishtha, Aravinda and Krounchapada which rise up from the hallowed plains of that sacred city, a man is absolved from all sins and of whatsover nature.

An offering of an obsequious cake to one's departed manes at Gaya, under the auspices of the continuance of the sun in the sign of the cancer or under that of a solar or a lunar eclipse, should be regarded as a piece of exceptionally rare good fortune.

Rare is the man in the three habitable worlds who is fortunate enough to cast obsequious cakes in honour of his departed manes at Gaya under the auspicies of the sun's continuance at the sign of the cancer, or under that of a solar or a lunar eclipse. A Shraddha ceremony performed at any of the seven following sites in Gaya, such as the great lake, the Koushiki, the Mulakshetra and the rock-hewn cave of the mount Gridhrakuta, etc., ensures an elevated status in the plain of astral existence to the soul for whose benefit the ceremony is celebrated. The man who performs a Shraddha ceremony at the place where flows the mighty stream of Maheshvari is supposed, to discharge all debts to his ancestors. The man who performs a Shraddha ceremony on the banks of the world-renowned stream of the sacred Vishala, acquires the merit of celebrating an Agnisthoma sacrifice and is translated to heaven after death. Similarly a Shraddha ceremony celebrated at the sacred shrine of Mashapada, as well as a rite of ceremonial ablution performed therein, ranks equal in merit with the celebration of a Vajapeya sacrifice. An obsequious cake offered at the shrine of the Ravipada, lifts up a fallen and benighted soul from the bottom of perdition.

The Pitris (departed manes of a person) acknowledge the sonship of a child and own him alone as their true offspring who resorts to the sacred precincts of Gaya for the sole purpose of benefiting them spiritually and offers them boiled rice by way of funeral oblation. The Pitris, afraid of the torments of hell, pray for the birth of a male child in their surviving family on earth, so that he might make a pilgrimage to Gaya, and succour their distressed souls from the gloom of the nether worlds. Verily do they rejoice over the advent of a son in Gaya, thinking that the water accumulated in the ruts of the streets of that sacred city and tossed off by his legs, might some day lead to the emancipation of their selves.

An obsequious cake offered to a departed spirit at Gaya by his son in flesh or by any other person, lifts him up to the region of the eternal Bramha. A similar pilgrimage to the sacred pool of Koti-Tirtham leads a man to the region of Vishnu.

The river, which is renowned in the three worlds by the name of Vaitarini, is descended from the region of the immortal gods and laves the shores of the sacred Gaya, absolving the souls of all departed beings. The man who performs a Shraddha ceremony, or offers an obsequious cake to, or makes the gift of a cow for the benefit of, his departed manes on the banks of that sacred stream, succours the souls of twenty-one generations of his ancestors.

A son, visiting the sacred sanctuary at Gaya in course of time, and for the spiritual benefit of his own departed forefathers, shall give a sumptuous repast to the local Bramhanas, as directed by the grandfather of the celestials. By worshipping his departed manes, a man acquires the merit of worshipping all the gods. The Bramhanas, on such an occasion, should be fed and propitiated according to the rules of a Havya Kavya ceremony.

Gaya is the best place for the religiously disposed to quit their mortal frames. The man who performs a Vrishotsarga ceremony at Gaya, the best of all sanctuaries, is sure to acquire the merit of a hundred Agnisthoma sacrifices. An intelligent man shall prospectively offer obsequious cakes to his own soul at Gaya, as well as to those of others without the customary admixture of sesamum with them. O Vyasa, such cakes should be duly offered at Gaya to the souls of one's all departed cognates, agnates and ancestors in the direct line of succession, as well as to their friends and relations.

By performing a ceremonial ablution in the sacred pool of Rama-Tirtham, a man acquires the merit of making a gift of a hundred cows at a time. A similar ablution in the lake of Matanga, is sure to enhance that merit ten-fold. The man who bathes at the confluence of the sacred Nishchira, leads his departed manes to the region of Brahma. By bathing at the hermitage of Vashista, the bather acquires the merit of performing a Vajapeya sacrifice. A residence near the sacred stream of Koushika ensures the merit of performing a Horse-Sacrifice. The hallowed fountain of Agnidhara rises from the lake sacred to the grandfather of the gods, and is usually known as the Kapila. The man who performs a Shraddha ceremony at or near this sacred stream, acquires the merit of performing an Agnisthoma sacrifice. By performing a similar ceremony near the fountain, sacred to the god Kumara, a man is sure to acquire the merit of performing a Horse-Sacrifice, whereas a visit to his divine image at the adjoining shrine, leads to the emancipation of one's self. An ablution in the sacred fount of the moon god, ensures one's residence in the region of that divinity after death. The man who offers an obsequious cake to his manes on the banks of the pool sacred to that god leads them to the region of Brahma.

CHAPTER LXXXIV.

BRAHMA said :—The man who is about to start on a pilgrimage to Gaya, shall only perform a Shraddha ceremony before setting out on his journey, circumbulate his native village in the garment of an anchorite, take up his residence in an adjoining village, live on the residue of obsequious cakes offered to his manes in the course of that Shraddha ceremony, and shall then go on his way, refraining from taking alms and charities on the road. The departed ancestors of a man commence to ascend each step of stairs to heaven at his each foot-fall on the way to that sacred city. The rules of fasting and shaving the head hold good in the case of all sacred pools and shrines, except Kurukshetra, Vishala, Viraja, and Gaya. A Shraddha ceremony at Gaya, does not wait for any particular part of the day for its performance, which may be gone through at any time in the day or night. By performing a Shraddha ceremony at Benares, or at the banks of the Shona, or the Mahanadi, a man is sure to ensure a felicitous residence to his manes in heaven. A pilgrimage to the sacred pool of Uttara Manasa at Gaya, grants the greatest success to the pilgrim in respect of his penances and penitential observances in general. By performing a Shraddha ceremony at the latter sanctuary, a man is sure to witness the fruition of all his desires and becomes an emancipated self after death. A man by observing a vow of silence and by offering an obsequious cake to his manes at the shore of the sacred pool of Dakshina Manasa at Gaya, stands absolved from the threefold obligations of human life.

The sacred pool of Kankhalam lies to the north of the shrine of Mundaprishtha at Gaya, and is the favourite haunt of the gods and the spirits of the immortal sages. The Siddhas delight to wade along the banks of this sacred fount; and serpents of dreadful appearance, guard its shores with their protruding tongues, inspiring terror into the hearts of the wicked and the unrighteous. An ablution in the waters of this sacred pool paves one's way to heaven, and a Shraddha ceremony performed at its shores is sure to bear immortal fruits. The pilgrim having duly made obeisance to the sun-god and having offered obsequious cakes to his manes, should recite the following prayer:—"Come, O ye high-souled Agnishvata and Vahirsadas, come O ye my heavenly manes whose drink is the juice of the ambrosial Soma, come and take me under your protection during my sojourn in this sacred city. I have offered obsequious cakes to the souls of my forefathers and to the spirits of those who had once been the members of my family on earth. I have come to Gaya for that express purpose."

Then having cast obsequious oblations to his manes as above indicated, he should resort to the sacred pool of the Phalgu and subsequently see the divine image of the celestial grandfather and that of the club-weilding deity, whereby he would be able to discharge all obligations, incidental to his birth. An ablution in the waters of the sacred Phalgu, as well as a visit to the divine image of the mace-bearing god, leads to the emancipation of a man after death and liberates the souls of his deceased cognates, even removed ten degress from him both in the ascending and descending lines of succession.

I have described the doings of a pilgrim in his first day at Gaya. On the second day, he should visit the holy forest of Dharmaranyam and offer obsequious cakes to his manes on the hallowed banks of the lake sacred to the god Matanga. A visit to the sacred forest of Dharmaranyam ranks equal in merit with the performance of a Vajapeya sacrifice. A pilgrimage to the sacred pool of the Brahma-tirthakam equals in merit with the performance of a Vajapeya or that of a horse-sacrifice. A Shraddha ceremony should be performed and oblations and libations of water should be offered to one's manes at any spot lying between the Yupa and the sacred well aforesaid (Brahma-tirtham).

The duty of the third day consists in paying a visit to the Brahmasada and in offering obsequious cakes and libations of water to one's departed manes, and in performing a Shraddha ceremony in their honour at a place midway between the Yupa and the sacred well. All beings, from the minutest animalculum to the creator of the universe, perpetually grace with their presence the holy pasturage known as the Goprachara, and a propitiation of those immortal spirits by a man, leads to the emancipation of his departed manes. By circumbulating the sacred Yupa, a man is sure to acquire the same merit as that of performing a Vajapeya sacrifice.

On the fourth day, having bathed in the sacred waters of the Phalgu, and having offered libations of water to the gods and his departed manes, and performed a Shraddha ceremony in their honour at the sanctuary of Gaya-Shirsha, O Vyasa, the pilgrim should offer cakes at the mouth and over the three foot-prints of the deity, as well as in the five sacred fires (Panchagni). A Shraddha ceremony performed at Gaya-Shirsha under the auspicious aspects of the sun and the moon in the month of Kartikeya, bears immortal fruits.

A Shraddha ceremony usually embraces the worship of nine different deities which should be made to include (Dvadasha-daivatam) three more, while performed within the sacred precincts of Gaya. A Shraddha ceremony in honour of one's deceased mother, should be separately performed on the occasion of an Anvastaka, or Vriddhi, or on the date of her death, as well as in Gaya, while on all other occasions, the ceremony should be performed jointly with that of his father.

The man, who having bathed at the Dashashvamedha, sees the image of the celestial grandfather and touches the foot of the god Rudra, is exempted from reverting to life and its miseries. By performing a Shraddha ceremony at Gaya-shiras, a man acquires the same merit which one gets by making a gift of the whole earth, covered over with threefold layers of gold. The obsequious cakes, to be offered at the sanctuary of Gaya-shiras, should be made to measure the leaves of a Shami tree in size, the occult energy of which may be unquestionably looked up to as the deliverer of the manes of the performer.

The god Mahadeva rested his foot on the sanctuary at Munda-prishtha and accordingly a man may achieve penitential success at the place with the least effort or exertion. Spirits in whose names obsequious cakes are offered at Gaya-shirsha, rise to heaven if doomed to the tortures of hell, or become emancipated selves, if already happened to be in the former place.

On the fifth day of his stay at Gaya, the pilgrim should perform a religious ablution at the sanctuary of Gadalola and offer obsequious cakes to his departed manes at the root of the sacred Vata tree, whereby he would succour the souls of his deceased ancestors from the gloom of the nether regions. Even by feeding a single Brahmana with boiled rice and prepared potherbs at the sacred Vata tree, a man would acquire the merit of treating a million of Brahmanas to a sumptuous repast. By performing a Shraddha ceremony at the root of the immortal Vata tree and by seeing the divine image of the celestial grandfather, a man is sure to ascend to the region of the immortals and to deliver a hundred generations of his departed manes from the shades of Hades. A father usually desires the births of many sons of his own loins, so that some of them might resort to Gaya, or perform a Vrishot-sarga Shraddha ceremony, or undertake a horse sacrifice for the welfare of his spiritual self after death.

Once on a time, a ghost met a certain merchant in the way and addressed him as follows :—

"Cast some obsequious cakes in my name at the sanctuary

of Gayashirsha, since both the offerer and the receiver of such cakes are liberated from the confines of the nether regions and are admitted into the abodes of the gods." The merchant did as he was requested to do by the departed spirit, and subsequently offered obsequious cakes to his own forefathers jointly with his younger brothers, who were immediatey released from the mansion of death. The merchant in his turn was blessed with the birth of a male child named Vishala. His wife Vishalá bore him that son. Vishala, who was childless up to that time, asked the Brahmanas, how he could beget children, and the Brahmanas replied that a pilgrimage to Gaya, would remove all impediments in the way of having offsprings of his own. Vishala went to Gaya and offered obsequious cakes to his departed fathers at the sanctuary of Gayashirsha. Whereupon a son was born to him. One day Vishala saw three shadowy images, white, red, and black reflected in the sky just before his eyes. He questioned them as to their identity and whereabouts, whereupon the white one replied. "I am thy father, O Vishala, and am at present residing in the region of Indra through the merit of my good deeds in life. O son, the red spectre thou findest is my father who killed a Brahmana in his human existence and was a man of the blackest inequity on earth. The black one is my grandfather who had taken by forcible hands the life of many a holy sages in their hermitage. They are now doomed to the torments of that particular quarter of the sea of hell, whose dire monotony is not broken by the rising of a single wave and which hides within its lethian and unfathomable depth an eternity of impious misery and wailing. Release them, O thou the offerer of our obsequious cakes, from the dismal confines of that infernal world and send them happy and emancipated to the region of the immortal gods."

Now Vishala did what he was requested to do by his father and assended heaven after a prosperous sovereignty on earth.

"May our departed manes who have been deprived of their obsequious cakes and libations of water, as well as the spirits of those who had been born in our family and died immediately after having been delivered of the womb, or without the rite of Chudakaranam done unto them, together with the souls of those whose earthly remains had not been cremated in the funeral pile, or whose earthly bodies had been consigned to the unconsecrated fire, be propitiated with the obsequious cake now offered by me, on the ground. This funeral oblation offered to the souls of my father, grandfather, great grandfather, mother, paternal grandmother, paternal great grandmother, or to those of my maternal grandfather, maternal great grandfather, maternal great great grandfather, maternal grandmother, maternal great grandmother, or maternal great great grandmother, or to the spirits of any other departed person or relation, furnish them with eternal satisfaction."

---:0:---

CHAPTER LXXXV.

BRAHMA said:—Then having performed a ceremonial ablution with the Varunastra Mantra, the pilgrim should offer obsequious cakes to his departed manes at the sanctuary of the hill of spirits (Pretashila) and invoke them as follows:—"On the blades of Kusha grass extended in my front, and with this libation of water containing sesamum, I invoke the presence of the souls of those who had been born in my family and subsequently died without any means of succour from the shades of the infernal region. I offer these obsequious cakes for the liberation of those spirits who had once born in flesh in the family of my father or mother. I offer this obsequious cake to those spirits, who had once taken their birth in the family of my maternal grandfather and who are divested of all means of liberation from their infernal confines. I offer this obsequious cakes for the release of those of my relations who had died in their mother's womb, or had found an untimely grave even without cutting a single tooth. I have offered this obsequious cake for the succour of those of my friends, whether born in my family or otherwise, and even whose names and spiritual clanship have escaped from my memory. I offer this cake to the souls of those who have committed suicide or met a violent death either by water, poison, blow, or strangulation. I offer this obsequious cake to the spirits of those who had been burnt to death, or devoured by lions and tigers, or killed by horned cattle, or expired under the bites of fanged or sharp-toothed beasts. I offer this obsequious cake to the spirits of those whose earthly remains had been cremated in unconsecrated fire, or had not been consigned to the flames of any fire at all, as well as to the souls of those who had been killed by thieves or lightning. I offer this obsequious cake for the liberation of those spirits who had been kept confined within the dark walls of the hells known as the Rourava and the Kalasutra. I offer this obsequious cake for the liberation of those spirits who are at present doomed to the tortures of those divisions of hell, which are known as the Kumbhipaka (hell of whirling eddies) or Asipatra Vanam (Forest of sword blades). I offer this obsequious cake for the liberation of spirits who are tortured in other quarters of hell. I offer this obsequious cake for the emancipation of those spirits who had re-incarnated as serpents, birds, or other lower animals, or had been consigned to the voiceless agonies of vegetable life. I offer this obsequious cake for the liberation of those spirits who under the ordination of the god of death, had been consigned to suffer eternal tortures in hell. I offer this obsequious cake for the elevation of those spirits in the astral plane who, for their countless misdeeds in successive re-births, and through the workings of the propulsions of ignoble passions turned into dynamics of fate, are perpetually getting down in the graduated scale of life, and to whom a working upward to to the plane of human existence has become a thing of rarest impossibility. May the souls of those who were friends to me in this life, or had been my friends in any other existence, or of those who are not related to me in that capacity and are utterly friendless for the present, be propitiated and liberated by this obsequious cake which I have offered at the present sanctuary in Gaya. May the souls of any of my forefathers, who might be staying at present in the shape of astral beings, derive perpetual satisfaction from the obsequious cake which I have offered. I have offered obsequious cakes for the satisfaction of all those spirits who had once taken their birth in the family of my father or mother, or who were related to my preceptors, or father-in-law or any other relations in life, or who had died without having any issue of their own, and accordingly stand, at present, divested of their specific shares of funeral cakes and libations of water, or who had been born deaf, dumb, blind, cripple or idiotic in life, whether they are any way related to me or not, or who had died in the womb without ever seeing the light of god, (whether do I know them or not), and may they derive eternal felicity from this cake which I have offered to them. May the gods and Brahma and Ishana, etc., in particular, bear testimony to the fact that I have come to Gaya, and effected the liberation of my fathers from the confines of the nether world. Witness, O thou mace-bearing god, that I have arrived at Gaya, done all the needful rites for the emancipation of my departed manes, and stand fully absolved from the three-fold debt of human existence."

The sanctity of the sacred field of Kurukshetra appertains to the Mahanadi, to the Bramhasada, to the Prabhasa, to the Gayashira, to the Sarasvati, to the Akshayavata, to the Dharmaranyam and to the Dhenukapristha at Gaya and these places should be deemed as equally sanctified as the memorable battle-field of the Kauravas.

—:o:—

CHAPTER LXXXVI.

BRAMHA said :—The well renowned hill of Pretashila lies detached in three places at Gaya, *viz.*, at the sanctuaries of Prabhasa, Pretakunda and the Gayashira. The hill rests on the shoulders of the god of virtue, and is supported by the aforesaid deity only for the elevation of the whole world. It is so called from the fact of its emancipating the departed spirits of one's parents, friends and relations in life, and thus fulfilling the initiative purpose of its own creation. The spirits of sages and potentates and canonised queens of old, perpetually grace with their presence the summits of the blissful Pretashila, and hence a Shraddha ceremony performed at the foot of this sacred hill, leads its performer to the region of Bramha, after death. The hill known as the Mundapristha is so called from the fact of its standing on the exact spot where fell the head of the demon Gaya at the time of his demise, and forms a sort of natural pantheon, visited by all the gods in the universe. The strip of forest which stretches along the foot of the hill of Mundapristha and is washed by the head waters of the sacred Bramhasara (the lake of Brâmha) is called the forest of Aravindam (Aravinda Vanâm). Partly hidden by the forest, the hill of Aravinda rears its lofty head and is seen looming at a distance. The hill is also known as the Krauncha-pada from the fact of its being impressed with the marks of a Krauncha's (a bird of the heron species) feet.

The spirit of the original deities, such as the mace-bearing god, etc., hovered over and lay inherent in that sacred hill, and hence it should be regarded as an elevation permeated with the respective essences of the aforesaid gods. The hill, pregnant with the spirit of the club-wielding god, had originally buried under its weight the head of the demon Gaya, but the divine spirit became patent and manifest in course of time, and the hill is to be looked upon as identical with his divine self. For the preservation of order and religion in the world, and for the suppression of evil-, and wrong-, doers, the birth and deathless Hari had incarnated in the shape of the divine fish, tortoise boar, Nrisinha (Man Lion), Vamana (Dwarf), Rama (Parashu Rama), Rama (the son of Dasaratha), Krishna, Buddha and Kalki, in the company of his celestial cohorts, the Ruddras etc. In like manner, the club wielding god, who was invisible and disembodied in the beginning, became patent and took shape at Gaya. And since he was worshipped at the outset (Adi) by such gods, as Bramha, etc., with offerings of flowers, perfumes, etc., he is called the original (Adi) club-wielding deity. Accordingly the pilgrim who pays a visit to his divine image, or worships him just after his arrival at Gaya (Adyam) with such offerings as Arghas, water for absolving his feet, perfumes, flowers, lamps, burning sticks of incense, garlands, sweets and edibles, garments, bells, mirrors, chowries, ornaments, boiled rice, obsequious cakes, etc., is blest with all the good things which wish can name in life, becomes the possessor of untold wealth and well-filled granaries, is enabled to live up to a ripe old age, honoured and revered as a man of knowledge and wisdom, and becomes the happy progenitor of a prosperous and fruitful race. Blest in the love of a true and devoted wife he is privileged to taste of an advance draught of heaven, where he is sure to be glorified after the close of his mortal career. From heaven he will reincarnate as the undisputed monarch of the whole earth, victorious in wars against his adversaries, courageous and noble in his thoughts and dealings, and so on through successive re-births until the final liberation or emancipation of his Self will be worked out. The man who performs a Shraddha ceremony at the present shrine, ascends to the region of Bramha with his departed manes, after death.

The man who worships at Gaya the divine image of Valabhadra, and that of his sister Subhadra, acquires wealth and wisdom in life, and goes to the region of Purushottama after death, leaving a large number of sons to mourn his loss. By casting obsequious cakes to his departed manes in the front of the divine images of Gana, Purushottama and the sun-god, a man is sure to lead their spirits to the region of Bramha. By devoutly making an obeisance to the god Kapardi Vignesha a man is sure to mount over all obstacles in life. The man who worships the god Kartikeya, is sure to be translated to the region of Bramha. A worship of the twelve Adityas, duly performed, is sure to prove curative in cases of all bodily distempers. A worship of the god of fire, imparts a healthful glow to the complexion of the worshipper. By worshipping the god Revanta a man becomes the possessor of a splendid stud of horses. The moon god, duly propitiated, grants the boon of unbounded wealth to the worshipper. A worship of the goddess Gouri confers affluence upon her votary. A worship of the goddess Sarasvati brings on wisdom to her suppliant, whereas the goddess Lakshmi increases the pecuniary resources of the man who duly supplicates her favour.

By worshipping the lord of the celestial birds (Garuda) one is sure to get over all impediments in the way to success, while the god Kshetrapala, duly propitiated, relents to nullify the evil influences cast by the malignant planets. The man who worships the sanctuary of the Mundapristha hill, lives to witness the realisation of all his desires. A man bitten by a serpent, is made sound and whole by worshipping the

Nagastakam. The man who worships the god Brahma, is translated to the region of Brahma after death. A worship of the god Valabhadra imparts health and strength to the votary, whereas a propitiation of the goddess Subhadra brings good fortune in its train. By worshipping the god Purushottama the best wishes of a man are sure to be realised. The man who worships the god Narayana is sure to extend his sway over the entire earth, and to become the undisputed monarch of the whole human race.

By touching, and making obeisance to, the image of the Nrisinha (man-lion) manifestation of Vishnu, one is sure to win victory in battle. The man who worships the image of the boar manifestation of Vishnu at Gaya, is sure to be crowned as a king and to acquire proprietory rights in lands. By touching the image of Vidyadhari, one is sure to acquire the status of a Vidyadhara (celestial musician). By worshipping the image of the original club-wielding deity, a man is enabled to witness the realisation of all his desires. A worship of the god Somanatha leads his votary to the region of Shiva. By making obeisance to the god Rudreshvara, a man is sure to be glorified in the region presided over by the Rudras. The man who makes an obeisance to the image of Rameshvara, becomes endeared to the people like the illustrious prince (Rama) after whom the god is named. The man, who hymnises the god Brahmeshvara, should be regarded as already a fit inmate for the region presided over by that divinity. By worshipping the god Kaleshvara, a man becomes invincible to decay. A worshipper of the Kedara manifestation of Shiva, is glorified in the region sacred to that divinity. The man who worships the god Siddeshvara, is sure to achieve penitential success and is belauded in the region of Brahma.

The man, who sees and touches the image of the original club-wielding deity at Gya (Adi Gadadhara) succours the souls of a hundred generations of his departed manes and is translated to the region of Brahma. By worshipping the same deity, a seeker of sovereignty is sure to acquire a kingdom, a suppliant for peace would enjoy divine tranquillity in his soul, a worker for the liberation of his self would undoubtedly see his labours crowned with success, a lover of virtue would be strengthened in his love, and a solicitor of creature comforts would have enough of good things in life. In short there is not a single blessing which the human wish can name, which is not promised to a votary of the club-wielding divinity. Similarly a female votary of the god would be blest with the pleasures of maternity, or would be rewarded with the undying love of her husband as her supplication might be.

The man who having worshipped the image of the club-wielding deity, makes a gift of water, or of boiled rice or of obsequious cakes at Gaya, is sure to ascend to the region of Brahma after death. Gaya is the most sacred of all the sanctuaries on earth, and the club-wielding god, transformed into stone at Gaya, is the foremost of all the deities that deign to visit our mortal globe. He who has seen the club-wielding god (maintainer of order and equity in the universe symbolised by his club or mace), has also seen his stone manifestation at Gaya, since He is the Universal Spirit who is all and runs through all.

——:o:——

CHAPTER LXXXVII.

SAID THE GOD HARI :—I shall enumerate the names of the different law-givers of the world (Manu) who flourished in the different cycles of time, as well as their sons and progenies such as Suka, etc. Sayambhuva was the name of the first law-giver of the world. He had seven sons named Marichi, Atri, Angira, Pulastya, Pulaha, Kratu, and Vashishta, who formed the brotherhood of the seven holy sages known as the Saptarishis. Twelve Ganas (regents or tutelary gods of the different quarters of the sky and of the physical phenomena as well) of that cycle of time, were named Jaya, Amita, Shukra, Yama, the four drinkers of the expressed juice of the Somaplant, Vishvabhuk, and Vamadeva. The latter was elected the lord of the celestials at the time. The Demon Vashkali invaded the kingdom of the then lord of the gods and the God Vishnu killed him with his own discus.

After him Svarochisa became the Manu or the law-giver of the world. His sons were named Mandaleshvara, Chaitraka, Vinata, Karnanta, Vidyata, Ravi, Vrihatguna, and Nabha. The seven holy sages who sanctified that particular age with their holy lives, were called Urja, Stambha, Prana, Rishabha, Nichala, Dambholi and Arvavira. The race of Paravatas then habited this terrestrial globe. The guardian deities of heaven were twelve in number. Vipaschit reigned as the lord of the celestials in that age and the demon Purukritsara was his antagonist. The god Hari assumed the shape of an elephant and killed that dreadful demoniac adversary of the contemporary Indra, and restored the moral order of the universe.

The names of the sons of Outtama, the third Manu or law-giver of the world, were Aja, Parushu, Vinita, Suketu, Sumitra, Suvala, Shuchi, Deva, Devavridha, Rudra, Mahatsaha, and Ajita. The seven sages who flourished in that age, were named Rathouja, Urdha-Vahu, Sharana, Anagha, Muni, Sutapa and Shanku. The sons of Outtama numbered twelve in all. The races of celestials who habited the region of heaven, were five in all and named as the Vashavartis, the Svadharmanas, the Shivas, the Satyas and the Pratardanas. Svashanti reigned over them all as their Indra or overlord. The demon Pralamva was the antagonist of the Indra of the age and the

God Hari in his Fish Incarnation had to kill that enemy of the gods.

The sons of Tamasa, the fourth Manu, were named Janu, Jangha, Nirbhaya, Nava, Khyati, Naya, Priya-bhritya, Vivikshita, Havu-Skandhi and Prostalaksha. The seven holy sages who flourished in that age, were named Jyotidharma, Dhrista-Kavya, Chaitra, Agni and Hemaka. The twenty five clans of celestials who peopled the region of paradise in that age, were named as the Suragas, the Svavhavyay, etc. There were four sun gods in those days and Shivi reigned as their Indra. The demon Bhimaratha disputed the suzerainty of heaven with the latter and was subsequently killed by Hari in his tortoise incarnation.

The sons of Raivata Manu were named as Mahaprana, Sadhaka, Vanavandhu, Niramitra, Pratyanga, Paraha, Shuchi, Dridhavrata, and Ketushringa. The seven holy sages who flourished in that age, were named Deva Shri, Veda Urdhavahu. Hiranyaroma, Parjanya, Satyanama and Svadharma. The four celestial clans which peopled heaven in that age, were named Abhuta Rajasa, Devashvamedhas, Vaikuntha and Amritas. The regents of the sky were fourteen in number, and Vibhu was the Indra or paramount soverign of them all. The demon Shanta was the antagonist of the contemporary lord of heaven. The god Vishnu assumed the shape of a swan and destroyed that molester of celestial peace.

The sons of Chakshusha Manu were named Uru, Puru, Mahavala, Shatadumnya, Tapasvi, Satyavahu, and Kriti. The names of the holy sages who practised penances in that age, were Agnishnu, Atiratra, Sudyumna, Nara, Havishmana, Sutanu, Shrimana, Sadharma, Viraja, Abhimana, Sahishnu, and Madhu-Shri. The five clans of the celestials were named the Aryyas, the Prasutas, the Bhavyas, the Lekhas, and the Prithukas, and Manojava ruled as their Indra. The demon Mahakala was the enemy of the contemporary king of heaven who was killed by the god Hari who had to assume the shape of a horse for the purpose.

The sons of Vaivasvata Manu were named Ikshaku, Nabha, Vishti, Sarjati, Lavishyanta, Panshunabha, Navishta, Karusha, Prishadra and Sudyumna. The seven sages who sanctified the age with their piety, were named Atri, the god like Vashista, Jamadagni, Kashyapa, Goutama, Bharadvaja and Vishvamitra. The wind gods (Marut) numbered forty-nine in all, and the celestial hierarchy which numbered fifteen in all, was divided into Adityas, Vasus, Sadhyas, Rudras, etc. There were eleven Rudras, eight Vasus, two Ashvins, ten Vishvedevas, ten Angirasas and nine divine Ganas in those days and Tejasvi was the Indra of them all. The demon Hiranyaksha was the sworn enemy of the then lord of the celestials and met his doom at the hand of the god Vishnu, incarnated as the primordial boar.

Now I shall enumerate the names of the sons of Savarni, the future Manu of the world. Their names would be Vijaya, Arvavira, Nirdeha, Satyavak, Kriti, Varishta, Garishta, Vachas and Sugati. The seven ages, who would grace the age with their advents, would be named Ashvathama, Kripa, Vyasa, Galava, Diptimana, Rishyashringa and Rama. The gods such as Sutapas Amritabhas, and Mukhyas, etc., would people the ethereal plains of heaven, and Vali, the son of Virochana would reign over them all as their Indra. The god Vishnu, incarnate as a Dwarf, would beg of him only three foot-measures of land. Vali would gladly grant him his behest, but would be deprived of his kingdom of the three worlds just at the time of ratifying his agreement, when the dwarf manifestation of god, would expand into his Infinite and eternal self to the consternation of all the on-lookers. Subsequently Vali would make over his sovereignty to the god and happily descend into the shades of the nether world.

Now hear me enumerate the names of the sons of Daksha Savarni, the ninth Manu or the law-giver of the world, their names would be Dhritiketu, Diptiketu, Pancha-hasta, Nirikriti, Prithushrava, Vrihatdumnya, Richika, Vrihata and Gana. The demon Kalakasha would be the enemy of the then lord of the celestials and would be destroyed by the Padmanabha manifestation of Vishnu.

The names of the twelve sons of Dharmaputra, the tenth Manu, would be Sukshetra Uttamouja, Bhurishrenya, Viryavana, Shatanika, Niramrita, Vrisha-sena, Jayadratha, Bhuridyumna, Suvarcha, Shantirindra and Pratapavana. The names of the seven holy sages who would sanctify that age with their holy lives, would be Aayomurti, Havishman, Sukriti, Avyaya, Labhaga, Apratima and Sourabha. The inmates of heaven would be divided into a hundred clanships at that cycle of time and would be called the Pranas, etc. The demon Vali would dispute the suzerainty of heaven with the then lord of the celestials, and the god Hari would slay him with one stroke of his mighty mace-weapon.

Now hear me enumerate the names of the sons of Rudraputra, the eleventh Manu. They would be called Sarvatraga, Susharma, Devanika, Pururguru, Kshetravarna, Dridheshu, Ardraka and Patraka. Havishman, Havishya, Varuna, Vishva, Vistara, Vishnu and Agniteja, would be the names of the seven holy sages who would flourish in that age. The inmates of heaven would be divided into different clanships, such as the Vihangamas (sky-coursers), Kamagamas (going anywhere they like), Nirmanas and the Ruchis. Members of the celestial family of Ruchi would rule over each of the other clans of heaven, and Vrisha would be the overlord of them all. The demon Dashagriva (ten-necked one) would contest the sovereignty of heaven with the then lord of the celestials, and would ultimately fall at the hands of the Shrirupa manifestation of Vishnu.

Hear me enumerate the names of the sons of Dakshaputra, the twelfth Manu of the world. They would be named as Devas, Anupdevas, Devashreshtha, Viduratha Mitravana, Mitradeva, Mitravindu, Viryavan, Mitravahu and Pravaha. Tapasvi, Sutapa, Tapomurti, Taporati, Tapo-dhriti, Dyuti and another, would be the names of the seven holy sages whose glorious advent would sanctify that particular cycle of time. The gods would be divided into different clans such as the Svadharmans, Sutapasas, Haritas, Rohitas, etc., and Retadhama or Bhadra would be their Indra or overlord. The demon Taraka would invade the territories of the then lord of the celestials. O Shankara, the god Hari, incarnate as a eunuch, would destroy that fell peace-breaker of the universe.

Now hear me enumerate the names of the sons of the thirteenth Manu of the world. They would be named as Chitrasena, Vichitra, Tapas. Dharmarata, Dhriti, Kshetravritti, Dharmapa, and Dridha. O thou possessed of handsome eyes, the seven holy sages who would grace the world with their advent in that age, would be called Dhritimana, Avyaya, Nisharupa, Nirutsaka, Nirmana, and Tattvadarshi. The celestials would be divided into thirty-three different clanships, such as the Svaromanas, the Svadharmanas, the Svakarmans, etc., and the god Divaspati would be the overlord of them all. The demon Tristhubha would dispute with him the suzerainty of heaven, and the god Madhava would kill him in the shape of a peacock.

Now hear me enumerate the names of the sons of Bhoutya, the fourteenth Manu of the world. They would be named as Uru, Gabhira, Dhrista, Tarasvi, Graha, Abhimani, Pravira, Jishnu, Sankrandana, Tejasvi and Durlabha. The seven holy sages who would flourish in that age, would be named Agnidhra, Agni-vahu, Magadha, Shuchi, Ajita, Mukta and Shukra. The gods would be divided into five clanships, each consisting of seven sub-groups, or families, such as the Chakshushas, the Karma-nisthas, the Pavitras, the Bhrajinas, and the Vachavrithas, and the god Shuchi, would be their

Indra or paramount ruler. The demon Maha-daitya would inimically intrude upon the rights of the then lord of the celestials, and the god Hari would slay him with his own hands.

The god Vishnu, incarnate in the shape of the holy Vyasa, would divide the one and the entire Veda, into four different parts, and subsequently compose the Puranas and the eighteen different branches of learning. The Vedas with their four kindred branches of study, the schools of philosophy known as the Mimansa, etc., the Puranas, the Dharma-Shastras, the Ayur-Vedas (science of medicine) the Arthashastrakam, the Dhanur-Veda (science of archery) the Gandharva-Vidyas (music and fine arts), etc., form the eighteen different branches of learning.

——:o:——

CHAPTER LXXXVIII.

SUTA said :—The God Hari related all about the different ages or cycles of time to the gods Hara, Brahma, etc. Now hear me narrate the Hymn known as the Pitri-Stotram which the holy Markandeya heard of yore from the lips of Krounchaki.

MARKANDEYA said :—Once in days of yore, the patriarch Ruchi, who was shorn of all vanity and attachment to world and its concerns, started out on a journey, free and friendless, with a view to see the different countries of the world. The departed Manes of the patriarch viewed him from their abodes, trudging the land houseless and alone, and passing his nights in bleak and unsheltered wildernesses without fire or friends to share in the perils of his journey. To him did they address as follows :—"O son, why hast thou foregone the pleasures of blessed matrimony, and why dost thou roam about cheerless and disconsolate without being bound in holy wedlock with an eligible bride? By duly propitiating the gods and one's departed Manes, and by attending to the wants of the needy and the holy sages, a householder, O son, becomes entitled to an elevated station after death. By uttering the Svaha Mantras (casting libations of clarified butter in fire), a householder is enabled to appease the gods, and a repetition of the Svadha Mantra leads to the propitiation of his departed Manes. Practice of free and hearty hospitality endears him to his guests, while servants and dependants eating his bread, look upon him as the mainstay of their lives. O thou holy one among mortals, from day to day, thus thou hast been incurring more and more debts to the gods. Thy obligations to us,—thy departed Manes, are getting heavier, and thy debts to the beings at large, as an inmate of the created universe, stand undischarged even up to the present moment. Where is the chance of thy working up to a better life, O my son, if you fail to marry and propagate children and to take to the life of an anchorite afterwards, as laid down in the books of the Shastra. Thy present conduct, therefore, brings thee nothing but misery and dooms thee to the pangs of successive re-births even after the cessation of the torments of that particular hell to which the souls of the "sonless are consigned."

To which Ruchi thus replied—Marriage is the parent of sin and misery, O fathers, and serves only to lower a man in the world to come. This thought alone has heretefore desisted me from being united with a wife. In a moment, it makes a man doubtful of his own spiritual life and therefore serves as a stumbling block in the way of his own salvation. Thinking of this I have hitherto refrained from marrying a wife. It is better that an unwedded person, though fondly attached to life and its cares, should wash his soul daily with the water of pure knowledge than that he would marry and forget all about his spiritual self, and become of the earth and earthly. It is imperatively obligatory on a man to subjugate his senses, and to constantly cleanse his soul of the mire, which his multifarious acts and promiscuous contact with a large concourse of created beings deposit upon it."

To which the spirits of his fathers thus replied :—" O son, certainly it is incumbent on all of us to wash our souls of all impurities by subduing our senses, still the way thou treadest, O darling, is not the proper road to salvation. The effects of good or evil deeds done by thee in a previous existence, would not fetter thy soul in the event of thy performing the five daily sacrifices peculiar to a householder (Pancha yajna) and practising penances and charities without any regard to their ulterior effects, and simply as a passive and involuntary instrument for the discharge of thy duties and for the absolution of thy daily sins. The effects of good or bad deeds done by a person in a prior existence, are constantly worn away by his actual experiences of pleasure or pain in this life. Wise men thus absolve their soul and protect it from being any way fettered with the bonds of Nescience. The soul thus guarded, can never be soiled with the mire of sin."

RUCHI said :—" Acts have been condemned in the Vedas by the celestial Brahman as the direct resultants of Nescience, and wherefore, O fathers, do you knowingly direct me to the path of action?" To which the spirits of his fathers thus replied :—"All is illusion in the universe and this universe itself is an illusion, O darling, and it is wrong to say that Nescience proceeds from action alone. On the contrary action primarily leads to the expansion of true knowledge and this brooks no contradiction. The good and the honest shun the evil incidental to the omission of a good act, and this self-imposed restraint leads to salvation. A restraint of a contrary nature tends to degenerate a soul. Thou hast considered it better to cherish pure thoughts in a pure soul.

but it avails thee nothing, my son, so long as any charge of neglect or omission of duty may be laid at thy door. Nescience, like an active poison, has its utility in the universe, which, being judiciously employed, rather serves to unfold the spirit than to tighten its shackles. Therefore do thou lawfully take a wife, O son. Otherwise in the absence of any provision for the future world, thy whole life would prove a miserable failure."

RUCHI said :—"I have grown old, O fathers, and who shall marry his daughter to an old man? Moreover marriage is a luxury which the poor can hardy afford to indulge in."

THE MANES said :—"Our descent into the lower regions as well as the degradation of thy own Self, is certain, O son, if thou dost not profit by our advice." Saying this the spirits of his (Ruchi's) fathers vanished in the air like a lamplight suddenly blown out by the wind. The holy sage Markendeya of mighty penance, narrated the entire discourse between Ruchi and his departed Manes to Krounchaki.

—:o:—

CHAPTER LXXXIX.

SUTA said :—Having again requested by Krounchaki the holy sage Markandeya resumed the thread of the narrative and related as follows :—"The holy sage of Bramhanic extraction being thus agitated by the words of his departed Manes, roamed over the whole earth in quest of a bride. But a bride he could not secure anywhere. The words of his fathers' spirits were burning like living fire in his heart. So he easily fell in that mood in which a man often holds colloquy with himself and began to discourse as follows :—"Where can I secure a suitable bride for myself and thus ensure an elevated station to my fathers and to my own self in the next world?"

Then having indulged in a similar strain of thought for a considerable time, the high-souled one resolved to realise his end by practising penance, and accordingly began to propitiate the lotus-origined Bramha with his austerities.

For a hundred years thereafter, the magnanimous sage practised austere penances in that forest, and meditated upon the self of his tutelary deity in perfect mastery over senses. Then Bramha, the progenitor of the different worlds with their inmates, manifested himself in his presence and asked him to name his wished-for, boon as he had been highly pleased with his penances. The holy sage laid himself prostrate at the feet of that appeased divinity and told the progenitor of the universe his intended course of action according to the directions of his departed Manes.

BRAHMA said:—"You shall be honored as a patriarch in the world. You shall be the progenitor of a mighty race of offsprings. O Brahman, it shall be your portion in this life to celebrate many a religious sacrifice and to rule the country in all the glory of a patriarchal sovereign, and then your penitential labours will be crowned with success. Be united with a handsome damsel in holy wedlock as your Manes had enjoined you to be. Worship and propitiate the spirits of your departed forefathers, and marry in fulfilment of their pleasant command. Your fathers, perfectly appeased, would grant you the fruition of all your desires. What is it that is not in the gift of one's departed Manes? Fathers, duly propitiated, bless their descendants with wives and children."

MARKANDEYA said:—Having heard these words of the divine Brahma, the eldest offspring of the Phenomenal Evolution, the holy sage offered libations of water to his departed Manes at the open and spacious foreshore of a river, and with his head bent down in devotion, and in a spirit, earnest, humble and contrite, he propitiated them with a hymn which runs as follows :—

RUCHI said :—With deep and unbounded devotion I make obeisance to the spirits of my fathers who sit beside the gods, and whom even the heaven-borns worship and propitiate with the Svadha-ending Mantras in the course of a Shraddha ceremony. I make obeisance to the Pitris, whom even the great sages, who are seekers after both salvation and earthly enjoyment, adore in heaven and propitiate with rites of purely mental Shraddha worship. I make obeisance to the Pitris, whom the Siddhas propitiate in heaven with offerings of celestial produce in the course of a Shraddha ceremony. I make obeisance to the Pitris, whom the Gujhyakas worship in heaven, with their whole soul merged in the contemplation of the former with a view to acquire infinite beatitude, and unparalleled and most exulted divine privileges. I make obeisance to the Pitris, who are worshipped in this mortal globe with the offerings of a Shraddha ceremony and who, when properly propitiated, bless its performer with a long line of sons and grandsons. I make obeisance to the Pitris, who are worshipped even by the twice-born ones in this world with a view to obtain their wished-for boons and who confer on their votaries the glories of an illustrious patriarch. I make obeisance to the Pitris, who are worshipped by the forest-dwellers of regulated diet, with fruits and flowers—the simple, though godly, offerings of the forest tress, sanctified with the occult energy of their well-practised Yoga. I make obeisance to the Pitris, who are worshipped and propitiated with the sacred energy of their Samadhi Yoga by Brahmanas exercising a perfect control over their senses, and the propulsions of whose minds have become one with the principles of virtue. I make obeisance to the Pitris, who are worshipped by crowned heads and potentates with various victuals of costly manufacture and who, when duly propitiated, bless their votaries with blessings which take effect both in this world and the next. I make obeisance to the Pitris whom the Vaishyas (members of the trading caste) who are always mindful of their own work, worship with flowers, incense-sticks, boiled rice and water. I make obeisance to the Pitris, who are worshipped even by the Shudras and are known as the Sukalinas. I make obeisance to the Pitris whom the great demons worship in the nether worlds, foregoing the pleasures of wine, bestial food, boisterousness and animalism. I make obeisance to the Pitris whom the various serpents worship in the nether world with a variety of costly oblations for the fruition of their heart-felt objects. I make obeisance to the Pitris whom the snakes worship with the gift of their incantations, etc.

I make obeisance to the Pitris who dwell in my presence, or on earth, or in the welkin, and to those who ramble in the glorious fields of heaven, adored by the lord of the celestials. May they deign to accept the offerings which I have made at this place. I make obeisance to the Pitris, who live in heaven as embodied beings, and who form the highest object of thought and contemplation, and whose satisfaction is the summum bonum of human existence, and whom the adepts in Yoga worship in a pure and unspotted heart for exemption from pain and miseries of successive re-births.

I make obeisance to the Pitris who dwell as embodied beings in heaven, living upon the libations of clarified butter cast in the course of a Shraddha ceremony in the accompaniment of the Svadha Mantras, and who are capable of granting all wished-for boons to their votaries; crown with success all ceremonial rites undertaken for the fruition of any definite object; and are the liberators from all undesirable situations. May my fathers in heaven be propitiated in the present Shraddha ceremony. May my Pitris, who grant all sorts of boons to persons soliciting them, and in whose gifts are the sovereignty of heaven, horses, elephants, cars, gem-studded dwellings and other paraphernalia of riches, be pleased with the present Shraddha ceremony celebrated for their satisfaction. May the spirits of my departed forefathers, who float in the moon-beam and ride on the white rays of solar light, be pleased with the present ceremony, and may they thrive on the offerings of flowers, perfumes, etc., offered in the course hereof. May the souls of my departed ancestors, who take delight in a well-kindled sacrificial fire blazing with the libations of clarified butter, and who, by temporarily residing in the bodies of the Brahmanas invited on the occasion, partake of what is offered to them in the course of a Shraddha ceremony, be pleased with the offerings of boiled rice and libations of water offered to them in the present ceremony. May the Pitris whom the gods worship with the flesh of a rhinoceros and the offerings of black sesamum of celestial origin, and whom the holy sages propitiate with dishes of cooked and prepared pot-herbs, known as the Kala Shaka, be pleased with the present ceremony undertaken for their propitiation. In the present ceremony I invoke the presence of the revered souls of my departed ancestors, who are extremely fond of obsequious cakes, in order they might receive the offerings of boiled rice, and perfumes, and libations of water to be offered to them at its close. May my departed Manes, who receive our loving homage every day and are worshipped every month on the occasion of an Ashtaka ceremony and at the close of each year under the auspicies of a Vriddhi Shraddha, be pleased with the present ceremony. May the departed Manes of the Brahmanas, who shine with the cool and mellow lustre of the moon-beam, and the departed Manes of the Kshatriyas, who shine with the dazzling effulgence of the noon-day-sun, and the departed Manes of the Vaishyas whose complexions are as the colour of molten gold, and the departed Manes of the Shudras whose complexions are deep blue, combinedly grace the present ceremony with their august presence, and be pleased with the offerings of flowers, perfumes, and edibles, etc., and the sweet exhalations of clarified butter cast in the sacrificial fire. Perpetually do

I make obeisance to the Pitris. May the Pitris, who partake of the obsequious cakes just after they had been eaten by the gods, and who, when duly appeased, confer prosperity upon their votaries, be pleased with the present ceremony. I make obeisance to them. May the Pitris, the mighty members of the celestial hierarchy, and revered by the gods, destroy the demons, and the monsters and the evil spirits and all other baneful visitations in the universe. I make obeisance to the Pitris.

May the different clans of the Pitris, such as the Agni-svattas, the Vahrishadas, the drinkers of clarified butter, and the drinkers of the expressed juice of the Soma-plant, be propitiated in the present Shraddha ceremony. I have propitiated the souls of my departed forefathers. May the members of the Agni-Svatta clan of the Pitris, guard my person in the east. May the members of the Vahrishada clan of that celestial order, protect me in the south. May the drinkers of sacrificial clarified butter, protect me in the west, and the drinkers of the expressed juice of the Divine Soma-plant, defend me in the east. May the Petris perpetually guard me against the malignant influences of ghosts, demons, monsters, and Pishachas.

The nine clans of Pitris are named as the Vishvas, the Vishvabhugs, the Aradhyas, the Dharmas, the Dhanyas, the Shubhananas, the Bhutidas, the Bhutikrids, and the Bhutis. The six other clans of the same celestial order, are known as the Kalyanas, the Kalyadas, the Kartàs, the Kalyatarashrayas, and the Kalyatahetu. The seven other clans of the same divine order, are called the Varas, the Varenyas, the Varadas, the Tushtidas, the Pushtidas, the Vishvapatas, and the Dhatas. The five clans of the same order, are named as the Mahan, the Mahtmas, the Mahitas, the Mahimavanas and the Mahavalas. The four remaining clans of the same order, are called the Sukhadas, the Dhanadas, the Dharmadas, and the Bhutidas, thus making thirty-one clanships in all, who guard the different approaches of the heaven, and are distributed all over the universe for the good of its inmates. May all of them be pleased with the present ceremony, duly inaugurated for their propitiation.

MARKANDEYA said:—While Ruchi was thus devoutly hymnising his departed Manes, a vast column of light suddenly shot across the heaven, and, behold, the universe stood entranced, wrapped in that mystic glow. Ruchi looked up and beheld that glorious phenomenon in mute wonder, and began to recite the following hymn on bent down knees.

RUCHI said:—Ever do I make obeisance to the Pitris, who are resplendent and disembodied spirits, endued with the faculty of spiritual vision, and always absorbed in the contemplation of the supreme Bramha. I make obeisance to the Pitris, who are the leaders of such celestial potentates as Indra, etc., and direct such holy sages as Daksha, Marichi, etc., who constitute the holy fraternity of the seven sages, in the path of truth and light, and who confer all boons upon their suppliants. I make obeisance to the Pitris who are the leaders of such mighty law-givers as Manu, etc., and who direct the sun and the moon in their path of heavenly duty. I make obeisance to the Pitris, who control the movements of the wind, guide the stars and planets in their orbits and sojourns, uphold the welkin, make the fire burn with its natural heat and glare, and fill in the earth and heaven and the space lying between them. With blended palms, I make obeisancce to Prajapati, to Kashyapa, to Soma, to Varuna, to the lord of all religious sacrifices. I make obeisance to the seven clans of the Pitris, who dwell in the seven regions or worlds. I make obeisance to the self-begotten Bramha whose vision is the light of Yoga (divine communion). I make obeisance to the Soma-drinking Pitris who are possessed of astral bodies. I make obeisance to the Moon God and the father of the universe. I make obeisance to the fiery-bodied Pitris, as well as to those whose persons are composed of the cooling principle in the universe. The two fundamental principles (fiery and cooling) run through all objects, and hence either they are fiery (heat making) or cooling (watery, albuminous) in their potencies. With a controlled heart I make obeisance to all the Yogins and the Pitris, who form the illuminating principle of light, and manifestly shine in the sun, in the moon and fire, and who are the models of creation and are identical with the Self of Supreme Bramha. May the Pitris who live upon the sweet exhalations of clarified butter cast in the sacrificial fire in the accompaniment of the Svadha Mantras, be pleased with the performance of the present ceremony.

MARKANDEYA said :—Having been thus propitiated by Ruchi, the best of the holy sages appeared to him in quick succession, illumining the ten quarters of heaven with the effulgence of their own spiritual bodies, and decked with the same sandal pastes and garlands of flowers which he had offered to them in the course of that Shraddha ceremony. Then Ruchi, having again made obeisance to them, addressed them for the second time as follows :—"With blended palms I make obeisance to each of you, O you Pitris!" Whereupon the Pitris, appeased by his devotion and humility, asked him to name his boon, to which Ruchi, with his head hung down in deep humility, replied as follows :—"I have been directed by the god Brahma to beget children and propagate my species. Accordingly most fervently do I pray for a noble and fruitful wife of celestial origin."

The FATHERS replied :—"O you, the best of the holy sages, this very day you shall be united with an extremely handsome wife. By her you shall have a son, O Ruchi, who would be named Rouchya after your honoured self, and who would rule the universe as a patriach and law-giver. He shall be the fore-runner of a mighty race of kings, high-souled and victorious, who would govern the whole Earth. You in your old age, would retire from the world, decked with the full glory of a pious and revered patriarch, and shall attain your penitential success and salvation. Blessed is the man who recites the aforesaid hymn for our satisfaction, for he will be blest with sons, and a long life of progeny, and all the creature comforts in this life. A suppliant for health, longevity and the blessings of fatherhood, shall do will to propitiate us with a recitation of the aforesaid hymn. A recitation of the hymn at the close of a Shraddha ceremony and before an assembly of Brahmanas sitting down at their meals, would bear immortal fruits through our intercession. Verily does its recitation make a Shraddha ceremony, endearing to us, even if it is not attended by Brahmanas well-versed in the Vedas (Shrotriyas), or is any way vitiated as to its precedure, or is celebrated with ill-gotten gain, or is attended by men who should not be invited on such an occasion, or performed at an improper place or time, or out of a spirit of bravado. The satisfaction which we derive from a Shraddha ceremony, in the course of which the hymn is recited, lasts us, O child, for a continuous period of twelve years. A single recitation of the hymn in the forepart of winter (Hemanta) gives us a satisfaction which lasts for twelve years. A single recitation of the hymn in winter gives us a satisfaction which continues for twice as many number (twenty-four) of years. The aforesaid hymn, recited in the course of a Shraddha ceremony performed in spring, furnishes us with a sense of repletion which lasts for a continuous period of sixteen years.

O Ruchi, a Shraddha ceremony, otherwise vitiated, or made defective as to its procedure, may be remedied by a single recitation of the hymn under discussion. O Ruchi, infinite is the pleasure which we derive from a recitation of the hymn during the rainy season. The satisfaction which we derive from a recitation of the hymn in autumn, lasts us for fifteen years. We grace a Shraddha ceremony with our presence in the event of its being performed in a room in which the hymn stands transcribed. Therefore, O you of mighty heritage, you shall recite the hymn before an assembly of Brahmanas invited on the occasion of a Shraddha ceremony and seated at their meals, whereby you would ensure infinite and eternal satisfaction to us, your departed Manes."

——:o:——

CHAPTER XC.

MARKANDEYA said:—The tranquil bosom of that lonely pool was stirred for a moment, and, behold, there appeared to Ruchi, Pamlocha, the slender-waisted water nymph of celestial beauty. The nymph solaced him with many a sweet and encouraging words and addressed him as follows:—Pushkara, the son of Varuna, the Ocean God, has begot on me a handsome daughter of uncommon beauty. Do you take her as thy lawful bride at my hands, O sage. By her you shall have a son of rare talents who would be the future law-giver of the universe.

MARKANDEYA said:—Then Ruchi, having consented to her proposal, drew that beautiful virgin out of the water of that lonely pool and duly married her on its green-clad bank. By her he had a son, named Rouchya after his honoured self, who had been a Manu (law-giver) of the universe, as narrated before.

——:o:——

CHAPTER XCI.

SUTA said :—The Manus, such as Svayambhuvas, etc, observe the rules of penance, worship, contemplation, and prayer, etc., recite the Mantras sacred to the God Hari, and meditate upon His eternal Self, which is shorn of body, senses, mind, intellect, vitality and the sense of egoism. The sky does not constitute His Self, nor does heat (light) enter into its composition. Water does not enter into the composition of His Supreme Self, nor do the attributes which characterise that material element, affect that eternal entity. Similarly, it is above all the fundamental principles of the earth matter, and is necessarily beyond the operative zone of virtues which specifically belong to that essential substance. Controller of all beings and becomings, he is the ever enlightened, ever wakeful One, the director and lord of all, the final receptacle of all force and energy, shorn of all illusion, and identical with pure consciousness. He is One, and without a second or companion, the supreme God, represented by light though void of fundamental quality of illumination (Sattva) and is hence beyond the necessity of practising any austerity. He is shorn of the quality of Rajas, and the three fundamental qualities of Sattva, Rajas and Tamas, do not affect his Supreme Self. He has no shape, is devoid of all action and desire, and is pure and incapable of sin and evil. Hankerings cannot assail him, nor griefs and ignorance can disturb the infinite serenity of His eternal Self. He knows no old age, death or decay. Without end or origin, he lies inherent in all,—the eternal witness to the process of phenomenal evolution and from whose vision nothing lies hidden or veiled and which nescience itself cannot clouden. He is the perfect and absolute truth, the Supreme God, one and indivisible, beyond all rules of ethics, nameless, and knows no sleep, nor dream, nor wakening. He is the only real factor in individual consciousness that makes the states of wakening, etc., possible. He is the personified peace, the lord of the gods and the celestials. He is real, and, as such, underlies the states of wakening, etc., void of the necessary categories of cause and effect. He is imaged in the phenomenal universe, and is accordingly seen by all. He is the most invisible of all invisible entities, and, as such, can be only perceived by means of pure knowledge, or through scriptural learning. He is the highest felicity, beyond all material process of creation or construction. He is shorn of intellect, and is beyond the process of intellection, and is identical with the fourth stage of pure consciousness (Turiya). He is the protector and destroyer of all. Beyond all virtues and attributes, he is the soul of all created beings. Without any receptacle to hold him in, he directs the universe in the path of light and benediction. He is Shiva (the blissful one, the highest bliss). He is Hari, the remover of all sin and misery. He suffers no change, nor knows any modification. He is known only through the teachings of the Vedanta philosophy. He is personified knowledge, the real substantial substratum whose attributes the senses inform us of. He is without the faculties of hearing, taste, touch, vision and smelling. He is without any origin, and lies inherent in the topmost cavity of the human brain, dawning upon the individual consciousness only to establesh its identity with his eternal Self, a fact which the human mind interprets in its experience of "I am He"

O thou, the supreme god, having realised this experience in mind, and having cast his whole self in the thought-mould of "I am He," a man should meditate upon the self of the supreme Brahman. He, who does this, is no other than the supreme One. I have disclosed to you the mode of contemplating the self of the supreme God. Now tell me, Rudra, whatever else you want me to speek about.

CHAPTER XCII.

RUDRA said :—Relate to me, O thou, the wielder of lotus, mace, discus, and conch shell, the mode of meditating upon the divine self of Vishnu, a knowledge whereof leads to salvation.

Said the god Hari :—Yes, I shall describe to you the mode of contemplating the divine self of Vishnu, which is of two sorts, according as the embodied or disembodied self of the god is meditated upon. O Rudra, in the preceding chapter I have discoursed on the latter mode, now hear me describe the process of contemplating the imaged or the embodied self of that deity. A seeker of salvation should meditate upon the god as burning with the combined effulgence of a million of suns, and moving about in the infinite space with the dignity of unquestioned prowess and unobstructed energy. The complexion of his divine body should be contemplated to be white as the hue of a Kunda flower. In the alternative, the god should be contemplated as burning with the combined effulgence of a thousand suns, and dreadful to look at through an excess of light, and as wielding a large and beautiful conchshell, a discus, a lotus flower, and a mace in his four hands, his face beaming with the calmness of divine peace. The crown or the head-gear of the god, should be contemplated as shining with the scintillations of a myriad of gems, and his attendants should be likewise contemplated as waiting upon his gracious divinity.

The mental picture, in the present instance, would not be complete without decorating the central figure with a garland of full-blown wild flowers. The image should be placed mentally on a full-blown lotus flower, decked with bracelets, necklace, etc., of celestial manufacture. The diamond Koustubha should be imagined as dangling over the region of his breast, grown over with the peculiar ringlets of hair, known as the Shrivatsam.

The imaginary person of this creator and destroyer of the universe, whom the gods and the holy sages contemplate in their celestial and sylvan retreats, should be contemplated as composed of the beatific attributes of Anima, etc., the different grades of conscious animalism, from the minutest animalculum to the mightiest Brahma, as having had their seats in the cardiac region of the image.

Thus the mental picture of the god should be completed, and the votary should worship it with the knowledge, that the deity imaged in his heart, is but the reflection of that primal light, the god of the gods, the absolute purity, the lord of all, and the only being equally compassionate towards all created life. He is the ever blissful lord, the regenator of the the human soul, and the destroyer of the threefold misery. He punishes the wicked, exhorts the good in the path of righteousness, is the soul of all, all-pervading, and the appeaser of all malignant stars. The beautiful circles of light which serve to relieve the darkness of the night, are his finger-rings. He is the primary source of all forms, and all shapes lie inherent in his disembodied spirit. He is the supreme god, the perfect beauty, the grand and final resort of all, the fountain-head from which equal felicity flows to all.

His body is decked with all sorts of ornaments, and is smeared with sandalpaste. The gods wait upon him in the spirit of loving servitude, and he does what the gods approve of. He does what is beneficial to them. He is Vasudeva, the lord of the universe. He looks after the universe. He looks after the good of all beings. He it is that shines in the sun. He it is that forms what is so wholesome in water. He is the only subject contemplated by all, the supreme ordainer in the universe, the supreme Vishnu, whom the seekers of salvation meditate upon.

"I am Vasudeva, I am He, the supreme soul," should be the form of thought in all who meditate upon the self of Vishnu. Those who contemplate him in this way, acquire the most exalted station after death. For having thus meditated upon the self of Vishnu, the holy Yajnavalkya, was honoured with the office of laying down the rules of conduct of his age. Therefore, O Shankara, O you, the lord of the celestials, always meditate upon the Self of Vishnu. Even he, who reads the present chapter, acquires the most elevated spiritual existence after death.

—:o:—

CHAPTER XCIII.

MAHESHVARA said :—Tell me, O Hari, O Madhava, O you who have destroyed the demon Keshi, what is it that led the holy Yajnavalkya, to lay down the rules of conduct in days of yore?

SAID THE GOD HARI :—Once on a time, the holy sages visited, in a body, the venerable Yajnavalkya in his hermitage at Mithila; and having duly made obeisance to him, they asked him about the rules of conduct to be observed by members of the different orders of society. Whereupon the self-controlled Yajnavalkya, meditating upon the self of Vishnu, replied as follows.

YAJNAVALKYA said :—Pious is the country where herds of black deer are found to roam about. Knowledge is in the Vedas, in the Puranas, in the different schools of philosophy such as the Nyaya, the Mimansa, etc., in the Dharma Shastras (Ethics and Social Economy) and in the books of money-making and temporal sciences : Manu, Vishnu, Yama, Angira, Vashishtha, Daksha, Samvarta, Shatatapa. Parashara,

Apastambha, Ushana, Vyasa, Katyayana, Vrihaspati. Goutama, Shankha, Likhita, Harita, and Atri, are the names of the fourteen holy sages, who, having worshipped the god Vishnu, were enabled to become the ethical dictators and law-givers (Dharma-Shashtrakaras) of the ages in which they lived.

A gift, made at a proper time and place, and to a deserving person in a true spirit of compassionate sympathy, carries the merit of all sorts of pious acts. Right conduct, self-control, charity, annihilation of all killing propensities, reading of the Vedas, and the performance of ceremonial rites therein enjoined to be performed, are the best of all pieties. Viewing of one's own soul through self-communion, is the highest and most imperative of all religious duties. The four Vedas together with the Trividyas form the branch of learning which is called the Para-Vidya (Supreme knowledge.)

The first three of the four social orders of Brahmana, Kshatriya, Vaishya and Shudra, are called the twice-born castes, and all rites, from nativity to death, should be done unto them in the accompaniment of the Vedic hymns and verses.

The rite of Garbhadhanam (*lit.*, rite for the taking of the womb) should be performed closely following upon the appearance of her first menses unto one's wife, and the rite of Punsavanam (rite for the conception of a male-child) just as soon as the movements of the fœtus in the womb would be felt by the mother. The rite of Sisanta should be done unto her in the sixth or in the eighth month of gestation, while the post-natal rites (Jatakarma) of the new-born babe should be performed after delivery.

The rite of naming (Nama-karanam) should be done unto the child on the eleventh day of its birth, while the rite of Nishkramanam (ceremonial taking of the child out of the room) should be done unto it, in the fourth month after delivery. The rite of Annaprashanam (first taking of boiled-rice by a child) should be done in the sixth month after its birth, while the rite of Chuda-karanam (tonsure) should be performed in accordance with the custom obtaining in the family. The sin, which attaches to the ovum and the semen, is absolved by the performance of the aforesaid rites, which should be omitted in the case of a female child, only on the occasion of whose marriage the Vedic Mantras should be recited.

—:o:—

CHAPTER XCIV.

YAJNAVALKYA said :—A Brahmana boy should be invested with the holy thread at the eighth year of his age, inclusive of the period of gestation, a Kshatriya child at his eleventh year, and a Vaishya child at an age as is customary in the family.

The preceptor, having duly invested him with the holy thread, shall first teach him the Maha-Vyahriti Mantras, and then the verses of the Vedas, as well as the rules of conduct and hygiene.

In the day, and at morning and evening, a member of any of the twice-born castes, shall pass urine with his face turned towards the north, while in the night he shall look towards the south under similar conditions, hanging the holy thread on his right ear at the time, whether in the day or in the night. He shall rise up from that sitting posture with the external organ of micturition firmly grasped with his fingers, and shall then wash the part with water kept ready for the purpose, or rub it with earth for the purpose of removing the characteristic smell. Then having sit on his haunches in a pool or a river, and with his face turned towards the north or towards the east, a member of any of the twice-born castes, shall wash and rinse his mouth with water, lifted up with that part of his palm which is called the Brahma-Tirtham. Regions about the first or the lowermost phalanges of the little, and the middle, finger, as well as the one lying about the root of the right thumb, should be held as sacred to the gods Prajapati, Pitri, and Brahma, which are accordingly called the Prajapati-Tirtham, the Pitri-Tirtham, and the Brahma-Tirtham.

A member of any of the twice-born castes, shall first take two draughts of water to rinse his lips with, and then cleanse his face with undisturbed and frothless water. The twice-born ones shall purify their breasts, throats, palates and umbilical regions with water. It will be enough for women and Shudras to purify their regions of back and umbilicus.

A member of the twice-born order, shall bathe every day, perform the rite of cleansing his body with the same Mantra as he shall recite at the time of ablution, practise the rite of Pranayama, invoke the Sun-god, and recite the Gayatri Mantra. After that, he shall mentally recite the Gayatri-shirah Mantra, and the Vyahritis with the holy Pranava prefixed to each part of its component parts. Then he shall thrice practise the rite of Pranayama (a peculiar mode of controlling the process of respiration) after reciting the three Riks for its purification, and shall then go on mentally reciting the Savitri-Mantra, till the appearance of stars in the evening sky.

The rite of morning Sandhya, should be commenced before dawn, and the twice-born worshipper, should sit self-controlled in his seat, reciting the Vedic Mantras enjoined to be read in connection with the aforesaid rite, till the rising of the Sun-God above the horizon. The rite of Agni-Karyam should be practised both morning and evening, after which the worshipper should visit and make obeisance to his elders by saying " I am That."

After that he shall visit his preceptor, and sit beside him humble, docile and self-controlled for the purpose of studying the Vedas. In the alternative, he should wait till sent for by his preceptor, and then learn his daily Vedic lessons from his lips. He shall make no secret of anything to his preceptor, and constantly look after his welfare, whether by word, or by thought, or by bodily toil.

He shall carry the anchorite's staff, put on the holy thread and a sable-coloured blanket, and girdle up his waist with the holy girdle made of the blades of the consecreted Kusha grass twisted together.

For the purposes of maintenance, he shall beg alms only of the householders of twice-born order, or of men of pure and unimpeachable character. The Vedic verses should be recited in the morning, evening and at noon, and a Brahmana shall beg alms only of persons of Kshatriya and Vaishya castes.

Having performed the morning Agni Karyam, the disciple shall sit down to his meal, in all humility and with the permission of his precep tor. He shall perform the rite of rinsing his mouth with water, and purify the plate of boiled rice served out to him before partaking of a single morsel, and shall eat his meal silently and without making any sort of reflection upon the nature of the food and its cooking. A Brahmana, who has subjugated his senses, and leads the life of a Brahmacharin, is at liberty to take a full meal of boiled rice on the occasion of a Shraddha ceremony, without incurring the risk of breaking his vow of asceticism. A Brahmana shall forego the use of wine, meat, curdled milk and its preparations. He is the Guru, who, having initiated the pupil into the mysteries of spiritualism, makes him conversant with the knowledge of the Vedas. He, who having duly invested his disciple with the holy thread, teaches him the holy Vedas, is called an Acharya. A tutor, living in the same village with his pupil, is called an Upadhyaya. A priest, officiating at a sacrificial ceremony, is called a Rittik. The person of each preceding one of these functionaries, is more venerable than that of the one immediately following it in the order of enumeration, and a mother is the most venerable of them all.

A pupil shall read each of these Vedas for a period of five or twelve years, and he shall live as a Brahmacharin with his Guru, up to the age of sixteen, twenty, or twenty-four years. The age of investing a child of the Brahmana, Kshatriya or Vaishya order, with the holy thread, has been laid down before; and a non-performance of the ceremony within the stated period, leads to his spiritual degeneration. A Brahmana, or a Kshatriya or a Vaishya child, thus degenerated as regards his Savitri initiation, is called a Vratya, the process of regeneration consisting in the performance of a Vratya-Stoma sacrifice.

The three twice born castes of Brahmana, Kshatriya and Vaishya, are, so called from the fact of their being born a second time through spiritual initiation (tieing of the sacred Mounji, 'or strings of deer skin and blades of Kusha grass twisted together, the symbol of Savitri initiation) after having been delivered of the mother's womb.

The Vedas are the highest depository of all sacrificial and penitential knowledge, and of all acts which conduce to the spiritual welfare of the twice-born ones. A member of a twice-born caste, shall offer libations of milk and honey to the gods and his departed manes. The libations should be offered from day to day, and the Vedic Ricks should be recited in connection therewith. A member of any of the twice-born orders, shall read the Saman, the Atharvans, and the Angirasam in the same manner, and shall appease the gods and his departed manes with similar libations. The gods and the Pitris are pleased with him who reads the Vedas, the Veda-Vakyam, the Puranas, the Gathikas, and the Itihasas, every day, to the best of his ability, and propitiates them with offerings of meat, and libations of milk and honey. The merit of performing a particular religious sacrifice can be acquired by reading the portion of the Veda which deals with that particular sacrifice, and the twice-born one who reads his Veda every day, acquires the merit of making the gift of a plot of land, as well as that of practising austerities.

A Brahmana disciple or pupil, pure in thought and conduct, and with an absolute control over his senses, shall sit beside his Acharya, or by the side of his wife or son in his absence, or in front of the sacred fire. The self-controlled one shall live according to the injunctions laid down above, whereby he will go to the region of Brahman after death, and will not revert to the chain of life.

———:o:———

CHAPTER XCV.

YAJNAVALKYA said :—Hear me, O holy sages, describe the duties which are obligatory on a house-holder. A householder, having made a money-gift to his preceptor, and having performed the rite of ceremonial ablution, shall wed a wife with all the auspicious marks on her person at the close of his life of asceticism. The wife should be a girl young in years and not previously married to any other husband, in the possession of sound health and having had uterine brothers of her own, and not related to him by any tie of Sapinda relationship, nor belonging to the same spiritual clanship (Arsha Gotram) as his own. She should be taken from any of the sixteen reputed families of the Shrotriyas, not related to the bridegroom within five and seven degrees in the lines of his mother and father respectively.

A bridegroom, well-versed in the knowledge of the Vedas, erudite and belonging to the same social order as herself, should be regarded as the only eligible one for a Brahmana bride. I denounce the practice of a Brahmana being united with a Shudra wife as he incurs the risk of taking birth in her womb in the shape of the child begotten by him on her person.

A Brahmana is at liberty to take a wife from any of the first three social orders, or to put it more explicitly, a Brahmana shall marry a girl either of his own caste, or one belonging to the warrior (Kshatriya), or to the trading (Vaishya) community. Similarly a Kshatriya shall marry a Kshatriya or a Vaishya girl, while a Vaishya shall take a wife from his own community, the marriage of a Shudra girl with a member of any of the twice-born castes being hereby absolutely forbidden.

A Brahma form of marriage is that in which the bridegroom is invited to take his bride, decked with ornaments as the means of her father would admit of, and an offspring of such a marriage purifies the members of both the families thus united, even removed from him to the twentieth degree in the ascending line. In the Daivam form, the daughter of a sacrificer (person on whose behalf a sacrifice is performed) is given away in marriage to the priest officiating at the ceremony (Rittik). In the Arsha form, the marriage is celebrated by making a gift of a pair of cows to the bridegroom. A child, who is the fruit of a Daivam marriage, sanctifies the members of both the united families to the sixteenth degree in the ascending line, while in the case of an offspring of the latter (Arsha) form, such sanctification extends to the sixth degree. The offspring of a nuptial union in which the bride is given away with the injunction "Live with him and discharge the duties of a householder," to one soliciting her hands, sanctifies the members of both the united families to the sixth degree in the ascending line. In the Asura form, the bride is received on the payment of a pecuniary consideration. In the Gandharva form, the union is effected on the mutual consent or agreement of the contracting parties. The Rakshasa form of marriage consists in taking away the bride by force, while in the Paishacha form the marriage is effected by practising a stratagem on the bride.

Only the first four forms of marriage are allowed in the case of a Brahmana. The Gandharva and Rakshasa forms are commended in the case of a member of the warrior caste, the Asura form in the case of a Vaishya, and the most condemnable form in the case of a Shudra.

A bride of the warrior caste, shall take hold of an arrow at the time of her marriage, a Vaishya girl shall hold a shuttle (Pratoda) in her hand at the time, while a Brahmana bride shall be formally united with her husband with a Vedani (sharp-pointed instrument) in her hands.

The father of the bride, or her paternal grandfather, or her uterine brother, or an agnate of her father's (Sakulya) or her brother, shall give her away in marriage, the right of such giving away being held as vested in each of these successive relations in the absence of the one immediately preceding it in the order of enumeration. The relations of a girl incur the sin of wilfully creating a miscarriage, or of killing a fœtus in the event of their failing to give her away in marriage before she has commenced to menstruate. A girl is at liberty to make her own choice, and to be united with a husband, in the absence of any such relation to give her away in marriage. A girl should be given only once in marriage and any one carrying away a married girl should be dealt with as a common felon.

Any one deserting a good and faithful wife, commits a crime punishable under the Code, while a wife possessed of contrary virtues, should be summarily discarded. The younger brother of a husband, may go unto a childless wife of his elder brother for the purpose of begetting an offspring on her person with the permission of his elders, first had and obtained in that behalf, and with his body annointed with clarified butter. A Sagotra (related by ties of consanguinity) or a Sapinda relation of the husband, may act in a similar capacity and for similar purposes. Such visits should be permitted only as long as there would remain any natural chance of conception, otherwise the visitor would be degraded in life. A child thus begotten, shall belong to the lawful husband of its mother.

A married woman found guilty of wilful incontinence to her husband, and again placed into his lawful custody, shall be made to wear dirty clothes, and to live on a single morsel of food (at the close of day), negligent of her toibette and sleeping on the bare ground instead of her usual bed. The Moon-God gave the women their sanctity, Gandharva gave them the sweetness of speech. Sacred is fire and sanctified is the person of a woman. She, who wilfully brings about an abortion, except for the purposes of purifying herself after having committed an act of adultery, commits the sin of killing her own husband born in her womb in the shape of the fœtus. Polluted is the person of such a murderess.

A husband is at liberty to summarlly discard a wife, addicted to the habit of drinking wine, or afflicted with an incurable disease, or found to be inimically disposed towards him. O ye holy sages, a wife, blest with the gift of sweetness of speech, tender, and graced with all those peculiar and excellent virtues which are found only in women, should be maintained and provided for at all hazards.

The threefold benediction of god reigns in the household where the husband and the wife live in perfect harmony; and paradise is the house which harbours such a true, loving and virtuous pair under its roof.

She, who does not take a second husband after the demise of her first one, achieves fame in this life, and lives in the same region with the goddess Uma in the next. Whoever discards a good and chaste wife, shall give her a third portion of her ornaments before formally effecting a separation. The sacred and imperative duty of a wife is to carry out the commands of her husband, and to live in perfect obedience to his wishes.

The menstrual period of a woman extends up to the sixteenth night after the the catamanial flow, each month, and her husband may visit her during that time on each even day, avoiding her bed side on the first three days of her unclearliness, as well as on days marked as Parvanas (days of full moon, new moon etc.,) in the Indian Calendar. The husband shall bide his time as a Brahmacharin before the actual meeting takes place. Days marked by such asterisms as the Magha, the Mula, etc., (when the moon is in such lunar mansions known as the Magha, Mula, etc.,) should be regarded as forbidden for the purposes of a sexual intercourse. He, who observes these rules in respect of visiting the bed of his wife, is sure to beget healthy children, marked by all auspicious features of the body and mind. In the alternative, a husband may visit the bed of his wife whenever he shall feel any propulsion for it, and he shall meditate upon the god of love during the continuance of the act of dalliance.

A man, true and faithful to his own wife, shall protect the female members of his family. The husband, or brother, or father, or the agnates, or the father-in-law, or the husbands' brother of a woman, shall maintain her with food, raiments and ornaments. A woman, who is economical in her habits, simple and not extravagant in her toilette, cleanly and ingenious in her household works, and is of a cheerful temperament, should be maintained by her friends (relations, Vandhus).

The wife of an absentee husband shall renounce all frolics, and forego the pleasures of mixing in society, or of sight-seeing and merry-making. She shall not smile, nor attend to her daily toilette, nor shall she stay in another's house till the return of her lord.

The father of a woman shall protect her in her infancy, the husband in her youth, and her son in her old age, in absence whereof the duty of maintaining her shall devolve upon his friends and relations. Day and night, a woman shall not quit the side of her husband.

The elder co-wife shall be the companion of her lord, inasmuch as the younger one does not enjoy that privilege. The husband shall personally attend to the cremation of the dead body of his own faithful wife with rites, as laid down under the head of an Agni-Hotra sacrifice, and is at liberty to marry a second wife with the same sacred fire. The wife, who devotes her whole self to the good of her husband, achieves fame in this life and goes to that particular connubial paradise after death, which is reserved for chaste matrons.

—:o:—

CHAPTER XCVI.

YAJNAVALKYA said:—Now I shall enumerate the names of the mixed castes, the offsprings of clandestime intercourse and unsacramental marriage, and describe the functions which the members of these hybrid communities, are expected to perform in the social economy.

A son begotten by a Brahman father on a Kshatriya mother, is called Murdhabhishikta, while a son by him on Vaishya woman, is called an Amvasta. A son by a Brahmana father on a Shudra woman, is called either a Nishada or a Parvata. O you, the best of erudite ones, a son begotten by a Kshatriya father on a Vaishya mother, is called a Mahishya, while a son born of a Shudra mother by a member of the trading community (Vaishya) is called a Karana.

A son born of a Brahman mother by a Kshatriya father is called a Suta, while a son begotten by a Vaishya father on a Brahmani woman, is called as Vaidehka. A son born of a Brahman mother by a Shudra father, is called a Chandala, the most abject of all social orders. A son born of a Kshatriya mother by a Vaishya father, is called a Magadha, while a son begotten by a Shudra father on a Kshatriya mother is called a Kshetrabama. A son begotten by a Shudra father on a Vaishya woman, is called a Ayogava. A son born of a Karana mother by a Mahishya father, is called a Rathakara. These hybrid castes, whether begotten by members of the twice-born castes on Shudra mothers, or the contrary (Pratilomaja and Anulomaja) are all unsanctified races without any right to the sacramental rites or knowledge.

The twice-born castes occupy the foremost place of all other social orders, as regards the glory of descent and sanctity, and a member, belonging to any of them, acquires the full privilege of his order at the fifth or at the seventh year of his age through his second birth in spirit.

A householder shall daily perform the rites laid down in the Smritis with the help of the sacred fire, first lighted on the occasion of his marriage, and all Vedic rites should be performed in the same, save and except on the occasion of making gifts. A member of the twice-born order shall leave his bed early in the morning, attend to the calls of nature, then wash and cleanse himself, specially cleansing the teeth with a crushed twig of any of the medicinal plants, and shall thereafter perform the rite of his daily Sandhya (worship). Then having cast libations of clarified fire in the sacred fire, he shall mentally repeat, in an unruffled spirit, the Mantras sacred to the Sun-God. Then having discoursed on the teachings of the Vedas, and discussed several topics of the kindred branches of study, a householder shall resort to his god with the object of attaining divine beatitude through the practice of Yoga.

Then having bathed, he shall propitiate the gods and his Pitris with libations of water, and worship them with the most heartfelt devotion. After that, he shall read several portions of the Vedas and the sacred Puranas. For the successful termination of his daily Japa-Yajna (divine meditation), he shall mentally recite the Adhyatmiki Vidyam. Offering of oblations to the created beings, to the gods, to the Pitris, and Brahma, casting of libations of clarified butter in the sacrificial fire, reading of the Vedic verses, and practice of hospitality to chance-comers, are the great daily religious sacrifices of all human beings. Libations of clarified butter should be cast in the sacred fire for the propitiation of the gods, and oblations of food stuff should be offered to the beasts (*lit.*, created beings). Boiled rice should be offered in the open, and on the bare, ground for the use of the crows and the Chandalas, and similar oblations of cooked food (*lit.*, rice), and libations of cold water should be daily offered to the gods and the Pitris.

A (twice-born) householder shall daily read his Vedas, and shall not cause any food to be cooked for his own exclusive use. He shall take his meal with his wife, after having fed all the infants, old men, invalids, and girls in the family and all chance-comers to his house. He shall eat his meals without finding any fault with it, and after having performed the rite of Homa to his vital (intestinal) fires.

He shall first feed the boys and infants in the house and observe moderation in eating. A householder is hereby enjoined only to take that sort of food which is wholesome in its digestionary reaction (Vipakam).

A member of the twice-born order shall convert his meal into ambrosia by performing the rite of Amritikaranam (transformation into ambrosia), and shall partake of the same in a covered place, screened from the view of the public.

He shall distribute food to the chance-comers to his house, and to the members of the remaining social orders, as his means would admit of. He shall not look upon a chance-comer to his house as an unwelcome intruder, nor try to identify him with another person, come on a previous occasion. Charities should be doled out to beggars and to men of commendable vows, and the Shrotriyas, and all comers should be treated with a sumptuous repast. The Snatakas (performers of ceremonial ablutions), Acharyyas and the princes, should be feasted each year.

A chance-comer, worn out with the fatigues of a long pedestrial journey, is called an Atithi, while a Brahmana, well-versed in the knowledge of the holy Vedas, is called a Shrotriya. A householder shall revere the Shrotriyas and the Atithis with a view to ascend to the region of Brahma after death.

A householder of the twice-born order shall feel no inclination for a food, cooked and prepared by another, nor shall he make any reflections on another man's conduct, except while deliberating a question of public interest in a council or meeting convened for the purpose. He shall not dangle his legs, nor listlessly move his arms, nor be hasty in his speech, and under no circumstance shall he indulge in the vice of over-eating. He shall escort a Shrotriya or an Atithi to the border of his land or village, after having fed him well in his own house. He shall pass the closing part of the day in friendly gossips with his trusted and well-meaning friends. A householder shall leave his bed early in the morning, and propitiate the gods and the Brahmanas with precious gifts. It is incumbent on a householder to ponder well over a matter before executing it (Vriddha-Pantha), to be godly and devoted to the service of the deity, like a man in disease (Arta-Riti), and not to suffer any delay in the execution of a work, when once he has chosen his line of action, like a load-carrier briskly running with his load in the way (Bharavahi-Riti).

The worldly duties of a Vaishya, or of a Kshatriya, consist in the celebration of religious sacrifices, and in the study and practice of charities, while performance of religious rites, study of the Vedas, acceptance of gifts, practice of charities, teaching and officiating at the religious sacrifices of others in the capacity of a priest, are morally obligatory to a Brahmana, living the life of a householder. The one and imperative duty of a Kshatriya is to protect the people from foreign invasions and civic or internal disturbances. Banking, merchandise, and rearing of large herds of cattle, are the functions which a member of the Vaishya (trading) community, is born to perform, while the sole duty of a Shudra is to render personal service to the foremost of the twice-born castes.

Truthfulness, annihilation of all killing or hostile propensities, non-stealing, personal cleanliness, and self-control, are the virtues, the practice whereof is equally obligatory on all human beings, irrespective of castes or functions in life. One should earn his livelihood by means proper to, and specifically enjoined in the Shastras for, the particular community one would belong to, which should never be crooked or deceitful.

He who is in the habit of taking rice, matured for more than three years, is alone fit to drink the holy Soma, while the person whose daily meals consist of boiled rice, not more than one year old, should perform the proper and necessary religious sacrifices before taking it.

A householder shall duly celebrate, each year, the Vedic sacrifices known as Soma, Pashu-Pratyayanam, Grahaneshti, and Chaturmashyam, in the failure whereof the one known as Vaishvanari, should be performed. A religious sacrifice, should not be celebrated with a number of articles or offerings, less than that laid down in the Shastras in that behalf. By celebrating a religious sacrifice with money or articles begged of a Shudra, a Brahmana is sure to reincarnate as a Chandala in his next existence. By stealing anything collected for the celebration of a religious sacrifice, the stealer becomes a crow or a Bhasa (bird) in his next birth. Of the four persons whose granary is filled with grains, who has got enough grain stored in his house to last him for three days, who has got sufficient only for a day's use, and the person who lives by picking up grains from the stubbles (Uncha-Vritti), the each preceding one is happier and lives in greater comfort than the one immediately succeeding him in the order of enumeration. A Brahmana is prohibited from adopting a profession which is caculated to interfere with his studies and divine contemplation, and who, in want of the barest necessaries of life, may be allowed to beg of a pupil, of a king, or of a fellow Brahmana. Any dishonest means of livelihood, or maintaining himself by passing off as a false prophet, or a false ascetic, is equally nefarious and criminal. It is sin for a Brahmana to earn money in pursuits of vanity.

A householder shall put on clean clothes, shave himself and pare off his finger-nails every day, and in short, must be cleanly in his habits. A man is enjoined not to sit down to his meals in the presence of his wife, and nor without being decently wrapped in his upper garment. A Brahmana should be always humble, and constantly wear his holy thread, nor shall he speak harsh to any body.

Micturation in a river-bed, in a shade, over ashes, in a pasturage, in water, or in the road, is forbidden, it being sinful for a man to pass urine while looking at the sun, or at the moon, or at the gloom of the evening, or at a woman, or at a Brahmana. One should not look at the blaze of fire, nor at any naked woman, nor at one sharing the bed of her husband, nor at any excreted matter, nor sleep with his head towards the west. It is forbidden to spit or throw blood, or poison, or any sort of excreta into water. It is injurious to bask one's soles in the glare of fire, or to leap over a blazing fire, or to drink of the blended palms of one's own hands, or to rouse up a sleeping person, or to play with any dishonest gambler, or to live in contact with any diseased person. Exposure to the smoke and vapours of a cremation ground, and residence on a river bank, should be avoided as harmful. One should not stand over torn hairs, husks of grains, and ashes, nor upon particles of any human cranium. A cow should not be disturbed while drinking, nor a chamber should be entered into by any passage other than its proper door. Money or any pecuniary help should not be asked of a greedy king, nor of a person who does not live according to the injunctions of the Shastras.

A rite of Upakarma (study of the Vedas after performing certain religious rites), should not be performed under the auspices of the full moon of Shravan, or of the asterism of Shravana and Hasta, nor on the fifth day of the moon's wane in the month of Shravan, nor on a day marked by the asterism of Rohini or Pushya, nor on the occasion of an Ashtaka. The stool, urine and other excreta should be put and deposited at a distance from one's dwelling-house.

The study of the Vedas should be discontinued for three successive days on the occasion of the death of one's disciple, priest, spiritual preceptor, or a male cognate relation. Cessation of Vedic study should be enjoined on the happening of an earthquake, or meteor-fall, or thunder-clap, or on the death of a Shrotriya Brahmana, and after finishing the recitation of a Veda and its allied Aranyakam by a student or pupil, duly initiated. A study of the Vedas is forbidden on days of the full and the new moon, as well as on the eighth or the fourteenth day of the moon's wane or increase, on the occasion of a lunar eclipse, after eating, at the meeting of two seasons, after taking any gift, at any Shraddha ceremony, and on the passing of a snake, hog, mungoose, dog, or cat between the pupil and the preceptor at the time of study. A study of the Vedas should be discontinued just as the reader would hear the bark, or howl, or braying or screeching, or crying, or moaning of a dog, or a jackal or an ass, or an owl, or an infant or a sick person, as well as on the near approach of a dead body, or a Shudra, or any morally degraded person. One should refrain from studying the Vedas at an unholy place, in the road, on hearing a thunder clap, after dinner, in wet palms, in water, at the dead of night; in storm, on the appearance of meteoric flashes in the sky, in dust storm, at evening, and during snowfall. The Vedas should not be studied from a preceptor in motion, and be stopped on the advent of a holy person in the house, or while the disciple is riding an elephant, a horse or a camel, or in a carriage, or climbing a tree or a hill, or crossing a river; these thirty-seven occasions of non-study of the Vedas should be regarded as contingent on the happening of particular events, and as limited by the period of their respective durations.

Acts enjoined in the Vedas, as well as the commands of a king or a preceptor, should be executed without questioning. The wife of another person, should never be polluted, and the shadow (of a person) as well as all excreted matter, and oils and cosmetics for human use, should never be leapt over and crossed. It is a sin to make light of a king or of a Brahmana, or of a snake, or of a disease lurking in the system. The refuges of tables and all sorts of excreta, should be shunned from a distance as impure. One shall not repent after executing any act approved of the Shrutis or the Shrastras, nor question its propriety or ethical fairness. A son or a disciple should be flogged, at times, for the purpose of discipline. Virtue should be perpetually practised and by all means, and vice should be repressed and refrained from. One should not angrily dispute with one's parents and guests (*lit*: chance-comers at one's house), even in the existence of a right cause for the same. One should not bathe in another's tank before lifting five handful of clay from its bed, which rule does not hold good in respect of lakes, springs and other natural reservoirs of water.

The bed of one should never be used by another, and the food prepared by one's own enemy, or by a Brahmana who is not a keeper of the sacred fire (Niragni), might be partaken of only in severe distress. A bad food, or the one prepared by a professional musician (*lit*: lute-player), or by a defiler of another man's bed, or by a person who lives by making breaches among friends and relations (Varddhushika), or by Brahmana who is the spiritual preceptor of prostitutes, or by a professional physician, or by a professional actor, or by a dishonest and furious person, or by a member of any of the twice-born castes, not formally invested with the holy thread (Vratya), or by an arrogant braggart, or by one who eats the refuges of others men's boards, or by one who lives by selling knowledge, or by an uxorious husband, or by a village priest, or by a cruel king, or by a traitor, or by a public executioner, or by a malicious person, or by an utterer of falsehood, or by a wine-seller, or by a bard (Vandi), or by a goldsmith, should never be taken. The flesh of an animal not sacrificed to a god, or boiled rice infested with worms and hairs, should never be partaken of.

An article of food, such as boiled rice etc, prepared on a previous day or night, or partaken of by another, or touched by a dog, or sprinkled over with water by a morally degraded person, or polluted by the touch of a woman in her menses, or squeezed by another, or smelled by a cow, or eaten by a bird, or trampled down with foot, should be shunned, as impure and unwholesome. A food (including boiled rice), prepared by a Shudra, should be unconditionally rejected with the exception of one made by a Dasa, Gopa, Kulamitra, Ardhasiri, Napita, or a Shudra, who has surrendered himself to a Brahmana, which may be eaten without any prejudice.

Boiled rice, prepared on a previous day and kept soaked with clarified butter, may be safely taken without any unwholesome effect. Articles made of wheat and barley, and without any admixture of clarified butter, should be rejected as food. The milk of a she-camel, or of any female animal with unbifurcated hoofs, should not be used. The flesh of any carnivorous bird or of a Dyatuha, as well as that of a dog, should never be eaten. The sin,—consequent on eating the flesh of a Sarasa, Hansa (Ekashapha), Valaka, Vaka or Tittibha, as well as the one originating from the use of Krishara, Pupa, Shankuli, etc., without dedicating them to one's guest, or from that of the flesh of a swan, Kurura, Bhasa, Khanjana, or Shuka,—may be expiated by a three days' fast. The use of garlic or onion in food, should be atoned by performing a Chandrayana penance. The use of any cooked meat on the occasion of Shraddha ceremony, and after dedicating it to one's departed manes (Pitris) does not entail any sin. The soul of the person, who wantonly kills any animal in this life, lives for as many number of years in hell after death, as there are hairs on the body of that slaughtered animal, and who may be only rescued, if the god Hari kindly listens to his constant prayers for expiation on the condition of his never killing any animal in his next re-birth.

—:o:—

CHAPTER XCVII.

YAJNAVALKYA said:—O Brahmanas, now hear me discourse on the means of cleansing or purifying the articles of daily use. All articles of gold, silver, conch-shell, or precious stones, as well as blankets and utensils are made pure by simply washing it with water. A spoon, or a laddle, as well as paddies, may be made pure by simply dipping them in hot water. An article, made of wood or horn, is made pure by the scraping off of a slice from its body, while the utensils to be used in a sacrificial ceremony, may be made pure by simply washing them with water. A blanket, or a cloth, made of sheep's hair or silk, is purified by dipping it in hot water, or by sprinkling drops of cow's urine over its surface. An article, obtained by begging, is made pure by being looked at by a woman, while a baked earthen pot is purified by a second burning. A pot of boiled rice, smelled by a cow, or dropped upon by a bunch of hair, or an insect, may be made pure by simply throwing a pinch of ashes over it. The ground is purified by rubbing it with water. An utensil made of brass, lead, or copper, is purified by rubbing it with alkali or any acid substance, an iron-made one by being rubbed with ashes, while a newly-gotten thing is always pure. The water of any natural reservoir of water, is made pure by being smelled by a cow, while a bit of flesh dropped from the beaks of any carnivorous bird in carriage, or from the mouth of a dog, or touched by a Chandala, does not lose its natural purity. The rays of the sun, fire, the shadow of a goat or a cow, the earth, a horse, a goat, a Brahmana, and a dewdrop (drop of water) are above all contamination. A man should change his clothes after bathing, drinking, sneezing, sleeping, eating, or returning from a walk, and by rinsing his mouth with water after having made an Achamanam. A Brahmana need not rinse his mouth with water after an act of sneezing, sleeping, spitting, wearing an apparel, or lachrymation. It is enough to touch his right ear under the circumstance, since all the gods, such as Agni, etc., reside in the Scapha of that organ of a Brahmana.

—:o:—

CHAPTER XCVIII.

YAJNAVALKYA said:—O you holy masters of excellent penitential rites, now hear me discourse on the method of making gifts. The Brahmanas are the fittest persons to make gifts to, foremost among them being those who regularly perform and celebrate the Brahminical rites and ceremonies. The best even among the latter are those who know the Supreme Brahma, and have devoted themselves to the cultivation of intellectual and spiritual knowledge.

Gifts of cows, proprietory rights in lands, food grains and gold, should be given to a Brahmana, who is every way worthy of receiving the same. A Brahmana who has neither erudition, nor is a seeker of spiritual knowledge, has no right to accept any gifts; and degrades the giver as well as his own soul by accepting any. A gift should be made every day to a worthy receiver, as well as on special occasions. A person is morally bound to give something in charity to a person in straitened circumstances, and soliciting his help, according to his own means and in a devout spirit.

A thousand of milch-cows with their horns cased in gold, and hoops bound with silver, may be given in gift to a Brahmana with thousand bowls of Indian bell-metal. The horn cases should be made of a Pala weight of gold (one Pala= eight tolas), the hoofs, of seven Palas of silver, and the bowls, of fifty Pala weights of bell-metal, each. A calf should be given with each of the abovesaid number of cows, or a sound and healthy calf, with a golden bowl, should be given with them.

By making a gift in the preceding manner, a giver is enabled to live in heaven for as many years as there are hairs on the body of each cow, gifted away. A cow of the Kapila species, gifted away in the preceding manner, succours the souls of the relations of her giver, removed to the seventh degree in the ascending line. A cow with the head and hoofs of a yet unborn calf just issued out of the passage of parturition, should be regarded as the embodied representative of the earth goddess; and the merit of making the gift of such a one at the time, is identical with that of making a gift of the whole world. A giver of a healthy and disease-less cow, whether with or without a calf, is glorified in heaven. By shampooing the feet of a tired and travel-worn person, by nursing the sick and the poor, by worshipping the god, or by washing the holy feet of a Brahmana, one is sure to acquire the same merit as that of making the gift of a cow. A man, by making the gift of a wished-for thing (desired by the receiver himself) to a Brahman, is glorified in the region of the gods. By making gifts of lands, lamps, boiled rice, cloths, and clarified butter, a man is sure to acquire opulence in his next birth. The merit of making the gift of a house, or paddy, umbrella, garland of flowers, or of a tree, or a carriage or of clarified butter, or water, ensures an exalted position to the giver in heaven. By making the gift of Vedas, a man is translated to the region of the supreme Brahma, unattainable even by the gods. By transcribing the Vedas, Yajna Shastras or the works on Dharma Shastras even for money, a man is elevated to the beatitude of Brahmaloka. The true signification of the Vedic verses, is to be gathered at all costs, since God created the universe on the basis of the immutable Vedas (knowledge). By making the gift of a well-transcribed work on Itihasa or Puranam, a man is glorified in the region of the supreme Brahma, and becomes doubly entitled to the privileges of heaven. It is sin for a Brahmana to join in any secular topic, or to lend his ears to any scandalous gossip, or listen to a speech, made in a vulgar, or in a Mlechchha tongue. He, who though being a fit and worthy receiver of gifts, studiously avoids accepting any, acquires the same relgious merit as a maker of gifts. Water, Kusha grass, milk, sandal wood, or any kind of edible roots or leaves, need not be refused when offered, it being not anywise impious to accept a gift from a dishonest person, voluntarily made and received without asking. Anything offered by a eunuch, by a man or woman of questionable morals, as well as the one offered by one's enemy, should be unconditionally rejected, except for the purpose of celebrating any religious ceremony, or performing the obsequies of one's own father.

——:o:——

CHAPTER XCIX.

YAJNAVALKYA SAID :—Now I shall describe the process of celebrating Shraddha ceremonies for the propitiation of one's own departed manes, whereby all sins are expiated.

A day of the new moon, Ashtaka, Vriddhi (occasion of the marriage of one's son) the advent of Pretapaksha (dark fortnight in the month of Bhádra) the passing of the sun into the sign of cancer or of capricornus, receiving of any kind of excellent meat, the advent of Brahmanas well-versed in the Vedas in ones's house, the two equinoxes, the passing of the sun into a zodiacal sign, the astral combination known as Vyatipata Yoga, Gajachchaya (Maghâ trayodashi—the thirteenth day of the moon's wane marked by the asterism Maghá) a solar or a lunar eclipse, are the occasions on which a Shraddha ceremony is to be performed.

Young Shrotriya Brahmanas well-versed in Vedic lore, astrologers, Trimadhus, the three Savarna friends the sister's son, the family priest, son-in-law, the preceptor, the father-in-law, the maternal uncle, daughter's son, the disciple, the wife's brothers, and friends and relations of the deceased, the three Nachiketas, and Brahmanas who officiate at the religious sacrifices or are the keepers of the sacred fire, or practise asceticism, or are fondly devoted to their parents, or strictly conform to the rules of Brahmanism, should be alone invited on the occasion of a Shraddha ceremony. A diseased or a maimed

Brahmana, as well as one born with an additional bodily appendage, or born in the unmarried state of his mother; or the issue of her second marriage, or any wise deviated from the execution of his true Brahminical duties, or ungodly (*lit.*, having no faith in the god Vishnu) in his conduct should not be invited on the occasion of a Shraddha ceremony. The Brahmanas, eligible to be present in the ceremony, should be invited on the day, previous to its celebration through other Brahmanas.

Then on the occasion of the ceremony, the performer of a Shraddha, should first humbly ask the invited Brahmanas to be seated in their respective seats, and then with his blended palms entreat them to arrange themselves in the following order, *viz.*, two Brahmanaas before the vessel containing offerings for the gods, with their faces turned towards the east, and three before the vessels containing offerings for the performer's departed manes and with their faces turned towards the north. Similar disposition of Brahmanas, should be made in respect of the vessels containing offerings for the performer's maternal ancestors. Then after having offered water to the Pitris for washing their hands with, and cushions of kusha blades to seat upon, the performer, with the permission of the Brahmanas officiating at the ceremoney, would invoke the presence of his departed manes in it, by reciting the proper Mantras, and scatter barley grains over the vessels containing the sacred knots of kusha grass (Pavitram). After that he shall offer water to the Brahmanas by reciting the "Shannodevi" etc., Mantra, barley grains by reciting the one, beginning with "Yavosi" etc., Mantra. Then with the permission of the Brahmanas, he shall invoke the presence of his departed manes in the ceremony by reciting the Mantra, running as "Ayantu nah Pitara" (Come, O our fathers) etc., by whirling his right hand over his head from the left. In offering Arghas to the Pitris, sesamame seed should be used instead of barley grains, and the performer of the ceremony shall then meditate upon their divine selves.

Then the vessel containing the offering for the Pitris shall be bent by reciting the Mantra running as "Pitribhyoh Sthanam-asi." Then boiled rice, soaked with clarified butter, should be taken in hand, and the permission of the Pitris should be obtained by reciting the Mantra, running as "Agnow Ķarishye," etc., after which the Gayatri Mantra and the one running as Madhuvátá, etc.,' should be thrice recited over it. Then after having recited the Mantra running as Yathásukham Vakjatah Sada (stay silently for a while as you please) etc., the performer of a Shráddha should mentally recite the sacred Mantras for a while during which period the Pitris should be contemplated as partaking of the oblations of boiled rice offered to them.

The performer should offer the Havishya oblations to his fathers, if desired, in an ungrudging spirit. He should mentally repeat the name of God or any other sacred Mantra, until the Pitris would finish their meal, and then recite the benedictory Vedic Verses, running as Madhu Vátá ritáyaté (may the sweet wind blow over the land), etc., and scatter the dedicated boiled rice over the ground by reciting the "Om, Triptah Stha" (Be you appeased) Mantra. After that, oblations of boiled rice, mixed with sesame seeds, should be offered near the vessel containing the refuge of the meals of the Pitris, the offerer looking towards the South at the time. Oblations should be thus offered to the souls of one's grandfather and great grandfather, both in the paternal and the maternal lines; and the rite of oblations should be closed by offering Achamaniyam (water for rinsing the mouth) to them.

A Brahmana shall utter the term "Svasti" in connection with all acts done by him in course of the ceremony, after which the Akshayyas should be given, and the Brahmanas officiating at the ceremony, should be remunerated with Dakshinas, as his means would admit of. Then he would ask the permission of the Brahmanas for uttering "Svâdha" with a recitation of the Mantra running as "Svadham Vachayishey" and the Brahmanas would express their consent thereto by uttering "Vachyatam" (speak out.) Then the sacred knot of the Kusha grass (Pavitram) should be untied with the permission of the Brahmanas, by reciting "Pitribhyah Svadhochatyâm," and he should sprinkle water over the ground with a similar permission of theirs with the Mantra "Om, Ashta Svadhâ." Then having again sprinkled water over the ground in accompaniment of the Mantra running as "Vishvédevah Priyantâm, etc. (May the Vishvédevâs be pleased with the ceremony), he should recite the one beginning with "Dâtaro Noh Abhivarddhantâm" (May our givers enjoy greater prosperity), whereupon the Brahmanas would reply "OM, Astu" (OM, be it so). Then the performer of the ceremony, would devoutly make an obeisance to the Brahmanas and dismiss them with sweet words. Then the Brahmanas in connection with the vessels known as the Pitri pâtras, etc., would be bidden adieu to by reciting the Mantra running as "Vajé," "Vajé," etc. Then the lid or the cover of the Pitri pâtra containing the Argha-sprinkled water, should be removed, and the performer would sprinkle a few drops thereof, and bid them (Brahmanas) farewell as before. He should circumbulate the ground or the site of the ceremony, and take the resdiue of the oblations dedicated to his manes. Both he and his wife, would practise a vow of continence for the night.

A Shrâddha ceremony, should be performed on the occasion of a marriage in the house in the aforesaid manner, with the exception that the term "Nândimukha" should be appended to the name of each of the performer's departed manes, and the oblations containing Vadari fruits, should be offered to them.

In a rite of Ekoddishta Shrâddhha, the vessel of oblation

known as the Daivapâtram, should be omitted, and the Pavitras, made of a single blade of Kusba grass, should be used. It is further distinguished by the absence of all invocation and "Agnoukaranam" rites, which should be performed with the upper sheet or garment (uttariya) being placed on the right shoulder of the performer (Apasavyavat). The Akshayyas (threads) should be given in the present rite by saying "Upatishtatâm" (Be pleased to get up) while the Brahmanas should be bidden adieu to by crying "Abhiramyatâm," whereupon the Brahmanas would say "Abhiramasva."

In a Sapindikarana ceremony, perfumed water containing sesame seeds, should be placed in four vessels at the time of offering the Argha, and one of them should be exclusively dedicated to the use of the Préta (departed mane for the salvation of whose soul the ceremony is performed). After that, the oblations and offerings offered to the latter (Préta) should be divided, by reciting the two Mantras beginning with "Ya Samâna," etc., and then mixed with those offered to the souls of the performer's grandfather. The forms of Shrâddha, known as Ekoddhista and Pârvana, jointly constitute what is known as Sapindikaranam.

Rice with pitchers, full of water, should be offered to the soul of a departed ancestor at the close of the year in the event of the Sapindakarana Shrâddha, it being performed within it. The oblations offered to one's departed manes in the course of a Shrâddha, should be given over to a cow, or to a goat, or to a Brahmana for eating at the close of the ceremony, or they should be cast in fire or water. The satisfaction resulting from a Shrâddha ceremny performed with Havishya (sun-dried rice boiled with any vegetable, and soaked with clarified butter) or with Pâyasha (sweetened porridge) in honour of one's departed manes, lasts them for a year, while the pleasure incidental to the performance of one with fish, or venison or mutton or Shakula fish, or goat's flesh, or with the flesh of a Prishata or an Ena or a Ruru (different families of deer), or of a boar, or of a hare, successively endures for a month more, in the order of enumeration.

A Shraddha ceremony should be celebrated each year, on the thirteenth day of the moon's wane marked by the asterism (lunar mansion) Magha. A Shraddha ceremony should be likewise performed each day, in honor of one's departed manes from the first day of the dark fortnight to its close (day of the new moon) in the month of Bhadra, known in the Sanskrit calendar as Pretapaksha (when the departed Manes are supposed to visit the earth), the benefit of such peformances being the birth of a daughter in the performer's family. Shraddha ceremonies for the salvation of souls who had quitted the world in consequence of any cut, blow or sword-thurst, should be celebrated on the fourteenth day of the moon's wane, in virtue of which the performer would be rewarded with wealth, offspring and valour in this life. By duly performing a Shraddha ceremony in honor of his departed manes, a performer is enabled to live a long life in the full possession of a good name, and a sound bodily health, suffers no bereavement in life, and attains an elevated status in the world to come. Knowledge spreads her store to such a man, the goddess of wealth pours down plenty over his fields, filling his chests and coffers with all sorts of precious metal, and the number of his cattle swells by daily additions. A similar benefit is derived from celebrating a Shraddha ceremony under the auspicies of any of the three asterisms (lunar mansion) calculated from the Krittika. The Pitris of a Brahmana, who performs a Shraddha ceremony with new water (water of the rainy season) or with newly harvested rice, confer upon him the blessings of longevity, fatherhood, opulence, erudition and sovereignity in this life, and a residence in heaven, and even salvation, after death in return.

—:0:—

CHAPTER C.

YAJNAVALKYA said :—Now hear me describe the symptoms which are exhibited in a person, struck by the malignant influence of a Vinayaka. The afflicted person dreams of water and fancies in dreams that he has been bathing in a lake or pool. The patient pines away in sorrow and silence, and all his undertakings end in dismal failures. A king under the influence of a Vinayaka, loses his sovereignty, a virgin cannot secure a husband, and a matron continues sterile or is deprived of the blessings of motherhood. The remedy consists in a ceremonial ablution effected in the following manner :—

The body of the patient should be first rubbed with a compound consisting of white mustard seeds and sandal wood pasted together with the admixture of clarified butter, his head being plastered with a paste of the drugs, known as Sarvoushadhi and Savagandha. Then he should be seated on a platform, as is generally raised on the occasion of a religious sacrifice; and the Brahmanas shall be asked to recite benedictory Mantras over his person. Then four earthen pitchers, all of the same colour, and filled with water fetched from the same lake or natural reservoir of water, and saturated with Rochona (yellow pigment), sandal paste, and Guggulu (aromatic gum resin) should be emptied over his head, the patient being seated on a red leather cushion, and the Brahmanas chanting the following Mantras at the time :— "We bathe thee with water which has been purified by the Sun-God and the Holy Sages. May the purifying element in the water, imparted to it by their sacred touch, cleanse thy spirit. May the gods Varuna, Indra, the Sun, the Wind, the concourse of the seven Holy Sages, as well as the Jupiter and the sacred person of the king, give back to thee thy lost splendour and fortune. May the ill fate which clings to thy hairs, forelock, head, temples, ears and eyes, be hereby dispelled and washed away." After that, mustard oil should be poured over his head and in his ears, and a Homa should be performed in the fire of lighted Kusha blades soaked with clarified butter, and held over his head. Libations of clarified butter, surcharged with powdered turmeric, should be subsequently cast in the sacrificial fire in honor of the gods, known as Kushmanda and Rajputra, by appending the term Svaha (obeisance) to their respective names, each time they are invoked in the course of the ceremony. Then blades of Kusha grass should be spread over a place where four roads meet, and the votary or the priest officiating at the ceremony, should sit upon them with a tray on his head, containing both ripe and unripe grains of rice, sweet-scented flowers of beautiful colours, the three kinds of wine, curd, sweet porridge, boiled rice, clarified butter, treacle and sweetmeats, and worship the goddess Amvica in that posture with blended palms and in a devout spirit. He shall dedicate those offerings to the goddess, and pray as follows:—"Grant me the boons of beauty and fame, O goddess, and make me happy in the delights of fatherhood."

Gifts of white cloths and white sandal pastes should be made to the Brahmanas at the close of the worship, and the spiritual preceptor of the patient's family, should be appeared with the gift of a pair of cloths, and the tutelary deities of the planets should also be propitiated with a worship.

—:o:—

CHAPTER CI.

YAJNAVALKYA said:—It is incumbent on a person, cast under the malignant influences of hostile planets, to celebrate a religious sacrifice for their propitiation, which is called a Grahayajna, and which a man, in quest of earthly prosperity and peace in life, shall do well to perform. The learned have designated the planets as the Sun, the Moon, the Mars, the Mercury, the Jupiter, the Venus, the Saturn, and the Nodes, both ascending and descending (Rahu and Ketu); and their respective malignant influences entail the wearing of copper, Indian bell metal, crystal, red sandalwood, gold, silver, iron, lead and Indian bell metal, by persons struck with them, on their bodies.

Now hear me, O holy sages, describe the respective colours of the aforesaid planets. The Sun is red; the Moon; white, the Mars, red; the Mercury and the Jupiter, yellowish; and the Venus, white; all the rest being black.

A person struck by the malignant influence of any of the planets, should be bathed with water containing bits of the metal, specifically held sacred to it, and libations of clarified butter surcharged with its particles should be likewise cast in the sacrificial fire in honour of its tutelary god. Offerings of gold, cloth and flowers, should be made to the antagonistic planet, and the worship should be conducted with flowers, perfumes, edibles and burning incense-sticks made of aromatic gum resin. The tutelary gods of the planets, as well as their subordinates, should be worshipped by reciting the Mantras respectively held sacred to them. The Rik running as "Akrishnnaa Rajasa," should be chanted during the worship of the Sun-God, the one beginning with "Imam Deva," etc., should be recited in worshipping the Moon-God. The Mars should be invoked by reciting the Vedic verse, running as "Agnimurdha," etc., while the Mercury should be addressed with the one beginning with "Udbudhyasva," etc. The Rik running as "Vrihaspati," etc., shall be chanted on the occasion of a worship of the Jupiter, and the Mantra of "Anyat," etc., on that of the worship of the Venus. The Saturn should be invoked by reciting the Rik running as "Shannodevi," etc., while the Nodes should be respectively addressed with the verses running as "Kayayana" etc., and "Kranvana etc."

The twigs of such sacrificial trees or plants such as the Arka, the Palasha, the Khadira, the Apamarga, the Pippala, the Oudumvara, the Shami, and Durva and Kusha blades, soaked with curd, honey and clarified butter, should be respectively cast in the sacrificial fire, in Homa ceremonies celebrated for the propitiation of the planets, such as the Sun etc., "Treacle and boiled rice, Payasa, Havishyannam (sun-dried rice cooked with any sacred vegetables and soaked with butter), boiled rice mixed with milk condensed and sweetened by boiling, curd with boild rice, clarified butter, cakes, cooked meat and Vichitrannam (some thing like our modern Pilaos) should be respectively dedicated as offerings to the planets beginning with the Sun. A cow, a conchshell, an ox, gold, a cloth, a horse, a black cow, iron and a goat, are the Dakshinas (honorarium), which should be paid to the Brahmanas officiating at the ceremonies respectively celebrated for the propitiation of the Sun, the Moon, the Mars, the Mercury, the Jupiter, the Venus, the Saturn and the Nodes. Even a king may derive many benefits from worshipping the planets.

——:o:——

CHAPTER CII.

YAJNAVALKYA said :—Hear me, O you holy sages, enumerate the duties of a householder, entering the life of a hermit at the close of his wordly career (Vanaprastha Dharma).

Having left his wife in the charge of his son, or in her company a householder, retired from the affairs of the world, shall enter the forest, and live the life of a forest-dwelling hermit (Vanaprastha). Putting his senses under perfect control, and banishing all procreative desires from his mind, he shall be a custodian of the sacred fire, revere the Brahmanas who shall belong to his own cult of fire worship, be hospitable to his guests, and propitiate his departed Manes with the celebration of Pitriyajnas. Self-controlled, he shall not attend to the embellishment of his own person, wear long hairs, and please or endear himself to his own servants. Accepting neither gifts nor charities, he shall refrain from pursuing all sorts of worldly pursuits, and live contented and happy in perfect mastery over his own self. Once only in a day or a month, he shall bestir himself about procuring the necessaries of life, and pass his time in meditation and goodly thoughts, wishing and doing good to all. He shall sleep on the bare ground, and all his acts shall be shaped to the fruition of one grand desire, *viz.*, the expansion of his spiritual self. Never angry, and ever contented, he shall practise Yoga amidst the fires (with blazing logs of wood on four sides and the Sun over head) in summer, in an open plain during the rains, and in wet clothes in winter.

—:0:—

CHAPTER CIII.

YAJNAVALKYA said :—Hear me, O you, the foremost of beings, narrate the duties of a Bhikshu (mendicant friar).

Having returned from the forest and performed the religious sacrifice, known as the Sarva-Veda Dakshinika, he shall celebrate a Prajapatya Vratam. Then humble, self-controlled, and doing good to all, he shall abstract the divine energy from the sacrificial fire and assimilate it in his own self. Now he shall be considered fit to reside in a village, living on alms voluntarily offered. Otherwise he shall stir abroad in the evening without any of the paraphernalia of begging, which characterise a common mendicant, and live contented on what will be obtained in a single stroll. He shall carry his bowl of gourd (Kamandula) and his Tridanda staff with him. He shall beg for the barest necessaries of life, and not out of any motive for gain. By practiseing self-control and regulation of breath, etc., a Bhikshu may attain the elevation of a Paramhansa, and ultimately emancipate his self at the completion of his Yoga. By practising Yoga and moderation in diet, a Bhikshu may acquire an elevated status after death. Even a householder may emancipate his self by dint of wisdom, hospitality and charity.

—:o:—

CHAPTER CIV.

YAJNAVALKYA said :—The soul of a sinner, after enduring the pangs of hell, is necessitated to revert to the lower plain of animal existence, and to incarnate in succession therein till the final extinction of the effects of his prior sinful acts. The killer of a Brahmana, after passing through the bodies of a dog, an ass and a camel, in succession, shall again work up its way to the plane of human life, and shall be born deaf and dumb in his first incarnation therein. A stealer of gold, shall take birth as a worm or an insect in his next existence. A person defiling the bed of his own preceptor or superior, shall vegetate as a blade of grass in his next incarnation. A killer of a Brahmana will be afflicted with an attack of Pthysis in his next life, a gold-stealer will have black teeth, and one seducing the wife of one's own preceptor, will have an attack of whitlow in his next birth. He who steals food-grain in this life, will be deprived of food in his next, while he who breaks the music at a duet, will be born dumb in his next existence. A grain-stealer is born with an additional limb, and is tormented with a fœtid smell in his nostrils, and a crooked nature, which can not bear the good fortune of others. An oil-stealer will be born as an insect known as oil worm in his next life, or as a mean, malicious person with fetour in his mouth. Those who have auspicious marks on their persons, will be rich and happy, while the opposite may be predicted of those possessed of contrary features.

—:o:—

CHAPTER CV.

YAJNAVALKYA said :—For commission of heinous and infamous acts, and omission of doing what is good and commendable, a person is sure to be condemned to the torments of hell. An unbridled gratification of the senses paves one's way to the gates of hell. Hence rites of expiation should be performed both for the cleansing of the spirit and the body. A performance of any expiatory rite restores the lost good name of its performer in society, and brings on that secret joy in the mind which is the true criterion of a reclaimed spirit. A non-repenting sinner, or the one not atoning for past iniquities with the performance of a proper expiatory rite, is sure to be doomed to the pangs of any of the different confines of hell, which are respectively known as Mahá-Rouravam, Támisram, Hansavanam, Lohitodakam, Sanjivana, Nadipatham, Mahá-Nilyayam, Kákolam, Andha Támisram, Avichi and Kumbhipákam, the doors of which are guarded by iron bolts and which are full of fœtid exhalations.

A wine-drinker, or an assaulter of the sacred person of a Brahmana, or a gold-stealer, or a person defiling the bed of, or calumniating, his own spiritual preceptor, as well as the one who speaks lightly of the Vedas, commits the same sin, both as regards extent and atrocity, as the killer of a Brahmana. By eating a food prohibited in the Shastras, by doing any thing low and deceitful, by kissing the lips of a woman in her menses, one commits the same sin as that which originates from the use of wine. The sin, which is attached to the stealing of a horse, is identical in all respects with what is committed by a theft of gold. By going unto the wife of a friend, or on a virgin daughter of one's own loins, or unto a girl of lowcaste, or unto a woman of one's own consanguinity, or unto a sister of one's own father or mother, or unto the wife of one's own maternal uncle, or by visiting the bed of one's own sister, or by living with a sister or a co-wife of one's own mother, or with the daugher or wife of one's own preceptor, one commits the same sin which is attached to the defilement of the bed of a preceptor. The male offending party should be killed by cutting off his genitals, as well as his female accomplice, if found to be a willing party to the incest under the circumstance.

The following sinful acts, *viz.*, cow-killing, robbing of a Brahmana, non-repayment of one's debts, and non-discharge of one's monitary obligations, non-keeping of the sacred fire by a Brahmana, or his engaging in any sort of trade or merchandise, marriage by a younger brother in the unmarried state of his elder, tutelage under one's own servant, or acceptance of any gift from him, going unto another man's wife, negotiation of the marriage of a younger brother before that of his elder, creating a breach among friends and relations for money, tuition for pecuniary considerations, sale of salt, murdering of a Kshatriya, Vaishya or a regenerated Shudra, infamous livelihood, misappropriation by a man of any property held in trust, breaking of a vow, selling of meat roasted on a gird iron, or of a cow, abandoning by one of one's own parents, selling of tanks, gardens, etc., dedicated to the use of the community, giving of one's daughter in marriage with a Parivinda (a younger brother marrying in the unmarried state of his elder), officiating as a priest in a religious ceremony celebrated by a person charged with the preceding guilt, selling by one of the ornaments of one's own daughter given her by her husband or friends, following of a crooked path in life, an attempt at defiling a religious vow or a penance of another, undertaking of any act for one's sole and exclusive benefit, drinking of any spirituous liquor, seduction of another man's wife, renunciation of the study of the holy Vedas, desertion of one's sons and relations, abandonment of the sacred fire, perusal of immoral literature, and selling of one's sons and wives, are included within the category of Upapatakas (minor moral delinquencies).

Now hear me describe the mode of performing the proper expiatory rites for the atonement of sins, enumerated before.

The killer of a Brahmana shall live on a spare diet, taking only as much food as is absolutely necessary for bare subsistence and roam about for a continuous period of twelve years, bearing a human skull on his head, and thereby making a contrite confession of his grave and unmitigated sin to the world at large. Paying no heed to the embellishment of his person and expressing the sincerest repentance both by his mind and mein, he shall not think of shaving himself and cast libations of clarified butter in the sacrificial fire by reciting the Mantra running as "Somebhyo Svaha," or in the accompaniment of the Mantras, sacred to the god Skanda. The sin which is attached to the killing of a Brahmana, may be expiated in the preceding manner. The sin which is incidental to the killing of a bird or a cow unsuspiciously reposing in a bush or a forest, though killed at the instance and for the benefit of, a Brahmana, is atoned for by reciting all the Mantras contained in the three Vedas, in the gloom of a lonely forest, or by worshipping the goddess Sarasvati (Minerva of the Hindu pantheon) and by making money-gifts to any worthy receiver of public munificence.

The sin, which is attached to the killing of a Kshatriya or a Vaishya while engaged in celebrating a religious sacrifice, may be atoned for by doing the same penances, as enjoined in the case of killing a Brahmana. The sin which is incidental to bringing about the abortion of a pregnant woman, may be expiated by doing a penance which is laid down in respect of an act of destroying a fœtus or a child of the same caste. The man engaged for the purpose, or one attempting to bring about such a miscarriage, shall perform a penance every way similar to the preceding one, even when the attempt will prove abortive. The sin which is attached to the killing of a Brahmana, while engaged in a rite of ceremonial ablution at the close of a religious sacrifice, may be atoned for by doing over again the penance previously enjoined in that behalf. A Brahmana who has wilfully taken any wine or spirituous liquor, shall expiate his sin by attempting self-immolation with potions of flame-coloured wine, water, cow's urine and clarified butter, or shall grow long hairs and pèrform, in tattered rags, the penances laid down in connection with an act of Brahmana-slaughter. All the Brahmanical rites such as those of tonsure, investiture of the holy thread, etc., should be done unto him after his purification through the performance of proper penances. A Brahmana woman polluted with any spirituous drink, or defiled by drinking semen or urine, is sure to be ousted of the eternal heaven of female chastity (Patiloka) and to reincarnate in the shape of a she-vulture, or as a sow or a bitch on earth. The expiation in the case of a Brahmana gold-stealer, consists in his being cudgled to death by his king with a club, voluntarily given by him to the latter with an express entreaty for the purpose, after having made a free and full confession of his own guilt, or in the alternative, he shall purchase his atonement by making a gift of gold of his own weight. A man ravishing a woman by taking advantage of her sleep in a lonely bed and chamber, shall atone for his crime by voluntarily cutting off his genitals and throwing them in the southwest quarter of the sky. A man defiling the bed of his preceptor, or going unto a woman bearing to him a relation-ship included within the category of Gurupatni previously described, shall expiate his sin with the performance of a Chándráyana penance, or with a continuous recitation of the Veda Sanhitas for an unbroken period of three months. A cow-killer, protected by the absence of any deliberate motive for the crime, shall practise self-control for a month, sharing the same shed with the cows, and leading them to pasturage, and drink by way of expiation the sacred compound, known as the Panchagavyam (*lit.*, the five things obtained from a cow, consisting of milk, curd clarified butter, cow's wine and cow-dung-serum). All crimes included within the list of Upapatakas (minor sins) may be expiated by performing a Chândráyana-Vrata, or by living on a milk-regime for a month, or by practising a Paraka-Vrata.

The sin, which is attached to the killing of a Kshatriya (a member of the military caste), may be atoned for by making the gift of a full-grown heifer with a thousand of young and healthy cows, or by doing for three years a penance enjoined to be performed for his expiation by a Brahmana-killer. Its duration shall be curtailed to one year only in the case of a person, who has killed a member of the trading community (Vaishya), whereas only a six months' practice of the penance, or a gift of ten cows, shall be the proper atonement for an act of killing a Shudra. A man who has accidentally killed his own good and unoffending wife, shall practise expiatory penances, as laid down in the immediately preceding instance.

The killer of a cat, or a lizard or a mongoose, or a toad, shall live on the milk regime for three days in sucession, or shall practise a Krichchha Vrata penance in addition thereto. The sin of killing an elephant, may be atoned for by making the gift of five blue-coloured heifers and a white calf of two years of age to a Brahmana. A gift of a single ox, will expiate the sin of one's killing a sheep, or an ass, or a goat, while in the case of a heron-killing (Crouncha) the animal of gift shall be a healthy calf of three years of age. The sin of tearing or uprooting a plant, or a shrub or a creeper, shall be expiated by mentally repeating a hundred Riks, while a Brahmacharin (a person who has taken the vow of celibacy) going unto a woman and thereby breaking his vow, shall touch an ass by way of atonement. The sin of eating a diet of honey and meat, may be expiated by practising a Krichchha Vrata or any other similar penance. In the death of a messenger in a foreign country, or at his destination, the sender of the message, or the person at whose instance he has been sent, shall practise the three penances designated with the term Krichchha An act of disobedience or insubordination to one's preceptor, is atoned for by doing his pleasure. The sin which results from doing an injury to one's enemy, is expiated by making a gift of paddies to the latter, or by winning his good graces in a friendly and affectionate discourse, after having banished all hostile and uncharitable feelings from the mind. Death is the only atonement for a Brahmana, found guilty of ingratitude, or of repaying good by evil. An utterer of falsehood or indecent language, shall live in perfect continence and practise self-control for a month, passing his time in a solitary place and without asking for food of any body. A man, going unto his brother's wife without any appointment from her husband, shall practise a Chándráyana penance. A person, going unto a woman in her menses, is purified by taking a draught of clarified butter at the end of a three days' fast. The sin of accepting a gift at the hand of an evil or a dishonest giver, is atoned for by his constantly repeating the Gáyatri Mantra, for a month in a cowshed or pasturage, and in perfect mastery over his senses. Three Krichchha Vratas should be performed for the expiation of the sin, incidental to the failure of a member of any twice-born order to be invested with the holy thread at the proper time (Vrátya), and a Brahmana, officiating at any religious ceremony undertaken by or on behalf of such person, shall do the same. The sin which originates from one's forsaking and deserting a person, who has asked one's protection, shall be atoned for by reading the Vedas to the best of his ability. A man while riding in a carriage drawn by an ass or a camel, shall thrice control his respiration in the manner of a Pránáyáma. A man, who has gone unto a woman in the day time, shall expiate his sin by bathing naked in a pool or a lake. The sin which is incidental to reprimanding one's elders or preceptors, as well as that which results from using abusive language towards a Brahmana, may be atoned for by regaining their favour, and observing a fast for a single day. A man aiming a blow at a Brahmana shall expiate his guilt by practising a Krichchha Vrata, while the expiation shall consist in the performance of the one known as Atikrichchha Vrata in the case of actual assault and battery.

The circumstances of the guilt, as well as the age, and physical capacity of a sinner, should be taken into consideration in determining the nature of his expiatory rite. Wilful miscarriage of a fœtus, and speaking ill of her husband, are the acts which degrade a woman, whose very presence should be shunned from a distance. A person of notorious guilt shall do his penances of atonement at a public place, and in conformity with the injunctions of his preceptor, while an atonement for a sin which has not got any publicity, shall be done in private. A killer of a Brahmana shall fast and recite the "Aghamarshana Shuktam" for three days standin water, after which he shall make the gift of a milch cow with milk. Then he shall recite the Rik beginning as "Obeisance to Soma," observing a fast on the day following, and cast forty times libations of clarified butter in the sacrificial fire, while standing in water. A wine-drinker or a stealer of gold shall fast for three days, recite the Mantra sacred to the god Rudra, and cast libations of clarified butter in the fire by chanting the KushmÂnda Mantra. A sin unwittingly committed by a Brahmana, as well as the one which he is unconscious of, is atoned for by his regularly attending to his Sandhya, thrice each day, whereas a sin may be expiated by reciting eleven times the RudrÂdhyÂya. The sin of defiling the bed of one's own preceptor may be expiated by mentally repeating the "Sahasra Shirsha" Mantra, whereas a sin of whatsoever denomination may be atoned for by practising PrÂnÂyÂma for a hundred times.

A person inadvertently taking any semen, urine or feculent matter, shall fast for the day, and drink water consecrated with the GÂyatri Mantra in the evening. No sin can assail the divine self of a Brahmana who has subjugated his senses, and lives in divine peace and contentment, daily reciting the holy

Vedas, and practising the five religious sacrifices, enjoined to be performed by a householder (Pancha-Yajna). All sins other than the one incidental to the killing of a Brahmana, are expiated by mentally repeating the Gâyatri Mantra for a thousand times. Practice of Brahmacharyya (continence), pity, contentment, contemplation, truthfullness, sincerity, annihilation of all killing propensities, non-stealing, sweetness of temperament and subjugation of senses, constitute what is technically known as Yama (self-control). Ablution, vow of silence, fasting, performance of religious sacrifices, reading of the Vedas, self-control, practice of austerities, non-irascibility, devotion to preceptors, and cleanliness, constitute what is called Niyama. A Brahmana, practising a Krichchha Santapana Vratam shall live on a milk regime on the first day, on curd on the second day, on cow's urine on the third, on cowdung on the fourth, and on clarified butter on the fifth, and fast on the sixth day, breaking the vow on the seventh. A vow practised for a week in the preceding manner is called the Mahâ-Santâpanam Vratam. In a vow of Parna-Krichchha, the observer shall successively live on the leaves of Oudumvara, Rajiva, and Vilva trees and on the washings of Kusha grass on the fifth. In the penance known as the Tapta Krichchham, the practiser shall successively live on warm milk, clarified butter, and water, observing a fast on the day of its close. A Pada-Krichchha Vratam consists in living on a single meal at day on the first day, on a single meal at night, obtained without asking, on the second day, followed by a day of fast. Any of the preceding penances practised for a thrice as much period, constitutes what is technically known as a Prajapatya, which may be converted into a Krichchhati-Krichchham, by its practiser's living on a palmful of water each day instead of the diet enjoined to be taken during the time by the scriptures. A continuous fasting for twelve days, constitutes what is called the Paraka Vratam. A diet of Pinyaka, Whey and powdered barley alternated with fast, constitutes what is called a Krichchha-Sáma, which being extended to a period of fifteen days, is called a Tulápurusha. A morsel of food to the size of a hen's egg, should be increased by one from the first day of the light fortnight to the day of the full moon, decreasing by the same number each day from the commencement of the dark one to the day of the new moon. This is what is known as Chándráyana Vrata.

Now hear me describe another mode of practising the same (Chándráyana) Vrata. The practiser of the penance shall thrice bathe each day, observing a regimen of diet as in the preceding case, recite the sacred Mantras, take morsels of food consecrated by reciting the Gayatri Mantra. A Chándráyana Vrata is the atonement for sins of all kinds and characters, and its performer is purified both in his body and spirit and goes to the region presided over by the Moon-God in the event of his undertaking the same out of a purely religious motive. A man practising a Krichchha Vrata for a similar purpose is rewarded with a boundless wealth.

——:o:——

CHAPTER CVI.

YAJNAVALKYA said:—O you, who are masters in the art of self-control, now hear me describe the funeral rites to be gone through in respect of the dead, according to the difference in age and social order. A dead child, who has been dead before completing his second year, should be buried instead of being cremated, and no sort of S'raddha or Udaka-kriyá (offering of libations of water to a departed spirit) is necessary in that case. The friends or relatives of a child, dead after completing its second year of life, shall carry its corpse to the cremation ground and exhume it in fire by mentally reciting the Yama Suktam. The relatives of a deceased person related to him within the seventh or tenth degree of consanguinity on the father's side, shall perform the rite of Udaka-kriyá with their faces turned towards the south, which rule shall be extended to include the funeral rite of one's departed maternal grandfather or preceptor's wife. Libations of water should be offered to the departed spirits of one's friend, son, father-in-law and sister's son, by mentioning their name and Gotra (spiritual clanship) in life. The rite of Udaka-kriyá in these cases is optional, and its non-observance does not entail any moral delinquency. A rite of Udaka-kriyá is forbidden in the case of a Brahmacharin, or of a degraded or sinful person, which in the case of a wife, dead after breaking her vow of chastity in life, is optional. The death of a suicide or of a wine-drinker, should not be mourned for, nor the rites of Udaka-kriyâ, etc., should be done unto their spirits. The death of any friend or relation or that of any man should not be mourned, nor should one indulge in an obstinate grief therefor, since life on earth is but transitory at the best. Having performed his funeral rites and paid the last honour to his earthly remains, the friends of a deceased person shall return to the house he has left behind for good, tear the leaves of a Nimva tree, and cross the threshold after having purified themselves with the touch of fire, cowdung, and white mustard seeds, perceded by acts of Achamanam. They shall strike their feet against a stone slab before entering the house. Similar procedure should be observed by all who might have touched the corpse, while the mere onlookers of the scene would be purified then and there without undertaking any religious ceremony for the purpose. The friends and consanguinous relations of a deceased person should be considered unclean till before their ablutions at the close of the funeral ceremony and until they would go through the necessary rites of Sanyama (self-control) in connection with the event. Returned from the cremation ground, they shall pass the day or night on fares purchased at a shop or a market, and lie down on the bare floor or ground, apart from one another. The performer of the incidental funeral sacrifice, shall offer oblations of boiled rice to the departed spirit for three successive days, for whose benefit an earthen vessel containing milk diluted with water, shall be as well kept in the open, during the period. The spirit should be invoked and worshipped in a lonely bower, and ceremonial rites (S'raddha, etc.,) enjoined in the S'rutis in that behalf, should be performed for his salvation.

The period of uncleanness in connection with the death of a child, expired before cutting its teeth, lasts for that day only, that incidental to the demise of one who has departed this life before attaining the age of tonsure, is one day and night, which extends to three days in the case of a boy who has been dead before attaining the proper age of taking the Brahminical vow (investiture with the sacred thread), while the death of a boy after that age entails a period of uncleanness for ten days in the case of a Brahmana. Persons standing in Sapinda relationship with the deceased, shall be deemed unclean for ten days after the occurrence, while those bearing only Sagotra relationship to him, shall so continue for three days (if Brahmanas). Both these kinds of relations shall be considered as clean on the very day of the event in the case of the death of the child happening before the completion of its second year of earthly existence, and only its mother shall bide the full time of uncleanness. In the case of two deaths ocurring successively in one's family (the second happening within the period of uncleanness entailed by the first) the period of uncleanness shall expire with the one resulting in consequence of the second without necessitating the observance of two full terms of uncleanness in sucession. The period of uncleanness incidental to the birth or death of a child of any cognate relation of a Brahmana, or of a Kshatriya or of a Vaishya, or of a S'udra, is ten days, twelve days, fifteen days and thirty days respectively.

Cleanness in connection with the death of a male infant or of an unmarried daughter, is restored on the expiry of a single day after the event. The period of uncleanness in connection with the death of one's preceptor, companion, maternal uncle, king, or of a son not of one's own loins, or of one's wife who has known another person, as well as that incidental to the death of a S'rotriya (a Brahmana well-versed in the S'rutis), or of one who has completed the study of his Védâ with its kindred branches of study, is one day only. The relations of a person, who has suffered death in execution of the sentence of a king or of a king's court, or killed by any horned cattle, or has committed suicide in private or by taking poison, shall not bide any period of uncleanness in consequence thereof. Uncleanness incidental to the death of a person addicted to the performance of a religious sacrifice, or while observing a religious vow, or of a Brahmacharin or a practiser of charities, or of a knower of the Supreme Brahma, or of one expiring while engaged in making gifts or celebrating a religious sacrifice, or fallen in battle or in a civic disturbance or political revolution, or killed by an act of God, shall expire on the very day of the occurrence. Fire, Time, good deeds, earth, air, Mind, knowledge, Meditation (divine) Repentence, fasting and practice of religious penances (Tapas) are the sources of all expiation and purification (cleansing) as the case may be. Charity is the atonement for all misdeeds and a river is purified by its current.

A Brahmana in distress, as well as the one fallen on evil days, may earn his livelihood by doing the office of a Kshatriya (a member of the military caste) or of a Vaishya (trader). One thus living by trade or merchandise, shall not sell any fruit, Soma, silk cloth (Kshouma), salt, edible shrub, curd, thickened milk, clarified butter, water, sesamum, boiled rice, mercury, alkaline preparation, honey, shellac. Aconite, requisites for a Homa ceremony, cloth, stone, wine, salads, earth (clay), leather-shoes, deer-skin, blanket, salt, flesh, levigated paste of any oil-seeds, edible roots or perfumes, however, may be sold for money only for religious purposes (celebration of a religious sacrifice, etc.,) in exchange of paddy and sesamum seeds. Even in most abject penury, a Bráhmana shall rather live by agriculture than engage in selling salt, and shall make it a religion never to sell a horse under whatsoever circumstance in life. Even in the absence of any means of livelihood, a Bráhmana shall fast for three days and abide by the decision of the king of the country regarding the choice of any new profession.

——:o:——

CHAPTER CVII.

SUTA said :—The holy Parâs'ara narrated to Vyasa the duties of the different social orders. Change is the law of the universe, and in each cycle the earth passes through the successive phases of origin, and decay, but the birthless ones (Vishnu, etc.,) suffer no modifications. The S'rutis, (*lit.*, things heard, are spiritual truths transmitted orally from generation to generation), Smritis (*lit* :—things remembered, are the unwritten laws of conduct, etc., subsequently collected into codes,) and the good institutions have their origin in the holy Védâs. It was Brahmá who first revealed the inspired rhapsodies of the Védás to the world at large, and the divine lawgivers of old, such as Manu etc, were the authors of the Dharma S'ástras (Institutes or Codes of Law, both moral and positive). Charity is the only virtue which would be practised in the cycle of Kali, and the votaries of all others would be scarce therein. Hence it is the only one virtue which should be practised for the redemption of human nature in that iron age. The kingdom of evil would come and vice would reign supreme on earth. Curses would take effect within one year of their making (giving). A pious conduct and a pure character would be the passport to all those merits in that age, which could have been secured only with the practice of the most austere penances in the preceding ones The six acts of necromancy (Shatkarma) would be the matters of daily undertaking and the rites of Sandhyá (recitation of a certain fixed portion of the Védâs by a Bráhmana) ceremonial ablutions, mental repetition of any sacred Mantra, Homa, worship of the gods and practice of hospitality, would be the stepping-stones to piety. Scarce would be the number of Bráhmana-Yatis in the Kali Yuga who would stick to the noble art of spiritual culture, and the Kshatriyas would rule the earth by conquering the armed forces of other sovereigns even in the absence of any legitimate cause for war, and simply out of a spirit of land-craving. The members of the mercantile community, should diligently ply on their respective trades and engage in agriculture, and the S'udras should live by serving the Bráhmanas in the age of Kali.

A man would degrade himself by stealing or by going unto a woman related to him in the category of a 'forbidden woman," or by eating any thing that is prohibited in the Shastras for the purpose. A Brâhmana engaged in agriculture, should not yoke a team of tired bullocks to his plough. The Brâhmanas even in the age of Kali, shall bathe at midday, practise trance for a while, and then feed the Brâhmanas assembled at his house. The five religious sacrifices enjoined to be performed by a Brâhmana householder, each day, should be likewise performed in the Kali Yuga, and sins and inequities should be held in contempt they deserve. A Brâhmana shall not sell sesamum and clarified butter for any pecuniary consideration. An agriculturist is absolved of all sins by giving a sixth part of the produce to his king, a twentieth part to the gods, and a thirty-third part thereof to the Brâhmanas. A Kshatriya, a Vaishya, or a S'udra agriculturist paying no such tithes as the preceding ones, stands charged with the guilt of theft.

A Brâhmana, who knows the Supreme Brahma, becomes clean on the third day of the event on the happening of any birth or death in his family, whereas the period of uncleanness, under the circumstance, shall extend to ten, twelve, and thirty days in respect of the Brahma-knowing Kshatriyas, Vaishyas, and S'udras respectively. On the contrary, persons belonging to the Brâhmana, Kshatriya, Vaishya and S'udra communities by mere accidents of birth, shall be respectively deemed pure at the expiry of ten, twelve, fifteen and thirty days after the event under the circumstance. The Sapinda relations of a deceased person or of a stillborn child, though not living in the same house, nor in commensality, shall bide the same full term of uncleanness, while those removed from him to the fourth degree of consanguinity shall be unclean for ten days, those removed to the fifth degree shall be judged unclean for six days, those removed to the sixth degree of consanguinity shall be regarded unclean for four days, and those removed to the seventh degree, shall be considered unclean for three days only from the date of the event under the circumstance. A child dead in a distant country does not entail any period of uncleanness to his relations beyond the moment the news is heard and delivered. The corpse of a child dead before cutting its teeth as well as that of a still-born one should not be cremated in fire, nor any funeral oblations and libations of water should be offered to it. In the case of a miscarriage or abortion of a fœtus, the period of uncleanness in respect of its mother, would extend to as many days as the age of the fœtus in months at the time of abortion. The period of uncleanness incidental to the death of a child, dead without the rite of Nâmakaran (nomenclature) having been done unto him, shall expire with the day of its occurrence, that on the occasion of one expired before the rite of tonsure shall continue for the whole day and night, while that incidental to the demise of a child, dead before having been invested with the holy thread, would last for three days from the date of its happening, and for ten days after that age.

An abortion of womb happening within the fourth month of gestation is called a Garbhasrâva, while the one occurring at a later period and in the fifth or sixth month of incubation, is called a miscarriage (Garbha-Tyâga). No such uncleanness can attach itself to the person of a Brâhmana who is a Brahmacharin or is a daily worshipper of the sacred fire, or has renounced all company and lives in solitude. The artisans, the mechanics, the physicians, and one's servants, male slaves, and female slaves, are incapable of catching such personal disqualifications (uncleanness incidental to the birth or death of a person). The persons of kings, S'rotriyas and custodians of the sacred fire, are perpetually clean. On the occasion of the birth of a child, its mother shall be considered clean at the close of ten days after the date of the event, while its father shall be clean again by an ablution on the receipt of the news. All acts should be suspended on the happening of the birth or death of a relation at the celebration of a marriage or a religious sacrifice or festivity, except those which have been actually projected and undertaken before the event. The mother of a child, dead within the period of uncleanness incidental to its birth, shall be clean again on the date of the event. The period of uncleanness incidental to the death of a person, dead in a cowshed, is only one day. By carrying the dead body of a friendless person to the cremation ground, a man shall remain unclean for a single day, while the period of uncleanness in respect of carrying the dead body of a Shudra, is three days only. The right of cremation is denied to a suicide, no matter whether the death has been brought about by self-poisoning or strangulation, as well as to one who has died of an insect-bite. A man, defiled by the contact of the corpse of a person, killed by any horned cattle or died of an insect-bite, is purified by practising a Krichchha Vrata.

He who forsakes a chaste and undegraded wife in her youth, is sure to incarnate as a woman, and to suffer the pangs of widowhood in his six successive re-births. By not visiting the bed of his wife during her menstrual period as enjoined in the Shástras, a man incurs the sin of infanticide, while a non-acommodating wife under the circumstance, is sure to be born as a sow in her next birth. An abstinence by the husband on the ground of being engaged in celebrating any Vedic rite or sacrifice at the time, deprives him of funeral libations, etc., after death. A son of one's own loins as well as the one begotten on one's wife by another under an appointment and hence related to one in that capacity, is equally entitled to offer oblations to one's departed spirit. A younger brother marrying in the unmarried state of his elder, as well as his bride shall practise a penance of Krichchha Vratam for the expiation of the crime. The person at whose hand the bride is taken, shall as well practise the penances respectively known as Ati-krichchha and Chándráyana Vratas. A younger brother is not prohibited from taking a bride even in the unmarried state of his elder, when the latter is found to be born a hunchback, or a dwarf, or impotent, deaf, blind, or dumb, or as an idiot, or as one incapable of distinct articulation. A betrothed girl may be married to another in any of the five following contingencies, *viz.*, in the event of no trace having been found of her appointed bridegroom, or in the event of his death, or of his taking to the life of a hermit, or on his loss of manhood or moral degradation. A wife immolating herself with the dead body of her husband at the same funeral pile, shall live in heaven for as many number of years as there are hairs on the human body. A man, bitten by a dog, or by an animal of the kindred species, is purified by mentally reciting the Gáyatri Mantra.

The dead body of a Bráhmana should be exhumed on a funeral pyre lighted with Loukikâgni (fire brought from a household). The bone of a Bráhmana, killed by a Chandála, should be washed with milk in order to impart to it the necessary purity before cremation, and burnt in fire with a recitation of the proper Mantras. An effigy of a Bráhmana made of Kusha-blades, should be burnt in the following manner in the event of his death having happened in a distant country. Six hundred Palasha-twigs, should be spread in the shape of a man over a piece of black deer skin, a Shami-twig being placed over the spot where the penis would be, an Arani (fire churning apparatus) at the region of its scrotum, a Kunda (vessel) at the region of its right hand, an Upabhrit (a sacrificial utensil) at its left, an Udâkhalam (a grain thresher) on either of its sides, a Mushala (threshing rod) at its back, a stone slab at the region of its breast, with rice, sesame and clarified butter at its mouth, a Prokshani on either of its ears, an Ajyasthali (vessel for clarified butter) on either of its eyes, and bits of gold in the orfices of its mouth, ears and eyes. Thus all the articles and utensils required in an Agni Hotra sacrifice, should be arranged along the different parts of the effigy of Kusha grass, which should be lighted with fire, and a single libation of clarified butter, should be cast therein by reciting the Mantra, "Asou svargáya lokáya sváhá" (obeisance to the Fre-God, may he ascend the region of heaven). By thus burning the effigy of a Bráhmana, dead in a distant country, his relation may ensure the residence of his soul in the region of Brahma.

The killer of a Swan, Sárasa, Heron, Chakravak, or a cock may regain the former purity of his self by fasting for a single day, which rule holds good as regards the killing of any other bird. The rite of expiation in connection with the killing of a quadruped, consists in fasting for a day and in mentally repeating any sacred Mantra. The proper atonement for inadvertantly bringing about the death of a Shudra, consists in practising a Krichchha Vrata, that for killing a member of the Vaishya caste, is the practice of an Ati-Krichchha Vrata. The penance to be practised for expiating the sin of killing a Kshatriya, is a Chándráyana, which should be practised twenty to thirty times by way of atoning for an act of Bráhman-killing.

——:o:——

CHAPTER CVIII.

SUTA (LOMAHARSHANA) said :—Now I shall discourse on the Science of Ethics and Expediency, a perusal whereof may benefit kings and commons alike, and enable them to secure long lives, and good names on earth, and exalted stations in heaven after death. A man wishing success in life, shall make it a point not to mix in vulgar companies, but to associate only with the best and the most virtuous in the land. Company of the wicked or of the inequitous, is neither good in this life nor in the one to come. A man should shun even any oral discourse with the wicked, avoid their presence and company, be on his guard against picking up a quarrel with his trusted friends, or against mixing with those who serve his enemies or are in friendly terms with them.

Even a learned man comes to grief by teaching a bad pupil, or by maintaining a bad wife. An evil company is but the high road to depravity. The very presence of an illiterate Bráhmana or of of a dastardly Kshatriya, or of a lazy Vaishya, or of a literate Shudra should be shunned from a distance. One should make a compact with one's enemies, or a breach with his friends at the right moment. Wise men bide their time out of motives of expediency and with a full regard to the cause and effect of their each act of conduct. It is Time that rears up all created beings. It is Time that brings about their dissolution. It is Time which sits up fully awake when all else is asleep. Hence Time is unconquerable, and suffers no slightness of his authority. It is Time that makes the semen flow in to its natural repository, and evolve itself in the shape of a fœtus in the womb. Time is the principal factor in the evolution of the universe, and it is Time that will bring about its final dissolution. Invisible is the flght of time, which becomes manifest at one place by the occurrence of gross phenomena, while in another it is too subtile to be detected.

The following synopsis of the rules of conduct was narrated by Vrihaspati to Indra, the lord of the celestials, whereby the latter acquired omniscience and was enabled to recover the kingdom of heaven from the hands of the demons. It is incumbent on the Bráhmanas and the Rájarshis to worship the gods, to propitiate the Bráhmanas and to celebrate Horse-Sacrifice for the atonement of sins of the most aggravated nature. A man by making an alliance with the good, as well as by discussing commendable topics with the learned and making friendship with the greedless, cannot possibly come to any grief. Incest or jesting with another's wife, taking of another's goods, and residence in another's house should be avoided. A well-meaning alien (enemy) is a friend and a hostile friend is an alien. A disease which originates in the body is an enemy, but a herb which grows in the forest (and outside of the body) is a friend. He who maintains a person is a father to him. He in whom confidence is reposed is a friend and the country which provides one's means of livelihood is one's true country. A servant who does the commands of his master, is a true servant, a seed which sprouts is a true seed; a child that lives is a true child, and a wife who speaks sweet is a true wife. He who has virtue is truly alive. He who has piety lives but in the true sense of the term. Futile is the life of him who is bereft of piety and commendable attributes. She who speaks sweetly to her husband and is a clever manager of household affairs, is a true wife. She who is one in spirit with her lord and devotes her whole self to his happiness, is a true wife. He whose wife decorates her person with sandal paste and perfumes her body after her daily ablution, talks little and agreeably, partakes small quantites of food, is ever fond of him and is constantly engaged in doing acts of piety and virtue with a view to bring happiness and prosperity in the house, and is ever ready to yield to the procreative desires of her lord, is not a man, but the lord of heaven.

A scolding wife, wild, querulous and argumentative, is but the blight of life (*lit.* :—old age itself). A wife, attached to another and fond of staying in an other man's house, and who is not ashamed of her own depravity, is but the curse of life. A wife who appreciates and honours the good qualities in her lord and lives in loving submission to his wishes, is satisfied with the little she gets, is alone entitled to be called a beloved. An unchaste wife, an insincere friend, an argumentative servant, and a residence in a snake-infested chamber, are but the preludes to death. Walk not in the path of the wicked, but sit in the assembly of the pious and the godly. Suffer not the transitory character of all mundane things to be absent for a moment from your mind, and be perpetually engaged in doing what is good and commendable. A woman who is deadlier than the fangs of a serpent, or one that is blood-eyed, black and fierce as a tigress, or is possessed of a cow-like tongue and becomes foul-mouthed in rage, or is eccentric in her habits, apathetic and fond of staying in an otherman's house, should not be courted by a wise man for matrimonial alliance He who lives in a snake-infested chamber, or whose disease has run into an incurable type, as well as the one who has passed through the three bodily stages of infancy, youth and old age, is undoubtedly in the grasp of Death. Where is the man who can retain his mental equilibrium under the circumstance?

—:o:—

CHAPTER CIX.

LOMAHARSHANA said :—Money should be saved for the time of distress, and a wife should be protected even at the sacrifice of a stored up treasure. A man should defend his own self even at the cost of his wealth and wife. It is prudent to sacrifice a individual for the protection of a family. The safety of an village should be purchased with the loss of a family, while that of a country should not be regarded too dear even at the sacrifice of a single village, it being imperatively obligatory on a person to save his own self even at the loss of the whole world. It is better to live in hell than to reside in a house of infamy. Extinction of the effects of his own misdeeds in life, sets free a condemned spirit from its doleful confines, whereas a person who has once resorted to a house of ill fame, can never be properly reclaimed. A wise man does not move one step by letting go his sure and former foot-hold. An old situation of trust and tested safety should not be given up without well ascertaining the nature of a new one. A man should renounce a country whose inhabitants walk in the path of inequity, give up his residence in a house found to be infested with dangers, avoid all connections with a niggardly prince, and forego the company of deceitful friends. Of what good is the gold which is in the greedy gripe of a miser? Of what worth is the knowledge which is wedded to a low cunning nature? What does mere personal beauty avail a person whose mind is not adorned with ennobling attributes? And what is the good of one's having a friend who forsakes one in days of adversity.

From unforeseen quarters friends gather round a man in power and prosperity. Even the very kins of one, out of office and fortune, turn their back as enemies in one's adversity. Friendship is tested in distress; valour, in battle; a wife, on the loss of fortune; and an agreeable guest in time of famine or scarcity. Birds forsake a tree whose fruits are gone. Herons visit not the shores of a dried pool. Courtesans smile not on (forswear the company of) a person whose purse is exhausted, nor Ministers flock round a king, bereft of his sovereignity. On the withered flowers the bees sit not with their melodious hummings, nor do herds of deer roam about in the forest which a wood fire has consumed. One person endears another simply out of motives of self-seeking. Is there any love for love's sake an earth?

The greedy are taken by gain, the proud by a show of humility, fools, by pleasing themes, and the wise by truth. The gods, the good and the Brahmans, are pleased with the exhibition of genuine goodness, the vulgar, with food and drink, and the erudite, with learned discourses. The good should be won over with marks of respect. The crafty should be won by creating a breach in their ranks, the low by making trifling gifts or concessions in their favour, and one's rivals by exhibiting equal prowess. An intelligent man shall enter into the good graces of persons he shall have to deal with through an accurate judgment of their likes and dislikes, and thus speedily win them over to his cause or side.

No confidence shonld be reposed in (the freaks of) rivers, horned cattle, clawed beasts, women, persons of royal blood and arm-bearing individuals (fully equipped soldiers etc.,) A prudent man should never give any publicity to any insult he might have suffered, to any deception that might have been practised upon him, to any heart-ache of his own, nor to an instance of female infidelity in his house. Movements in a low or wicked company, a long separation from her husband, excessive and indulgent fondling, and a residence in another's house are the factors which excite a wife to break her plighted faith. Who is he who can boast of a spotless pedigree? Where is the man who has never been assailed by any malady? Who is he whom danger doth not beset in life? Who can be sure of the perpetual favours of fickle fate? Who is he whom opulence filleth not with pride? Who is he who standeth above all probability of danger? Where is the man who is impervious to female charms? Who is he whom a king doth love in his heart? Who is he whom Time doth not sway? Who is he whom begging doth not lower? Who is he who being netted with the guiles of the crafty, has come off unscathed? Perpetually in distress is the man who has no friends or relations of his own, nor endowed with a sharp intellectual faculty and incapable of putting a success to better advantage. Wherefore should a wise man engage in a pursuit, success in which does not bring in any profit, and failure whereof is fraught with dangerous results. Quit the country where you can find neither friends nor pleasures, nor in which is there any knowledge to be gained.

Acquire that wealth which kings or thieves can neither extort nor steal and which follows a person even beyond the grave. Your successors, after your demise, shall inherit and divide among themselves the wealth which has cost you life-long and killing toils to acquire.

The soul only enjoys the fruits of the sins and inequities involved in the acquisition of wealth which, again, forms the portion of others who come next. A miser, earning and hoarding up gold without knowing its proper use, is like a mouse which steals from other men's granaries, and is only troubled with the care of defending his ill-gotten gain. A miser, naked, wretched and lamenting the loss of his fortune by striking his hand against his forehead, shows but the evil effects of not making any gift (proper use of money). A miser, continually crying for fresh hoards, and stretching out his palms in greed, demonstrates but the plight in which a non-giver would stand in his next birth. May you never be in such a predicament. Money hoarded up by a miser simply for the pleasure of hoarding, without being spent in the celebration of a hundred Horse-Sacrifices, or in relieving the want of the wise and the erudite, ultimately finds its way into the coffers of thieves and king's courts. The wealth accumulated by a miser, never comes to the use of the Brahmanas, nor to that of his own relations; is never spent for any religious purpose, nor in purchasing his personal comforts, but is consumed by fire, thieves, and law-courts.

May that wealth which is acquired by vicious ways, or by excessive toil, or by bowing down to one's enemies, be never yours.

Non-cultivation thereof, is a blow to one's learning; a shabby dress is a blow to a woman; eating after digestion is a blow to a disease; and cleverness is a blow to one's enemies. Death is the penalty for theft, a separate bed is the punishment for a wife, a cold greeting is the punishment for deceitful friends, and non-invitation is the punishment for Brahmanas. Rogues, artisans, servants, badmen, drums, and women, are softened and set right by beating. They do not deserve good behaviour. A mission is the true test for the efficiency of one's servants; adversity, for the sincerity of one's friends; and loss of fortune is the proper occasion to test the fondness of one's wife. A woman takes twice as much food, is four times as much cunning, six times as much resourceful, and eight times as much armorous, as a man. Sleep cannot be conquered by sleeping. A woman knows no satisfaction in sexual matters. Fire cannot be conquered with logs of wood, nor thirst, with wines. Amorous fancies in women, are roused up by a meat diet and emulsive fares, by good apparels, flowers, perfumes and wine. Verily do I say unto you, O Shounaka, that even an ascetic Brahmacharin, becomes fascinated [at such a sight], and the sexual organ of a woman, is moistened at the sight of a handsome and well-dressed youth, even if he happen to be connected with her in the relationship of a father, a brother, or a son. A woman as well as a river, let alone, is sure to take the downward course. A woman, under the circumstance, brings down the honour of her family, while a river tumbles down her banks. A free woman, or an unchecked stream of water, is sportive in her course. Fire is never satisfied with fuels; nor an ocean is satisfied with receiving rivers. Death knows no satiety; and a woman knows no gratification in matters sexual. A man knows no satiety in discoursing with good and sincere talkers; pleasure never palls; and a man knows no satisfaction as regards the increased duration of his life and increased number of his progeny. A king knows no gratification in the acquisition of wealth, nor is an ocean satisfied with the increase of its tributaries. A learned man knows no content in discoursing, nor the eyes suffer any satiety with their feasts of royal sight (sight of the king).

Those excellent men, who live by plying any honest trade, and rest contented with money honestly earned and obtained, are true to their own wives and pass their time in intellectual pursuits, practise hospitality to all comers, and are the lords of their own senses, attain liberation even in their own homes. Residence in a brick-built house of one's own, in the company of a beautiful and loving wife, bedecked with ornaments, and in elysian felicity, should be ascribed to the dynamics of good deeds done in one's prior birth. A woman baffles the best wisdom of the wise. She is incorrigible and simply incomprehensible, being incapable of being won with flattery, jewels or frankness, or of being cowed down to submission with threats of violence, and sets at naught the injunctions of the S'astras. Little by little a man should acquire learning. Little by little a mountain should be climbed. Little by little desires should be gratified, and virtues acquired. These five things should be gradually performed.

Eternal are the effects of divine worship and contemplation. Through all eternity runs the merit of the gift to a Brahmana. Eternal is the happiness which a good friend and a good education confer on a person. Pitiable, indeed, are they who have got no education in their childhood. and fail to secure any wealth and wives in their youth. They may be likened unto the beasts that roam about in the world in the guise of human beings. A student of the Shastras, shall not constantly indulge in thoughts of eating, but travel even to a distant clime for his study with the speed of the celestial Garuda (the bird of conveyance of the divine Vishnu). Like the lotus in winter, those who have not studied out of playful tendencies in their infancy, and have defiled their souls with the follies of youth, shall be withered up in their old age, overwhelmed with griefs and cares.

Disquisitions on Religion and Godhead are as old as the human race, yet the S'rutis could not come to an agreement anent those subjects. There is not a Rishi but propounds a theory of his own. True religion lies hid in a cave. The path of the masters is the true path in life.

The latent, or hidden workings of a man's mind, should be gathered and ascertained from his mien, demeanour, and the contortions of his face and eyes. A wise man can catch the significance even of an unarticulated speech. The function of the intellect is to read the language of demeanours, etc. Even a beast can understand the meaning of an articulated speech. Do not horses, elephants, etc., execute the biddings of their drivers? Tumbled out of a fortune, one should start on a pilgrimage to a distant shrine. Deviation from the path of truth leads to Rourava (a hell of that name), deprived of the privilege of trance (occult sight). One should bide his time with truth and patience. Ousted of his kingdom, a king should go out on a hunting excursion in the forest.

——:o:——

CHAPTER CX.

SUTA said:—He who rejects a certain good in quest of one which is uncertain and remote, loses both the certain and the prospective one. Like erudition in the dumb, like swords in the hands of cowards, a beauty wedded to a blind husband, loses the significance of her life. A good appetite with plenty to eat, a healthy sexual potency with a bevy of handsome wives, and opulence with a heart that unstintedly gives to the poor, are the effects of a prior-life Tapasya of no mean order. The high prerogative of reading the immutable Vedas (revelations) is the fruit of performing the Agnihotra sacrifices. Good both in this world and the one to come, is the fruit of one's moral living in this existence. Offsprings and sexual pleasure are the fruits of marriage, and charity and enjoyment are the fruits of wealth. One should marry a girl of noble descent even bereft of personal attractions, in preference to a handsome one with spacious and well-formed hips but of low and obscure parentage.

Covet not the riches of the mighty who would meet such efforts with condign punishment. Who on earth will stretch out his hand to rob a cobra of the jewel which shines on its hood? Clarified butter may be taken even from a house of divine service, and good words may be considered, even if spoken by a child. Gold may be taken from a person of impure descent, and a good and virtuous wife, even from a family of questionable morals. Friendship with a king is an absurdity. Absurdity is a serpent without venom, and absurd is the lasting good name of a house in which female children are born. One should engage a devoted person in one's own house, engage one's sons in pursuit of knowledge, keep one's enemies engaged with dangers, and engage one's own Self in the pursuit of God. Servants and ornaments should be kept and worn in their proper places. No one puts on a head-gear around his ankle, nor a servant thinks that he is the master. Head is the natural place for fire, ocean, king and head jewels. They should never be touched with the foot even through inadvertance.

Even in their own homes, liberation awaits those free and foremost of men, who are true to their wives and the commandments of the scriptures, and live content with their honest gain, practising hospitality and self-control and dedicating themselves to the services of the God and the Brahmanas. Paradise on earth is the residence in a splendid mansion in the company of a pleasant, handsome, and gem-bedecked wife, which can result only from the dynamics of good deeds done by a man in his previous existence. Neither by gift alone, nor by simple respect, courtesy, nursing, chastisement, etc., nor with knowledge alone that a woman can be conquered. Gradually knowledge should be acquired. Little by little a fortune should be built up. By degrees a mountain should be climbed (difficulty should be surmounted). Little by little desires should be gratified, and litttle by little virtues should be acquired, graduated efforts being enjoined to be made in these five things.

For all eternity lasts the merit of divine service, while that of making a gift to a Brahmana endures for good. Eternal are the fruits of knowledge wedded to a noble nature; and eternal is the friendship which is roused up in a lofty soul. Pitiable are those human mammals in life who neglect their studies out of excessive fondness for play in their childhood; and fail to secure good friends, wives, and fortunes in their youth. They are but beasts in human shapes. Like the petals of a flower, only two alternatives are open to a man of true vigour, either to be placed on the heads of men, or to drop down withered and unnoticed in a lonely forest. A gem which is fit to be worn on the head, set in a fitting ornament of gold, shines none the less if it is tied around the ankle. But censurable is the man who puts it in such a low and wrong position. Great is the difference between a horse and an elephant, wood and iron, stone and sliver, and a man and a woman. The lofty aspirations and ennobling virtues of a truly great man who is vanquished, are not jeopardised in his disgrace; the tongues of a flame (fire), never cease to point upward even when held in an inverted position. A good horse brooks not the touch of a whip; nor a lion, the roar of an elephant; nor a true hero, the boastings of his rival. Seek not the service of the wicked, nor beg of the mean and the vulgar, even if thou chancest to be fallen on evil days. A lion, even under the pangs of hunger, eateth not grass but drinketh the hot blood of an elephant's heart. A reunion with a friend who has once betrayed himself, is fatal to a person like conception to a she-mule. A wise man shall not spare the offsprings of his enemy, even if courteous and sweet-mouthed inasmuch as they can prove themselves fatal like cups of poison. One enemy should be got rid of through the help of another one by a favour, as a thorn, pricked into the sole of the foot, is extracted with the help of one taken hold of by the hand. No means is necessary to be devised for the fall of a person whose constant theme is the downfall of others, as he meets his own overthrow in the usual course of things, like a tree which grows on the bank of a treacherous river. The harmful appear as good and the good as harmful, when fortune frowns. A man, under the circumstance, is inevitably drawn on towards the evil which leads to his doom. Good propensities return with the smile of Fortune, and a man, perceiving the errors of his judgment and conduct, forthwith turns aside from the path of evil. No sense of false delicacy should be observed in matters of learning, pecuniary transaction and mutual dealing. Live not in a country which can not boast of these five factors, namely, a king, rich men, S'rotriyas (scholars well-versed in Vedic lore), a river and a physician. Live not in a place, even for a single day where these five things, such as, prospect of earning a livelihood, sense of shame, dread of law, mercy, and charity, exist not. Live not in a place which is devoid of these five things, such as, an astrologer, a S'rotriya, a king, a river, and a true anchorite. O S'ounaka, perfect knowledge does not culminate in any particular individual, since every one knows not all, nor there can be found an omniscient being among men. None is omniscient in this world, nor is there one entirely devoid of knowledge. Wise men make such distinctions as Erudite, Idiot and Average Intellect, according to a relative standard of knowledge possessed by the individual members of a society.

—:o:—

CHAPTER CXI.

SUTA said :—Now I shall deal with the commendable traits in kings, and servants in regal employ, which a king should keep a constant eye upon, during their entire period of service. A king should rule his kingdom according to the tenets of true religion, and in the light of truth and justice, and protect the country from the inroads of foreign invaders. Like a florist who makes a festoon by culling flowers from flower-bearing trees without uprooting them, a king should collect a tithe of the income of his subjects by the way of imperial revenue, without creating any hardship on, or grinding, them with an unbearable taxation. As a milk-man milches a cow without exhausting the supply in, or cutting away, her teats, so a king shall justly tap the resources of an enemy's country brought under his sway, without draining it dry or carrying fire and sword through its entire length. Hence a king should rule the world for the advancement of order and prosperity, since the Earth with the fame, valour and strength which follows a just and vigorous rule, belongs to her protector.

That king, who, having bridled his senses, dedicates himself to the service of God and the well-being of the world (Es) and the Brahmanas, is alone capable of justly ruling his subjects. Even amidst when flushed with victory and prosperity, a king should devote his Self to the pursuit of virtue, since the riches of the world are always liable to decay, whereas the opulence of the soul knows no perishing. Pleasant indeed it is to gratify one's desires. Pleasant, indeed, are the riches of the world, but they are fickle and transitory as the flurried and wistful glances of an amorous damsel.

Old age, like a tigress, is lying in wait just to spring upon a man; and Diseases, like victorious enemies, are consuming his limbs—and life, like water in a leaky vessel, is fast ebbing away. Ah, wherefore should he not attend to the well-being of his own Self? Why do you continue in complacent quietitude, oh men? Why do you allow yourselves to be smitten with the amorous glances of youthful maidens? Why do you not think of what will befall you after death? Life is transitory; and each moment, the Ghati-yantra (a time-measuring apparatus somewhat like our modern clock) of the heart ticks out the footfalls of approaching Death.

He, who looks at another's wife as his own mother, at another's goods as (worthless) brickbats, and upon all men as similarly susceptible to impressions of pleasure and pain as his own self, sees but right. Kings desire realms, O lord of the Bráhmanas, only for the end that their commands might not be frustrated. Kings collect money only to leave its residue at the disposal of the Bráhmanas after first providing for their own legitimate wants. Omkár is the natural sound of the Bráhmanas. Recitation of Omkar leads to the expansion of the suzerainty of a king and contributes to his health and prosperity in life.

Even the Munis, though otherwise incapable of earning, are found to make provisions for times of scarcity, and hence it is doubly incumbent on a sovereign, who rules his liege subjects in a paternal spirit, to keep his treasuries well-replenished at all times. He who has money, has many friends. He who has money, has many relations—he who has it is a learned man. He only is really worthy who has a long purse at his command. Friends, wives and sons forsake a man in distress and fall off in his days of adversity. They return to him with the return of fortune. Hence money is the only true friend a man may have in this life. Blind is the king who is bereft of knowledge. A blind prince may see through the eyes of his spies, but an ignorant king is always in the dark. Transient is the sovereignty of the prince whose sons, servants and priests

42

are not always on the alert, and whose senses have lost their wonted vigour. The king who has conquered the hearts of his friends, sons and servants may already count upon the sovereignty of the whole ocean-girdled earth with the homage of the potentates of her different divisions. The king, who defies the dictates of reason and the injunctions of the Shastras, is dead both in this world and the next. Even in defeat or discomfiture a king should not give vent to grief or despondency. Equally indifferent to pleasures and pain, he shall always try to preserve his equanimity. The wise grieve not at the loss of fortune. Does not the moon come back resplendent out of the jaws of the Rahu? Fie to him who thinks only of his body and its comforts. Grieve not at the loss of flesh and muscular strength. Whoever has not heard it that the sons of Pándu managed to retrieve their fortune even amidst almost insurmountable difficulties?

A king shall protect the courtesans by hearing their songs and witnessing their dances and theatrical performances, and his subjects with the cultivation of sciences of money-making and warfare. An unjust and groundless chastisement of his servant by a king is often retalliated by an attempt at poisoning him. A king shall renounce all fickleness in his dealings and be always truthful and pleasantly disposed to his servants, subjects and the Bráhmanas. A king, who being elated by the fealty of his friends and relations yields to the snares of gossip and falconry, is easily conquered by his adversary. A king shall not always roar nor frown, but protect his servants without infringing the rules of state-craft. Pleasures and luxurious habits are the two things which should be foresworn by a king. The luxurious and the voluptuous are easily defeated by their enemies in battle. Even the gods stand in dread of him who is possessed of energy, daring, fortitude, strength, valour and intelligence. It is an evil providence that mars the success of an energetic exertion, still a man must exert and command success.

CHAPTER CXII.

SUTA said :—There are three kinds of servants, good, bad and indifferent, who shall be posted to offices best suited to their capacities. Presently shall I describe in detail the traits which are to be commended in the character of each of them, as narrated in the works on Social Economy. Gold is tested by touch, cutting, striking and melting, whereas a servant is known by his conduct, character, parentage and acts. A man of noble birth and character, who is further graced by the qualifications of truthfulness, honesty of purpose, handsome features and a broad catholicity of views, should be entrusted with the management of a realm. He who can rightly assay gold, silver and precious stones, should be alone appointed as the jeweller to his king. An officer, who understands the comparative strength or weakness of the enemy's forces and can at once detect the point of vantage in a field of battle, should be alone confided with the martialship of the realm. He, who can read the mind of his master by his looks and gestures, and is strong vigilant, and handsome, and can successfully deal or pair off a blow, should be appointed as a warder. The king's writer or secretary shall be a man, who is intelligent, wise, truthful and self-controlled and is well-read in all the branches of the Shastras. The royal ambassador shall be a man of profound intelligence and clear comprehension. An adept in the art of simulation, he must be capable of reading what passes in other men's minds and of giving the right reply at the opportune moment. The high priest of the realm, should be a man of vast erudition and perfect self-control—a hero in soul and virtue. The royal cook should be a man whose father and grandfather had served in the same capacity before and who is truthful, hardy and cleanly in his habits. He, who has acquired a mastery in the science and practice of medicine and is virtuous, frank and friendly to all—beaming with the glow of health and kindness which virtue sheds only on the face of her sincere and ardent votary, shall be the royal physician. The royal priest should be a man who has studied the Védás and the Védángas, and constantly meditates upon the divine Self, and celebrating Homa ceremonies and pleasing the whole world in his weal and woe. A king shall dismiss from the royal service any writer (secretary), astrologer, computer, and the head of any civic corporation, etc., any way found wanting in their respective duties.

Double-tongued are the snakes and the malicious; their cruel mouths are the source of many an evil to man. Avoid the company of an erudite miscreant: Is not the serpent that bears a gem on its hood doubly dangerous for the stone? Who is he that dreadeth not the malicious who work mischief without any provocation and who are but the serpents in human form? Words of spite drop down from the mouths of the malicious; the fangs of serpents secrete deadly venom. The king, who ruins a servant, who is equally rich, powerful and influential as himself and holds a divided sway over the country, escapes ruin in his turn. They bode no good—those servants who show themselves silent, valarous, truthful, self-controlled and capable at the outset, and exhibit contrary qualities in the course, of the service. Rare are the servants who are contented, laborious, vigilant, equally devoted for good or for evil, and capable of being readily roused up from their sleep. A man bereft of all fortitude, character and honesty as well as the one who is arrogant, gluttonous, dishonest, spiteful, should be excluded from the royal service. A king shall take recourse to his fortress for the purpose of destroying his enemy as soon as he can secure a well-replenished treasury and a well-equipped arsenal. A king shall bide in peace with his adversary under a treaty, for six months or a year at the outside, and shall give battle thereafter as soon as he will be able to fully recoup his losses. Infamy, frustration and Hell are the three dire consequences which befall a prince that employs a foolish and illiterate man in his service. The subtle dynamics of good or evil deeds determine the prosperity or ruin of a sovereign, and therefore he shall ponder well over a thing before undertaking it. Hence a king should constantly dedicate himself to the good of the cows and the Bráhmanas.

—:o:—

CHAPTER CXIII.

SUTA said :—Try to secure the services of the qualified and reject the incapable from the list inasmuch as all virtues grace the mind of the erudite, and an illiterate fool is, at best, but the embodiment of all evil propensities. Sit in the assembly of the honest; combine with those that are good and virtuous; nay seek out a noble enemy where enmity can be helped and have nothing to do with the wicked and the unrighteous. Even in bondage thou shalt live with the virtuous, the erudite and the truthful; but not for a kingdom thou shalt stay with the wicked and the malicious. Good can come only out of a work that has been rightly carried through; and therefore thou shalt leave no work unfinished. A king shall tap the resources of his dominion just as a bee culls honey from a flower without killing it. He shall milch a cow or the earth, leaving some sustenance for her offsprings. A bee culls honey from flower to flower without fully draining any particular one, and a king shall collect his revenues, bee-fashion, from his subjects without creating hardship on any. Day by day the royal granary and treasury should be replenished and filled as an ant-hill, a bee-hive, and the phases of the moon in a light fortnight are increased. A little ink (used every day in writing) writes a good volume in the long run. By little fresh accretions, each day, an ant-hill reaches to a pretty good height. A little study, a little virtue, a little act of charity practised, each day, may serve to make the life unbarren at its close.

Desires assail the worldly-disposed even amidst the solitude of a wilderness and the subjugation of his senses by a man even amidst the tumults of the world and domesticity constitues true penitence and meditation. The house of a man who has abjured evil and killed all desires, is the true hermitage. Piety is preserved by truthfulness; knowledge, by constant cultivation; courtesy, by humility; and a family good name, by the character of its members. Better it is to dwell in the howling Vindhya forest, better it is to die of starvation, preferable it is to live in a snake-infested chamber, infinitely preferable is a leap in a well or in a whirlpool where sharks and other dreadful water-animals abound, than to say "help me" to one's friends and relations. Enjoyment does not consume the opulence of a man, it is the end of his good luck that leads to his ruin. The effects of his deeds in a prior birth has a hand in hewing his destiny in this as in other things.

Knowledge is the ornament of the Bráhmanas; the king, is that of the Earth. The moon is the ornament of the heaven; and a good character is a decoration and distinction to all and everywhere.

The valorous Bhimasena and his brothers Arjuna, etc., were all heroes of royal descent. They were truthful and resplendent like the mid-day sun and enjoyed the direct tutelary protection of Keshava. Even they, under the influence of a malign fate, were bound to live in penury and beg their bread from door to door. What can a man achieve in life without destiny? It is fate that makes us fulfill our own destiny on earth according to the effects of our own deeds in a prior life. Obeisance to Karma that has fixed Brahma in this globe of the universe (*lit.*,—region of Beconing) which is perpetually revolving like a potter's wheel—that has consigned the divine Vishnu to the pangs of ten successive incarnations on earth—that has sent out the immortal Rudra in the guise of a common mendicant with an alms-bowl of human cranium in his hand—and that has driven the Sun-God as a blazing, burning itinerant across the plains of heaven. The good king Vali made a gift of the whole earth amidst the best of the Bráhmanas to the god Murári, who stood as a supplicant for it at his door; and in consequence he was incarcerated for good in the gloom of the nether worlds—Obeisance to Fate, the creator of all anomalies. Which way will trend the thoughts of a being whom the supreme god has begotten on Lakshmi, the goddess of opulence? What wonder is there that good fortune will preside at his nativity. We enjoy or suffer the effects of our own good or bad deeds of our past birth. A man is the creator of his own fate, and even in his fœtal life he is afflected by the dynamics of the works of his prior existence. Whether confined in a mountain fastness or lulling on the bosom of a sea, whether secure in his mother's lap or held high above her head, a man cannot fly from the effects of his own prior deeds. Rávana had his fortress on the summits of the mount Trikruta, moated by the deep sea; and innumerable hosts of valiant Rákshasas were ever ready to lay their lives for him. The wise sage Ushaná (Shukrácháryya) himself tutored him well in ethics, politics and social economy. Time has killed even that mighty Rávana. Whatever is to befall a man on any particular age or time, will surely overtake him then and on that date. Scale the heavens, or plunge into the nether regions, or enfilade the quarters of the skies, a thing, which you have once given away, can never be yours. Knowledge acquired by a man in his prior birth, wealth given away in charity in his prior existence, and works done by him in a previous incarnation, go ahead of his soul in its sojourn. A person's Karma is the principal factor in determining his happiness or unhappiness in life, inasmuch as Janaki, though joined in wedlock under the auspices of blissful asterisms by the holy Vashishta himself, had nothing but misery for her portion in life. [A good physiognomy does not necessarily ensure a happy life on earth.] Ráma was round-thighed, Lakshmana was fleet-coursing as the wind, and Sitá had a crown of fine, thick-set hair, yet they were all unhappy. A son cannot relieve the misery of his father's spirit by performing proper obsequies, nor a fond father, with all his anxious care for his good and due performance of his paternal duties, can lead him in the path of happiness. This human body entombs a Self which is nothing if not emphatically a worker. It is the works of this Self in a prior existence which determine the nature of its organism in the next, as well as the character of the diseases, whether physical or mental which it is to fall a prey to. Shafts discharged even by strong-armed archers fall to the ground and wise men even with their knowledge and fore-thought are sometimes vanquished. Hence all projects should be carefully judged and deliberated in the light of the Shastras. A man reaps that at that age, whether infancy, youth or old age, at which he had sowed it in his previous birth. The Karma of a man draws him away from a foreign country and makes him feel its conseqnence even in spite of his will. A man gets in life what he is fated to get, and even a god cannot make it otherwise. Thus neither do I wonder nor mourn my lot, O Sounaka. What is lotted cannot be blotted.* A frightened mouse runs to its hole ; a scared serpent, to a well ; a terrified elephant, to its stake—but where can a man fly from his Karma ?

Knowledge imparted is knowledge gained. Fresh water springs up from beneath the well that has been bored out.

* Different reading.—" What is mine cannot be others."

Riches earned honestly and fairly, are true riches; opulence acquired by honest means, is true opulence:—Do not lose sight of the fact, when you try to acquire any thing in life. The amount of hardship which a man undergoes in order to earn his bread, is infinitely greater than what is necessary for acquiring religious merit which can grant him an immunity from such troubles in his births to come.

Of all cleanliness, cleanliness of food, is the best. Truthfulness is the cleanliness of speech. A clean mind denotes a clean spirit. Subjugation of the senses is the only true cleanliness of the flesh. Kindness to all constitutes one sort of cleanliness of which cleansing by water forms the fifth method. Heaven is open and easily accessible to a man of truth; and he who lieth not, is holier than a horse-sacrifice. Impure is the person of a miscreant or of an evil-thinker which cannot be cleansed, though a thousand times rubbed with clay, or a hundred times washed with water. He who has subjugated his mind and acquired knowledge, fame and a full control over his hands and feet, and has practised penance and meditation as well, acquires for himself the merit of a pilgrimage. Not to be jubilant over a mark of honour or distinction, nor to take umbrage at any humiliation, as well as forbearance from using any abusive language are the qualities which mark a truly virtuous man. A man can never come to any grief by listening to the sweet admonitions of a wise, though poor man at the opportune moment. Neither by prowess and wisdom, nor by magic and incantations can a man attain to that which he is not fated to receive:—What is there to mourn for in this? Sometimes I have got a thing without seeking it. Sometimes my fervent prayer for a thing has rested unanswered. A thing goes there where it is wanted:—What is there to mourn for in this? Bevies of birds pass the night on the boughs of the same tree only to be dispersed on the break of day:—What is there to mourn for in this? What is there to mourn for in the fact, if one or two out of an innumerable host, all permeated with the same purpose and proceeding to the same destination, reaches the goal a little earlier? Our life comes from the unseen and goes to the unseen, its middle part being only patent and manifest:—What is there to mourn for in this, O Shounaka? A man dies not before the appointed time, even if he is riddled with shafts. A wound from the tip of a Kusha sprout proves fatal at the right moment. A man receives that which he is fated to receive, goes only there where fate leads him to, and finds only that much pleasure or pain what he is destined to meet in this life:—What is there to mourn for in this life? Flowers bloom and fruits ripen in their appointed time and of their own accord without waiting for any body's bidding; and the effects of one's Karma, O Shounaka, bide their time and become patent only on the right occasion. Birth, education, conduct, character, virtue or connection avails not a man in this life. The effects of one's Karma and penance, done in a prior existence, fructify, like a tree at the appointed time in the next.

The Karma of a man forcibly draws him to the place where death or fortune waits him. The effects of deeds (Karma) done by a man in a prior existence overtake and choose him out in the next, as a calf seeks out its own mother out of a thousand cows. Thus one's Karma blinds one for good or for evil. Pleasure or pain, happiness or misery is the direct result of one's good or bad deeds in a prior birth. Why do you make such a heavy stock of misery out of it, O you foolish one?

The vile are ever prone to detect the faults of others, though they be as small as mustard seeds, and persistently shut their eyes against their own, though they be as large as Vilva fruits. I come to the conclusion after much deliberation, O thou twice-born one, that pleasure exists not where desire or affection has a room to be. True happiness lies in the extinction of all emotions. Apprehension is where affection is. Where there is affection there is misery. Pain has its root in love or affection. Renounce affection and you shall be happy. This human body is a theatre of pleasure and pain, and they come into being *pari passu* with the self of a man. Dependence or Bondage is misery. Liberty or Emancipation is the only happiness vouchsafed to man. Learn this to be a general synopsis, O Shounaka, of the rules of pleasure and pain. Misery follows happiness and happiness follows misery like the spokes of a wheel. What is gone is gone for good. What is future is still remote. He who acts only in the living present, knows no affliction.

—:o:—

CHAPTER CIV.

SUTA said :—No body is no body's friend. No body is no body's enemy. Friendship or enmity is bounded with each other by a distinct chain of cause and effect (self-interest). A source of solace in grief, a succour in distress, and a repository of happiness and confidence :—O who has created the two letters, "Mitram" (friend) which are more precious than a mine of gems! By the single utterance of the two letters "Hari" a fettered Self makes a step towards emancipation. A man does not repose so much confidence in his sons, wives and brothers as he implicitly places in his own natural friend. Gamble not and make no pecuniary transactions with a man, nor see his wife in his absence; these three being the essentials of a permanent amity. Never stay in a lonely place with your own daughters, sisters or step-mothers. The fiend of lust takes advantage of solitude and pleads evil counsel to the heart to which the learned have been known to yield. How absurd is the love God in his frolics! A man naturally shuns a woman who loves him and is easily available to him, and covets one whose touch is the forfeit of life. Easier it is to determine the velocity of a horse or of a storm, or even the depth of an unfathomable ocean; but how puerile is the attempt at sounding a heart that loves not. It is the absence of a nook of vantage, or the want of leisure or of a person making love-overtures to her, O Shounaka, that mainly accounts for the chastity of a woman. It is only rarely, O Shounaka, when a couple is fondly attached to each other that the wife is true at heart. A son should not think, out of a sense of decorum, what is done by his mother in a passion of love.

A courtesan is a dependant even in respect of her sleep, the sole aim of her life being to regale the hearts of her visitors as long as they can decently bear their wine. She is a sort of perpetual smiling machine, being obliged to hammer out a horse-laugh, even with the weight of a life-long grief, misery and futility lying heavy on her heart. Her person is sold to others for money, while she often meets a violent death. Fire, water, a king, a woman, a fool, or a serpent used or provoked by another, should be regarded as fatal. What wonder is it that a man well-versed in letters will pass as an erudite one? What is surprising in the fact that a king who is learned in the science of politics will rule justly as a virtuous prince? What is there to wonder, if a young and beautiful woman, proud and conscious of her charms, leads a gay and fast life? What is there to surprise, if an indigent person commits a crime? Let not your neighbour know of your weakness, but rather observe his weak points unseen, like a turtle, from your own housetop. Amorous fancies spontaneously occur even in the mind of a girl, who has been incarcerated from her infancy in a moated castle in the nether worlds. Who can pretend to conquer a woman? O Shounaka, an intelligent brother-worker of yours can do you more harm, if inimical, than a professed enemy who is not in your line. He who can preserve his children in health, please the ladies of his household with money, propitiate the heavens with his penances, and win the good opinion of the public with his urbanity, alone deserves the epithet of a learned man. Those who try to coerce a man to friendship or to win a woman with brute force, and seek knowledge without any effort and prosperity, by working the ruin of others, cannot be called wise. It is foolishness to cut down a tree for its fruits. A tree or a project that yields good fruits, should never be uprooted, O Vipra. How can I believe that a rich man to be an anchorite, and a drunken woman chaste? Trust not the untrustworthy nor confide any secret in your friend, lest he might betray you in a fit of anger. A vast, deep and child-like faith in all, a universal clemency, and a close and watchful veiling of his own god-like inherent virtues, are the traits which mark a noble soul. The doer of an act does alone feel its consequence. Hence all works should be coolly pondered over before execution. The six things, such as the use of a new wine or Trimulakam (*lit.*,—horse radish in its three different forms), the partaking of curd in the night, or of dried meat, sleep during the day, and the bed of an elderly woman, should be abjured.

A family is a poison (ruinous) to a poor man. A young wife is a poison (fatal) to an old man. Poison is an ill-acquired knowledge, or a food that cannot be digested. Sweet is charity to a man of bountiful spirit, sweet is social elevation to a man who has risen from the ranks, bounties are sweet to the indigent, and by far the sweetest of them all is his youthful bride to a man of advanced years. Excessive water-drinking, constant use of hard seats or cushions, loss of vital fluid, repression of any natural urging of the body, sleep by the day and vigils in the night, are the six exciting factors of disease. Exposure to the rays of the sun when he stays in the sign of Virgo, sexual excesses, exposure to the smoke of a cremation-ground, the heating of the palms of one's hands, and the sight of a woman in her menses, tend to shorten life. Dried meat, exposure to the rays of the autumn, sun (in Virgo), curd of more than two days' manufacture (Tarunam Dadhi), intercourse with a woman older than one's own self, and sleep and coitus in the morning are the six depletive agents that tend to reduce strength and vitality. The six things such as, butter manufactured and clarified very same day, grapes, a young wife, a milk potion, tepid water and the shadow of a tree, instantaneously contribute to the formation of strength in the human organism. The water of a well, the shadow of a Vata tree, and the breasts of a youthful maiden, become warm in winter and cold in summer.

The three following, *viz.*, a young wife, an annointment with oil, and a wholesome, toothsome meal instantaneously tend to impart strength to the organism. A fatiguing journey, an act of sexual intercourse and an attack of fever are the three factors which instantaneously diminish the strength of a man. Dry meat should not be taken with milk, nor a man should sit down to a meal in the company of his friends and wives, or with the king of his country, inasmuch as such a conduct might lead to a rupture and misunderstanding. Torn and filthy clothes, voracious eating, rough speaking and sleep at dusk and dawn, are the factors which may bring bad luck to the God Chakrapáni, the lord of the wealth goddess. The cutting of weeds with nails, the digging of earth with toes, the bandying and beating of legs against each other, the wearing of filthy garments and dirty clotted hairs, sleeping both at day-break and night-fall, and without the wearing cloth, the beating against one's back and belly to keep time with music, a voracious appetite and boistrous laughter are the causes which may destroy the opulence even of the god Keshava himself. A cooled and well-washed head, the well-cleansed extremities, an intercourse with a virtuous woman of commendable features except on the nights of the new and the full moon, and sleeping in the night with the usual wearing cloth on, are the acts which may retrieve one's long-lost fortune. The wearing of any flower, and of a white flower in special, on the head, bars the advent of Bad Luck which has her favourite haunts in the back shadow of a bedstead, or in that of a cushion or lighted lamp, and at the pools where washer women wash their dirty linens. A man with any love of life and health shall avoid exposure to the autumnal sun (*lit.*, staying in the sign of Virgo), or to the smokes and exhalations of a cremation ground, or to the sweepings of a chamber, and coition with woman who is his older in years, and the use of putrid curd technically known as Tarunam Dadhi. The particles of dust brushed off from the sides of a horse, of a cow, of an elephant, or of a chariot are auspicious, while those obtained from the body of an ass, of a sheep, or of a camel are unholy. Paddy-dusts as well as those which stick to the body of one's own child or cow, are holy and sin-expiating in their contact. Dusts which are brushed off from the sides of a goat, or of an ass, as well as those which are raised by a sweeping broom are unholy and unhealthy. The wind wafted by a winnow, the washings of hair and nails, the dribblets from one's bathing cloth and bath-pitcher, as well as the dusts which float before a sweeping broom, have the power of destroying the pieties of a man acquired even in a previous existence.

You must not walk between two rows of Bráhmanas, nor between a fire and a Bráhmana, nor between a man and his wife, nor between two bulls or elephants. What wise man will believe in a woman, in a serpent, in a king, in the services done by his own enemy, in the infallible nature of his own knowledge and memory and in the enjoyment of the worldly pleasures, even for once in life? Trust not those who are unworthy of credence. Do not repose unbounded faith even in the trustworthy, lest they might bring about your ruin and overthrow by betraying it.

He who rests confident after having made a reconciliation with his enemy, is sure to a fall one day like a man who peacefully reposes on a tree-top. Be not too mild nor too fierce, but subdue a mild enemy with a mild means and a fierce one with fierce measures. Be not too straight nor too crooked. Crooked trees are left standing while the straight ones are felled by a forester. Trees that are laden with fruits are bent under their burden, a heavy rain-cloud seems to touch the ground with the weight of its charge; but a fool and a dry wood breaks under pressure but knows no bending. Pleasure and pain come and go without asking. Men, like cats, are ever ready to pounce upon happiness. Many a happiness walks before and after a virtuous man, the contrary being the case with the inequitous. A counsel heard by six ears (discussed among three men) is soon divulged; heard by four it is kept secret for a while. He who keeps his own counsel baffles the scrutiny of the god Brahmá.

Of what use is the cow which does not conceive and give milk? Of what good is the son who is not wise and virtuous? A single moon illumines the heaven; a single son, virtuous and erudite, sheds lustre on the family. A single tree in blossom purfumes the whole wood land; a single good son gives fragrance to the whole family tree. A single erudite son is the light of the whole family, a family of a hundred illiterate ones is but a grand noodledom. A single moon dispels the darkness of the heaven which hundreds of stars are incapable of doing. A child should be only fondled for the first five years, and ruled or tutored for the next ten. A son of sixteen should be looked upon in the light of a friend and adviser by his father. A son, as soon as he is born, monopolises (robs his father of) the love of his mother. Coming into age he usurps his father's estate. His doleful look is a death to the parent. A son is the worst enemy a father may possibly have. There are deer-mouthed tigers and tiger-mouthed deer in this world; an implicit confidence in them is the best means of drawing out their nature, on each occasion. The only defect of a pardoning spirit is that its toleration is often mistaken for its weakness or incapability. I do not know what other defects it has. Know all enjoyments in life to be transitory, and do not build your happiness on the foundation of a frail heart's affection; since whom you love most, may be taken away the next morning. The eldest brother, O Shounaka, is a father to the younger ones after the demise of their progenitor. Hence he shall look after them all with the same loving and anxious care. The younger brothers should be devoted to their eldest, and he shall look upon them as his own begotten children. Strong is the combination of small and insignificant men. Straws, strung together into a rope, may be strong enough to fetter an elephant. Benevolence with stolen or ill-gotten wealth, leads to hell; the merit is of him to whom the money rightfully belongs. The family of one who robs the gods and the Bráhmanás or humiliates a member of that sacred order, is degraded. The sin which is attached to wine-drinking, to theft, to a broken vow, or to a Bráhmana-slaughter may be atoned for. There is no expiation for ingratitude. The gods and manes accept not the offerings by a person who is uxorious, or who connives at the whoredom of his own wife or at her illicit amours under his own roof. The dishonest, the wicked, the crooked and the invalid, form the four classes of Chandálas, the fifth being by the accident of birth. An enemy or an evil propensity, however small, should not be neglected. A tiny spark of fire may eventually spread and consume the whole world. Self-control in youth is the only genuine thing; continence is the natural offspring of old age. A public woman, like the right of passage on a public thoroughfare belongs to the whole community; and hence she should not be suffered to be molested or insulted.

O thou the foremost of the Bráhmanás, the vital principles of the body are dependent on consciousness (*lit.*, mind). The body perishes when the mind is extinct for good. Hence the equilibrium of mind should carefully preserved. A healthy mind is the nursery of healthy thoughts.

—:o:—

CHAPTER CXV.

SUTA said:—A false wife, a false friend, a false prince, a false relation, and a false country, should be shunned from a distance. Virtue will fly from the earth in the Kali Yuga; Truth will be taken down from her altar and pilloried in the market; Earth will lose her fecundity; Craft will usurp the throne of ethics; Greed will be the god of the Bráhmanás; men will be slaves to their wives' fancies; and the low and the vile will be elevated in the world. Blessed are they that die early in that iron age. Blessed are they that witness not the ruin of their own house or country, or live not to see their wives making love to others and their sons walking in the path of infamy. Countless are the ways in which a bad son torments his father. What love can there be for a false wife, what confidence in a false friend? What guarantee of life and living can there be in the realm of a false prince? To eat another man's bread, to be a hangeron on another man's purse, to lie in another's bed and with another's wife, and to lodge in another man's house are the iniquities which may send even an Indra (lord of the celestials) to go a-begging in the world.

Sinful contagion spreads from man to man by conversation, by touch, or by company of the impious, or by sharing same beds and cushions with them. A woman is ruined by her beauty; a penance, by anger; a cow, by straying far out of the fold; a Bráhman, by partaking of a meal cooked by a S'udra. Sin spreads from man to man by contagion as water passes off from one pitcher to another by syphoning. Fondling of a son by his father is fraught with many an evil consequence. Innumerable are the benefits which accrue from chastisement. Hence a son or a disciple should be birched and not fondled. A long pedestrial journey is old age (proves exhausting) to men (*lit.*, organic beings.) Water is death to a mountain, the abjuring of her bed by her lord spells death to a wife, and heat is death to clothes. Sensuality is the idol of the vulgar; good men long for peace, and the best covet honour which is the true wealth to the noble. Honour is the culminating stage of wealth. Why do you covet wealth when you have honour? What is wealth to a man who has suffered in his honour and prestige? The vulgar seek only wealth; good men, riches and honour; the best only strive for honour which is the wealth of the noble. A hungry lion do not flap his ears, nor bend down his head to look at his armpits. A noble man in indigence, does not stoop to mean things.

A lion does not wait for being anointed, or a crowned king of the forest by any body. The right of sovereignty is inherently vested in valour; and the chivalrous are the born rulers of men. A dishonest merchant, a haughty servant, a luxurious friar, a poor voluptuary, and a scolding beauty are the anomalies in the world. A poor, benevolent person, a rich miser, a wild disobedient son, a service under the wicked or the vulgar, and the ruin of a person in a philanthrophic cause, are the five anomalies in life which illustrate the examples of living death. The death of one's own dear wife, humiliation at the hands of one's own relations, a debt—unpaid and undischarged, a service of the low and the vulgar and desertion by friends in one's evil days, are the five things which though not fire in themselves, consume one's vitals. The thoughts of a starving family, of a scolding wife, of dissensions with one's own brothers, and of suffering humiliation at the hands of a mean, sordid wretch, are the four thoughts which are like sword blades to the heart, out of the hundred that agitate or ruffle the human mind. A good obedient son, a knowledge that helps one to earn money, a sound health, the company of the virtuous, and a loving sweet speaking wife, are the five things which dispel misery in the world. The bear, the elephant, the fly, the bee, and the fish are the five animals which destroy one another in the universe in their order of enumeration; but man deals death to all of them. Why should he not be killed by his fully gratified senses by way of divine retribution? The presence of a poor, ill-clad, rough-haired Bráhmaná, though otherwise erudite like the holy Vrihaspati, passes unnoticed in the mansions of the rich. The longevity, desting, character, erudition and death of a child are the factors, which should be reckoned at the time of its nativity. Commendable is the character of the man who succours a drowned man from his watery grave, or one fallen in climbing a hill, or in a local feud, or is attacked by a wild bull in a pasturage, or any way degraded in society.

The shadow of a cloud, the love of the malicious, an intimacy with another man's wife, youth and opulence, are the five equally transitory things in the world. Life is transitory. Transient are the youth and opulence of a man. Wives, children, friends, and relations are but passing shadows in the phantasmagoria of life. Only virtue and good deeds endure. Even a centenarian has but a short space of life, the one-half of which is covered by the night, the other half being rendered fruitless by disease, grief, imbecility and toil. Night covers the one-half of the hundred years allotted to man and is spent in sleep. Infancy and boyhood cover the half of the other moiety, a part of its remaining half being cloudened by grief, misery and service.

The rest is but changeful and transient like a wave of the ocean. Ah, what is the end of life? What does glory, fame, or honour signify? Death with his attendants Day and Night is perpetually travelling the world in the guise of Old Age, and is devouring all created beings, as a serpent gulps down a gust of wind.

At rest, or while moving about, in sleep, or while awake, always try to do good to the world. Good deeds are the wages of life. He who seeks only his own good, is an animal. The man who has lost all conscience, lets himself be carried away by many an ignoble and worldly care at the time of divine service, and is troubled only with the cares of pampering his belly, is an animal. The man, who has acquired no fame in respect of piety, penance, benevolence, and learning, is but the excrement of his own mother. A good life, lived even for a short while by a man in the fame of his learning, valour or manliness, is called right living by the wise.—Does not a crow eat and live to term? A life without wealth or fame is a failure. What is the use of an ally who constantly apprehends evil and falls back at the wanted time? Cast not doleful looks, but live like a hero, O Shounaka, even a crow gets its food in the world and is plagued with the toil of simple continunance from day to day. Of what use is the life of a man who does not come to the help of his servants, relations, friends or the needy? Does not a crow eat and live to term? He who passes his days without earning fame, piety, and wealth, is like the belows of an Ironsmith which breathes out wind but does not live. An independent living is success in life, a dependent existence is the false rendering of life's inner meaning. They who are servanted to others, are the monuments of living death. Cowards are they who rest satisfied with the fulfilment of their own personal wants.—Does not the mouse in the hole gets his bellyful? Cowards grumble most but are contented with a little.

The shadow of a cloud, the wild-fire, the service of the vulgar, the water in a rut, the love of a courtesan, and the friendship of the malicious, are the six things which are transient like the bubbles of water. A good advice is always unpalatable. Life is leased on honour. What remains when truth is broken? The king is the strength of the weak. The strength of a woman lies in her tears; silence is the shield of the ignorant, and falsehood is the refuge of the thieves. Study a science so that you may have your own light on the subject, that is the only right kind of study. While staying in a country do what is done by its inhabitants, combine with them, win their favour and thereby serve your own interest. A man is ruined by his greed, lust or undue confidence. Hence these three should be averted. A dread is to be dreaded so long as it does not come; when once present, a man should meet it with a bold front. The undischarged residue of a debt, the unextinguished residue of a fire, and the unconquered residue of an enemy, may increase and grow stronger. Hence they should be totally extinguished. Repay good by good and evil by evil, O Shounaka, I do not think it bad politics. Avoid a friend who speaks sweet in your presence and slander you behind your back. A good man is ruined by an evil company; clear water is made turbid with clay. Whatever is enjoyed by a Bráhmaná, is put to right use. Hence a Bráhmaná should be feasted at all costs. He who eats the residue of the dishes of a Bráhmaná, eats only in the right way. He who commits no sin, is clever. A friend is he who speaks good of you behind your back. A good deed done without bragging, is piety. It is no assembly where there is no old man. They are no old men who do not uphold what is virtuous. What does not contain truth, is no virtue, and a truth which is a half truth, is no truth at all.

The Brâhmanás are the noblest of mankind; the sun is the most resplendent of the stars; the head is the most important of all organs; and truth is the highest of all vows. A thing which instantaneously affects the mind as good, is good. Living, without serving any body's will, is true living. True earning is that which is enjoyed by one's relations. He who has been abandoned by his enemy in a battle-field, is abandoned. A wife who is not proud of her charms, is a true wife. He who has abjured all desires, is happy. He is a friend in whom confidence is reposed. The man who has subjugated his senses, is a man. He who brags of his own virtues and holds a very exalted opinion of himself, should not be loved, nor be made a friend. The sources of rivers, fire-worshippers (Agni-hotris) and the race of Bhárata should not be tried to be discovered, as it may lead to the discovery of many an unpleasant thing. The sea is the final goal of a river, one's love-making ends with the illicit amours of one's own wife; and a mischievous propensity is checked by a healthy public opinion. The effect of wealth is misery. The prosperity of a king may be ended by the curse of a Bráhmana; decency and cleanliness, by living close to the dwelling of a Ghosa; and a family is ruined where women reign supreme. All accumulations are followed by waste. All risings end in fall; combinations, in dissolutions; evolutions, in involutions; and life, in death. Proceed not far with haste in a business so that you may easily retrace your steps. Walk not far with your guest from a place where you intend to return. A friend or a preceptor should be bid adieu to by following him up to the border of a pool, or under the shade of a tree of pleasant foliage. Dwell not in a country where there is no law, or in which the central government is vested in a more than one responsible head, or which is governed by a woman or an infant. A woman is protected by her father in infáncy, by her husband in youth, and by her son in old age. She has no separate and independent living. A man is at liberty to marry a second wife in the event of his first having had no issue after eight years of wedlock; after nine years of that of one whose children die in their infancy; after eleven years of the marriage a wife that has given birth to daughters only, and instantly when the first is foul-mouthed and tries to give him a bit of her mind. A man of honest purpose and entrusted with the duty of feeding many mouths, never suffers any humiliation on account pecuniary difficulties. A noble forethought for providing for the wants of many and a sacred dread for being found wanting in his duties, makes him a ready master of resources and of ways and means under difficulties. A suppliant never returns half-fed from his door. The family is a seminary of applied ethics. Fatherhood is a synopsis of the moral economy of the universe and marriage is the pledge (*lit.*,—a pawn) for its realisation on earth, serving as a grand citadel of man on the border land of mental affections where the light begins to fail and the kingdom of darkness begins.

A wise man should keep at a respectful distance from a tired horse, a wild (excited) elephant, a cow after her first parturition and a toad squatting on the dry ground. A suppliant for money has nither friends nor relations. A voluptuous man has neither shame nor dread. A care-worn man is a stranger, to sleep and happiness, and a starving man wants no salt but nutrition. Sleep is forbidden to the poor, to the slaves, to thieves and to those who are in love with their neighbours' wives. Soundly do they sleep who are healthy, free, or owe no money-debts, or are not plagued with the love of a woman. A servant is honoured in proportion to the social elevation of his master; the height of a lotus lily is proportionate to that of the water level of the pool it grows in. The sun and Varuna (water) serve as friends to a water-lily in its days of bloom and prosperity, but they cause it to wither and petrify when it is severed from its stem. The friends who flock round a man in office turn his enemies when he is ousted of it. The sun who gladly unfolds the petals of a water-lily on its stem in water, scorches it when it is culled and taken out of its element. Men are respected for their office and position. Men's hair and nails are fostered in their natural seats and shunned as obnoxious excrescences when severed from them. Conduct shows the birth or parentage of a man; and his speech, his country. Deference or regard bespeaks affection; and the body, the nature and quantity of one's food. Useless is the rain to the sea; a good meal is a useless superfluity to a well-fed man. Useless are the gifts to the rich; and kind acts, to the mean. He who is close to the heart, can never be really absent. A wide gulf separates a couple when hearts are estranged, even, though they may sit side by side.

A distorted face, a low sunk voice, a clammy sweat, and a sense of vague dread are the symptoms which mark the dying and the begging men alike. A man of honour prefers a snake-bite or a stroke of paralysis, or a life-long physical deformity, or a second birth by self immolation, to begging. Who is he that is not lowered by begging? Even the Supreme God (Vishnu) suffered a diminution of stature by playing the role of a supplicant in the religious sacrifice celebrated by Vali.

The parents of a child are but his enemies when they fail to educate him properly in his boyhood. An illiterate boy, like a heron amidst swans, cannot shine in the assembly of of the learned. Learning imparts a heightened charm to a homely face. Knowledge is the best treasure that a man can secretly hoard up in life. Learning is the revered of the revered. Knowledge makes a man honest, virtuous and endearing to the society. It is learning alone that enables a man to better the condition of his friends and relations. Knowledge is the holiest of the holies, the god of the gods, and commands the respect of crowned heads; shorn of it a man is but an animal. The fixtures and furniture of one's house may be stolen by thieves; but knowledge, the highest treasure, is above all stealing. This synopsis of ethics, was first related to S'aunaka by Vishnu. The god Hara learnt it from S'aunaka and related it to the birthless Vyasa who has illumined our minds on the subject.

—:o:—

CHAPTER CXVI.

SUTA said :—I shall now deal with the mode of practising those religious vows and penances, O Vyasa, by which a man may win the good graces of the god Hari to the extent that he may be pleased to answer all his prayers. The god should be worshipped in all months of the year and in all days of the week, and under the auspicies of all lunar phases and astral combinations. The votary shall observe a fast or take a single meal in the night, or live upon a fruit regimen on the day of the vow, and make gifts of money and paddy for the satisfaction of the god Vishnu, for which he will be blest with the birth of a son and the ownership of fresh landed estates. The gods Kuvera and Vaishvánara, worshipped under the auspices of the first phase of the moon's wane, grant wealth and opulence to their votary. On the same day, the votary shall fast and worship either the god Brahmá which will be rewarded with opulence and a number of mares. The deities Yama, Lakshmi and Náráyana, worshipped on the second day of the fortnight, grant wealth to their votaries. The three deities Gauri, Vighnesha and S'ankara, should be worshipped on the third day of the fortnight. The god Chaturvyuha should be worshipped on the fourth day of the moon's wane and the god Hari on the fifth; the Sun God and Kartikeya, on the sixth; and the god Bhaskara on the seventh.

The goddess Durgá with her female cohorts and the guardians of the different quarters of the heaven, should be worshipped on the eighth and the ninth day of the fortnight for a pecuniary boon; the Moon-God, on the tenth; the Rishis, on the eleventh; the god Hari, on the twelfith; and the god Maheshwara on the thirteenth day of the moon's increase which is known as the Madana-Trayodashi. The god Brahmá, and the Pitris, worshipped on the fourteenth and the fifteenth day of the fortnight, give wealth to their votaries. The presiding deities of the different days of the week, as well as the sun god and the asterisms, etc., worshipped on the day of the new moon, give all that they are supplicated for by their votaries.

——:o:——

CHAPTER CVII.

SUTA said:—O Vyasa, the vow of Ananga-Trayodashi falls on the thirteenth day of the moon's increase in the month of Margas'irsha; and the god S'iva should be worshipped on the day with the offerings of Dhustura flowers and tooth-brushes of Mallikâ twigs. The votary shall live on honey on the day of the worship in the month of Pousha and make offerings of a variety of confectionaries to the god of love, and worship the god Yoges'vara (S'iva) with Vilva leaves, tooth-brushes of Kadamva twigs, sandal-paste and S'uskulis (Puris and Kachouris). The god Nateshvara should be worshipped with Kunda flowers; and strings of pearls and offerings of Purikas and of Plaksha twigs as tooth-brushes should be made to him. The god Vires'vara should be worshipped with Maruvaka flowers in the month of Phálguna and offerings of sugar, pot herbs and Mandas should be made to him,

O holy sage, together with the twigs of a Chuta tree as tooth-brushes. The votary shall take nothing but camphor on the day of worship in the month of Chaitra, when the Surupa manifestation of the god shall be propitiated with the offerings of S'uskulis and tooth-brushes of Vata twigs. In the month of Vais'áka, the god S'ambhu should be worshipped with the offerings of Modakas and As'oka flowers and confections made of treacle as well as tooth-brushes of Audumvara twigs, and nutmeg should be dedicated to him by reciting the Mantra which reads as, "Obeisance to Maharupa." The god Pradyumna should be worshipped with Champaka flowers in the month of Jaishtha; and tooth-brushes of Vilva twigs should be offered to him. The votary shall take nothing but cloves on the day of the Puja in the month of Ashída and worship the god with the flowers of Apámárga. Tooth-brushes of Agaru twigs should be offered to the god by reciting the Mantra which runs as "Om, Obeisance to the god Umá-bhadra. The god should be worshipped with the offerings of Karavira flowers, clarified butter and cushions in the month of S'rávana, and tooth-brushes of Karavira twigs should be dedicated to him with the repetition of the Mantra which reads as "Om, Obeisance to the mace-bearing god who is without any origin." In the month of A's'vina the god should be worshipped with the offerings of Vakula flowers, cakes and tooth-brushes of Madhavi twigs which should be dedicated to him by reciting the Mantra which runs as, "Obeisance to the god who is the source of perpetual genesis." The Surádhipa (the lord of the celestials) manifestation of the god, should be worshipped in the month of A's'vina when offerings of Champaka flowers, Modakas, and tooth-brushes of catechu twigs should be dedicated to him. The god Rudra should be worshipped in the month of Kárt'ika with the offerings of tooth-brushes of Vadari twigs. At the year's end, the Puja should be closed with the offerings of milk, pot herbs and lotus flowers to the deity.

The votary who has been living a life of strict continence from a few days before the date of the worship, shall worship the image of the god of love on a golden throne with the offerings of flowers, perfumes, etc.; and a thousand oblations of Vrihi and sesame seeds should be cast into the sacrificial fire in his honour. The votary shall pass the night in songs and festivities and again worship the god on the morrow, making gifts of bed, cushions, umbrellas, shoes, clothes and metal-utensils filled with seeds, to the Bráhmanas. After that, he shall feed the cows and the Bráhmanas and think himself as a man who has accomplished the ends of his life. The vow should be thus practised for a year, after which it should be closed. The Vratam under discussion is called Ananga-Trayodashi, a due performance of which is rewarded with health, opulence, a beautiful wife and the blessings of paternity.

—:o:—

CHAPTER CXVIII.

BRAHMA said:—Now I shall describe the mode of practising the Akhanda-Dvâdashi-Vratam, the merit attending it performance enables the votary to enjoy divine beatitude in life. The votary shall take nothing but the Panchagavyam (the five kinds of articles obtained from a cow such as, milk, etc.,) on the day previous, and fast on the twelfth day of the moon's increase in the month of Márgas'irsha, spending it entirely in the worship of the god Vishnu. Five metal vessels filled with Vrihi corn, should be gifted away to the Bráhmanas each day for the four successive months commencing from the date. The votary shall pray as follows:—"May the merit of all good and pious acts done by me in my seven prior incarnations, continue one and indivisible, O lord. May all my pieties continue whole and undivided as the universe is, and just as thou art the one and indivisible spirit which runs through all." Vessels filled with powders of freed barley corns, should be gifted away by him in the month of Chaitra ; and bowls filled with clarified butter, in the month of S'rávana. Earthly bliss and the pleasures of fatherhood are the rewards of the vow in this life, and an elevated status in heaven, in the next.

—:0:—

CHAPTER CXIX.

BRAHMA said :—Now I shall describe the mode of practising the Agastyárgha-Vratam. The vow should be celebrated on the three days immediately before the sun passes into the sign of Virgo. O thou holy sage, an image of Agastya, should be made of Kásha flowers, and worshipped inside a water-pitcher. The Argha offering should be duly made to it and the votary shall pass the night in vigil and divine contemplation. He shall fast that day and worship the image with the offerings of curd, sesamum, fruits and flowers and formally dedicate the vessel containing the Argha offering to the god. The vessel should be tinged with five colours (containing rice powders of five colours) and filled with bits of gold and silver and the seven kinds of cereals, technically known as the Saptadhányam, besmeared with curd and sandal paste. The Argham should be finally offered by reciting the Mantra which reads as follows :—" I make obeisance to thee, O Agastya, who art the offspring of Mitrá and Varuna, and hence retain in thy self the principles of ether and water. I make obeisance to thee, (O Agastya,) who art hoary as the Kásha flower and wast born in a pitcher."

Even women and S'udras are admitted to the privilege of practising the vow as above described. The votary shall forego all fruits, rice meals, and vegetable juices during the observance of the vow, which should be closed by feasting and making gifts of water-pitchers with bits of gold to the Bráhmanas. The successive observance of the vow for seven years is rewarded with the realisation of one's all wished-for ends.

—:o:—

CHAPTER CXX.

BRAHMA said :—Now I shall deal with the mode of practising the Rambhá-Tritiyá-Vratam which brings good luck, and opulence to the votary and blesses him with the pleasures of fatherhood, etc. The votary shall fast on the third day of the moon's increase in the month of Márgas'ira, procure water and the blades of the sacred Kusha grass, and worship the goddess Gouri with the offerings of Vilva leaves and tooth-brushes made of Kadmavá twigs. In the month of Pousha he shall take nothing but camphor on the day of the Vratam and worship the goddess Girisutá (the mountain-daughter) with the offerings of Kuruvaka flowers, Krisharas and tooth-brushes of Mallikâ twigs. In the month of Mágha, the votary shall live on a butter regimen on the day of the penance and worship the goddess Subhadrá with the offerings of Kalhára flowers, Mandas, and imaginary tooth-brushes formed of the spirit of song and harmony (Gitimayi). In the month of Phálguna, the votary shall take nothing but barley gruel after the Puja on the day of the vow, and worship the goddess Gomati with the offerings of S'askulis and tooth-brushes of Kunda stems. The goddess Vis'álákshi should be worshipped with the offerings of Mádhavi flowers and Krishras, and the votary shall take curd after that and dedicate tooth-brushes of Tagara twigs to the goddess. The S'rimukhi manifestation of the deity should be worshipped with Karavikara flowers in the month of Vais'áka, the votary eating nothing but the polens of As'oka flowers and dedicating tooth-brushes of As'oka twigs to her, therafter. The Nárayani manifestation of the goddess should be worshipped in the month of Jaishtha with the offerings of treacle (khanda) and lotus lilies; and the votary shall take nothing but cloves after the Puja on the day. The goddess Mádhavi should be worshipped with the offerings of Vilva leaves in the month of A'shad'a. The goddess S'ri should be woshipped in the month of S'rávana with the offerings of Kshiránnam and tooth-brushes of Audumvara twigs. The votary shall take nothing but sesame seeds and offer tooth-brushes of Tagara twigs, after that, to the goddess. The goddess Uttamá should be worshipped in the month of Bhádra with the offerings of tooth-brushes of Malliká twigs. The votary shall take nothing but S'ringada after the Puja on the day. The goddess Rájaputri should be worshipped in the month of A's'vina with the offerings of Javá flowers; and the votary shall eat nothing, but Jiraka on the night of the Vratam. The goddess Padmajá should be worshipped in the month of Kárt'ika with the offerings of Játi flowers, fruits, viands, and Krisharás and the votary shall take nothing but the Panchagavyam, that day. The Vratam should be thus celebrated for a year and closed by feasting a Brahmana pair and distributing confections made of clarified butter to the Bráhmanas. After that, Umá and Mahes'vara should be worshipped with the usual ceremonial rites; and gold, silver, confectionaries, clothes, and umbrellas should be given to the Bráhmanas, the night of the final celebration being spent in songs and revelry.

CHAPTER CXXI.

BRAHMA said :—Now I shall describe the mode of practising the Cháturmásyam Vratam. The vow should be first undertaken on the eleventh day of the moon's increase in the month of Ashád'a, or on the day of the full moon therein, after having duly worshipped and supplicated the god Hari as follows :—" May the Vratam which I have, this day, undertaken in thy presence, O lord, come to a successful termination, by thy grace and will. Kindly deem it complete, O Janárd'ana, even if I be not spared to fulfil it as now vowed for."

Thus having worshipped and addressed the god, the votary shall get himself initiated into the acts of subsequent meditation and penitence. The sins of a man, who wishes to practise this vow for the satisfaction of the god Hari, are annihilated. He who bathes and takes a single meal each day during the four months under discussion, ascends, a pure and undefiled spirit, to the region of Vishnu. A Bráhmana, who is well-versed in the Védás and abjures oil, wine, women, and animal food for these four months, goes to the region of Vishnu, by practising the present Vratam, and attains to that stage of self-liberation which is called Sâyuyayam (*lit.*—to be in perpetual touch with the Supreme Self). Even by fasting for a single night during the season, a man is transformed into a god, after death.

By fasting for three consecutive days during the season, a man is sure to be translated to Shveta-dvipa, after death. An unsolicited emancipation waits the man who practises a Chándráyana Vratam during the period. By practising a Prájápatyan during the period, a man attains to the region of Vishnu. The performance of a Paráka Vratam under the circumstance, is attended with the same result. The votary shall live on powdered barley (Shaktu), barley gruel, milk, curd or clarified butter, or on alms during the entire term of the vow, which may be substituted for cow's urine, barley gruel or the Panchagavyam. He shall forego the use of all pot herbs, fruits, roots and vegetable juices. He who practises the vow as above indicated, shall attain to the region of Vishnu.

——:o:——

CHAPTER CXXII.

BRAHMA said :—Now I shall describe the mode of practising the vow of a month's privation, which is the best of all penances. It is imparatively obligatory on women, anchorites and forest-dwelling hermits to practise the penance. The votary shall undertake the vow, first on the day of the eleventh phase of the moon's increase in the month of As'vina, and which is to be continued for the next consecutive thirty days. He shall invoke the help of the god Hari for the successful termination of his vow by reciting the prayer which reads as follows :—"I undertake this vow in thy presence, O Vishnu. From this date, I shall worship thee fasting continuously for a month each day until the day of thy rising from slumber. I shall practise this vow from the twelfth day of the moon's increase in the month of As'vina to the corresponding day of the month of Kârtika. May I not be accused of the sin of a broken vow if I die in the interim, and may my Vratam be deemed complete by thy grace even under the circumstance."

The penitent shall thrice bathe each day, and worship the god Hari with the offerings of perfumes, etc., during the term of the Vratam. He shall abjure the use of oil and unguents during the period, and break his vow on the day of the twelfth phase of the moon's increase in the month of Kârtika. The god should be worshipped at the close of the Vratam; and the Brâhmanas, sumptuously feasted; after which the penitent shall break his fast. Milk may be taken by the penitent in the case of his fainting during the fast, without any apprehension of breaking his vow, the reward of its observance being enjoyment of creature comforts in this life, and residence in heaven in the next.

—:0:—

CHAPTER CXXIII.

BRAHMA said :—I shall now enumerate the Vratas which are to be practised in the month of Kártika. A votary of Vishnu shall take his ablution and worship his deity each morning. The votary shall take a single meal each] day, or shall live on alms in connection with the practising of any Vratam in the month of Kártika. In the alternative, he shall live on vegetables or on a milk regimen, whereby he shall be exonerated from all sins, will witness the realisation of all his wished-for objects, and ascend, a stainless spirit, to the region of heaven after death. A Vratam, practised at any time in honour of the god Hari, ranks foremost in respect of merit; and specially so is the one, performed when the sun is in the winter solstice. The Chaturmásyam is the greatest of all annual Vratas, while the one, practised in the month of Kártika and known as the Bhishmapanchakam, is better than the former. The Bhishmapanchakam Vratam should be practised on the day of the eleventh phase of the moon's increase in the month of Kârtika, in connection with which the practiser shall thrice bathe each day, worship the god Hari, and propitiate his departed manes with the offerings of barley corn. Further he shall observe a vow of silence; perform the rite of ceremonial ablution, with a solution of Panchagavyam in sacred water, unto the god Hari; and annoint his image with camphorated unguents. A Brâhmana votary, under the circumstance, shall continuously burn, for five days, incense sticks made of Guggulu and clarified butter, and dedicate viands, edibles and Paramânnas (a kind of sweetened rice porridge) to the god, and cast hundred and eight libations of clarified butter into the sacrificial fire by repeating the Mantra which runs as, "Om, obeisance to the god Vâsudeva."

On the first day, the feet of the divine image (Vishnu) should be worshipped with lotus flowers; its knees, with the Vilva leaves on the second; its navel, with sandal paste on the third; its shoulders, with the Javâ flowers and Vilva leaves on the fonrth; and its head, with the Malati flowers on the fifth. The votary shall lie down on the bare ground during the entire term of the Vratam and successively take the five components of Panchagavyam, *viz.*, one on each day of the worship, taking the entire compound (Panchagavyam) on the fifth night. By practising the vows as above described, a man becomes entitled to the pleasures of the two worlds.

The performance of the Ekádasi Vratam is imparatively obligatory on all, a breach being sinful and degrading. A man shall observe a fast on the eleventh day of the fortnight, whether light or dark, inasmuch as it tends to absolve him of all sins, precludes the chance of his ever visiting the shades of Haydes and makes him entitled to the beatitude of the region of Vishnu. A man observing a fast on the eleventh day of the fortnight, shall break it on the twelfth, and resume his usual mode of living on the night of the thirteenth. A day entirely marked by the eleventh phase of the moon, should be regarded as permeated with the blessed Self of Hari. The day on which the moon is both in her tenth and eleventh phases, should be regarded as consigned to the demons. Hence fasting on such a day is prohibited.

The votary shall break his fast on the twelfth day of the fortnight. The performance of an Ekádasi Vratam is never affected by the personal uncleanness incidental to the death or birth of one's agnates. Fasts, which are to be made on the fourteenth, or on the first day of the fortnight, should be respectively observed on a day when the moon exists for a while in her preceding phase. The same rule holds good in respect of Dvitiyá, Tritiyá, Chaturthi, Panchami and Shashthi Vratras.

—:o:—

CHAPTER CXXIV.

BRAHMA said :—I shall now describe the mode of practising the S'ivarátra Vratam, the performance of which confers all wished-for blessings on the practiser. The goddess Gouri learnt it of yore from the god Mahâdeva, the lord of all created beings. The god said :—" He who keeps a vigil and worships the god Rudra on the night of the fourteenth phase of the moon's wane which comes between the months of Mágha and Phálguna, becomes entitled to the pleasures of life and the liberation of self. The god Mahâdeva emancipates the votary from the chain of necessary existence in the instance, as the god Kes'ava does on the occasion of an Ekâdasi Vratam.

Once upon a time, the vicious Sundara Sena, the king of the country of Arvuda, went out, with his dogs, on a hunting excursion in the forest. But the day wore on and night came without any game even being sighted. The hunter, hungry and jaded with the day's trouble, sat down weary and watchful in a bower on the bank of a pool on the hill-brow. But lo, there happened to be a phallic emblem in that bower, and the leaves of the Vilva tree, which was shaken by the impact of the hunter's body as he strove to lie down on the ground, rustled and fell in heaps over the emblem, without his knowledge. The fowler fetched water from the pool and sprinkled it over the floor of the bower to lay down the dust; and drops of water thus dribbled down over the head of the emblem from the tips of his fingers. Suddenly there fell down a shaft from his quiver on the ground, and the fowler crawled on his all fours to lift it up, when unknowingly he touched the emblem with his chest. Thus he touched and bathed and worshipped a phallic emblem on the night of the Vratam, which he passed in a vigil, though for quite a different purpose.

The fowler returned home on the following morning and took his meal with his wife and children. So years came and years went away, and the fowler died a natural death at the end of his appointed days, when the emissaries of Death came to take his unclean spirit in fetters to the mansion of their lord. But lo, my own warders sprang upon them, and overpowered them in the scuffle that ensued, and finally brought him, a free and unfettered spirit, to my own special region of bliss (S'iva-loka) in the company of that faithful dog which watched by him on the night of the chase in the bower."

The votary shall practise self-control on the day of the thirteenth phase of the moon's wane, and worship the god Rudra by praying as follows:—"Next night, I will keep a vigil in thy honour, O lord, and worship thee and meditate on thy divine self. I undertake to perform a Homa ceremony and give alms to the poor for the glorification of thy honoured name. I will fast on the day of the fourteenth phase of the moon's wane, and break it on the day following for the emancipation of my self. Be thou my help in that, O thou, the originless, all-pervading deity. The phallic emblem should be bathed with the compositions known as the Panchagavyam and the Panchámritam, and worshipped by reciting the Mantram running as, " Om, obeisance to S'iva." Libations of clarified butter containing rice, Vrihi, sesame seeds and little morsels of the cooked sacrificial porridge should be cast into the fire, after which the closing libation should be cast. The votary shall hear the legend of the Vratam recited by the priest, and worship the god once in each quarter of the night and recite the sacred Mantra till the break of dawn, when he shall bid farewell to the deity by asking his pardon as follows :—" I have safely and peacefully fulfilled this vow by thy grace, O thou the lord of the three worlds. Most humbly do I dedicate the merit of these performances to thy self. I supplicate thy grace, O lord, I have invoked thee on the occasion of my Vratam, now I beseech thee, O lord, to go back to thy mansion from whence thou hast come. Thy very presence has absolved me of all sins. Graciously accept my humble offerings, O thou the god of the gods, who art the origin, stay and goal of all created beings, and kind and compassionate to all."

Thus the Vratam should be practised for twelve consecutive years, the reward of which is fame, opulence, kingdom and progeny in this life and residence in the region of S'iva after death. The Vratam may be practised as well on the same night in each month of the year, and should be closed by feasting a dozen hermits and by illuminating the temple of the deity, by which a perpetual residence in heaven may be ensured.

——:o:——

CHAPTER CXXV.

SAID THE DIVINE GRAND FATHER :—The king Mandhata managed to be the undisputed lord of the three worlds by by practising the Ekádas'i Vratam of yore. Hence one shall fast both on the eleventh days of the light and dark fortnights. The queen Gándhari fasted on the day of the tenth phase of the moon, and lost her hundred sons in consequence. Hence one shall not fast on the eleventh day of the fortnight. Even in spite of the dictum that the god Hari presides over the day when the moon is both in her tenth, and eleventh, phases, one should fast on the day of the twelfth phase of the moon, and break it on the day following. One shall fast on the day marked even by a Kalâ of Ekdâashi, or on the day when the moon is successively in her eleventh, twelfth, and thirteenth, phases. The king Rukmángada used to keep vigils on the nights of the two Ekâdas'is and hear the Purânas recited to him by the holy sages, in consequence whereof he was liberated from the trammels of life and ascended to heaven after death.

—:o:—

CHAPTER CXXVI.

BRAHMA said:—Now I shall describe a mode of worship which entitles the votary to the highest beatitude, as well as to the pleasures of this life and to the joy of self-emancipation. The votary shall psychically locate the mystic Mandalam (a trancendental figure) in the mystic nerve phlexus in his heart and mentally worship the deities Gangá, Jamuná, Mahánadi, Dháta, and Vidháta at its different approaches. The deities, such as, S'ri, Danda, Prachanda and Vástu-Purusha, should be likewise worshipped at its exterior lives, while the mystic tortoise (smybol of universal evolution and involution,) the universal receptacle and eternity, should be worshipped at its centre.

After that, the attributes, location, virtue, knowledge, non-attachment, splendour, impiety, non-knowledge, bondage, and the pollens, stems, and bulb of the mystic lotus lily should be worshipped. After that, the petals and stamens of that mystic flower, as well as the qualities of illumination, action, and nescience, the solar world, the lunar world, the region of fire, and the divine energies such as, Vimalā, etc., should be worshipped in that psychic diagram over that mystic nerve plexus of the heart. Similarly, the deities Durga, Ganes'a, Sarasvati and Kshetrapāla, should be worshipped at the four cardinal points of the Mand'alam. After that, the pedestal and the embodied image of the God should be worshipped followed by a similar puja of Vāsudeva, Valabhadra, and the God of Love. After that, Aniruddha and Nārāyana with his weapons and conch-shell should be worshipped, and the votary should practise the rite of Shad'ānganyāsa (psychic attraction and localisation of certain universal categories and attributes in the different parts of the human organism) in the usual orthodox way. Then having worshipped the deities, beauty, growth and Garud'a, he should worship the guardian deities of the different quarters of the heaven and the god Brahmā, above, and the god Ananta, below. After that, the god Vis'vaksena should be worshipped at the north-east angle of the Mand'alam.

He, who can thus worship the god even for a single time in his life, is freed from the chains of successive re-births. The Pund'arika and Gadādhara manifestations of the deity should be as well meditated upon in connection with the present form of worship.

—:o:—

CHAPTER CXXVII.

BRAHMA said :—The renowned Bhimasena of yore fasted on the day of the eleventh phase of the moon's increase (Ekādas'i) marked by the Asterism Hastā, in the month of Māgha; and behold, he was instantly exonerated from his obligations to the Pitris in consequence. Accordingly the Vratam is called Bhaimi Ekādas'i. This Bhaimi Dvādas'i is renowned for the fact of its increasing the piety of men. He, who observes a fast on this Ekādas'i and breaks it on the following day, acquires merit in the eyes of heaven. One should fast on that Ekādas'i in the month of Māgha even if it be not marked by the above-named asterism, and even by so-doing one would be freed from the sins of a Brāhmana-slaughter. This Ekādas'i Vratam destroys all sins as surely as a bad son brings ruin on his family, a false wife brings death and disgrace to her husband; a false minister brings confusion to his king, and a pious act dispels the gloom of iniquity. As knowledge dispels nescience, as purity removes the impurity of the heart; as truth conquers untruth; and reverence, irreverence; so this Vratam annihilates all kinds of sin. As surely as cold removes heat, as profligacy destroys a stored up treasure, asbragging of it destroys the merit of a gift, as worldliness destroys penance, the Ekādas'i Vratam destroys all sin. As surely as a son is ruined without good education, cattle are destroyed by straying far from the folds, as a peaceful temperament is ruffled by anger, and as expenditures without income destroy one's wealth, so the Ekādas'i Vratam destroys all kinds of sin. As surely as a motive destroys the merit of an act, as knowledge destroys nescience, this Vratam destroys all kinds of sin. The sin, which is attached to the acts of Brāhmana-slaughter, wine-drinking gold-stealing and defiling the bed of a preceptor, when simultaneously done, are absolved by performing the Ekādas'i Vratam in its true spirit. The dreadful astral combination, known as the Tripushkara Yoga, can annihilate the progeny and relations of the man, who dies under its influence, but cannot destroy his sins, which may be expiated by performing the Ekādas'i Vratam.

Neither the holy shrines of Kuru-Kshetra, Prabhāsa and Naimisha, nor the sacred rivers, the Ganges, the Yamunā, the Kālindi and the Sarasvati, can rank equal in merit with the Ekādas'i Vratam. Neither the practice of charity and philanthropy, nor meditation and burnt offerings can vie with the Vratam under discussion, in respect of merit and sanctity. The merit of an Ekadas'i Vratam weighed in balance with that of making a gift of the whole world, immensely outweighs the latter. This Bhaimi Ekādas'i is by far the most sacred of all the other sacred Ekādas'is in the year.

A golden image of the Varāha manifestation of the god should be worshipped inside a copper vessel placed on the top of the sacrificial pitcher. The image should be covered with a clean sheet of white linen, and worshipped with the offerings of lighted lamps of gold, and a variety of costly viands. The lower extremities of the image should be worshipped by reciting the Mantram, "Om, obeisance to Varahā;" its lips, by reciting the one which reads as "Om, obeisance to Krodhākriti;" its navel, by reciting the Mantram, "Om, obeisance to the deep-voiced one;" its chest, by reading the Mantram, "Om, obeisance to S'rivatsadhāri;" its arms, by reciting the Mantram, "Om, obeisance to the thousand-headed one;" its neck, by reciting the Mantram, "Om, obeisance to the lord of all;" its face, by reciting the Mantram, "Om, obeisance to the soul of the universe;" its fore-headed, by reciting the Mantram, "Om, obeisance to the Universal Master," and its hair, by reciting the Mantram, which reads as, "Om, beisance to the hundred-mouthed deity."

Having thus duly worshipped the god, the votary should pass the night in a holy vigil, and hear the glorious exploits of his Varāha manifestation on earth from the Puranam, which deals with them. Gifts should be made to the beggars and the Brāhmanās, the next morning; and wearing apparels containing bits of gold should be given to the Brāhmanās in special. After that, the votary should break his fast and take only a few morsels of food instead of eating too much. He, who practises the Vratam in the afore-said manner, suffers not the pangs of re-births, and is exonerated from the three-fold obligations which a man incurs at his birth. The performance of the Vratam grants the merit of performing all other vows, and makes the performer, the happy possessor of all his wished-for objects.

—:o:—

CHAPTER CXXVIII.

BRAHMA said:—O Vyāsa, hear me discourse on the mode of performing a variety of Vratas, which can win the good graces of the god Hari, who blesses the performer with all his cherished boons in return. A Vratam signifies an act of living in conformity with the rules of conduct and self-control, as laid down in the S'āstras. The Vratam is but another name for penance (Tapasyā). AVrati (performer of a Vratram) is under the obligation of observing sepecific rules of conduct and self-control. He should bathe, thrice every day, during the entire term of the Vratam, and sleep on the bare ground, contented, and controlled in his mind and senses, and renouncing all talk with women, S'udrsā, and degraded persons. He should make burnt offerings of the five sacred articles, as his circumstances would admit of. A Vrati wishing to acquire the full merit of his vow, should practise the above-named austerities, and undergo double the hardship, in the event of his wearing long hair during the entire term of the Vratam. He should not take any thing out of a bowl of Indian bellmetal, nor consume any potherbs, nor take honey, grain, and Koradushaka, nor chew any betel leaf on the day of breaking his fast, not take his meals in another's house on the occasion. A fast is vitiated by using flowers, perfumes, unguents, collyrium, a tooth brush, a new cloth, or an article of ornament. A Vrati should wash his mouth with the Panchagavyam in the morning before breaking his fast. The merit of a fast is destroyed by gambling, by indulging in day-sleep or in sexual intercourse, and by constantly drinking water on the day of its breaking. Forbearance, truthfulness, clemency, charity, cleanliness of body and mind, and subjugation of the senses, divine worship and Homa celebration are the ten cardinal virtues, which should be practised in connection with the performance of every Vratam. A meal after a whole day's fast and taken after the rising of the evening star is technically called a night-meal (Nakta Bhojanam), which must not be interpreted to simply mean a meal in the night. Take of a Pala weight (eight tolās) of cow's urine, a half thumbful of cowdung, seven Pala weights of milk, three Pala weights of curd, one Pala of clarified butter, and one Pala of the washings of Kus'a grass and mix together. The resulting compound is called be the Pancha-gavyam. A person about to practise the Brahmakrichchha-Vratam should take Pancha-gavyam after purifying its component cow's urine by reciting the Gāyatri Mantram; cowdung, by reciting the Gandha Dvāra, etc., Mantram; curd, by reciting the Dadhikravya, etc., Mantram; milk, by reciting the Apyayasva, etc., Mantram; clarified butter, by reciting the Tejoshi, etc., Mantram; and the washings of the Kus'a grass, by reciting the Devasya, etc., Mantram.

Celebrations of such religious ceremonies as, Agnyādhānam (*lit.*, first kindling of the sacrificial fire), installation of a divine image, a religious sacrifice, Vedavrata, rite of tonsure, investiture with the sacred thread, Vrishotsarga (the rite of the setting free of a sacrificial bull), as well as acts of charities and penances should not be made in a month, which contains two new moons (Malamāsha).

A Sāvana month consists of thirty days counted from one new moon to another. A Saura (solar) month is computed from the passing of the sun from one zodiacal sign to another. The time taken by the twenty-seven asterisms (lunar mansions) to make one complete revolution round the earth, is counted as an astral (Nākshatra) month, which consists of twenty-seven days. The Saura mode of computation should be adapted in respect of celebrating marriages; and the Sāvana style, in respect of celebrating religious sacrifices. The second and the third, the fourth and the fifth, the sixth and the seventh, the eighth and the ninth, the tenth and the eleventh, the twelfth and the thirteenth, the fourteenth and the fifteenth phases of the moon's wane or increase are called Yugmādara to each other. A Tithi Vratam performed on a day when that Tithi (lunar phase) meets its Yugmādara, is doubly meritorious. A female vowist menstruating after taking the vow is not disqualified from practising it to term in consequence. The Vratas may be practised through a proxy, but penances must be personally performed. A vow broken through anger, greed, or incontinence, should be atoned for by a three days' fast and a clean shave of the head. The performance of a Vratam may be delegated to one's son in case of one's ill health. A Brāhmana, swooning away in course of a Vratam, should be enlivened with milk, and cold applications.

—:o:—

CHAPTER CXXIX.

BRAHMA said:—Now I shall describe the mode of practising the Vratas, which should be performed on the days of the first phase of the moon, etc. A votary should take a single meal on the day of the first phase of the moon, and make the gift of a cow of the Kapila species, the next morning. The Vratam is called S'ikhi Vratam, the merit of which leads the performer to the region of the Fire-God, after death. The Vratam should be commenced from the month of Chaitra, and the God Brahmā should be worshipped with offerings of perfumes, flowers, and flower-garlands. The worship should be closed with a rite of Homa, and the votary should think himself as to have been already possessed of the good he covets in life. A person seeking personal beauty in his next re-birth, should worship the god with the offerings of flower-garlands, etc., on the day of the sixth phase of the moon's increase in the mouth of Kārtika, and thenceforth on the same day, each month, for a year. The S'ridhara manifestation of Vishnu should be worshipped in the company of his consort Lakshmi, on the day of the third phase of the moon's wane in the month of S'rāvana. Beds, bedsteads, and fruits, etc., should be gifted to the Brāhmanās at the close of the worship, which should be conducted by reciting the Mantras, which respectively run as, "Om, obeisance to S'ridhara;" and "Om, obeisance to S'ri." The God S'iva and his consort Umā should be as well worshipped on the third day of the fortnight in the month of Chaitra. Offerings of viands and Madanaka should be made to the deities. The Vratam, which should be commenced from the month of Chaitrā, should be practised, for a year for the fruition of the end for which it is undertaken. The God S'iva has given this injunction to his divine consort. A Vrati should formally abjure the use of salt in his meals, on the day of the third phase of the moon in the month of Phālguna, and refrain from using any, for a year. The Vratam should be closed by making gifts of beds and furnished dwelling houses to the Brāhmanās. A married couple belonging to the same social order should be sumptuously feasted on the occasion as the prototype of the divine man and wife, and addressed as, "Be thou propitiated, O thou the consort of the god of becoming, etc." He, who performs the Vratam as above described, is translated to the region of Gauri after a prosperous career on earth. The different manifestations of energy such as, Gauri, Kāli, Umā, Bhadrā, Durgā, Kānti, Sarasvati, Mangalā, Vaishnavi, Lakshmi, S'ivā and Nārāyani, should be successively worshipped on the day of the third lunar phase, each month, whereby the performer would never know the pangs of separation and bereavement. The Vrati should fast on the day of the fourth phase of the moon's increase in the month of Māgha, and give measures of sesame seeds to the Brāhmanas, taking nothing but sesame water that day. The Vratam should be performed on the same day, each month, for a period of two years, the reward of its performance being a peaceful and undisturbed life on earth. "Gah Svāha" is the principal Mantram, which should be used in the worship, and the rites of Shadanganyāsa, etc., should be duly performed. The Gāyatri Mantram sacred to the god of this worship (Ganapati) reads as follows, "Om, let us know the long-eared deity; let us meditate upon the Self of the god with protruted lips, may the tusked-one lead us to do the same." Burnt offerings of sesame seeds should be made to the god, and his divine cohorts should be likewise worshipped as follows:—"Obeisance to Gana, obeisance to Ganapati, obeisance to Kushmānd'aka, obeisance to Amogholka, obeisance to Ekadanta, obeisance to Tripurāntaka-rupi." After that, S'yamadanta, Vikarālāsya, A'haves'a, and Padmadanshtra, should be worshipped. After that, the votary should laugh, and clap his hands and dance round the divine image for the propitiation of the god. The reward of thus worshipping the god, for a year, on the day of the fourth phase of the moon's increase, each month, is erudition, opulence, fame, longevity, and a large progeny. The God Gana should be worshipped on a Monday marked by the fourth phase of the moon's increase, and rites of Japa and Homa should be duly performed thereafter, the reward of the performance being an immunity from the calamities of the world, and a glorious residence in heaven after death. By worshipping the god Vignes'vara on the day of the fourth phase of the moon's increase with offerings of sugar, *laddukas* and other articles of confectionary, a man becomes the happy possessor of all earthly good things in life. By worshipping the god with the offerings of Damanaka flowers, the votary is blest with the pleasures of fatherhood. The God Gana may be worshipped under the auspices of the fourth phase of the moon in any month of the year by reciting the Mantra which reads as, "Om, obeisance to Ganapati." The Mantra specifically sacred to the deity, should be as well recited on the occasion; and libations of clarified butter, cast into the fire, the reward of the performance being an immunity from all earthly calamities and the enjoyment of all good things, which this life can possibly offer. The man, who worships the image of the God Vināyaka and addresses him in any of the following names, *viz.*, the worshipped one of the gods, the one-tusked deity, the god with the protruted lips, the three-eyed or the three-mouthed one, the blue-necked celestial, the large-bellied god, the dreadful one, the lord (succourer) of distress, the dusk-coloured deity, the young moon Vināyaka, the lord of the Ganges and the elephant-faced one, attains to an elevated status after death, and becomes entitled to the privileges of heaven in the capacity of a liberated Self. The intelligent votary, who worships the true import of any or all of the abovesaid epithets, witnessess the realisation of all his heartfelt objects.

The divine serpents Vâsuki, Tahṣhaka, Kâliya, Manibhadraka, Airâvata, Dhritarâshtra, Karkataka, and Dhananjaya, should be bathed with clarified butter, etc., in either of the blessed month's of Shrâvana, Bhâdra, A's'wina or Kârtika and under the auspices of the fifth phase of the moon's increase. The serpents named Ananta, Vâsuki, S'ankha, Padma, Kamvala, Karkotaka, Shankhaka, Kâliya, Takshaka, and Pingala, should be worshipped in each month of the year. A votary by worshipping these eight celestial serpents in the light fortnight of Bhâdra, is liberated from the trammels of rebirth. The pictures of these celestial serpents should be drawn on each side of the door of the house under the auspices of the fifth phase of the moon's increase in the month of Bhâdra, and the household should invoke and worship the divine snakes by name, in each of them. Milk and clarified butter should be offered to the images of snakes on the occasion, inasmuch as it would ward off the danger of snake bites in the household. The Vratam is called Dashtoddhâra (prophylasis against snake bites) Panchami.

——:o:——

CHAPTER CXXX.

BRAHMA said :—Similarly, the god Kârtikeya should be worshipped under the auspices of the sixth phase of the moon's increase in the month of Bhâdra. Acts of ceremonial ablution, etc., performed on that day, bear immortal fruits. The votary should break his fast the next morning, after having worshipped the Sun-God and sumptuously feasted the Brâhmânas. The Mantra to be recited in connection with the solar worship on the occasion, reads as follows :—" Om,

O Sun, O thou the first and permanent light-meteor, that illumineth the vast expanse of heaven, the parent of all life on earth and emblem of eternal life, beest thou my friend and guide in the universe. Humbly do I lay myself prostrate before thy godly presence." The votary should break his fast thereafter on the day of the eighth phase of the moon's increase, and eat nothing but pepper that day. The Vratam is called Maricha Saptami, the reward of its performance being the attainment of all objects in life.

The votary having bathed and lived as an anchorite on the day of the seventh phase of the moon's increase in the month of Bhādra, should worship the Sun-God and make gifts of fruits to the Brāhmanās. His food that day should consist of nothing but Matulungas or cocoanuts. The fruits should be gifted to the Brāhmanās on the occasion by reciting the Mantra, "Be pleased, O Sun-God." The Vratam is called Phala-Saptami. It makes its performer the happy possessor of all good things he covets in life. The votary having worshipped the Sun-God under the auspicies of the seventh phase of the moon's increase in Bhādra, should make offerings of sweet porridge (Pāyasa) to the god, and feast the Brāhmanās with that article of food. He should take nothing but milk on the day of the Vratam, and pay money remunerations to the Brāhmanās, who have been feasted on the occasion with food, drink, lambatives, etc., which should be foregone by the votary himself. The Vratam is called Anodana-Saptami, which brings wealth, progeny and creature comforts to its performer. A person wishing victory in life should take nothing but air on the occasion of the Vijaya-Saptami, whereas a person with the realisation of any definite object in his heart, should live on Arka leaves on the day. The performance of the Vratam is rewarded with the fulfilment of all desires of the votary, who is enjoined to refrain from using all kinds of cereals, honey-cakes, utensils made of stone, or of Indian bell-metal, unguents, oils, meat, etc. Moreover he should foreswear his cup and the bed of his wife on the day of the Vratam, which enables its performer to witness the realisation of all his desires.

—:o:—

CHAPTER CXXXI.

Brahma said :—O Brāhman, the deities S'iva, Gauri, Ganesha, and Durvā should be worshipped with offerings of fruits and flowers under the auspicies of the eighth phase of the moon's increase in the month of Bhādra. Offerings consisting of fruits and Vrihi seeds, should be made to the deities S'ivā and S'ambhu. The presiding deity of the eighth phase of the moon, should be invoked as follows :—"O thou, the eighth phase of the moon, who art begotten of the divine ambrosia and whom this bunch of grass represents in its primeval verdure and spreading roots (the symbols of perpetual life), dost thou enable me to realise all my desires." The performance of the Vrata under discussion is rewarded with the fruition of one's all desires. By performing this Vrata and foregoing all cooked food during the day, a man is exonerated from the sin of killing a Brāhmana.

Rohini-Ashtami Vratam :—The God Hari should be worshipped, at mid-night, on the day of the eighth phase of the moon's wane in the month of Bhādra. The Vratam, which consists in worshipping the deity, should be performed on the aforesaid day marked by the asterism Rohini, and even if the moon continues in her seventh phase for a few hours, that day. The performance of the Vratam absolves its performer from the sins of his three previous re-births. The votary should worship the gods fasting, and break his fast after the moon has entered her next phase and mansion. The rite of ablution should be done unto the god by reciting the Mantra. "Obeisance to Yoga, to the lord of Yoga, to the god of Yoga, and to Govinda," (the stay of the universe).

The Mantra, which should be recited during the worship, runs as, "Obeisance to sacrifice, to the lord and god of sacrifice, and to the one begotten of the merit of celebrating a religious sacrifice." The god should be laid down in bed by reciting the Mantra, "Obeisance to the lord and god whose embodiment the universe is, and who is the main stay of the universe." The Moon-God with his consort Rohini should be worshipped on the sacrificial sand-cushion, and the deity should be addressed, on the occasion as, "O thou, the universal spirit, that is in all, and runs through all, and determines all becoming and is the support of all." An Argha offering composed of fruits, flowers, sandalpaste, and water should be kept in a conchshell, and the votary should offer the same, on bent knees, to the Moon-God by reciting the Mantra, which runs as follows:—"Accept this offering, with thy consort Rohini, O Moon, who came out of the primordial ocean of water and sprang from the eyes of Atri. Similar Argha offerings consisting of fruits should be separately made to S'ri, Vāsudeva, Nanda, Vala and Yashodā. The god should be addressed as follows:—"I make obeisance to the eternal spirit that shines in the sun. I bow down to the great Vāsudeva, the greatest self-conscious individuality, and who, though grand yet beyond all comprehension, had born as a dwarf on earth. Salutation unto the god Madhava (*lit.*, the husband of beauty), who killed the demon Madhu, and who is also called Hrishikes'a, and whose abode is in the heart of faith that doubts not. Obeisance to the lotus-eyed one, to the great boar and Nrisinha manifestations, the slayers of demons. Salutations unto Dāmodara, Kes'ava, Padmanābha and to the one on the pinnacle of whose car sits the mighty

Garuda. I make obeisance to Govinda, the seed of the universe, the supreme cause of all creation, continuance and dissolution. Salutation unto the eternal spirit, which the eye seeth not and which is absolute and irresistible and suffers no decay. I bow dow down to Vishnu, the supreme lord of the three regions, who is without end or origin. I make obeisance to Nārāyana, the four-armed one, who is clad in a gold-coloured garment and wields a mace, discus, and a conchshell in his hands. Salutation unto S'ridhara, S'ripati, and Hari, on whose spacious breast there are curls of hair and on which hangs a garland of wild flowers. I make obeisance to him whom Vasudeva begot on his wife Devaki for the safety of the earth and Brāhmanās."

After having addressed the god as above, the votary should pray as follows :—"Take me across this ocean of existence, O Hari, absolve my sins, and succour me from the sea of grief and misery. He, who utters your name even once in life, he who calls Vishnu, the all-pervading one, even for a single moment, is rescued, howsoever great a sinner he may be. Deeper and deeper do I plunge in the ocean of misery and nescience. O lift me, lift me up, O lord! who else will run to my rescue! Salutation unto the self-origined Vāsudeva, to Krishna and to Govinda, who sees the good of the Brāhmanās and the universe. May the divine light fall on my soul, may I find bliss in this life, may my fame, wealth and possessions increase."

———:o:———

CHAPTER CXXIII.

BRAHMA said :—One should perform a Vratam, on the day of the eighth phase of the moon, and break his fast on the night of the vow. He, who continually practises the Vrata for a year, and closes it by making the gift of a cow to a Brāhmana, is elevated to the status of an Indra, after death. The Vratam is called *Sadgati Vratam*. The same Vratam practised on the day of the eighth phase of the moon's increase in the month of Pausha, is called the *Maha Rudra Vratam*. Such a Vratam practised in my honour is ten thousand times more meritorious than the one practised for an ordinary end. The Vratam should be specially performed if the proper day of its celebration happens to fall on a Wednesday, inasmuch as its performance would ensure endless prosperity to the votary. A seeker after self-emancipation should take nothing but eight pinchfuls of cooked rice on the occasion, and live as devout and pure as possible.

By taking Kalamvicā treated with acid and enshrouded with the blades of Kusha grass, on the occasion, a man is sure to acquire all wished-for objects. The god Mercury should be worshipped in a pool with the five kinds of offerings, and a *Karkari* (a kind of small water pot) full of rice, should be given to a Brāhmana by way of Dakshinā. The god should be contemplated as armed with a bow and an arrow, shining with the greenish golden hue of his complexion, and worshipped on the petals of the mystic Mandalam by reciting the "Vang, etc.," Vijam. The votary should then hear the legends of the Vratam recited by a Brāhmana, which is as follows :—"Once upon a time there lived in the city of Pātaliputra a good Brāhmana whose name was Vira. Vira had a wife named Rambhā, a daughter named Vijayā, a son named

Kaushika, and a bullock named Dhanapāla. One hot day in summer, Kaushika, oppressed with the scorching heat of the sun, took the bullock to the Ganges to give him a much-needed ablution. While he was himself bathing, several cowboys came and decamped with the bullock before he could raise the necessary alarm. Kaushika came out of the river and began to wander in the forest in grief and despair. It so happened that his sister Vijayā came to fetch water from the Ganges at the time and saw her brother in that sad predicament. So she joined him in the wood and went on rambling in quest of the bullock. Thirsty and worn out with the fatigues of the day, Kaushika went down to a pool of water to fetch some dark lotus stems for his sister, when, behold, there appeared to him on the green grassy bank of that limpid pool a bevy of celestial nymphs engaged in practising the Vudāshtami Vratam. Kaushika, hungry and exhausted asked them for food. The nymphs in their turn directed him to first practise the Vratam. Kaushika called his sister and did as directed Kaushika and Vijayā practised the Vratam, he with the object of recovering his lost bullock, and she with the motive of securing a suitable husband for herself. They took their meals out of two mango leaves as served out to them by the nymphs; and the nymphs vanished after their repast. Kaushika recovered his lost bullock through the merit of performing the Vratam. The thieves voluntarily restored the same to him in the morning, and Kaushika and his sister went home with their boons.

"Now the good Brāhmana Vira had past an anxious and sleepless night, and he was glad when his son and daughter saluted him in the morning. Now Vira was anxious to secure a suitable husband for his daughter as she had attained a marriagable age. There were idle speculations for many long days of suspense and domestic quarrel. At last Vijayā, the daughter, disgusted with the peremptory way in which her father wished to dispose her off, broke her silence and said "I shall be wedded to the God of Death." Now Death was the bridegroom she had chosen for herself, and the merit of the Vratam had entitled her to have the husband of her choice. So the Lord of Death appeared to Vira and sued for the hand of his daughter. Irrevocable is the decree of heaven, and the gods brook no equivocation of terms. So there could be no refusal, and the marriage of fair Vijayā with the Lord of Death was contracted with the seal of fate. Vira and his wife Rambhā were translated to heaven, and the son Kaushika was rewarded with a kingdom at Ayodhyā. Kaushika celebrated the marriage of his sister in a style quite in keeping with his new dignity, and the Lord of Death took away his bride to his mansion in the nether world. After his installation as the Queen of Yama (the God of Death), Vijayā was suddenly roused up, one day, from her revery by the agonised cries of her own mother. She saw her spirit, chained and fallen from heaven, and about to be consigned to the pangs of hell. Vijayā performed this Vratam for the liberation of her mother's spirit and asked it to do the same after it had been liberated. The mother again ascended to heaven through the merit of performing this Vratam, and lived there happy in the company of her husband.

——:o:——

CHAPTER CXXXIII.

BRAHMA said :—He, who eats eight buds of As'oka flowers on the eighth day of the moon's increase in the month of Chaitra marked by the asterism Punarvasu, suffers no bereavement in life. The Mantra, which should be recited on the occasion, is as follows :—" I bereaved and miserable, eat thee, O As'oka, who art a favourite with the God Hara.

Dost thou make me griefless in life. Thus the process of performing As'okāshtami is described."

BRAHMA said:—The ninth day of the moon's increase, marked by the asterism Uttarāshāda, is called Mahānavami. A gift or a ceremonial ablution made under the auspices of this astral combination bears immortal fruits. The Goddess Durgā worshipped on that day grants infinite piety to her votary. The Gods S'ankara and others worshipped her on that day and acquired infinite piety. A king wishing victory over his royal adversaries, should practise an Ajāchita Vratam from the previous sixth day of the moon's increase, and close it on the abovesaid day with rites of Japa and Homa, and by feasting the unmarried virgins. The worship should be conducted by reciting the "Durgā, Durgā, Rakshini Svāhā" (Oh, Durgā, Durgā, obeisance to Durgā, the protectress) Mantra. The rites of Hridinyāsa etc., should be performed by appending the terms "Namah, Svaha, Vasat, Hum, Voushat and Fat" to the principal Vija-Mantra. The Puja should be concluded by performing the "Angushtha-Kanishtha Nyāsa." A new wooden temple should be constructed, and a golden or silver image of the Goddess Durgā should be worshipped therein, on the eighth day of the moon's increase. As an alternative, the Goddess should be invoked and worshipped at the head of a spear, or at a sword-blade, or in a book, picture or a mystic diagram. The Goddess should be contemplated as respectively holding a human skull, a dagger, a bell, a mirror, a Tarjani, a bow, a banner, a small drum, and a noose in her left hands, and a spear, a club, a trident, a thunderbolt, a sword, a mace, an arrow, a discus and a rod in her right. The goddess should be worshipped fully equipped as described before. The different manifestations of the Goddess, such as, Ugrachandā, Prachandā, Chandogrā, Chandāvati, Chandarupā and Atichandikā should be as well worshipped on the occasion. Of these Ugrachandā is coloured like yellow pigment. Prachandā is coloured like rosy dawn; Chandogrā is sable; Chanda-nāyikā is blue;

Chandarupā, yellow; and Atichandikā, grey. Each of these divinities should be contemplated as standing sidewise on a lion, with her left leg elevated and thurst out. A furious centaur (half man, half buffalo) should be contemplated as charging the deity, who has got a sword in one hand and has caught hold of the hair of the centaur in the other. The Mantra, which consists of ten letters (Dashākshari) and is sacred to the Goddess, should be mentally recited by the votary; after which the trident of the Goddess should be worshipped. The votary should observe a fast on the eighth day of the moon's increase after having worshipped the Goddess in an image, or in a divine sandal, or in water. A bull buffalo, five years old, should be sacrificed at the close of the night, and the blood of the offering should be offered by duly reciting the "Kali, Kali" Mantra. The blood should be dedicated to Puṭanā in the south-west; to the sin demoness in the north-west; to Chandikā, in the north-east and to Vidarikā, in the south-east; quarter of the heaven.

—:o:—

CHAPTER CXXXIV.

BRAHMA said:—Now I shall recite the Mahā-Kaushika Mantra, which ranks foremost in respect of merit. [Here follows a recitation of the Mahā-Kaushika Mantra.]

An animal consecrated with the Mahā-Kaushika Mantra should be sacrificed at the south-west angle of the sacrificial ground, and the rite of ceremonial ablution should be done unto the king in front of the sacrificial offering. The king should cut with one blow of his sword a rice-paste image of his adversary, bits of which should be dedicated to Skanda and Vishikha. The Mātrikās should be worshipped in the night by reciting the Mantra, which runs as, "Obeisance to Bramhāni, Maheshi, Kaumāri, Vaishnavi, Varāhi, Māhendri, Chāmundā, Chandikā, Jayanti, Mangalā, Kāli, Bhadrakāli, Kapālini, Durgā, S'ivā, Kshamā, Dhātri, Svāhā, and Svadhā." The image of the Goddess should be bathed with milk, and virgins, maidens, Brāhmanās and Chandālās should be sumptuously feasted and propitiated with money gifts. By worshipping the Goddess with the offerings of banners, poles, cars, cloths, etc., under the auspicies of the Mahā-Navami, a votary can win kingdoms and victories in war.

—:o:—

CHAPTER CXXXV.

BRAHMA said:—A votary having fasted on the day of the ninth phase of the moon's increase in the month of A's'vin, should worship the Goddess and the Brāhmanās, and mentally recite, a hundred thousand times, the Mantra which is held as principally sacred to her. This Vratam is called Vira Navami.

BRAHMA said:—By worshipping the goddess with the offerings of Damanaka twigs on the day of the ninth phase of the moon's increase in the month of Chaitra, a man acquires enough merit to be above all desires, sufferings, and defeats in life. Such a man bears a kind of charmed life against sword cuts, etc., and is immune from the horrors of violent or premature death. This Vratam is called Damanaka Navami.

BRAHMA said:—A votary should worship the Goddess Durgā on the day of the tenth phase of the moon's increase in the month of A's'vin. The Vratam thus undertaken should be practised for a year under the auspices of the same lunar phase, each month. It should be concluded by making a gift of ten cows and the golden images of the presiding Deities of the quarters of heaven to the Brāhmanās. The merit of the performance entitles its practiser of the suzerainty of the universe. This Vratam is called Digdas'ami.

BRAHMA said :—For worshipping the Rishis on the day of the eleventh phase of the moon with various kinds of offerings, a man is rewarded with wealth, beauty and progeny, and is glorified in the region of the celestial saints. The Rishis such as, Marichi, Atri, Angirasa, Pulastya, Pulaha, Kratu, Prachetā, Vas'ishta, Bhrigu and Nārada should be worshipped in the month of Chaitra with garlands of Damanaka flowers. I have finished describing the Ashokāshtami, Vira-Navami, Damanaka-Navami, and Digdas'ami Vratas.

—:o:—

CHAPTER CXXXVI.

BRAHMA said :—I shall now deal with the mode of performing S'ravanā-Dvādas'i Vratam, a practice whereof grants enjoyment and salvation to the person who practises it. The day of the eleventh or twelfth phase of the moon's increase, marked by the asterism S'ravanā is called Vijayā. A Pujā done unto the God Hari on that day bears immortal fruit. A night meal, or a single meal in the day time, or a meal voluntarily offered to the votary without any solicitation on his part and taken by him on the occasion, does not vitiate the vow of Dvādas'i Vratam. He should refrain from using any utensil of bell-metal, honey, lentil and collyrium, and renounce all false talk, greed, physical exercise and sexual intercourse.

The day of the twelfth phase of the moon's increase in the month of Bhādra marked by the asterism S'ravanā, is called Mahati Dvādas'i. A fast observed under the auspices of this astral combination, bears immortal fruits. Great is the merit of a ceremonial ablution performed at a junction of streams on the occasion, specially if the combination happens to fall on a day when the moon is in opposition with the Mercury. Gems should be immersed in water contained in a pitcher of gold which should be covered with a pair of cloths, and the god Vāmana should be worshipped with offerings of umbrella, shoes, etc. Naividyas consisting of Pāyasam and clarified butter should be offered to the God, and the votary should pass the night in a holy vigil, and make gifts of Modakās and water-pitchers to the Brāhmanās. Then having bathed and taken some light refreshments (water according to others,) on the day following, he should again worship the Dwarf Manifestation of the God, and address him as follows :—

"Salutation unto Govinda, who is the presiding Deity of of the asterism S'ravanā, and who is also called the Mercury. Expiate my sins, O lord, and bless me with all the pleasures and comforts of this life. Be pleased with me, O thou the God of the gods." The Vratam may be as well performed on the bank of a river.

——:o:——

CHAPTER CXXXVII.

BRAHMA said ;—The god (S'iva) should be worshipped with the offerings of Damanaka leaves, etc., on the day of the thirteenth phase of the moon's increase, which is held sacred to the God of Love. The merit of the Pujā would make the votary a favourite with the fair sex, and enable him to live happy and prosperous, free from all pain and bereavement.

Thus the description of the Madana Trayodas'i is finished. By worshipping the God S'iva on the eighth, and the fourteenth, day of the fortnight, each month, for a year, the votary is freed from the chains of necessary re-births. By making the gift of a well-furnished room on the fullmoon night in the month of Kārtika, and by observing a fast for three days previous thereto, the giver is translated to the region of the Sun, after death. Libations of water should be offered to the Pitris on the day of the new moon, and on each day by mentioning its name. The votary should fast the whole day and take his meal in the night, whereby he would be entitled to all the pleasures of life. The God Hari should be worshipped on a day in the month of Agrahāyana, marked by the asterism Mrigas'irā, by addressing him as, "O Kes'ava, etc." He should be addressed as Nārāyana and worshipped in the month of Pausha on a day marked by the asterism Pushyā. Similarly, he should be invoked by the epithet Mādhava and worshipped in the month of Māgha on a day marked by the asterism Maghā. He should be invoked by the name of Govinda in the month of Phālguna and worshipped on a day marked by the asterism Purva Phalguni. The name by which he should be invoked on the day of the Pujā in the month of Chaitra, which should be under the auspices of the asterism Chitra, is Vishnu. Similarly, "Madhusudana, Tribikrama, Vāmana, S'ridhara, Hrishikes'a, Padmanābha, and Dāmodara," are the epithets by which he should be invoked and worshipped on the days in the months of Vaishākha, Jaishtha, A'shāda, Shrāvana, Bhādra, A's'vin, and Kārtika, respectively marked by the asterisms Vis'ākhā, Jestha, Purvāshāda, Shravanā, Purva-Bhādrapada, As'vini, and Krittikā. Offer ings of Pāyasha, etc., should be made to the God in the months of A'shāda, etc., and the Brāhmanās should be sumptuously feasted therewith. Only Brāhmanās well versed in the knowledge of Pāncha-Rātra school of philosophy should be invited on the occasion. The Vratam should be practised for a year, at the close of which the God Vishnu should be worshipped and addressed as follows:—

"O thou who sufferest no decay, O thou who art the supreme Brahmā make infinite the good which I covet in this life. Absolve my soul from all sins which I have wittingly or unwittingly committed, O lord, who can not be measured by any standard of measurement. Grant all my prayers, O thou, the eternal immeasurable stay of the universe, whom decay afflicteth not and who art the foremost of beings." A person seeking beauty, possession, or longevity, should practise the Vratam for seven years in succession. The Gods Kuvera, Agni and As'vis should be worshipped on the first; the Deities S'ri and Yama, on the second; the Goddess Pārvati, on the fifth; the Nāgas, on the sixth; the Sun-God on the seventh; the Mātris, on the eighth; Takshaka, on the ninth; Indra and Kuvera, on the tenth; the holy sages, on the eleventh; the God Hari, on the twefth; Mahes'vara on the thirteenth; and Brahmā, on the fourteenth day of the fortnight. The Pitris should be worshipped on the days of the new and full moon. The day of the thirteenth phase of the moon on which the god Mahes'vara should be worshipped is known as Kāma-Trayodas'i.

CHAPER CXXXVIII.

:o:

SAID THE GOD HARI:—Now I shall describe the geneology of the princes of the blood royal, as well the exploits done by each of them. The God Brahmā sprang from the navel of the eternal Vishnu. Daksha, the father of all created beings sprang from the thumb of Brahmā. Daksha begat Aditi, and Aditi was the father of the Sun-God. The Sun God created

Manu, and Manu was the father of Ikshāku, Sharyāti, Mriga, Dhrishta, Prishadhra, Narishyanta, Nābhaga, Dishta, and Shashaka. Manu, the son of the Sun God, had a daughter named Ilā, who was subsequently known as Sudyumna. Mercury, the son of the Moon God, had a sexual congress with Ilā and begat on her person the three sons named Rājāh, Rudra and Puraravā. In the character of Sudyumna Ilā had three sons named Utkala, Vinata and Gayā. Prishadhra, a son of Manu, killed a cow, and so he was degraded to the status of a S'udra. After that, the race of the Kshatriyās that sprung from Karusha, is called Kárusha. Dishta, a son of Manu, had a son named Nabhāga, who became a Vaishya. Nabhāga had a son named Bhanandana, and the son of Bhanandana wasVatsapriti. Subsequently the said Bhanandana begat two other sons named Pānshu and Khanitra, and Khanitra had a son named Kshupa. Vinsha was the son of Kshupa and Vivinsha was the son of Vinsha. Vivinsha had another son named Khaninetra, and Khaninetra had a son named Vibhuti. Vibhuti begat Karandhama, and Karandhama begat Abikshita. Abikshita had a son named Marutta, and Marutta was the father of Navishyanta. Tamas begat Rájvardhana, Rájvardhana begat Sudhriti, and Sudhriti begat Nara. Nara had a son named Kavela who was the father of Dhundhumāna. Dhundumāna begat Vegavan, who was the father of Budha.

Afteawards Budha begat a son named Trinavindu and a daughter named Ailavilā. The said Trinavindu begat on Alamvushā a son named Vishāla. Vishāla had a son named Hemchandra who in his turn begat Chandra. Chandra begat Dhumráshva who begat Srinjaya; and Srinjaya had a son named Sahadeva who was the father of Krishāshva. The name of the son of Krisháshva was Somadatta who begat Janamejaya. Janamejaya was the father of Sumantri. All these princes ruled in the city of Vishālā.

Sharyayāti had a daughter who was married to the holy Chyavana. Sharyayāti had a son named Ananta, and Ananta was the father of Devaka. Afterwards Revata had a son who was called Baivataka and a daughter named Revati. The son begat by Dhrista, the son of Manu, was called Dhárstaka who though born a Kshatriya, took to the life of a Vaishya. Amvarisha was the son of Nabhāga, a son of Manu. Amvarisha begat Virupa, Virupa begat Prishadashva, Prishadashva begat Rathinara, who was firmly devoted to Vásudeva.

Of the three sons of Ikshākshu, the first was named Vikukshi, the second was called Nimi; and the third Dandaka. Vikukshi ate the hare kept for sacrificial purposes and hence he was called the hare-eater (S'as'ada). This S'as'ada had a son named Puranjaya who begat Kákutstha. Kákutstha had a son named Anenā, and the son of Anenā was named Prithu. Prithu had a son named Vishvarāta who was the father of Ardra. Ardra begat Yuvanās'va who begat S'rāvanta. S'rāvanta had a son named Vribadās'va, who was the father of Kuvalayās'va, who had a son called Dridās'va, and who was better known by the epithet of Dhundumāra. This Dridās'va had three sons, *viz.*, Chandrās'va, Kapilās'va and Haryās'va. Haryās'va begat Nikumbha. Nikumbha begat Hitāshva who was the father of Pujās'va. Pujās'va had a a son named Yuvnās'va. The son of Yuvanās'va was called Māndhātā who had a son named Vindu Mahya. Vindu Mahya had three sons named Muchukunda, Amvarisha and Purukutsa. The aforesaid Vindu Mahya had fifty daughters who became the wives of the holy sage Sauvari. Amvarisha begat Yuvanās'va who begat Harita. The son begotten on Narmadā by Purukutsa was called Trasadasyu. Anaranya was the son of Trasadasyu, and the son of Anaranya was called Haryayas'va. Vasumanah was the son of Haryayas'va and Tridhanvā was the son of Vasumanah. Tridhanvā had a son named Trayāruna who was the father of Satyarata. This Satyarata became famous by the name of Trishanku. The son of Trishanku was named Harish Chandra, who was the father of Rohitās'va. Harita was the son of Rohitās'va and Chanchu was the son of Harita. Chanchu begat Vijaya, and Vijaya begat Ruruk, and Ruruk begat Vrika. Vāhu was the son of Vrika and he became a king. Sagara was the son of Vāhu who had sixty thousand sons by his wife Sumati, and a son named Asamanjasa by his wife Keshini. Anshumana was the son of Asamanjasa, and Dilipa was the son of Anshumana. Bhagiratha was the son of Dilipa, and he brought down the Ganges on earth. S'ruta was the son of Bhagiratha, and the son of S'ruta was named Nābhāga. Nābhāga had a son named Amvarisha who was the father of Sindhudvipa. Ajutāyu was the son of Sindhudvipa, and the son of Ajutāyu was Rituparna. Sarvakāma was the son of Rituparna, and Sudasa was the the son of Sarvakāma. The son of Sudasa became famous by the name of Mitrasaha. Sudasa begat a son on his wife Damayanti who was called Kalmāshapāda. Kalmāshapāda begat As'vaka, and As'vaka begat Mulaka, and Mulaka begat Das'ārha who was the father of Ailavila. The son of Ailavila was named Vishvasaha, who was the father of Khattānga. Khattānga had a son named Dirghavāhu who was the father of Aja. The son of Aja was Dasharatha who had four sons, *viz.*, Rāma, Bharata, Lakshmana and S'atrughna. All of them became famous in history for prowess and glorious achievements. Kus'a and Lava were the sons of Rāma. Bharat's sons were named Tārksha and Pus'kala. Chitrāngada and Chandraketu were the sons of Lakshmana, while the sons of Shatrughna were named Suvāhu and Surasena. Kus'a had a son named Atithi who was the father of Nishāda. Nala was the son of Nishāda, and Nabhasa was the son of Nala. Pundarika was the son of Nabhasa, and Kshemdhanvā was the son of Pundarika. Devānika was the son of Kshemadhanvā, and Ahinaka was the son of Devānika. Ahinaka begat Ruru, and Ruru begat Pāripatra, and Pāripatra begat Dala, and Dala begat Chhala. Vuktha was the son of

Chhala and Vajranabha was the son of Vuktha. The son of Vajranābha was Gana who was the father of Ushitās'va who was the father of Vis'vashaha. Hiranyanābha was the son of Vis'vasaha, and Pushpaka was the son of Hiranyanābha. The son of Pushpaka was Dhruvasandhi who was to father of Sudars'ana. Sudars,ana begat Agnivarna who was the father of Padmavarna. Padmavarna begat S'ighra, and S'ighra begat Maru, and Maru begat Pras'ruta who was the father of Udāvasu. Nandivardhana was the son of Udāvasu. Suketu was the son of Nandivardhana. Suketu had a son named Devarāta who was the father of Vrihaduktha. Vrihaduktha had a son named Mahāvirya who was the father of Sudhriti. The son of Sudhriti was Dhristaketu who was the father of Haryayas'va. The son of Haryayas'va was Maru who was the father of Pratindhaka. Pratindhaka begat Kritiratha, and Kritiratha begat Devamidha who was the father of Vivudha. The son of Vivudha was Mahādhriti who was the father of Kritirāta. The son of Kritirāta was Manoromā who was the father of Svarnaromá, whose son was Hrasvaromá, whose son was Siradhvaja who had a daughter named Sitā. Kushadhvaja was the brother of S'iradhvaja who had a son named Bhānuman. S'atadyumna was the son of Bhánuman and S'uchi was the son of S'atadyumna. S'uchi begat Urja. Urja begat Sanadhvāja whose son was Kuli. The son of Kuli was Ananjana who was the father of Kulajit. The son of Kulajit was Adhinemi who was the father of S'rutāyu. The son of S'rutāyu was Supārs'va who was the father of Kshemāri. Kshemāri begat Anená who was the father of Rámaratha. Rámaratha begat Satyaratha; and Satyaratha, Upaguru. Upaguru begat Upagupta whose son was Svagata. Svagata had a son named Svanara, who begat Suvarcha, who begat Supārs'va, who begat Sus'ruta. The son of Sus'ruta was Jaya who was the father of Vijaya. Vijaya begat Rita, and Rita begat Sunaya, and Sunaya begat Vitahavya, who was the father of Dhriti. The son of Dhriti was Vahulās'va who was the father of Kriti. Two different races sprang from Janaka who were all addicted to Yoga.

—:o:—

CHAPTER CXXXIX.

HARI said :—I have finished describing the solar race, now hear me narrate the genealogy of princes who were the descendants of the Moon-God. Brahmā, the son of Nārāyana created the holy Atri. From Atri sprang the Moon-God who became the consort of the beatiful Tārā, the favourite wife of Vrihaspati, the preceptor of the celestials. The Moon-God begat on the person of his beloved Tārā a son named Budha, who in his turn begat Puraravā.

The son of Budha begat on the nymph Urvasi six sons who were named S'rutātmaka, Vis'vāvasu, S'atāyu, A'yu, Dheemān, and Amāvasu. Bhima was the son of Amāvasu, Kānchana was the son of Bhima, Kānchan's son was Suhotra who was the father of Janhu. Janhu's son was Sumanta and Sumanta's son was Apajāpaka. The son of Apajāpaka was Valākās'va, who was the father of Kus'a. Kus'a had four sons named Kus'ās'ava, Kus'alābha, Amurtaraya and Vasu. The son of Kus'ās'va was Gādhi who was the father of the celebrated Vis'vāmitra. Gādhi had a daughter named Satyavati, who was given in marriage to the holy sage Richik. The son of Richik was Jamadagni, who was the father of Paras'urāma. The sage Vis'vāmitra had a large family of sons such as Devarakta, Madhuchchhanda, etc.

A'yu (a son of Budha) had a son named Nahusha who had four sons named Anenā, Rāji, Rambhaka and Kshatra

Vriddha. The son of Kshatra Vriddha was Suhotra who had three sons, *viz.*, Kāshya, Kāsha, and Gritsamada. S'aunaka was the son of Gritsamada, and Dirghatamā was the son of Kās'ya. The son of Dirghatamā was Dhanvantari who took the profession of a physician. Dhanvantari had a son named Ketumān who was the father of Bhimaratha. Divodāsa was the son of Bhimaratha, and Patardana known to history as S'atrujit (conquerer of enemies) was the son of Divodāsa. The son of Pratardana wās Ritadhvaja, who was the father of Alarka. Alarka's son was Sannati and Sunita was Sannati's son. The son of Sunita was Satyaketu who was the father of Bibhu. The son of Bibhu was Subibhu, the father of Sukumāra. Sukumāra begat Dhristaketu, and Dhristaketu begat Vitihotra who had a son named Bharga. The son of Bharga was Bhargabhumi. All these magnanimous princes were firmly devoted to Vishnu and ruled in Kāshi.

Rāji (a son of Nahusha) had five hundred sons who were killed by the God-Indra. Kshatra Vriddha (a son of Nahusha) had another son named Pratikshatra who was the father of Sanjaya. Sanjaya begat Vijaya whose son was Krita. Krita begat Vrishadhana, and Vrishadhana begat Sahadeva whose son was Adina who begat Jayat Sena. The latter had a son named Satkriti whose son was Kshatradharma. Nahusha had a family of another five sons who were called Yati, Yayāti, Sanyāti, Ajāti and Kriti. Out of these, Yayāti begat on his wife Devayāni two sons who were named Yadu and Turvusu, and three sons on his wife S'armisthā who were called Drahyu, Anu and Puru. Yadu had three sons named Sahasrajit, Kroshtumāna and Raghu. The son of Sahasrajit was S'atajit who was the father of Haya and Haiheya. The son of Haya was Anaranya who was the father of Dharma. Dharma's son was Dharmamitra, whose son was Kunti. Kunti's son was Sahanji whose son was Mahishman. Mahishman's son was Bhadras'renya whose son was Durdama. Durdama's son was Dhanaka who had four sons named Kritavirja, Kritāgni, Kritakarmā and Kritogu. All of them were of mighty prowess.

Kritavirja had a son named Arjuna whose sons were S'urasena, Jayadhvaja, Madhu, S'ura and Vrishna. All these five sons of Kritavirya were princes of excellent conduct. Jayadhvaja's son was Tālajangha whose son was Bharata. Madhu was the son of Vrishana, and from him (Madhu) sprang the race of Vrishni. Ahi was the son of Kroshta and his son was Ashanku. The son of As'anku was Chitraratha whose son was S'as'avindu. S'as'avindu had two wives. By his first wife he had a hundred thousand sons, while by his second he had ten hundreds of thousands, such as Prithukirti, etc. Prithukirti had three sons, *viz.*, Prithujaya, Prithudana and Prithus'ravā. Prithus'ravā begat Tama, Tama begat Ushanā, Ushanā begat S'itagu, and S'itagu begat Rukmakavacha. Rukmakavacha had five sons *viz.*, Rukma, Prithurukma, Jyamagha, Palita and Hari. The son of Jyamagha was Vidarbha whose wife's name was S'aivyā. Vidarbha begat on his wife S'aivyā three sons whose names were Krutha, Kanshika, and Romapāda: Romapāda's son was Babhru, and Babhru's son was Dhriti. The son whom Kaus'ika begot was named Richi whose son was Chaidya. Chaidya begat Kunti, and Kunti begat Vrishni and Vrishni begat Nibriti, who was the father of Das'ārha. The son of Das'ārha was Vyoma whose son was Jimuta. The son of Jimuta was Vikriti, who was the father of Bhimaratha. Bhimaratha begat Madhuratha whose son was S'akuni, who begat Karambhi, who was the father of Devamata. The son of Devamata was Devakshatra whose son was Madhu, whose son was Kuruvans'a. Kuruvans'a begat Anu. Anu begat Puruhotra. who begat Ans'u whose son was Sattvas'ruta, who was the father of Sattvata.

Bhajina, Bhajamāna, Andhaka, Mahabhoja, Vrishni, Divya, Aranya, and Devavrita were the sons of Sattvata.

Nimi, Vrishni, Ayutajit S'atajit, Sahasrajit, Vabhru, Deva, and Vrihaspati were the sons of Bhajamāna. Bhoja was the son of Mahabhoja, and Sumitra was the son of Vrishni. Svadhājit was the son of Sumitra, and S'ini and Animita were the sons of Svadhājit. Nighna was the son of Anamitra, and S'atajit was the son of Nighna. The other two sons of Anamitra were Prasensa and S'iva. Satyaka was the son of S'ivi, and the son of Satyaka was Sātyaki. Sanjaya was the son of Sātyaki, and the son of Sanjaya was Kuli who was the father of Yugundhara. All these princes were the votaries of the God-S'iva.

Vrishni, S'aphalka, and Chitraka were the sons that graced the line of Anamitra. S'aphalka begat on the person of Gāndhini a son named Akrura, who was firmly devoted to the God-Vishnu. Upamudga was the son of Akrura, and the son of Upamudga was Devadyota. Akrura had two other sons who were called Devayāna and Upadeva.

Prithu and Viprithu were the sons of Chitraka, who was of the race of Anamitra, and S'uchi was the son of Andhaka the son of Sattvata. Kukkura and Kamvala Varhisha were the sons of Bhajamāna. Kukkura had a son named Dhrista, and Kapotaromaka was the son of Dhrista. Viloma was the son of Kapotaromaka, and Tumvuru was the son of Viloma. The sons of Tumvuru was Dundubhi who was the father of Punarvasu. Punarvasu had a son named Ahuka, and a daughter named Ahuki. The sons of Ahuka were Devaka and Ugrasena. The daughters of Devaka were named Devaki, Vrikadevā, Upadevā, Sahadevā, Sarakshitā, Shridevi, and S'āntidevi, who were all married to Vasudeva. Sahadevā had two sons named Deva and Upadeva. Ugrasena had several sons named Kansa, Soluma and Chavata.

Viduratha was the son of Bhajamāna, a son of Andhaka. The son of Viduratha was S'ura, who was the father of S'ami. Pratikshatra was the son of S'ami, and the son of Pratikshatra was Svayambhoja, who was the father of

Hridika. The son of Hridika was Kritavarma. The son of Shura, the son of Viduratha, were Deva, Shatadhanu, and Devamidusha. Shura had another wife named Mārishā, who became the mother of five daughters named Prithā, Shrutadevā, Shrutakirti, Shrutashravā and Rājādhidevi; and of two sons such as Vasudeva, etc. Prithā was filiated to Kuntiraja who married her to Pāndu. The God of Virtue begat on the person of Prithā, a son named Yudhisthira, while the Wind-God and Indra successively begot on her two sons named Bhimasena and Arjuna. The king Pāndu had another queen named Mādri, who became the mother of two sons named Nakula and Sahadeva, begot on her person by the Ashvis Nāsatya and Dasra. Kunti had another son before marriage who was named Karna. Shrutadevā was the mother of Dantavakra who was valiant in battles. The king of Kekaya begat on the person of Shrutakirti five sons such as Shantardhana, etc. Rājādhidevi had two sons named Vindhu and Anuvindha. Damaghosa begat on the person of Shrutashravā a son named Shishupala. Vasudeva had several wives named Pauravi, Rohini, Madirā and Devaki, etc. Of these Rohini became the mother of Balarāma. Balarāma begat on his wife Revati several sons such as Sarana, Shatha, Nishatha, and Ulmaka, etc.,

Devaki became the mother of six sons, who were named Kirtimāna, Sushena, Udarya, Bhadrasena, Rijudaša, and Bhadradeva. King Kansa destroyed all these six sons of Devaki. Sankarshana or Valarāma was the seventh son of Devaki, and Krishna was her eighth. Krishna had sixteen thousand wives, of whom Rukmini, Satyabhāmā, Lakshmanā Chāruhāsini, and Jāmvavati were the eight principal ones. Krishna had a large family of sons by these wives, of whom Pradyumna, Chārudeshna, and Shāmva were famous. Pradyumna begat on his wife Rati a son of mighty prowess who was named Aniruddha. Aniruddha had by his wife Subhadrā, a son named Vajra. The son of Vajra was Prativāhu, and the son of Prativāhu was Chāru.

Vanhi was a scion of the race of Turvasu. The son of Vanhi was Bharya, whose son was Bhima, the father of Karandhama. Karandhama's son was Marut.

Now hear me describe the race of Druhya. Druhya's son was Setu, whose son was Arandha, whose son was Gāndhāra, whose son was Gharma. The son of Gharma was Ghrita, whose son was Durgama who was the father of Prachetā.

Now hear me describe the progeny of Anu, whose son was Svabhānara. The son of Svabhānara was Kālānala, whose son was Srinjaya, whose son was Puranjaya. The son of Puranjaya was Janamejaya, whose son was Mahāshāla, who was the father of Mahāmanā better known by the appellation of Ushinara. The son of Ushinara was Shivi, whose son was Vrishadarbha. Mahāmanā had another son named Titikshu whose son was Rudraratha. The son of Rudraratha was Hema, whose son was Sutapa, whose son was Vali. This Vali was the father of several sons who were called Anga, Vanga, Kalinga, Andhra, and Paundra. The son of Anga was Anapāla, whose son was Diviratha, who was the father of Dharmaratha. The son of Dharmaratha was Lompāda, whose son was Chaturanga, whose son was Prithulakshya, who was the father of Champa. The son of Champa was Haryaksha, whose son was Bhadraratha, whose son was Vrihatkarmā, who was the father of Vrihadbhānu. The son of Vrihadbhānu was Vrihatmanā, whose son was Jayadratha, whose son was Vijaya, who was the father of Dhriti. The son of Dhriti was Dhritavrata, whose son was Satyadharma, whose son was Addiratha who was the father of Karna. The son of Karna was Vrishasena. Now I shall describe the race of Puru.

—:o:—

CHAPTER CXL.

Hari said :—The son of Puru was Janamejaya, whose son was Manushya, whose son was Abhayada, whose son was Sambhu, who was the father of Vahugati. The son of Vahugati was Samjāti, whose son was Vatsagati, who was the father of Randrāshva. Randrāshva had several sons, who were named Riteyu, Sthandileyu, Kaksheyu, Kriteya, Jaleyu, and Santateyu. Of these the son of Riteyu was Ratinara, whose son was Pratiratha. The son of Pratiratha was Medhātithi whose son was Ainila. The son of Ainila was Dushmanta, who by his wife Shakuntalā, had a son named Bharata. The son of Bharata was Vitatha, whose son was Manyu, whose son was Nara, whose son was Samkriti, who was the father of Gardha. The son of Gardha was Amanyu, whose son was Shini. The mighty Nara, the son of Manyu had another son named Urukshaya. The son of Urukshaya was Trayāruni, whose son was Vyuhakshetra, whose son was Suhotra, who had three sons Hasti, Ajamida and Dvimida. The son of Hasti was Purumida, and the son of Ajamida was Kanva. Medhātithi sprang from this Kauva, who was the progenitor of the Kānvayana clan of Brahmanās. Ajamida had another son named Vrihadishu, who was the father of Vrihatdhanu. The son of Vrihatdhanu was Vrihatkarma, whose son was Jayadratha, whose son was Vishvājit, whose son was Senajit, whose son was Ruchirāshva, who was the father of Prithusena.

Puru was the son of Prithusena, whose son was Dvipa, whose son was Samara. Prithusena had another son named Sukriti. The son of Sukriti was Vibhrāja, whose son was Ashvaha. The said Ashvaha had a son by his wife Kriti, named Brahmadatta, whose son was Vishvaksen. Dvimidha, the son of Suhotra had a son named Yamina. The son of

Yamina was Dhritimāna, whose son was Satyadhriti, whose son was Dridhamuni. The son of Dridhamuni was Suparshva, whose son was Sannati. The son of Sannati was Kritu, whose son was Ugrāyudha, whose son was Kshema, whose son was Sudhira, whose son was Puranjāya, who was the father of Viduratha.

Ajamidā had a wife named Nalini, who gave birth to Nila. The son of Nila was Shānti, whose son was Sushānti, whose son was Puru, whose son was Arka, whose son was Haryashva, who was the father of Mukula. This Mukula became the ruler of the country of Pānchāla. He had five sons named Yuvanira, Vrihadbhānu, Kampilla, Srinjaya and Sharadvāna. This Sharadvāna was firmly devoted to Vishnu. Sharadvāna begat a son on Ahalyā, who was called Divodāsa, the socond. Divodāsa had a son named Shatānanda. Satyadhriti was the son of Shatānanda. Satyadhriti lost control over his senses at the sight of the nymph Urvasi, and a son named Kripa and a daughter named Kripri were born out of his emitted seed. Kripri was married to Dronāchāryya, and Ashvathvāmā was the fruit of this union.

The son of Divodāsa was Mitrāyu, whose son was Chyavana, whose son was Sudāsa, who was the father of Saudāsa. The son of Saudāsa was Sahadeva, whose son was Somaka, who had two sons named Jantu and Prishata. The son of Prishata was Drupada, through whom Dhrishtadyumna came into being. The son of Dhrishtadyumna was Dhrishtaketu.

The aforesaid Ajamida had a son named Riksha. The son of Riksha was Shamvarana, who was the father of Kuru, Sudhanu, Parikshit and Janhu. The son of Sudhanu was Suhotra, whose son was Chyavana, who was the father of King Kritaka. The son of Kritaka was Uparichayavasu, the father of Vrihadratha, Pratyagra, Satya and others. The son of Vrihadratha was Kushāgra, whose son was Rishabha, whose son was Pushpanābha, who was the father of king Satyāhita. The son of Satyāhita was Sudhanvā, whose son was Janhu.

The said Vrihadratha had another son named Jarāsandha. The son of Jarāsandha was Sahadeva, whose son was Somāti, who was the father of Bhimasena, Ugrasena, Shrutasena and others.

The abovesaid Janhu had a son named Suratha. The son of Suratha was Viduratha, whose son was Sārvabhauma, whose son was Jayasena, who was the father of A'vādhita. The son of A'vādhita was Ayutāyu, whose son was Akrodhana, whose son was Atithi, who was the father of Riksha. The son of Riksha was Bhimasena, whose son was Dilipa, whose son was Pratipa, who was the father of Devāpi, Shantanu, and Valhika. Somadatta owes his paternity to King Valhika. The son of Somadatta was Bhuri, whose sons were Bhurishravā and Shāla.

Shāntanu begot on the person of Gangā, a son named Bhishma, who was noted for his piety. The said Shāntanu had two other sons named Chitrāngada and Vichitraviryya. Vichitraviryya had two wives named Amvikā and Amvālikā. The holy Vyāsa begot on Amvika, a son named (Dhritarāshtra; on Amvālikā, a son named Pāndu; and on the person of a slave girl, a son named Vidura. Dhritarāshtra had by his wife Gāndhāri, a hundred sons named Duryyodhana, etc., while Pāndu had five sons named Yudhishthira, etc. By their common wife Draupadi, Yudhishthira had a son named Prativindhya; Bhima, a son named Shrutasoma; Arjuna, a son named Shrutakirti; Nakula, a son named Shatānika; and Sahadeva, a son named Shrutakarma. Yudhisthira and his five brothers had a number of wives; such as, Yandhayi, Hidimvā, Kaushi, Subhadrā Vijayā and Renumati, who respectively became the mothers of Devaka, Ghatatkacha, Abhimanyu, Sarvaga, and Suhotra. Abhimanyu was the father of Parikshit, whose son was Janamejaya.

Now hear me enumerate the names of kings who came after Janamejaya.

—:o:—

CHAPTER CLXI.

—:o:—

HARI said :—The son of Shatānika was Ashmedhadatta, whose son was Adhisimaka, whose son was Krishna, whose son was Aniruddha, whose son was Ushana, whose son was Chitraratha, whose son was Shuchidratha, whose son was Vrishnimana, whose son was Susena, whose son was Sunitha, whose son was Arichakshu, whose son was Mukāvana, whose son was Medhāvi, who was the father of Jaya.

The son of Nripanjaya Pāriplava, whose son was Sunayá, whose son was Medhāvi, who was the father of Nripanjaya, The son of this Nripanjaya was Hari, whose son was Tigma, whose son was Vrihadratha, whose son was Shatanika who was the father of Sudānaka. The son of Sudānaka was Udana, whose son was Anninara, whose son was Dantapāni, whose son was Nimittaka, whose son was Kshemaka who was the father of Shudra.

Now hear me narrate the genealogy of princes, who would grace in future the life of Vrihadvala of the race of Ikshāku. The son of Vrihadvala would be Urukshaya, whose son would be Vatsavyuha, whose son would be Vrihadashva, whose son would be Bhānuratha, whose son would be Prativya, whose son would be Pratilaka, whose son would be Manudeva, whose son would be Sunakshatra, whose son would be Kinnara, whose son would be Antarikshaka. Antarikshaka would beget Suparna, who would beget Kritajit, who would beget the pious Vrihadbhraja, who would beget Kritanjaya, who would beget Dhananjaya, who would beget Sanjaya, who would beget Shâkya. Shâkya would beget Shuddhodana, who would beget Vâhula, who would beget Senajit, who would beget Kshudraka, who would beget Samitra, who would beget Kudava, who would beget Sumitra.

Now hear me narrate the genealogy of the princes of Magadha. The son of Jarâsandha was Surâpi, whose son was Shrutashravâ, whose son was Ayutâyu, whose son was Niramitra, whose son was Svakshetra, whose son was Karmaka. The son of Karmaka was Shrutanjaya, whose son was Senajit, whose son was Bhuri, whose son was Shuchi, whose son was Kshemya, whose son was Suvrata, whose son was Dharma, whose son was Shmashruma, whose son was Dridhasenaka, whose son was Sumati, whose son was Savala, whose son was Neeta, whose son was Satyajit, whose son was Vishvajit, whose son was Ishanjay. All these princes were of the race of Vrihadratha. After this, impious Shudra kings, who would stick at nothing to gain their ends, would be the rulers of the world, and oppression, duplicity and falsehood would be the only recognised principles of statecraft.

The eternal Nârâyana, who suffers no change nor decay, is the creator, protector and disintegrator of the cosmic Universe. This Pralaya or dissolution of the cosmos admits of being grouped under three different heads; such as, the Naimittika (accidental or contingent, and conditional); Prâkritika (physical and cosmic); and lastly, A'tyantika (final, and without any chance of the re-integration and re-combination of its molecules). The different categories of cosmic evolution will merge in one another in the inverse order of their enumeration, *viz.*, the solids will dissolve into the liquids, the liquids will be absorbed in the gaseous or the heat, the heat will die away in the ether, the ether will be merged in the etherine, the etherine, in the category of Ahankāra (Egoism); the Ahankāra in the principle of Intellection, (Buddhitattva); the Intellection in the Self or Jiva, and the Jiva in the unmanifest Brahma. Vishnu, the Soul of the Universe, is the only deathless Reality in the Universe, which makes itself patent in the shape of Nar Nārāyana (the Divine Man.) The universe is transient and illusory. Many kings there had been in the world and many more will come and pass away as fitful shadows. Therefore walk ye not in the paths of the unrighteous. Abjure sin and work out the purity of thought, for in such thoughts consists the salvation of a man; and such thoughts lead to the blissful Hari.

—:oo:—

CHAPTER CXLII.

BRAHMA said :—The God Hari incarnated on earth and protected the seed of the A'ryyas. His advent on this fleeting world was for the destruction of the kingdom of the Asurās and the propagation of the religion of the Vedās. His several incarnations were in the forms of Fish Tortoise, etc. The God Keshava incarnated himself as the Fish in the primordial ocean, carried the immutable Vedās on his back, killed the demon Hayagriva, and protected the patriarch Manu and others. Incarnated as a Tortoise, he carried the Mount Mandāra on his back, wherewith the gods and demons churned the primordial ocean for ambrosia. As the fruit of that churning, Dhanvantara, the first of the propounder of the medical science, came out of its troubled waters, carrying the pitcher of divine ambrosia in his hand. Dhanvantari related to Sushruta the science of Ayurveda with its eight subdivisions, and the God Hari, assuming the shape of a girl of fascinating beauty, doled out the ambrosia to the gods. Incarnated as the Divine Boar, the God Hari killed the demon Hiranyāksha, lifted up the submerged earth on his tusks from beneath the waters of the enshrouding ocean, and protected the gods and patriarchs. Incarnated as the redoubtable Nrisinha (half-man, half-lion), the God Hari destroyed the demon Hiranyakashipu with his sinful allies, and vindicated the religion of the Vedās. After that, the lord of the universe was incarnated as Parashurām, a son of Jāmadagni. For twenty-one times in succession he extirpated the race of the wicked Kshatriyās, killed the dreadful Kārtaviryārjuna, made a gift of the whole earth to Kashyapa, and finally settled himself on the summits of the Mount Mahendra. After that, the subduer of the wicked divided his divine self into four parts and came into the world as Rāma, Bharata, Lakshmana and Shatrughna, the four sons of king Dasharatha. Jānaki was the wife of Rāma, who, for the good of his step-mother Kekayi, and for the performance of a promise made her by his father, resorted, as a voluntary exile, to the forest of Dandaka. He cut the nose of Surpanakhā, killed the monsters Khara and Dushana, and destroyed the dreadful Rāvana, who had carried away his wife Sitā. After the fall of Rāvana, Rāma installed Vibbishana, a brother of Rāvana, on the throne of his kingdom Lankā, and returned to his own capital in the aerial car, Pushpaka, in the company of Hanumāna, Sugriva and his faithful Sitā. In the bliss of his consort's love, Rāma ruled his kingdom for the good of his people and the gods, and performed a Horse-Sacrifice to commemorate his suzerainty over the earth.

Sitā, though passed a long time in the house of Rāvana, did not betray his lord either in deeds or thoughts. Sitā was as chaste as the virtuous Anasuyā, the beloved wife of Atri. Now hear me narrate the excellence of Sitā's chastity and the exalted station which virtuous and faithful wives occupy in the economy of the universe.

Once on a time there lived in the city of Pratisthāna, a leper Brahmana whose name was Kaushika. His wife, who was firmly devoted to him, used to adore and worship her lord as a god without even thinking for a moment that he was afflicted with such a foul and loathsome disease. But Kaushika was a cross and peevish husband, and never missed opportunities to abuse his wife, who, though often chastised, never ceased to pay him god-like veneration and love. One day, Kaushika took a fancy to visit a courtezan in the city, and expressed that desire to his wife. Whereupon she took him on her shoulders and safely carried him to that house of ill fame. Nor did she forget to take with her a considerable amount of money which the courtezan might ask for her nefarious trade.

Now it happened that the Sage Māndavya was then undergoing punishment on the top of a pointed mace, as he was unjustly sentenced by the authorities on a false charge of theft. The faithful wife, on her way to the house of the courtezan, touched with her feet the body of that afflicted sage, who, in his agony, cursed her with the pangs of widowhood on the break of day. The wife, on the other hand, forbade the Sun to rise in order that the curse of the Sage might not take effect. The Sun-God, over-powered by the energy of conjugal chastity, was afraid to show his face, and creation was enshrouded in a pall of dark-ness. Ages past without the Sun in the sky. The frightened gods resorted to Brahmā for help and advice. Brahmā said, " It is the energy of Chastity that has overpowed the energy of asceticism, and obstructed the advent of the Sun. Go, ye gods, to Anasuyā, and she will plead, on your behalf, to the wife of Kaushika." The gods did as they were told to do.

Anasuyā saw and propitiated her with the boon of a long life and perfect health to her lord, and lo and behold, the Sun-God again appeared in the sky.

—:o:—

CHAPTER CXLIII.

BRAHMA said:—Now I shall narrate the celebrated *Rāmāyanam*, hearing which a man is absolved of sin. Brahmā sprang out of the lotus-navel of Vishnu, and Marichi was the son of Brahmā. Kashyapa was the son of Marichi, and the Sun-God was the son of Kashyapa. Manu was the son of the Sun-God. Ikshāku was the son of Manu, in whose line Raghu of mighty prowess was born. Aja was the son of Raghu, and Dasharatha was the son of Aja. Dasharatha had four sons, each of mighty prowess, of whom Rāma was born in the womb of Kaushalyā, Bharata in the womb of Kaikeyi, and Lakshmana and Shatrughna in the womb of Sumitrā. Rāma, the beloved of his parents and firmly devoted to them, learned the use of arms and weapons from the holy Vishvāmitra, and was thus enabled to kill the monstress Tādakā. He killed the monster Subāhu, while defending the sacrificial platform of Vishvāmitra, whence he accompanied that holy Sage to witness the celebration of a religious sacrifice by Janaka, whose daughter Jānaki he married. Lakshmana married Urmilā; Bharata married Māndavi, and Shatrughna married Shrutakirti. After the celebration of their marriage ceremony, Rāma and Lakshmana stayed with their parents at Ayodhyā, while Bharata and Shatrughna went to live with their maternal uncle, Yudhājit. When the two princes Bharata and Shatrughna were away from the city (Ayodhyā), the king (Dasharatha) attempted to instal his favourite Rāma as the Crown-Prince of his dominion, when his consort Kaikeyi asked him to send Rāma in exile for a period of fourteen years. For the spiritual edification of his father, Rāma renounced the kingdom as a thing of little consequence and went out as a voluntary exile, in the company of his beloved Sitā and Lakshmana, to the city of Shringabera. He renounced the use of his car, and travelled on foot to the city of Prayāga from whence he sojourned to the Mount of Chitrakuta.

King Dasharatha, in agony of separation and in bitter remorse for what he had done, died and ascended to heaven. Prince Bharata performed the funeral rites of his father Dasharatha, and then went to Rāma with a large army to welcome him back to his kingdom and heritage. Rāma did not return to his capital, but gave his sandal to Bharata instead, to be installed on the throne of his kingdom as a royal insignia. Whereupon Bharata justly ruled the kingdom in the name of his sovereign Rāma. Thus dismissed by Rāma, Bharata did not return to Ayodhyā, but fixed his residence in the town of Nandigrama, while Rāma thereafter sojourned to the hermitage of Atri from the Mount Chitrakuta. Thence having made obeisance to Sutikshna and Agastya, Rāma entered the forest of Dandaka, where the Monstress Surpanakhā attempted to devour (Sitā). Rāma disgraced her by cutting her ears and clipping away her nose. Thus disfigured and insulted, Surpanakhā prevailed upon the Monsters Khara, Dushana, and Trishirā to attack Rāma simultaneously from three different sides. The three Rākshasa heroes, with an army of fourteen thousand Rākshasa soldiers drawn up in a battle array, attacked Rāma in battle, but Rāma with the help of his deadly shafts, consigned them all to the mansion of death. Rāvana, through the instigation of this Rākshasi (Surpanakhā), resolved to carry away Sitā by fraud; and for that end, he despatched before him a Rākshasa named Māricha to lure away Rāma in the forest in the magic-guise of a golden stag. Sitā entreated Rāma to chase the golden deer and to secure that golden query for her. Rāma chased and killed that magic deer with his arrow, and the disguised Monster expired shouting, "Help, O Sitā, help, O Lakshmana!" Lakshmana importunated by Sitā, ran to the rescue of Rāma, and beheld him in the forest. Rāma said, "O Brother, these are the wicked charms which the Rākshasas practise in this dense and lonely forest, and surely they have carried away Sitā by fraud." In the meantime, Rāvana appeared before the cottage of Rāma, and carried away the beloved bride of Rāma vainly struggling on his lap. The mighty Jatāyu, the king of the birds, assailed the dark-souled miscreant on the way, but Rāvana was more than a match for him. So in the battle that ensued Ravana completely defeated the bird-king Jatāyu, and returned victor with his beautiful prize to his capital at Lankā, and kept her well guarded in a shady garden of Ashoka trees.

Rāma and Lakshmana returned to their forest-retreat, their hearts foreboding all sorts of dire mishaps,—and found it lonely and deserted. Oh, the first stifled sobs of widowed love that almost broke the all-conquering soul of Rāma in their repression! Lakshmana wept like a child in the first-gloom of a dire calamity in which suspense metamorphises itself into a torrid noon of burning shame, and a robust stream of molten affection suddenly broke forth, in his heart, into a deathless volcano of vengeance and retaliation, for the consummation of which all eternity expanded its bloated bosom and hypothecated itself to the prospective realisation of that spiritual wrath.

Rāma and Lakshmana followed the trail of their stolen goddess—sombre and ominous like a summer thunder cloud. On and on they went, weary and footsore, and traversed many a mile of that sylvan solitude when they stumbled upon the wounded body of the brave though dying Jatāyu. That gallant bird-king narrated the whole history of Sitā's forcible carrying away by the benighted Rāvana, and breathed his last in the presence of the divine brothers (Rāma and Lakshmana). They collected the cast off leaves and twigs of the forest, exhumed the dead body of the godly Jatāyu, performed the last earthly rites to his mortal remains, and trended their way to the South.

While there, Rāma entered into a friendly compact with Sugriva, the brother of the monkey-king Vāli, and showed his skill in archery by shooting through the trunks of seven Tāla trees. Then he killed Vāli and made over the sovereignity of the monkey-land Kishkindā to his brother Sugriva, and quartered himself with his beloved Lakshmana in the outskirts of the Mount Rishyamukha. Then Sugriva commissioned the leaders of his monkey-troops to search for Sitā in all directions, and the huge monkey-generals, with their bodies mountain high, went out north, south, east and west in quest of the sunny bride of the solar race. In vain did they search every stream or river bank, hill or dale, forest or hamlet, and at last while deliberating suicide in despair, they saw Shampāti. Hanumān, the greatest of the monkey-generals, having got the information from Shampāti, leapt over the sea, which is hundreds of miles wide, and forms the abode of monsters. He saw the lovely Jānaki imprisoned in the forest of Ashoka trees, chastised by its female guards who had been pressing her hard to share the bed of Rāvana, and harshly rousing her up from her revery of Rāma's company. The monkey-general dropped down to Sitā the signet ring of Rāma, and asked her about her health. "Do not be dejected, O Maithili," observed that gallant monkey, "but rather give me something of yours which my master Rāma might cherish as a sweet memento of love. Do not be frightened, O Maithili, for I am the servant of Rāma." Whereupon Sitā unfastened a jewel from her chignanon, made it over to Hanumān, and asked him to request Rāma to succour her immediately after his return to Rāma's residence (at Rishyamukha). Hanumān gladly assented to her request, and thereafter began to destroy the pleasure-garden of Rāvana, killing prince Aksha and many a Rākshasa-soldier in the act. A Brahmāstra cast by Indrajita hit him hard and left him a captive in the hands of Rākshasās, who dragged him in fetters to the presence of Rāvana. Hanumān said. "I am a servant of Rāma. Return to him, O miscreant, his faithful Maithili." Rāvana, madly infuriated by these observations ordered to burn the tail of the monkey general, and Hanumān, by wildly lashing his burning tail against the thatched roofs of Lankā, instantaneously set the whole city on fire. Having consumed Lankā with fire, the monkey-general returned to the side of Rāma and reported to him of his having eaten mango, and of the general conflagration that broke out in Lankā through his own instrumentality. He made over to him the head gem of Sitā, and Rāma with Lakshman, Hanumān and his monkey-army with its generals and officers, marched in the direction of Lankā.

Meanwhile, Vibhishana slighted by his brother Rāvana, went over to Rāma's side and made a common cause with him. After that, Rāma caused a bridge to be built across the ocean with the help of the monkey-general Nala, and crossed over with his whole army and officers to the Isle of Lankā. He viewed the splendid prospect of the Island from the summit of the Hill Suvela, where he fixed his quarter for the day. Then the monkey-generals Nila, Angada, Nala, Dhuma, Dhumrāksha, Jāmvuvāna, Manda, Dvividha and others set to demolish the fortifications of the city (Lankā) and killed many leaders of the Rākshasa-army. Rāma and Lakshmana destroyed, with the help of their monkey-army, many an eminent Rākshasa-hero of gigantic stature and black as the sable collyrium of death, such as Vidyutjihva, Dhumrāksha, Devāntaka, Narāntaka, Mahodara, Mahāpārshva, Atikāya, Kumbha, Nikumbha, Matta, Makarāksha, and

Akampana. After that, Lakshmana defeated and killed in a single combat, the redoubtable Indrajita, and Rāma having severed with his arrows the twenty arms of Rāvana, subsequently killed him in battle.

Sitā gave ample proof of her chastity, and came unscathed out of an Ordeal of Fire. Sitā, thus purified by Fire, ascended the aeriel car with her beloved consort, and the whole monkey-army, jubilant, and elated with victory, followed its gracious leader to his capital at Ayodhyā.

Rāma ruled the country for eleven thousand years, and protected his subjects with paternal love and care. He undertook and accomplished the celebration of ten Horse-Sacrifices in succession, and offered oblations to his departed manes at the shrine of Gaya-Shirsha. He was blessed with two sons named Lava and Kusha. It was in his reign that the holy Sage Bharata first organised dramatic performances, and Shatrughna killed the demon Lavana. Rāma heard the origin of the Rākshasas narrated to him by the holy Agastya. Having made over the sovereignty to his sons Lava and Kusha, Rāma made his exit from the world at the close of a glorious though chequered life, dedicated exclusively to the furtherance of good therein.

—:oo:—

CHAPTER CXLIV.

BRAHMA said:—Now I shall narrate the family history of Hari which teems with the sanctified exploits of Krishna. Vasudeva begot Krishna and Valadeva on the person of Devaki for the edification of the righteous and annihilation of the wicked. The eternal God was incarnated on this mortal globe in the shape of Krishna. The Monstress Putanā was engaged by the tyrant Kansa to put an end to his life, in infancy, with the pretext of suckling him. But Krishna sucked her poisoned nipples with a force that verily killed her on the spot. The mighty prowessed Krishna overturned the car-demon, felled the two tree-monsters named Jamalā and Arjuna, and destroyed the serpent Kāliya and the monster Dhenuka. At this time, he supported the mount Govardhana on the tip of his finger, and was honoured and worshipped by the God Indra for this exploit. He relieved this sinful earth of its weight of sin, and pledged himself to protect the five sons of Pāndu in their days of trouble and distress. The demon Arishta fell an easy victim to his prowess, and he cheered the Gopās and Gopa-maidens of Brindāban by slaying the monster Keshi. He dragged down the demon Kansa from the platform, and killed the wrestlers Chānuka, Mushtika and Malla, who guarded the person of that detestable tyrant.

Krishna had eight principal wives, such as Rukmini, Satyabhāmā, etc., besides a seraglio of sixteen thousand other wives. By them he got hundreds, nay thousands of sons and grandsons. By Rukmini he had a son named Pradyumna, who killed the demon Shambara. The son of Pradyumna was Aniruddha, who married Ushā, the daughter of king Vāna. There ensued a deadly conflict between Krishna and the God Shankara, when the elopement of Ushā with Aniruddha was detected and made known to the world. Krishna cut down the thousand arms of king Vāna with the exception of two. Once upon a time, he killed the demon Naraka and carried the flower Pārijāt from the garden of heaven. Shishupāla, Vala, and the monkey, named Dvibidha, were also among the victims, who fell at the stroke of his mighty discus.

The son of Aniruddha was Vajra, who became the king of Mathura, when Krishna was translated to heaven. In order to please his preceptor Sandipani, Krishna brought back the soul of his son from the mansion of death, and brought back to life the son of that holy sage. For the furtherance of the divine cause, he installed Ugrasena as king on the throne of Mathurā.

—:o:—

CHAPTER CLV.

Brahma said :—Now hear me narrate the story of the Mahābhāratam. It is so called (Bharatam) from the fact of Krishna,s espousing the cause the Pāndavas in battle, for relieving the earth of its weight of sin (Bhubhāra). Brahmā sprang out of the lotus navel of Hari. The son of Brahmā was Atri. The son of Atri was the Moon-God, and in the line that sprang from him was born Pururava, who begot on the nymph Urvasi a son, named A'yu. Yayāti, Bharat, Kuru, and Shāntanu were of the race of A'yu. The divinely wise Bhishma was the son of Shāntanu by his wife Gangā. This Shāntanu had two other sons named Chitrāngada and Vichitravirya by his wife Satyavati. This Chitrānguda was killed in battle by a Gandharva of the same name. The secoud son, Vichitravirya married Amvicā and Amvalikā, the daughters of the king of Kāshi. After the death of Vichitravirya, the holy Vyāsa begot sons on the wives of Vichitravirya. Amvikā became the mother of Dhritarāshtra; Amvālika, of Pāndu; and Bhujisyā, of Vidura. Dhritarāshtra had a hundred sons by his wife Gāndhāri such as Duryodhana, etc., while the five sons, who were begotten on Kunti and Mādri, the two wives of Pāndu, were Yudhishthira, etc.

By a preordinance of fate there sprang up a bitter animosity between the Kurus (sons of Dhritarāshtra) and the Pāndavās (sons of Pāndu). Duryodhana, a man of fickle temperament and unstable principles, was not slow to devise means for harrassing the Pāndavās. He attempted to kill them by burning them down in a house of shellac. The guileless Pāndavās, saved through the merit of their faith and innocence, sojourned to the village of Ekachakrā, and took shelter in the house of a Brāhmana. These mighty Pāndavās stayed for a while in the house of that Brāhmana, and, while there, the redoubtable Bhimasena killed the monster Vaka. Thence they went to the country of Pānchāla and married Draupadi, the princess of that country, whose hands had to be won by a competition in skilful archery, and by showing matchless proficiency in that art.

In the meantime, Dhritarāshtra, who had been prevailed upon by Bhishma and Drona to grant them the sovereignty of half the kingdom, called the Pāndavās over to his capital, and installed them as kings in the city of Indraprastha. Then the self-controlled Pāndavās caused a splendid pavilion to be raised at Indraprastha, and there they celebrated the Rājasuya sacrifice. At Dvārakā, Arjuna wedded his bride Subhadrā, the sister of Krishna, and secured the friendship of that great personage, who stood by him as his staunchest ally all through life. From the Fire-God Arjuna obtained a car named Nandighosa, the invincible bow named Gāndiva, the inexhaustible quiver, and a suit of unpierceable armour. With Krishna as his second, and with the help of this invincible bow, Arjuna was able to appease the hunger of the Fire-God. In his campaigns of world-conquest, Arjuna defeated many kings, and made over their treasures to his brother Yudhishthira, the master of politics and statecraft. In a fraudulent game of dice, Duryodhana managed to win all that belonged to Yudhishthira, and, through the machination of the evil-souled Karna and Shakuni, pursuaded him to continue the play, pledging a residence incognito for one year out of an exile of twelve as his stake. Yudhishthira lost this last stake, and went out as a voluntary exile in the company of his faithful and devoted brothers and their beloved Draupadi, Dhaumya and a concourse of other holy sages. For one year, they lived incognito in the house of the king of Virāt, serving as cowherds and menials in his household. After one year, they declared themselves, and asked for their moiety of the country, or a proprietary right in only five villages in its stead, which Duryodhana, in an evil hour and through the machination of his evil-grained courtiers, refused to grant.

The five brothers, thus insulted and ousted of their legitimate birthright, began to collect troops and secure powerful allies. With an army of seven Akshauhinis of soldiers they met Duryodhana at the head of eleven Ashauhinis at the field of Kurukshetra. So there ensued a cruel and dreadful war between the Kurus and the Pāndavās, similar to the one that was waged by the gods against the demons of yore. Bhishma was the leader of Duryodhana's forces just as the hostilities commenced, while the armies of the Pāndavās were led by Shikhandi.

Shikhandi chose out Bhishma, the commandant of the Kaurava-forces as his opponent in battle, which lasted for ten consecutive days, the archers posted against archers, and swordsmen and spearsmen picked against soldiers similarly equipped as themselves. Bhishma, pierced through and through by the arrows of Shikhandi and Arjuna, saw that the sun had just then entered the summer solstice, and having meditated upon the divine self of the mace-bearing Deity and discoursed on many a topic of ethical and political philosophy, propitiated his departed Manes with suitable oblations; and the spirit of that brave and righteous soldier, who had never swerved from truth in his life, joyfully abandoned its earthly tenement and merged itself in that infinite joy, knowledge and purity, which the wise men worship as the Supreme Brahma.

Then Drona, the preceptor ot the race of Kuru, took up the command of the Kauravā's army, and went out to fight the valiant Dhrishtadyumna, the commander of the Pāndavā's troops. For five days the battle raged furious and undecided, and many gallant chiefs fell on both the sides like sear leaves before the winter wind. Drona sadly dejected by the news of his son's death, fell an easy victim to the sword thursts of Dhrishtadyumna. After that, Karna became the leader of the Kuru's forces, and picked out Arjuna as his opponent in battle. For two days the battle raged furious, and victory oscillated between the banners of the Kurus and the Pāndavās. At last, Karna, tossed about like a weed in the seathing sea of Arjuna's arrows, breathed his last and entered the region of the Sun-God. After that, Salya was elected commander of the Kuru's forces and fell at the hands of Yudhishthira at the middle of the day of battle. Then Duryodhana, mad with despair and ignominy, ran, club in hand, towards the redoubtable Bhimasena, like the God of Death bent on stifling out the life of Time and Space. But the redoubtable Bhimasena proved too much of a match for him and killed him quick with one stroke of his deadly club.

After that, Ashvathamā, the son of Drona, determined to storm the Pāndavā's camp by surprise at night, and to annihilate the Pāndavā-army while peacefully lulled in the lap of sleep. Bent on avenging the death of his father Drona, he stealthily entered the Pāndavā's camp, and brooding over the death of his illustrious progenitor, he severed with his sword the heads of Dhrishtadyumna and the five sons of Draupadi. Arjuna, maddened by the agonising wailings of Draupadi, took the fugitive miscreant a captive, and cut out of his (Ashvathaman's) head the famous gem with the means of his Aishika-weapon. Arjuna consoled the widows of the killed warriors and performed funeral obsequies in honour of his departed friends, relations and cognates. Yudhishthira, consoled and advised by Bhishma in his last moments, ascended the throne, and ruled the kingdom according to the injunctions of the Sciptures. He propitiated the God Vishnu by celebrating a Horse-Sacrifice, and having heard of the annihilation of the race of Jādavā by that cursed club, made over the sovereignty to his grandson Parikshita, and ascended to the region of Vishnu in the company of his brother, while repeating the sacred name of that Deity.

After that, for the furtherance of the divine good, as well as for the punishment of the wicked and elevation of the righteous, the God Vasudeva was incarnated on earth. He comes down on earth, at intervals of centuries and in the shape of man, to chastise the wrong-doers and to set right the path of truth and piety. In the twentieth Manvantara (age of the twentieth Manu), he sprang out, in the guise of Dhanvantari, of the ocean of milk, as it was churned by the gods and demons for the divine ambrosia, and taught the science of life (Medical Science) to Sushruta, the son of Vishvāmitra. He, who hears of the genesis (evolution) of this grand idealist and his adjunct ideas, goes to heaven after death.

—:o:—

CHAPTER CXLVI.

DHANVANTARI said :—O Sushruta, now I shall deal with the nosology pathology, pathogeny and symptomology of all the diseases as related by the holy Atreya to the' sages of yore, The terms *Roga*, *Pápma*, *Jvara*, *Vyadhi*, *Vikára*, *Dushtam*, *Amaya*, and *Yakshmá* are the synonyms of disease. The five essential categories in respect of a disease may be described as its (Nidānam) pathology (*lit*., exciting factors), preliminary or incubative stage (Purvarupa), manifestation of characteristic indications (Rupa), amelioration (Upashaya), location (Samprapti), Diagnosis (Vijnanam). Reason, cause, pathogney, exciting factors are the synonyms of the term Nidānam. The stage in which an uncertain kind of *malaise* is complained of by the patient in the absence of any particular characterestic triat of any given disease, is called its incubative stage, which points to the certain genesis of the disease but does not furnish any clue to its name and character—Manifestation (Rupa) of a disease indicates the stage in which its distinguishing and characterestic traits or symptoms become patent. The terms Samsthānam (fixity), Vijnam (distinctive traits), Lingam (differentiating features), and Lakshanam (symptoms) are the synonyms of Rupam. Upashaya signifies the amelioration of the morbific diatheses in a particular disease, effected with the help of drugs which are contrary in character to the *esse* of the disease, or are contrary in virtue to its exciting factors, or are contrary both to the *esse* of the disease and its exciting factors, or are similar in character to the *esse* of the disease (pathogenetic principle), or are similar in virtues to its exciting factors, or are similar both to the *esse* of the disease and the elements that favour its genesis, or with the help of proper diet and conduct.*

The genesis or appearance of a disease in a particular part of the human body, either through the upward, downward, oblique, or transverse movement of the morbific principles, such as the deranged nerve force (Vāyu), defective metabolism (Pittam), or disordered secretary or execretory process (Kapham) concerned in the case and determining location of the disease, is called its Samprāpti (Pathogeny). The terms Agati, and Jati are the synonyms of Samprāpti. The contrary of amelioration is called aggravation, disease or

---

* The A'yurveda recognises both the laws of similars and contraries in the domain of practical therapeutics. The fact that a drug, which can induce a disease similar in character to the one under observation is curative to it, was discovered by the savants of Indian medicine long before the birth of Hanemann, or of Homœopathy in Europe.

incongeniality. The mode of this pathogeny differs according to the nature of the prevailing season of the year and the number nature, strength, predominance, or neutrality of the different morbific principle involved in the case. The genesis of the eight different types of fever owing to the varied strength, and several or combined actions of the three morbific principles of Vāyu, Pittam and Kapham, may be cited as an example of the foregoing dictum. The number of types into which a disease may be divided, or which is usually detected in practice, is called its *Sankhyâ* (number). The relative preponderance of any of the pathogenic principles involved in a disease, is called its *Vikalpa*. The virulence or serious character of a disease is proportionate to the combined or several actions of the morbific principles acting as its exciting factors. The relative virulence or strength of a disease should be ascertained with a due regard to its pathology, and the import of its indications, etc. Deliberations as to the aggravation or manifestation of a disease whether in day or night, or whether before or after a meal, or during summer or winter, etc., help the determination of its periodicity (Kāla Nirupanam). Thus we have briefly described the outlines of pathogeny (Nidânam), etc., which shall be more elaborately described later on. A vareity of injudicious conduct tends to enrage the fundamental organic principles of Vāyu, Pittam and Kapham. Ingestion of a large quantity of hot, astringent acid, pungent, and parchifying articles of fare, heavy meals, or voracious eating, running, climbing, lifting, loud-talking, night-keeping, vigorous and energetic action, fright, mental and physical labour, and sexual intercourse are the factors, which enrage or aggravate the bodily Vāyu, which becomes spontaneously aggravated in summer and after meals, aud at the close of the day or night. Ingestion of pungent, acid, sharp, hot, fetid, or indigestible articles of food, and indulgence in irascible feelings are the factors which tend to enrage the Pittam, which becomes spontaneously aggravated in Sharat (months of Kārtika and Agrahāyana according to the Ayurvedic calender), at the middle part of the day or night, as well as when the food undergoes an acid reaction in the stomach after digestion (Videha). Ingestion of sweet, acid, saline, demlucent, heavy (of digestion) and cold articles of fare, as well as of those which increase the humidity of the system, a long sitting at one place, want of sleep, day-sleep, and indigestion are the factors, which tend to enrage the Kapham, which becomes spontaneously aggravated in spring (Baishākha and Jaishtha), in the forepart of the day or night, and immediately after eating or vomiting*

Now I shall discourse on the combination of the deranged Vāyu, Pittam and Kapham. Ingestion of insufficient, indigestible, irregular and incompatible meals, use of stab wine, dried potherbs, green radish, and fetid or dry fish, sudden change of food and drink, contrary or unnatural seasons, exposure to the east wind, sudden change of one's mode of living, partaking of raw, uncooked food accumulation of phlegm in the body, malignant influence exerted by one's natal star, false dealings and evil doings, non-gratification of any mental or bodily hankering, and the pucrperal conditions of women are the factors, which help the combination and concerted action of the deranged Vāyu, Pittam and Kapham. In each disease, the Vāyu, Pittam and Kapham produce chemical changes in the blood according to the nature of the disease they give rise to and their characterestic symptoms.

* The term Váyu, Pittam and Kapham have been very loosely used by the Ayurvedic Physiologists to designate two different sets of substances. In one acceptance, Váyu, Pittam and Kapham mean nerve force, metabolism, and unutilised products of the body; while in another, they signify gas, bile and phlegm.—T. R.

54

CHAPTER CXLVII.

DHANVANTARI said :—Now I shall describe the Nidānam of fever, with the help of which a fever of whatsoever type may be correctly diagnosed. The terms, the lord of diseases, the sinful one, the lord of death, the devourer, and the finisher are the synonyms of fever. Sprung from the upper eye of the wrathful and insulted Rudra in the sacrifice which was celebrated by Daksha, this dreadful and sinful disease attacks all species of animals, through their injudicious conduct. Unconsciousness heat and delirium being its principal characteristics. Manifest in the body of an elephant, it is called Pākala. The type of fever which is peculiar to the horse, is called Abhitāpa, In dogs, it is called Alarka ; in clouds, it is called Indramada ; in water, Nilika ; in cereals, Oshadhi ; in soil, Ushara.

The type due to the action of the deranged Kapham, is marked by nausea, vomiting, cough, numbness of the body, coldness of the skin, and appearance of rashes or eruptions on the body. As birth, growth, and death are natural to all created beings, so aggravation and amelioration are natural to all types of fever. Indigestion with a non-relish for food, numbness of the body, lassitude, a burning sensation in the region of the heart, restlessness (the patient finding no relief in any position whatsoever), non-evacuation of stool and other deranged principles, salivation, nausea, loss of appetite, tasteful moisture in the mouth, heat and gloss of the skin, heaviness of the body, constant urination, and natural fulness of the body, are the symptoms, which mark the type known as A'ma-Jvara, (*i.e.*, the stage in which the deranged humours have not been digested or resolved). Rousing of the appetite, lightness of the limbs, abatement of the bodily temperature, and evacuation of the contents of the bowels after the eighth day of the attack, are the indications, which show that the deranged humours have been digested or have undergone resolution. Symptoms, which are peculiar to the several deranged humours combinedly mark the type of fever which is the product of their concerted action. Headache, swooning, vomiting with a burning sensation in the body and parchedness of the throat, aching pain in the joints, insomnia, fright, horrification, yawning and delirium, are the symptoms which characterise the type of fever due to the combined action of the deranged Vāyu (nerve-force) and Pittam (metabolism). Small heat, with a non-relish for food, pain in the joints and headache, low breathing, cough, and discolouring of the skin are the indications of the type due to the combined action of the deranged Vâyu and Shleshmā (Kapham). Fitful shivering, numbness of the body, perspiraton with a burning sensation of the body, thirst, restlessness, vomiting of mucous and bilious matter, stupefaction, drowsiness, clamminess and a bitter taste in the mouth, are the indications of the type due to the combined action of the deranged Pittam and Kapham. All the symptoms combinedly mark the type which is due to the concerted action of the deranged Vāyu, Pittam, and Kapham in addition to the following specific ones, *viz.*, alternate fits of shivering and burning sensation in the body, vertigo, sleepy in the day, sleeplessness in the night, constant sleepiness or complete insomnia, excess or absence of perspiration, singing, dancing, laughing, stoppage of the natural functions of the organs, with sunk, redshot, watery eyes, and drooping eyelids, accumulation of grity wax at the corner of the eyes, pain at the head, sides, joints and calves of the legs, vertigo, ringing in the ears, pain, violent shivering or absence of shivering, sooty colour of the tongue which becomes as black as charcoal and rough as that of a cow, heaviness and looseness of the joints, vomiting of bloody or blood-streaked bile, rolling or tossing about of the head, violent unquenchable thirst, eruptions of warts or circular rushes on the skin, pain at the heart, purging or scanty evacuations of stool, glossiness of the face, prostration of strength, loss of voice, delirium, deep heavy somnolence, and a croaking or wheezing sound in the throat. The type which is marked by the foregoing symptoms is called Abhinyasa Sannipāta. It destroys the principle of Ojas in the body (protoplasmic cells). In the Sānnipātika type of fever, the deranged Vāyu produces the constriction of the throat, and the deranged Pittam consumes the vital principle of the organism. The deranged Pittam, on account of its expansive character, finds an outlet through, and tinges the conjunctiva with its own characteristic colour (yellow). Hence the yellowness of the eyes in a case of Sānnipātika fever. A case of Sānnipātika fever in which the deranged Vāyu, Pittam and Kapham, being extremely aggravated, impair the digestive heat and thereby help the full development of all its characteristic symptoms, proves incurable. In all other events, a Sānnipātika fever can be made amenable to medicine only with the greatest difficulty. There is a different type of Sānnipātika fever in which the deranged Pittam, separately enraged and aggravated, gives rise to a burning sensation in the skin and the stomach (*lit.*, the abdominal cavity), the burning sensation coming on either with the commencement or with the abatement of the paroxysm, and being first experienced either in the stomach or in the skin. Similarly, the aggravated Vāyu and Kapham produce rigor in Sānnipātika fever, which being preceded by a burning sensation in the body indicates an unfavourable prognosis and is more dangerous of the said two types. In a case of Sānnipātika fever in which the rigor comes on first owing to the action of the deranged and aggravated Pittam, the Kapham is set free and corrected, and with the abatement of the action of the aggravated Pittam comes on fainting, with swooning, vertigo, and thirst, etc. Somnolence, langour and vomiting manifest themselves in succession at the close of the paroxysm, which is ushered in with a shivering sensation. Fevers caused by the effects of a hurt or a blow, or contracted through any foul contagion, or engendered through the potency of any spell, magic, or incantation, as well as those which are due to burns or scalds, are usually grouped under the traumatic head of fevers and owe their origin to extrinsic causes. Extreme fatigue or exhaustion brings on a type of fever in which the enraged and aggravated Vāyu affects the vascular process of the organism, and produces pain, swelling and discolouring of the skin. Anger, fright, bereavement, passion of love, exhalations of poisonous drugs, dusts of flowers, narcotics and the baneful influence cast by malignant planets may engender types of fever, which may be grouped under the traumatic head, and in which the patient laughs, weeps or raves like a maniac in succession. The type of fever caused by the odours or exhalations of any drug or cereal is marked by headache, vomiting, epileptic fits and wasting, etc., while the one, due to the effects of any poison, develops dysentery, epilepetic fits, vertigo with a yellowish black clour of the skin, and a burning sensation in the body.

Palsy and pain in the head are the symptoms, which mark the case of fever due to anger, while delirium and palsy characterise the one due to the conjoint effects of fright and rage. Fever, which has its origin in the ungratified sexual desire, develops such symptoms as loss of consciousness or absent-mindedness, with somnolence, impatience, shyness, and a non-relish for food. In fever due either to the influence of malignant stars, or to the concerted action of the three morbific principles of Vāyu, Pittam and Kapham (Sānnipāta) both the Vāyu and the Pittam of the organism are simultaneously enraged. The types of Sānnipātika fever caused through the dynamics of a curse or an incantation, are simply unbearable in their intensity. In cases of spell-origined fever the patient should be basked in the glare of the sacrificial fire (Homāgni) into which libations of clarified butter should be cast by reciting the

Abhichāra-Mantram. The two last named types of fever are usually ushered in by the appearance of a large crop of bilious eruptions on the skin, great restlessness, fainting fits, and the absence of any distinctive knowledge regarding the different quarters of the heaven. The patient tosses about in the bed in intense agony, and the heat goes on increasing day after day. Thus the premonitory symptoms of the eight forms of fever have been briefly described.

All types of fever are either mental or physical, superficial or affecting the deeper principles of the organism, and mild or virulent. Similarly they may be grouped under two broad sub-divisions such as mature or immature, and Epidemic or sporadic.*

A paroxysm of bodily fever first affects the body, whereas it first invades the mind in a case of the mental type. In cases of fever due to the action of the deranged Kapham (cold or catarrhal fever), the deranged Vāyu, in conjunction with the deranged Kapham, produces rigor and horripilation, whereas the combination of the deranged Pittam in such cases is witnessed as the burning sensation in the body. Contrary symptoms such as hyperperaxia with loose motions of the bowels are manifest in a case of Sānnipātika fever only on account of the simultaneous derangement of the different morbific principles of the body of a contrary character. In cases of Vahirlinga Sānnipāta all the symptoms are restricted to the external or superficial principles of the organism, and therefore they become fully patent.

The organic Vāyu becomes deranged during the rainy season (Bhādra and A'shvin), the Pittam in autumn (Kārticka and Agrahāyana), and Kapham in spring (Phālguna and

---

* A case of fever, which is caused by the deranged morbific principle which is naturally enraged and aggravated during any particular season of the year, is said to be seasonable (Prakrita) when it breaks out in that season. It is called Vikrita (unnatural) when contrary is the case.

Chaitra)* Hence a case of fever which is due to the deranged Vāyu is said to be natural when it breaks out in the rainy season. Similarly, cases of Pittaja or Kaphaja fever breaking out in autum or spring are said to be natural. In fever due to the action of the deranged Pittam and which breaks out in autum, the Kapham lies subservient to the deranged Pittam. Accordingly the patient may be safely advised to fast in the case of fever which is due to the concerted action of the deranged Pittam and Kapham. In spring, the deranged and aggravated Kapham, in conjunction with the deranged Vāyu and Pittam, gives rise to a type of fever in which the two last named morbific principles of the body remain subordinate to the enraged Kapham.

A paroxysm of fever unattented with any supervening or dreadful symptoms and appearing in a person of unimpaired strength readily proves amenable to medicine, while the one which is accompanied with grave symptoms, and evinces the concerted derangement of all the three morbific principles of the body often finds a fatal termination. The holy sages of yore have thus opined on the subject. The presence of a large concourse of distressing symptoms together with a sense of constant *malaise* and aching pain in the limbs, constant micturition, intene heat of the body, loss of appetite, non desire for food, and impairment of the digestive function mark a case of immature fever (A'majvara or the stage of fever before the resolution of the different morbific principles which lie at its root). Heat, hyperperaxia, waterbrash, delirium, motions of the bowels, vertigo,

* In certain parts of India.

भाद्रपादाश्वयुयौ वर्षा, कार्त्तिक मार्गशीर्षौ शरत् ।
फाल्गुन चैत्रौ वसन्तः ।
सुश्रुत संहिता । सूत्रस्थानम्
६ अः १० ।

and rapid breathing indicate that the fever is approaching its crisis (*lit.*,—is being matured). Rice meal should be prohibited and a light diet should be enjoined in its stead for seven days in cases where there would be reasons to apprehend the immature (unresolved) state of the deranged organic principles in fever.

The holy sages have classified the Sānnipātika fever into five different kinds according to the nature of the morbific principles which serve as its exciting factors, its periodicity or time of attack, and the strength or weakness of the patient (the line may be likewise interpreted to mean according to the virulence or mildness of an attack). These five types of fever are respectively named as Santata (remittent), Satata (intermittent), Anyedyushka (appearing on every alternate day), Tritiyaka (tertian) and Chaturthaka (quotodian). The morbific principles such as the deranged Vāyu, Pittam and Kapham, enraged and aggravated by their own enraging and aggravating factors, lie stuffing the ducts which carry the feces, urine, and sweat, etc., and invade as well the fundamental organic principles of the body and give rise to heat and pyrexia. The disease (fever) affects the lymphchyle (blood or the vascular system) and grows in strength and intensity without knowing any remission or abatement. It is simply unbearable in its virulence. The disease runs its course in seven, ten or twelve days according to the predominance of the deranged Vāyu, Pittam or Kapham, on which days the morbific diatheses are either fully resolved and eliminated (Malapāk) thus bringing on an unfavourable crisis; or the fundamental principles of the body are dried up through the agency of fever-heat and predict a fatal termination. This is the opinion of the holy Agnivesha. But according to Hārita, the critical days in a case of Sānnipāta-fever are the seventh, the ninth, the eleventh, and the fourtenth. The patient either dies on any of these days, or passes into a state of convalescence. The course of the disease is shorter or longer according as the affected fundamental principles of the body are purified and brought back to their normal state, sooner or later. Even a small quantity of morbific diatheses present in the organism of a weak or emaciated person of unwholesome living, is augmented by, and gains in intensity from, the cumulative strength of the other morbid matter continuing therein, and thus leads to a gradual wasting of the body. Thus by causing the general wasting of the body, it brings on a type of fever which baffles all medical skill. The fever thus aggravated leads to a general break down of the constitution. On the other hand, the disease, if checked by any kind of medicine, soon suffers an abatement, the small residue of fever still remaining being absorbed in the lymph chyle. With the absorption of fever in the lymph chyle, cachexia, sallowness of complexion and lethargy also vanish. In the meantime, owing to the dilation of the vessels that carry the lymph chyle, the morbific diathesis is set free, and eliminated through the natural outlets of the body without being able to spread through the whole organism. The type of fever, which continues without remission for a certain number of days, is called Santata (remittent). The type in which there are periods of distinct intermission or abatement is called Satata (intermittent). The type known as Vishama has no definite periodicity, nor any fixed term of continuance, and its attacks are usually nocturnal. Any morbific diathesis taking lodgment in the blood, produces Santata-type of fever. In the type known as Anyedyushka, the paroxysm comes once within twenty-four hours at the juncture of the day and night. In the Tritiyaka-type (Tertian), the vessels containing fat and carrying the essential principle of flesh are contaminated. In this fever the patient suffers from an excruciating headache through the action of the deranged Vāyu and Pittam, from an aching pain in the sacrum (extending to the coccyx) through the action of the deranged Kapham and Pittam, and from a pain along the spinal column through the action of the deranged Vayu and Kapham. The type called Chaturthaka, fever results from the contamination of either the fat, marrow, or any other secretion of the body by any of the morbific diatheses. Moreover the quotodian-fever which is confined to the marrow, makes itself manifest twice a day. In the first-named type, the paroxysm is ushered in with a numbed pain in the knee-joints and calves of the legs, while an excruciating headache markes the advent of the last-named one. The type known as the Chaturthaka-Viparyaya, has its seat in the bone and the marrow. The paroxysm comes on the first day and continues for three days in succession, completely going down on the fourth. Owing to the virulence of the morbific diatheses through injudicious diet and conduct of the patient, the deranged morbific principles are not eliminated in well-digested condition, hence arises the necessity of foregoing rice-meal and observing a light diet for seven days in this type of fever. The mind and physical acts of the patient are equally affected; and in consequence of its invading the deeper principles of the organism and the concerted action of the deranged Vayu, Pittam and Kapham therein and their equality in virulence and intensity, a case of the Chaturthaka-type of fever soon runs into an incurable one. The morbifiic diatheses go on accumulating in the remote and minute bloodvessels of the body, in consequence whereof the body does not suffer any attenuation, though the patient complains of a little heat and an uncertain kind of *malaise*. The disease, not checked with proper medicines at this stage of its incubation, manifests itself in nightly paroxysms of pyrexia, and other serious symptoms. The fever slowly infiltrates into the succcessive fundamental principles of the organism in proportion to the diminution of the bodily strength of the patient; and a short while after, the angry morbific diathesis incarcerated in the organism begins to work mischief and brings on its own peculiar cachexia. As a seed sown in a congenial and well-watered soil does not wait long to sprout, so the morbific diatheses, the seeds of diseases, incarcerated in a disordered human organism and nourished by their own exciting or aggravating factors, do not take a long time to take shape and manifest themselves in the form of a particular disease. As an extraneous imbibed poison carried down into the stomach, gains in strength from its own aggravating factors, and produces its harmful effects in due course of time, so the different types of Satata-, and Santata-, fever are originated in the human body.

The symptoms, which mark the type of fever restricted to the organic principle of lymph chyle, are water brash, nausea, a feeling of heaviness in the limbs, dejection, aching pain in the limbs and yawning. together with vomiting, difficult breathing and a marked non-relish for food. The following symptoms are developed in the type in which the fever invades the circulatory system (blood). *viz.*, spitting of red (arterial) blood, thirst, and appearance of crops of dry, hot eruptions on the skin, together with a redness of the skin, vertigo, delirium, a sense of intoxication and a burning sensation of the body. Thirst, lassitude, emission of semen, an internal burning sensation in body, vertigo, jerky movements of the limbs, and fetour of the skin are the symptoms which characterise the type in which the fever invades the flesh. Perspiration with an unquenchable thirst, vomiting, fetid smell of the skin and impatience are the symptoms which mark the type in which the fever affects the fat. The type in which the fever invades the organic principle of marrow, manifests such symptoms as evacuation or elimination of the morbific matter from the system, sleeplessness, dyspnœa, convulsive movements of the limbs, together with difficult respiration and a sensation of heat in the inside, and cold on the surface of, the body. Vanishings of sight, severance or disunion of the Marmas (vulnerable bone-joints or venal, neural or arterial anestomoses), numbness of the male organ of generation, and non-emission of semen are the symptoms which are exhibited in the type in which the fever attacks the principle of semen. Each of these five types of fever are respectively more difficult to cure than the one immediately preceding it in the order of enumeration. A case of seminal fever usually ends in death. The types in which the fever affects the marrow or the semen are absolutely incurable.

The type known as Pralepaka is marked by rigour, delirium, a comparatively lower temperature of the body, and heaviness of the limbs. The patient feels as if his whole organism has been plastered with a coat of phlegm.

In the Angavalasaka-type there is small heat with numbness of the limbs, parchedness of the skin, and rigour. The patient feels as if his whole body has been stuffed with phlegm (mucous). The fever is persistent in its character and may be cured only with the greatest difficulty. In the Haridrabha-type (yellow fever), the skin, urine and feces of the patient become yollow. It is fatal as death itself. In the type known as Ratrijvara. both the deranged Vāyu and Kapham of the patient's temperament become equally dominant owing to the Pittam being considerably reduced. There is but little pyrexia in the day which is increased in the night with the aggravation of the paroxysm. The deranged Kapham (phlegm) in the patient's body is naturally dried up by the rays of the sun as well as by the heat originated through the movements of his body during the day. Hence the small rise of the bodily temperature during day in this type of fever, which persists as a remnant of the night's paroxysm only through the action of the deranged Vāyu. When the Kapham continues in the patient's stomach, which is its natural seat, and the deranged Pittam in the abdomen, the upper part of the body remains cold, while its lower part is felt hot to the touch during a paroxysm-fever. On the contrary, when the deranged Kapham is located in the extremities, and the deranged Pittam is incarcerated in the trunk of the body, the hands and feet are felt hot, and the latter cold.

The fever, which invades the principle of lymph chyle, blood, flesh or fat, is easily curable, while the one, which affects the bone or marrow, and is detected from the atrophy and discolouring of the locality affected, can be made amenable to medicine only with the greatest difficulty. This type of fever is further characterised by unconscious or sub-comatose of the patient, hyperpyrexia, frequent loose motions of warm muco-billious matter, and an angry look of the eyes.

Subsidence of heat and pain, appearance of sordes on the teeth or of herpetic eruptions on the lips, perspiration, with a desire for food and an unruffled state of the mind, and healthy functions of the organs of sense-perceptions are the symptoms which indicate that the fever has perfectly gone down.

—:o:—

CHAPTER CXLVIII.

DHANVANTARI said :—Now I shall discourse on the Ætiology and symptoms of Raktapittam (Hæmorrhage). The bodily Pittam deranged through such factors as excessive ingestion of Kodrava and Uddalaka (grains) or extremely hot, bitter, acid, or saline things, or of those which are followed by an acid re-action in the stomach, or through the agency of those which accelerate the process of metabolism and increase the metabolic heat in the organism, deranges, in its turn, the liquid bile which by gradually contaminating the blood, courses with it throughout the system. Owing to a similarity which exists between the blood and the bile, in colour, smell, origin and morbific effect, this bile-charged blood in Hæmorrhage is called blood in the parlance of the Ayurveda.* The blood in Hæmorrhage rises from the spleen, liver, bloodvessels, and the receptacle of blood. Heaviness of the head with a non-relish for food, desire for cold things and cool contracts, vertigo, darkness of vision, nausea, vomiting with a belching sensation, cough, laboured or difficult breathing (dyspnœa) with a sensation of fatigue or exhaustion, a fishy smell in the mouth, redness of the face, redness, blueness or yellowness of the conjunctiva, inability to distinguish a red colour from the yellow or blue, dreams of insanity in sleep and an absence of fever are the symptoms which mark the premonitary stage of Raktapittam. There is hæmorrhage either from any of the super-clavicular cavities of the body, such as the ears, the nose, or the eyes, or from any of the downward passages. such as the anus, penis or vagina. Sometimes the deranged blood flows out in jets through the pores of the skin. Hæmorrhage from any of the superclavicular passages of the body, readily yields to medicine inasmuch as the deranged Kapham which serves as the exciting factor of the disease in these cases, may be easily curbed with the help of purgatives. In such cases, a medicine which helps the purging of the deranged Pittam (bile) is a far better remedy than that which arrests its secretion, more so because the deranged Kapham which invariably acts in concert with the disordered Pittam in such cases, gets the chance of being eliminated from the system. Drugs of a sweet or astringent taste, as well as those which generate Kapham in the system, or increase glandular secretions of the organism, or are bitter or pungent, should be deemed beneficial in these cases.

Palliation is the only remedy possible in cases where Hæmorrhage occurs from any of the downward passages

* In the Ayurvedic physiology blood and bile are but the modifications of the lymph chyle under different degrees of metabolism (Rasapaka).—*Tr.*

of the body, since the administration of emetics is the only treatment admissible. The patient in such a case should be looked upon as a person whose days are numbered. A little of any of the drugs which help the elimination of the deranged Pittam, and a little other medicine to subdue the concomitant symtoms may be given to a Raktapitta patient of unimpaired strength and of not much disordered Pittam. Sweet and astringent substances are good for patients of the foregoing type. Cure is almost hopeless in the case of a patient in whom both the derenged Vāyu and Kapham act in concert with the deranged Pittam and serve as the exciting factors of the disease. A case of Raktapittam, in which Hæmorrhage occurs from both the upward and downward passages of the body, baffles all medicine since purgatives and emetics are the only two remedies which can be given with benefit in this disease. In short, emetics may be given with advantage even in a case of Raktapittam where the morbific principles act in concert. It is needless to say that the last-named type of the disease is fatal as a spear-dart of the God Shiva, since many a distressing and unfavourable symtoms are found to supervene from the outset.

—:o:—

CHAPTER CXLIX.

DHANVANTARI said:—I shall first deal with the ætiology of cough, inasmuch as this disease fast affects the entire organism, and speedily runs its course. The disease admits of being grouped under five sub-heads according as it is brought about through the deranged action of Vāyu, Pittam, or Kapham, or as the outcome of consumption, or ulcerative Endocarditis.

Any of these five types of cough, being neglected at the outset, may run into a case of Pthisis, and each of them is successively more virulent than the one immediately preceding it in the order of enumeration. An itching, tickling sensation in the throat, and a non-relish for food are the symptoms which mark the premonitory stage of every type of cough. Parchedness of the throat and mouth, and a sensation of dryness in the cavity of the ear are the symptoms which characterise the type due to the action of the deranged Vāyu. The wind, which courses through the lower parts of the body, violently rushes upward and presses upon the larynx and the bronchi. The agitated wind fills the vessels causing the sides to heave up in spasms, and the eyes seem as if starting out of their sockets. The voice becomes weak and a sound resembling that of a broken belmetal gong is perceived in the mouth and larynx. The patient complains of a bruised pain at the sides, attended with a violent headache, and an aching pain about the region of the heart. Aphonia, hurried breathing and swooning may be also present, and a sort of dry spasmodic cough constantly harrasses the patient who finds a little relief only by hawking a kind of dry mucous out of the throat, which often causes horripilation. These are the symptoms which mark the type due to the action of the disordered Vāyu (Nervous, spasmodic cough).

A bitter taste in the mouth accompanied with fever, vertigo, billious vomitting, and yellowness of the conjunctiva, as well as blood-spitting, thirst, aphonia, darkness of vision, etc., mark the billious type, and the patient sees bright rings of fire floating before his eyes during a fit of cough. In the type due to the action of the deranged Kapham, the patient complains of a slight dull pain in the chest, and a heavy numbness in the head and cardiac region, and feels as if the throat has been plastered with a coat of sticky mucous, which cannot be scraped out with efforts. Vomiting, and horrifibation, attended with a fluent coryza secreting a thick glossy mucous, and a non-relish for food are the symptoms, which further characterise this type of cough.

The local Vāyu enraged through such factors as inordinate and overfatiguing physical exercise, lifting of heavy loads, etc., which give rise to ulcers in the chest, becomes united with the aggravated Pittam, and produces a type of cough in which the patient coughs out bloody or blood-streaked mucous, or spits out a sort of brown, yellowish, dry, knotty, or angry-looking mucous. The patient feels pain in the throat at the time of coughing, and complains of heat and an aching, piercing pain in the heart while spitting, or hawking out the phlegm. Fever with thirst, shivering, and dyspnœa, and hoarseness with a breaking pain in the joints, supervene; the voice becomes small, weak and resembles the cooing of a dove; the sides ache; the digestion is impaired; and palour and weakness go on increasing every day. In this stage all the specific symptoms of Pthisis are developed. There is extreme prostration with bloody micturition, dyspnœa and a catching pain at the back and sacrum. A pthisis patient generally coughs out a greenish, bloody, or blood-streaked, fetid, pus-like, mucous; and complains of diverse kind of pain even in bed. The heart seems as if it is being boiled; and the patient, without any ostensible reason, complains of heat; and evinces a desire for cool things and heavy meals. Prostration goes on increasing; the eyes, teeth, and face of the patient assume a glossy peaceful look; and all the specific symptoms of wasting supervene.

A case of consumption (Rāja Yakshmā) or Ulcerative Endocarditis (Urah-kshata) may be arrested, if not radically cured, under a judicious medical treatment resorted to at the very commencement of the disease. Both these diseases in a strong and young patient, may be expected to be cured, if well-cared for from the outset. All those forms of ailment which admit only of a palliative treatment, as well as the maladies of old age may bring on dyspnœa, cough, consumption, vomiting, Aphonia and a host of other distempers, if not well-cared for, at the outset. Thus ends the Ætiology of Cough.

—:o:—

CHAPTER CL.

DHANVANTARI said:—Now I shall discourse on the Nidānam of Dyspnœa (Shvāsa). A case of chronic or aggravated cough may run into one of Dyspnœa, or the enraged morbific principles of the body may likewise give rise to this diseased condition. Difficult breathing may also mark the sequel of A'mātisāra (mucous dysentery), vomiting, chlorosis, fever, or poisoning, or may be produced as the effect of an exposure to dust storm, smoke, cold wind, or of a blow on any of the vulnerable amestomoses of nerves, arteries, etc., (Marmas). Dyspnœa may be divided into five different kinds such as Kshudraka, Tamaka, Chhinna, Mahān, and Urdha-Shvāsa. The Vāyu (nerve-force), that courses all through the organsim, affects the channels of food-carrying, water-carrying and breath-carrying ducts in the event of its own vessels being obstructed by the deranged Kapham (mucous deposits), and remains incarcerated in the cardiac region, producing dyspnœa from the lower end of the stomach. An aching pain about the heart and the sides, contrary direction of the breath-wind, long drawn breaths, paln at the temporal bones, and tympanites are the premonitory symptoms of this disease. The Vāyu, enraged and aggravated by the toils of overeating, and over fatiguing physical labour, obstructs the vessels by enraging and aggravating the deranged Kapham, coursing through them in a contrary direction, and produces the form of difficult breathing known as Kshudra-

Shvāsa. The enraged Vāyu, by exciting the deranged Kapham, lies catching at the head, neck and cardiac region, and produces an aching pain at the sides. A wheezing sound is heard in the throat, and catarrh with fits of fainting and a non-relish for food supervene. The aggravated Vāyu increases the difficulty of breathing, and the patient is seized with a violent fit of cough, feeling a little relief when a little mucous is coughed, or belched out. He is obliged to sit up, as a lying or recumbent posture tends to aggravate the pain and difficulty of breath. The eyes are turned upward and beads of perspiration break out on the forehead of the patient, testifying to the intense agony he suffers from in this form of disease. The lining membrane of the cavity of the mouth gets dry and parched up by constant drawing in of the breath-wind, and the patient evinces a strong desire for hot drinks or food. Winter, rain, east-wind, and partaking of phlegm-generating food, are set down as the aggravating factors of Asthma.

The type known as Tamaka Shvāsa is curable only in a strong patient, but the paroxysm does not speedily abate in the event of there being fever, epiliptic fits, rigour, etc., in its company. In this type both cough and dyspnœa are marked by their virulence. The patient becomes emaciated, and complains of a cutting pain at the chest and the Marmas. Perspiration, fainting fits, and tympanites with a burning sensation in the bladder are its further characteristics. The eyes become red, swollen, and glossy, and are turned downward. The patient complains of a dryness in the throat, and drops down unconscious, moaning in a low, piteous voice.

In the type known as Mahā-Shvāsa (cerebral dyspnœa) the patient breathes very hard and upward (with upturned nose) like an infuriated bull. The breathing is hard, rapid and hurried, and the patient lies senseless and almost speechless with eyes turned upward, and stool and urine are entirely suppressed. The throat is dry and parched, respiration becomes hard and rapid, drops of perspiration appear on the forehead; and the patient complains of an excruciating pain at the head and the temples. All chance of recovery should be given up if the patient is found to continue in this state for a while. In this type the mouth and ears of the patient are found to be stuffed with mucous, and the eyes under the influence of the aggravated Vāyu, are found to roll about in their sockets or are fixed in an upward stare. The heart seems as if being torn asunder, and the patient moans for a while and then lies speechless in death. Medical treatment may be useful in this tye of dyspnœa until the preceding symptoms appear, in which case the physician should think it prudent to retire.

—:0:—

CHAPTER CLI.

DHANVANTARI said :—Now I shall discourse on the Nidānam of Hiccough. Hiccough and dyspnœa result from similar causes, and its preliminary symptoms, as well as the number of types in which it is ordinarily divided by pathologists, are same as those mentioned under dyspnœa. The several types of hiccough are named as Vakshyodbhavā, Kshudrā, Yamalā, Mahati, and Gambhirā. The wind in the stomach, enraged and aggravated by hasty and injudicious eating, partaking of sharp, unwholesome and parchifying substances and such like causes, produces a kind of hiccough which is never loud, and which abates with the eating of the evening meal. This type of hiccough is called Vakshyodbhavā or Annajā. The low and mild hiccough, which is caused by the wind enraged by fatiguing physical exercises, is called Kshudrā. It rises from the root of the throat, becomes aggravated through labour, and abates with the partaking of food. The type in which hiccoughs rise in couples, and which, though mild at the outset, becomes violent in course of time, and in which the head and the neck are simultaneously shaken, is called Yamalā. Delirium, vomiting, dysentery, yawning, and distortion of the eyes are the symptoms that are found to supervene with the advancement of this type of hiccough. In the Mahāhiccā-type the eye-brows droop down, the temples are sunk, consciousness vanishes, a peculiar pain is felt in all the sense-organs, the spinal bone is arched down, and an aching pain is felt about the heart. This kind of hiccough violently rises from the bottom of the abdomen, or from the région of the umbilicus, in quick succession and accompanied by a loud report and an excruciating pain. Yawning and spasmodic jerks of the limbs, are its characteristics. This type of hiccough proceeds only from fatal and deep-seated organic disorders, and the remedies administered to subdue the same, must be likewise deep-acting in their potency. The two last-named types should be abandoned as incurable, while the one, which is not ordinarily fatal, should be regarded as indicating an unfavourable prognosis as soon as it develops all the afore-said grave symptoms. Any of the types of hiccough, afflicting an old man, or one of impaired digestion, or one that is extremely run down from sexual excesses, may have a fatal termination. Any disease of whatsoever type and denomination, may prove fatal, but the only two maladies, that portend an impending danger, are hiccough and dyspnœa.

—:o:—

CHAPTER CLII.

DHANVANTARI said :—Now I shall discourse on the Nidnam of Raja Yakshmā (pulmonary consumption). The terms

Rāja Yakshmā, wasting (Kshaya), Shosha (atrophy, *lit.* withering up), and Rogarāt (king of maladies) are all synonymous terms. The Moon-God, the King of the Brāhmanas and Asterisms, had an attack of pulmonary consumption in days of yore, and as it first appeared in that King (Raja) of Heavens, it has since been honoured with the proud designation of King of Maladies.*

The disease may appear as a sequel to any other disease, and certainly runs as the harbinger of many. The disease is called Kshaya from the fact of its causing a general wasting of the body, as well as from the incapacity of any medicine in arresting that waste. It is called Shosa (Atrophy) from the fact of its withering up the fundamental organic principles of lymph chyle, blood, flesh, fat, bone, marrow, and semen in succession. Rash feats of strength, over-fatiguing physical exercise, loss of semen, albumen or any other albuminous principle of the organism, voluntary suppression of any natural propulsion of the body, and irregular or insufficient food may be set down as the exciting factors of Rāja-Yakshmā. The Vāyu, enraged by any of the preceding causes, affects the process of metabolism all through the organism, and hence the unutilised products of the body

---

* With a view to emphasise the facts of a gradual wasting of the fundamental principles of the body and formation of cavities in the lungs in pulmonary consumption, onr Ayurvedic pathology, in which science has been sublimized to chime in harmony with the universal poetry of Brahmanic genius, has made use of the gradual waning of the moon's disc in the dark-fortnight and the existence of dark caves in the lunar continent as representing the typical picture of the organic, lesions and changes in the human body in Pthisis. The Moon-God has been punished with this disease in the Puranas for his ardent and sinful passion for his preceptor's beautiful wife (Tárá), and it may not be incorrect to assert that originally the lesion, as handed down to posterity, might have some connection with mental dejections and sexual excesses.—*Tr.*

(Kapham or Vyartham), which becomes increased in consequence, are carried into the unions of bodily members and appendages (such as amestomoses of veins and arteries) and dilate or contract the orfices of the principal ducts of the body, giving rise to pain in regions above, below, about and across the heart.

Salivation with fever, hyperperaxia and a sweet taste in the mouth, dulness of appetite, a gluttonous desire for food and drink, a thought of uncleanness in things clean and pure, a feeling as if his food and drink have been studded with bits of hair or flees' wings, nausea, vomiting, a non-relish for food, extreme whiteness of the eyes, chest, palms of the hands and soles of the feet as well as of the armpits, and expectoration of thick mucous even without bathing, are the symptoms which mark the premonitory stage of this disease. The patient experiences a pain in the tongue and arms, learns to abhor his body, becomes unreasonably fond of wine and women or loathes their sight, and suffers from giddiness. Hairs, and nails of toes or fingers become marked by their rapid and excessive growth, and sleep become chequered with fearful dreams. The patient dreams of lizards, serpents, monkeys, or of savage birds or beasts darting upon his head, or as if he is climbing a hill of ashes, hairs, paddy husks, or a withered tree. He sees deserted hamlets and homesteads in his sleep, or dreams of burning forests, and dry and empty river-beds. Catarrh, dyspnœa, cough, headache, loss of voice, a non-relish for food, updrawn breath, emaciation, vomiting, fever, and pain at the sides, chest and joints are the eleven specific symptoms of the disease under discussion. The distressing symptoms, which are invariably found to supervene, are a breaking pain in the throat, yawning, aching pain in the limbs, spitting of blood, impaired digestion, and a foul-smell in the mouth. Of these, headache, aching pain at the sides, and in the limbs, constriction of the throat, hoarseness, and kindred symptoms should be attributed to the action of the deranged Vāyu, while to the deranged Pitta [illegible] ascribed the burning sensation in the shoulders and extremities dysentery, blood-spitting, foul-smell in the mouth, fever, and the general excited condition of the body. Vomiting cough, feeling of heaviness in one half of the body, water-bash, catarrh, dyspnœa, aphonia, and impaired digestion with a non-relish for food are the symptoms, which owe their origin to the action of the deranged Kapham in Rāja Yakshmā. The enraged morbific diatheses, such as, the Vāyu, Pittam and the Kapham, produce a general anasarca in these cases only on account of the impairment of digestive capacity. The burning sensation in the cardiac region, which is usually experienced in these cases, is only for the diminution which the fundamental principles of lymbh chyle, and blood, suffer on account of the obstructed orfices of the vessels of the vascular system. The food undergoes a sort of acid reaction in the stomach, for which reason the food ingested by a pthisis patient cannot contribute to the formation of a healthy lymph chyle, and hence cannot make good the waste which incessantly goes on in the body. Accordingly, a pthisis patient may be described as living by drawing upon the reserve capital of life, and his body, in the absence of healthy nutrition and assimilation, becomes emaciated from day to day. A prudent physician should not take in hand a pthisis patient whose sense-organs have been affected even before the development of most of the specific symptoms of the disease. The disease occurring in a strong and young patient and well cared for from the outset, may not develop more unfavourable symptoms, and may ultimately prove amenable to medicine. Once its specific symptoms have been fully developed, the disease should be regarded as past all cure. The voice becomes weak or rough in this disease owing to the loss of the organic principle of fat. In the type due to the action of the deranged Vāyu, the body loses its gloss and heat, and the patient feels as if his throat has been studded with the bristles of Shuka Shimvi leaves. The gradual wasting of the body, and the burning sensation in the throat and palate, in these cases, should be ascribed to the action of the deranged Pittam. The sensation of a sticky mucous, together with the specific wheezing sound, in the throat is due to the action of the deranged Kapham. Vertigo, darkness of vision, and symptoms peculiar to the deranged Kapham are invariably present. Wasting of the body is accelerated by an unwholesome diet and injudicious and intemperate living in Rāja-Yakshmā. This disease is seldom curable, and a wise physician should abandon the patient just as its specific symptoms would be but partially developed.

—:o:—

CHAPTER CLIII.

DHANVANTARI said :—Now hear me, O Sushruta, discourse on the Nidānam of Arochakam (Non-relish for food). The several morbific diatheses of Vāyu, Pittam, and Kapham, by finding lodgment in the tongue and the heart, give rise to three different forms of Arochakam. The fourth kind owes its origin to their concerted action, while the fifth is usually brought about through a perturbed condition of the mind. The patient complains of an astringent taste in the mouth in the Vāyu-origined, of a bitter taste in the Pittaja, and of a sweet taste in the Kaphaja type. In the type due to grief, fright, or anxiety, all things seem vapid and tasteless. The vital Udāna Vāyu flings up the morbific principles from the bottom of the stomach, and thus carried up into the cavity of the mouth, they give rise to waterbrash with a saline taste in the mouth, annihilate all desires for food, and bring a host of other discomforts in their train. The patient suddenly feels a pain at the back and about the umbilicus, and the ingested food is thrown up in the side of his stomach, causing him to belch out a scanty, frothy, and astringent chylous matter.

In the Vāyu-origined type of this disease there are loud eructations, and painful and violent vomitings after that, bringing cough, parchedness of the mouth, and hoarseness in their train. In the Pittaja type, the patient vomits a kind of greenish, or yellowish, blood-streaked acid matter of a bitter and astringent taste, resembling alkaline water—thirst, fainting, and a burning sensation in the body being its further characteristics.

In the type due to the action of the deranged Kapham, there is expectoration of thick glossy, yellowish, ropy mucous of a sweetish saline taste, attended with a copious salivation, and horlipilation. Symptoms such as, swelling of the mouth, somnolence, cough, and nausea with a sweetish taste in the mouth, are found to supervene. In the type due to the concerted action of all the three morbific principles of Vāyu, Pittam and Kapham, the patient finds no pleasure even in the most congenial topics, which, according to Vishnu, ought to be discussed in a gentle assembly. All sights and sounds are hateful to him. The disease is aggravated with the aggravation of any of the abovesaid morbific principles in the body. The type due to the presence of worms in the intestines, or to the ingestion of any stale or unwholesome food, manifests colic, shivering, and nausea, etc., as its specific indications.

CHAPTER CLIV.

DHANVANTARI said :—O Sushruta, now I shall discourse on the Nidānam of Hridroga* which admits of being grouped under five sub-heads according as the deranged Vayu, Pittam and Kapham, either severally or concertedly lie at the root of the disease, or as any parasitic growth in the heart serves as its exciting factor. In the type due to the action of the deranged Vāyu, the patient complains of a vacuum in his heart, which seems dry, numbed, and as if being broken or turn asunder. He cannot bear the least sound or noise, and is frightened, or feels dejected, or indulges in grief without any apparent reason. Insomnia becomes markedly patent, and the patient suffers from difficult breathing, shivers, and lapses into fits of unconsciousness. The bilious type develops such symptoms as thirst, fatigue with a burning sensation in the body, perspiration, acid eructations, vomiting of acid or bilious matter, fever and darkness of vision. The symptoms, which manifest themselves in the type due to the action of the deranged Kapham, are a sensation of numbness in the heart, impairment of digestive faculty, distaste in the mouth, cough, pain in the bones, expectoration of mucous, somnolence, and fever with a non-relish for food. The type, which is due to the concerted action of the deranged Vāyu, Pittam and Kapham, exhibits symtoms which are peculiar to the form which are respectively brought about by each of these morbific principles. A blackish (dull) yellow

* The term Hridroga of the Ayurvedic pathology, which is a usually translated as diseases of the Heart, includes palpilation of the heart, Angina Pectoris and kindred disorders, such as aneurism of the thoracic auorta, but does not signify any structural or valvular disorder of the heart.—*Tr.*

colour (brownish) of the conjunctiva accompanied by vertigo, nausea, waterbrash, œdema, expectoration of mucous, and an itching sensation in the limbs form the specific indications of the type of Hridroga which is of a parasitic origin. The patient feels as if his heart is being sawed with a sharp-toothed saw. The medical treatment of a case of any of these types of Hridroga should be commenced almost simultaneously with the manifestation of any of its specific indications, inasmuch as it is often found to run into one of the incurable types, and speedily runs its course, terminating fatally in most instances. The sixth form or type of Hridroga is fouud to result as a supervening symptom of any other pre-existing distemper in which any of the vital principles of the organism, such as, blood, lymph-chyle, albumen, etc., has suffered an abnormal loss or diminution. In almost all the types of Hridroga, there occurs a loss of any of the abovesaid vital principles of the body in consequence of which both the Vāyu and Pittam are enraged. Hence an abnormal derangement of the Vāyu and Pittam, causing spasmodic jerks in all the limbs, rigour, palpitation of, and a burning sensation in, the heart, and fits of unconscious should be looked for in all the types described above. The water-crrying vessels, which traverse the throat, palate, lungs and the root of the tougue, become dry and parched up, giving rise to a short of unquenchable thirst which is common to all the forms of Hridroga. An unquenchable thirst attended with dryness of the mouth (the patient craving for more water each time), loss of voice, roughness of the throat, lips and palate, difficulty in protruding the tongue, delirium, mental aberrations and loud eructations, are the further characteristics of this disease. Prostration, dejection of spirit and vertigo with a breaking pain in the temples, loss of smell, dulness of hearing, and insomnia with a vapid taste in the mouth, are the symptoms which are developed through the action of the deranged Vāyu in Hridroga. A little increase of reactionary acidity in the stomach after digestion accompanied by a bitter taste in the mouth, redness of the eyes, a burning sensation in the body, dryness of, and a feeling as if fumes are escaping through, the skin, and fainting are the symptoms which should be specifically attributed to the action of the deranged Pittam in the present disease. In the Kshayaja type the aggravated Kaphah chokes up the passages of Vāyu in the heart, and the sticky mucous accumulated in those vessels absorbs heat, like thickened slime. Somnolence, and a sensation as if the lining membrane of the throat has been studded with the bristles of a Shuka insect, together with a sweetish taste in the mouth, are the symptoms which should be attributed to the action of the deranged Kapham in this disease. A sensation of heaviness and numbness in the head, vomiting, lassitude, indigestion with a non-relish for food, and tympanites, are the symptoms, which should be attributed to the concerted action of the deranged Vāyu, Pittam and Kapham in a case of Hridroga. Owing to the obstructed course of blood and generation of mucous in the system in this disease, both the deranged Vāyu and Pittam are inordinately aggravated, and for this the patient, though suffering from an intense heat in the body, is suddenly seized with a rigour which shakes him to the very bones.

The type of Hridroga, which is caused by the Pittam being obstructed in the thorax through the agency of thirst, should be regarded as of a bilious origin. Similarly, a kind of aching pain is felt in the heart through drinking large quantities of water inasmuch as heavy drinks naturally dissolve the albuminous constituents of the body and help their digestion in the usual way. The kind of thirst, which is generated through taking acid, saline or emolient things, should be regarded as caused by the deranged Kapham. The kind of thirst which follows from the loss of lymph-chyle (any vital organic principle) is but an indication of wasting or consumption. The thirst, which is experienced during a paroxysm of fever or in consumption, should be regarded as a mere supervening symptom.

CHAPTER CLV.

DHANVANTARI said :—Now I shall discourse on the Nidānam of Madātyayam (diseases which result from the abuse of wines and spirits) as formerly described by the holy Rishis of yore.

Wine is sharp, acid (gives rise to an acid digestion), dry, parchifying, light, fatiguing and its potency at once pervades the minutest capillaries of the organism, and tends to vitiate the fat of the body. All the preceding properties of wine such as sharpness, etc., tend to produce a disturbed state of the mind, and clouden the intellect. Excessive drinking may even prove fatal. The primary property of wine is to injuriously affect the ten organs of sense-perception of a man; and wine, though heat-making and stimulating in its primary action, deteriorates the strength of the organism in its reaction. The use of the first two kinds of wine is always injurious. It is only the fools of fortune that find pleasures in cups. A drunkard, even if he happens to be a king, cannot maintain the dignity of his position, and only cares for drink in this world. A drunkard king, like a fanged and uncaged serpent, is capable of committing any mischief in the world. Wine is the progenitor of filthy speeches, and the only royal road to wretchedness and misery. In the third stage of drinking there comes unconsciousness. A drunkard suffers more than death-pangs in life, and loses all distinction of virtue and vice, honour and dishonour, or pleasure and pain. He indulges in fits of grief or senseless laughter at intervals, or falls down unconscious in convulsive spasms. A strong man after a hearty meal may bear his wine well. The deranged Vāyu, Pittam and Kaphah may also serve as the exciting factors of the disease known as Madātyayam. Intoxication, pain at the heart, loose motions of bowels, thirst, unstability of gait, fever with a non-relish for food, vanishings of sight, cough, dyspnœa, insomnia, excessive perspiration, œdema, and tympanites are the general symptoms of the disease.*

The patient in such a case remains in a drowsy state, and talks garrulously even without being spoken to. Fever with a burning sensation in the body, perspiration, distraction of the mind, and fits of fainting are the symptoms, which mark the bilious type of Madātyayam, while vomiting, nausea somnolence, and tympanites are developed in the one which owes its origin to the deranged Kapham. All tbe above said symptoms are exhibited in the Sannipātika type of Madātyayam. Nothing can be distasteful or disagreeable to the person who indulges in cups even with a full knowledge of its baneful consequences. Such a person only courts mental imbecility and wilfully kills his mind and intellect. A Madātyaya-patient cannot tell the difference between a chip of wood and an article of fare in respect of taste.

Expectoration of mucous, dryness of the throat, somnolence, incapability of bearing the least sound with a distracted state of the mind and shooting pain in the limbs,

---

* The Ayurvedic Materia Medica recognises three different kinds of stages of wine, such as Sattvika, Rajasika and Tamasika though Sushruta recognises a fourth stage or form of drinking called Atitámasa.

चतुर्थेंतु मदे मूढ़ो भग्नदार्विवनिष्क्रियः ।
कार्य्याकार्य्याविभागा ज्ञो मृतादपि परोमृतः ॥

सुश्रुत संहिता ।

diseases of the heart and larynx, epileptic fits, dyspnœa, thirst, vomiting and fever, are the supervening symptoms of the type of Madātyayam, which owes its origin to the disordered Vāyu. The self-controlled person, who intelligently foregoes the pleasures of wine, defies all diseases whether of the body or of mind. Intoxication, Epilepsy, and Palsy (corea), are the three diseases which result from the derangement of the vascular and lymphatic systems and are usually found to afflict a person of injudicious diet and living and of an irascible or lymphatic temperament of mind. Each of these diseases is respectively stronger than the one immediately following it in the order of enumeration. This kind of Madātyayam has its origin in the impure blood, or results from the presence of wine (alcohol) in the system, or from any other idiopathic causes such as aggravation of any of the morbific principles of the body. In the Vātajatype of Madātyayam the complexion becomes pale or sallow on account of the anæmic condition of the body, or assumes a dry, reddish, or brownish hue, and the patient is tormented with a kind of listlessness, and takes recourse to acts of low cunning. In the Pittaja type, the skin of the body asumes a reddish yellow colour, and the patient becomes irritable and querulous. Somnolence, delirium or loose talks mark the type which owes it origin to the deranged Kapham. All the abovesaid symptoms are exhibited in the Sannipātika type of Madātyayam. The specific symptoms of the deranged Pittam are usually found to be present in almost all the types of Madātyayam. The patient fails to recognise even the most familiar voices, and palsy, somnolence, and above all, a feeling of exhaustion (prostration) gradually supervene. A languid circulation, or obstruction of the blood in certain parts of the body, and a partial paralysis of the limbs may be witnessed in the Sannipātika type. In the Vātaja type of Madātyayam the patient beholds the sky as enveloped in a blue, red, or black colour, and faints away, regaining consciousness very soon after. Shivering, vertigo, cough with a pain about the cardiac region, epileptic fits, and a brownish or reddish colour of the skin during the fit are the further characteristics of this type. In the Pittaja type the patient faints away seeing the sky wrapped in red or blue, and regains consciousness oppressed with thirst, perspiration and a burning sensation in the body. The complexion becomes blue or yellow during the paroxysm of fainting, the eyes become red or yellow, and the patient complains of a breaking pain in his body and talks incoherently. In the Kaphaja type of Madātyayam the patient sees the welkin enshrouded with a cloud like pall, and falls down unconscious. Consciousness returns late in this type, and the patient suffers from nausea and salivation after being restored to his senses. Owing to the sensation of numbness and heaviness in the limbs, the patient falls down all on a heap like a goat. All the aforesaid symptoms are combinedly exhibited in the Sānnipātika type of Madātyayam. Moreover, the patient suffers from epileptic fits in this Sānnipātika type, and falls down unconscious through the aggravated condition of the morbific principles of his body, even in the absence of any frightening or anæsthetic agent. The fit passes off spontaneously as soon as the dynamics of the morbific diathesis spends itself in the body, and the patient regains his consciousness even without the help of any sense-restoring medicine. The functions of the mind as well as of the sense organs, and the faculty of speech are jeopardised in this disease, and the patient, though otherwise of an unstable and impaired mind, acquires a kind of increased physical strength through the disorder of the nervous system. A sudden derangement of the respiratory system brings on a swoon in Madātyayam, which may terminate fatally, and in which the patient lies stiff and rigid, like a log of wood, with a bluish, shrunken, cadaverous countenance. A little delay in calling in medical help in these cases is often followed by a fatal consequence. It is morally obligatory on a physician to rescue a man from drowning in the ocean of Madâtyayam, which, like any other ocean abounding in dreadful sea-monsters, is full of many serious symptoms. There is a dictum in the Vedas to the effect that a drunkard feels merry or irritated at intervals. Vices described before should be considered as appertaining to wine improperly taken or used. "Wine paves the road to hell" is a prohibitory aphorism, which should be interpreted as interdicting the abuse or injudicious use of wine. Wine properly and judiciously taken is same as the divine ambrosia. It gives health, strength and beauty to persons using it, and ultimately leads to their salvation.

—:o:—

CHAPTER CLVI.

DHANVANTARI said:—O Sushruta, I shall now discourse on the Nidânam of Hæmorrhoids. Fleshy condylomatous growths are found to frequently crop up on the body. Polypi, that appear in the region of the rectum obstructing its orfice, are called Arshas (Hæmorrhoids). The enraged and aggravated morbific principles of the body such as, the deranged Vâyu, Pittam, etc., give rise to these growths of diverse shape in the anal region by vitiating the local skin, fat (adipose tissue) and flesh, which the learned call Hæmorrhoids. These growths may be divided into two classes such as, the congenital and post-natal ones. They are either dry, bleeding or jagged, and are situated in the region of the rectum. The passage of the rectum measures five fingers' widths and a half in length, and hæmorrhoids are found to appear within the length of three fingers'-widths and a half from the external orfice of the anus. Bleeding occurs from the veins which run through these internal piles or hæmorrhoids, while the external ones are found to be situated in the region of the anus within the length of a finger's-width of its external orfice. Another kind of polypi crop up in the region about a finger and a half distant from the anus, aronnd the outskirt of which the hairs grow.

The congenital hæmorrhoids are attributed to injudicious conducts of its parents during the period of gestation and the bodily discomfort of the child during its inter-uterine life. The Sānnipātika form of hæmorrhoids owes its origin to the concerted action of the deranged morbific principles of the body, and to the curse of gods as well. Congenital piles, like any other congenital disease, are incurable, and they are dry, ugly-looking, pointing inward, of a pale (yellowish) colour, and are attended with all the dreadful supervening symptoms. Hæmorrhoids may be divided into six different forms, *viz.*, those which are severally due to the action of the deranged Vāyu, Pittam, or Kapham, of Vāyu and Pittam, of Vāyu and Kapham, of Pittam and Kapham, and of Vāyu, Pittam, and Kapham combined.

The polypi, which are due to the action of the deranged Vāyu and Kapham, are dry, while those which owe their origin to the concerted action of the Vāyu and Pittam, are moist and exuding. The factors, which tend to aggravate the morbific principles of the body in this disease, have been described before, and likewise, impaired digestion, accumulation of feces in the intestines, and sexual excesses may be set down as conditions which help the growth of these polypi. Similar vegetations of polypous growths may appear in the throat, eyes, bladder, uterus, lips, etc., through a pressure, or friction, or rubbing of those localities with fingers, or with any other hard substance, or through the agency of a small cough, or choking cough during a drink. Constant contact of extremely cold water, long and frequent rides, voluntary repression of any urging toward micturition or defecation, violent straining at the time of bearing down the stool, or of passing water, daily ingestion of loathsome food, lienteric diarrhœa, fasting, pulls that involve a heavy strain on the muscles, acts that involve a heavy strain on the female organs of generation, and miscarriage are factors which tend to enrage the Apāna Vāyu (Genito-urinary and illiac nerve force) of the organism. The feces lie incarcerated in the grooves (flexus) of the rectum owing to the disordered condition of this angry Apāna, giving rise to a sort of congestion in those localities which help the vegetation of hæmorrhoids.

The symptoms, which mark the preliminary stage of this disease, are impaired digestive capacity, loss of appetite, distension of the abdomen, aching pain in the loins and calves of the legs, vertigo, a burning sensation in the eyes, œdema, and loose motions, or constipation, of the bowels. The wind incarcerated about and below the umbilicus, is passed with the greatest difficulty, and attended with loud reports and bleeding.

The aggravated Vāyu, by producing a parched condition of the intestines, gall and urinary bladders, gives rise to all kinds of hæmorrhoid growths. The patient gradually becomes thinner and more dejected. The complexion becomes pale and sallow; the strength of the body is markedly diminished; and, the whole organism becomes sapless as a worm-eaten tree. The pain in the regions of the Marmas specifically described under Yakshmā is found to supervene with cough, thirst, dyspnœa, lassitude, vomiting, œdema, fever, deafness, and a disagreeable taste in the mouth. An aching pain in the limbs, anus, groins, umbilicus, and the region of the heart may be also present. The patient constantly spits and evinces no desire for food, and remains drowsy all day long. A kind of bilious discharge, resembling washing of meat, is secreted from the rectum.

In some cases the vegetations remain dry, while in others

they are found to suppurate and burst. In the type due to the action of the deranged Pittám, they become yellow, suppurate, spontaneously burst, and bleed. In the type due to the action of the enraged Vāyu, the polypi are marked by their small growth and absence of any secretion. They are found to be rough, uneven, sharp-pointed, hard, and of a reddish or brownish colour, with their external ends, cracked and severed, resembling a Vimba, Kārkandu, Kharjura, or Kārpāsa seed in shape. Some of them grow in the shape of Kadamva flowers, while others are found to resemble mustard seeds in size and shape. An excruciating pain in the head, sides, shoulders, thighs and inguinal regions, salivation, eructation, distension of the abdomen, cough, dyspnœa, vertigo, noise in the ears, impaired digestion with a catching pain in the heart, and an extreme nonrelish for food are the symptoms, which mark the Vāyu-origined type of hæmorrhoids. The patient in this type passes hard, knotty, slimy. stool with loud flatus and much straining. The skin, nails, feces, urine, eyes and face of of the patient assume a black (dep blue) hue, and splenic dropsy, internal glands (Gulma) and mucous tumours make their appearance with the progress of the disease. In the Pittaja type, the heads of the polypi assume a blackish, bluish, or yellowish red colour. They are felt soft to the touch, emit afleshy smell, and secrete a thick bloody discharge from their elongated ends. Some of them are either like the tongues of parrots, or resemble the mouths of leeches in shape, or are shaped like the liver. A burning sensation of the body together with suppuration of the growths, perspiration, epileptic fits and an extreme repugnance for food are the symptoms which are found to supervene. The patient passes a kind of hard undigested feces which are coloured green, yellow, or bloody at intervals. The polypi are thick at the middle like barley corns, and the skin, nails, feces, urine, eyes, etc., of the patient assume a yellow color in this type of the disease. In the Shleshmaja type, the hæmorrhoid growths are thick and flat at their base and are found to vegetate over a considerable area around the anus. They are white, slightly painful, glossy, unyielding, firm, smooth, globular in shape, and are felt soft to the touch. An itching sensation is invariably experienced in the affected region. and the patient feels an irresistible desire to constantly handle the growths, which seem heavy and as if enshrouded with a wet compress, resembling either the Kantaki seeds, bamboo sprouts, or the teats of a cow in shape. The patient complains of a catching, binding pain in the inguinal regions, and of a drawiug pain either in the bladder, rectum, or in the umbilical region. Cough, dyspnœa, nausea, vomiting, catarrh, repugnance for food, strangury, heaviness of the head, rigour, fever, increased sexual desire, mucous dysentery, dulness of appetite, and urethral and urinary disorders are the symptoms which are likewise found to supervene. In this type the patient passes stool in large quantities with much straining. The stool is found to be largely charged with thick, lard-like mucous, and the polypi are marked by the absence of bleeding or of any kind of slimy discharge. They look grey and glossy, and do not burst or crack even under the pressure of hard feces. The type of hæmorrhoids, which owes its origin to the concerted action of the deranged Vāyu, Pittam, and Kapham, exhibits symptoms which are respectively peculiar to the three kinds described above. Hæmorrhoids, which result from a cotaminated (lit: enraged) condition of the blood, resemble Gunja berries, or coral or Vata sprouts in shape and colour, and are attended with all the symptoms specifically described under the Pittaja type. The polypi, under the pressure of hard stool, violently bleed in this type, and in consequence of such copious hæmorrhages the complexion of the patient becomes pale and yellowish like the skin of a yellow frog, not to speak of hosts of other distempers which result from the loss of blood. The patient gets thinner and feebler every day. The complexion becomes pale and sallow, the organs fail to perform their proper functions, and the spirit becomes gloomy and dejected. The Vāyu enraged and aggravated through the ingestion of gram, mudga, bamboo sprouts and such like stuff, takes lodgment in the region of the rectum, and obstructs the downward passage of the body by absorbing moisture from the urine and stool, which becomes extremely hard in consequence. Thus incarcerated in the system they give rise to an excruciating pain in the sides, abdomen, back, and sacral and cardiac regions, bringing on tympanitis, ascites, salivation, colic in the urinary bladder, œdematous swelling of the cheeks, and an obstinate constipation of the bowels with the progress of the disease. The deranged Vâyu, if happens to take an upward direction in the system, in this disease, produces vomiting, repugnance for food, fever, palpitation of the heart and kindred complaints, diarrhœa, dysentery, suppression of urine, deafness, dyspnœa cough, coryza, fecal disorders, thirst, internal glands (gulmas), cephalagia and a violent obstinate headache, etc., which are usually attributed to its aggravation and disturbance. Asthma or any other form of dyspnœa, and entire suppression of the stool and urine with tympanitis are the distressing symptoms, which are usually found to supervene, causing death of the patient in unfavourable instances. Even in the absence of foregoing exciting factors, rectal hæmorrhoids may grow from quite idiopathic causes in persons whose abdominal chamber has been invaded by the deranged and incarcerated Vāyu of the body. The congenital form of the disease, as well as the one in which the polypi are found to vegetate upon the inner groove of the rectum soon becomes incurable. Palliation is the only treatment possible in these cases in the event of the digestive faculty of the patient being sound and unimpaired. A case of hæmorrhoids in which the polypi vegetate on the second groove of the rectum may lapse into an incurable one in the event of their not being remedied within the first year of their growth or appearance. A case of hæmorrhoids in which the polypi are of recent growth and are found to vegetate on the outer or external groove of the rectum, and in which only a single morbific principle of the body serves as the exciting factor, may yield to medical treatment. Polypi, which are found to crop up on the generative organs (condylomatous growths), or on the region of the umbilicus, are slimy and felt soft to the touch like the mouth of an earth-worm. The deranged Vyāna Vāyu of the system, by forcing out the deranged Kapham through the skin, gives rise to a kind of pappilatous growths on the surface of the body which are called Charmakilas, which are firm and rough to the touch. In the Vataja type of Charmakilas, a piercing pain is felt in the growths; in the Pittaja type they are found to be black capped, while in the Kaphaja type they become glossy, concurrent, and of the same colour with the surrounding skin. An intelligent person should resort to good medical treatment from the very first appearance of this disease in his organism, in as much as a little delay or neglect might bring in a host of other rectal disorders and ascitis.

—:o:—

CHAPTER CLVII.

DHANVANTARI said :—Hear me now, O Sushruta, discourse on the Nidānam of Atisāra (dysentery) and Grahini (Lienteric diarrhœa.) The three morbific principles of the body such as the Vayu, Pittam, and Kapham, as well as their combinations and fright and grief may be set down as the exciting factors of Atisāra, which admits of being divided into six different types. Drinking of large quantities of water, ingestion of dry food, or of inordinate quantities of lard, oil, butter, or cakes, and excessive indulgence in cups may be likewise set down as the exciting causes of the disease. The bodily Vāyu (nerve force), disturbed on account of either day-sleep, keeping of late hours, presence of worms in the intestines, and voluntary repression of any natural urging of the body, etc., takes lodgment in the intestines and impairs the digestive function, causing a rush of blood to the nether regions of the body. The Vāyu by continuing in the intestines with the feces and ingested food, serves to liquify the stool and give rise to the disease which is called Atisāra. A breaking pain in the rectum, abdomen and cardiac region, together with a sense of lassitude and constipation of the bowels are the premonitory symptoms of Atisāra. Distension of the abdomen, together with indigestion, scanty ejections of the contents of the stomach without any sound or report, frothy turbid stool, or constant passing of knotty, slimy feces, and a burning, cutting pain about the anus mark the Vātaja-type of Atisāra. Fever is absent in this type of Atisāra. The anus is constricted, or the patient suffers from prolapsus ani together with dyspnœa and horripilation. Constant passing of yellow, black, yellowish, greenish or blood-coloured, fetid smelling stool, together with thirst, epileptic fits, and a burning sensation in the body mark the Pittaja-type. An aching, burning pain in the region of the anus, together with constant passings of thick, slimy, scanty stool, characterises the Kaphaja-type of Atisāra. All the abovesaid symptoms together with nausea, vomiting, a sense of heaviness about the anus and in the abdomen, and horripilation are the characteristics of the Sānnipātika-type. The patient loses all consciousness in this type, and thinks what he has done as undone.

The bodily Vāyu enraged through the effect of fright upon the mind liquifies the stool which is immediately passed out in hot or warm jets. In the Vāta-Paittika-type symptoms respectively described under the Vātaja and Pittaja-types of

Atisāra are combinedly exhibited. The specific symptoms of Atisāra brought about through the action of grief are identical with those described under the fright-born type.

The disease admits of being further grouped under two broad subdivisions such as, the Sāma (with mucous) and Nirāma (without mucous). In the first named type (Sāma) the stool emits a very fetid smell, and nausea with distension of the abdomen, and suppression of urine are also present. A case exhibiting symptoms other than the foregoing ones should be included within the Nirāma group. A marked predominence of the deranged Kapham in the body during the term of Atisāra leads to death. A case of Atisāra neglected at the outset may run into one of Grahini (Lienteric diarrhœa). Ingestion of a large quantity of articles, that impair the digestive function, brings about either Ama or Nirāma type of fever. Incarceration of undigested food in the stomach is sure to be followed by an attack of Atisāra of the Sāma-type. The disease is so named from the fact of one's passing large (Ati) quanties of stool during its attack. This disease naturally and invariably proves fatal. A case of Amātisāra usually follows from indigestion and on account of the incarceration of undigested fecal matter in the intestines. A case of old and persistent Atisāra runs into one of Grahini, which may be divided into four different types such as, Vātaja-Grahini, Pittaja-Grahini, Kaphaja-Grahini, and Sānnipātika-Grahini. A sense of lassidude in the limbs and constant emission of flatus together with salivation, and a distaste in the mouth, thirst, vertigo, repugnance for food, colic, vomiting, and buzzing in the ears are the general indications of Grahini. Weakness and emaciation of the body, hot eructations, dyspepsia fever, epiliptic fits, a sensation of numbness in the head and cardiac region, œdematous swelling of the extremities, drowsiness, parchedness of the palate, darkness of vision, noise in the ears, pain (crams) in the neck, thighs, sides and inguinal regions, and cholera are the symptoms, which are found to supervene. All these symptoms are aggravated in a weak patient, thirst and hunger being specially and oppressively increased.

The abdomen gets distended close upon the completion of digestion, and the patient finds a little relief immediately after eating. Palpitation of the heart, with pain in the cardiac region and kindred complaints, internal glands (gulmas) rectal hæmorrhoids, splenic enlargement, Chlorosis and loss of consciousness should be regarded as the distressing and supervening troubles in a case of Vātaja-Grahini. The stool is frequent, and either loose, hard or frothy and is passed with loud report, causing pain about the anus as well as cough and dyspnœa. In the Pittaja-type, the stool is either yellowish, or bluish yellow. Acid eructions, with a burning sensation in the heart and throat, repugnance for food, and an unquenchable thirst are the further characteristics of this type of Grahini. Painful motions of the bowels, difficulty of digestion, vomiting, reprugnance for food, burning sensation in the mouth, salivation, cough, nausea, catarrh, distension and heaviness of the abdomen, sweet eructations, lassitude, and horripilation are the specific features of the Kaphaja-type. The patient passes thick stool charged with mucous All the abovesaid symptoms are exhibited in the Sānnipātika-type. Epilepsy, stone in the bladder, Leprosy, Gonorrhœa, Ascites, fistula in ano, hæmorrhoids, and Grahini should be regarded as great maladies (Mahā Roga) and cures in these cases are extremely difficult.

——:●:——

CHAPTER CLVIII.

DHANVANTARI said:—Now, hear me, O Sushruta, discourse on the Ætiology and symptoms of Mutraghāta (suppressed or scanty urination) and Mutrakrichchha (strangury). The urinary bladder, with its neck or region of outlet, as well as the penis, the hip, the testes and the rectum are covered with one and the same peritonium, and are situated within the pelvic cavity. The urinary bladder is placed with its cervix (neck) hung downward and is filled with the help of the two ureters which open obliquely at the base of its fundus. The morbific principles of the body such as, the deranged Vāyu, Pittam and Kapham, may enter the minute nerve vessels that transverse this membranous sac of the body, and may give rise to twenty different forms of disorder. Both Prameha and Mutraghāta attack the Marma or the vulnervable part of the pelvis where the penis (urethra), inguinal ligaments, and ligaments of the pelvic bones meet one another, and in both these diseases, the patient constantly passes a very small quantity of urine with pain in the aforementioned localities. In the Vātaja form of Mutraghāta the urine is scanty and is constantly emitted with the greatest pain. In the Pittaja form the patient passes a high coloured or bloody urine attended with a burning sensation and pain at the external orfice of the urethra. In the Kaphaja type the patient complains of swelling and heaviness in the urinary bladder and the urethra (lit.—penis). The face of the patient assumes a withered, bluish aspect in the case where the deranged and aggravated bodily Vāyu serves as the exciting factor of this disease (Mutraghāta). The preponderance of the deranged Vāyu, Pittam, and Kapham in a given case of Mutraghāta is marked by the scanty emission of urine charged with sperm, bile matter, or mucous. The deranged Pittam in a case of the Pittaja type of Mutraghāta may generate urinary calculi or concretions to the size and colour of Gorochanā (hard biliary concretions occasionally obtained from the gall bladder of an ox.) The deranged and aggravated Kapham should be regarded as underlying all cases of urinary concretions (lit :—stone in the bladder).

A distended condition of the urinary bladder with an excruciating pain in regions around that organ is the premonitary symptom of a case of stone in the bladder—accumulation of urine in that membraneous sac, difficult and painful micturition, fever with a repugnance for food, and a pain about the umbilicus, bladder and the perineal suture, and headache being its general characteristics. These urinary concretions obstruct the external orfice of the bladder, and the patient passes a clear, crystal-coloured urine with extreme pain and difficulty A long retention of the urine in the bladder in these cases may produce local congestion followed by bleeding and a pain in the urethra. In the Vātaja-type, the patient gnashes his teeth violently, and shakes. The incarcerated urine in this type of Ashmari produces an excruciating pain about the umbilicus, and the patient passes a sort of hot, frothy stool accompanied by emission of flatus, and the urine is dribbled out in drops with pain. In the Vātaja type the urinary concretions become rough, and of a tawny-brown colour, and are found to be studded with thorns (crystaline.) In the Pittaja-type, the patient complains of a burning pain in the urinary bladder, and the concretions are found to resemble the stones of Bhallātaka fruit, or become of a red, yellow, or white colour. In the Kaphaja type of urinary calculi, an excruciating pain is experienced in the bladder, and the concretions are felt to be cold and heavy. Urinary calculi found in the bladders of infants, usually become, small, heavy, white or honey-coloured. These calculi should be extracted from the bladder before they can grow in size, or attain their fullest development.

A stream of semen, anywise obstructed in its emission, may give rise to the genesis of dreadful seminal concretions. The deranged and aggravated Vāyu of the locality dries up the drops of semen, thus disloged from its proper receptacle, and keeps them ensconced in the shape of hard crystals within the spermatic chords in the scrotum. The concretions are called Shukrāshmaries, which produce a painful swelling of the bladder and difficulty in passing urine. The formation of semen in a man is at once arrested immediately upon the formation of seminal concretions in his spermatic chords.

An attack of fever, or an obstinate cough may tend to transform these urinary concretions into gravels or Sharkarās. These calculi, being split and crushed by the force of the aggravated bodily Vāyu in the locality, may pass off with the urine in its normal course. Taking a contrary or upward direction they lie incarcerated in the urinary bladder, producing a kind of irritation in its cervix, which impedes the free emission of urine, and causes it to dribble out. The deranged Vāyu, thus aggravated, fills up the cavity of the bladder, and thence it gradually permeates the peritonium of the abdomen, causing it to be distended and producing painful spasms in its inside, as well as tympanites.

The enraged and aggravated bodily Vāyu by taking lodgment in the urinary bladder causes the urine to flow out in drops. The urine is invariably emitted in broken or obstructed jets. The disease, thus engendered, is called Vātavasti. This disease is extremely hard to cure, and becomes much more difficult when it is associated with the deranged Vāyu. The deranged and aggravated bodily Vāyu taking lodgment in that part of the perineum which lies between the rectum and the urinary bladder may give rise to a kind of thick, knotty, round, raised concretions which is called Vātashthila. It brings on profuse micturition and copious evacuations of the bowels. The enraged bodily Vāyu is coiled up, and produces an excruciating pain, in the urinary bladder without in any way interfering with the flow of urine, but giving rise to vertigo, a sensation of numbness and heaviness in the limbs, and nausea.

The type of disease, which is known as Vātakundalikā, and which is but an offspriug of enforced continence or voluntary suppression of semen, is characterised by a scanty though constant urination. The urine suppressed in these cases produces a slight pain at the external orfice of the urethra. The suppressed flow (of urine), forced to recoil back upon itself through the obstruction of the enraged Vāyu, tends to distend the abdomen from below the umbilicus, and gives rise to a kind of intolerable pain in the locality accompanied by tympanites and loose motions of the bowels. The enraged Vāyu, in this disease, tends to send up the urine higher up in the abdominal cavity, whence results the scantiness of that fluid. The said enraged Vāyu finds lodgment either in the intestines, urinary bladder, or in the umbilical region, giving rise to a constant, and, sometimes slightly painful, micturition. The urine is emitted in gusts (*lit.* in unbroken jets) and the residue of the fluid lies pent up in the scrotum, producing a sensation of heaviness in the scrotal sac. Sometimes, the urine, accumulated and pent up little by little in the bladder, gives rise to a kind of local nodular growths, which somewhat resemble urinary calculi in shape, and are called Mutragranthis. A sexsual intercourse in these urinary diseases, enrages the local Vāyu, which may tend to dislodge and draw up the spermatic fluid from its receptacle. The semen, under the circumstance, is found to be emitted either before, or with the flow of urine, resembling washings of ashes. The disease is called Mutra Shukra (a type of spermatorrhœa).

The enraged Vāyu, by bringing down fecal matter into the urinary channel of a weak, emaciated patient of parched temperament, causes the disease which is called Mutra-

Vighāta. The disease is characterised by loose motions of the bowels with tympanites, and emission of urine in drops, smelling like fecal matter. The bodily Vāyu, enraged through the agency of the aggravated Pittam, inordinate physical exercise, excessive ingestion of sharp and acid substances, and retention of urine in the bladder, causes a disease, called Ushna Vāta, its specific symptoms being an extreme burning sensation in the bladder, scanty urination followed by emission of hot bloody urine, or hematuria. The deranged Pittam and Vāyu finding lodgment in the urinary bladder of a person of exhausted and parched up constitution, give rise to a disease which is called Mutrakshaya, characterised by scanty, painful, burning urination. When the local Vāyu is affected by the deranged Pittam and Kapham, it produces a disease which is called Mutrasāda. The urine is either red, yellow, or white and thick, attended with burning, or resembles the colour of oxbile, or powdered conch-shell. The urine may be entirely absent in some cases, or may assume any of the aforesaid colours. Thus all diseases affecting the flow of urine have been described in detail.

—:o:—

CHAPTER CLIX.

DHANVANTARI said :—Now hear me, O Sushruta, discourse on the causes and symptoms of Pramehas.

Twenty different forms of Prameha are recognised in practice. Of these, ten are due to the action of the deranged Kapham, six are caused through the agency of the deranged Pittam, and four have their origin in the aggravated condition of the bodily Vāyu. The semen, fat, and urine, surcharged with Kapham, should be looked upon as the immediate exciting factors of the several types of Prameha.

A patient suffering from Haridrā-Meha passes hot stool and urine, having the colour of turmeric. A person attacked with Manjishthā-Meha passes urine like the solution of Mangishthā (yellowish red). The urine in a case of Rakta-Meha is either pure blood, or hot, bloody and saline, while that in Vasā-Meha is either a jet of fat, or is found to be coloured like lard. A person suffering from Majjā-Meha passes urine, which resembles, or is charged with, marrow, A patient in this disease, like a wild and infuriated elephant, does not constantly pass urine, but passes a copious flow whenever urinating. The urine in Hasti-Meha is copious and found to be largely charged with slimy mucous. A Madhu-Meha patient passes urine which resembles honey. The obstruction of the channels of the bodily Vāyu (nerves) by the deranged Pittam and Kapham in an organism, which has suffered a considerable loss in its fundamental, vital principles, may be likewise set down as the exciting factor of Madhu meha. The morbic principles, which usher in the disease in a given case, soon exhibit their specific symptoms.

A case of Prameha spontaneously exhibits symptoms of amelioration or aggravation without any apparent reason, and soon runs into one of the most difficult and obstinate type. All types of Prameha, neglected at the outset, may run into Madhu-Meha in course of time. The urine in Madhu-Meha becomes sweet like honey. All cases of Prameha in which the bodily excretions of the patient acquire a sweetish taste, should be regarded as cases of Madhumeha.

Indigestion, with a non-relish for food, vomiting, somnolence, cough, and catarrh are the distessing symptoms, which are found to supervene in a case of Meha due to the action of the deranged Kapham. A pricking pain in the urinary bladder and urethra, bursting of the scortum, fever with a burning sensation of the body, epilcpsy, thirst, sour risings, and loose motions of the bowels are the distressing symptoms, which supervene in a case of Maha due to the action of the deranged Pittam. Suppression of stool, flatus, and urine, shivering, a catching pain about the heart, with a desire for (pungent, bitter or astringent) food), colic, insomnia, cough, dyspnœa, and wasting are the distressing symptoms, which mark a Vātaja type of Prameha.

The ten kinds of carbuncles, or abscesses, which mark the sequel of Prameha are called Sarāvika, Kachchhapikā, Jvālini, Vinatā, Alaji, Masurikā, Sarshapikā, Putrini, and Vidārikā. The ingested food in combination with the deranged Kapham of the system usually ushers in an attack of Prameha, and the deranged Kaphah, in most cases, may be set down as the primary and exciting factor of the disease. The urine in every type of Prameha becomes slimy, acid, sweet or saline, heavy (in respect of its specific gravity), oily and cold. Use of newly harvested rice, new wine, meat-soup, meat, sugarcane, treacle and milk in excessive quantities, and sharing the same bed or cushion with a Prameha-patient may be set down as the exciting factors of this disease. The deranged Kaphah located in the urinary bladder liquefies the fat and myosin of the body like excrementitious discharge. The aggravated Vāyu, on the subsidence of the action of the deranged Kapham, augments the action of the Pittam, and brings on congestion of blood in the urinary bladder, thus producing the disease, which is called Prameha.

The prognosis in a case of Prameha should be determined in consideration of the nature of the morbific diatheses underlying the attack. A continuance of the Vāyu, Pittam, and Kapham in their normal state (in the patient's body) points to a happy prognosis, while the reverse is indicated when their natural equilibrium is in any way disturbed. The patient, in each type of Prameha, passes a copious, turbid urine, which should be regarded as one of the general characteristics of the disease. As a variety of colours may be produced through a combination of those that are white, yellow, black or red, so the deranged Vāyu, Pittam and Kapham, in combination with the different organic principles of fat, flesh, etc., may serve to give a variety of colours to the urine in this disease.

In the type known as Udaka-Meha (poluria), the patient passes a copious, transparent, water-like or slightly turbid, slimy, cold, and odourless urine. In a case of Ikshu-Meha, the patient passes a sweet, vinegar-like urine.

In Sāndra-Meha (Chyluria), the patient passes a thick urine, which resembles stale rice-boilings. In Pishta-Meha, the patient passes urine like a solution of pasted rice attended with horripilation. In Surā-Meha, the patient passes urine like wine, which is transparent in its surface but leaves a sediment at its bottom. In Sukra-Meha (Spermatorrhœa), the patient passes urine highly charged with semen, or resembling semen in colour. In Sikatā-Meha, the urine becomes turbid, and is found to leave a sediment resembling hard grains of sand. The urine becomes cold, sweet, and copious in S'ita-Meha, while it dribbles out or is emitted in successive and broken jets in S'anair Meha. In Lālā-Meha, the urine becomes slimy and shreddy like saliva, while in Kshāra-Meha, it assumes an alkaline character, or resembles an alkaline solution in taste, touch, smell and appearance. In Nilameha, the patient passes a bluish urine, while in Kāla Meha, the urine becomes black as ink.

A case of Prameha, neglected at the outset, may be followed by the appearance of one of the ten aforesaid types of abscess at a fleshy part of the patient's body, or about any of his bone-joints, or about any anastomosis of veins, arteries, etc., (Marmasthānam). Of these, the type of abscess known as S'ara'vikā, is raised or elevated at its margin and dipped in its centre, characterised by the absence of any pain or discharge, and resembles a saucer in shape. An abscess appearing about the seat of the body, and characterised by an intolerable, burning sensation in its inside, and resembling a tortoise in shape, is called Kachchhapikā. An abscess, which is of a considerably large size and assumes a bluish colour, is called Vinatā. An abscess, which develops a kind of intolerable, burning sensation in the skin during its stage of incubation, is called Jvālini. An abscess of the present type becomes extremely painful. An abscess, which is tinged either red or white, is studded with belbs or blisters, and is characterised by a sort of burning sensation, is called Alaji. Postules to the size of lentil seeds are called Masurikā, while those that crop up like small mustard seeds on the tongue in the latter stage of Prameha, attended with an extreme pain and local suppuration, are called Sarshapikā. Abscesses, that crop up covering a considerably extensive area, marked by a comparatively smaller elevation, are called Putrini. An abscess, which is hard and round like the root of a Vidarikā, is called Vidarikā. An abscess, which is marked by features peculiar to erysipelas, is called Vidradhikā. Of these, the types known as Putrini and Vidāri are characterised by an excessive deposit of fat, and a kind of intolerable pain. Other kinds of abscesses may mark the sequel of a case of Prameha, marked by an extremely aggravated condition of the deranged Pittam. The deranged Vāyu, Pittam and Kapham in connection with a case of Prameha give rise to abscesses peculiar to their respective aggravated conditions in the body of a person of vitiated fat, even without an attack of Prameha, but their specific natures can not be ascertained till their characterestic colours are developed. A case in which a person passes an extremely high-coloured urine, like washings of turmeric or blood, without the specific features of urine in Prameha as described before, should be diagnosed as a case of Raktapittam (urethral hæmorrhage) Perspiration, with a bad smell in the body, lassitude of the body with a kind of gone feeling in the limbs, inclination to sleep, eating, and repose, a burning sensation in the heart, eyes, tongue and ears, growth, and thickness, of the ends of finger-nails and hairs, fondness for cool things and cooling measures, and dryness of the palate, with a sweet taste in the mouth and burning sensation in the extremities are the symptoms, which mark the premonitory stage of Prameha. Ants are found to infest the urine of a patient during this stage of Prameha, and thirst, and sweetness of the urine, etc., are the symptoms, which are developed with the progress of the disease. The body having been permeated with deranged Kaphah, the bodily Vāyu gets the upper hand of the other morbific diathesis in the body, and produces the Va'taja type of Prameha. Types of Prameha, due to the action of the deranged Pittam or Kapham, fully exhibit their charateristic symptoms, while those, which are due to any impure contact, take time to develop all their specific features, and are contaminated from one person to another. Types of Prameha, due to the action of the deranged Pittam, may be checked, if not cured. A case of Prameha may be expected to be cured only before the specific symptoms are fully developed.

—:o:—

CHAPTER CLX.

DHANVANTARI said :—Hear me, O Sushruta, now discourse on the ætiology and symptomology etc., of abscesses, (*Vidradhi*) and *Gulmas* (internal glands). Ingestion of stale, dry, parchifying, or extremely hot food may be set down as the primary cause of *Vidradhis* and *Gulmas*. The blood vitiated through such factors as gratification of carnal propensities by unnatural means, use of hard and uneven beds, etc., vitiates, in its turn, the skin, flesh, fat, and bones of the body, and takes refuge in the abdominal cavity, causing a round or extended swelling to appear either in the inside or on the surface of the body, attended with an excruciating, aching pain, which is called a *Vidradhi*. The morbific principles of the body, such as the deranged Vāyu, Pittam and Kapham, either severally or combinedly, may give rise to an abscess, which may likewise occur in any part of the body, which has been profusely bled. An external abscess appearing at any part of the body as an outcome of profuse blood-letting is found to have a knotty formation. An internal tumour, on the other hand, is always found to be deep-seated, compact as an internal gland *(Gulma)* and chequered with orfices, like an ant-hill, through which secretions are exuded. The patient complains of impaired digestion in this internal type of *Vidradhi*, which proves fatal in many instances.

The spleen, liver, lungs, heart, urinary bladder, intercostal, and inguinal regions principally form the seats of these internal abscesses. A heavy palpitation of the heart, enhancing the pain, is experienced when an abscess occurs in that locality. The abscess assumes either a blackish or bluish red colour, is slow in its growth and suppuration, and regular in its formation. Loss of consciousness, vertigo, tympanites with suppression of the stool and urine, and bleeding, attended with a kind of indistinct report, are the distressing symtoms which are found to supervene. An abscess orignated through the action of the deranged Pittam assumes either a red, copper, or black colour, and is attended with fainting, fever and a burning sensation. The abscess is rapid in its growth, and suppuration sets in early in the Pittaja type. An abscess of the Kaphaja type is tinged grey, and is attended with an itching sensation, and shivering. Numbness of the affected part, yawning, and heaviness of the limbs, with a non-relish for food are the symptoms which further characterise this Kaphaja tyye. An internal abscess of the Sannipa'ta type, like an external one of the same kind, is slow in growth and suppuration. It assumes a black colour, becomes studded over with belbs, and is attended with an intolerable burning pain, with fever and loose motions of the bowels. The external abscesses have all their origin in the deranged condition of the Pittam. There is another kind of external abscess which is peculiar to women. The blood, enraged by a blow or hurt, may give rise to another kind of *Vidradhi*.

The blood in any part of the body, that has been wounded, becomes agitated through the action of the local Vâyu (nerve force). The enraged blood, failing to find out an outlet, mixes with the deranged Pittam, and produces a kind of abscess, which is attended with all the symptoms peculiar to the deranged Pittam and vitiated blood.

Different symptoms are exhibited according to the variation in the seat of an abscess in the body, as for example, an internal abscess, occurring about the region of the umbilicus, brings on an obstinate tympanites, while the one, which appears in the urinary bladder, produces painful micturition. An abscess of the spleen brings on dyspnœa, and an unquenchable thirst. An abscess in the lungs produces constriction of the larynx, while the one in the heart produces a pain all over the body. An abscess, occurring inside the intercostal region, produces vertigo, fainting, a digging pain in the heart, and the peculiar form of dyspnœa known as Tamaka S'vâsa (described before). An abscess, occurring inside the inguinal regions, about joint of the thighs, or about the union of the back and waist (sacrum), produces the incarceration of the wind and a kind of intolerable pain.

The non-suppurated, suppurating, and suppurated stages of an abscess should be ascertained in the manner of any other swelling. An internal abscess, occurring in the region above the umbilicus, with its head pointing upward, bursts out in the stomach, and evacuates its contents through the passage of the anus. An internal abscess, occurring in the rectum, mouth, or the umbilicus, and exuding its (peculiar) secretion, should be regarded as indicating a painful prognosis. An internal abscess of the *Sannipâta* type appearing in any of the aforesaid localities in the body produces an alteration in the composition of the local tissues, while an external one, occurring about the umbilicus, or in or above the urinary bladder, runs to suppuration and bursts. An internal abscess, fully developed, is always found to suppurate, while the one, that is not well developed, gives rise to many a supervening, distressing symptom in its immature stage.

A peculiar kind of abscess is found to occur in the uterus of wicked women, who are addicted to the sinful practice of effecting miscarriage of their pregnancy. The swellings in the uterus, caused by frequent abortions, become compact and condensed, and are thus transformed into abscesses. A mammary abscess should be regarded as an external one to all intents and purposes. An internal abscess can never occur in any of the reproductive organs of a girl, owing to the comparatively greater thinness of blood that courses in the female economy, during childhood. It is the aggravated and obstructed Vāyu (nerve force) that should be regarded as the primary cause of all swellings. The local Vāyu, any wise aggravated, courses down from the region of union between the penis and the scrotum, finds lodgment in the spermatic chord of the testes, presses upon the local vessels, and produces a swelling of the scrotum by vitiating the fat of the locality. The disease is called *Vriddhi Roga*, which admits of being divided into seven different types. A preponderance of the deranged Vāyu in a *Vidradhi Roga* of this type, whether external or internal, is followed by copious micturitions. In the Vātaja type of this *Vriddhi Roga*, the swelling (scrotal tumour) becomes inflated, parched and rough to the touch, marked by a burning sensation in its inside. In the Pittaja type, the swelling assumes a vermilion tint like that of a ripe Audumvara fruit (Ficus Indica), and is attended with heat, burning, and suppuration. In the Kaphaja type, the swelling becomes cold, heavy, glossy, and slightly painful, attended with an itiching sensation. In the Raktaja type (Hematocele) (due to the action of the contaminated blood), the swelling becomes compact, and is covered with a crop of belbous eruptions on its surface, its other features being one with those described under the head of Pitaja type of *Vriddhi*. The swelling in the type originated through the action of the deranged fat and Kapham becomes soft and rounded like a palm fruit. The type known as Mutraja Vriddhi (Hydrocele, usually appears in those who are in the habit of voluntarily suppressing their urine. The patient leads a sort of quiscient life, and does not evince any desire for any thing in special. The swelling becomes distended with serous accumulations, and suffers a perceptible diminution in size, if its fluid contents are in any way evacuated.

Cold ablutions and use of articles of fare, that tend to aggravate the bodily Vāyu, are the factors which produce a kind of ring-like swelling at the bottom of the scrotum, producing painful micturition. The Vāyu aggravated by voluntary repression of natural urgings of the body to urination or defecation, or by violent physical exercise or straining of the lower limbs in any unnatural posture, or suck like aggravating factors, tends to produce a determination of blood to the lower limbs and inguinal regions, instantaneously causing the appearance of a ring-like glandular swelling (hernia) in the groin. Neglected at the outset, a case of this type of *Vriddhi Roga* may run into one of *Gulma*, attended with tympanites, pain, and hosts of other distempers. Firmly pressed, the ring-like, protuberant, swelling rises upward, making a distinctly audible report. The type (Rakta Vriddhi) is incurable, while the swelling in a case of Vātaja Vriddhi continues in the same size, traversed by a net-work of dry, bluish red veins. The aforesaid diseases may be divided into eight different types according as the morbific principles of the deranged Vāyu, Pittam, and Kaphah severally or combinedly act as their exciting and underlying factors.

The eighth kind of abscess (Vidradhi) is that, which occurs in any of the generative organs (ovary or uterus, etc.) of women of impaired menstrual functions. Even a strong patient (during an attack) is afflicted with fever, dysentery, vomiting, rigor, and hunger, and gets emaciated. A Vidradhi-patient, who partakes of boiled rice, or drinks copiously, or bathes, or fasts, during an attack, is soon overwhelmed with fits of fainting. Diaphoretic or emolient measures should not be resorted to in a case of Vidradhi, and expedients calculated to promote a free and healthy circulation of blood should be at once tried, no matter whether the morbific principles have been eliminated from the body of the patient with the help of suitable purgatives, or not.

In a case of Vātaja *Vidradhi*, the wind and the filthy matter are either combinedly emitted from the abscess, or they may be separately emitted at different times. The aggravated Vāyu, coursing through the capillaries, sometimes gives rise to bloody discharge from a Vātaja abscess, while obstructing the upward and downward passages of the body it brings on a violent aching pain.

A *Gulma* (internal gland) is tangible (can be caught hold of with the hand) like a stone, hot, and glandular in shape. The Vayu, aggravated through fasting, suppression of stool or urine, or obstruction of the channels of the body, finds lodgment in the abdominal cavity, and dries up, in virtue of its own parchifying property, the feces and mucous accumulated therein in the shape of a hard lump, which is called *Gulma*.

The deranged Vāyu continuing in its own locations acts independently, while located in the seat of any other morbific principle of the body (such as the Pittam and Kaphah) it acts subservient to that principle. The consolidated lump of Kapham, solidified in combination with mucous, and which is found to occupy the region either about the umbilicus, sides, or thoracic or abdominal cavity, is called a *Gulma*.

In the Vātaja type of *Gulma*, fever with an excruciating headache, enlarged spleen, a rumbling or croaking sound in the intestines, loose motions of the bowels, a pricking pain in the limbs, and difficult or painful urination are the symptoms, which are invariably exhibited. The patient suffers from an œdematous swelling of the face and extremities, or from a general anasarca. The ball-like tumour rolls about, or shifts from one place to another, in the region of its location, the skin of the patient becomes parched and dark, the pupils of the eyes are dilated, and the sight is perceptibly impaired. The patient complains of a creeping sensation in the *Gulma*, as if hosts of ants are traversing its inside, and the ball-like tumour is perceived to be shifting from place to place.

In the Pittaja type, symptoms such as Epilepsy, acid eructations with loose motions of the bowels and a burning sensation in the body, perspiration, thirst, chlorosis, and anasarca are found to be mainfest. In the Kaphaja type, the *Gulma* becomes hard, heavy, and fixed, attended with insomnia, or fretful sleep at irregular hours, obesity, nausea, white or dark colour of the skin, heaviness of the head, and a sensation, as if the body has been packed with a wet compress, with a non-relish for food are also present. The deranged Kaphah in the system is aggravated or suffers a diminution at times without any apparent reason, scorching its specific seats in the organism. The distressful concomitants in this desease such as, hæmorrhage etc., soon manifest themselves through the deranged condition of the specific organs they are found to attack, thus bringing on a complication which invariably proves fatal. The type known as

Rakta-gulma (ovarian tumour) which occurs in women is found to be hard, raised and compact. The type should be attributed to the concerted action of the deranged Vāyu, Pittam and Kaphah, etc., and is marked by an excruciating pain and rapid suppuration.

A long exposure to the wind by a woman, during her menses, or by one suffering from any kind of uterine or vaginal disease, tends to augment and aggravate the Vāyu in her system. The Vāyu, thus aggravated, obstructs the orfice of the menstrual duct, and the blood accumulated, each month, in her abdominal cavity, produces all the symptoms of pregnancy. Nausea, appearance of milk in the mamme, and a fretful mood are the symptoms, which characterise this disease in which the patient becomes fastidious in her taste, and evinces her desires for various kinds of food, as in true pregnancy. The deranged Pittam, in contact with the aggravated Vāyu, leads to the accumulation of blood in the uterus, and the Gulma, generated in consequence thereof, manifests symptoms which are peculiar to both of them (Vāyu and Pittam). The accumulated blood in the uterus produces an intolerable aching pain in that viscus, attended with pain in the vagina, and a fetid, water-like, vaginal discharge, or leucorrhœa. The gulma in this type sometimes develops all other symptoms of pregnancy. All these types of Gulma should be regarded as having their origin in excessive or unnatural gratification of sexual propensities.

The food long remains undigested in the stomach of a Gulma-patient, and the growth and progress of an abscess are arrested as soon as a Gulma makes its appearance in the body of the patient. A *Vidradhi* (abscess) is so called from the fact of its soon running to suppuration. A Gulma, occurring in the abdominal cavity, is marked by a burning sensation in the pelvic cavity, and a pain in the inside of the Gulma like that, which is experienced in an enlarged spleen. The complexion of the patient becomes pale and sallow, the strength of the body is diminished, the digestion is impaired, and the stool and urine are suppressed. External symptoms develop themselves, and the patient complains of a pain in his limbs and abdomen, or about the umbilicus, while the reverse is the case (*i e.*, in cases where the preceding symptoms are not exhibited). Cough, palour, bulging out of the abdomen, rumbling sound in the intestine, tympanites, and an excruciating pain in the abdomen are the symptoms, which are found to supervene. When in combination with the preceding symptoms, emission of flatus or rising of eructations are stopped, the disease is called *A'na'ha*. A thick, raised, knotty, and stone-like gland, appearing in a case of Gulma, is called *Ashthihá*. When the Vāyu incarcerated in the stomach gives rise to an excruciating pain, accompanied by all the foregoing symptoms, the disease is called *Pratya-shthilá*. Bulging out of the abdomen, suppression of stool, dulness of the senses with a rumbling sound in the intestines, tympanites, and distension of the abdomen are the symptoms, which mark all types of Gulma.

—:o:—

CHAPTER CLXI.

DHANVANTARI said :—Hear me, O Sushruta, now discourse on the Nidanam of *Udaram* (Ascites). All diseases are but the offspring of impaired digestion, and it is but superfluous to add that *Udaram* has its origin in the deranged condition of the digestive function. An accumulation of feces in the intestines may give rise to indigestion or to any other form of dyspepsia or disease, and the deranged up-coursing and down-coursing Vāyus of the system, being obstructed in their course, make the intestines (*Prabahini)* inoperative.

The Prana Vāyu (nerve-force of the respilatory centre) brings about the derangement of the Apana Vāyu (pneumo-gastric nerveforce), and keeps them incarcerated in the union of the skin and flesh (faces), thus giving rise to a distended condition of the abdomen, which is called *Udara-Roga* (Ascites.)

The disease admits of being divided into eight types according as it is engendered through the several, or concerted action of the morbific principles of the deranged Vāyu, Pittam, and Kapham, or through the enlargement of the spleen, or abdominal glands, etc., or is produced as the outcome of a wound in the abdomen, or is ushered in through an accumulation of serous fluid in the abdominal cavity. Dryness of the lips and palate, distension of the abdomen, diminution of strength and appetite, incapacity for all kinds of work, bulging out of the abdomen, and a cadaverous look are the premonitory symptoms of Ascites. Loss of appetite with a non-relish for food, which, if retained in the stomach, gives rise to an acid reaction are the further characterestics of ascites during its period of incubation. He, who does not experience a proper digestion of his ingested food, should do well to live on a wholesome diet. The strength of the patient is diminished, every day, and he feels tired after the least exertion. He becomes incapable of fixing his attention to any definite subject, and the least thinking distresses his mind. The limbs becomes emaciated, and the patient feels despondent and complains of a breaking pain in the pelvis, even after the scantiest meal. Somnolence, lassitude, loose motions of the bowels, fondness for seclusion, impaired digestion with a burning sensation in the body, anasarca, and tympanites are the symptoms, which indicate the accumulation of water (serous fluid) in the abdomen. A case of Ascites invariably ends in death, and it is futile on the part of the patient's relations to mourn his death under the circumstance. A rumbling sound is heard in the intestines, and the surface of the abdomen becomes chequered with a net-work of veins. The intestines and the region of the umbilicus becomes stuffed (with wind) in this disease, and an urging towards defication vanishes as soon as it is experienced. In this Vātaja type, the patient experiences a pain in the groins, heart, and other parts of the body, as well as about the waist, anus, and umbilicus. Flatus is olten emitted with a loud report, and urine becomes scanty. All desire for food vanishes in this type of the disease, and the patient complains of a bad taste in his mouth. Œdematous swelling of the face, abdomen, and extremities, a breaking pain in the abdomen, or about the waist, sides, back, or other parts of the body, dry cough, pain in the limbs, heaviness of the nether regions of the body, suppression of stool, varied taste in the mouth, and a reddish or blackish colour of the skin are the further characteristics of the Vātaja type of Ascites. A breaking, piercing, pain is likewise experienced in the abdomen in this type, and the surface of the abdomen becomes covered over with a fret-work of blue or black veins. The abdomen gets distended, and a variety of sound is heard within its cavity. The deranged bodily Vāyu, which courses all through the organism, gives rise to various sounds and and diverse kinds of pain in the different parts of the body.

Fever, epileptic fits, a bitter taste in the mouth, and a burning sensation in the body, vertigo, dysenteric stools, yellowness of the skin, and greenness of the skin of the distended abdomen are the symptoms, which mark the Pittaja type of Ascites. Yellow or copper-coloured veins appear on the skin of the patient, who imagines as if fumes are escaping out of his body, and complains of constant vanishings of sight. Perspiration becomes copious which does not relieve the intolerable burning sensation in the body. The abdomen is felt soft to the touch and speedily supperates in this (Pittaja) type of Ascites.

Lassitude of the body, perspiration, œdematous swelling

of the limbs, heaviness of the body, somnolence with a non-relish for food, dyspnœa, cough and whiteness of the skin and conjunctivæ are the features, which mark the Kaphaja type of Ascites. The skin of the protruded abdomen becomes glossy, and fretted with messes of black or white veins. On the excessive accumulation of water (serous fluid) in the abdominal cavity, the abdomen becomes hard, heavy, immoveable, and cold to the touch. In the *Tridoshaja* type the symptoms peculiar to each of the three aforesaid types manifest themselves in unison.

All the morbific principles of the body, in combination with the vitiated blood and accumulated fecal matter, find lodgment in the cavity of the abdomen, giving rise to vertigo, Epilepsy, and emaciation in a form of Ascites in which symptoms peculiar to the three morbific diathises of Vayu, Pittam, and Kaham are combinedly developed; and suppuration sets in early in the distended abdomen. The disease shows signs of aggravation in cold and windy days, and is extremely hard to cure.

The spleen, which is situated in the left side of the abdominal cavity, is disloged (hangs down) from its seat through the ingestion of inordinate quantities of food, mental anxiety, or excessive riding or drinking, or through the abuse of emetics (excessive emisis).

In the alternative, the spleen may increase in bulk through the accumulation of fat or engorgement of blood in its body. It becomes hard and raised like the back of a tortoise, and gradually fills a greater part of the abdominal cavity, bringing on dyspnœa, cough, thirst, fever with a bad taste in the mouth, distension of the abdomen, yellowness of the skin, epileptic fits, vomiting, fainting, and a burning sensation in the body in its train. In abdominal dropsy due to enlargement of the spleen, nets of red, blue, or yellow veins are found to appaer on the skin of the abdomen, and tympanites with suppression of stool and flatus, vertigo, and fever with a burning sensation in the region of the heart are found to supervene.

Similarly, the liver, which is situated in the upper part of the right side of the abdominal cavity, is pressed down from its natural position either through a voluntary and constant repression of any natural urging of the body, or through the heaviness of any of the surrounding appendages, or through eating without any relish for food, or in reason of its own indurated condition, gives rise, like the spleen, to a peculiar form of abdominal dropsy, which is called *Yakritodaram* (lit Dropsy of the enlarged liver). The feces remain obstructed in the rectum of the patient as soon as the process of suppuration is established in the liver, producing dyspnœa, tympanites, etc. The enraged and aggravated Vāyu, in this disease, arrests the secretion of bile, and those of the glands of the intestimes, thus obstructing the expulsion of the feces. The *Apâna* Vāyu, thus incarcerated in the abdominal cavity, brings on fever attended with cough, dyspnœa, a gone feeling in the thighs, headache, an aching pain at the sides, in the limbs, or about the umbilicus, constipation of the bowels, vomiting and a non-relish for food. The enraged bodily Vāyu should be regarded as the principal agent in engendering this, as well as every other, form of abdominal dropsy. Blue or red veins are found to appear permanently on the skin of the dropsical abdomen, and the dropsy extends in the form of a cow's tail transvesely above the umbilicus, marked by crow-feet marks.

The visceras of the abdominal cavity supparate in the event of any bone or foreign matter being pricked into the cavity of the abdomen. The abdominal dropsy engendered in consequence thereof is called *Chhidrodara* or *Parisrâvyodara* (Peritonites) according to others The Vāyu and Kapham in the system of an emaciated person, or of one of impaired digestive function or addicted to the habit of drinking large quantities of water, become enraged through such injudicious conduct, and arrest the discharge of the acid secretions of the stomach, giving rise to an accumulation of water in the abdomen. Thirst, prolapsus ani, pain, cough, and dyspnœa with a non relish for food. are the symptoms which are exhibited during the extremely aggravated stage of this disease. The surface of the distended abdomen becomes covered over with a net work of veins. The abdomen is found to fluctuate under pressure, and is felt soft to the touch. In some cases the abdomen is felt to be firm and glossy like the abdomen of a heron, and the disease is found to invade the intestines. Th patient suffers from alternate fits of heat and rigor. In all types of Dropsy, neglect at the outset leads to the further liquefication of the serous accumulations of the abdomen, which are diffused all through the organism, causing œdamatous swelling of the face, joints etc., and facilitating the accumulation of serous fluid in the vessels of the body.

An obstruction of the ducts of the body that carry perspiration may help the accumulation of water in the abdomen. Purging or loose motions of the bowels precede an attack of this type of Ascites. The dropsy becomes firm, heavy, and spherical, and does not give the characteristic sound under percussion. The patient gets weaker, every day, and the disease becomes incurable as soon as it invades the internal vessels of the abdomen. A case of Ascites, in which the appearance of veins on the surface of the bulged out abdomen is obliterated, should be regarded as of a Sānnipātika origin.

Of the different types of dropsy such as, the Vātaja, Pittaja, Kaphaja, Plihaja (Dropsy of the enlarged spleen) and Sānnipātika (due to the concerted action of the deranged Vāyu Pittam, and Kapham), and Dakodara (Ascites), each preceding one should be regarded as more difficult to cure than the one immediately following it in the order of enumeration. All types of Dropsy, attended with the symptoms of obstructed (flow), become incurable after a fortnight from the date of their attack. A case of congenital Ascites invariably proves fatal.

—:o:—

CHAPTER CLXII.

DHANVANTARI :—Hear me, O Sushruta, now discourse on the *Nidânam* of chlorosis (*Pându*), Œdema and Anasarca (Shotha). The morbific principles of Vāyu and Kaphah, in combination with the Pittam extremely aggravated through their respective aggravating factors, are carried upward in the region of the heart, the deranged and aggravated Vāyu supplies the motive power in these instances, and the aggravated Pittam, through the channels of the ten *Dhamanis* (nerves) which branch out from that locality, spreads all through the organism. The deranged Pittam vitiates the Kapham, blood, skin, and flesh of the body, imparting a varied hue to its skin. As the colour of the skin largely becomes yellow (*Pându*) like turmeric in this disease, it is called *Pându Roga* (Jaundice).

In the *âmaja* type of Jaundice, the fundamental principles of the body become lighter and considerably lose their consistency. The patient suffers from a marked anæmia, the functions of the sense organs are impaired, the limbs become loose and flabby, the quantity of fat is diminished in the body, and the bones are deprived of their substance. The limbs get thinner and thinner every day, a clammy perspiration is felt in the region of the heart, a burning and aching sensation is experienced both in the conjunctiva and sockets of the eyes, and the mouth becomes filled with saliva. Thirst is conspicuously absent. The patient cannot bear the least cold, and abhors all cold things, and a persistent fever of equal intensity, attended with dyspnœa. earache, vertigo, vanishings of sight, impaired digestion and horripilation on the skin of the head are found to supervene.

The disease admits of being grouped under five subheads according as it is engendered through the several, or concerted action of the morbific principles of the body. A peculiar type of chlorosis is caused by eating earth, and the premonitory stage of all types of Jaundice develops such symptoms as, perspiration about the region of the heart, dryness of the skin with a repugnance for food, yellowness and scantyness of urine, or absence of perspiration.

The Vâtaja type of Chlorosis is marked by lassitude of the body, a stupour like that of a drunkard, and an excruciating pain in the limbs. The veins, finger-nails, feces, urine, and conjunctive assume a black colour, or loook dry and coloured like vermilion, and œdematous swelling of the limbs and dryness of the feces and of the mouth and the nostrils are the symptoms which further characterise this type of the disease. In the Pittaja type the veins become either yellow or greenish coloured, and fever with thirst, fainting, vanishings of sight, heat, and emaciation of the body with a bitter taste in the mouth and longing for cold things are found to supervene.

Diarrhœa, acid risings, a burning sensation in the body, clamminess of the cardiac region, somnolence, a saline taste in the mouth, cough, and vomitting are the features which mark the *Kaphaja* type of Jaundice, which is very distressing in its effect. The expectorated mucous in this disease acquires a pungent or sweetish taste either through a preponderance of the deranged Vâyu or Pittam. The deranged phlegm vitiates the fundamental principles of fat etc., of the body, and produces a condition of parchedness in the organism which results in hæmorrage. The deranged Kaphah, as before described, obstructs the internal vessels of the body, and thereby produces its general emaciation. In Jaundice, the face of the patient gets thinner, the scrotum and the muscles of the calves and abdomen are withered up, and the patient passes stool which is mixed with blood and mucous, and contains hosts of little intestinal worms.

An injudicious use of extremely Pitta-generating food by a Jaundice-patient is followed by an attack of *Kâmalâ* (Chlorosis). The deranged and aggravated Pittam, in this disease, coming out of its seat in the abdominal cavity, scorches up the flesh and the blood. The urine, eyes, skin, face and feces of the patient assume a yellow colour, and thirst, and indigestion with a burning sensation in the body are found to supervene. The patient lies like a bloated toad, weak in all his limbs and organs. The unassimilated Pittam, in this disease. gives rise to a kind of general anasarca, which, being neglected, may run into a case of *Kumbha Kâmalâ.* The undigested bile produces greenness of complexion, the deranged Vāyu and Pittam give rise to vertigo and thirst, and a low fever with fondness for female company, somnolence, extreme lassitude, and impaired digestion are the symptoms which mark the premonitory stage of *Hali mak.*

I have already, told you, O Sustruta, that *Sotha* is one of the most dreadful diseases, now hear me discourse on the Nidānam of that disease. The deranged Vāyu, by driving the deranged Kapham (phlegm), Pittam and blood to the external vessels of the body, make them incarcerated in the local skin and flesh, giving rise to a raised and compact swelling which is called a *Sotka.* The disease may be divided into nine different types according to the difference of the morbific principle acting as its exciting factor, inclusive of those which are of extraneous origin, or are caused by ardent sexual passion. The last named kinds of S'otham extends all over the body. The swellings may be divided into three classes according as they are extended, raised and pointed, or knotty and concurrent in shape. The several actions of the deranged Vāyu, Pittam and Kapham may be set down as the exciting causes of all forms of swellings, and they are often found to invade persons emaciated with disease, over work, or fasting. Ingestion of inordinate quantities of pot herbs, or of extremely cooling, saline, acid or alkaline articles of fare, drinking of large quantities of water, and excessive sleep or wakefulness may likewise serve to bring on an attack of S'otha. Suppression of any natural urging of body, ingestion of dry meat, or of heavy and indigestible articles of fare, or excessive riding are the factors which tend to obstruct the orfices of the vessels of the body, thus causing the appearance of an œdematous swelling about the locality of obstruction, dyspnœa, cough, dysentery, hæmorrhoids, ascites, leucorrhœa, fever, tympanites, vomiting and hiccough may be manifest as supervening, distressing symptoms in a case of œdema. The morbific principles of the deranged Vāyu, Pittam and Khpham, finding lodgment in in the upper, middle, or lower part of the body, or in the urinary bladder, may give rise to an œdematous swelling about the seat of their lodgment, while spreading all through the organism they may give rise to a general anasarca. An increased temperature of the body, heaviness of the limbs, and a kind of breaking, expanding pain in the veins are the symptoms which mark the premonitory stage of œdema.

In the Vātaja (nervous) type of œdema, the swelling is found to be shifting in its character. It assumes a blackish or reddish colour, and is felt rough to the touch. The hairs about the base of the swelling become rough, and the patient complains of a breaking pain about the temporal bones or in the urinary bladder, pelvis and the intestimes, and suffers badly from insominia. The swelling is speedy in its growth and even in its formation, and perceptibly yields to pressure, entirely disappearing after massage. After the application of a mustard plaster to it, a sort of tingling sensation is experienced inside the swelling, which increases in size during the night and markedly subsides during the day.

In the Pittaja type, the swelling assumes a black, red or yellow colour, and is marked by a burning sensation in its inside; the swelling does not readily subside, and an intolerable burning sensation of the body indicates its advent. Fever with thirst and a burning sensation in the skin, perspiration, vertigo, stupor, and loose motions of the bowels are its distressing concomitants. The swelling emits a peculiar fetid smell, yields to pressure, and is felt soft to the touch.

In the Kaphaja type, the swelling assumes a grey colour and becomes cold, glossy, firm and hard-skinned. An itching sensation is experienced in its inside, and somnolence, aching pain and impaired digestion are the symptoms which manifest themselves with the progress of this type of the disease.

An œdematous swelling may appear as the effect of a stroke, blow, cut, or wound, or as the outcome of an exposure to cold winds, or see-breezes, or that of being rubbed with a *Kapikachchhu* berry or with the juice of *Bhallâtakam*. It may also appear in the body of a person after a long pedestrean journey. All these kinds of swelling are marked by extreme heat, and exhibit symptoms peculiar to the Pittaja type. Similarly, the touch of a venomous reptile, or that of its excretions, or a bite by a venomous animal, or an exposure to a breeze blowing over poisonous trees, smelling of dusts and pollens of poisonous flowers are the factors which may likewise produce swellings of the body. These swellings are soft and shifting, and usually appear about the lower part of the body. A swelling of recent origin, unattended with any of the distressing symptoms, may be easily cured, while one of the opposite kind should be regarded as incurable.

——.o.——

CHAPTER CLXIII.

DHANVANTARI said:—Hear me, O Sushruta, now discourse on the *Nidânam* of *Visarpa* (Erysipelas). To some extent, œdema (S'otha) and Erysipelas may be attributed, to the same causes; and a wound, in no small number of cases, has been known to bring about an attack of this disease. Erysipelas usually attacks those parts of the body which have been already described as the peculiar seats of œdematous swellings; and fright and exhaustion, like the voluntary suppression on any natural urging of the body, may be enumerated as the exciting factors of cases of External Erysipelas. Of the several (Vātaja, Pittaja, Kaphaja, Sannipātaja) types of erysipelas, each preceding type is more difficult to cure than the one immediately following it in the order of enumeration. The morbific principles of the deranged Vāyu, Pittam, and Kapham, aggravated through their respective aggravating factors and specially through the ingestion of articles of fare which are followed by a reactionary acidity after digestion in the stomach, penetrate deep into the organism from their locations in the superficial principles of the body. An unappeased thirst, or a voluntary repression of any natural urging of the body, under the circumstance, again throws them up to the surface of the skin, bringing on an attack of external erysipelas.

In the Vātaja type of erysipelas, symptoms peculiar to the Vātika fever manifest themselves, a throbbing sensation is experienced in the belbs, and an aching, picreing pain is felt in the swelling, attended with horripilation. In the Pittaja type, the erysipelas shifts from one place to another, and the patches assume an extremely red colour, attended with fever. In the Kaphaja type of erysipelas, an itching sensation is felt in the affected parts, which assume a glossy aspect, and symptoms peculiar to Kaphaja (cattarrhal) fever exhibit themselves. In the Sānnipātika type of erysipelas, symptoms peculiar to the there above said types manifest themeelves in unison, and the belbs are characterised by diverse kinds of pain. In the type due to the concerted action of the deranged Vāyu and Pittam (Agni *Visarpa*) fever, vomiting, fainting, diarrhœa, (or dysentery), thirst, and vertigo soon develop themselves. A breaking pain is experienced in the joints, the digestion is inpaired, all desires for food are gone, and the patient suffers from vanishings of sight, and feels as if his whole body has been covered with live charcoal. The erysipelas swiftly shifts from one part of the body to another, leaving blue or black, burn-like, stains at its former seats. The disease gradually invades the vital principles of the body (such as the marrow etc.,) giving rise to an aching pain in the limbs; and unconsciousness, insomnia, dyspnœa, and hic-cough add to the trouble of the patient. The patient finds no relief in any posture whatsoever, and vainly tosses about on the ground in quest of relieving coolness. Stupor or unconsciousness gradually creeps over his mind, out of which the patient can be hardly roused up, until death comes and relieves him of his trouble. This disease is called *Agni Viarpa.*

The deranged Kapham, obstructed by the aggravated Vāyu, is divided into many parta, and gives rise to a kind of round, extensive, painful, thick, rough and confluent patches of erysipelas by vitiating the blood, skin, veins, ligaments, and blood (in the flesh) of a man of sanguinous (temerament in combination with the aggravated Vāyu of his system. The erysipelas, thus generated is called *Granthi Visarpa.* Fever, dyspnœa, cough, dysentery, parchedness of the mouth, hiccough, vomiting, vertigo, drowsiness, epileptic fits, dullness of complexion, pain in the limbs),and impaired digestive faculty are the symptoms, which mark this type of

Erysipelas, which is due to the action of the deranged Vāyu and Kapham.

The type of Erysipelas, known as *Kardama* (sloughing) *Visarpa*, which is due to the action of the deranged Kapham and Pittam, develops such symptoms as numbness of the body, excessive sleep or somnolence, headache, weakness, jerky movements of the limbs, delirium, vertigo, repugnance for food, epileptic fits, impaired digestion, a breaking pain in the bones, thirst, dullness of the senses, passing of undigested fecal matter, and deposit of mucous in the internal ducts of the body. The stomach is the seat of the Kapham and Pittam, hence, the disease (Erysipelas), first originating in the stomach, spreads and confines itself to any particular part of the body. A slight pain characterises this kind of Erysipelas (kardama) which becomes studded over with red, yellow, or grey coloured pustules. The Erysipelas assumes a glossy, black, blackish, or variegated colour. It becomes hot and heavy, marked by much swelling which exudes a slimy secretion, and suppuration takes place in its deeper strata. The Erysipelas, when bursts, emits an extremely offensive smell, attended with sloughing of flesh, which exposes the veins and ligaments in its inside. This kind of erysipelas (Kardama *Visarpa*) is so called from the fact of its secreting a copious slimy discharge which emits cadaverous smell.

The Vāyu, enraged by a blow or hurt, vitiates the blood and Pittam in the incidental wound, and produces a kind of Erysipelas about its locality which becomes studded with crops of belbous eruptions, resembling Kulattha pulse. This kind of erysipeals is called Kshataja Visarpa, and is characterised by fever with a pain and burning sensation in its inside. The blood in this type assumes a blackish red colour. A case of Erysipelas, originating through the action of any of the several morbific principles of the deranged Vāyu, Pittam and Kapham, is curable; cases at the root of which two such morbific principles lie as their exciting factors, and which are without any complication may yield to medical treatment, while those which are of a Sānnipātika origin and emit a cadaverous smell, are situated at any of the Marmas, and are attended with sloughing, laying bare the internal veins and ligaments, should be regarded as incurable.

—:o:—

CHAPTER CLXIV.

DHANVANTARI said:—The principles of the deranged Vāyu, Pittam, and Kapham, aggravated through the agency of injudicious diet and conduct, or through the dynamics of sinful acts or *Karma*, are sent coursing through the vessels of the body, which thereby vitiating the blood, fat, flesh, and skin of the locality, are kept incarcerated in the surface of the skin, bringing about a discolouring of the skin. These diseases are called Kushtham (cutaneous affections). Neglected at the outset, these Kushthas spread all over the body, gradually invading the fundamental principles of the organism, whether external or internal. The affected parts become contracted, and are characterised by the absence, or discharge, of a clammy perspiration. Later on parasites are found to germinate in those localities, which gradually attack the skin, hairs, and vessels of the part. In the type known as *Vahaya* (external) *Kushtham*, the body of the patient appears as if it has been dusted with ashes.

The disease (Kushtham) admits of being divided into seven kinds according to the several, duplicate, or concerted actions of the morbific principles of the deranged Vāyu, Pittam, and Kaphah, such as the Vātaja, Pittaja, Khapaja, Vāta-pittaja, Vāta-Shleshmaja, Pitta-shleshmaja, and Sānnipātika types. In each type of Kushtham the deranged Vāyu,

Pittam and Kapham are found to act in unison, though the action of any one of them may predominate therein.

The type of Kushtham, which is due to the action of the deranged Vāyu, is called Kapāla; that which is due to the deranged Pittam is called Audumvura; and that which has its origin in the deranged Kapham is called Mandala. Besides these, the types known as Vicharchikā and Rishyajihva originate through the action of the deranged Vāyu and Pittam, the types known as Charmakushtha (Prurigo), Kitima (Keloid tumour), Alasa and Vipādikā owe their origin to the deranged Vāyu and Sleshma, while the types known as Dadru (Ring worm), Shataru, Pundarika, Vishphota, Pāmā Shidhma (leucoderma) and Charmadala Impertigo) are brought about through the action of the deranged Pittam and Kapham. Of all these types of Kushtham, Dadru and Kākana Kushthas should be regarded as most common (Prathama).

The seven types such as the Pundarika etc., are called Maha Kushthas (Leprosy). The affected patches in this disease become soft and rough. Perspiration may be entirely absent, or a kind of clammy perspiration may be felt in these localities. An itching, burning sensation in the skin, attended with complete anæsthesia and contraction of the spots, marks the premonitory stage of this desease, and the patient suffers from vanishings of sight. A large number of ulcers or patches are found to appear at a time in this disease, which become permament (refuse to be healed), and an aching pain is constantly experienced in their inside. The patches, just after their appearance, are felt rough to the touch, and the deranged Vāyu, Pittam and Kaphah in these spots are extremely aggravated even at a slight exciting cause. Thinness or poverty of blood, and horrlipilation are the premonitory symptoms of all types of Kushtham. The forehead of the patient, during this stage, becomes blackish, or reddish, then dry and rough. The disease which extensive patches covered over with hairs, and attended with an excruciating pain, are found to appear in certain parts of the body, is called Kapāla Kushtham, which should be considered as one of the most dreadful types of leprosy. In the type known as Audumvara, the ulcerated patches assume the colour of a ripe Audumvera (ficus Indica). They become rounded in size, attended, with pain and burning, and exude a copious discharge. They appear in detachad patches and never burst, although parasites are found to germinate in their midst. The ulcerated patches, in this disease, become thick, firm (non-shifting) and glossy, and are found to exude a red and white discharge. In the type known as Mandala Kushtham (Erythema) the pitches are found to be raised, confluent, soft and yellowish marked by an itching sensation and the germniation of parasites in their inside. The type of Kushtham in which crops of black, itching, excuding postules are found to appear on the skin is called Vicharchikā. These patches become of a twaney brown colour, and are felt a little raised and rough to the touch. The type in which lepirous patches, resembling the tongue of a (Rishya) deer in colour and shape, are found to appear on theskin of the body, is called Rishyajihva, marked by the germination of large number of parasites in their inside. The type in which the skin of the patient becomes dry and rough like that of an elephant is called Charmākhyam. The type in which the patches becomes hard and shining like the scales of a fish, dry, itching, flame coloured, can not bear the least touch, and is marked by the absence of perspiration, is called Kitima (keloid tumour). In the Sidhma type, the ulcers become rough in their inside and glossy on the surface. A kind of dust-like effiorescences is obtained by rubbing these patches which are found to be extremely thin and transparent, and are felt flower-like soft to the touch, marked by the absence of perspiration.

The form of Kushtham in which the patches are marked with red marks, being thin at their upper ends, and characterised by an extremely itching sensation, and which appear usually at the hands and legs are called Vipādikā. An excruciating pain and an in tolerable itching sensation mark the several types of Kustham which become studded with red pustules and spread like the roots of Durva grass, tinged with a colour like that of an Atasi flower. In the type known as Dadru (Ring worm), the patches are found to be a little elevated, distributed in ring-like grooves and are attended with an itching sensation. In the type due to the concerted action of the deranged Vāyu, Pittam and Kapham, the patches are found to be thick at the base, marked by bleeding and a burning sensation in the incidental ulcers, which break out in large numbers. Grey, or red coloured, circular patches, attended with pain and burning, appear on the skin of the patient in this type of Leprosy. The type in which raised, reddish, patches, like dried leaves, studded over with white or red-coloured vesicles, appear on the skin, is called Pundarikam. In the type known as Pāmā, the patches are marked by a pain and itching sensation, and assume a reddish or dusky hue, covered over with dry, erysipilatous eruptions, and usually appear about the elbow, hands, and the lumbar region. An excruciating pain and an intolerable burning sensation mark the types known as Kākana, Charmadala etc., The colour of the patches in the Kākana type is at first red which changes into black, resembling the washings of Triphalā. The patches in all tyes of leprosy may subsequently assume a black hue through the agency of their respective exciting factors. The exciting factor in each case should be ascertained with regard to the colour of the leprous patches and the symptoms, specifically developed therein. A case of Kustham originated through the action of any particular morbific principle should be abandoned as incurable, as soon as its complication with the other two of the morbic principles of (Vâyu, Pittam and Kapham) would be detected. A cases of Kushtham in which the virus is found to invade the organic principles of bone, or semen, should be considered as extremely hard to cure. With the help of suitable medicines, the disease may be suppressed, for the time being, in cases where the virus affects the fat only, while a radical cure may be expected in those in which only the fish and bones are affected. Cases of Kushtham, originated through the action of the deranged Vâyu and Kapham, should be regarded as incurable, like those which are confined only to the skin, and do not secrete any discharge or cast any sediment.

Discolouring and dryness of the skin are all that characterise a case of Kushtham confined only to the skin, while perspiration, heat, and swelling at and of the palms of hands and soles of feet, appearance of belbous ulcers about the joints, and an extreme pain are the symptoms which become manifest in cases in which the virus attacks the blood. The adipose tissues of the body seem as if being crushed, and suffer a marked deterioration through the virulence of the deranged Vāyu, Pittam, and Kapham, in this disease. The voice becomes sunk and hollow, the eye sight is impaired, and bones, fat and marrow are destroyed with the progress of this dreadful scourge. The parasites destroy the organic principle of semen in the patient, disqualifyinghim to discharge his conjugal duties. All the abovesaid forms of Kushtham with their respective specific symptoms may attack even the lower animals.

The disease known as S'vitram (Leucoderma) as well as the dreadful Kilâsa originate from the same cause as Kushtham. Both these forms of disease are non-bleeding, and involve the concerted action of the three morbific principles of the deranged Vāyu, Pittam, and Kapham. In the Vâtaja type of S'vitra, the patches become dry and vermil-coloured, while in the Pittaja type they are found to be copper-coloured, like lotus leaves. A burning sensation is present in these patches, and the virus attacks the hairs of the affected parts, causing their entire destruction (them to fall off) in this type. In the Kaphaja type of S'vitra, the patches become thick and white, attended with an itching sensation. The virus gradually and successively attacks the organic principles of blood, flesh, and fat in both these diseases, which become more and more difficult to cure as it invades these succcessive principles. Both S'vitra and Kilāsa (Psoriasis) originate from the same cause, and the patches in similar types of both of them are found to assume the same colour. Cases of recent origin in which the patches are not confluent, and the local hairs have not become white, and which are not the results of burns or scalds, may be expected to be cured, the rest should be given up as incurable. Cases of Kilāsa even of recent origin, in which the spots (patches) are found to appear on the lips, or on the palms of hand, or on the soles of feet, or about the anus, should be specially given up as incurable. All diseases, and cataneous affections in special, are contagious; and are contaminated from one person to another through the use of the same bed, seat, unguent, apparels etc., with a diseased person.

—:o:—

CHAPTER CLXV.

DHANVANTARI said:—Bodily parasites may be divided into two classes according as they are external or internal in their origin. The external parasites of the body, again, may be divided in their turn into four species according as they germinate from mucous secretions, bodily excrements, fecal matter, or blood of the body. Twenty varities of parasites, each with a corresponding epithet of its own, have been enumerated (in the A'yurveda).

The external bodily parasites are but the offspring of the excrementitious matter of the body—vermin of the shape and colour of mustard seeds that usually infest the hairs and wearing apparels of persons of uncleanly habits. Although of extremely attenuated size, they are provided with a large number of tiny legs, *Yukas* and *Likhyas* being the representatives of these species. Two of these species should be regarded as the cause of two different diseases such as Urticaria (*Kotha*) and Itches (*Kandu*). All types of cutaneous affections (*Kushtham*) should be attributed to the presence of parasites in the skin. The external parasites originate from the mucous discbarges or secretions of the body. The deranged Kaphah in the system, augmented through ingestions of incompatible articles of fare as treacle, sweet rice, milk, milk-curd, fish or newly harvested rice, give rise to the germination of a kind of worms, which, when fully developed, spread therefrom all through the organism. Some of them are circular in shape like the solar disc, some of them are shaped like common earth worm, some are long and transparent, while others are like newly sprouting paddy. Some of them are white and striated in shape, while others are copper-coloured. There are seven varieties of internal worms which are respectively named as the *Antrâda* (Gnawer of the intestines), *Udaravesta* (encompasser of the abdomen), *Hridayâda* (eater of the heart), *Mahaguda* (the great rectal one) *Chyura*, *Darbha-Kusuma* (Darbha flower) and *Sugandha* (Odoriferous one). The presence of any of these kinds of parasites in the human system is marked by nausea, water brash, indigestion, swoonings, vomiting, fever, tympanites with suppression of the stool, flatus and urine, emaciation of the body, purging and running at the nose. The extremely small parasites, which are found in the blood or blood-carrying vessels, are round, copper coloured, and are devoid of legs. Several varieties of these parasites are so small as to be invisible to the naked eyes. Six of these species, which have been named as *Kes'âda* (hair-eater), *Roma-Vidhvansa* (destroyer of bodily hairs) *Udamvara* (figcoloured), *Roma dvipa*, *Saurasa*, and *Mâtri* should be regarded as the primary cause of Leprosy and of cutaneous affections in general.

The worms, which grow out of the feces in the intestines, usually travel in a downward direction to the anus, but when fully developed they ascend into the stomach, imparting a smell like feces to breaths, and eructations. Some of these varieties are elongated in shape, some are round, some are extremely attenuated in size, some are white, some black, some yellow, and some brown. They are respectively known as Kakerukas, Makerukas, Sansuradas, Kasulākhyas and Lalehas. Travelling in contrary directions, these intestinal worms produce purging, colic, tympanites, emaciation of the body with dark rings round the eyes, palour, horripilation, impaired digestion, and an itching sensation about the anus.

——:o:——

CHAPTER CLXVI.

DHANVANTARI said :—Hear me, O Sushruta, now discourse on the *Nidânam* of the diseases of the nervous system (*Vâta-Vyâdhi*). A disturbance of the normal equilibrium among the different fundamental principles of the organism is the root of all bodily distempers. The bodily Vāyu, deranged through any unknown or invisible factor, makes the body inert and inoperative. A man should always endeavour to keep his body in health in conjunction with the efforts of Bis'vakarmā, (the architect of the universe), Vis'varupa (the shaper of the universe), Prajāpati (the lord of created beings), Srashtā (creator), Vibhu (lord), Vishnu (the all pervading one) Samhartā (destroyer) and Mrityu (Dealth) to that end.

A correct knowledge of physiological and pathological (*Prâkrita* and *Vaikrita*) processes is necessary for a correct diagnosis of a disease. The combined and several actions of the morbific principles should be taken into consideration in arriving at a correct diagnosis. *Nidânam* (Ætiology), premonitory symptoms, specific features, spontaneous aggravation or amelioration, and the exciting causes are the five factors which are included within the *Prâkrita Karma* (physiological cogitations). I shall now discourse on the causes and symptoms of *Vâta Vyâdhi* (diseases of the nervous system) in the light of this *Prâkrita Karma.* One should at once abjure the use of articles that tend to destroy any fundamental principle of the organism whenever there may be symptoms to indicate that the bodily Vāyu has been agitated or affected by their use. The deranged Vāyu chokes up the orifices of the vessels and keeps them stuffed. The vessels, thus stuffed up with the morbific principles of the body, send the deranged Vāyu to its surface, which, in its turn, chokes up the pores of the skin, causing colic, tympanites, rumbling in the intestines, suppression of the stool, loss of voice, and obstruction of sight, with a catching pain at the waist and back, as precursors to more dreadful diseases.

Vâta Vyâdhi located in (diseases of the nerves of) the stomach gives rise to vomiting, dyspnœa, cough, violent purging, itching sensations and diverse kinds of diseases above the region of the umbilicus. Similarly, the deranged Vāyu, located in the internal ducts (*Srotas*) of the body, produces cracking and dryness of the skin, excruciting pain, sallowness of complexion, symptoms of poisoning, tympanites with a non-relish for food, emaciation of the body, vertigo, glandular growths, and roughness of the skin. The body seems heavy and painful as if it has been violently beaten with a cudgel, and an aching pain is felt in the bones, and vertebraæs. The pain in the bones and vertebraæ becomes so intense as to leave no repose to the patient, who sits up waking in the night. The emission of semen becomes rapid or involuntary when the nerves (Vāyu) of the genito-urinary tracts are affected in this desease, which in a pregnant woman leads to an abortion or miscarriage, and brings on constipation of the bowels with an excruciating head-ache in both the sexes. Swelling and inflammation are found to set in about the place where the enraged Vāyu lies incarcerated, first determining the locality of *Vâta Vyâdhi*, and causing an intense pain to the patient. The body appears like a full water-drum, and the enraged Vāyu, by entering into the joints of the body, produces local atrophy. Lying stuffed through the whole organism, the enraged Vāyu produces an aching pain, throbbing, breaking of skin and bones, numbness of the body, convulsive movements of the limbs, somnolence, and palsy.

When the enraged Vāyu courses through the nerve of the body it produces constant convulsions of the limbs, and the disease, thus generated, is called *A'kshepakâ* (convulsions). The enraged *Vâyu*, any wise obstructed in its downward course, recoils back upon itself, and goes upward, pressing the heart and the templar bones, and the cranium. Thereafter it (Vāyu) spreads through the whole organism, causing the cheek bones of the patient to hang down, numb and paralysed, and producing distortion of the whole face.

The eyes remain permanently open, and the patient suffers from difficulty of breathing, and lies unconscious, moaning indistinctly like a pigeon. This disease is called *Apatantraka*, and is one of the most difficult of difficult diseases to cure. The patient sometimes feels a little respite when the enraged Vāyu with the *esse* of the disease descends into his heart and left nostril, and feels troubles at other times.

A case of paralysis, which is the outcome of a blow or fall, should be regarded as indicating an unfavourable prognosis, or almost beyond the pale of medicine.

The enraged Vāyu, taking lodgment in the internal vital principles of the organism, produces suppression of locomotion, obstruction of the sight, yawning, dirty deposits on the teeth, and loss of energy. This disease is found to further develop the symptoms of numbed pain at the external sides, catching pain about the cheekbones, numbness of the back, headache, curvature or bending of the body on the posterior side, and sensation of heaviness at the back and cardiac region. The patient constantly suffers from fits of vertigo, the shoulders drop down, and the teeth and face of the patient suffers discolouring. A patient, suffering from numbness of the jaws and external curvatare of the body, should be set down as suffering from at attack of *Vâta vyâdhi.* The enraged *Vâyu* in this disease takes lodgment in the blood and excrements of the system, causing the morbific principles to surcharge the whole economy, and producing ulcers, exhaustion, and palour. In all forms of *Vâta Vyâdhi* the patient derives a little comfort from massage.

Ingestion of extremely hot food, and excessive scraping of the tongue are the factors which tend to enrage the local Vāyu, which produces paralysis of the cheek bones and mandibles, causing the closing of the mouth, or keeping it fixedly open and gaping. Chewing of extremely hard substances, and constant speaking in an overloud tone are the factors, which, by enraging the local Vāyu, and causing it to be incarcerated in the nerves traversing the organs of speech, bring about a paralysis of the tongue, which ultimately spreads to the muscles of the cheekbones and mandibles. In cases of paralysis of the tongue, digestation of food, drinking, and articulation of speech become seriously hampered or almost impossible. Carrying of extremely heavy loads on the head, loud laughters, loud talkings, resting of head on a hard and uneven pillow, and chewing of extremely hard articles of fare are the factors that tend to enrage the local *Vâyu,* which takes lodgment in the upper part of the body. Similarly, the face of a man may suffer permanent distortion through loud laughing, or looking suddenly with extremely dilated eyes, or through injudicious straining of the eyes. In this type of (faceal) paralysis, the tongue loses the faculty of speech, and the eyes become numbed and motionless. Gnashing of the teeth, loss of voice, impairment of hearing and sight, loss of smell and memory, fright, anguish and dyspnœa are the distressing supervening symptoms which are manifested in almost all types of *Vâta Vyâdhi*; ptyalism, pain at the sides, incapacity of closing the eye-lids with an excruciating pain in the upper part of the body and hemiphlegia being its further characteristics. Several autherities call the first named disease as *Arditam* (faceal paralysis) and the last named one as *Ekânga Vyâdhi* (Hemiphlegia)

The enraged Vâyu, by interfering with the flow of blood in the arteries, and specially in those that traverse the head, produces a kind of hemicrania in which rough, black veins appear on the regions of the temple. This type of head-ache is incurable. The enraged Vâyu, by affecting the nerves and ligaments of the body, produces a kind of disease that strikes down either half of the body. The disease is called *Paksha-Vadha* in which the organs and members of the affected side become inert and inoperative, and lose all sensations. This disease is also called *Kaksha-roga* by several authorities. Similarly, the disease, in which the enraged Vâyu instead of striking down either half of the body paralyses the whole of it, is called *Sarvânga Roga*. Cases of paralysis, which are due to the action of only the enraged Vâyu, are curable, while those which are complicated with the presence of two of the morbific principles (*Doshas*), together with those in which all the characterestic symptoms are fully developed, should be regarded as incurable, as they invariably prove fatal. The disease, in which the course of the Vāyu, acting in concert with the deranged *Kapham*, is obstructed by mucous, and which is characterised by the loss of sensation, is called *Dandápatánaka*. The disease, in which the enraged Vāyu contracts up the muscles that start up from behind the shoulder blades and in which all movements of the arms are lost, is called *Avaváhuka* (Ebb's paralysis).

The disease in which the enraged Vāyu paralyses the *Kandará*, that runs down the back of the arms, extending to the tips of the fingers, is called *Vis'vachi*. The disease in which the enraged Vāyu, taking lodgment in the region of the waist, draws up the great sacral muscles, producing lameness, is called *Khanja*. The disease in which both the knees are deprived of their strength and become inoperative is called *Pangu*. The type of *Váta Vyádhi* in which the patient walks in a tottering gait and the joints of the legs seem loose and unsteady is called *Kaláya Khanja*. The deranged Kaphah in conjunction with the fat gets augmented through the ingestion of extremely cold, hot, dry, fluid, heavy (indigstable) or emulsive articles of fare, or through excessive or extremely fatiguing physical labour immediately before or after the digestion of a meal, or through the effect of a blow, hurt or mental anguish, or through excessive night keeping, and the deranged Kaphah tends to defile the other fundamental principles of the organism as well. The deranged Kaphah, by being stuffed about thigh bones, produces numbness in the locality, which results in looseness of the thighs, which are felt cold to the touch. The complexion assumes a dull twany brown hue; the patient feels as if he has been packed in a wet blanket, and fever, somolence, epileptic fits with a non-relish for food supervene. This disease is called *Uru-stambha*, while several authorities designate it as *Váhya Vátam*. An extremely painful swelling occurring about the locality between the thigh and the knee joint is called *Kroshtuka-*

Sirsha. A false step made at the time of walking, or a long pedestrian journey may give rise to an excruciating aching pain in the insteps which is called *Vâta Kantakam.* This disease is due to an aggravated condition of the deranged Vāyu of the locality. An extremely aching pain produced by the deranged bodily Vāyu in the toes, in the sides of thighs, and about the regions of throat and umbilicus is called *Gridhrasi* (sciatica). The disease in which the deranged Vāyu and Kaphah produce a complete anæsthesia in the lower limbs, which become insensible to pinches and are characterised by constant horripilation, is called *Pâdaharsha.* The disease in which through the agency of the deranged Vāyu and Pittam being combineed with blood, the patient complains of an intolerable burning sensation in the lower limbs, which is little alleviated on locomotion, is called *Pâdadâha.*

——:o:——

CHAPTER CLXVII.

DHANVANTARI said :—Now hear me, O Sushruta, discourse on the *Nidânam* of *Vâta-raktam.* The blood and the bodily Vāyu of a person, enraged and aggravated through ingestion of incompatible articles of fare, or through indulgence in day sleep or extreme irascibility, or through excessive night keeping, produces the disease known as *Vâta Raktam.* Persons of soft or delicate physical temperament, as well as fat men and persons of luxurious living are extremely susceptible to an attack of *Vâta-Raktam.* Similarly, a blow or an injury to any part of the body, may lead to vitiation of blood, and the bodily Vāyu, deranged through ingestion of extremely cold, phlegmagoguic articles of fare, follows a wrong path ; or on the other band the Vāyu obstructed in its course by the blood, vitiated through aforesaid causes, first produces its own specific symptoms. The disease is so named from the fact that the bodily Vâyu is first deranged. Profuse perspiration (in most cases), emaciation of the body, anæsthesia, or an excruciating pain in a pre-existing ulcar, looseness of the joints, lassitude with a gone feeling in the limbs, pustular eruptions with an aching, breaking, piercing, throbbing pain in the thighs, knee-joints, and calves of legs, and about the sacrum and joints of the extremities, heaviness and loss of sensation in the foregoing parts and numbness of the body, itching sensation in the affected localities, heaviness of the limbs, pain in (the affected parts) which vanishes at intervals, discolouration of the skin and appearance of circular patches on the skin are the symptoms which mark the premonitory stage of Vâta-Raktam.

In the Vâtaja type of this disease the patient suffers from an extremely excruciating pain in the affected parts, which become further characterized by an aching, throbbing pain. The swelling is felt rough to the touch and assumes a black or reddish-brown hue, spontaneously increasing or decreasing at intervals. The body seems numbed and extremely painful, the joints and vessels of fingers become contracted, and the patient evinces a repugnance for cold which fails to give any relief whatsoever. The numbness of the body becomes prominent, and the patient suffers from rigour and a complete anæsthesia in the affected parts.

In the type marked by predominant action of the enraged and vitiated blood, the swelling is marked by a greater aching pain, and becomes copper coloured. The disease does not yield to emulsive or parchifying measures (such as fomentation etc.,) and is marked by a tingling sensation. The patient feels an irresistible tendency to scratch the patches which exude a slimy discharge. In the Pittaja type of Vâta-Raktam, perspiration with a burning sensation in the body, vertigo, epileptic fits, thirst and distraction of the mind are the symptoms which manifest themselves. The swelling can not bear the least touch, becomes red and hot, and is ultimately found to suppurate.

In the Kaphaja type of Vâta-Raktam, heaviness, coldness, and anæsthesia of the affected parts become manifest. The swelling looks glossy, is marked by a slight pain and an itching sensation, and seems as if it has been tied with a wet compress. Types of Vâta-Raktam, which are connected with the action of any two of the *Doshas* (morbific principles of Vâyu, Pittam and Kaphah), exhibit symptoms which are respectively peculiar to types brought about through their several actions, while the type, which is due to the concerted action of all the three *Doshas*, combinedly develop the symptoms, severally belonging to the Vâtaja, Pittaja and Kaphaja types of Vâta-Raktam.

The virus, like the poison of a mouse, first affects the lower parts of the legs, or is seen to invade the extremities of hands in certain instances, and thenceforth spreads over the whole organism. A case of Vâta-Raktam, which has extended upward to the thighs, and in which the skin of the affected part breaks and exudes a discharge, and in which the patient suffers from loss of strength and flesh, or which is complicated with a host of other distressing symptoms, should be regarded as incurable, while palliation is the only treatment in a case of more than a year's standing. Similarly, cases of Vâta-Raktam marked by such supervening distresses as, insomnia with a non-relish for food, dyspnœa, sloughing of flesh, hemicrania, epileptic, fits, vertigo, pain, thirst, fever, loss of consciousness, rigour, hiccough, maimedness of gait, erysipelas, suppuration (of the affected parts), langour, curvature of the fingers, crops of pustular eruptions with a burning sensation in the body, and tumours with a catching pain at any of the nerve-unions, bone-unions, or vein-unions, as well as the one which is accompanied by epileptic fits alone, should be understood as incurable. Cases of Vâta-Raktam, uncomplicated with any distressing, supervening symptoms, are curable, while those attended with a few concomitants admit only of palliative treatment. Cases of Vâta-Raktam originated through the action of a single *Dosha* (morbific principle) are curable, while those of recent origin, and at the root of which only two *Doshas* lie, admit of palliative treatment. Cases of Vâta-Raktam of which the three *Doshas* conjointly act as the exciting factors, as well as those which are connected with a host of other complications, should be regarded as incurable.

—:o:—

CHAPTER CLXVIII.

HEAR me, O Sushruta, now discourse on the Nidânam of Mukhoroga. Ingestion of such incompatible articles of fare as milk, mild-curd, and fishes living in swamps, in inordinate quantities, tends to enrage the *Doshas*, which give rise to a number of diseases in the mouth. A predominance of the deranged Kaphah should be understood as the exciting factor of all these distempers. The lips seem numbed and hard, are felt rough to the touch, and are characterised by a kind of bursting, thrashing pain in their body, through the aggravation of the deranged Vâyu. In the Pittaja type of this disease, the lips assume a yellowish hue, become studded with crops of painful pustules, and are characterised by a burning sensation. In the Kaphaja type of this disease the lips assume a colour peculiar to that morbific principle (Kaphah) and become cold, glossy and slimy. In the Sânnipâtika type of this disease the lips assume a varied colour, successively changing from black (blue) to yellow and from yellow to white, and become studded with crops of pustular eruptions. In the type brought about through the agency of vitiated blood, crops of pustular eruptions, coloured like ripe date fruits, are found to appear on the lips, which bleed and are marked with streaks of blood. In the type due to the vitiation of the local flesh, the lips become thick and heavy, and are gathered up in knots like condylomatous growths. Vermins, which are often found to germinate in the affected lips, drop down from the two corners of the mouth. In the type due to the action of the deranged fat (areolar tissues) the lips assume a colour like that of the surface layer of clarified butter, and become heavy and marked by an itching sensation, and secrete a copious secretion of cold, crystal-like, white fluid. An ulcer occurring in such diseased lips can never be healed, nor it may be softened with the help of any medicine. In the traumatic type the lips seem as if they are being chopped with an axe.

Now hear me discourse on the Nidânam of diseases that affect the gums of teeth. The disease in which the gums are found to bleed without any apparent reason, and in which they become spongy, black and shiny, and emit a fetid smell, and begin to slough off, is called S'itâda. This disease is attributed to the action of the deranged blood and Kaphah. The disease in which large swellings (boils) appear about the root of two or three of the teeth is called Dantapupputaka, which is attributed to the action of the deranged Kaphah and blood. The disease, in which the teeth move and become loose, and the gums are found to bleed and to secrete pus, is called Danta-Veshta, of which the vitiated blood acts as the (sole) exciting factor. A painful swelling brought about through the agency of the deranged Kaphah and Vâyu and appearing over the gums, accompanied by salivation and an itching sensation, is called S'aus'ira. The disease in which the teeth move about in their sockets, the gums slough off, the roof of the palate cracks and bursts open, and the lining membrane of the cavity of the mouth is inflammed is called Mahâ Saushira. This disease is engendered by the concerted action of the deranged Vâyu, Pittam, and Kaphah. The disease in which the gums become thin, and the patient spits blood, is called Paridara which is due to the action of the deranged blood, Pittam and Kaphah. The disease in which a burning sensation is felt in the gums which are ultimately found to suppurate, and the teeth become loose in their sockets, which when moved about with the hand, seem slightly painful and bleed, and in which the gums swell and a fetor comes out of the mouth if that bleeding is arrested, is called Supakusha, of which the deranged blood and Pittam act as the exciting factors. The disease in which inflammation occurs about the gums, if in any way rubbed, and the teeth are found to move about in their sockets, is called Vaidarbha, which should be regarded as of a traumatic origin. The disease in which the enraged and aggravated Vâyu serves to force up an additional tooth, accompanied by an excruciating pain, and in which the pain subsides on the perfect cutting of that additional tooth, is called Khalivardhana. A large swelling occurring about the gums, attended with pain and a burning sensation, is called Danta-Vidradhi (abscess of the gums), which, when lanced off, secretes blood and pus. A large and extremely painful swelling occurring about the posterior side of the last molar tooth is called Adhimânsaka. This disease is due to the action of the deranged Kaphah and is marked by a copious salivation. The sinus of the gums developes the same characteristic features as the five kinds of ordinary sinuses.

Now hear me, O child discourse on the Nidânam of diseases that affect the teeth. The disease in which a bursting pain is felt in the bodies of the teeth, is called Dâlana, which is due to the action of the deranged Vâyu. The disease in which black holes are made into the teeth, which become loose, and in which an extremely painful inflammation occurs about their roots, which is aggravated by an exposure to air, is called Krimi Dantaka. The disease in which the face is distorted and the teeth are broken is called Bhanjana. This disease is due to the action of the deranged Kaphah and Vâyu. The disease in which the teeth become incapable of bearing the least wind or the touch of any dry, cold or acid substance is called Dantaharsha (tooth-edge), of which the deranged Vâyu and Pittam act as the exciting factors. The disease in which the deranged Vâyu, by taking recourse to the teeth, make them jagged and uneven is called Karâla, which should be regarded as incurable. Deposits of refuge (calcareous) matter on the teeth, dried up and hardened through the action of the Vâyu and Pittam, become crystalised like sugar. These Crystals are called Danta-Sharkarâs. When these crystalised deposits are extracted they invariably destroy the teeth. This disease is called Kapâlika from the resemblance of the cracked deposits with bits of skeletal bones *(Kapâla)*. The disease in which the teeth, burned through the action of the deranged Pittam and blood, assume a black or blue colour, is called Shyâva-Dantaka.

Now hear me discourse on the Nidânam of Mukha-Rogam which invades the tongue. In diseases of the tongue due to the action of the deranged Vâyu, the tongue is cracked and covered over with a greenish deposit, resembling the paste of S'aka leaves. In diseases of the tongue, due to the action of the deranged Pittam, the tongue becomes studded over with yellowish or red-coloured papillæ attended with a burning sensation in its body. In diseases of the tongue, due to the actionof the deranged Kaphah the tongue becomes heavy and is covered over with a large number of fleshy growths (papillæ) resembling the throns of a Shâlmali tree. A deep swelling, occurring on the lower side of, and paralysing the tongue, is called Alasa, which is due to the action of the deranged Kaphah and blood. A swelling, resembling the tip of a tongue in shape, and occurring about the root of the tongue, so as to raise it up, is called Upajihva. This disease is due to the action of the deranged Kaphah and blood, and is attended with profuse salivation and a burning sensation in the inside of the tongue.

Now hear me discourse on the Nidânam of diseases that affect the palate. An extremely large and elongated swelling, due to the action of the deranged Kaphah and blood, and occurring about the root of the palate is called Kantha-Sunthi. The swelling assumes the shape of an inflated bladder, and thirst, cough, and dyspnœa are found to supervene. A thick swelling occurring at the root of the palate, attended with burning and suppuration, is called Tundakeri by the wise. A swelling of the palate due to the action of the vitiated blood is called Dhrushuna. It is of slow growth and is attended with fever and an extreme pain. A swelling, due to the action of the deranged Kaphah and occurring about the palate, raised like the back of a tortoise, is called Kachchhapa. This swelling is very slow in its growth. A circular swelling at the palate, characterised by all the specific features of a blood-tumour is called Tâlvarvuda. Painless condylomatous growths, brought about through the agency of the deranged Kapbah, are called Mânsa-Sanghâta. A jujube like fixed growth at the palate, unattended with pain, is called Tâlupupputa. In the disease known as Talupâk the palate is cracked, a dry parchifying (arid) sensation is experienced therein, dyspnœa is present tbrough the agency of the deranged Vâyu, and the deranged Pittam induces suppuration.

Now hear me discourse, O child, on the Nidânam of diseases peculiar to the throat. The deranged Vâyu and Pittam, by lying incarcerated in the throat, vitiates the local flesh and blood, and gives rise to membranous growths, which resemble paddy sprouts in shape and produce constriction (choking) of the passage of the throat, which results in death. This disease is called Rohini. The type of Rohini in which the entire tongue becomes numbed and extremely painful, and in which membranous growths, obstructing the passage of the throat, are formed, attended with the specific symptoms of the deranged and aggravated Vâyu, should be regarded as belonging to the Vâtaja type. In the Pittaja type of Rohini the membranous growths are rapid in their formation and speedily suppurate. Fever becomes intense and symptoms peculiar to the deranged Pittam are found to supervene. In the Kaphaja type of Rohini, the membranous growth are fixed and do not obstruct the passage of the throat (larynx). The type due to the concerted action of the deranged Vâyu, Pittam and Kaphah should be regarded as incurable in as much as suppuration sets in in the deeper strata of the membranous growths in this type. In the type due to the vitiation of blood, the membranous growths become studded with crops of red pustules and prove amenable to treatment, the other characteristics of this type being common with those of the Pittaja class. A fixed nodular growth in the throat, to the size of a jujube-stone, brought about through the action of the deranged Kaphah is called Kantha Shâluka. The patient in this disease feels as if his throat has been studded with the bristles of a S'uka insect or thorns have pricked into it. The growth is rough to the touch and should be removed only with the knife. A swelling of the shape of the tip of the tongue, streaked with blood, is called Adhijihva. This disease is attributed to the action of the deranged Kaphah, and a patient suffering from Adhijihva should be abandoned as soon as suppuration would be found to have been established in the swelling. A circular (ring-like) elevated swelling around the passage of the throat, threatening to constrict the orifice of the œsophagns, is called Valaya. This disease is incurable and a patient suffering from Valaya should be given up as lost from its very out-set. A swelling caused by the deranged Vâyu and Kaphah in the throat, and which is attended with pain and dyspnœa, is called Valása. Expert physicians stand in dread of this disease, and pronounce it incurable. A raised and circular swelling in the throat caused by the deranged Kaphah and blood is called Ekâvrindâ. The swelling but scarcely suppurates and is felt a little soft to the touch, itching and burning sensations in the swelling being the further characteristics of this disease.

A thick, stick-like growth in the throat, studded over with fleshy papillæ and attended with diverse kinds of pain, is called Shataghni. This disease is attributed to the concerted action of the deranged Vâyu, Pittam and Kaphah, and invariably proves fatal. A fixed growth in the throat to the size of an Amalaka seed, brought about through the agency of the deranged Kaphah and blood, is called Shilâyu. This disease in which the patient thinks that a morsel of food lies stuck into the throat is a purely surgical one. An extensive swelling, covering the entire passage of the throat and characterised by an uniform pain all through its inside, is called Gala-Vidradhi. This disease is due to the concerted action of the deranged Vâyu etc. An extensive swelling in the throat, due to the action of the deranged Kaphah, which obstructs the deglutition of food and water, and closes the orifice of the larynx, is called Galaugha. This disease is always attended with high fever. The disease in which the patient, with a parched throat and mouth, suffers from difficult breathing owing to the choking of the bronchial tubes with mucous and which is further characterised by epileptic fits and hoarseness is called Svaraghna. An extremely pendent painful swelling with membranous offshoots, which gradually tends to close the passage of the throat, is called Mânsatâna. This disease is brought about through the concerted action of the deranged Vâyu, Pittam and Kaphah and invariably ends in death. An extensive copper-coloured swelling in the throat and mouth attended with an aching pain and a burning sensation, and in which the flesh of the affected part is found to slough off, is called Vidâri. This disease is attributed to the deranged Pittam and affects the same side of the throat on which the patient usually lies.

Now I shall describe the Nidânam of diseases that affect the entire cavity of the mouth (Sarvasara). In the Vâtaja type of Sarvasara Mukha-Roga (stomatitis) pustules attended with an aching pain appear all over the cavity of the mouth. In the Pittaja type of this disease red or yellowish pustules are found to crop up over the entire lining membrane of the mouth in which a burning sensation is also felt, while in the Kaphaja type painless, itching pustules appear on the lining membrane of the mouth. The type of Ostha-prapâka due to the action of the vitiated flesh and blood as well as the one due to the concerted action of the deranged Vâyu, Pittam and Kaphah, should be given up as incurable. Of diseases of the gums, sinuses, due to the concerted action of the deranged Vâyu, Pittam and Kaphah should be pronounced incurable; of diseases affecting the teeth those known as Shaushira and Bhanjana should be regarded as incurable. Of diseases of the throat Svaraghna, Valâsa, Vrinda, Shataghni, Vidâri and Rohini should be regarded as incurable. Of diseases of the tongue Valâsha and Tâlvârvuda should be regarded as incurable.

—:o:—

CHAPTER CLXIX.

Now hear me, O Sushruta, discourse on the Nidânam of Karnaroga (diseases of the ear). The deranged Vâyu, by coursing through the vessels of the ears, produces an extremely aching sensation therein which is called Karna-shula (Otalgia). The vessels in their turn are choked up by the morbific principles (doshas) in this disease when the deranged Vâyu lies incarcerated in the ducts of the ears. The patient hears a variety of sounds such as of drums, trumpets, etc.

When the deranged Vâyu affects the sound-carrying nerves of the ears, deafness is the result in as much as they are choked up with the deranged Kaphah. The deranged Vâyu in conjunction with the deranged Pittam produces a flute-like sound in the ears. This disease is called Karna-ksheda. The disease in which on account of a hurt or injury to, or through the effect of long keeping the head immersed in water, or through the suppuration of a (local) abscess, pus is discharged from the ears, is called Karna-pâka.

The deranged local Vâyu in conjunction with the deranged Kaphah produces an itching sensation in the ducts of the ears which is called Karna-kandu. The deranged Kaphah, dried up by the heat of the Pittam, is transformed into a waxy substance called Karna-Guthakam. The same waxy substance, when melted, enters into the cavities of the mouth and nostrils and gives rise to a disease which is called Karna-Pratinâha, which is characterised by an aching sensation in the half of the body. The disease in which parasites or vermins, exist or germinate in the ducts of the ears is called Krimi-karnaka by the wise. Insects and Shatapadis by entering into the cavities of the ears produce a buzzing sound and pain therein. An extremely aching pain is felt when the insect moves about in the ear, which subsides when the insect lies still and quiet. Abscesses may also grow in the ears through the effects of blows or injuries, or through the agency of any of the deranged morbific principles, secreting a reddish or yellowish coloured discharge accompanied by a burning, sucking sensation. The patient feels as if fumes are escaping out of the affected ear-duct. The waxy deposit in the ears melted through the agency of the aggravated Pittam tends to set up a flow of pus from the ducts of the ears. Similar secretions from inflammed ear-ducts may be established as a consequence of a bursting abscess. The disease in which fetid pus is discharged from the ears is called Puti-karnam. The Nidânas of Abscesses, hæmorrhoids, Arvuds or other pappilatous growths in the ear-ducts are same as those described under their respective general heads.

In the Vâtaja type of the disease of the ears, the patient hears a variety of sounds in his ears which become extremely painful. The waxy deposits in the ears are dried up and a thin fluid is discharged from the ears, with loss of the faculty of hearing. In the Pittaja type of ear-disease red coloured swellings attended with a burning sensation crop up in the ears, which are found to discharge a fetid yellow coloured pus. In the Kaphaja type of this disease, the ears lose the faculty of correctly locating the sound or to catch it correctly, an itching sensation is experienced and hard swellings appear in the ears, which discharge a white glossy fluid, attended with a slight pain. In the Sânnipâtika type, the specific symptoms of all the several types of ear-diseases (Otalgia) enumerated above conjointly manifest themselves, and the predominant morbific principle (Dosha) in these cases impart its peculiar colour to the secretion, and tends to determine its nature as well.

Swelling and inflammation of the soft appendages of the ears (ear-lobes) brought about in consequence of an attempt at getting them elongated, and which burst out and assume a blackish (bluish) colour, should be attributed to the action of the deranged and aggravated Vâyu of the locality. The disease is called Paripolaka. A red or reddish brown swelling of the ear-lobes, brought about through actions of the Doshas in the part, or through the effect of wearing heavy ear-ornaments attended with a burning sensation and suppuration and pain is called Upapâka. This disease is attributed to the action of the enraged blood and Pittam of the locality. A slightly painful swelling occurring about the lobulus through the effect of forcibly drawing it, attended with an itching sensation and a little numbness is called Unmathaka. This disease is attributed to the action of the deranged Vâyu and Kaphah of the locality. A swelling of the earlobes attended with an itching, burning sensation and pain in consequence of their perforation, or of their being violently pulled or attempted to be elongated is called Duhkhavardhanam, which should be attributed to the concerted action of the three morbific principles of the body (Sânnipâtika).

Parasites (krimi), offspring of the deranged Kaphah and vitiated blood, give rise to swellings about the ear-lobes attended with pain and itching, burning sensations. These pustular eruptions, engendered through the action of the deranged Kaphah and vitiated blood are gradually found to spread over and invade the concha and lobes of the ears. This disease is called Parichi.

—:o:—

CHAPTER CLXX.

Now hear me, O Sushruta, discourse on the Nidânam of the diseases of the nose. In the disease known as Pinasa or Apinasa the nostrils (passages of the nose) seem to be stuffed with the Vâyu-dried Kaphah, and the patient complains of warm vapours escaping out of his nostrils. The faculties of smell and taste are affected in this disease, which, like nasal catarrh (Pratisyâya) should be attributed to the action of the deranged Vâyu and Kaphah. The disease in which the Vâyu aggravated through the several actions of the Pittam, Kaphah and blood, and finding lodgment in the larynx and the root of the palate, is emitted with a fetid smell through the nostrils is called Putinasyam (fetid-nose) by the wise. The disease in which the deranged Pittam, lodged in the nose, gives rise to inflammation and crops of pustular eruptions in the nostrils, or in which the nostrils alternately becom edry and moist (with a mucous discharge) is called Nâsâpâka. The disease in which blood-mixed pus is discharged from the nostrils through actions of the morbific principles of the body, or through the effect of any blow or injury on the forehead, is called Puya-raktam. The disease in which the deranged and aggravated Vâyu, by taking recourse to the Sringâtaka Marma in the nose, is expelled with mucous through the nostrils, is called Kshavathu (sneezing). Ingestion of irritating articles of fare (such as mustard, etc.,) smell of any strong-smelling or irritating substance, looking at the sun, tickling of the septum of the nostrils with a thread, etc., are the factors which may likewise produce sneezing. The disease in which thick mucous, previously accumulated in the head, is liquefied and acquires a saline taste on account of being exposed to the heat of the deranged Pittam, and is emitted through the nostrils, is called Bhransakam. In the disease known as Diptam the patient complains of an intolerable burning sensation in the nose and thinks as if hot fumes are escaping out of his nostrils. The disease in which the deranged Vâyu and Kaphah tend to choke up the passages of the nostrils, is called Pratinaha. The disease in which a thick or thin, white or yellow mucous is discharged from the nostrils, is called Nâsâsrâva (fluent coryza). The disease in which the natural moisture of the mucous membrane of the passages of the nose, absorbed through the action of the deranged Vâyu, and heated (parchified) through the action of the deranged Pittam, produces difficulty of breathing is called Nâsa-S'osa. In the acute or immature stage of Pinasam (nasal catarrh) the patient suffers from heaviness of the head and feels a repugnance for all kinds of food. The voice becomes weak, and the discharge (from the nostrils) thin and constant. The mature stage of the disease is marked by all these symptoms with the exception that sound becomes clear and pronounciation of words more distinct, and the mucous discharges from the nostrils are thickened and remain stuck to the walls of the nostrils. The disease known as Pratis'yâya admits of being grouped under two heads such as Sadya (brought on the very day the exciting factors are present) and that which is brought on after the accumulation and aggravation of the morbific principles lying at the root of the disease. Voluntary repression of any natural urging of the body and indigestion, vapours and particles of dust getting into the nostrils, excessive talking or irascibility, unnatural seasons, night-keeping, day-sleep, use of extremely cold water, exposure to frost or mist, coition, weeping, and any thing, that engenders heat in the head, are the factors which tend to thicken the mucous in the head. The Vâyu, enraged and aggravated in consequence, instantaneously brings on Sadya Pratis'yâya.

The different morbific principles of the body, gradually accumulating in the head, and by being aggravated by their respective exciting factors, bring on the second form of Prastis'yâya. Sneezing, heaviness of, or a numbed feeling in, the head, aching of the limbs, horripilation, feeling as if hot fumes escaping out of the nostrils, burning in the palate, lachrymation and running at the eyes are the symptoms which mark the premonitory stage of this disease. In the Vâtaja type of Pratis'yâya, the nostrils seem choked or stuffed and a discharge of mucous flows out from the nostrils, the lips, palate and throat seem dry or parched, a pricking pain is felt in the regions of the temples, sneezing becomes constant and the voice hoarse or week, and a vapid taste is felt in the mouth. In the Pittaja type of Pratis'yâya a flow of hot or yellowish mucous is discharged from the nostrils, the complexion becomes pale and sallow, the patient begins to lose flesh and complains of heat in the body and feels as if hot fumes are escaping out of his nostrils. In the Kaphaja type of Pratis'yâya there is a profuse discharge of grey mucous from the nostrils. The eyes and complexion of the patient become white. There is a tight feeling around the head and the patient complains of an itching sensation in the lips and throat, and about the palate.

Cases of Pratis'yâya, whether mature (Pakka) or immature (Apakka), which know many relapses after being spontaneously subsided, and in which the specific symptoms of the three several Doshas manifest themselves in unison, should be regarded as of a Sânnipâtika origin. The type of Pratis'yâya in which there is a fetid smell in the breath and the patient loses the faculty of smell, and in which the apertures of the nose seem dry or moist, stuffed or dilated at intervals, is called Dushta (bad) Pratis'yâya (catarrh). Cases of this type of nasal catarrh are extremely hard to cure. In the type known asRakta-Pratis'yâya the nose bleeds, the eyes assume a bloody or blood-shot aspect, the breath exhales a fetid smell, the faculty of smell is lost or impaired, and the patient suffers from a pain about the chest. Neglected or not properly remedied at the outset, all cases of nasal catarrh may run into those of Dushta Pratis'yâya type, which are extremely hard to cure, or prove irremedible in certain instances. Small parasites are found to germinate in the mucous discharge in Dushta Pratis'yâya (Rakta-Pratis'yâya according to others) which serve to produce symptoms which ordinarily characterise cases of S'iroroga (diseases of the head, Cephalagia). Discharges of thick mucous which are the specific features of chronic cases of Pratis'yâya may bring on blindness, deafness, loss of smell, impairment of the digestive faculty, cough, and a host of other diseases of the eyes. Seven forms of tumours, four kinds of œdematous swellings, four kinds of polypous growths and four types of Hæmorrhage (Rakta Pittam) are found to invade the nose in addition to diseases described above.

CHAPTER CLXXI.

Now hear me, O Sushruta, discourse on the Nidánam of the diseases of the eyes. Plunging into water when the body is extremely heated, straining of the eyes to observe objects which are extremely small, or remote, excessive sleep or wakefulness, injudicious emesis, suppression of urgings towards vomiting, particles of dust or beads of perspiration dropping into the eyes, or exposure of the eyes to dust and glare, ingestion of large quantities of liquid food in the night, voluntary suppression of urgings towards urination or defecation, continuous weeping, indulgence in grief, or in anger, irascibility, injury to the head, excessive use of wine, contrary seasons, over-fatiguing physical labour, sexual excesses, and looking through mists or vapours are the factors which tend to derange the local Vâyu, Pittam and Kaphah which bring on a host of occular affections. The Vâyu, Pittam, Kaphah and blood serve as the exciting factors of the four several types of Opthalmia (Abhishyanda) which may be described as the parent of all kinds of eye-diseases. An aching, pricking pain in the eyes, horripilation, dryness and a sense of irritation in the eyes, heat in the head and flowing of cold tears are the symptoms which mark the Vátaja type of Abhishyanda. Burning and inflammation of the eyes, relief after cold contact, feeling as if hot fumes escaping out of the eyes, yellowness of the conjunctiva and flow of hot tears are the symptoms which mark the Pittaja type of Abhishyanda. Relief after warm contact, heaviness and swelling of the eyes, profuse deposit of sticky mucous in the corners of, and an itching sensation in, the eyes, and constant lachrymation are the symptoms which mark the Kaphaja type of Abhishyanda. Flow of copper-coloured tears from the eyes, redness of the conjunctiva, appearance of red veins upon sclerotic, as well as symptoms which mark the Pittaja type of Abhishyanda manifest themselves in the type due to the action of the enraged and vitiated blood of the locality.

Cases of Abhishyanda, aggravated by the aforesaid causes, and not properly cared for and remedied, soon run into those of Adhimantha (conjunctivitis) of which an excruciating pain in the eyes forms the chief characteristic. The eyes seem as if they are being thrashed and plucked out; and half of the head seems as if being hammered. These are the specific features of Adhimantha. A case of Kaphaja Adhimantha destroys the eye-sight within seven days. In a case of Raktaja Adhimantha the sight is destroyed within five nights. In a case of Vâtaja Adhimantha the sight is destroyed within six nights, while in a case of Pittaja Adhimantha the eye-sight may be destroyed on the very day of the attack, if the regimen of diet and conduct is not properly observed. During the immature (acute) stage of Adhimantha the redness, swelling, and aching pain in the eyes continue unabated. The pricking sensation as well as irritation in the eyes remain undiminished and lachrymation is markedly profuse. During the mature (Pákká) stage, the inflammation, pain, and itching sensation in the eyes are diminished, lachrymation is arrested and the eyes are found to resume their natural colour. The disease in which the eyes are inflammated and assume the colour of ripe Audumvara fruits, attended with heat, lachrymation, and an itching sensation in their inside is called Netrapâkah, which is due to Kaphah. The disease in which the enraged Vâyu, by taking recourse to the vessels of the weak or impaired eyes, withers them up like withered lotus-flowers, and destroys the eye-sight, is called Hatádhimantha, which should be regarded as incurable. The disease in which the enraged and aggravated Váyu alternately gives rise to diverse kinds of intolerable pain in the eyes and about the eye-brows is called Vátaparyáya.

The disease in which the eye-lids remain closed and a burning sensation is felt in the eyes and the vision becomes cloudy, and in which the patient feels an excruciating pain in opening the eye-lids is called S'ushkákshi-páka. The disease in which the enraged and aggravated Váyu, lying incarcerated about the Manyâ (muscles of the neck) and Avatu, gives rise to extreme pain in the eyes and about the eye-brows is called Anyatováta by experts in eye-diseases. In the disease known as Amladhyushita, the middle of the eyes assume a bluish hue and the corners become red-coloured, attended with swelling, lachrymation, and a burning sensation in their bodies. This disease is due to the enragement of the deranged Pittam through the ingestion of large quantitics of boiled rice. In the disease known as S'irotpáta the vessels (veins) of the eyes are marked either by the presence or absence of pain and become either copper-coloured or discoloured. Neglected at the outset this disease may run into one, known as S'irapraharsha, in which thick copper-coloured tears are found to be discharged from the eyes and the patient becomes incapable of seeing anything.

A depressed white spot like the puncture of a needle, occurring on the iris, attended with pain and warm discharge, is called Savrana Sukta. Such Savrana Suktas, not occurring too close to the pupils, nor in couples, and unattended with pain and discharge, are curable, otherwise they are incurable. Non-ulcerative opaque spots are likewise found to appear on the iris. They are coloured either like conch-shells, or Kunda flowers and resemble thin shreds of white clouds in shape. They are easily curable. Non-ulcerative opaque spots, affecting two or three successive layers of sclerotic, should be regarded as incurable, But such opaque spots, which are perforated in the middle owing to the bursting of their centres, or which are deep or indented, or are covered with fleshy over-growths, or are covered with shreds of red-coloured veins which are found to pulsate, or affect the two coats of the sclerotic, or threaten to destroy the eye-sight should be regarded as incurable. Opaque spots in the eyes, attended with hot lachrymation and crops of pustular eruptions resembling Mudga pulse in shape, should be regarded as incurable. The disease in which the entire surface of the iris is covered over with such opaque spots is called Pakshapákátyayam. This disease should be attributed to the concerted action of the three Doshas and regarded as incurable. Reddish, fatty growths covering the entire surface of the iris, like dry excrements of goats, and attended with extreme pain, and a thick, shiny, copper-coloured discharge, is called Ajakajátam. This disease has its seat in the third coat of the sclerotic. Objects appear dim when the morbific principles lie incarcerated about the pupils. Optical illusions result from the incarceration of the morbific principles in the second coat of the sclerotic. Moats in the sun-beam, halo round the sun, and insects' images are seen to fly before the eyes when the second coat of the sclerotic is thus affected. Things remote appear near, and things near appear remote, and it becomes impossible for a person, thus afflicted, to thread a needle. The patient loses the faculty of seeing downward although having the capacity of observing anything situated higher up, when the Doshas lie incarcerated in the third coat of the sclerotic. Even large objects appear indistinct as if enshrouded in a sheet, and features of persons around seem distorted (lit. nose-less ear-less etc.). Each of these morbific principles, thus incarcerated in the third coat of sclerotic imparts its characteristic tint to the object of vision. The patient fails to catch the vision of a near object when the morbific principle is lodged in the lower parts of the pupils, while the remote objects remain invisible when the morbific principle is lodged in the upper part of the eyes. The patient cannot see objects that are at his sides when the Doshas are lodged in the sides of the pupil, while he can not catch the vision of any object at all when the morbific principles extend over the whole of the pupil. Bifurcated images are seen when the Doshas in the pupils lie cleft in twain, while multiple images are perceived when the Doshas lie multifariously divided in the pupil. The morbific principles lodged in the fourth coat of the sclerotic get the denomination of Timira, when they tend to obliterate the vision of the eyes, which ultimately destroy the faculty of sight. At this stage the disease is designated as Linganâsha. Effulgence of the sun, moon and lightning, and lustres of gems become visible to the patient so long as the morbific principles do no reach down into the deeper tissues of the eyes. This disease is also known by the name of Nâlikâ or Kâcha.

In the Vâtaja form of Linganâsha, reddish, cloudy and distorted images are seen by the patient. In the Pittaja form of Linganâsha, sparks of fire flies, flashes of lightning, effulgence of the sun, and images of rain-bows and dancing peacocks are seen to flash about before the vision. In the Kaphaja form of Linganâsha, small objects appear thick and large, things in general appear white and glossy, cloudless skies appear overcast with clouds, and the earth seems as if laid under a sheet of water. In the Raktaja form of Linganâsha, objects appear red to the vision and spots of darkness float about in its range, inverted images of objects are seen, and things appear white, black, or yellow-coloured to the eyes. In the Sânnipâtika form of Linganâsha, bifurcated, double or triplicate images of objects are seen. Persons appear deformed, or possessed of additional limbs or bodily members to the eyes, and sparks of light are seen to float about all round. The Pittam, deranged in conjunction with tbe blood which is the purified essence of the former, brings on a disease of vision, which is called Parimlâyi. The quarters of the heaven, sparks of fire-flies, and rays of the sun appear yellow to the vision, and leaves of trees appear studded with particles of sparkling diamonds. The six forms of Linganâsha described above impart the characteristic colour of their exciting factors (Doshas) to the objects of vision. In the Vâtaja Linganâsha the pupils appear like thick, rosy lenses of glass. In the disease known as Parimlâyi the pupils appear blue and lustre-less. The faculty of sight is sometimes found to be restored on the subsidence of the deranged morbific principles ushering in the disease. The pupils appear dry, quick and rose-coloured through the action of the deranged and aggravated Vâyu ; bluish or yellowish like that of bell metal, through the action of the deranged and aggravated Pittam ; and thick, glossy, and white, like conch-shells, or Kunda flowers, or shifting water drops on lotus petals, through the action of the deranged and aggravated Kaphah. In the type due to the action of the enraged blood, the pupils seem to move about when the eyes are rubbed with the hands.

Objects appear yellow to the vision, when the vision is affected by the deranged Pittam. The patient loses the faculty of sight during the day and regains it in the night, when the morbific principles lie incarcerated in the third coat of the eyes. This regaining of the eye-sight is brought about through the subsidence of the action of the deranged Pittam during the night. To a person, whose sight has been affected by the deranged Kaphah, every thing appears white. A little of the morbific principles, lying in all the three coats of the eyes, produces night-blindness. The patient regains his faculty of sight in the day on the subsidence of the action of the deranged Kaphah through the heat of the solar rays. He, who, through grief, or through the effects of a long fever, or of an injury to the head, sees every thing dusky, is said to be a Dhumra-darshi. In the disease known as Hrasva-Jâdyam the patient sees with difficulty during the day and large objects appear diminutive to the vision. The disease in which the sight glows like that of an ichneumon during the day in consequence whereof the patient beholds things as multi-coloured and which is due to the spreading of the morbific principles all over the pupils, is called Nakulândhyam. The pupils, affected by the enraged Vâyu, become contracted and extremely painful in their inside and bring on distortion of vision. This disease is called Gambhirikâ. The loss of eye-sight (Linganâsha) may be brought about through two causes, *viz.*, Sanimitta and Animitta. Derangement of the local morbific principles through their respective aggravating factors or the effects of a badly-handed conjunctivitis may be included within the first named (Sanimitta) cause, while the sight of celestial Rishis, serpents, etc., are included within the Animitta causes of the loss of eye-sight. The pupils look blue and sparkling in cases brought about through the last named causes.

A thin, extensive, brown or reddish, screen-like fleshy growth on the sclerotic is called Prastaryârma. Soft, whitish, expanding, screen-like excrescences of slow growth appearing on the sclerotic are called Suklármas. Soft fleshy growths, coloured like the rosy lotus-petals and appearing on the sclerotic are called Raktármas. Thick, soft, extensive, fleshy excrescences, either black or liver-coloured, and appearing on the sclerotic, are called Adhimánsármas. Hard, extensive, non-secreting, fleshy screen-like growths appearing on the sclerotic are called Snáyavármas. Brown or flesh-coloured spots, or spots coloured like oyester-shells, appearing on the sclerotic are called S'uktikas. A single spot, coloured like a drop of hare's blood, and occurring on the sclerotic, is called Arjuna. A white circular, raised, fleshy swelling resembling a patch of rice-paste and appearing on the sclerotic is called Pishtaka. A Pishtaka looks like a faded mirror. Nets of hard, red-coloured veins appearing on the sclerotic, are called Sirájálas. White pustules, appearing on the part of the sclerotic, adjacent to the iris and covered over with nets of veins are called Sirâja Pidakás. Hard, white spots, slightly elevated, and looking like drops of water and having the colour of bell-metal are called Valásas. Swellings appearing about the unions of the pupils, marked by an aching pain and suppuration and discharge of pus, are called Puyálasas. A large nodular swelling appearing about the union of the pupil and iris, attended with a slight pain and an itching sensation, and which is found but to partially suppurate, is called Upanâha. The morbific principles by taking recourse to the lachrymial sacs of the eyes, affects the four places of unions in that organ. This desease is called Srâva-Roga, or Netranâdi, according to others. A swelling, which occurs about any of these places of union, and which suppurates and secretes pus, is called Puyasráva. This desease is due to the concerted action of the deranged Váyu, Pittam, and Kaphah. A similar swelling, which suppurates and discharges thick, slimy and white-coloured pus, is called Sleshma-Sráva. A similar swelling that discharges blood is called Raktasráva, which is due to the action of the enraged blood. A similar discharge of hot, thin, watery, yellow-coloured fluid is called Pitta-Sráva. A thin, circular, copper-coloured swelling attended with an aching pain and burning sensation and appearing about the meeting of the iris and sclerotic is called Parvani. Alajis appear about the same places of union, and their symptoms have been described before (Vide, chapter on Meha). Parasites germinating in the folds of the eyelids and about the blending of the eyelids and sclerotic gradully tend to affect the entire organ of vision.

Now I shall discourse on the Nidânam of diseases that affect the eye-lids. Thick, copper-coloured Pustules appearing on the lower lids attended with an itching sensation, and with their heads pointed inward and full of pus, are called Utsanga Pidakâs. These pustules are attributed to the concerted action of the deranged Vâyu, Pittam, and Kaphah. Pustules appearing at the ends of the eyelids, and resembling

Kumbhikâ fruit in shape, which burst and are again filled with pus, are called Kumbhikâs. Pustules to the size of red mustard seeds, which appear on the eye-lids, attended with pain, heaviness, discharge and an itching sensation, are called Pothakis. Thick and rough pustules appearing on the eye-lids, surrounded by a crop of small pustules, are called Vartma-Sharkarâs, which vitiate the eye-lids. Pustules, to the size of Ervâruka seeds, and with pointed heads, and which are glossy and attended with a slight pain, are called Arsho-Vartmas. Hard, long, pappilous growths, devoid of discharge and occurring within the eye-lids, are called Sushkârshas. Soft and copper-coloured pustules occurring within the eye-lids, attended with a burning sensation and an aching pain, are called Anjana-námikás. In the disease known as Vahulá Vartma, the eye-lids become studded over with hard pustules, of the same colour with the surrounding skin. The disease in which the eye-lids cannot be opened in consequence of the appearance of a slightly painful and itching swelling therein, is called Vartma-Vandhaka. The disease in which the eye-lids suddenly become soft, and red or copper-coloured, attended with a little pain and discharge, is called Klishta-Vartmaka. If a discharge is set up in the eye-lids in consequence of the aggravation of the deranged blood and Pittam, the disease is called Vartma-Kardama. The disease in which the both sides of the eye-lids assume a twany brown colour and are attended with an aching pain is called S'yáva-Vartma. The disease in which the exteriors of the eye-lids become marked by a slight pain and swelling, and the interiors are characterised by a discharge is called Praklinna-Vartma. The disease in which the eye-lids, whether washed or unwashed, become agglutinated, is called Aklinna Vartma. In the disease known as Vâtâhata Vartma the eyes are found to squint owing to the looseness of the unions of the eye-lids and sclerotic. A slightly painful, rose-coloured tumour (cyst), irregular in shape and rapid in its growth, is called Vartmârvuda. In the disease known as Nimesha (squinting) the morbific principles, by taking recourse to the nerves controlling the closing of the eye-lids, make them shut in quick succession.

A hard, thick, slightly painful, itching, slimy tumour, occurring on the eye-lid, is called Lagana. The disease in which the deranged Vâyu, Pittam and Kaphah produce swellings on the exterior sides of the eye-lids, and a series of perforated sores in their inside is called Visa-Vartma. The disease in which the morbific principles, by taking recourse to the eye-lids, make them contracted, is called Kunchana. The disease in which the eye-lashes, affected by the morbific principles of the body, get into the eye-lids, producing irritation of and swellings on the iris and sclerotic is called Pakshakopa. This disease is of a Sânnipâtika origin, and falling off of the eye-lashes forms one of its specific features. The disease, in which the deranged Pittam, ensconced in the eye-lids and sclerotic, tends to destroy the eye-lashes and produces an itching, burning sensation in the eyes, is called Pakshapáta.

—:o:—

CHAPTER CLXXII.

HEAR me, O Sushruta, now discourse on the Nidánam of S'iro roga. There are several types of Shiro-roga, such as those due to the several actions of the deranged Vâyu, Pittam and Kapha, Suryâvarta, Anantavâta, Ardhâvabhedaka and Shankhaka, as well as those which are brought about through the concerted action of the deranged Vâyu, Pittam and Kaphah, or are due to the action of parasites, or to the loss of any fundamental principle of the body, or to the vitiated condition of the blood. In the Vâtaja type of Shiro-roga a pain is suddenly experienced in the head which is aggravated in the night and relieved on pressure, or on application of oil to the head. In the Pittaja type, the patient feels as if his head is burning with live charcoal and fumes escaping out of his ostrils. The disease shows signs of amelioration after night-fall, and after cold applications to the head. In the Kaphaja type of Shiro-roga the head is felt cold to the touch and seems heavy and tight, as if closely tied with a compress. Swellings about the sockets of the eyes form one of its special characteristics. In the Sânnipâtika form all the symptoms of the three aforesaid types manifest themselves in unison. In the Raktaja type all the symptoms of the Pittaja one are manifested, and the head, in special, cannot bear the least touch. The type known as Kshayaja is brought about through the loss of fat, blood, or of Kapham (mucous) of the head. This is one of the most distressing and virulent types of S'ira-roga and is extremely hard to cure. Applications of medicated oils, bleeding, errhines, emetics, etc., fail to give any relief in this type. Vertigo with a gone feeling in the limbs, and epileptic fits form the specific features of this disease. The patient feels as if needles are being pricked into his head which rolls about. In the type due to the action of the parasites, the patient suffers from a fluent coryza mixed with pus. The parasites gnaw at the membranes of the skull, the head throbs, and a pricking, piercing pain is felt in its inside. This disease is extremely hard to cure. In the type known as Suryávarta a slight pain about the eyes and eye-brows is commenced to be felt from the sunrise in the morning which increases as the sun travels towards the zenith, the pain reaching its climax at midday. With the decline of the sun in the west the pain shows signs of amelioration, entirely subsiding after night-fall. This disease is attributed to the aggravated action of the deranged Vâyu, Pittam and Kaphah, and si extremely hard to cure.

The disease, in which the bodily Vâyu, aggravated through the ingestion of parchifying articles of fare, or in consequence of eating before the digestion of a previous meal is completed, or enraged through an exposure to cold or east wind, or in consequence of over-fatiguing physical exercise, or aggravated through the suppression of any natural urging of the body, either alone or in unison with the deranged Kaphah, gives rise to an excruciating pain extending over the half of the head (Hemicrania) and affecting only one ear, one eye, one eye-brow, and one half of the region of the temple or neck, is called Ardhâvabhedaka. The affected half of the head seems as if it is being cut with a knife, or is being churned in the manner of fire-churning (Arani). The disease in which the enraged blood, Pittam and Váyu, being augmented, and accumulated in the temporal regions, give rise to a swelling attended with a burning sensation, redness, and an intolerable pain is called S'ankhaka by the wise. The disease soon spreads to the head with the rapidity of a poison and brings on constriction of the larynx. It invariably proves fatal within three nights. A patient, not succombing within this period, may rally under an extremely cautious and judicious treatment.

—:o:—

CHAPTER CLXXIII.

HEAR me, O Sushruta, now discourse the Nidánam of diseases that are peculiar to the opposite sex. Ingestion of incompatible articles of fare, eating before the digestion of a previous meal, indigestion, abortions, sexual excesses, excessive travelling in carriages, or riding on horse-back etc., exhaustion through excessive grief or anguish, lifting or carrying of inordinately heavy weights, local-injuries and day sleep may be described as the exciting factors of Asrigdara (uterine or vaginal catarrh) of which a bruised or aching pain in the limbs forms the specific concomitant. Weakness, vertigo. epileptic fits, mental distraction, somnolence, delirium with a burning sensation in the body and various other nervous distempers manifest themselves on the aggravation of the discharge. There are four different types of Pradara, brought about through the several actions of the deranged Vâyu, Pittam, and Kaphah and through their concerted action as well. In the type of Pradara (leucorrhœa) due to the action of the deranged Kaphah, the discharge becomes greyish and slimy, or resembles the washings of meat in colour. In the Pittaja type of leucorrhœa, the discharge becomes hot and assumes a yellowish, bluish, blackish or reddish colour, and other specific symptoms of the deranged Pittam are found to supervene. In the Vâtaja type of leucorrhœa the discharge is frothy and scanty, and resembles the washings of meat. It is ejected in small quantities, attended with the other specific affections of the deranged Vâyu. In the Sânnipâtika type of leucorrhœa the discharge assumes the colour of honey, clarified butter, yellow oxide of arsenic (Haritála) or of marrow, and gets a cadaverous smell. This Sânnipâtika form of leucorrhœa should be ragarded as incurable, and a physician, with any regard to his personal fame, should not prescribe any medicine in cases of this type. A case of leucorrhœa, attended with fever, thirst, weakness, poverty of blood, and a copious and constant discharge with a burning sensation in the body, should be regarded as beyond all cure. Catamenial blood which follows a regular periodicity as regards its out-flow and flows out for five days, each month, unattended with any pain or burning sensation, and which is neither exceedingly thin nor slimy, should be regarded as the indication of sound health in a woman. Catamenial blood, which is coloured either like the washings of shellac, or the blood of a hare, and which leaves no stain on the linen after washing, should be likewise regarded as pure (healthy.)

Twenty different varieties of vaginal diseases are recognised in practice, O Sushruta, of which injudicious and unwholesome food, menstrual disorders, congenital taints, and dynamics of acts done by a woman in her previous births act as the exciting factors.

In the variety known as Udávartâ (dysmenorrhœa) frothy catamenial blood is emitted with the greatest pain. In the disease known as Vandhyâ (sterility) the menstrual flow is either absent or suppressed. In the disease known as Viplutâ, an intolerable pain is felt in the reproductive organs. In the variety known as Pariplutá (Vaginitis) an excruciating pain is felt in the vagina during an act of sexual congress. In the variety known as Vâtalâ-yoni, the vaginal canal is felt rough and numbed, attended with an aching. piercing pain. In all these four varieties of vaginal complaints the pain experienced is of a nervous (Vátaja) character. A female reproductive organ, which loses blood (bleeds, attended with a burning sensation in its inside, is called Lohita-Kshayá. In the disease known as Vámini, a large number of ova is ejected with blood, accompanied by loud reports. In the disease called Prasransini, the vagina is displaced from its natural seat (prolapsus of the Vagina), while the disease known as Kshobhitá precludes the possibility of conception on account of the extremely agitated condition of the local nerves. In the disease known as Putraghni, the patient may conceive at close intervals, but the pregnancy is often destroyed though the emission of uterine blood, which is facilitated by a weakened condition of the local nerves which is one of the specific features of this disease. In the disease known as Pittaláyoni, fever with a burning sensation and suppuration in the vagina is found to supervene. These four foregoing types of Yoni-roga should, be regarded as marked by a predominance of the deranged Pittam, and of symptoms peculiar to that morbific diathesis. In the disease known as Atyánandá the patient knows no satisfaction in respect of sexual pleasures (nymphomania). In the disease known as Karnini, polypi grow in the vaginal canal through the agency of the deranged Kaphah and blood. In the disease known as Acharaná, the woman spends herself before her husband during an act of sexual congress, while in that called Atichará the woman is never satisfied, hence in both these diseases the seeds of man and woman never meet. In the disease known as Shleshmalá-yoni, the vaginal canal is felt cold and slimy and is marked by an itching sensation. These four forms of Yoni-roga should be regarded as marked by the predominance of the deranged Kaphah. A woman in whom the catamenial flow and the mammæ do not appear, and whose vaginal canal is perceived rough during acts of sexual congress is called a Shandi. An immature girl by holding sexual intercourse with a fully developed and exceedingly large-limbed man suffers from evils which are called Andalis. A vagina with an extremely dilated vulva is called Mahá-yoni, while that with an extremely constricted (external) orifice is called Suchi-Vaktrá. These four last-named types of Yoni-roga should be regarded as due to the concerted action of the deranged Váyu, Pittam, and Kaphah, and hence incurable.

The deranged Váyu, Pittam and Kaphah of the vaginal region, aggravated through such exciting factors as day-sleep, excessive irascibility, over-fatiguing physical exercise, sexual excesses, bites, and scratches, give rise to excrescences in that locality which assume a colour, blended of those of pus and blood, and resemble Lakucha fruit in shape. These vaginal growths or excrescences are called Kandas. In the Vátaja type of this disease the growths become rough, discoloured and cracked. In the Pittaja type they are marked by redness and a burning sensation.

In the Kaphaja type they are coloured blue like Atasi flowers and are marked by an itching sensation. In the Sánnipátika type they are marked by all the aforementioned specific symptoms.

—:o:—

CHAPTER CLXXIV.

Now, hear me, O Sushruta, discourse on the Nidánam of Mudhagarbha. Carrying or lifting of inordinately heavy loads, hurt (to the womb or uterus), and excessively hot, or irritating food or drink are the factors which tend to bring about an abortion of pregnancy, which is ushered in by such symptoms as show of blood and an aching pain in the uterus. The fætus continues in a liquid state (undifferentiated limbs) up to the fourth month of gestation, while it is aborted in a solidified (lit, with developed limbs) state in the fifth or sixth month of gestation. Hence, an abortion of pregnancy taking place after the fifth month of gestation is called miscarriage. As a fully ripe fruit may be felled down from a true by shaking it, so a hurt to the womb, fever, and irregular eating may bring on miscarriage of pregnancy in a woman. The enraged Váyu, by lying stuffed in the maternal passage, produces suppression of urine and an aching pain in the uterus and vagina, and obstructs the child in its passage out of the channel of parturition. Such an obstruction of the fætus is called Mudha-garbham (difficult parturition or false presentation). Cases of false presentation (Mudhagarbha) although admitting of being grouped under a large number of heads, are usually classified into four or eight forms, according as the child lies obstructed at the head of the maternal passage on account of its head proving too large for the latter, or as the bloated belly of the child proves the cause of obstruction, or as the arched back of the child hinders its downward passage, or as the child, with its one hand or both hands raised up, lies obliquely obstructed across the passage of parturition, or as the child, with its arched neck, and chin pressed on its breast, or with its sides contorted, lies stuffed in the vaginal canal. On the other hand, all these different forms of false presentation may be grouped under four sub-heads such as Sankilaka, Pratikhura, Parigha, and Vijagati. The form of false-presentation in which the child, with its hands and legs uplifted and pressed upon its head, lies obstructed in the maternal passage, is called Sankilaka. The form of false-presentation in which the two hands and legs of the child together with its head are passed out and its body lies obstructed in the passage of parturition is called Pratikhura. The form of difficult labour in which the hands and the head of the child are passed out and the rest of its body lies obstructed in the passage of child-birth is called Vijaka. In the form known as Parigha, the body of the fætus lies obliquely across the passage of parturition, in the manner of a Parigha (bolt). An *enciente* whose head droops down on the advent of the pain of child-birth, and who forsakes all modesty during the time, and whose body becomes cold, and on the surface of whose abdomen blue veins are found to appear, should be regarded as indicating an unfavourable termination of the labour. Absence of pain of child-birth, or of urination, defecation, etc., which invariably usher in the labour, as well as non-throbbing of the womb indicates an unfavourable prognosis. The complexion of the *enciente* becomes sallow, she complains of a cadaverous smell in her breath, and symptoms of tympanites present themselves on account of the bloated condition of the belly of the dead fætus in the womb. Loss of friends or of fortune, assault, and injury to the uterus are the factors that are usually calculated to bring on abortion of pregnancy. Constriction of the vulva, rigidity of the external orifice of the uterus, obstruction of the child in the maternal passage and the presence of a colicky pain in the uterus (Makalla*) are the factors which accelerate death in cases of difficult labour.

—:o:—

CHAPTER CLXXV.

NOW hear me, O Sushruta, discourse on the Nidânam of 'diseases of parturient women (Sutikâ Roga)

The enraged and aggravated bodily Vâyu, by arresting the flow of uterine blood in a parturient woman, produces a peculiar kind of aching pain in her pelvic and cardiac regions, as well as in the region of her head, which is called Makallam. An aching pain in the limbs, fever with shivering, thirst and a sensation of heaviness in the limbs, œdematous swellings of the limbs, diarrhœa and colic are the symptoms which mark a case of Sutikâ-roga. Inadequate food, want of proper rest and physical comforts, irregular diet, and indigestion serve to bring in a host of diseases in parturient women, of which the following are usually met with (in practice) viz., Fever, dysentery, œdema, colic, constipation of the bowels, weakness, somnolence with a non-relish for food, water-brash and diseases that originate through the interference of the deranged Vâyu and Kaphah. These diseases occurring in

* Makalla literally means after-pain, or false pain after child-birth. In the Sushruta Samhita, Makalla is described as

प्रजातायाश्चोत्तरं कालं नो रूक्षैर्विशोषितं शरीरं मक्कल्लं करोति ।

The term "cha" in this aphorism includes any kind of uterine colic, hether occurring in a parturient or non-parturient woman.

weak and emaciated women after parturition, as well their supervening symptoms are extremely hard to cure.

I shall now describe, O child, the diseases of mammary glands. The morbific principles of the deranged Vâyu, Pittam and Kaphah, by affecting the mammæ, whether charged with milk or otherwise, vitiate the flesh and blood of the breast. Five different kinds of mammary diseases are known in addition to the one named Raktaja Vidradhi, whose symptoms are quite in common with those of an external abscess. Bad or indigestible food in parturient women, by enraging the morbific principles of their breasts, tends to vitiate their breast milk, which forms the source of many diseases in their children. Breast-milk, vitiated by the deranged Vâyu, becomes thin and watery and acquires an astringent flavour; that vitiated by the deranged Pittam tastes either pungent, acid or saline, while that vitiated by the deranged Kaphah is thick and slimy and sinks in water when thrown into it. Good breast-milk speedily mixes with water, is colourless, and has a sweet taste. The use of such breast-milk alone is recommended.

—:o:—

CHAPTER CLXXVI.

NOW hear me, O Sushruta, discourse on the Nidânam of diseases, peculiar to infant-life. A child sucking its mother's milk, vitiated by the deranged Vâyu, suffers from diseases of the deranged Vâyu, hoarseness, emaciation, and suppression of the stool, urine and flatus being its chief characteristics. A child sucking milk, vitiated by the deranged Pittam, suffers from Pittaja affections, of which loose motions of the bowels, chlorosis, thirst, heat in the body and perspiration form the principal symptoms. A child sucking breast-milk vitiated by the deranged Kaphah suffers from diseases of the deranged Kaphah, and salivation (water brash) somnolence, running at the nose, flow of tears, vomiting of undigested breast-milk etc., form its main features. Diseases of infants, brought about through the agency of any two of the morbific principles of Vâyu, Pittam, etc., exhibit symptoms which are peculiar to each of them. In the Sânnipâtika forms of diseases of infant life, the symptoms of all the Vâtaja, Pittaja and Kaphaja types become manifest in unison. The intensity of pain in the body of a child should be inferred from the pitch of its cry-sound. The use of bad breast-milk produces a kind of itching sensation in the eye-lids of infants which is called Kakunaka. Profuse tears run down from the eyes, and the child constantly rubs its forehead, nose and eyes, and becomes incapable of looking at the sun, or of opening its eye-lids. Through the use of breast-milk of pregnant mothers infants are found to suffer from a peculiar form of indigestion (lit, impaired digestion) attended with cough, vomiting, somnolence, vertigo, and bloatedness of the abdomen with a non-relish for foood which is called Paribhava. The deranged and aggravated Kaphah, by lying incarcerated: about the root of the palate, produces a kind of disease in infants which is called Tâlu-Kantaka. The part of the head parallel to the roof of the palate is found to sink in this disease, the roof of the palate looks as if it hangs down, and the child refuses to be weaned at the breast. Deglutition becomes painful, the neck of the child droops down, and belching of milk, loose motions of the bowels, thirst, and pain in the mouth, throat and the eyes, are the symptoms which are found to supervene. A kind of Erysipelas, resembling the petals of red lotus in shape, are found to appear on the scalps, or about the pelves of infants which invariably finds a fatal termination. The Erysipelatous patches are either found to descend from the head to the breast by the way of the temples, or to ascend from the pelvis to the head by the region of the breast. Symptoms of fever etc. affecting infants are identical with those described before under their respective heads. In addition to these, several diseases of supernatural origin, such as Skandâpsmâra, S'akunigraha, etc., are found to afflict infants. In the form known as Skanda-Graha, either the right or the left eye of an infant becomes full of tears, perspiration becomes profuse, the child shakes more or less as in palsy, the eyes look upward, the face is contorted, a kind of bloody smell is emitted from its body, and the child gnashes its teeth, or looks terrified, or cries a little and refuses to take at the breast.

In the disease known as Skandâpasmâra, the child vomits frothy matter in an unconscious state, or writhes about in convulsive fits. Roused from swoon it cries and refuses to be consoled, and a peculiar smell, blended of those of blood and pus, is perceived to be emitted from its body. In the disease known as S'akuni-graha, the affected child suffers from looseness of the joints and a gone feeling in the limbs, and rouses up terrified. An odour like that which is perceived in the body of a bird is exhaled from its limbs, which become covered over with patches of secreting ulcers, and crops of belbous eruptions, attended with suppuration and a burning sensation, are found to appear on its body. In the disease known as Revati-graha, the body of the affected child becomes covered over with ulcers or belbs, which are found to readily bleed. The body of the child emits a pecular miry odour, and fever with loose motions of the bowels and a burning sensation in the body is likewise found to supervene. In the disease named as Putaná-graha the affected child suffers from fever and dysentery, the eyes are directed obliquely upward, and the child looks agitated and refuses to be lulled down to sleep. In the disease called Andhaputaná, the affected child suffers from vomiting, dysentery, fever, thirst, cough, and a disinclination to take the breast. The cries become extremely pitious and a smell like that of clotted blood is emitted from its body. In the disease known as S'eeta Putaná, the child coughs and shakes, emaciation of the body, vomiting, dysentery, and running at the eyes being its further characteristics. In the disease named as Naigameya Graha, the affected child violently gnashes its teeth with its eyes turned upward, and vomiting, rigour, dryness of the throat and mouth, and epileptic fits are the symptoms which are found to supervene. In the disease known as Mukha-Mandaliká-Graha, the complexion of the affected child becomes bright and clear, and large veins are found to appear on its body, which emits a smell like urine. The child craves for more and more food in this disease.

—:o:—

CHAPTER CLXXVII.

Now hear me, O Sushruta, discourse on the Nidánam of Upadansa. Sexual congress with women who have observed a long vow of perfect continence, or with those, the external orifices of whose reproductive organs are extremely narrow or constricted, or the canals of whose reproductive organs are studded with patches of hairy growths, promiscuous intercourse, neglect in cleansing the parts after coitus, vaginal diseases in women, visited, bites or pinches at the genitals, washing of the parts with hot or alkaline water, carnal acts with beasts, and masturbation etc., are the factors which tend to produce the five forms of Upadansa in the genitals. In the type of Upadansa due to the action of the deranged Váyu, the (primary) pustule assumes a black hue and is produces an aching, piercing pain about the frenum. In the Pittaja type of Upadansa the (primary) pustules assume a yellowish colour and are attended with discharge and a burning sensation. In the type of Upadansa due to contamination of blood the pustules assume a black or flesh-like colour, and readily bleed. Symptoms peculiar to the Pittaja type of Upadansa also manifest themselves in this one. In the Kaphaja type of Upadansa, the swelling becomes extremely great and the pustules (incidental sores) are found to secrete a thick copious discharge. Cases of Sánnipátika, type of Upadansa of which a varied colour and character of the discharge form the chief specific features, should be regarded as incurable. A physician should renounce the medical treatment of a patient whose genitals have been entirely eaten away by parasites, leaving only the balls to dangle. The foolish one, who does not resort to proper medical treatment at the outset, ultimately dies of this disease, with his genitals extremely emaciated, or attended with swelling and suppuration, or eaten away by parasites. Condylomatous growths, resembling crests of cocks in shape and occurring upon or about the glanpenis, or between the integuments of the scrotum, or about any other joints of the body, are called Lingârsas. They are painless and slimy in character, and are of a Sánnipátika origin, whence their incurablity.

Foolish persons, who get their reproductive organs swollen and elongated by means other than those described in the works of the holy Vátsáyana, etc., or by pricking bristles of S'uka insects into the cavernous tissues of their reproductive organs, suffer from any of the eighteen forms of the malady designated as Shukadosha. These eighteen forms of malady are respectively known as Sarshapikâ, Ashthilikâ, Kumbhikâ, Alaji, etc. Pustules to the size of white mustard seeds, and occurring over the penis through the aggravation of the local Vâyu and Kaphah, in consequence of the bristles of S'uka insects lying pricked into its body, are called Sarshapikâs. Hard pustules, resembling pea-seeds and occurring over the penis, through the aggravation of the enraged local Vâyu, are called Ashthilas. Patches of thready pustules occurring over the penis, through the action of the deranged Kaphah, are called Grathitâs. Hard black pustules over the penis, resembling seeds of black berries and having their origin in the aggravation of the deranged Pittam and blood, are called Kumbhikâs. Alâjis, which are found to crop up on the penis in this disease, are quite identical in character with those described under Prameha. Pustules attended with swelling of the part, which are found to appaer on the penis in consequence of rubbing it, in this disease, through the aggravation of the local Vâyu, are called Mriditâs. Pustules, which appear on the penis in consequence of pressing it with the hands for the purpose of introducing the bristles of S'uka, in this disease, are called Sanmuda Pidakâs, which are due to the aggravated condition of the local Vâyu. Long pappilous pustules, which crop up on the penis, owing to the introduction of S'uka-bristles into its body and which burst at their centre and give rise to pain and horripilation, are called Adhimanthas. These pustules should be attributed to the action of the aggravated Kaphah and blood in the locality. In the form of S'ukadosha known as Pushkarikâ, round roseolar patches, resembling petals of red lotus in shape, appear upon the penis, surrounded by small pustular eruptions. The local blood, vitiated by the virus of S'uka bristles, produces a kind of anæsthesia in the body of the penis, which is called Sparsha-hâni.

Repeated introduction of the bristles of S'uka insects into the cavernosa of the penis for the purpose of getting it abnormally swollen and elongated gives rise to a kind of red pustules on its body, which are called Uttamas, which resemble Mâsha or Mudga pulse and owe their origin to the vitiated condition of blood and the Pittam. Nets of sieve-like sinuses, which are found to invade the male organ of reproduction owing to the injudicious insertion of Suka-bristles into its body, are called S'ataponakas. These sores result from the deranged condition of blood and of the bodily Vâyu. An inflammatory suppuration is established inside the skin and prepuce of the penis owing to the injudicious use of Suka, which is called Tvakapâka. A disease of the male organ of generation, resulting from the same cause as above, in which it becomes studded with black pustules and belbous eruptions, attended with an extreme pain, is called Shonitârvuda. Fleshy tumours, which crop up on the body of the penis owing to its being roughly handled after the insertion of Suka-bristles into its body, are called Mânsârvudas. The disease in which the flesh of the penis is found to slough off through the agency of the above-said exciting factor (S'uka dosha) is called Mânsapâka, which should be attributed to the concerted action of the three Doshas. Abscesses appearing on the male organ of reproduction exhibit the same symptoms as are manifested in connection with the Sânnipâtika ones. An inflammatory suppuration of the same organ owing to the introduction of the bristles of poisonous, black, or multicoloured Suka insects, and in which the organ becomes, shrivelled, or emaciated, or is entirely destroyed, is called Tilakâlaka, which is of a Sânnipâtika origin. Of these diseases of the male organ of generation, Mânsârvuda, Mânsapâka, Vidradhi and Tilakâlaka should be regarded as incurable.

Impotency and loss of virile power often mark the sequel to Upadansha. A person incapable of discharging his conjugal duties is called a Kliva (impotent), and impotency may arise from a variety of causes, mental, physical, traumatic, etc. Non-erection of one's virile organ owing to one's holding sexual congress with a woman whom one detests, or the incapacity of that organ to respond to the call of desire on account of grief or fright are cases which illustrate the mental cause of impotency. Excessive loss of semen through ingestion of extremely saline, pungent, or acid articles of fare, or through such like factors which are calculated to aggravate the deranged Pittam may bring on impotency which may be called Pittaja impotency. Similarly, sexual excesses without using any kind of aphrodisiac medicines may be followed by the same result. Voluntary suppression of erotic propulsions, severance of the spermatic chords, not to speak of congenital deformities, such as absence of the testes, etc., may give rise to impotency. Congenital impotency, as well as that due to the severance of the spermatic chords, should be regarded as incurable.

—:o:—

CHAPTER CLXXVIII.

Now hear me, O Sushruta, discourse on the Nidânam of Masurikâ (Variola), etc. Ingestion of pungent, saline or alkaline articles of fare in inordinate quantities, use of incompatible articles of food, eating before the digestion of a previous meal is digested, use of stale food, Simbi seeds, and Madhvâlukas, exhalations from poisonous trees, marshy grounds, etc., use of vitiated water for drinking purposes, exposure to winds charged with poisonous miasm, and influences of malignant planets are the factors which tend to aggravate the morbific principles in the human organism, and these pathogenetic factors, in combination with the consequently poisoned blood, bring on an attack of Masurikâ (small-pox). The disease is so named from the fact of the resemblance of its eruptions to lentil seeds. Eruptive fever with lassitude and a desire to stretch the limbs, vertigo and a distaste for all things and concerns of life, discolouring and swelling of the skin (eruptive rashes) and redness of the eyes are the symptoms, which mark the premonitory stage of Masurikâ. In the Vâtaja type of Masurikâ the pustules become hard, rough, and reddish brown, attended with an excruciating pain in the limbs. These pustules are very slow of suppuration. In the Pittaja type of Masurikâ a breaking pain is experienced in the limbs. Cough, rigour, apathy, lassitude, parchedness of the palate, lips, and tongue, and thirst with a non-relish for food are its symptoms. The pustules become white, red, or yellow, attended with a kind of extreme pain and burning sensation, and suppuration is found to set in later. In the Raktaja type of Variola, loose motions of the bowels with an aching pain in the limbs, thirst with a non-relish for food, stomatitis, and inflammation of the conjuctivæ with a high fever are the symptoms which speedily manifest themselves in conjunction with the other specific features of the Pittja type of this disease. Water-brash, a non-relish food, heaviness of the limbs, headache, a sensation as if the body has been tied with a wet compress, somnolence and physical languor are the symptoms which mark the Kaphaja type of Masurikâ. The pustules are found to be white, thick, glossy, and marked by a little pain and an itching sensation about them, taking time to be fully suppurated. In the Sânnipâtika type of Masurikâ the pustules assume a bluish colour, are dipped at the centre, and look elongated like thrashed paddy. They are very slow to suppurate, being attended with an extreme pain and a copious fetid discharge. The type of small pox, known as Charmadala, in which constriction of the larynx with a non-relish for food, numbed pain in the limbs, delirium, and want of comforts are developed, should be regarded as incurable. Red eruptive rashes of the same elevation with the follicles of bodily hairs, due to the aggravated condition of the deranged Kaphah and Pittam, of which cough, fever and a repugnance for food mark the premonitory stage, are called Romanthikâ (measles).

The eruptions in cases of Tvakgata Masurikâ (Chicken pox) are found to be belbous in their character, which secrete a water-like fluid when they burst. These eruptions have their origin in the vitiated condition of the serum. Those which have their origin in the vitiated condition of the blood assume a blood-red colour. The cuticles of these pustules are exremely thin. They bleed when burst, and prove curable if the blood is not extremely poisoned. In the type which has its origin in the diseased condition of the flesh, the pustules become hard, and glossy, and are possessed of thick cuticles. They suppurate later and thirst and fever with an aching, itching sensation in the body are found to supervene. In the type which has its origin in the diseased condition of the bodily fat, the eruptions are soft, slightly elevated, and circular in shape, attended with an extremely high fever. Hyperperaxia, mental aberration and delirium are also developed and scarcely its victim escapes with life. In the type which has its origin in the diseased condition of the marrow, the pustules become small sized and of the same colour with the surrounding skin, and are slightly raised and flat like thrashed paddy. There is loss of consciousness, nerve and vein amestomoses and regions about the unions of bones and ligaments (Marmas) seem as if being torn asunder and the bones seem as if being bored with drills. This disease is highly fatal, the patient expires on the very day of the attack. In the type which is due to the diseased condition of the semen, the eruptions look as if they are suppurated, while in fact they are not. They are small, glossy and extremely painful. Epileptic fits, loss of consciousness, and insanity with a burning sensation in the body and superficial coldness and heaviness of the limbs form the specific symptoms of this type of Masurikâ, which invariably proves fatal.

Of the several types of Variola, those that are respectively due to the action of the deranged Pittam, Kaphah, or Pittah and Kaphah combined, or have their respective seats in the lymph chyle or blood speedily yield to medicine. Those which are due to the deranged condition of the bodily Vâyu, or of the Vâyu and Pittam, or of the Vâyu and Kaphah, are comparatively more difficult to cure, while cases of Sânnipâtika origin should be abandoned as incurable.

In the Sánnipátika type, the eruptive pustules are either coloured like the red corals, or like the ripe Jambolin or Tamála flowers, or like iron-dust. Cough, hiccough, mental aberrations, hyper-peraxia, delirium, convulsions, thirst, hæmorrhage from any of the upper apertures of the body, a wheezing sound in the chest and violent fits of vertigo are the symptoms which point to an unfavourable prognosis in Variola. A small-pox patient affected with excessive thirst, or with any nervous disease, such as Apatanaka (hysterical convulsion) and found breathing through the mouth, should be regarded as already within the clutches of death. A painful œdematous swelling about the wrists, elbows or shoulder-blades marks the sequel to an attack of small pox. These swellings are extremely hard to cure.

——:o:——

CHAPTER CLXXIX.

Now hear me, O Sushruta, discourse on the Nidánam of Kshudra Roga. Painless, shiny, erythematous eruptions of the same colour with the surrounding skin and to the size of Mudga pulse, which are often found to attack infants, are called Ajagallikás. They are due to the action of the deranged Váyu and Kaphah. Confluent erythematous eruptions, resembling barley corn and cropping up from underneath the flesh are called Yavaprakshas. This disease is due to the action of the deranged Váyu and Kaphah. Thick, raised, circular patches of erythematous pustules marked by the presence of a little pus in their inside and brought about through the agency of the deranged Váyu and Kaphah, are called Antrálajis. Pustules resembling ripe Audumvara fruits in colour, and characterised by dilated mouths and an intolerable burning sensation are called Vivritas, which are due to the action of the deranged Pittam. Crops of five or six pustules which are hard, confluent and resemble the back of a tortoise in shape, are called Kachchhapikás. Pustules with pointed and jagged tops like those of an ant-hill and appearing on the shoulders, neck and extremities, or about the armpits are called Valmikas, which should be understood as of a Sánnipátika origin. Crops of pustular eruptions, arranged in the manner of lotus seeds and brought about through the agency of the deranged Váyu and Pittam are called Indraviddha (Herpes) The disease in which circular patches of painful and elevated pustules appear on the skin are called Gardhavikas which are due to the deranged Váyu and Pittam. A hard, glossy, slightly painful swelling, appearing about the mandibles, is called Páshána Gardhava (Parotitis) which is due to the deranged Váyu and Kaphah. Firm and extremely painful pustules, which appear within the ducts of the ears, are called Panasikas. A thin (non-elevated) and non-suppurating swelling, attended with fever and a burning sensation, which shifts from one part of the body to another in the manner of erysipelas, is called Jála-Gardhava. A nodular boil, attended with fever and extreme pain which appears on the head through the concerted action of the three Doshas, is called Irivelliká. Black and extremely painful belbous eruptions on the arms, sides, or shoulders, or about the arm-pits are called Kakshas. Such belbous eruptions occurring singly on the skin are called Gandha málá. Both these diseases are of a Pittaja origin. Belbous eruptions about the armpits, which cause the sloughing off of the local flesh and which are attended with fever and an intolerable burning sensation in their inside are called Agni Rohinis, which should be understood as of a Sânnipâtika origin, which usually terminate in death on the seventh, tenth, or fifteenth day of the attack. The disease of the flesh of the finger-nail caused by the deranged Váyu and Pittam, and which is characterised by the inflammation and suppuration of the affected parts is called Chippa (onycha). Large, nodular abscesses resembling a Vidarikâ in shape and occuring in the femoral regions or about the arm-pits, are called Vidárikás. They are of a Sânnipâtika origin. The deranged Vâyu and Kaphah, by taking recourse to the flesh and veins, produce a kind of tumours, which, bursting, secrete a kind of secretion resembling a compound of honey and sugar in colour. They are called Sharkárârvudas. Long pedestrian journeys tend to enrage the Vayu of the feet which produces cracks in the soles. This disease is called Pádadári. Constant contact of mire or of mud produces a kind of painful exyma in regions between the toes which is called Alasa. The deranged Vâyu and Pittam, by finding lodgment in the follicles of hairs, tend to cause their falling off and to prevent their reappearance. This disease is called Indralupta (alopacea). In the disease known as Dárunaka (dandruff) the scalp becomes rough and encrusted. Crops of profusely secreting pustular eruptions on the scalp due to the action of the deranged Kaphah, or of parasites or diseased blood in the locality, is called Arunshikâ. In consequence of grief, fright or of over-fatiguing physical exercise, the increased bodily heat and the aggravated Pittam, by taking recourse to the head, tend to produce premature greyness of hair. This disease is called Pálityam. The deranged Váyu and Kaphah, as well as the diseased blood, give rise to a kind of pustular eruptions on the faces of young persons which are called Mukha-dushika's (acne). Circular patches of itching, grey-coloured pustules on the skin, resembling the thorns of lotus stems, are called Padmini Kantakas (Lupus). Black, glossy, painless, and slightly elevated spots on the skin, which are mostly congenital, are called Jutumanis (moles). More or less extensive areas of painless, black or twany coloured spots on the skin are called Nyachchhas (Chlasma). Brown or twany brown coloured spots on the skin of the face are called Vyangas (Tans). The disease in which the prepuce is found to entirely encase the glan penis in consequence of the aggravation of the Váyu through onanisám or coitus is called Parivartika (Phymoses). Sexual congress with girls with extremely narrow or constricted vulva, or with those who have not attained puberty, leads to bursting or retro-flexion of the prepuce, leaving the glan-penis exposed. This disease is called Avapâtika (paraphymosis). The deranged Váyu, by taking recourse to the prepuce, makes it closely adhere to the glan penis, completely covering the Meatus. This disease is called (stricture of the urethra) Niruddha-prakásha in which the urine dribbles out with pain. Voluntary suppression of urgings towards defecation tends to enrage the Apana Váyu which produces constriction of the rectum. This disease is called Sanniruddha Guda (Rectal constriction) in which scanty stools are expelled with the greatest difficulty. Urine, perspiration and particles of fecal matter lying deposited about the anus of infants in consequence of the neglect to cleanse the parts give rise to a sort of Erythematous eruptions which are called Ahiputanas (Erythema). They are apt to become confluent and secrete a kind of discharge on scratching. Dusts and other filthy matter lying deposited in the integuments of the scrotum give rise to a sort of erythematous eruptions which are called Vrishana Kachchhu. Violent purging of stool, or excessive straining at the time of bearing down the stool, produces protrusion of the anus in a weak subject.

This disease is called Guda-Bhransa (Prolapsus Ani.) An excruciating pain with an itching sensation about the protruded part in the same disease, attended with fever and suppuration of the anus, constitutes what is known as Shukara-danshtra in the parlance of the Ayurveda.

—:o:—

CHAPTER CLXXX.

NOW hear me, O Sushruta, discourse on the Nidánam of Bhagandara (fistula in ano). Within a space of two fingers' width about the anus an extremely painful pustule, which bursts and is transformed into a kind of sinus, is called Bhagandara. This disease admits of being divided into five different types such as the Vátaja, Pittaja, Kaphaja, Sánnipátika, and Shalyaja (traumatic).

In the Vátaja type of Bhagandara, which is also called Shataponaka (sive-like), ingestion of astringent and parchifying articles of fare serves to enrage and aggravate the bodily Váyu. The deranged Váyu, thus aggravated, gives rise to a pustule in the region above described, which, if not properly attended to at the outset, becomes suppurated and exudes a vermil-tinted, frothy discharge on bursting. A large number of sinuses is formed into the incidental sore through which semen, urine and feces are found to be discharged. In the Pittaja type of Bhagandara, which is also designated as Ushtragriva, a red pustule is produced in the region of the anus through factors, which are calculated to enrage the deranged Pittam. It is rapid in suppuration and discharges a warm, fetid pus. The disease is so named from the fact of the pustule assuming an arched shape like the neck of a camel in its immature stage. In the Kaphaja type of Bhagandara, which is also called Parisrávi, the pustule becomes hard, white, and slightly painful, attended with an itching sensation and marked by a thick, cold discharge. The Shalyaja (traumatic) type of Bhagandara is also designated as Unmárgi. A sore about the anus owing to the pricking of any thorny substance into that region, if not properly cared for from the outset, is converted into a tyne of Bhagandara which is called Unmárgi. All types of Bhagandara are extremely painful and obstinate. A case of Bhagandara in which flatus, stool, urine, semen and parasites are found to be ejected through the incidental sinuses should be regarded as incurable.

Incidentally I shall deal with the Nidánam of Nádi Vrana (sinus), O Sushruta. The pus in a fully suppurated abscess or swelling, if not evacuated at the proper time, begins to infiltrate and burrow into the underlying tissues, producing sinuses, which constantly discharge pus. In the Vátaja type of Nádi-Vrana the sinuses become narrow, provided with extremely narrow orifices, and are attended with an aching pain in their inside. A frothy pus is discharged more in the night than in the day from these sinuses. In the Pittaja type of Nádi Vrana, fever, thirst and an intolerable burning sensation in the sinuses are found to supervene. A hot, yellow pus is discharged from these sinuses, more in the day than in the night. In the Kaphaja type of Nádi Vrana the sinuses become hard and are marked by an itching sensation and an extreme pain, exuding a large quantity of thick, white, slimy pus in the night. In the Sánnipátika form of Nádi-Vrana, the characteristic symptoms of all the three preceding types, together with fever, dyspnœa, epileptic fits and a burning sensation manifest themselves in unison. In the traumatic type, any foreign matter lying concealed in the incidental sore may give rise to sinuses, which are marked by a constant pain, and are found to excude a frothy, blood-streaked, churned-like pus. Sinuses of the Sánnipátika type scarcely yield to medicinal treatment.

CHAPTER CLXXXI.

Now, Hear me, O Sushruta, discourse on the Nidánam of poisoning. Poisons may be divided into two classes such as Vegetable and animal. Poisons obtained from bulbs of plants etc., may be called vegetable poisons, while those dropped down from the fangs of venomous snakes, etc., are called animal poisons.

Somnolence, drowsiness, lassitude with a burning sensation, horripilation, swelling (œdema) and dysentery are the symptoms, which mark the action of vegetable poisons in general, while fever, tooth-edge, hic-cough, pain in the throat, vomiting of frothy mucous, dyspnœa, epileptic fits and a marked repugnance for all kinds of food are the symptoms, which generally walk in the trail of animal poisons. Delirium, unconsciousness and a thrashing or bruised pain in the limbs are the general features, which mark the action of poisons obtained from the roots of poisonous plants or trees. Yawning, shivering, and dyspnœa are the symptoms which result from the ingestion of leaves of poisonous trees (lit, leaf-poisons). Dryness of the mouth with a burning sensation in the body and a distaste for food are the symptoms which result from the ingestion of a fruit-poison. Vomiting, tympanites and epileptic fits are the features which mark the action of a flower-poison. Roughness of the body, head-ache and salivation with a bad smell in the mouth are the symptoms which mark the action of a bark-poison or of a sap-poison. The use of milky exudations of poisonous trees develops such symptoms as a feeling of heaviness in the limbs, emission of frothy mucous from the mouth and violent purgings. Cardiac difficulties, epileptic fits, and a burning sensation about the palate are the symptoms, which are exhibited in cases of poisoning with any metallic poison.

These nine kinds of poison, anywise imbibed by a person, may ultimately prove fatal, if not instantaneously so. A wound from a poisoned weapon ,is marked by bleeding. It suppurates on the very day it is inflicted and shows signs of putrefaction, the black putrid flesh sloughing off day by day. The patient suffers from thirst, fever, and an intolerable burning sensation in the body until titanus is developed. All these symptoms may be exhibited in connection with any other kind of poisoned wounds. Yellow or black-coloured stool and vomiting of frothy mucous are the specific features of cases of poison-imbibing.

Venomous serpents are divided into three different groups such as, the Bhogis (Hooded ones), Mandalis (spotted with ring-like marks on their bodies) and Rájilas (marked with stripes). Of these, the Bhogis possess a temperament of dominant Váyu, the Mandalis possess a temperament of dominant Pittam, and the Rájilas possess a temperament of dominant Kaphah. From these species of snakes many have originated by hybridisation, and their offspring possess temperaments blended of the specific traits of their parents. A bite by a snake of the Bhogi species imparts a black tint to the skin of the bitten part and the specific symptoms of the deranged Váyu begin to manifest themselves in succession. A bite by a snake of the Mandali species gives a yellow tint to the space about the punctures made by its fangs, which becomes soft and marked by a burning sensation in its inside, and other specific symptoms of the deranged Pittam are found to supervene. Likewise, a bite by a snake of the Rájila species imparts a greyish tint to the seat of the wound, which becomes hard, glossy and slimy, the blood discharged from the punctures being found to be exceedingly thick. Symptoms peculiar to the deranged Kaphah are moreover exhibited in cases of bites by Râjila snakes.

A bite by a snake at the root of an Ashvaththa tree, or in a temple, or at a cremation ground, or near an ant-hill, or at the crossing of two roads, or at evening, or under the influence of the asterisms, Bharani, Ardrá, Ashleshá, Maghá and Mulá invariably proves fatal. Poisons of hooded serpents (Darbikaras) instantaneously prove fatal. Heat enhances the virulence of all kinds of poison. Poisons prove instantaneously fatal in infants, old men, pregnant women, lepers, and hungry or weak persons, as well as in those suffering from any kind of urinary disease or ulcer-cachexia. Persons bitten by snakes in whose body an incision fails to draw any blood (is not followed by bleeding), or strokes of lashes do not leave any marks on the skin, or in whom sprays of cold water do not produce any horripilation, should be abandoned as already in the clutches of death. A snake-bitten person whose face is distorted, nose is sunk down, neck is bent and jaws are locked up, and whose hairs may be easily pulled up, and in whom the punctured wounds of the bite assume a red or blackish hue, should be already counted with the dead. Emissions of ropy mucous from the mouth, and hæmorrhage from the upward or downward apertures of the body point to an unfavourable prognosis in a case of snake-bite. Similarly, four fang-marks on the seat of the bite, as well as loss of voice, inability to walk, or loss of the power of locomotion, blackness of complexion and bending of the nose are symptoms, which portend impending evil in cases of snake-bite.

An animal or a vegetable poison, made to part with any of the ten specific qualities of instantaneous expansiveness etc., or weakened by time, or through the exposure to air and light, or through contact with any neutralising vegetable agent, is called a Dushi Visha. A slow (dushi) poison, by reason of its weakened potency, lies over-powered by the mucous secretion, which its presence in the organism engenders, and fails to exercise any fatal effect, but long continues un-eliminated in the system. The presence of such a poison in the organism is indicated by loose stools, sallowness of complexion, a fetid smell in the body and a distaste in the mouth, with thirst, vertigo, epileptic fits, vomiting, indistinctness of speech, mental and bodily inertia, and a host of other distempers owing to the impairment of the normal physiological functions of the body. The presence of a slow poison in the stomach gives rise to diseases, which are due to the action of the deranged Váyu and Kaphah.

Continuing in the intestines, it brings on disorders which originate from the deranged action of the bodily Váyu and Pittam, falling off of the hair being one of its specific traits. Lodged in the lympchyle (Rasa) it produces indigestion, fever, nausea, jaundice, diseases of the heart, an aching pain in the limbs, a feeling of heaviness of the body and a distaste for food. Located in the blood (affecting the vascular system) it engenders cutaneous affections, erysipelas, pustular eruptions, specks and tans on the face, alopecia, abscesses, hæmorrhoids, tumours, menorrhagia, hæmorrhage, and splenic enlargement. Affecting the flesh it begets scrofula, scurvy, Osthapáka, ranula, tonsilitis, tumours, hæmorrhoids, etc. Deranging the fat it brings on glandular enlargements, tumours, Ostha-prokopa, diabetes and abnormal perspiration. Attacking the bones it produces such diseases as bad nails, Adhidanta, bone-ache, Adhyasthi, etc. Lodged in the marrow it begets darkness of vision, vertigo, epileptic fits, heaviness of the joints and opthalmia, etc. Lodged in the semen (affecting reproductive apparatus) it brings on impotency, seminal concretions in the urethra and spermatorrhœa, etc.

Increased sleep, heaviness of the limbs, yawns, looseness of the joints, horripilation and an aching pain in the body mark the premonitory stage of the aggravation of a slow poison in the system. A feeling of mandagore after eating, indigestion, with a distaste for food, appearance of circular rashes on the skin, or urticaria, loss of flesh, œdematous swelling of the extremities, epileptic fits, vomiting, dysentery, thirst, dyspnœa, fever, and dropsical swelling of the abdomen are the symptoms, which mark the stage when the effects of a slow poison becomes fully patent after the necessary period of incubation. One kind of slow-poison produces insanity, another brings on tympanites, a third begets seminal disorders (losses), a fourth engenders indistinctness of speech, a fifth brings on cutaneous affections, a sixth brings on carbuncles and erysipelàs, and so on. A residence in a swampy, or in a marshy country, cloudy days, ingestion of preparations of barley corn, and day-sleep are the factors, which tend to rouse up the latent action of a slow poison. Cases of slow-poisoning of recent origin and occurring in ungreedy and judicious persons are curable, such cases of nearly a year's standing can only be suppressed, while those occurring in persons of immoderate habits are incurable.

Wicked women, with a view to enthrall their lovers or husbands, mix the dirty rubbings of their bodies, or catamenial blood, or such like poisonous organic refuges with their food and drink, or men's enemies administer some sorts of slow poison through these vehicles out of a spirit of retaliation with the effect that the lovers or enemies to whom they are administered become afflicted with jaundice, emaciation, impaired digestion, dropsical swelling of the extremities, tympanites, ascites, diarrhœa, pthisis, consumption, fever or intestinal glands.

Once on a time king Vishvâmitra went to the hermitage of the holy Vashishta and attempted to forcibly drag away his cow (Káma dhenu). The beads of perspiration, which the wrath of that insulted sage engendered on his forehead, dropped on the bundles of cut grass (Lunas) stacked near at hand, and, behold, they were transformed into hosts of venomous spiders, called Lutás. Lutás (spiders) are so called from the fact of their originating from the drops of wrathful perspiration of the holy Vashistha which fell upon the bundles of cut grass (Luna's. There are sixteen different species of spiders, of which the bites by Sauvarnikas etc., prove fatal, while those by Trimandalas etc., obstinately resist the action of curative agents. Sloughing and putrefaction of and bleeding from, the seat of the bite, fever with a burning sensation in the bowels, appearance of large circular rashes and pustular eruptions on the skin, and red or brown-coloured, soft, extensive, and shifting swellings on the limbs form the general features of bites by venomous spiders. Bites by venomous spiders of Trimandala or allied species give a twany brown colour to seats of the bite. The wounds become covered with net works of false membranes and evince a tendency of shifting upward, attended with fever, swelling and discharge. The poison of a spider of any of these species undergoes a long incubation after which its action becomes patent in the organism. A bite by a venomous spider of any of the eight species, such as Sauvranikas etc., is marked by a swelling about the seat of the bite and the appearance of white, black, red or yellow pustular eruptions on the skin. Fever, dyspnœa, and hiccough with symptoms of cephalagia are also present and the patient succumbs to the virulence of the poison.

A bite by a poisonous rat is marked by bleeding from the seat of the bite, appearance of grey-coloured rashes on the skin, fever with a distaste for food, horripilation and a burning sensation in the body. A bite by a rat, which is fatally poisonous, gives rise to epileptic fits, a rat-like swelling about the seat of the bite, discolouring of skin, deafness, fever, salivation, vomiting of red blood, heaviness in the head and exudation of slimy fluid from the wound. A bite by a lizard (Krikalâsa), is marked by unconsciousness, loose motions of the bowels, and a varied colour of the skin of the seat of the bite. The poison of a centipede first produces an intolerable burning, breaking pain, and courses upward in the organism after which it returns to the seat of the bite and continues therein. A bite by a centipede at the tip of the tongue or nose, or at the region of the heart, happening to develop such symptoms as painful sloughing of the parts, should be regarded as presaging a near death. A bite by a venomous insect of the Kanabha species gives rise to erysipelatous eruptions, œdematous swellings, colic, fever, vomiting and sloughing of the seat of the bite. A bite by a poisonous cricket (Uchchitinga) is followed by horripilation and numbness of the genitals of its victim. An indescribable pain is felt in the body, which seems cold, as if packed in a wet sheet. Venomous frogs are usually found to bite with a single fang, swelling of, and pustular eruptions about, the seat of the bite, thirst, vomiting and somnolence being its specific characteristics. A bite by a venomous fish, is characterised by pain, swelling and a burning sensation. A bite by poisonous leeches develops fever, epileptic fits, swelling and an itching sensation. A bite by a domestic lizard develops perspiration, burning, swelling and a pricking pain. A bite by a venomous mountain-mosquito proves fatal as a Lutâ-bite of the incurable type. A bite by a fly of the Sthagika species proves instantaneously fatal, the wound being characterised by a constant discharge. Pustular eruptions appear on the skin, and fever, convulsion and a burning sensation in the body supervene. A bite or a scratch by a tiger or an ourang-outang gives rise to inflammation and suppuration in the wound. A bite by a rabid dog or a jackal develops tetanus, fever, etc,. Subsidence of the deranged and aggravated morbific principles of the body, restoration of the fundamental principles of the body to their normal condition with a desire for food, emission of stool and urine, normal functions of the organs, a healthy colour of the complexion, and a cheerful frame of mind of the patient are the symptoms from which a physician should infer the full elimination of a poison from his system.

——:o:——

CHAPTER CLXXXII.

Now hear me, O Sushruta, discourse on the Nidánam of Shlipadam (Elephantiasis).

A swelling attended with fever, which first occurs in either of the inguinal regions and ultimately extends to the legs, is called Shlipadam (Elephantiasis). Similar swellings may occur of the ears, hands, nose, lips and genitals. In the Vátaja form of Shlipadam (Elephantiasis) the skin of the swelling becomes rough and assumes a black colour. The skin of the affected part breaks, and a diverse kind of pain is felt in the affected regions without any apparent exciting cause. In the Pittaja form of Elephantiasis the swelling becomes soft, attended with a burning sensation in its inside, and the skin of the swelling assumes a yellowish colour. In the Kaphaja form of Elephantiasis the swelling becomes cold, compact, and white, glossy or grey. A case of Elephantiasis, which is of more than a year's growth, and is grown over with nodular excrescences in the manner of an anthill, should be given up as incurable. All these three forms of Elephantiasis should be understood as marked by a predominant action of the deranged Kaphah, inasmuch as heaviness, and swelling can not originate through the agency of any other morbific principle than the deranged Kaphah.

Now I shall discourse on the Nidánam of Vriddhi-Roga (Hernia, Hematocele). The enraged and aggravated down-coursing Váyu, by descending from the inguinal regions into the scrotum and pressing upon the chords of the testes, gives rise to enlargement of the scrotum, attended with fever, and an aching pain, etc., Vriddhi-Rogas may be divided into seven types according as the different deranged morbific principles attack the blood, fat, urine, or the colon. Of these Mutraja Vriddhi (Hydrocele) and Antra-Vriddhi (Hernia) are brought about through the aggravation of the deranged Váyu, though they are classed as two different diseases according to the difference of their regions of locations. In the Vátaja form of Vriddhi-Roga the tumour looks like a full bloated air-bladder and a variety of nervous pain is felt in its inside. In the Pittaja form of Vriddhi Roga the (scrotal tumour) assumes the colour of a ripe Audamvara fruit, and is marked by heat and a burning sensation. In the Kaphaja form of Vriddhi-Roga the tumour is félt hard and becomes cold, glossy, white or grey-coloured and slightly painful. In the Raktaja form of Vriddhi Roga (Hematocele), black belbous eruptions appear on the skin of the tumour and symptoms peculiar to the Pittaja form are likewise found to supervene. In the form of Vriddhi Roga, which has its origin in the diseased condition of the bodily fat, symptoms peculiar to the Kaphaja type are exhibited and the tumour looks big and brown like a ripe Tála fruit.

—:o:—

CHAPTER CLXXXIII.

Now hear me, O Sushruta, discourse of the Nidánam of Galaganda, (goitre) scrofula, and glandular swellings etc. A large or small, pendent swelling (growth) at the neck is called Galaganda (Goitre). The morbific principles of the deranged Váyu, and Kaphah, as well as the deranged fat, by taking recourse to the Manyás (muscles of the neck) severally give rise to different forms of Goitre, marked by their respective specific symptoms. In the form of Goitre originated though the action of the deranged Váyu, the swelling (growth)) assumes either a vermilion or a twany brown colour, covered over with nets of black veins, and is attended with an aching pain in its inside. Suppuration is markedly absent or is seldom established in the swelling in this form of Galaganda. A vapid taste in the mouth, together with a feeling of parchedness of the throat and the palate, is the specific concomitant of the type of Goitre which has its seat in the deranged Kaphah. The swelling is felt cold and firm to the touch, and becomes heavy and glossy in this type of the disease. A sweet taste in the mouth, together with the feeling of a sticky mucous-deposit lying on the lining membranes of the throat and the palate, forms the specific features of the type of Goitre which is brought about through the agency of the deranged fat. The swelling, which is marked by the presence of a little pain and an excessive itching sensation, becomes heavy, looks grey and glossy, and is found to be markedly slow in its growth and suppuratfon. It emits a kind of offensive smell and hangs down short-based from the neck (of the patient) like a pendent gourd, decreasing or increasing in size as the patient loses or gains flesh. The face of the patient looks glossy with a sort of oily deposit on the skin of the cheeks and forehead, and a sort of croaking sound is heard inside the body of the goitre. A patient with a goitre of more than a year's growth and afflicted with dyspnœa, weakness, aphonia, looseness of the limbs and a distaste for food should be abandoned as beyond all cure.

Strings of glandular swellings to the size of Karkandhu or Jujube stones, and occurring about the arm pits, inguinal or submaxillary regions or about the nape of the neck etc., through the agency of the deranged fat and Kaphah are called Gandamálás. These swellings are found to be very slow of suppuration. The disease in which some of these glands are found to suppurate and to spontaneously burst and secrete their contents, immediately followed by fresh crops of such glandular swellings in the affected region is called Apachi (scrofula). Cases of scrofula in which the glandular swellings do not appear in strings* are curable, while those in which the strings of glands are affected in succession and which exhibit the supervening symptoms of fever, cough, catarrh, pain at the sides pleuro-dynia), vomiting etc., baffle the ingenuity of even the best of physicians (Vaidyas.)

The morbific principles of the deranged Váyu etc., by vitiating the flesh, blood, fat and the vessels of the body, give rise to isolated nodular swellings, which are marked by their considerable elevation. These swellings are called Granthis. In the Vâtaja form of Granthi, the swelling seems as if it is being drawn about or burst open, or as if a scorpion has been stinging into it, or as if its contents are being churned about. It assumes a black colour and looks like an inflated bladder although fluctuating under pressure,† and secretes a kind of thin, transparent fluid, on bursting. In the Pittaja form of Granthi, the glandular swelling assumes a reddish or yellowish colour, and a variety of sucking, burning, tearing pain is felt in its inside. It secretes a thin, transparent, hot fluid on bursting. In the form of Granthi, which has its origin in the deranged Kaphah, the glandular swelling becomes slightly painful and hard like a stone. It is marked by a greyish tint or by the absence of any colour at all. The specific itching sensation of the deranged Kaphah is experienced, and the swelling, which is remarkably slow in its growth and suppuration, secretes a kind of thick, cold, white discharge, on bursting. In the type of Granthi, which is due to the deranged condition of the bodily fat the swelling decreases or gains in size with the emaciation or fattening of the body of the patient. It looks glossy

---

* Sushruta has *Analparupa* (not extremely increased or aggravated) —Tr.

† Dallana Mishra in his recension of the Sushruta Samhita reads Amridu (hard)—Tr.

and large, marked by a little pain and a considerable itching sensation and secretes a discharge of the colour of sesame-cake, on bursting. The deranged bodily Váyu, aggravated through over-fatiguing physical exercise and such like aggravating factors, finds lodgment in the veins and nerves, and gives rise to elevated nodular swellings by contracting, contorting (drawing up) and withering them up. Such swellings are called S'iraja Granthis (varicose veins, Neuroma) which happening to be shifting and painful, should be regarded as incurable. A varicose vein about any of the Marma Sthánas (described before), even if happening to be painless and non-shifting in its character, should be regarded as incurable.

The mobific principles of the deranged Váyu, Pittam, etc., by lying incarcerated in any part of the organism and by affecting the flesh and blood, give rise to firm, painless, round, large sized, short-based growths, which are very slow of growth and suppuration. These growths are found to be considerably deep-seated in the flesh of the affected region and are called tumours (Arvudas). The several types of tumours recognised in practice have their respective seats in the deranged Vâyu, Pittam, Kaphah, blood, flesh, and fat, and the specific features of each of these types are identical with those of Granthis brought about through the agency of each of these morbific principles of the organism. Now hear me, O Sushruta, describe the symptoms of the types of tumours, which originate from a vitiated condition of the flesh and blood.

The deranged Pittam and vitiated blood, by drawing up and contracting the veins, give rise to a kind of tumours, which are marked by secretion and a partial suppuration. They are very rapid in their growth, and are found to constantly bleed. These tumours are called Raktárvudas. Jaundice results from constant bleeding in cases of Raktárvudas. The flesh of any part of the body, affected through the effect of a hurt or injury, produces a kind of firm (non-shifting), hard, glossy, painless, or slightly painful swelling (tumour) of the same colour with the surrounding skin which is marked by little or no suppuration. These tumours are called Mánsárvudas. The exciting factor in all cases of Mánsárvudas should be regarded as the deranged Váyu. A deep seated Mánsárvuda appearing in persons, who are in the habit of taking meat diet, each day, through the vitiation of flesh, should be regarded as incurable. Even Mánsárvudas of curable types appearing about any of the Marmas and marked by copious discharges, as well as those which are firm and crop up in any of the external ducts of the body, should be regarded as incurable. A tumour, which appears on a pre-existing one, is called Adhyarvudam by the wise. A tumour suddenly or gradually appearing on a pre-existing one through the agency of any two of the morbific principles of the body should be likewise regarded as beyond the province of medicine. Suppuration is never found to set in in tumours owing to the presence of excessive Kaphah or fat in their inside, as well as in consequence of the morbific principles of the organism continuing therein in an unresolvable condition.

——:0:——

CHAPTER CLXXXIV.

Now hear me, O Sushruta, discourse on the Nidánam of Chhardi-Roga (vomiting). The enraged and aggravated Váyu, Pittam and Kaphah, as well as their concerted action, and the sight or smell of obnoxous things are the factors, which tend to produce vomiting, which may be grouped under five subheads according to the difference of its exciting factors.

Drinking of inordinately large quantities of fluid, ingestion of excessive quantities of emolient food, or of offensive, unwholesome, unaccustomed, or incongenial articles of fare, hasty eating, excessive physical labour, anxiety, indigestion, worms in the intestines, pregnancy and kindred conditions of the body are the factors which tend to set the morbific principles of the deranged Váyu, Pittam and Kaphah in motion, which, in their turn, are violently expelled through the mouth, producing a sort of breaking pain in the joints. The aggravated Váyu leads to the opening of the diaphragm of the chest, which makes the expulsion of the contents of the stomach through the mouth possible. This disease is called Chhardi (vomiting).

Nausea, suppression of eructations, water brash, and an extreme repugnance for food or drink are the symptoms, which are exhibited immediately previous to an act of vomiting. In the form of vomiting due to the action of the deranged Vâyu, pain at the chest and the sides, dryness of the mouth, aching pain in the head and about the umbilicus, cough, hoarseness, and a pricking pain in the body are the symptoms, which manifest themselves.

In the Pittaja form of vomiting thirst with epileptic fits, dryness of the mouth, heat in the head and eyes, vertigo and vanishing of sight are the symptoms, which manifest themselves. A kind of yellow, green, or reddish black, hot matter, which leaves a bitter taste in the mouth, is ejected and the patient complains of a burning sensation in the throat at the time of vomiting. Somnolence with a sweet taste in the mouth, water brash and a sense of repletion, drowsiness and a distaste for food and a feeling of heaviness of the limbs form the characteristic traits of the Kaphaja type of vomiting (Emisis). A thick, glossy, sweet and white coloured matter is belched out in this type, attended with horripilation. This type of vomiting is the least painful of all other types. Colic, indigestion with a repugnance for food, thirst, dyspnœa with a burning sensation in the body and epileptic fits are the symptoms, which are prominently exhibited in the Sánnipâtika form of vomiting, and the patient constantly belches out a hot, thick, blue or red-coloured matter with a saline taste. The accumulated bile and mucous in the stomach of the patient, as well as the other waste matters of the organism, vitiated by the deranged and aggravated Vâyu, are carried up and violently ejected through the mouth, when the enraged and aggravated bodily Vâyu, by obstructing the ducts of stool, urine and perspiration etc., abnormally courses in an upward direction within the organism. The ejected matter smells of stool and urine owing to the obstruction of the intestines and urinary ducts by the deranged Vâyu. Thirst, dyspnœa, and hic-cough are soon found to supervene and death comes and speedily closes the scene.

Vomitings severally induced by the sight or smell of an obnoxous object, as well as those due to uterine irritation as in pregnancy, or to the presence of worms, or of accumulated mucous in the intestines, should be all regarded as of a traumatic origin, the symptoms indicating the predominance of any particular morbific diathesis (such as the deranged Vâyu, etc.,) in the system should lay down the course of medical treatment to be adopted in each case. There is a persistent nausea with an intolerable colic in the type of vomiting due to the existence of worms in the intestines, and symptoms peculiar to a case of Hrid-roga of a parasitic origin are likewise found to supervene. Extreme prostration, and the colour of the ejected matter resembling that of the crest of a peacock's plume, as well as the fact of its being marked with shreds of blood or pus are symptoms which point to an unfavourable prognosis in vomiting.

Now hear me, O Sushruta, discourse on the Nidánam of the burning sensation in the body (Dáha). The heat of the Pittam, augmented through the abuse of wine, lies pent up in the blood and bile, and is afterwards thrown up to the surface-layer of the bodily skin, causing an intolerable burning sensation therein which is known as "wine's-burning." Blood, which courses through the whole organism, being conjested in the head, produces a kind of burning sensation in the body, attended with thirst and a copper-coloured complexion. The eyes assume a blood-shot aspect, an iron-like smell is emitted from the mouth and the patient feels as if being surrounded with a circle of blazing fire. All other symptoms of bilious fever become patent in this type of burning in which the same course of medical treatment should be followed as laid down in connection with bilious fever. Unappeased thirsts, by bringing about a diminution of the watery parts of the bodily constituents through the agency of the augmented Pittam, produce a kind of burning sensation both in the surface of the body and its inside in which the lips, throat, and palate seem as if parched up and the patient shakes and protrudes his tongue. Accumulation of blood in any of the chambers or cavities of the body (such as the the thorax) in consequence of a deep-seated sword-cut, or arrow-wound gives rise to a kind of intolerable burning sensation in the body in which all the symptoms of the type due to the congestion of blood are found to supervene. A loss of any of the fundamental principles of the body is followed by a burning sensation in the body which brings on epiliptic fits, thirst, aphonia, and stupour, which, if not speedily remedied, may terminate in death. A blow on any of the vulnerable Marmas of the body, such as the heart, bladder, head, etc., may bring on an intolerable burning sensation in the body which defies all medicinal remedies. A wise physician should not take in hand the medical treatment of a patient, who complains of a burning sensation in the body when it is felt cold to the touch.

CHAPTER CLXXXV.

NOW hear me, O Sushruta, discourse on the Nidánam of Shitapitta (Urticaria) etc,. The Kaphah and Váyu of the body, deranged through the contact of (exposure to) currents of cold air, invades the skin and blood in combination with the deranged Pittam, and produces the disease known as Shitapittam. Thirst with a burning sensation in the body, nausea with a distaste for food, feeling of physical languor, and heaviness of the eyes are the symptoms, which mark the premonitory stage of Urticaria. Eruptions like wasp-stings appear on the body both in urticaria and the disease known as Urdada. An itching, pricking pain is felt in these eruptions, and fever with vomiting, etc., becomes manifest. A preponderance of the deranged bodily Váyu acts as the exciting factor of Urticaria, while a preponderance of the deranged Kaphah lies at the root of a case of Urdada. The distinctive traits of the eruptions of Urdada are that they are dipped at the centre, being marked by an itching sensation, and are arranged in circular patches. Unsatisfactory exhibitions of emetics, by arresting the ejection of bile, mucous and ingested food from the system, cause a large number of itching, circular rashes to appear on the skin, which spontaneously disappear a short while after their appearance.

Now hear me, O Sushruta, discourse on the Nidánam of Amlapittam (acidity). Ingestion of incompatible articles of fare, use of unwholesome food, ingestion of acid substances, or of those which give rise to a re actionary acidity (Undergoes an acid transformation after digestion) in the stomach, or of those which extremely aggravate the Pittam are the factors, which hinder the assimilation of the Pittam (bile) accumulated in the digestive apparatus of a man, and this undigested or unassimilated bile brings about the disease known as Amla-Pittam (acidity).

Indigestion of the ingested food, lassitude, nausea, risings of bitter eructations, or a feeling of heaviness in the limbs with a burning sensation in the throat or epigastrium, as well as a marked distaste for food are the symptoms which form the characteristic features of Amlapittam. Loose motions of green, yellow, or various coloured stool, together with thirst, vertigo, epileptic fits, cloudy perception, nausea, absent-mindedness, Urticaria, impaired digestion, horripilation, yellowness of the complexion and abnormal perspiration, together with a burning sensation in the body form the specific symptoms of the type of Amlapittam in which the undigested food in the stomach finds a downward outlet. In the type of which vomiting forms the primary and specific trait the ejected matter is found to be either green, yellow, red, or blue, mixed with a kind of slimy, transparent mucous. It has bitter or acid taste. Imperfect digestion of ingested food in the stomach is sometimes followed by the rising of bitter or acid eructations or belching out of a bitter acid fluid. A burning sensation in the throat, epigastrium and the sides, headache, heat in the body, an extreme repugnance for food, fever which has its origin in the deranged condition of the Kaphah and Pittam, pustular eruptions on the skin and a host of other distempers are usually found to follow in the wake of Amlapittam. Even cases of acidity of recent origin require special care to be radically cured, and a temporary palliation is the only relief that can be expected from a judicious course of medical treatment in old or chronic cases, although instances are not wanting where a radical cure has been effected inspite of the age and chronic nature of the ailment. Cases of Amlapittam are usually divided into three classes such as Vátaja, Kaphaja, and Vata-Kaphaja, according to the predominance of any of these three morbific principles in those under treatment, and they are very apt to confound even an expert physician in matters of diagnosis. Shivering, delirium, epileptic fits, tingling sensations in the limbs, lassitude, neuralgic pain, darkness of vision, vertigo and mind-wanderings are the symptoms, which mark the Vátaja type of Amlapittam. In the type marked by the dominant action of the deranged and aggravated Kaphah, symptoms such as expectoration of mucous, heaviness of the limbs, lassitude with a distaste for food, and shivering with a gone feeling in the limbs manifest themselves. In the type due to the combined action of the deranged Vâyu and Kaphah, drowsiness, together with the specific symptoms of the two abovesaid types, forms the specific feature. Bitter or acid eructations, with a burning sensation in the throat, sides and the epigastrium, vertigo, swooning, vomiting, lassitude with a distaste for food, headache, salivation, and a sweet taste in the mouth are the symptoms, which mark the Kaphaja type of Amlapittam.

—:o:—

CHAPTER CLXXXVI.

Now hear me, O Sushruta, discourse on the Nidánam of Shula (Colic, etc., and neuralgic pain). Over-fatiguing physical labour, excessive riding, or pedestrian journey, sexual excesses, late hours, drinking of extremely cold water, ingestion of extremely parchifying articles of fare, such as peas, Mudgapulse, etc., eating before a previous meal is digested, hurt or injury, eating of bitter or astringent articles in exclusion of those of any other taste, as well as of incompatible food-stuff, suppression of any natural urgings of the body, grief, fasting, and excessive laughter or talk are the factors, which tend to enrage the bodily Váyu, which, in its turn, produces colicky (neuralgic pain) in the chest, sides, back, sacrum and pelvis. Eight different forms of Shula are recognised in practice according as the different morbific principles of the deranged Váyu, Pittam, etc., either severally or jointly bring on an attack, although a dominant action of the deranged Váyu should be regarded as lying at the root of each case of neuralgic (Shula) pain or colic.

The Vátaja type of Shula is spontaneously aggravated after the completion of the process of digestion, at nightfall (evening), in cloudy days and in winter and the rainy season. The pain subsides and comes on at close intervals in this type of the disease, the emission of stool and flatus is suppressed, and the patient complains of a pricking or breaking pain in his limbs, which is relieved by fomentation, massage, oily applications, and the use of hot food.

Ingestion of excessively hot, irritating, alkaline or indigestible articles of fare (that undergo an acid reaction in the stomach after digestion), use of fermented liquors or of extremely acid 'food, anger, exposure to heat or to the sun, sexual excesses, and over-fatiguing physical labour are the factors, which tend to derange the Pittam, which, in its turn, brings on a peculiar kind of Shula (colic) about the umbilicus, which is usually known as Pittaja Shula. Thirst, delusion (feeling of intoxication) with a burning sensation in the body, perspiration, epilepsy, vertigo, and a scorching heat in the body are the further characteristics of this type of Shula, which is spontaneously aggravated at noon, at mid-night, during the process of digestion and in autumn, and is ameliorated in winter and by cold measures and applications.

Use of the cooked flesh of aquatic animals, or of those that frequent swamps or live in marshy places, drinking of milk, milk-curd or the expressed juice of sugarcane in inordinate quantities, and factors that tend to aggravate the Kaphah should be regarded as the exciting causes of a kind of Shula in the stomach (Kaphja Shula) of which nausea, cough, lassitude of the body, salivation with a distaste for food, numbness of the stomach and heaviness of the head form the specific features. This disease is intensely aggravated at morning, and in spring and winter, and immately after a meal. In the type due to the concerted action of the deranged Váyu, Pittam and Kaphah, a colic is experienced in the chest, back, sacrum, sides, abdomen and the pelvis and death may result within a very short space of time. The type of Shula, which is due to the incarceration of mucous in the intestines (Amaja), tympanites with a rumbling sound in the abdomen, nausea, vomiting, heaviness of the limbs, suppression of stool and urine and salivation and a feeling of being packed in a wet sheet together with other specific symptoms of the Kaphaja type speedily manifest themselves.

In the type of Shula, due to the incarceration of mucous in the intestines, nausea, vomiting with a rumbling sound in the intestimes, suppression of stool and anus, salivation with a feeling as if the body is packed in a wet sheet, and other specific features of the Kaphaja type of this disease are also present. In the types of Shula respectively due to the combined actions of the deranged Váyu and Kaphah, Pittam and Kaphah, and Váyu and Pittam the pain is confined to regions of the urinary bladder (Pelvis according to certain authorities) heart, sides and the back, to the inguinal, umbilical and cardiac regions, and to those of sacrum, pelvis heart sides, back and umbilicus respectively, an intense fever and an intolerable burning sensation in the body being the further characteristics of each of them. Cases of Shula (neuralgia) brought about through the several actions of the deranged Váyu, Pittam and Kaphah readily prove amenable to medicine, those due to the combined action of any two of the said Doshas are comparatively more difficult to cure, while those which are due to their concerted action (Sánnipátika) baffle all medicinal remedies.

The deranged bodily Váyu, aggravated by its own exciting factors, produces a kind of Pre-digestionary colic, which is called Parináma Shula (Gastralgia). This disease is so named from the fact that the colic is brought on after the ingested food is considerably digested in the stomach and close before the completion of the proceess of digestion. The nature of an attack, which is usually experienced at the advanced stage, and before the completion, of the process of digestion, may be determined with regard to the predominance of the deranged Váyu, Pittam, or Kaphah, acting as its exciting cause. In the Vátaja form of Parináma Shula tympanites with a rumbling sound in the belly, suppression of the stool and urine, malaise and rigour are the symptoms that are usually developed. The pain in this type is relieved by the use of hot, emulsive food. Ingestion of pungent, acid, or saline articles of fare may be set down as the exciting cause of a case of Pittaja type of this disease, which is characterised by thirst, malaise, and perspiration with a burning sensation in the body. It shows signs of marked amclioration under cold applications and cooling measures in general. Nausea, vomiting, and epileptic fits are exhibited in the Kaphaja type of this disease. The pain continues long and becomes persistent and is relieved by the use of bitter, pungent articles of fare. The presence of specific features of any two of the deranged Váyu, Pittam, etc., in a particular case of Parináma Shula, indicates its origin through the agency of those two morbific principles of the body, while that of the specific features of all the there Doshas points to its Sánnipátika origin, a case of the latter type being always regarded as incurable, in as much as it produces emaciation of the body and entirely impairs the digestive faculty of the patient. The type of colic which comes on simultaneously with the commencement of the digestion of the ingested food, or after the completion of the digestive process, or just after the ingested food is carried down into the stomach and before it is fully converted into chyme, and which does not show any sign of amelioration even with a strict regimen of diet and conduct, is called Anna-Drava-Shula (lit colic of undigested chyme or chyle). Ejection of the contents of the stomach and the consequent assimilation of the deranged bile give relief in this type of Gastralgia.

——:o:——

CHAPTER CLXXXVII.

DHANVANTARI said :—Now hear me, O Sushruta, discourse on the Nidánam of Svara-Bhanga (aphonia). The deranged Váyu etc, aggravated by loud talking, loud chanting of the Vedas and loud recitations of verses, etc., affect the vocal chords, and give rise to Svarabhanga (aphonia) which may divided into six different types. In the Vátaja form of aphonia the stool, urine, face and the eyes of the patient assume a black colour and the voice somewhat resembles the harsh brayings of an ass. The stool, urine, face and the eyes of a patient, suffering from an attack of Pittaja aphonia assume a yellow colour, and a burning sensation is experienced in the larynx at the time of speaking. In the Kaphaja type the voice becomes small and weak owing to the obstruction of the larynx with mucous, which, when it melts under the influence of the solar heat during the day, allows the patient to speak in a stronger and clearer voice.

CHAPTER CLXXXVIII.

DHANVANTARI said:—Now hear me, O Sushruta, discourse on the Nidánam of Udávarta. Suppression of urgings towards sneezing, yawning, defecation, urination or of any other functions of the body, unnatural non-gratification of hunger, thirst, etc., should be regarded as the exciting factors of Udávarta. The type of Udávarta, ushered in through a voluntary retention of flatus, is marked by tympanites with suppression of stool and urine, lassitude and a pricking, aching pain in the intestines. A deranged and aggravated condition of the bodily Váyu should be regarded as one of the essential causes of Udávarta, and measures calculated to restore the deranged Váyu to its normal course and condition should be considered as the primary remedies in all types of this disease. In the type due to the voluntary retention of stool, an aching pain with a rumbling sound in the intestines, a cutting pain about the anus, suppression of stool and urine and rising of eructations are the symptoms which manifest themselves, and sometimes the fecal matter is found to be ejected though the mouth. The type of Udávarta, which originates from a voluntary retention of urine, is marked by an aching pain in the bladder and urethera, strangury, and a drawing pain in the inguinal regions. The body seems extremely painful and the patient finds relief only in a recumbent posture. In the type ot Udávarta resulting from a voluntary suppression of an urging towards yawning, stiffness of the muscle of the neck (Manyá) with a numbed pain in the throat, headache and a host of other diseases of the eyes, ears, nose and mouth are developed. Similarly, the type of Udávarta, which is brought on through a voluntary suppression of tears, is amrked by an excruciating headache, catarrh and affections of the eyes. Voluntary suppressions of urgings towards sneezing may bring on a type of Udávarta, which is marked by an excruciating headache, stiffness of the neck, faceal paralysis, hemi-crania and impaired organic functions in general. The type of Udávarta, which is induced through voluntary suppressions of yawns, gives rise to a sense of fullness in the throat and mouth, an aching pain with a rumbling sound in the intestines, a croaking sound in the throat, indistinctness of speech, dyspnœa, hic-cough, and other disorders of the deranged Váyu. The type of Udávarta, which is caused through the voluntary suppression of vomitings, is marked by urticaria, itching eruptions on the skin, with a distate for food, cutaneous affections, nausea, and erysipelatous ulcers on the skin. In the type ushered in through a voluntary suppression of emission of semen, a cutting pain in the scrotum, rectum, penis and bladder, together with a swelling about any of these localities, dribbling of urine and semen, suppression of urine, and seminal concretions are the symptoms that are exhibited. Unappeased hunger brings on drowsiness, lassitude with a distate for food and an aching pain in the limbs and impaired faculty of sight. An ungratified thirst produces parchedness of the throat and mouth, pain about the cardiac region, and obstruction of the faculty of hearing. Suppression of sighs after a fatiguing physical labour or exhaustion may bring on diseases of the heart, loss of consciousness, intestinal glands, yawning, with an aching pain in the limbs, heaviness of the head and the eyes, and drowsiness.

The bodily Váyu, deranged and aggravated by the ingestion of bitter, astringent, or parchifying articles of fare, invades the digestive apparatus, and by taking recourse in the abdominal cavity, gives rise to Udávarta. The deranged Váyu, thus aggravated, by stuffing the vessels of blood, fat, stool and urine, etc., absorbs the humidity of the feces and makes them dry and hard as stone. The patient tosses about in agony, afflicted with nausea, pain about the heart, and an aching pain in the urinary bladder, and the flatus, stool and urine are emitted with the greatest difficulty. Dyspnœa, cough, catarrh with a burning sensation in the body, thirst, epileptic fits, fever, vomiting, hic-cough, mental aberrations, headache and other distempers, which originate from the deranged Váyu, gradually manifest themselves with the progress of the disease.

The feces and the undigested lymph-chyle gradually accumulated in the stomach and obstructed in their downward course by the deranged and aggravated Váyu, gives rise to Anáha, which is characterised by thirst, catarrh with a burning sensation in the head, gastralgia and a sensation of a weight in the stomach, and suppression of eructations, etc. In the type due to the accumulation of fecal matter in the intestines a feeling of numbness at the back and sacrum, suppression of stool and urine, colic epileptic fits, vomiting of fecal matter, œdema, and other distempers of the obstructed Váyu are found to be manifest.

—:o:—

CHAPTER CLXXXIX.

DHANVANTARI said :—Now hear me, O Sushruta, discourse on the Nidánam of Sadyo Vranas (traumatic ulcers). Wounds inflicted with weapons of variously shaped edges, necessarily assume a variety of shape. Wounds may be described as cut (Chhinna). Incised (Bhinna), Pierced (Viddha), Kshatam (ulcerated), Pichchhitam (thrashed) and Ghrisam (bruised or contused). Now hear me describe the characteristic features of each of them. A straight or oblique, extensive cut in which the local flesh is entirely cut away is called Chinna. A piercing of any of the chambers or viscera of the body with a fine-topped weapon of the nature of a spear, etc., furnishes the example of a pierced or incised (Bhinna) wound, which is usually found to be attended with a discharge. The stomach, the abdomen, the liver, the spleen, the heart, the urinary bladder, the kidneys, the lungs, and the cecum are called the Koshthas. A perforation of any of these Koshthas usually exhibits the following symptoms, *viz.*, fever with a burning sensation in the body, hæmorrhage from the nose, mouth anus or the urethra, epileptic fits, dyspnœa, tympanites, with a disinclination to take any food, suppression of the stool urine and flatus, parchedness of the body even inspite of a copious perspiration, emission of an iron-like smell from the mouth, as well as of an offensive smell from the skin, and an aching pain at the sides and about the cardiac region. Now hear me describe the detailed and specific symptoms of perforation of each of the Koshthas. Vomiting of blood follows the accumulation of blood in the stomach, and an excruciating colic and excessive distension of the abdomen are found to instantaneously supervene. Pain and heaviness of the limbs are developed when the blood is accumulated in the abdominal cavity, coldness of the lower extremities being one of its specific and distinctive traits. A wound caused by the piercing of a sharp-topped substance into any part of the body, whether with or without the piercing substance lying within its inside, is called a Biddha (pierced) wound. A wound, which is neither a cut nor an incision, but partakes of the nature of the both and whose cavity is of an irregular shape, is called a Kshata. Any part of the body thrashed with the underlying bones by beating, and becoming smeared with blood and marrow furnishes the examples of a Pichchhita (thrashed) wound. An abraded wound is called a Ghrishta Vrana. Secretion of hot serum and breaking of the local skin form its principal characteristics. A traumatic wound with any extrinsic matter (shalyam) lying imbedded in its cavity is marked by a swelling of tawny brown colour, studded over with pustular eruptions and constant bleeding and a pain about its seat, which becomes extremely sensitive and can not bear the least touch. A Shalyam (extrinsic matter), which is pierced into any of the aforesaid Koshthas of the body, by passing through the layers of the local skin, or through any of the local veins and arteries, produces symptoms that have been described before in this connection. A wise surgeon (Vaidya), having any regard to his professional good name, should not take in hand the treatment of a patient with a pierced Kostha, whose eyes have become blood-red, whose breath, face and extremities have become cold, whose complexion has assumed an ashy colour, and from the cavity of whose wound the piercing dart has not been extracted and the accumulated blood has not been let out. Vertigo, delirium, prostration, unconsciousness, languor, heat, looseness of the limbs, epileptic, fits, Urdhavâta, pain and other distressing symptoms of the deranged Váyu, discharge of blood resembling the washings of meat, and cessation of all organic functions of the body are the general symptoms, which are exhibited in connection with perforation of any of the bodily Marmas. Ulcers produced through the agency of two of the morbific principles of the body, or brought about through the concerted action of all of them, exhibit symptoms which are respectively peculiar to each of them. Ulcers appearing in young persons of judicious and moderate habits and in a season of the year in which the morbific principles acting as their exciting factors are spontaneously aggravated, and occurring in parts of the body which are easily accessible, readily yield to medicinal treatment. Ulcers possessed of features other than the foregoing ones, are very hard to cure. Ulcers brought about through the concerted action of the three Doshas and attended with the abovesaid supervening distresses baffle all medicimal treatment. A putrid condition of the cavity of an ulcer, as well as a discharge of blood or pus from its inside, and exhalation of an offensive odours therefrom indicate that it is not yet asepsised. An ulcer whose cavity has assumed a tongue-like colour, studded over by healthy granulations, should be regarded as a cleansed (Shuddha) ulcer. An ulcer, which is marked by the absence of any discharge, and whose cavity has assumed a colour like that of a pigeon, and which has become firm, surrounded by crops of pustular eruptions, should be regarded as being granulating. Ulcers whose cavities have been entirely filled up and which are marked by the absence of any pain or swelling and whose cicatrixes have become of the same colour with the surrounding skin, should be regarded as healed up ulcers (Rudha Vranas). Ulcers appearing in lepers and in persons affiicted with diabetes or pthisis as well as in those suffering from the effects of any poison, or those which appear on pre-existing ulcers should be regarded as extremely hard to cure- An idiopathic ulcer secreting a discharge of fat, clotted blood, or of marrow should be regarded as beyond all cure, whereas a traumatic ulcer attended with a similar discharge may prove amenable to medicine. Exhalation of a smell like that of wine, Eagle wood, clarified butter, Champaka or lotus flowers, or of any other celestial or fragrant smell from an ulcer indicate the impending death of the ulcer patient. In cases of piercing of the arteries the bleeding becomes excessive. The discharged blood has a colour like that of a cochineal insect and the deranged and aggravated Vayu of the incidental wound produces blindness, convulsions etc., Piercing of any ligament (Snáya) produces curvature or archedness of the affected part of the body, with a gone feeling in the limbs, loss of functions of the part of the ligament affected and an intolerable pain, the incidental wound taking a long time to be healed up. The piercing of any fixed or moving bone-joints of the body is followed by an excessive and extremely painful swelling about, and loss of function of, the affected joint. Whereas in a case of piercing of a bone-shaft the pain continues without respite during the whole day and night, and the patient fails to find relief in any posture whatsoever, Erysipelas, paralysis, stiffness and numbness of veins or arteries, convulsions, swooning, mania, fever with an excruciating pain in the wound, excessive thirst, paralysis, of the mandibles, cough, vomiting, dysentery, hic-cough, dyspnœa, and shivering are the sixteen distressing and dangerous concomitants of Sadyovranas.

—:o:—

CHAPTER CXC.

DHANVANTARI said:—Now hear me, O Sushruta, discourse on the Nidánam of Shárira Vranas. (Idiopathic ulcers). Vranas may be divided into two classes such as the Sharira and Aguntaka (traumatic) ones. Ulcers originating through the agency of the aggravated morbific principles of the body, are called Sharira (Idiopathic) ulcers, while those that are due to the effects of blows with sharp-edged weapons are called Agantukas.

Ulcers due to the action of the deranged and aggravated Váyu is marked by an aching, throbbing pain and a scanty discharge. It becomes hard and assumes a twany brown colour. Pittaja ulcers are marked by a fetid smell and a discharge of fetid pus and give rise to thirst, and fever with a burning sensation in the body and an excited state of mind like that of intoxication. Kaphaja ulcers are characterised by a numbed pain and a greyish colour. They secrete a copious quantity of slimy discharge and are very slow to suppurate, a sensation of heaviness about their locations being also one of their specific traits. Ulcers, which have their origin in the vitiated blood, are marked by a copious bleeding, while those, which are engendered through the concerted action of the three Doshas, or which appear on any of the Marma Sthânas of the body and are marked by an intolerable burning sensation within, although they are felt cold on the surface, or which are attended with cough, emaciation, prostration of the bodily strength and a distaste for food with a copious fetid discharge from their inside, should be regarded as incurable. Ulcers, which do not show any sign of healing inspite of the applications of proper remedial agents and measures, should be pronounced as incurable.

——:o:——

CHAPTER CXCI.

DHANVANTARI said :—Now hear me, O Sushruta, discourse on the Nidânam of fractures of bone-joints (Bhagnas), which may be divided into six kinds such as, the Utpishtam (Fractures brought about through the friction of two bones), Vishlishtam (dislocation), Vivartitaṁ (Retroversion), Tirjakgatam (obliquely turned up), Kshiptam (displacement from sockets) and Adhah-kshiptam (such displacement in a downward direction). Bone-shafts lying between two bone-joints are called Kândas, and twelve different kinds of fractures of bone-shafts (Kânda-Bhagnas) have been recognised in practice, which are called Karkataka (crab-like), Ashvakarna (horse-ear), Vichurnita (Smashed), Pichchhita (flattened) Chhallikâ (splintered), Kânda-bhagna (bone-fractures), Atipâtitam (hung down), Majjâgatam, Sphutitam, Vakra (bent) and the two kinds of Chhinnam.

Incapacity of stretching or flexing the affected limb and its inability to bear the least touch (extreme sensitiveness) form the general characteristics of all kinds of fractured bone-joints.

The fracture of a bone-joint owing to the friction between its parts is called Utpishtam, which is marked by swellings on its both sides and a constant pain, which is aggravated in the night. An excruciating pain about each side of the fractured joint forms the specific trait of a case of the Vivartitam type. An excruciating pain is experienced about the bone-joint where a bone is dislodged from its joint and remains in an oblique position (Tirjakgatam). An aching pain is experienced in the case where a bone is severed from its joint and is directed upward. An intolerable pain is felt about the affected bone-joint, and the two shafts of the bone are felt to be uneven and unequal in length in the Kshipta type of fractured bone-joint. Similarly, a broken bone, hanging down from its socket, furnishes the example of one of the Adhahkshiptam type. An aching pain is felt about the affected part and the one bone of the broken joint can be rubbed against the other.

The names of the twelve different kinds of fractured bones signify the shape and nature of the fracture in each. Looseness of the affected limb, pain and swelling about the fractured bone, a creaking sound on pressing the seat of the fracture, together with an aching, pricking pain in its inside, form the general features of all types of fractures. Impairment of digestion in a fracture-patient of a nervous temperament, fever, tympanites, suppression of the stool and urine, and want of proper care in reducing the fracture at the outset are the factors, which hinder the cure in fracture cases. Dislocation and fracture of the bones of the sacrum, as well as smashing of the bones of the thighs should be regarded as irremediable. Cases where the fractured bones have been wrongly reduced and reset at the outset should be likewise regarded as beyond all cure. The Bhanga (lit, fracture) of a bone of the Taruna class (gristle) consists in its bending or curvature, that of a bone of the Nalaka kind (hollow like tibial bones) consists in its bursting, that of a bone of the Kapâla kind (like that of the forehead) consists in its breaking, while that of one of the Ruchaka kind (as a tooth) consists in its cracking or splintering.

——:o:——

CHAPTER CXCII.

DHANVANTARI said :—Now hear me, O Sushruta, discourse on the recipes of medicinal compounds of infallible efficacy, which I shall shortly enumerate for the good of all creatures. Ingestion of astringent, pungent, bitter, acid or parchifying articles of fare, anxiety, sexual excesses, physical fatigue, fright, grief, late hours, loud talking, carrying of inordinately heavy weights, undue application to any kind of work and fasting are the factors, which tend to aggravate the bodily Vâyu, which is naturally aggravated during the rainy season, after the digestion of food, and at the close of day. Similarly, ingestion of hot, acid, saline, alkaline, pungent and indigestable articles of fare in general, exposure to heat, and indulgence in cups and anger are the factors, which tend to aggravate the Pittam, which is spontaneously aggravated during the process of digestion, in summer and autumn, and at the middle part of the day or night. Ingestion of sweet, acid, saline, emulsive, cold, or heavy (of digestion) articles of fare, use of newly harvested rice, or of the flesh of animals that live in pools or in marshy places, want of physical exercise, day sleep, and sedentary habits in general are the factors, which tend to aggravate the Kaphah, which is spontaneously aggravated in the morning, just after eating and in the spring time Roughness of the skin, contraction of the limbs, an aching sensation, tympanites, anæsthesia, horripilation, atrophy or numbness of any part of the body, looseness of the limbs with a twany brown complexion, increase of physical strength, or extreme prostration are the specific traits of the deranged and aggravated Vâyu, as well as of diseases due to its agency. Heat with a burning sensation in the body, redness and inflammation of the (affected part), exhalation of an acid, pungent, or cadaverous smell from the body, perspiration, thirst, vertigo, and epileptic fits, as well as jaundice or chlorosis form the specific features of the deranged Pittam. Gloss of skin with a sweet taste in the mouth, a sense of being packed in a wet sheet, œdema, coldness, heaviness, itching, somnolence, and a delayed crisis are the symptoms, which indicate the action of the deranged Kaphah. The presence of the combined symptoms of any two of these Doshas in a disease points to its Bi-doshaja origin, while a combination of all the three Doshas in a disease indicates its Sánnipátika origin. The human body is the receptacle of Doshas, Dhâtus (fundamental organic principles) and Malas (excreta.) A normal equlibrium among them is called health, while an increase or decrease of any of them is called disease. Blood, fat, flesh, myosin, bones, marrow and semen are called Dhátus; the deranged Vâyu, Pittam and Kaphah are called Doshas, while stool, urine, etc., are called Malas. The Váyu (nerve energy) is cold, light, subtle, parchifying and mobile; the Pittam (bile) is acid, pungent and hot, and brings on suppuration and diseases of the albumen and Glycogen; Kaphah (mucous) is sweet, heavy, slimy, shiny and emulsive. The Vâyu is principally located in the rectum and pelvis; the Pittam, in the digestive apparatus; and the Kaphah, in the stomach and head and about the bones (synovia). Things of pungent, bitter or astringent flavour aggravates the deranged Váyu; saline, acid and pungent things aggravate the deranged Pittam, while sweet, saline and hot things aggravate the deranged Kaphah. Proper antidotes to these, administered in diseases, lead to their subsidence, while they contribute to keep the normal equilibrium among the fundamental organic principles in health. A sweet taste improves the eye-sight and increases the quantity of Dhâtus and lymph chyle, while an acid taste is digestant, appetising and relishing. A saline taste is purgative, emetic, digestant, and liquefacient. A pungent taste is digestant, appetising, anti-toxic, anti-corpulent, and exciting. A bitter taste is a febrifuge, and is appetising, laxative, and refrigerant. An astringent taste is liquefacient, choleric, aperient and absorbant. A drug is the receptacle of taste, potency, and digestive transformation. The potency of a drug is either cooling or thermogenic. Digestive transformation (reaction undergone in the stomach by a thing after digestion) is either sweet or pungent. A physician, patient, nursing attendant and medicine form the four legs of a medical treatment, and an absence of any of these makes it abortive or impossible. The season of the year, the place (of residence), age, digestive capacity, physical temperament of the patient, as well as the state of his body and its strength, things he is accustomed to, and the nature of the disease and of the curative drug to be employed should be taken into consideration before commencing a medical treatment.

A well watered, well drained, hilly country, well shaded by forests, is called a *Jángala* country in which hæmorrhage is found to be the prevailing disease. A marshy place, or a swampy country, in which Váyu and Kaphah are naturally aggravated, is called an A'nupa country. A country, which partakes of the physical traits of both these kinds, is called a Sádhárana country. Infancy extends to the sixteenth year of a person, youth extends thence forward to the seventieth year, and after that is the old age. The Kaphah predominates in infancy; the Pittam, in youth; and the Váyu, in old age. Surgical operations should be done with the help of cauterisation of both kinds (fire and alkali) on infants and old men. An emaciated frame should be tried to be made stout; a corpulent body should be tried to be reduced in bulk An active, muscular frame is all that is to be desired in life. The strength of a person should be inferred from his sustaining power, physical work and cheerfulness of mind. A healthy man is possessed of an indomitable energy and courage. Even food and drink, which are ordinarily calculated as unwholesome, should be regarded as congenial to persons in whom they fail to produce any distressing symptoms. Váyu-generating, Pitta-generating, or Kapha-generating food, exclusively taken by a person, makes his physical temperament marked by a preponderance of Váyu, Pittam, or Khaphah, hence one should partake of a mixed kind of diet. A man of Vátika temperament has a sinewy frame and sparse hairs, is of a volatile disposition, and talks much in dreams. The hair of a man of Pittaja temperament becomes prematurely grey. He is irritable and fair-complexioned, easily perspires and dreams of fire in sleep. A man of Kaphaja (phlegmatic) temperament is possessed of a crown of glossy hair, is of a somewhat sluggish disposition, and dreams of water in sleep. A man of a bi-humoural temperament is possessed of mental and physical traits peculiar to each of those humours. The digestive capacity of a person is either sluggish, sharp, irregular, or normal; and of these four kinds the normal one is to be preferred. In the irregular kind measures and remedies calculated to subdue the deranged Váyu should be employed, while in sharp and sluggish forms, Pitta-subduing, and Kaphah-destroying remedies should be respectively employed. Indigestion is the parent of all diseases, and there are four forms of indigestion such as, the A'ma, Amla, Rasa, and Vishtambha. In the A'maja form vomiting should be induced with the administration of Vacha and salt.

In the Amla form of indigestion, which is marked by the non-emission of semen, vertigo, swoonings, etc., the remedy consists in drinking cold water, and inhaling cold air.

In the indigestion of undigested lymph chyle (Rasa), which begets an aching pain in the limbs, with a numbed, confused feeling in the head and a distaste for food, the patient should be advised to forego all food and drink, and to take a sleep in the day. In the Vishtambha form of indigestion, which is marked by tympanites, colic, and suppression of stool and urine, diaphoretic measures should be employed, and solution of common salt should be internally administered. The three forms of indigestion (A'ma, Amla and Vishtambha) should be regarded as respectively due to the actions of the deranged Kaphah, Pittam, and Váyu. A prudent man, (suffering from indigestion), should plaster his abdomen with a paste of Hingu, Trushana, and rock salt, and enjoy a siesta in the day, inasmuch as these measures are found to be curative in all forms of indigestion. Hosts of bodily ailments result from the use of unwholesome food, hence one should refrain from taking any food that proves incongenial to one's system. A potion of honey and warm water acts as a digestant, and milk is incompatible with Karira, fish and milk-curd. The group of drugs, which is known as the major Pancha Mulam and which consists of Vilva, Shonyâka, Gâmbhâri, Pâtalâ, and Ganikarikâ, is appetising, and subdues the deranged Váyu and Kaphah. The group of drugs, which is known as minor Pancha Mulam, and which consists of Shâlaparni, Prishniparni, Gokshura, Vrihati and Kantakâri, is restorative and subdues the deranged Váyu and Pittam. These two groups of drugs jointly form what is called Dasha Mulam, which forms curative in Sánnipátika forms of fever, cough, asthma, aching pain at the sides, and somnolence. Medicated oils and Ghritas, cooked and prepared with the aforesaid Dashamulam, as well as Dashamula plasters and pastes cure Sánnipátika forms of diseases. Take water four times as much as the drugs, boil it down to its quarter part, add oil or Ghrita, four times as much as this drug-decoction, and milk to the weight of the oil or Ghrita, and drug-paste to a quarter weight of the latter, and boil and cook it in the usual way. The medicated oil or Ghritam of Dashamulam, properly prepared (neither over nor under-cooked), should be employed as potions and clysters; that, which is over-cooked, should be used as unguents, while that which is under-cooked should be used errhines. This is the usual practice. A cure denotes the restoration of the gross body and its internal organs to their normal condition or functions, and a patient, whose vital energy is not at its lowest ebb, should be alone medicinally treated. A patient, who becomes hostilely disposed to his friends, elders, and physicians, and fondly attached to his enemies, and the functions of whose sense-organs have become perverted, should be looked upon as on the point of death. A patient, the bones of whose ankles, knee-joints, fore-head, jaws and cheeks have become loose and look hung down, would soon give up his ghost. A black tongue, sunk eyes and nose, black hung down lips and a fetid exhalation from the mouth are the symptoms, which indicate an approaching death.

Dhanvantari said :—For the knowledge of what is good or evil, I shall now discourse on the rules of food and drink. The red species of Shâli paddy (rice) destroys the three-Doshas, allays thirst, and arrests perspiration. Mahâshâli is highly restorative, and Kalabha is anticholeric and phlegmagougic, while Shastika is heavy (of digestion) and cooling, and destroys the three Doshas. Shyâmaka is parchifying, absorbant, anticholeric, and phlegmagougic, and generates Vâyu in the organism. The species of food grain such as Priyangu, Nivâra and Koradushas, etc., are possessed of the same properties as the latter (Shyâmaka), Yava (barley) is cooling, anti-choleric, phlegmagougic and highly Vâyu-generating, while wheat (Godhuma) is constructive, cooling, palatable and Vayu-destroying. Mudga pulse is light, sweet, astringent, anti-choleric, phlegmagougic and alterative. Mâsha pulse is heavy (of digestion), aphrodisiac, extremely strengthening and engenders the Pittam and Kapham. The species known as Rájamásha is non-aphrodisiac and destroys the three D shas. Kulattha pulse cures dyspnœa, hic-cough and intestinal glands, and subdues the Váyu and Kapham. Kushthaka is cooling, astringent febrifuginous and styptic; and Chanak (gram) generates the Váyu, destroys the Pittam, Kapham and blood (sic), and diminishes virile potency. Masura (lentil) is sweet, cooling (in its potency), astringent, and subdues the Kapham and Pittam. Sathina pulse is extremely Váyu-generating. Adhaki destroys Kapham and Pittam, Kapikachchha is highly spermatopoetic, Atasi is Pitta-generating; and Siddhârtha, Kaphah and Váyu-destroying. Tilah (sesame has a sweet and alkaline taste, and is emulsive, tonic, thermogenic and choleric. The rest of the seeds (*lit.* food grains) are parchifying or cooling in their potency and serve to impair the strength of the organism. Chitraka, Ingudi, Nálika, Pippali, Madhu-Shigru, Chavya, Nirgundi, Tarkári, Káshamarda and Vilva are vermifuginous, appetising, light (of digestion), anti-choleric and phlegmagougic, Varshâbhu and Markara destroy the Váyu, and Vâyu and Kapham in combination. Eranda is bitter and laxative, Kákamâchi destroys the three Doshas, Chángeri destroys the Váyu and Kapham, while Sarshapa, like Kaushambha, aggravates all the Doshas. Rájika engenders the Váyu and Pittam, Nadicha destroys the Kaphah and Pittam, Chuchchu is sweet and cooling, Padmapatram destoys the Doshas, Tripátam is extremely Váyu-generating, Kâkshara destroys all the Doshas, Vastuka is extremely relishing, Tanduliya, like Pálankya and Choudrika, is antitoxic, raw Mulakam generates the Doshas and Mucous in the intestines, while cooked it destroys Vâyu and Kapham. Mature Karkotakam, like Vârtakam, Patolam and Kârabillam, destroys the three Doshas, is delicious, and improves the voice; Kushmándam is diuretic and relishing, destroys all the Doshas, and proves curative in cutaneous affections, urinary complaints, fever, cough, asthma and diseases of the Kapham and Pittam. Kalinga Alâvuni is anti-choleric and Vâyu-generating, Trapusha and Ervâruka are anti-choleric and generate the Vâyu and Kapham, Vrikshâmla destroys the Kapham and Vâyu, and Jamvira destroys the Kapham and Vâyu. Dâdima (pomegranate) is astringent and Vâyu-destroying ; Nâgaranga-phalam is heavy of digestion, while Keshara and Mátulunga are appetising and tend to destroy (the deranged) Kapham and Vâyu. Másha destroys the Vâyu and Pittam, while its rind is emolient, heat-making and Vâyu-destroying. Amalakam is sweet, relishing, constructive and aphrodisiac ; Haritaki is relishing, appetising and favourably compares with the divine ambrosia. Like Aksha phalam, it is liquefacient and laxative, and tends to destroy all the Doshas. Tintidiphalam (tamarind) is liquefacient, laxative, acid (in its flavour) and subdues the deranged Vâyu and Kapham. Lakucham is sweet and pathogenic, Vakulam, is Vâyu and Kaphah-subduing, and Vijapurakam is anti-spasmodic, proving efficacious in intestinal glands, cough, bronchitis and diseases of the deranged Vâyu and Kaphah. Kapittham (horse-apple) is astringent, anti-toxic, and anti-pathogenic, ripe Kapittham is heavy of digestion. Immature Amram (mango) generates the Kapham and Pittam, raw-mango aggravates the Pittam, while ripe mango subdues the deranged Vâyu, and is tonic, cosmetic and spermatopoetic. Jamboline fruit is astringent, takes time to be digested, engenders the Vâyu and destroys the deranged Kapham and Pittam. Tinduka is Kaphah and Vâyu-destroying, Vadaram destroys the Vâyu and Pittam, Vilvam engenders the Vâyu, and continues long undigested in the stomach, while Piyâlam subdues the deranged Vâyu. Tâlam, Râjâdanam, Mocham, Panasam and Narikelam (cocoanut) are sweet, emolient, heavy (of digestion) tonic, and spermatopoetic. Drâksha, Madhuka, Kharjuram and Kunkunni pacifies the enraged blood and Vâyu, while ripe Mâgadhis are sweet, laxative and curative of bronchitis and diseases of the deranged Pittam. Ardrakam is relishing, appetising and subdues the deranged Kaphah and Vâyu, while Shunthi, Maricha and Pippali conquer the deranged Kapham and Vâyu. Maricha is anti-aphrodisiac, though several authorities attribute a contrary virtue to it. Hingu (asafœtida) conquers Kapham and proves curative in colic, intestinal glands, and tympanites. Yamâni (Ptychotis), Dhânyakam (corriander seeds and Ajâji (cumin seeds) are highly Vâyu and Kapha-destroying. Saindhavam (Rock salt) is aphrodisiac, improves the eye-sight, and destroys the three Doshas. Saubarchal salt is heat making in its potency and cures tympanites and angina pectoris. Vid salt is sharp and heatmaking, anti-spasmodic and Vâyu-subding. Romakam Salt is heavy, relishing and Vâyu-subduing and leaves a slimy deposit in the vessels of the body. Yavakshâra (impure Nitrate of Potash) improves the digestive faculty, and proves curative in Jaundice and diseases of the heart and throat. Sarjikshâra (barilla) is sharp, caustic, appetising, and is used in bursting absceses. Atmospheric water is light, refreshing, anti-toxic and Dosha-destroying. River water is parchifying (in its effect) and Vâyu-generating; tank-water, sweet and light; Vapi-water Kapha and Vâyu-subding; and Tadâga water, Vâyu-generating. Fountain water is palatable, digestant, phlegmagougic, light and parchifying (produces a condition of parchedness in the organism); well water generates the Pittam and is appetising; water that springs up from beneath the soil is Pitta-subduing; water that is kept exposed to the sun, whole day, and is cooled by the moon beam, all night, acquires virtues identical with those of atmospheric water. Hot (boiled water) is beneficial in fever, bronchitis, and corpulency, and subdues the Vâyu and Kapham. Water, which is boiled and subsequently cooled down, destroys the three Doshas, while that, which is collected over night, generates or aggravates them (Doshas) in the system. Cow's milk is heavy, emulsive, rejuvenating, and Vâyu and Pitta-subduing; that of a she-buffalo is heavier and more emulsive than the former, and impairs the digestive faculty;

that of a she-goat proves curative in blood-dysentery, cough, bronchitis, asthma and diseases of the deranged Kapham. Woman's (breast) milk has a saline taste and proves beneficial in hæmorrhage and diseases of the eyes. Milk-curd is tonic, and aphrodisiac; it destroys the Vâyu and generates the Pittam and Kapham in the system. Cream, churned out of curdled milk, destroys the Doshas and cleanses the ducts of the body (Sratovishodhanam). Newly made butter cures lienteric diarrhœa (Grahani), hæmorrhoids, and faceal paralysis, while preparations of stale butter are heavy of digestion and beget Keloid tumours and other cutaneous affections. Takram (a kind of whey), whose creamy substance has been removed, subdues the three Doshas and cures lienteric diarrhœa, œdema, hæmorrhoids Jaundice, dysentery and effects of any slow poison retained in the system. Clarified butter (Ghritam) is sweet, constructive, nerve-tonic, anticholeric and phlegmagougic; Ghritam made out of cow-butter improves the intellect and eye-sight, while a properly prepared and medicated Ghritam serves to destroy the three Doshas. Old Ghritam proves curative in hysteria, insanity, and epileptic fits. Ghritam made out of goat's butter, or of any other butter should be regarded as possessing identical virtues with that milk. Urine is an antitoxic vermifuge and subdues the deranged Kapham and Vâyu. Sesame oil is tonic, improves the growth of hair, subdues the deranged Vâyu and Kapham, and proves beneficial in Jaundice, Ascitis, cutaneous affections, hæmorrhoids, œdema, intestinal glands and urinary complaints. Mustard oil is anti-corpulent, vermifuginous, and phlegmagougic and cures Jaundice and the deranged Vâyu. Linseed oil impairs digestion, and destroys the Vâyu and Pittam. Oil expressed out of Aksha seeds is anti-choleric, and phlegmagoguic, it improves the growth of hair and soothes the skin and the eyes. Honey destroys the three Doshas, and generates Vâyu in the system, and proves curative in hic-cough, bronchitis, vomiting, urinary complaints, thirst, intestinal worms and effects of poisoning. Sugarcane is tonic and constructive, generates the Kapham, and cures hæmorrhage, hymoptisis, etc. Phánitam (boiled sugarcane juice) is sharp and Pitta-generating, while Matsandikâ (surface layer of treacle) is white and light, and Khanda (a kind of unrefined sugar) is emolient, constructive, and sweet, and proves curative in hæmorrhages and disorders of the Vâyu. Treacle is constructive, Kaphah-generating and Vâyu and Pitta-subduing. Old treacle is extremely wholesome, subdues the Pittam and soothes the blood. Treacle-sugar is constructive and cures hæmorrhage, hymoptisis, etc. All kinds of urine generate the Pittam, which, through its acid taste, conquers the Kapham and Vâyu. Wines of the Sauvira species are sharp and aggrgvate blood and the Pittam. Manda made of fried rice is appetising and digestant. Peyâ (Gruel) is light, diuretic and restores the deranged Vâyu to its normal condition. Peyás made with whey, pomegranate, and Vyosha, or with treacle, Amala and Pippali prove curative in cough, bronchitis and diarrhœa. Páyasa is tonic and phlegmagoguic, Krishara, is Vâyu-destroying. Soup being cooked in combination with bulbs, roots, fruit or Ghritam becomes heavy and constructive. A Supa (salted soup), well-cooked and taken lukewarm, forms a light diet. Shákas, well-cooked and with their watery parts squeezed out, and seasoned with any oily or fatty substance, forms a wholesome dish. Jusha (unsalted soup) made with Amalaka and pomegranate improves digestion, destroys the Vâyu and Pittam; made with Mulaka it proves efficacious in cough, bronchitis, catarrh and diseases of the deranged Kapham. Jusha of barley, Kola and Kulattha pulse is beneficial to the voice and subdues the deranged Vâyu. Juice made with Amalaka and Mudga-pulse is astringent and conquers the deranged Kaphah and Pittam. Milk-curd with treacle is Vâyu-destroying, fried barley-powder (Shaktu) is parchifyiug and Vâyu generating. Shuskalis (something like Kachauries) prepared with Ghritam are aphrodisiac and heavy (of digestion), and improve the digestive faculty. Articles of fare made with cooked meat are constructive and tissue building; cakes are heavy of digestion, those, which are baked with oil, impair the eyesight, while those which are boiled with water are extremely hard to digest. Warm Mandakas are extremely wholesome; cold they take a long time to be digested. Drinks and after-potions (Anupânas) are refrigerant, and those, who follow the proper rules as regards drinks and Anupânas, know no disease and enjoy a sort of immunity from poisoning. The taste or touch of a cold poison, resembling the neck of a peacock in colour, produces mental anguish and discolouring of the complexion of a patient anywise handling it. The smell of such a poison produces obstinate occular affections, yawning, shivering, etc., which baffle the skill of even the best of physicians.

—:o:—

CHAPTER CXCIII.

DHANVANTARI said :—There are eight forms of fever, in consideration of their Dosha-born or traumatic nature, as well as of cases in which the deranged Váyu, Pittam and Kaphah act in couples or in entire concert. Water cooked with Musta, Parpata, Ushira, Chandana, Udichi and Nágara and subsequently cooled down should be given to a fever-patient for the alleviation of heat and thirst.

A febrifuge decoction of Nágaram, Devadáru, Dhányakam, Vrihati and Kantakâri should be given to a fever patient. A decoction (Páchanam) of the Aragvadha, Musta, Tikta, and Granthika proves efficacious during the immature stage of fever attended with colic. A compound of Madhuka pith,

Sindhuttha, Vacha, Usana, and Kaná taken in equal parts and pounded together should be given as an errhine for rousing up the patient from an unconscious state. A purgative decoction of Trivrid, Vishala, Triphalá, Katuká and Aragvadha, saturated with an alkali, proves curative in all types of fever. A decoction of Mahaushadha, Amrita, Musta, Chandana, Ushira, and Dhanyakam, administered with the addition of sugar and honey, cures tertian ague. Clusters of Apármárga flowers tied with seven strings of red thread round the waist of a patient on a Sunday, cures tertian ague (Tritiyakam.) A recitation of the Mantra, "a sonless ascetic died on the north bank of the Ganges, I offer libations of water with sesame seeds unto him," proves curative in Aikáhika form of intermittent fever. A Ghritam properly cooked with the expressed juice and paste of Guduchi, Triphalâ, Vrisha, Mridvikâ and Valâ acts as a good febrifuge. Similarly, a decoction of Dhâtri, Shivâ, Kaná and Vanhi cures all forms of fever. Now hear me discourse on the drug-compounds, which prove remedial to Jvaratisâra (fever with dysentery). A decoction of Prishni-parni, Valá, Vilva, Nâgaram, Utpalam, Dhânyakam, Pâthâ, Indrayava, Bhunimva, Musta, Parpata and Mahaushadham cures fever with mucous dysentery. A decoction of Nâgaram Ativishâ, Musta, Bhunimva, and Vatsaka proves curative in all forms of fever and dysentery. Water boiled and cooked with Musta, Parpatâka, Udichya, and Shringavera, and subsequently cooled down, may be advantageously given as a drink in all forms of dysentery. Similarly, Shâlaparni, Prishniparni, the two kinds of Vrihati, Kantakârika, Valâ, Shvadanstrâ, Vilva, Pâthâ, Nágara, and Dhányakam may be administered with diet in all forms of the same disease. Bela fruits or the inner pulps of mango-stones, taken with treacle or honey, or Kutaja bark taken with Kanâ proves beneficial in dysentery. A decoction of Vatsaka, Ativishâ, Vilva, Kanâ and Kasháyaka cures dysentery with bloody mucous stool, attended with an extreme griping pain.

Now hear me discourse on the therapeutics of Grahanî (lienteric diarrhœa) Grahini results from the impairment of the digestive faculty. A medicated Ghritam cooked with the paste and decoction of Chitrakam is appetising, and proves curative in intestinal glands, œdema, Ascites, splenic enlargement, colic and hæmorrhoids. The five kinds of salt such as the Sauvarchala, Saindhavam, Vid, Audbhidam, and Sâmudram should be added to the foregoing medicine. Medicines, surgical operations, and potential and actual cauteries are the four remedies to be resorted to for the purposes of curing piles. Newly made Takram (a kind of whey) proves remedial to piles. Pippali taken with treacle, Haritakis fried with clarified butter, or Trivrit with acid Lonikâ may be used with advantage in piles. A compound of sugar-cane juice and sesame proves beneficial in piles and cutaneous affections. A decoction of the Panchakola group of drugs with Maricha and Tryashunam improves the digestive faculty. Haritakis, taken with Nâgaram, treacle or rock-salt, are extremely appetising and stomachic. A decoction of Triphalá, Amritâ, Vásâ, Tiktâ, Bhunimva, and Nimvaja taken with honey cures Jaundice and Chlorosis. A confection prepared with Trivrit, Triphalá, Shyámá, Pippali, sugar and honey cures hæmoptisis and Sánnipátika forms of fever. As long as there exists a Vásâ plant in this word, why should a hæmoptisis, bronchitis, cough or pthisis patient despair of his life. A decoction of Atarushaka, Mridviká, and Pathyâ taken with sugar and honey proves remedial to cough, bronchitis, and hæmoptisis. The expressed juice of Vâsâ, taken with sugar and honey arrests hæmorrhage. The expressed juice of Sallaki, Vadari, Jamvu, Piyâla, Amra, Arjunam, and Dhava, severally taken with honey and alkali, exercises a styptic virtue. A patient suffering from ulcerative endocarditis, by taking a Ghritam, cooked and medicated with the expressed juice of the bark and leaves of Nirgundi, gets rid of the disease and acquires a godly health. A confection made of Haritaki, Kanâ, Shunthi, Maricha and treacle, removes cough, thirst and a distaste for food. A Prastha measure of Ghritam cooked with a thirty Pala weight each of the expressed juice of Kantakári and Guduchi cures cough and improves the digestive faculty. A decoction of Krishnâ, Dhátri, Sitâ and Shunthi, taken with honey, cures hic-cough, whereas a patient suffering from asthma should take Bhârgi and Vishvâ through the medium of warm water. A person suffering from hoarseness should keep catechu soaked in oil, or powdered Pippali and Pathyâ, or Pathyá and Nágaram in his mouth. A powdered compound of Vidanga, Triphalâ and Vishvâ taken with honey arrests vomiting, or a decoction of Amra or Jâmbu may be taken with Mákshikam for that end. The last named compound allays thirst and arrests vomiting, Triphalá taken with honey or milk conquers vertigo, epileptic fits, etc. Potions of Panchagavyam are remedial to hysteria and diseases due to the influences of malignant planets. Ghritam medicated with the expressed juice of Kushmânda and Yashthikam possesses the same efficacy. Old Ghritam medicated with the addition of Vacha, Kushtham, Shankhapushpi, and the expressed juice of Brâhmi cures insanity and the nervous diseases known as Grahâpsmâra. A medicinal Ghritam cooked with the expressed juice of Ashvagandhâ and four times as much milk is constructive, aphrodisiac, and remedial to nervous diseases and sterility. Powders of Nili and Mundarika taken with honey and clarified butter, as well as the decoction of Chhinnâ creeper proves curative in the worst type of Vâtaraktam. Five Haritakis taken with treacle cure nervous diseases and cutaneous affections; the paste, powder, or decoction of Guduchi possesses the same efficacy. A medicinal Ghritam cooked with the expressed juice of Kâla, Guduchi and milk cures cutaneous affections, heat in the body and diseases of the deranged Vâyu. Triphalâ taken with Guggula cures epilepsy and Vâtaraktam;

Guggulu taken with cow's urine conquers that form of nervous disease which is known as Urustambha.

A decoction of Dashamula, Gokshura, Shunthi, Eranda, Rásna and Nágara proves curative in Rheumatism and an aching pain in the limbs. A decoction of Valâ, Punarnavâ, Eranda, Vrihati, Kantakári and Gokshura, taken with castor-oil, subdues even the most vilurent cases of nervous disorders. A solution of common salt, taken with asafœtida, proves curative in flatulent colic. An infusion of Triphalâ, Nimva, Yashtika, Katuka and A'ragvadha should be given with honey for the alleviation of colic, or of a burning sensation in the body. Triphalâ-water taken with Yashthikam cures the type of colic known as Parinâma Shula. A lambative made of iron-rust purified with cow's urine and Triphalá-powder, honey, and clarified butter proves curative in all types of Shula (Gastralgia.) A pill consisting of two parts of Trivrit, four parts of Krishná, and five parts of Haritaki, taken with an equal quantity of treacle, removes constipation of the bowels. A compound consisting of powdered Haritaki, Yavakshâra, Pippali and Trivrit taken with clarified butter proves curative in Udávarta (tympanites with suppression of the stool and urine). Pills consisting of Trivrit, powders of Haritaki and Shyámá soaked with the expressed juice of Snuhi and then dried in the sun (Bhâvita), and taken with cow's urine, forms the best purgative and cures even the worst cases of A'náha. A medicinal Ghritam, duly prepared with a paste of Tryashunam, Triphalâ, Dhánya, Vidanga, Chavya and Chitrakam, and taken with alkali, proves curative in the Vâtaja form of Gulma. Roots of Nâgavalâ taken with milk, as well as Sauvarchala salt taken with half as much of Shivá-Ghritam should be regarded as a potent cure for all forms of diseases of the heart. A compound consisting of powdered Kaná, Páshánabheda, Elá and Shilâjatu taken with treacle and washings of rice is a potent remedy for all forms of strangury. A decoction of Amrita, Nágara,

DhÂtri, VÂjigandhá and Trikantakam may be given with advantage to patients suffering from strangurv, colic, or any disease of the deranged Váyu. YavakshÂra (impure carbonate of potash) taken with an equal quantity of sugar is almost a specific for all forms of strangury, in which the expressed juice of NidigdhikÂ may be also advantageously taken in combination with honey. Triphalá-paste taken with rock-salt removes the suppression of urine in which disease a stick of camphor may be introduced into the urethra for inducing the flow. Decoctions of Shigru-roots administered lukewarm lead to the disintegration and falling off of stones in the bladder, or of urinary concretion s The expressed juice of DhÂtri and NishÂ taken with honey is almost a specific remedy for all forms of urinary complaints (Mehas). A decoction of TriphalÂ, DÂru, DÂrvi, and Avja taken with honey proves beneficial in all types of Meha. Wishing to be stout a person should renounce late hours, sexual congress, physical exercise, and anxiety. Food into the composition of which barley or ShyÂmaka grains largely enter, as well as sweet drinks contribute to the stoutness of the body. Hot food or hot Mandas, or fried barley-powder taken with honey, or compounds made of Chavya, Jiraka, Vyosha, Hingu, Sauvarchala salt and Amala are anti-corpulent in their effects. A medicinal Ghritam duly cooked with four times as much water, twice as much Chitrakam and Utpalam, and cow's urine should be internally administered to an Ascites-patient. Ten Haritakis, successively increased, each day, and taken for ten days with milk, prove curative in Ascites. Use of such a thousand Haritakis while living on a milk, Yashthika, or rice diet prove curative in dropsy due to splenic enlargement. They are extremely constructive and life-prolonging in their efficacy. A medicinal Ghritam cooked with the admixture of the expressed juice of Punarnavá should be regarded as a potent cure for œdema and anasarca. An œdema or Anasarca-patient should do well to take Pippali through the vehicle of milk or cow's urine, or Abhyayâ and treacle. Castor oil, taken with a decoction of Valá cures hernia, attended with distension of the abdomen and an aching pain. Oil of black Uravaka cooked with the paste of Pathyâ and taken with Krishnâ and rock salt proves efficacious in Vriddhi Roga. The expressed juice of Nirgundi roots used as an errhine cures Scrofula; fomentations with decoctions of Snuhi and Gambhiriká leads to the resolution of tumours. Plasters of pasted Hasti-Karna and Palâsha prove curative in scrofula; plasters composed of Dhushra, Eranda, Nirgundhi, Varshábhu, Shigru and Sarshapa pasted together are known to cure cases of long-standing Elephantiasis. Plasters of Hingu, Shobhânjana and Sindhuttha cure Vidradhis (abcesses). Plasters of Sharapunkha made with honey bring about the healing of an ulcer; plasters of Nimva leaves help its asepcision. A wise physician should employ a decoction of Triphalâ, Khadira, Dárvi, and Nyagrodha for washing all cuts, ulcers or Sadyao Vranas attended with an aching pain. Plasters of Yashthimadhu mixed with warm clarified butter would prove efficacious in all forms of traumatic ulcers. In all traumatic ulcers (cuts, wounds, etc.) cooling measures should be at once resorted to for alleviating the heat of the enraged blood and deranged Pittam of the locality, for which purpose the part may be washed with a decoction of Bamboo-bark, Eranda and Shvadanstrá, mixed with honey; a solution of Hingu with rocksalt, or a decoction of Yava, Kola, and Kulatha pulse without the addition of Ghritam, internally administered, lets out the blood incarcerated in any of the wounded Kosthas (chambers) or viscera of the body. Arishta (medicated wine) of Karanja, or the expressed juice of Nirgundi proves curative in ulcers and worms in the intestines. Pills made of powdered Triphalâ and Guggulu remove constipation of the bowels and cure ulcers. A medicated oil cooked with the expressed juice of Durvâ grass, Kampilla, and the paste of Darvitvacha is one of the most potent healing remedies in ulcer cases.

—:o:—

CHAPTER CXCIV.

DHANVANTARI said :—Now hear me, O Sushruta, discourse on the nature of the medical treatment to be adopted in cases of sinus. Sinuses should be first opened with the knife, after which remedial measures mentioned in connection with ulcers should be employed. A medicated Ghritam cooked with the admixture of Guggula, Triphâlâ, Vyosha and Mânsa cures sinus, fistula in ano, bad or malignant sores, as well as colic. A medicated oil cooked with the admixture of the expressed juice of Nirgundi cures sinuses, and malignant ulcers; used both internally and externally this oil proves efficacious in Páma. Pills consisting of three parts of Guggulu, five parts of Triphalá, and one part of Krishnâ prove curative in œdema, intestinal glands, hæmorrhods and fistula in ano. In cutting of the vein of the penis, as well as in syphilis, suppuration of the sore is to be primarily guarded against in as much as suppuration in these cases may ultimately lead to the sloughing off of the organ. A decoction of Guduchi, Maricha, Nimva and Patola leaves may be advantageously given with catechu and bdellilium in Syphilis. Burn down Triphalá to ashes in an iron pan, charred Triphalá applied with honey to syphilitic sores brings about their healing almost that very day. A medicated Ghritam cooked with the admixture of a decoction or paste of Triphalá, Nimva, Bhunimva, Karanja, and Khadira proves curative in syphilis and in diseases of syphilitic origin. In a case of fracture of the bone, the seat of the fracture should be first ascertained, which should be first washed with cold water then plastered with mire and bound with blades of Kusha grass. Milk, clarified butter, meat-essence, meat-soap, or soup of sesame seeds should form the diet of a fracture-patient. A patient suffering from the dislocation, fracture, or crushing of any bone would do well to live on a regimen of garlic and fried paddy, mixed with honey and sugar. Take equal parts of Ashvattha, Triphalâ and Vyosha, and Guggulu equal to their combined weight, and mix. This compound has the virtue of setting broken bones. Bleeding, and use of emetics and purgatives are recommended in all forms of cutaneous affections. A decoction of Vacha, Vâsá, Patola, and Nimva, or Phalini-bark, taken with honey, subdues the deranged Vâyu, and is a good constructive remedy. Purgings should be induced with the administration of a compound of Trivrit, Danti and Triphalâ. A medicated oil cooked with the admixture of realgar and black pepper proves efficacious in all forms of cutaneous affections, and plasters composed of these two drugs may be used in all forms of Kustha (skin disease) with advantage in which the patient should take every day five Myrobalans in combination with treacle. Plasters composed of Karanja, Tagara, and Kushtham pasted together with cow's urine, and rubbing of the affected part with Karavira after anointing it, prove curative in cutaneous affections. Similarly, plasters composed of Haridrá, Malayam, Râsna, Guduchi, Tagara, A'ragbadha and Karanja, or of realgar, Vidanga, Vâguji, Karanja and Sarshapa, pasted together with cow's urine, destroys cutaneous affections as the sun destroys darkness. A plaster composed of Vidanga, Airagaja, Kushtha, Nishâ and Sindhuttha pasted together with eow's urine cures Ring-worm. Plasters composed of Prapunnâd-seeds, Dhâtri, Sarjarasa and Snuhi pasted together with Sauvira wine may be advantageously used in rubbing the patches in cases of Ring-worm.

Plasters composed of A'ragvadha leaves pasted with A'ranâlam proves curative in ring-worms, keloid tumours, and psoriasis. A compound of Tilam, Triphalâ, Vyosha, Bhallátaka, sugar, honey and clarified butter taken in equal parts, is highly possessed of constructive and aphrodisiac properties, which may be given with benefit to patients, suffering from any form of cutaneous affections. A lambative consisting of Vidanga, Triphalâ, and Krishnâ pounded and pasted together with honey covers urinary complaints (Mehas), skin diseases, intestinal worms, sinuses, and fistula in ano within the range of its therapeutic application. He, who takes Abhayârishtam (urine of Myrobalan), or Amalaka and Nishâ for a month, is sure to get rid of all kinds of skin deseases. Burn to ashes the sprouts of Amra and Khadira trees in an iron pot. Ashes thus prepared together with powders of Aksha, taken through the medium of honey and the expressed juice of Dhâtri, proves curative in all forms of cutaneous affections. This medicine is also possessed of a good rejuvenating efficacy. A decoction of Dhâtri and Khadira taken with Valguja speedily cures even the most obestinate type of leucoderma. Oil of Bhallâtaka taken for a month cures all forms of leprosy; solution of catechu taken every day with food or drink cures all forms of skin-diseases. A medicated Ghritam cooked with a decoction and paste of Vâsâ, Guduchi, Triphalâ, Patolam, Karanjakam, Nimva, Asanam, and Krishna Vetasam proves curative in all forms of skin diseases, and enables its users to live up to a hundred years. This Ghritam is called Vajrakam Ghritam. Take the expressed juice of Durvâ grass and four times as much oil, cook it in the usual officinial method; external applications of this oil cures itches, Pámâ, etc. An oil duly cooked and prepared in combination with Druma-bark, Tvak, Arka, Kushtham, rock salt, Gamviriká, and cow's urine proves curative in ulcers and skin diseases. A decoction composed of Vásá, Amrita, Parpatakam, Nimva, Bhunimva, Markara, Triphalá, and Kulattha pulse, taken with honey, cures Amlapittam (acidity). A decoction of Triphalá, Patolam, and Tikta, taken with sugar and Yashtimadhu cures fever, vomiting and acidity. Vâsá-Ghritam, Tiktaghritam, Pippali-Ghritam and Guda-Kushmândam should be employed in Amlapittam. Pippali taken with honey cures acidity, a confection made of Pathyâ, Pippali, and treacle conquers impaired digestion and diseases of the deranged Kapham. Cook a Ghritam in the usual way with a paste of Ajáji, and and Dhányakam. This Ghritam cures impaired digestion with a non-relish for food, as well as vomiting and diseases of the deranged Pittam and Kapham. A decoction of Pippali, Amrita, Bhunimva, Vásaka, Arishta. Parpata and Khadira proves curative in carbuncles with fever. Clarified butter in admixture with the expressed juice (Rasa) of Triphalâ and Trivrit should be given as a purgative in Erysipelas with fever. A decoction of Khadira, Triphalá, Arishta, Patolam, Amrita, and Vâsaka, proves curative in measles and small pox. Dusting of the affected part with garlic-powder proves beneficial in carbuncles, Erysipelas, itches, Mashaka and other cutaneous affections. In Charmakilas, Jatumanis, Mashaka (described before) the affected part should be first scarified and then cauterised with fire or alkali. Plasters composed of Nili, and Patola leaves cures Pâshana-Gardhava (parotitis), oil cooked with Gunja berries and the expressed juice of Bhringarája cures the form of cutaneous affection known as Kapála Kushtham. A compound consisting of the inner pulps of mango stones, Triphalâ, Nila, Bhringarâja, Kandupâk and iron dust mixed with Kânjika imparts a black gloss to grey hair. Cook a Kudava measure of oil with two Prastha measures of the expressed juice of Parna leaves, milk, Isha and Arka. The oil thus prepared removes the greyness of hairs even of old men. Gargles of Triphalâ-decoction, or of one consisting of chamber soot, nitrate of potash, Pâthâ, Vyosha, and Rasânjanam should be held in the mouth in stomatitis and affections of the mouth. Honey saturated with powders of Lodhra, Triphalá, and Chitrakam, held in the mouth, cures diseases of the throat and the teeth. Gargles consisting of a decoction of the five astringent leaves *viz.*, Leaves of Patola, Nimva, Jamvira, A'mra, and Mâlati, should be regarded as the best in diseases of the mouth. The expressed juice of Lasuna, A'rdrakam, Shigru, Pârula, Mulakam, or Kadali, administered lukeworm, forms the best ear-drop in Otalgia. In acute Otitis, attended with noise in the ears and a shiny discharge, the expressed juice of Snuhi should be poured into the tympanum, after dusting it with powdered rocksalt. Oil cooked with the expressed juice of Jâtipatram, as well as Shunthi-oil, or warm mustard oil proves most efficacious in relieving earache. Milk cooked in combination with the drugs of the Panchamula group, as well as a compound of Chitrakam, Haritaki, and treacle, or a Shadanga soup (jusa) proves curative in cases of catarrh. By taking a light diet (lit. fasting) for five days in succession a man can get rid of the disorders of digestion, catarrh, fever, ulcer and inflammatory diseases of the eyes. Drops of the expressed juice of Dhâtri, poured into the eyes, allay the local inflammation, and the same result may be obtained by using honey and rocksalt with a solution of Shigru, Dârvi, and Rasânjanam pasted together. A plaster composed of Haridrâ, Daru-Haridrâ, Rasânjanam, Gairikam and rock-salt pasted together and applied around the eyes relieves occular affections. Plasters of Abhayâ fried with melted butter, or of Triphalâ pasted with milk, or a luke-warm solution of a paste of Sunthi, Nimva leaves and an extremely small quantity of rocksalt poured into the eyes in the manner of an eye slave, proves efficacious in all forms of occular complaints. A decoction of one part of Abhayâ, two parts of Aksha, and one part of Amritam, or a lambative of these drugs made with the admixture of honey and clarified butter, and sticks made of Chandana, Triphalâ, Puga, Palâsha and Tarumula pasted together with water cure all forms of Timira.

Plasters of Maricha pasted with milk curd and applied in the manner of a collyrium cures all forms of Timira. A Ghritam cooked with the admixture of a paste and decoction of Triphalâ and milk, and taken at the evening, speedily cures all forms of Timira. Pills made of Pippali, Drâkshâ, iron-powders and rocksalt, pasted with the expressed juice of Bhringarája, prove efficacious in hæmorrhoids, cataract, urticaria and occular affections. Pills made of Trikatu, Triphalâ, rock-salt, Manah-shila Ketakam, Shankhanábhi, Jâti flowers, Nimva, Rasânjanam and Bhringarâja, pasted together with milk, honey and clarified butter, prove curative in all forms of occular affections. Eranda-roots or Muchukunda flowers, pasted with milk or Kânjikam, and applied as plasters over the forehead, instantly cure headache. A medicinal oil cooked in combination with Shatânga, Eranda-roots, Ugra, Chakra, and Vyâghri, each weighing a Pala weight, and used as an errhine, proves curative in Timira, in diseases of the deranged Vâyu and Kapham, and in diseases of super-clavicular regions. A compound of Vishvam, Pippali and rock-salt, taken with salt and treacle, proves curative in Bhuja-stambha (Ebb's paralyais?) and diseases of the super-clavicular regions. Errhines should be freely employed in combating all forms of Suryâvarta (a type of Cephalagia). A decoction of the drugs of the Dashamula-group mixed with rock-salt and clarified butter should be employed as an errhine in Suryâvartam, A woman suffering from an attack of leucorrhœa of the Vâtaja type should take a compound of Sauvarchala salt, Ajâji, Madhukam, and Nilotpalam, pasted together with milk-curd, and sweetened with honey. In the Pittaja form of leucorrhœa the expressed juice of Vâsaka, or Guduchi or Amalaka seeds pasted with water and sweetened with honey and sugar should be administered. For the alleviation of Pându type of leucorrhœa a woman should take the expressed juice of A'malakam, and honey, or that of the Kârpâsa roots in combination with the washings of rice.

A paste of Tanduliyakam roots and Rasânjanam taken through the vehicle of rice-washings and honey cures all forms of leucorrhœa. Kusha roots pasted with rice-washings and taken through the same medium conquer all forms of leucorrhœa.

——:o:——

CHAPTER CXCV.

DHANVATARI said :—Now hear me, O Sushruta, discourse on the threapeutics of diseases peculiar to the female sex. In all forms of Yoni-vyâpat (such as Vaginitis, etc.,) measures calculated to subdue the deranged Vâyu (soothe the irritated nerves) should be at once resorted to. A compound of Vacha, Upakunchikâ, Jâti, Krishnâ, Vâsakam, rocksalt, Ajamodâ, Yavakshâra, Chitrakam and sugar pasted with water and well stirred, and fried with clarified butter, alleviates pain at the sides and in the vagnia, and removes hæmorrhoids and intestinal glands (Gulmas). A plaster of pasted Vadari leaves applied to the affected locality proves curative in rupture of the perineum and vagnia; a plaster of Lodhra and Tumvi-phalam gives firmness to the vaginal muscles. A medicinal Ghritam prepared with the admixture of the expressed juice of Pancha-pallavas, Yashti, Arka, and Mâlati flowers, heated in the sun, removes the bad odours of the vagina and cures leucorrhœa. Javâ flowers pasted with Kânjikam, a Prastha measure of Jyotishmati leaves pasted with the same substance, Durvâ grass pasted with water, Chitrakam pasted with sugar and water, and powders of Dhâtri, Anjana and Abhayâ taken with water arrest the catamenial flow. Errhines or potions of milk and Lakshanâ-juice during the menstrual period (four to twelve days after the suppression of the flow) lead to the conception of a male child. A half A'dakam measure of milk cooked with Ashvagandhâ and clarified butter should be taken by a woman desiring male offspring ; by taking Vyosha and Kesharam with clarified butter even a a sterile woman may enjoy the pleasures of motherhood. Milk cooked in combination with the roots of Kusha, Kâsha, Urubak and Gokshura and sweetened with sugar should be employed for the alleviation of uterine or abdominal colic of pregnant women. Plasters of Pâthâ, Lângali, Apâmârga, or Kutaja applied to the surface of the reproductive organ of an *enciente* lead to a speedy and easy parturition. Potions containing Yavakshâra and decoctions of Dashamulam tend to remove all post-parturient pain. Powders of Shâli rice taken with milk should be regarded as possessed of a highly galactogougic virtue. For the purification of the milk of a wet nurse the expressed juice of Vidâri flowers or of Kârpâsa roots, or Mudga soup, which acts as an elixir, may be given with advantage. A lambative composed of Kushtha, Vach, Abhayâ, Brâhmi, and Madhukam pasted together and mixed with honey and clarified butter should be given to a babe for the purpose of improving its intellect and complexion, and of increasing the duration of its life. In the absence of mother's milk, goat's milk or cow's milk may be safely given to a child ; and a swelling about its umbilicus should be alleviated by fomenting the part with a piece of heated clay. A compound of iron, Mustakam, and Ativishâ should be administered in fever with cough and vomiting ; a decoction of Musta, Shunthi, Vishâ, Aruna, and, Kutaja proves curative in dysentery. A compound of Vyosha, Mâtulunga and honey cures hic-cough and vomiting. A compound of Kushtham, Indra-yava, Siddhârtha, Nishâ and Durvâ proves efficacious in all forms of cutaneous affections ; and a bath in a decotion of Mahâmunditikâ and Udichyâ proves beneficial in deseases due to the influences of malignant planets. The body of such a patient should be smeared with a paste of Saptachchhada, Abhayâ, Nishâ, and Chandanam, or he should be made to wear Vachâ, Rudrâksha, lotus seeds, Shankha, or iron on his person. Magical practices and offerings etc., for the good health and well being of a child, should be done by reciting the Mantra, Om, Kam, Tam, Pam, Sham, obeisance to Vainateya. Om, Haum, Ham, Hah. Om, Hrim, O ye malignant planets (disease-spirit), that afflict a child, graciously accept these offerings and renounce your hold upon the child. Shirisha-roots taken with the washings of rice tend to neutralise the effects of an imbibed poison; while white Varshábhu taken through the same medium proves curative in cases of snake-bite. A compound of Tanduliyam, chamber-soot, Nishâ, and rock salt, pasted together with milk curd and taken with honey, acts as a good anti-toxic remedy. The expressed juice of Ankota-roots mixed with clarified butter acquires a good anti-toxic virtue. A medicine, which arrests disease and decay, is called a Rasâyanam. Persons desiring to use a Rasâyanam should take Abhayâ (Myrobalans) with rock salt, sugar, Shunthi, Râsna, honey and treacle respectively during the rains, autumn, winter, spring and summer. A single Abhayâ taken after the completion of digestion, two Vibhitakis taken immediately before eating, and four Dhâtris taken with honey and clarified butter immediately after eating enable their users to live up to a hundredth year. Ashvagandhâ taken with milk and clarified butter conquers a host of bodily ailments. By taking the expressed juice of Mandukapadi, Vidâri, Amritâ, as well as sesame, Dhâtri and Bhringarája, one is able to live up to a hundredth year. A compound of Trikatu, Triphalâ, Vanhi, Guduchi, Shatâvari, Vidanga, and iron-powders (oxide of iron) taken with honey serves to kill a host of diseases. A compound of Triphalâ, Kanâ, Shunthi, Guduchi, and Shatâvari, treated in the manner of a Bhávaná with the expressed juice of Bhringarâja etc., acts as a general prophylaxis against disease. By daily taking Vidâri-powders with honey, a man is enable to visit ten women, each night. A medicinal Ghritam cooked with the addition of ten times as much milk, or a Shatâvari-paste taken with sugar, honey and Pippali, acts as a good stomachic and digestant. Massage, lubrication of the body with oil or Ghritam, and applications of errhines, emeties and purgatives constitute what is technically known as the Pancha Karma. There are six seasons of the year, and each season lasts for a period of two months, in which warming one's self in fire or basking in the sun, and use of honey, milk or its modifications should be respectively used. Sexual congress is beneficial in winter (December, January); day sleep is injurious in spring (April and May). Exposure to moon-beams in Sharat (october and November) and excessive sleep during the rains should be avoided. Shâli rice, Mudga pulse, rain water and boiled water are always wholesome. Oil expressed out of Nimva, Atasi, Kusumbha, or Shigru seeds, as well as mustard oil, Mula oil, and Jyotishmati oil prove efficacious in cases of intestinal worms, cutaneous affections, urinary and kidney complants and the type of Cephalagia due to the action of the deranged Váyu and Kapham. Dâdima, A'malaki, Kola, Karmarda, Piyâlakam, Jamvira, Nâgaram, A'mrâtakam, and Kapittham generate the Pittam, destroy the Váyu, and produce diseases, which are caused through the agency of the deranged Kapham. Kála Jimuta, Ikshâku, Kutaja, Kritabadhanam, and Dhámárgava combinedly form one of the most potent of emetic compounds, and should be always used for the purpose of inducing vomiting. A compound consisting of Vacha, Indrayava and Madana may be used for emetic purposes in the morning. Easy (loose) motions of the bowels should be attributed to the action of the (deranged) Pittam, normal motions of the bowels indicate a state of normal equilibrium among the fundamental principles of the organism, while constipation of the bowels is brought about through the agency of the deranged Vâyu and Kapham. In cases, which indicate the predominance of the deranged Pittam, purgings should be induced with the help of Trivit. A compound consisting of Trivrit, Nâgaram, and rock salt pounded together and taken with sugar and honey, or that composed of Haritaki and Vidanga pounded together and administered through the vehicle of cow's urine acts as a purgative. Eranda oil in combination with a decoction of Triphalâ, twice as much as the former, acts as a good purgative. In diseases indicating an extreme predominance of the deranged Vâyu, the patient should be first fed and then caused to belch out the ingested food. Hollow bamboo, stems, to the lengths of six, eight, and twelve fingers respectively, and with apertures to the girth of a Karkandu fruit, should be cut out and used for the purpose of applying enematas; the patient to be thus treated should be laid on his back during the application. This rule should be likewise observed in applying enematas of the Niruha class. The full, middle, and small doses of clysters (fluid to be syringed into the rectum) must not exceed six, three, and a half Pala weights respectively. One part of Pathyâ, two parts of Aksha, and four parts of Dhâtri pounded together and treated with the expressed juice of Shatâvari and Bhringarâja in the manner of a Bhâbanâ cure all distempers of the body.

—:o:—

CHAPTER CXCVI.

DHANVANTARI said:—The group of drugs known as Madhurâdi Gana, which are possessed of disease-killing properties, consists of Shâli, Yashthika, wheat, milk, clarified butter, honey, marrow, Shringâtakam, barley corn, Erbâru, Gokshuram, Gâmbhâri, lotus seeds, raisins, dates, Valâ, cocoanut,

A'tmaguptâ, Vidâri, Piyâlakam, Madhukam, Tâla, and Kushmândam. They alleviate epileptic fits and a burning sensation in the body, soothe the six organs, and being partaken of in exclusion of all other things, generate the Kapham, and worms in the intestines, and bring on cough, dyspnœa, with a sweet taste in the mouth, hoarseness, tumours, goitres, and elephantiasis, etc.

Dâdima, A'malakam, A'mram, Kapittha, Karmarda, Mâtulunga, A'mrâtakam, Vadaram, Tintidi, milk curd, whey, Kânjikam, Lakucham, Amla-Vetasam and Amla-lona form the acid group. The last named one, taken with Shunthi, acts as a good digestant, and stomachic. These acid fruits generate the Vâyu in the system, give rise to an increased secretion of the mucous membranes of the body, take a long time to be digested, and are possessed of considerable constructive properties. The acid taste exclusively partaken of produces tooth-edge, looseness of the limbs, a burning sensation in the heart and epigastrium, and establishes suppuration in excised or incesed wounds, like a living fire.

The different kinds of salt, Yavakshâra (nitrate of potash) and barilla etc., form the saline group, which acts as a laxative, liquefacient and digestant agent, and gives rise to increased mucous secretion, and its potency readily expands through the whole organism. The saline taste exclusively partaken of tends to obstruct the vessels of the body, brings on resolution of tumours, and begets urticaria, œdema, erythematous eruptions, discolouring of complexion, Rakta-Vâtam, Pitta-raktam, virile inpotency and diverse kinds of pain in the body. Vyosha, Shigru, Mulakam. Devadâru, Kushthakam, Lashuna, Valguja-phala, Musta, Guggulu, and Lângali, are pungent, appetising, cleanse the system of the morbific diatheses (Shodhi, it may also mean laxative) and conquer itches, skin-disease and the deranged Kapham. These things, exclusively taken, reduce corpulency, bring on physical lassitude, act as good vermifuginous agents, reduce the quantity of fat and semen in the system, and produce a burning sensation in the body. Kritamâla, Karira, Haridrâ, Indrayava, the sweet Kantakam, the sweet Vetram, the two kinds of Vrihati, Shankhini, Guduchi, Dravanti, Trivrit, Mandukaparni, Karavellakam, Vârtâku, Karavira, Vâsaka, Rohini, Shankhapushpi, Karkota, Jayantikâ, Jâti, Varunakam, Nimva, Jyotishmati, and Punarnavâ, are bitter in flavour, tend to set flow the arrested serum (free the venal circulation), are relishing, refrigerant, and laxative, improve the digestive capacity, and conquer fever, epileptic fits and itching sensations. These drugs, exclusively taken, dry up the excrementitous matter of the organism, and prove remedial in cases of wry neck, convulsion, cephalagia and ucler. The group consisting of Triphalâ, Shallaki, Jamvu, A'mrâtakam, Vata and its kindred species, Tindukam, Vakulam, Shâlam, Pâlankam, Mudga, and Chillakam are astringent, and absorbant, arrest local secretions, and produce granulations in ulcers. Exclusively taken, these drugs beget pain at the chest, fever, parchedness of the mouth, distension of the abdomen, and wry neck. Haridrâ, Kushtham, salt, Meshashringi, the two kinds of Valâ, Kachchura, Shallaki, Punarnavâ, Shatâvari, Agnimantha, Brahmadandi, Shvadanshtrâ, Eranda, Yava, Kola, Kulattha, Karshâshi, and Dashamulam, these drugs, whether severally or in combination, destroy the deranged Vâyu, and subdue the deranged Pittam and Kapham. The group consisting of such drugs as Shatâvari, Vidâri, Vâlakam, Ushira, Chandanam, Durvâ, Vata, Pippali, Vadari, Shallaki, Kadali, Utpatam, Padma, Audumvara and Patolakam acts as a good phlegmagogue. Haridrâ, treacle with Kushthakam, Shatapushpi, Jâti, Vyosha, A'ragvadha, and Lângali are possessed of the same virtue as the foregoing ones; clarified butter, oil, myosin and marrow are the best of all lardaceous substances. Persons desiring to improve their memory, intelligence and digestive capacity should regularly take clarified butter; Ghritam unmixed with any thing should be given in diseases of the deranged Pittam, in combination with salts in diseases of the deranged Vâyu, and in admixture with Vyosha or alkalis in glandular affections, sinuses, worms in the intestines, and diseases brought about through the agency of the deranged Vâyu, or through the predominance of the deranged Kapham. Oil, which imparts lightness and firmness to the body, should be internally administered to patients suffering from extreme constipation of the bowels, to those whose fundamental organic principles have suffered a diminution through sexual excesses, carrying of inordinately heavy loads, excessive physical labour, and exposure to wind and water. It should be used in vaginal enematas, after cautérising a vein, in obstruction of the vessels of the body, for removing a parched condition of the organism, after fatiguing physical labour, and for making up any loss in the system. In connection with emulsive medicinal decoctions the full dose of oil should be understood as a Palam weight; three Aksha weight is the middling dose, and a half Palam weight is the smallest (Jaghanyam) dose. Hot water should be given with Ghritam, while it should be separately given [to patients to whom oil may be prescribed. A man feeling himself thirsty after taking any kind of Ghritam or oil should drink hot water. Measures calculated to restore the deranged Vâyu to its normal condition should be resorted to with the help of any emulsive substance in respect of patients of good digestive capacity. Diaphoretic measures should be employed in respect of persons of extremely parched temperament, while parchifying measures should be adapted in cases of over-dose of an oil or Ghritam. A compound of Shyâmaka, Koradusha, or boiled rice, or Pinyâkam, pasted with whey and made warm, should be used in fomenting the body of the patient, in diseases of the [deranged Váyu and Kapham, or in those of the deranged Vayu, or in those of the deranged Kapham. Extremely corpulent, or weak patients, as well as those of parched temperament, or suffering from epileptic fits should not be fomented at all.

—:o:—

CHAPTER CXCVII.

DHANVANTARI said:—Hear me, O Sushruta, who art well-conversant with the nature of diseases, discourse on the preparations and efficacies of different medicinal oils and Ghritas. Cook a Prastha measure of clarified butter with an Aksha measure of each of the following drugs, *viz.*, Shankha-pushpi, Vacha, Soma, Brâhmi, Brahma, Suvarchala, Abhayâ, Guduchi, Atarushaka and Vaguchi, in combination with a Prastha measure of the expressed juice of Kantakâri. and the same quantity of milk. This Ghritam is called Brâhmi Ghritam. It improves the intellect and memory. Cook a Ghritam with Triphalâ, Chitrakam, Valâ, Nirgundi, Nimva, Vâsaka, Punarnavâ, Guduchi, the two kinds of Vrihati and Shatâvari, or with as many of them as are available. This Ghritam may be used with benefit in all forms of disease. Cook half an A'dakam of oil with a decoction of a hundred Valâs and a paste of Madhukam, Manjishthâ, Chandana, Utpalam, Padmakam, Sukshmelâ, Pippali, Kushtham, Tvak, Elâ, Aguru, Keshara, Ashvagandhâ, and drugs of the Jivaniya group; cook it over a gentle fire, and keep it in a silver pitcher after cooking. This Ghritam, which is named as Râja-ballabham, proves highly efficacious in all diseases of the deranged Vâyu, no matter what fundamental principle of the organism it might have affected, as well as in diseases of the deranged Kapham. Cook a Prastha measure of clarified butter with a Prashtha measure of the expressed juice of Shatâvari and a Prastha measure of milk, as well as with the addition of the paste of a Karsha of each of the following drugs, *viz.*, Shatapushpâ, Devadâru, Mânsi, Shaileyakam, Valâ, Chandanam, and Tagaram. Hanch backs, dwarfs, maimed persons, deaf ones, or those suffering from Vyanga or Kushtham, as well as those who suffer from distortions of limbs in consequence of the enargement of the bodily Vâyu, or meet disappointment during the middle part of an act of sexual congress, persons suffering from the imbecilities of old age, or from tympanites or dryness of the mouth, or from diseases affecting the skin, veins and ligaments have got a splendid remedy in this Nârâyana Tailam, the killer of all diseases, the recipe of which was formerly disclosed by Vishnu himself. Oils or Ghritas may be separately cooked in admixture with each of the following drugs, *viz.*, Shatâvari, Guduchi, Chitrakam, Vyosha, Nimva, the expressed juice of Nirgundi, Prasârini, or Kantakari, Varshâbhu, Valâ, Vâsaka, Phalatrikam, Brâhmi, Eranda, Yashthika, Bhringarâja, Mushali, Dashamulam, Khadira and Vata. Confection, pills, or pulverised compounds of the foregoing drugs, taken with honey, sugar, and clarified butter, or with water, prove curative in all diseases. The intelligent one should cook a medicinal oil in combination with Chitrakam, Trivrit, Pâthâ, Malapum, Hayamârakam, Sudhâ, Vacha, Lângalakim, Saptaparnam, Suvarchikâ, and Jyotishmali. This oil is called Syandanam Tailam and should be employed for the purpose of asepsising and healing ulcers, and especially in fistula in ano. The medicinal oil of great efficacy, which is called Chitrakâdyam Tailam, cures all diseases; cook mustard oil in combination with Ajamodâ, Sindura, Haritâlam, the two kinds of Nishâ, the two kinds of Kshâra, Phena, A'rdrakam, Sarala, Indra-Varuni, Apâmârga, Kadala and Kandala taken in equal parts with the addition of the usual quantity of goat's urine. This Tailam should be cooked over a gentle fire and with the admixture of cow-milk. The oil thus cooked and prepared is called Ajamodâ Tailam, which proves highly efficacious in scrofula and scrofulous sores. It induces satisfactory suppuration in indurated or partially suppurated sores, and cleanse the suppurating ones. Healing, granulation and softening of ulcers may be brought about with the help of this Ajamodá oil, which is one of the most efficacious of medicinal oils, and cures a host of bodily distempers.

—:o:—

CHAPTER CXCVIII.

SUTA said :—Thus the holy Dhanvantari, who is an incarnation of Vishnu, discoursed on many a medicinal compound of infallible potency, which (Hari) formerly disclosed to Hara.

HARI said :—O Shankara, in all types of fever the patient should be made to fast and kept in a room protected from the wind. Boiled water should be given to him for drink. Dry fomentations prove efficacious in all forms of fever ; a decoction of Musta and Guduchi proves antidotal to the Vátajá type. A decoction of Durálabhá cures Pittaja fever, and hear that, a decoction of Shunthi, Parpata, Musta, Válaka, Ushira and Chandana proves remedial in the same type. A decoction of the Shunthi and Durálabhá taken with ghritam proves curative in the Kaphaja type of fever. A decoction of Shunthi, Válakam and Prapatam proves curative in all forms of fever. A decoction of Tiktá, Eranda, Guduchi, Shunthi, and Mustaka cures Pittaja fever ; now hear me enumerate the other medicinal compounds of infallible efficacy. A decoction of Válaka, Ushira, Páthá, Kantakári, Mustaka, and Devadáru acts as a good febrifuge remedy. O Shankara, a decoction of Dhányákam, Nimva and Musta taken with honey, or a decoction of Triphalá, Guduchi, and Patola leaves, internally administered, acts as an appetising, Vâyu-subduing, and febrifuge medicine. Powders of Haritaki, Pippali, Amala and Chitrakam taken with a decoction of Dhányakam, Ushira and Parpatam, or a decoction of A'malaki, Gudachi, and Chandanam taken with honey proves curative in all forms of fever. Now hear me, discourse on the medicinal compounds, which have the efficacy of subduing the Sánnipátika forms of fever. A decoction of Haridrá, Nimva, Triphalá, Mustakam, Devadáru, Katurohini and Patola leaves destroys Sánnipátika fever. Powders of Nágavalá, taken with a decoction of Guduchi, Pushkara, Nágaram and Kantákari subdues cough, asthma, etc. Hot water should be given for the alleviation of thirst in fever due to the action of the deranged Váyu and Kapham. Cooked Shâli rice reduced to the consistency of a soup, rice gruel, or Mudga soup should be given to a fever-patient for the subsidence of fever. Water boiled with Vishva, Parpatakam, Ushira, and Chandanam, and subsequently cooled down, should be given for the alleviation of fever, thirst and vomiting. A decoction of the drugs of the Panchamulam group proves remedial to Vátaja fever. A decoction of Pippali-mulam, Guduchi, and Vishva-bheshajam conquers Vátaja fever. A decoction of Nimva and Parpatakam, taken with honey, proves curative in Pittaja fever. The forehead and soles of the feet of a fever-patient, who can not be restored to consciousness even with the employment of ordinary restorative measures, should be cauterised with an iron rod. A purgative decoction consisting' of Tiktá, Páthâ, Patola, Vishálá, Triphalá, and Trivrit, taken with boiled milk ,proves curative in all forms of fever.

—:o.—

CHAPTER CXCIX.

THE DEITY said :—Plasters of the ashes of elephant's tusks and Rasánjanam pasted with goat's milk and applied for seven days in succession, contribute to the growth of beards and mustachios. Oil, cooked with its quarter part of the expressed juice of Bhringarája and Gunjá-powders, helps the growth of hair. For the cure of baldness (alopacea), first rub the scalp with a paste of Elá, Mánsi, Kushtham, and Murá, and then apply a plaster of pasted Guuja berries over it. Applications of plasters of the powdered pulps of mango stones impart a thickness and silky gloss to the hairs and prevent their falling off. Anointment of the head with a medicinal oil cooked with Vidanga, Gandha-páshána, and Manah-Shilá and with the admixuture of cow's urine, four times its own weight, destroys lice and dandruff. O thou bull-riding deity, applications of freshly burnt conch-shell powders mixed with rubbings of lead and water to the scalf impart a raven like blackness to the hair. A hair dye composed of Bhringá-rája, iron-dusts, Triphalâ, Vijapurakam, Nili and Karaviram boiled with an equal quantity of treacle make the grey hairs of old men black again. Pulps of mango-stones, Triphalâ, Nili, Bhingarâja, steel-powders, dissolved in Kânjika make a good hair-dye. Plasters of Chakramarda-seeds, Kushtham and Eranda-roots pasted with warm Kânjikam and applied to the scalp prove curative in all diseases of the head (cephalagia). A medicinal oil cooked with its quarter part of cow's urine and with the addition of rock salt, Vach, Hingu, Kushtham, Nâgeshvaram, Shata-pushpâ, and Devadâru, poured into the ears, relieves earache. Similarly, ear-drops composed of rock salt and lamb's urine prove beneficial in otalgia with a fetid discharge, and germination of parasites in the tympanum.

Pourings of the expressed juice of the Mâlati leaves, and cow's urine arrest fetid discharges from the ears. Rubbings of a plaster composed of Kushtha, Mâsha, Maricham, Tagaram, Pippali, Apâmârga, Ashvagandhâ, the two kinds of Vrihati, and mustard, Yava, and Tilam pasted with honey and rock-salt remove the numbness of the penis and the arms. Mustard oil cooked with the admixture of Bhallâtakam, the two kinds of Vrihati, and the fruit and barks of Dâdima trees should be prescribed for the purpose of getting the male reproductive organ elongated.

—:o:—

CHAPTER CC.

HARI said :—The expressed juice of the leaves of Shobhânjanam mixed with honey, and poured into the eyes, undoubtedly relieves all forms of occular affections. Make a pill with the flowers of black sesame, Jâti flowers, Usha, Nimva, Amalâ, Shunthi, Pippali, and Tanduliyakam pasted together with rice-washings and dried in the shade. Rub this pill with honey and reduce it to a paste, apply this paste to the eyes in the manner of a collyrium. It cures blindness (Timira). Take black pepper and Nimva leaves, reduce them to a paste with the addition of cow's urine. It cures Timira, Patalam and night-blindness. Take four parts of powdered conch-shell, two parts of realgar and one part of rock-salt, reduce them to a paste with the addition of cold water, make them into pills and dry them in the shade. A pill, thus prepared, and pasted with water and applied along the eyes in the manner of a collyrium cures loss of sight, Patalam and agglutination of the eyes with slimy mucous (Pichchhitam). A plaster composed of Trikatu, Triphalâ, Karanja seeds, the two kinds of Rajani, and rock salt pasted with the expressed juice of Bhringarája and applied in the manner of a collyrium cures loss of vision, etc. Atarushaka roots pasted with Kânjikam and thickly plastered over the eyelids relieve aching sensations in the eyes. Decoctions of Shatadru, and Vâdâri roots internally administrated relieve pain in the eyes. An Anjanam composed of mustard oil, rock-salt and Apâmârga roots pasted together with milk and Kânjikam and prepared in a copper vessel, and applied to the eyes in the manner of a collyrium, removes, O Shankara, the agglutination of the eye-lids with mucous. This Anjanam (eye-salve) applied by reciting the *Mantrah*, Om, Dadru Sara, Krim, Hrim, Thah, Thah, Dadru Sara, Hrim, Hrim, Om, Um, Um, Sara, Krim, Krim, Thah, Thah, brings the A'dyas under the control of the applier. The application of an eye-salve composed of Vilvakam, and Nili-roots pasted together with water instantly cures the loss of vision. A stick made of Pippali, Tagaram, Haridrâ, A'malakam, Vacha and Khadira pasted together with water and applied to the eyes, proves curative in occular affections. Dash cold water over the eyes while holding water in the mouth at morning, each day. This measure cures many an occular affection. Fomentations of the eyes with vapours of warm goat's milk cooked in combination with the roots and leaves of white Eranda prove curative in the Vâtaja form of eye-diseases. A compound of Chandanam, Saindhava, Vriddha, Palâsha, Haritaki, Patola flowers, and Chakrikâ pasted together with water, or Gunja-roots pasted with goat's urine and applied to the eyes in the manner of a collyrium removes blindness (Timiram). Lubrication of the body of a Chlorosis-patient with clarified butter containing rubbings of gold, silver and copper rods tends to bring about a cure. Smelling or eating of Ghoshâphalams proves curative in chlorosis. Errhines composed of a soluble compound of Haritaki, Alaktakam, Durvâ and Dâdima-flowers pasted with their own expressed juice cure nasal polypi and Vâtaraktam. O Thou blue and red bodied one, O Thou bull-riding deity, errhines composed of Jingini-roots pasted with their own expressed juice lead to the falling off of nasal polypi. A medicinal oil prepared with the admixture of Siktham saturated with the expressed juice of Dhushturam and Dhânyakam, and mixed with

Sarjarasa, Gairikam, rock-salt and Ghritam made out of cow butter proves remedial in ulcers, as well as in sloughing and splintering of the lips. Jâtipatram unmixed with Ghritam should be chewed by one, for the alleviation of the diseases of one's mouth; chewing of Kosha-seeds imparts a firmness even to loose teeth. Chewing of a compound consi t-ing of Mustakam, Kushtham, Elâ, Yashthikam, Vâlakam, Dhânyakam and honey removes fetour in the mouth. Daily ingestions of bitter, pungent, or astringent Shâkas fried with oil remove the bad smell from the mouth and prove beneficial in cases of ulcerated gums. Gargles of Kánjikam mixed with oil, as well as those containing ashes of burnt betel lives prove curative in affections of the mouth. Chewing of Shunthi, as well as eating of a compound of Mâtulunga leaves, Ela, Yasthimadhu, Pippali and Jâtipatram pounded together, leads to the secretion of mucous from the mouth. Chewing of the clustered sprouts (Jatâ) of Shephâlikâ proves curative in Goitre; O Shankara, errhines of the expressed juice of Gihvika arrest hæmorrhage from the nose or the brain. A medicinal oil cooked with the admixture of the expressed juice of Shirisha seeds, and Haridrâ, four times as much as that juice, should be employed as errhines for the extinction of diseases of the head and throat. Chewing of Gunja-roots leads to the extinction of worms in the teeth. A decoction of Kâka-Janghâ, Snuhi, and Nili, sweetened with the addition of honey, kills worms that might have originated in, or invaded the teeth. Rubbing of the teeth with a Ghritam cooked in combination with milk and the expressed juice of Karkata-pâda prevent their gnashing (destroys the tendency of gnashing the teeth). As an alternative, O Shiva, a paste of Karkatapâda alone should be applied to the teeth, or Jotishmati fruits pasted with water alone should be applied to them for three weeks in succession, or the pith (marrow) of white myrobalans pasted with water should be applied for removing the black or yellow colour (tan or tartar) of the teeth. A cosmetic composed of Lodhra, Kumkum, Manjisthâ, Loha, Kâleyakam, barley, rice, and Yasthimadhu pasted together with water should be used by ladies for beautifying their complexion. Cook a Prastha measure of oil with two parts of goat's milk and a Karsha of each of the following drugs, *viz.*, Rakta-Chandanam, Manjishthâ, Lâkshâ, Yashtimadhu, and Kumkum. This Tailam is highly possessed of cosmetic properties; a week's application will impart a beautiful tint to one's complexion. A decoction of Shunthi, powdered Pippali, Guduchi, and Kantakârikâ, acts as a good digestant and stomachic remedy, and tends to alleviate, O Thou, the lord of benighted spirits, the aching (rheumatic) pain brought about through the agency of the deranged Vâyu. A decoction of Karanja, Karkata, Ushiram, the two kinds of Vrihati, Katu-Rohini, and Gokshuram, internally administered, tends to relieve the sense of exhaustion or fatigue, and proves curative in Pthisis, consumption, Epileptic fits and Pittaja fever with a burning sensation in the body. Milk cooked with powdered Pippali and taken in combination with honey, sugar and clarified butter cures cough, heart disease, and chronic intermittent fever. A Karsha measure of the combined drugs should be taken in preparing all kinds of drug-decoction; O thou bull-riding one, the dose of such decoctions should be determined in consideration of the age of the patient under treatment. The expressed juice of Kâka-Janghâ, as well as the serous fluid extracted from cow-dung, taken with warm milk, proves curative in chronic, intermittent fever. Milk cooked with Shunthi acts as a good febrifuge. Errhines composed of Yashthimadhu, Musta, Vrihatiphalam and rock salt pounded together is possessed of highly soporific properties. Similarly, errhines composed of Maricha pasted with honey, O Shiva, are possessed of the virtue of inducing sleep. O Shiva, Kâka-jangha roots are possessed of good soporific properties, and a medicinal oil cooked in combination with Kânjikam and Sarja-rasa, applied with the admixture of cold water, instantly allays heat and burning sensation, and should be employed in alleviating the burning sensation of the body which characterises fever of contaminated blood (fever induced through blood-poisoning or Septecimia). A decoction of Shâli, Shaivâla, Agnimantha, Shunthi, Pâshâna-Bhedakam, Shobhânjanam, Gokshuram, Shobhânjanam roots, or Varuna and Chhannam, taken with Yavakshâra and Hingu, proves antidotal to diseases of the deranged Vâyu. O Shiva, a decoction of Pippali, Pippalimulam, and Bhallâtakam, internally administered, proves curative in colic and convulsions. External applications of a plaster composed of the earth of an ant hill cooked in combination with Ashvagandhâ, Mulakam and water alleviate the form of rheumatism known as Urastambha. Decoctions of Vrihati root internally administered cure Sanghâta-Vâtam. The expressed juice of the roots of A'rdrakam and Tagaram, taken with whey, cures the form of neuresthesnia whose specific trait is a tingling sensation, O Shiva, as the thunder bolt of Indra cleaves a tree. The expressed juice of Asthi-Samhârakam taken with a single meal, each day, or with meat soup cures nervous diseases and brings about the setting of broken bones. Powders of fried barley corn reduced to a paste with the addition of goat's milk and clarified butter, and applied to the soles of the feet, tend to ally the burning sensation of those localities. Plasters composed of honey, clarified butter, rock salt, treacle, Gairikam, Guggulu and Sarja rasa prove beneficial in cases of cracked soles of women and children. O thou bull-riding deity, clay-eaten soles of feet should be lubricated with mustard oil and heated over a smokeless fire. A medicinal Ghritam cooked with the admixture of Sarja-rasa, Siktham, Jivakam and Haritaki, and applied to scalds or burns alleviates the incidental pain. Sesame-oil saturated with the ashes of burnt barely corn proves remedial to belbs, blisters caused by a burn or scald. Plasters of Tilam, and Bhallâtam pasted with milk and mixed with buffalo butter, prove beneficial in ulcer cases; applied over the chest, or employed as errhines they alleviate angina pectoris and cardiac colic. O Shankara, bruises caused by blows of one's enemies are remedied by bandaging the spots with strips of clean linen saturated with cow-butter and powdered camphor. Sword cuts and arrow wounds, filled with the expressed juice of Amra-roots, are adhesioned and united by the first instance without producing any pain, pus, or inflammation. Similarly, sprays of clarified butter poured into freshly made sword-cuts or wounds bring about their adhesion and asepsision. Cuts and wounds are healed by applying plasters of Sharapunkha, Lajjâluka, Pâthâ, Chasa (the Bengal edition reads Vâsâ) and Mulakam pasted with water. The expressed juice of Kâkajangha, poured four three nights in succession in a granulating ulcer, brings about it asepsision and alleviates the inflammation, and prevents the production of of Pus in its cavity.

Rubbing of the body with water and the expressed juice of Apâmârga instantly alleviates the bruised pain caused by thrashing. O Shankara, a compound of Abhayâ, Shunthi, and rock salt pasted with water and internally administered cures all forms of indigestion. Nimva roots tied round the waist relieves an aching pain in the eyes; dry Haridrâ, white Sarshapa, Mulakam and Mâtulunga seeds, pounded together, should be used in cleansing the skin of all its impurities, a week's use of this compound imparts a brighter hue to the colour of the skin. Errhines composed of the expressed juice, white Aparâjitâ leaves and Nimva leaves should be employed for the purpose of delivering patients from the influences Dâkinis, Mâtrikas and other malignant spirit. O thou bull-ensigned deity, errhines of Madhuka piths are possessed of the same efficacy. Cull the roots of white Jayanti, or white Aparâjitâ, Arka,

Chitrakam or Mulakam under the influence of the asterism Pushyâ, reduce them to a paste with the addition of water and divide the mass into pills, A pill thus prepared and applied as a Tilaka mark on the forehead of a man has the magical virtue of enthralling the hearts of young maidens. Learn, O Rudra, that powders of killed iron, Pippali, Shunthi, A'malakam, rocksalt, sugar and honey, taken in equal parts, pasted together, and made into pills, to the seize of an Audumvara, should be taken for seven days in succession by a man, desiring a healthful life of a hundred years.

The Mantra, Om, Tha, Tha, Tha, should be employed in connection with all acts of charming. Collect the nest of a crow from a tree, burn that nest in the fire of a blazing funeral pile. The ashes of this burnt crow's nest cast on the head of a person makes him distracted and compels him to abandon his hearth and home. O Shankara, hear me enumerate such other measures of black magic. Let a man cast the excreta of his enemy on the skin of a wild rat and tie that skin round his waist, thereby he will be able to cause a suppression of his stool. A man or woman whose name is written on a mango-leaf with the blood of a raven and is cast amidst heaps of filthy substances is sure to be devoured by crows. O Hara, a compound consisting of goat's milk, Tilam, Gokshuram sugar and honey, taken in equal parts and internally administered, proves curative in cases of loss of manhood and virile impotency. A hundred Vilva twigs soaked with the blood of a raven and an owl and cast in the fire by uttering the names of two different persons are sure to create a bitter animosity between them. A medicinal oil cooked with the addition of the flesh of a Jhasa and Rohita, treated with the milk of a she-bear in the manner of a Bhâvanâ, may be prescribed for anointing the body of the patient in any kind of disease. Solutions of Chandanam, employed as errhines, facilitate the re-appearance of hairs. He, who holds a Lângalikâ bulb in his hand, [or smears his body with a paste of that plant, is sure to break the arrogance of the strong-bodied ones, even in his old age. O Thou blissful one, peacock's blood is fatal even to snakes residing in their holes. Burn down to ashes the dead body of an Ajagar (Boa constrictor) in the fire of a cremation ground. By casting these ashes before one's enemies one is sure to confound them, almost instantaneously. The *Mantra*, which should be recited on the occasion, runs as Om, Tha, Tha, Tha, Cháhi, Cháhi, Svâhâ, Om, Udaram, Páhihi, Páhihi, Svâhâ. Sudarshaná roots culled under the influence of the asterism Pushyâ and kept in a chamber drive the serpents from its inside and bar their re-occupation of the same site. Torches made of linen soaked with the expressed juice of Arkaplants and lighted to illumine a road way serve to drive away all snakes from that roadside. Smear the body of a rat with Haritâlam soaked in the serum of a cat's excreta and pasted with goat's urine. The sight of such a rat is sure to scare away all its kindreds from that house. For the extinction of mosquitos in a chamber, fumigate it with the vapours of a compound consisting of Triphalá, Arjuna, Bhallátakam, Shirisham, Vidanga, shellac, resin, and bdellium pounded together and cast in a smokeless fire.

—:•:—

CHAPTER CCI.

HARI said :—Let a woman administer a compound of Brahmadandi, Vacha, Kushtham, and Nágakesharam, with a prepared betel leaf to a man she loves by repeating the *Mantra*, Om Náráyani Svaha. The man to whom such a betel is given becomes the slave of its beautiful giver. After giving it (betel) let the woman recite the *Mantra*, Om, Hari, Hari, Sváhá. The man on whose head is cast powders of dried crow's tongue and Godanta Haritalam is sure to be under the influence of their giver. This influence is neutralised by keeping a garland of white mustard seeds hung in the chamber of such a hypnoti-ed man. By placing Shâkotaka and Vaibhataka branches with their leaves unstripped off at the door of one's house you can create dissensions, O Rudra. among its inmates. Powders of dried Khanjirataka's (a kind of bird) flesh pasted with honey should be applied as a plaster to her own re-productive organ during the menstrual period by a woman, desiring to enslave her lord. By fumigating one's body with the vapours of a compound consisting of Aguru, Guggulu, Nilotpalam and treacle one can become a favourite in a royal court. With a Tilak mark, on his forehead composed of white Aparájitá roots pasted with Gorochoná a man is sure to domineer the mind of the person he sees in a royal court. A totem on the forehead composed of Kákajangha, Vacha, Kushtham, Nimva leaves and Kumkum pasted together with one's own blood gives one a gift of fascination. Take a few drops of the blood of a wild cat, mix it with Karanja Tailam in the method of a Bhábanâ. Prepare a collyrium therewith on a lotus leaf over the fire of a burning funeral pile (Rudrágni). By applying this collyrium to the eyes one can remain invisible to others.

The Mantra to be recited in connection with this charm reads as follows: Om obeisance to the Commander in Chief of the Yakshas who wields a sword and a thunder bolt in his hands. Om Rudram, Hrám, Prim, the science of Tvaritâ, the repository of all spiritual and occult power. A'm, may the Mâtris stupefy you all. Mahâsugandhika root tied round the waist arrests the emission of semen. Karavira flowers seven times enchanted with the recitation of the Mantra, Om Namas Sarva—Sattebhyoh. Namas, Siddhim Kura

Kuru Svâha. These flowers whirled round before a woman are sure to hypnotise her. A compound of Brahmadandi, Vacha and Patram pasted together with honey, and applied as a plaster to one's reproductive organ during an act of coitus will enthral the affections of the woman to such an extent that she will desire no other husband.* Clumps of Brahmadandi kept in the mouth arrests the emission of semen. Jayanti root kept in the mouth imparts victory to a man in respect of an act of sexual congress. Bhringarâja roots pasted with semen and applied along the eye-lids in the manner of a collyrium exercises a fascinating influence. Aparâjitâ clumps given with Nilotpalam to a man through the medium of a prepared betel leaf serve to exercise a good fascinating (hypnotising) effect. Toes, legs, calves of legs, knee-joints, thighs, umbilicus, breasts, sides of the abdomen (groins,) arm-pits, neck, cheeks, lips, eyes, forehead, and head are the regions where the Chandrakalá (erotic centres) are located in the organism. They are located in the right side of a male body and in the left side of a female one. By exciting these centres by tickling, etc., one can rouse up erotic propulsions. The different centres from the head downward should be respectively excited on the different days of a light fortnight, whereas the centres from the toes upward should be respectively excited on the different days in a black one. Sixty-four measures of fascination have been enumerated in the Káma Shâstra (Erotic Science). Virgins or maidens may be fascinated by an embrace. A totem composed of Rochoná, Gandhapushpâ, Nimva leaves, Priyangu, Kumkum and Chandana pasted together with water and put on the forehead is potent enough to fascinate the whole world. The Mantrah to be recited in connection with this charm runs as, Om, Hrim, O Thou, Goddess Gouri,

* One Edition reads Kushtham; and another, Nimvam instead of Patram.—*Tr.*

grant me good fortune and secure me the obedience of sons. Om, Hrim, O thou goddess, Lakshmi, grant me all good fortune and the power to fascinate the three worlds. Smearing of the body with a paste of Sugandhâ, Haridrâ, and Kumkum, O Rudra, as well as its fumigation with the vapours of burning Sugandhi flowers gives one the power of fascinating other people. By applying a plaster of Durálabhâ, Vacha, Kushtham, Kumkum, ShatÂvari, pasted together with sesame-oil, to her vaginal canal, a woman is sure to enthral the affection of her lover. By fumigating her private part with the vapours of burning Nimva wood, a woman is enabled to become a favourite with her husband, and to captivate his affection for good. Similarly, a plaster composed of Yashthimadhu and Kushtham pasted together with buffalo-butter and applied to the same organ brings good luck to a girl. Take Yashthimadhu, Gokshuram, and Kantakârikâ in equal parts and boil them with water. This decoction boiled down to its quarter part should be taken by a woman desiring conception inasmuch as it is one of the most potent remedies that accelerate pregnancy in a woman. Soak Mátulunga seeds in milk, by drinking this milk a woman is sure to conceive. A woman desiring the birth of male-child should take Eranda-roots and Mátulunga seeds in combination with clarified butter. Milk cooked in combination with a decoction of Ashvagandhá (acts as an agent) that leads to the conception of a male-child. A woman, desiring to get rid of menstruation and pregnancy, should take Palásha-seeds pasted with honey, during the period of her monthly flow.

CHAPTER CCII.

HARI said :—Take Haritálam, Yavakshâra, Patrángam, Rakta-Chandanam, Jâti flowers, Hingulakam, and Lâkshâ; pound them together and reduce the compound to the consistency of a paste with the addition of boiled oil. First rinse the teeth, O Rudra, with a decoction of Haritaki, and after that, apply this plaster to the teeth whereby they would be tinged red. Scorch a Mulakam in a slow fire, and squeeze out its juice. This juice poured into their cavities tends to arrest the discharge from the ears. Take Arka leaves, and warm them over a gentle fire. The juice squeezed out of these Arka leaves, being poured into the ears, cures earache. A medicinal oil cooked in combination with Priyangu, Yashtimadhu, Dhátaki, Utpalam-leaves, Manjishthâ, Lohram, Lákshá and the expressed juice of Kapittha, and employed as vaginal enemetas, arrests leucorrhic discharges. A compound of the ashes of dry Mulakam and Shunthi, Hingu, Mahaushadham, Shatapushpá, Vacha, Kushtham, Dâru, Shigru, Rasâyanam, Sauvarchalam, Yavakshara, Sarjakam, Saindhavam, Granthi, Vidam, Mustatakam, with four times as much honey, as well as a medicinal oil cooked in combination with the expressed juice of Mâtulunga and Kadali, undoubtedly arrests all kinds of discharge. Pourings of mustard oil into the ears tend to destroy the local parasites. O Hara, take Haridrá, Nimva-leaves, Pippali, Vishvabhesajam, Maricham, Vidanga, Bhadram and Musta, pound them together, reduce them to the consistency of a paste with the addition of cow's urine, and divide the mass into pills. One pill of this compound is potent enough to cure indigestion, two of these pills cure cholera. Taken with honey these pills destroy Patola-roga; taken with cow's urine they prove beneficial in tumours. External applications of these pills, which are called Shánkari Vartis, prove curative in all forms of occular affections.

CHAPTER CCIII.

Hari said :—Take Vacha, Mânsi, Vilvam, Tagaram, Padmakesharam, Nâgapushpam and Priyangu, in equal parts, pound them together, and make this compound into sticks with the addition of water. A man, who fumigates his body with a burning fumigating stick of this kind, is sure to roam about in this world as Eros incarnate. A plaster composed of Devadáru-powders and camphor pasted with honey and applied to the male re-productive organ is sure to fascinate a woman during an act of sexual congress. "Om, Rakta-Chandiké, bring such and such a person under my control." O Shankara, by putting a totem composed of Gorochanâ (ox-gall) pasted with one's own blood on one's forehead and by ten thousand times reciting the foregoing Mantra, one is sure to fascinate the whole world. A plaster composed of Saindhava, Krishna Lavanam, galls of fishes, and sugar pasted together with honey and clarified butter may be applied by a woman to her own private parts before sharing the bed of a man. The man, who will know her thus, will never visit any other woman in his life. A plaster composed of Shankhapushpi, Vachâ, Mânsi, Somarâji, and Phalgukam pasted together with buffalo butter imparts a firmness to vaginal muscles and removes the flabbiness of the organ. Padmas, culled with their stems, should be pasted with milk and clarified butter and divided into pills. A dry pill, thus prepared and inserted into the maternal passage of a mother of ten children, will again make her as a virgin.

A fumigation with the vapours of a compound consisting of Sarshapa, Vacha, Madana-phalam, cat's excreta, Dhushram and a woman's hair proves antidotal to fever due to the malignant influences of Dákinis. Vapours of a compound consisting of Arjuna flowers, Bhallâtaka, Vidanga. Valâ, Sarjarasa, and Sarshapa, pasted together with Sauviram and burnt in a room, destroys snakes, mosquitos, flees, and lice. Plasters of powdered Earth-worms applied to, or introduced into, the reproductive organ of a woman, produce a paralysis of the vaginal walls.

——:o:——

CHAPTER CCIV.

HARI said :—The expressed juice of betel leaf, clarifid butter, honey, salt and milk rubbed in a copper vessel relieve aching pain in the eyes. Vibhitaka seeds, Haritâlam, and Manah-Shilâ pasted together with goat's milk remove all kinds of occular affections. A collyrium made of Mâlati flowers applied to the eyes instantaneously cures the form of eye-disease known as Pushpanâsha. A lambative consisting of Haritaki, Vacha, Kushtham, Hingu and Manahshilâ pasted together with clarified butter and taken through the medium of honey proves efficacious in cough, hic-cough and asthma. A pulverised compound of Pippali and Triphala taken with honey relieves cough, catarrh and acute bronchitis and asthma. O thou bull-ensigned deity, Pippali powders, and the ashes of Chitrakam burnt with its roots, taken with honey, proves curative in asthma, cough, and hic-cough. The expressed juice of Nilotpalam taken with sugar, or Madhukam and Padma taken in equal parts and administered through the vehicle of rice-washings, arrests hæmorrhage (lit affections of blood). Shunthi powders taken with sugar and honey instantaneously make one's voice sweet and clear. A compound of Haritâlam, and conch-shell powders, and the ashes of the plantain bark pasted together with water acts as a good hair-dilapidator. Rock-salt, Haritâlam, and powdered Tumbi-fruit pasted together with the solution of Lâkshâ forms a good hair-dilapidator. Take Sudhâ, Haritâlam, ashes of conch-shells, Manah-shilâ and rock-salt, pound them together and reduce them to the consistency of a paste with the addition of goat's urine. The paste thus prepared acts as an instantaneous hair-dilapidator. Paste powders of conch-shells, Amalakam, Patram and Dhâtaki flowers together with milk. A week's keeping of this compound in the mouth imparts a pearly lustre and whiteness to one's teeth.

—:o:—

CHAPTER CCV.

HARI said :—The use of milk curd is forbidden in autumn summer, and spring (computed according to the Ayurvedic calendar), whereas its use is recommended in fore-winter (Hemanta), winter and the rainy season. Butter and sugar, taken after a meal, tend to improve the intellect. O Hara, by taking a Palam of common treacle, each day, for a year, a man is enabled to visit a thousand women and to acquire an enormous bodily strength. By taking Kushtham-powders, each night, at bed time, in combination with Ghritam and honey, a person is enabled to withstand the ravages of time such as grey hair and a shrivelled, wrinkled skin of the body The intelligent man, who rubs his body with a cosmetic compound composed of Atasi, Mâsha and Godhuma pounded together and mixed with clarified butter, walks about charmingly, O Shankara, like an incarnation of Cupid. Pills composed of Yava, Tilam, Ashvagandhâ, Mushali, Sarala and Gudam act as splendid rejuvenating and constructive remedies. A decoction composed of Hingu, Sauvarchalam and Shunthi boiled together with water cures indigestion and the type of Gastralgia known as Parinâma Shulam. Make a paste by adding milk to powdered Dhâtaki; by taking this medicine an emaciated person is sure to gain flesh and to be stout again. A strong person should lick a lambative composed of butter, sugar and honey; a person suffering from any kind of wasting disease should take a goodly quantity of milk whereby his health and intellect would be improved. Powders of crab shells taken with milk prove curative in Pthisis or consumption. A medicinal oil cooked in combination with Bhallâtakam, Vidanga, Yavakshâra, Saindhava, Manah-shilâ, and powdered conch-shells acts as an infallible hair-dilapidator. Paste leeches with the expressed juice of Mâlura; by applying this paste to the palms of one's hands one is enabled to hold fire in his hands. Take the expressed juice of Shâlmali mixed with the urine of an ass; this compound. cast in the fire acts as a potent fire-extinguisher. Take the belly of a female crow, reduce it to powder, and then into a paste with the addition of frog's blood. Beat this mass into pills. By casting these pills in the fire, while repeating the Mantrah, Om, Agnistambhanam, Kuru Kuru (paralyse this fire), the intelligent one is sure to neutralise (lit benumb) its heat. By chewing a compound consisting of Munditakam, Vachâ, Mustam Maricham or Tagaram, a person is able to lick the flame of a fire with his tongue. Rain may be arrested by reciting the mystic formula, which runs as, Om Namo Bhagavate Jalam Stambhaya, Stambhaya, Sam, Sam, Sam, Keka, Keka, Chara Chara. By burying a cow-bone, vulture's bone and Nirmâlyam underneath the threshhold of one's enemy, one is enabled to bring about his death. A Tilak-mark compossed of five red flowers of different species, Kumkum, and one Palam of Rochanâ pasted together with his or her own blood, and put on his or her forehead by a man or woman, exercises a fascinating influence. Brahmadandi administered through his food or drink to a person under the auspecies of the asterism Pushyâ brings him under the control of the giver. A Palam of Yashtimadhu taken with warm water, relieves, O thou the supreme deity, constipa- of the bowels, as well as an aching pain in the chest. Recitations of the Mantra, which runs as Om, Hrum, Jah, destroy all kinds of scorpion poison. Pippali, Shringavera, rock salt, and Maricham mixed with butter and milk curd and employed as a potion or an errhine act as a potent anti-toxic remedy. Decoctions of Triphalâ, A'drakam, Kushtham and Chandana taken with clarified butter, or these drugs applied as plasters with the addition of the same substance tend to neutralise the effects of poison A compound of Haritâlam, Manah-shilâ and pigeon's eyes destroys the effects of a poison as Garuda destroys the serpents. O thou bull-ensigned deity, a plaster composed of Saindhava and Tryashunam pasted with milk-curd and applied to the seat of the bite with the addition of honey and clarified butter, proves curative in a case of scorpion-bite. Trikatu-powders taken through the vehicle of a decoction of Tilam and Brahmadandi prove remedial to Gulmas and tend to set flow the blood incarcerated or accumulated in any part or organ of the body. Milk taken with honey tends to arrest hæmorrhage. Apply a plaster of pasted Atarushakam roots to the pelvis, umbilicus and exterior re-productive organ of a woman for the purpose of effecting a speedy and painless parturition. O thou, bull-riding celestial, washings of rice, taken with honey and sugar, prove curative in blood-dysentery.

CHAPTER CCVI.

HARI said:—O thou moon-crested deity, a decoction of Maricham, Shringaveram, Kutaja, and Tvacham, internally administered, cures lienteric diarrhœa (Grahini). A compound consisting of Pippali, Pippali-mulam, Maricham, Tagaram, Vachâ, and Páthá, pasted together with milk and the expressed juice of Devadâru, proves curative in cases of dysentery. An Anjanam composed of Maricham and sesame flowers pasted together and applied to the eyes cures chlorosis. O Rudra, treacle and Haritaki, taken in equal parts and given in combination with honey, act as a good purgative remedy. A compound of Triphalâ, Chitrakam, Chitram, and Katu-Rohini boiled together with water and internally administered forms a good purgative, and relieves the form of Rheumatism known as Urustambha. A decoction of Haritaki, Shringaveram, Devadâru, Chandana, and Apámárga-root boiled together with goat's milk, and taken for a week, undoubtedly alleviates a rheumatic aching pain in the thighs, and proves curative in Urustambha as well. Reduce to fine powder Ananta and Shringaveram, and add to it equal parts of treacle and bdellium. Beat it up into a mass and divide the mass into pills. These pills alleviate stiffness and aching of the ligaments, and improve the digestive capacity. Cull a Shankapushpi creeper with its leaves, roots and flowers. Reduce it to a paste with the addition of goat's milk; by taking it one is relieved of hysteric fits. Take equal parts of Abhayá and Ashvagandhá through the medium of water, and rest assured of a radical cure of hæmorhhage (Raktapittam). Take a mouthful of a pulverised compound of Haritaki and Kushtham, and gulp it down with water for the cure of vomiting. A decoction of Guduchi,

Padmaka, Arishtham, Dhanyákam and Rakta Chandanam proves curative in the Pittaja type of fever, attended with thirst, vomiting and a burning sensation in the body. Shankhapushpi, mystically dynamised with the recitation of the Mantra, Om, Hum, Namas, and tied round the ear of a fever-patient, acts as a sure febrifuge remedy. O Rudra, put into the hands of a fever-patient eight hundred flowers, each consecrated with the mystic formula, Om Jambhini, Stambhini (destroying and paralysing goddess), Mohaya (make spell-bound) Sarva Vyádhin (all diseases) Mé (of mine), Vajréna Thah Thah Sarva Vyâdhin Vajrena (dissipate with the thunder-like mystic potency of "Tha" Mantra the morbific energies of all diseases), Phad (obeisance), and touch the tips of his finger-nails. All forms of fever and specially quotidian ague may be destroyed by practising this fever-charm. Fumigation of the body of the patient with the vapours of a burning febrifuge-stick composed of Jamboline fruits, Haridrâ and the cast off skin of a snake, pasted together and dried, proves curative, O Rudra, in all forms of fever, and in quotidian ague in special. A medicinal oil cooked in combination with Karabira, Bhringa-leaves, rock salt, Kushtham. Karkatam, and cow's urine, four times as much as its (oil's) actual weight, proves remedial to ulcers and Pámá, Vicharchiká and other kindred diseases of the skin. O Rudra, Pippalis taken with honey, or the use of Shurana and other sweet articles of diet would prove beneficial in cases of splenic enlargement. A compound of Pippali and Haridrá pasted together with cow's urine and inserted into the rectum leads to the falling off of rectal hæmorrhoids (piles). Goat's milk admixtured with the expressed juice of A'rdrakam should be prescribed for the cure of splenic enlargement. Plasters of Nimva leaves pasted with cow's urine, or of those composed of Saindhavam, Vidanga, Somaráji, Sarshapa, Visham and the two kinds of Rajani (Haridrá and Dáru-Haridrá) pasted together with cow's urine, and applied to the skin, prove highly beneficial in all forms of cutaneous affections.

—:o:—

CHAPTER CCVII.

HARI said:—Plasters of Rajani and the ashes of plantain bark pasted together with water, or one part of Kushtham and two parts of Pathyá taken with hot water relieve an aching pain about the waist and sacrum. Abhayá taken with water, or Pippali taken with sugar, cures rectal hæmorrhoids. Cook a Ghritam with powders, and the expressed juice, of Atarushakam leaves. Plasters of this Ghritam are highly beneficial in cases of rectal hæmorrhoids. Potions of Triphalá-decoctions taken with Guggulu will bring about the cure in a case of fistula in ano. The cream (surface layer) of milk curd cooked in combination with Ajáji and Shringaveram and taken with salt removes strangury. Solutions of sugar and Yava-Ksháram (impure carbonate of potash) prove remedial in strangury and suppression of urine. Make a collyrium with the excreta of a Khanjana, Shobhânjanan, and the foam of a horse's mouth over the fire of a cremation ground. By applying this collyrium to his eyes, a person remains invisible to the celestials, not to speak of purblind human beings. Plasters of burnt barley corn pasted with sesame oil relieve the burning sensation in cases of scald or burn. Plasters of Lajjálu and Sharapunkha pasted together with clarified butter relieve the heat in cases of scald or burn. These plasters should be applied by reciting the mystic formula running as, Om Namo Bhagavate, Tha, Tha, Chhindi Chhindi Jvalanam, Prajvalitam Náshaya Náshya, Hrum Fut. Nirgundi-roots tied round the wrist destroy fever. A root of white Gunjâ divided into seven pieces and tied 'round the arms of a patient undoubtedly cures rectal hæmorrhoids. Smearing of the body with a plaster composed of Vishnukrântâ pasted with goat's urine gives an immunity from the attacks of thieves and tigers. All magical acts may be practised with the help of a Brahmadandi root. Triphalá-powders taken with clarified butter relieve all forms of cutaneous affections. Powders of Punarnavá, Vilva and Pippali pounded together and taken with clarified butter remove cough, hic-cough and asthma; administered to women they facilitate conception. The foregoing drugs, cooked in combination with milk or clarified butter and taken with the same adjuncts, acquire a splendid spermatopoetic property. Take Vidanga, Madhukam, Pâthá, Mánsi, Sarjarasam, Haridrá, Triphalâ, Apâmárga, Manah-Shilá, Audumvara, and Dhátaki. Pound them together and reduce this pulverised compound to the consistency of a paste with the addition of sesame oil. By plastering their own reproductive organs with this paste, a man and a woman become extremely enamoured of each other. The lubrication of the organs should be followed by the recitation of a mystic formula running as, Namasté Isha Vardáya A'karshini, Vikarshini Mugdha svaha (obeisance to the god who is the grantor of boons, obeisance to the goddess who attracts draws and fascinates every creature). Such enamoured pairs shall rub the palms of their hands with a compound of the seeds of Punarnavá, Amritá, Durvá, Kanakam, and Indravâruni, pasted together with the expressed juice of Jâtika. The killing of Rasa (mercury) consists in rubbing the mineral with the seeds of the foregoing drugs pasted together with the expressed juice of Jâti as described in the preceding line, and then in boiling it in a closed crucible.

Milk taken in combination with honey and clarified butter arrests the advent of premature old age. Copper, burnt in combination with honey, clarified butter, treacle and the expressed juice of Kâravella, is soon converted into silver. Now hear me describe the method of converting a base metal into gold. A Palam weight of lead burnt in combination with a Palam weight of yellow Dhustura flower and twigs of Lângalikâ is easily converted into pure gold. By burning Dhustura oil in a lamp, while seated in Samâdhi Yoga, a Yogin can remain invisible even to the sky-scaling divinities. A clay figure of a bull, moulded in the attitude of killing a frog, O Shankara, will commence to bellow as a living one, on being fumigated with the vapours of the aforesaid Dhustura oil. Mustard oil burned in a lamp tends to destroy fire-flies. Fire-flies and mustard oil burnt together in a lamp will produce a glaring light like a conflagration. Burn down the powders of the cropse of a dead rat; plaster any part of the body with this burnt powder, and it will be found to be burnt in its turn, which may be alleviated with plasters or potions of pasted sandal wood. O Shiva, by personally applying a collyrium to the eyes of an infuriated elephant, a man is sure to win a victory in battle and turn out a valorous hero. By retaining the skin of a Dundubha snake in his mouth, a person can stay under water as confortably as on land. By smearing his body with a compound of the teeth, bones and eyes of a crocodile pasted with the blood and fat of that animal, a person may comfortably stay under water. By smearing his body with a compound consisting of the eyes of a crocodile, the heart of a tortoise and the bones of a rat pasted together with rat's lard and that of a porpoise, a man can stay under water as easily as in a chamber of his own house. Powders of iron taken with whey prove curative in jaundice. Roots of Tanduliyakam and Gokshuram, pasted together and administered through the medium of milk, cure chlorosis and affections of the mouth. Jâti roots or Kola roots, taken with whey, reileve indigestion. Kusha roots or Vâkuchi roots taken with Kânjikam relieve diseases of the teeth. Roots of Indra-Vâruni taken with water exercise an antitoxic virtue; the roots of Surabhikâ prove remedial to diseases of the nervous system. Plasters of Gunjâ-powders pasted with Kânjikam and applied to the scalp prove remedial to diseases of the head (cephalagia). By a taking a compound (decoction) of Valâ, Atívalâ, and Yashti, sweetened with the addition of Sugar and honey, even a sterile woman is sure to conceive. A plaster composed of white Aparâjitâ roots, Pippali and Shunthi, pasted together with water and applied to the scalp, proves curative in Cephalagia (head-ache). O thou blissful one, Gunja-roots pasted with Kânjikam and applied to the scalp, relieve headache. Aratnikâ roots boiled with water impart a pleasant colour to the palate. Decoctions of clustered sprouts of Nirgundikâ prove curative in scrofula. Ashes of burnt Ketaki leaves taken with treacle, or Sharapunkhas taken with whey, cure splenic enlargement. Exudations of Mâtulunga taken with treacle and clarified butter relieve the type of colic (Gastralgia) due to the actions of the deranged Vâyu, and Pittam. Decoctions of Shunthi taken with Sauvarchala and Hingu prove antidotal to diseases of the heart.

——:o——

CHAPTER CCVIII.

HARI said:—Om, Gam Ganapatayé Sváhá (obeisance to the lord of the Ganas). By eight thousand times repeating this Mantram, and by tying up the tuft of hair on one's crown in a knot subsequent to that, one is sure to come victorious out of a royal court of justice and to be a favourite with kings. O Rudra, a thousand and eight libations of clarified butter containing black sesame should be cast in the fire with the recitation of this opulence-giving (Ganapati) Mantra for acquiring a mastery over the minds of kings and ladies.

Having fasted, and worshipped the lord of impediments under the auspices of the eighth or the fourteenth day of a lunar month, one should cast a thousand and eight oblations of sesame and white mustard seeds in fire, whereby one would be invincible in battle, and all the inmates of the world would be brought under one's control. Having tied up the tuft of hair on his crown into a knot after eight thousand and eight hundred times repeating the Mantram sacred to this divinity, a man would return victorious from a royal court or tribunal. The man, who repeats the Hrinkâra Mantra appended with a Visarga, each morning, by psychically projecting and locating it in the forehead of a woman, is sure to bring her under his control. By psychically projecting and locating the same Mantram in the reproductive organ of a woman, one can make her mad with amorous propulsions. He, who in a pure and tranquil mind casts ten thousand libations of clarified butter in fire by repeating this Mantram, is sure to bring a woman under his control at the first sight. A Tilaka mark composed of realgar, saffron, ox-gall and Patrakam pasted together and put on his forehead by a man enables him to fascinate the members of the softer sex. A Tilaka mark composed of white Aparájitá, Bhringarája, Vachá and Sahadevâ pasted together and put on his forehead by a man enables him to charm the three worlds. A Tilaka mark composed of fishes' gall and ox-gall pasted together and put on his forehead by a man with the tip of his left small finger, enables him to fascinate the three worlds. A Tilaka mark composed of oxgall treated with her catamenial blood in the manner of a Bhâbanâ and impressed on her forehead by a woman enables her to fascinate a man at the first sight. O thou supreme deity, a fumigation of the body with the vapours of a (burning) fumigating compound composed of Nâgeshvaram, Shaileyam, Tvak, Patram, Haritaki,, Chandanam, Kushtham, red Shâli and small Elâ pounded together gives a man the power of fascination. O thou supreme deity, O thou beloved of Pârvati, let a man, during an act of sexual congress, take his own seed, and smear the left leg of the woman therewith with his left hand, whereby he is sure to bring her under his control. O thou supreme deity, the application of a plaster composed of pigeon's dung and rock-salt pasted together with honey by a man, before an act of coitus, to his own reproductive organ, enables him to bring the woman under his control. Take five red flowers of different species, and Priyangu, equal in weight with these flowers; and paste them together. The plastering of his reproductive organ with this paste, before an act of sexual union, gives a man the power of fascinating the woman. A plaster composed of Ashvagandhâ, Manjisthâ, Mâlati-flowers and white Sarshapa pasted together and applied as the preceding one makes its applier endeared of women. Kâkajanghâ roots taken with milk prove curative in pulmonary consumption. By regularly taking a compound of Ashvagandhâ, Nâgavalâ, Mâshapulse and treacle, an old man may be young over again. O Rudra, powders of Triphalâ and iron, taken with honey, relieve the type of Gastralgia known as Parinâma Shula. Use of boiled water containing alkalis made of burnt Shambuka (a species of mollusc) shells, or of the ashes of a burnt stag-horn through the vehicle of clarified butter, proves efficacious, O Shiva, in cases of aching (neuralgic) pain at the chest and back. O thou bull-ensigned deity, water boiled with Hingu, Sauvarchalam, Shunthi, and Mahaushadham relieves all forms of colic. Apamarga roots taken with sea-brine cures all forms of indigestion and colic. O Rudra, O thou blissful one, sprouts of a Vata tree rubbed with the washings of rice should be administered for the purpose of curing any form of dysentery. A half Karsha measure of Ankata roots taken with the washings of rice relieves all forms of dysentery. A compound consisting of Maricham, Shunthi, twice as much as Maricham, and Kutaja-bark, twice as much as Sunthi, taken with treacle, tends to alleviate all forms of dysentery.

O Shiva, pills composed of Haridrâ, Tandulam, Apâmârga, Trikatu, and the roots of white Aparâjitâ pasted together with Siktham, undoubtedly alleviate all forms of cholera. A compound consisting of Trikatu, Triphalâ, Shilâjatu, and Haritaki pounded together, and taken with honey, proves curative, O Shankara, in all forms of urinary complaints (Meha). Take one Palam of Manah-Shilâ, one Palam of Maricham, and one Palam of Sinduram; pound them together and keep them soaked in a Prastha measure of sesame oil and the milky exudations of Arka plants in a copper vessel. Dry this compound in shade; this compound, as well as rock-salt taken with the milky exudations of a Snuhi plant, would be found to be highly efficacious in relieving all forms of colic (and neuralgic pain as well.) Take Trikatu, Triphalá, Alaktam, sesame oil, Realgar, Nimva leaves, Jâti flowers, goat's milk, Shankha-nâbhi, Chandana, and goat's urine, mix them together and make the mass into a stick. An application of this stick, pasted with water, to the eyes in the manner of a collyrium, cures loss of vision, cataract, and kindred occular affections. Powders of Vibhitaka seeds taken with honey relieve all forms of asthma; a compound of Triphalâ, Pippali and rock-salt pounded together and taken with honey proves beneficial in all forms of fever, cough, catarrh, asthma (bronchites) and Pthisis. Soak Deva-dâru powders with goat's urine, and dry them in shade, do this twenty-one times in succession; the application of this medicine to the eyes in the manner of a collyrium proves curative in night-blindness, Loss of vision, and falling off of the eye-lashes. O Rudra, a compound consisting of Pippali, Ketakam, Haridrâ. Amlakam and Vacha pounded together and applied to the eyes with the addition of milk proves beneficial in all forms of occular affections. O Shiva, roots of Shigru and Kâkajanghâ kept in the mouth or chewed together tend to relieve all diseases of the teeth.

CHAPTER CCIX.

HARI said :—The expressed juice, or sulphate of, Guduchi, taken with honey, cures all forms of Meha (urethral or urinary complaints). A decoction of Gohâlikâ roots and sesame, taken through the vehicle of milkcurd and clarified butter, tends to set flow the suppressed urine. The same docoction taken with Sauvarchala salt relieves hiccough. Roots of Goraksha and Karkati pasted with Vasya water and taken for three days in succession relieves caries of the teeth and Danta-Sharkarâ. Mâlati roots (culled in summer) and pasted with goat's milk should be administered for inducing urination, as well as for the cure of Chlorosis and urinary concretions. Plasters of Brahmadandi pasted with rice-washings should be applied to scrotal tumours, scrofulous glands, and goitres. This plaster mixed with the powders of Haritaki and Rasânjanam should be applied to the genitals in cases of loss of manhood, or of virile impotency. O Rudra, a plaster composed of Pugaphalam and Karavira roots pasted together with water would remove virile impotency. A plaster composed of Danti roots, Haridrâ, and Chitrakam pasted together should be employed for the cure of fistula in ano. In treating a case of fistula in ano, first apply leeches to the affected part, then wash it with a solution of Triphalâ, and then apply a plaster of pasted cat's bone to it, whereby the discharge of blood from the locality would be undoubtedly arrested, O thou bull-ensigned deity, soak Haridrâ with the milky exudations of Snuhi plants and dry them in shade, do this many times in succession. Applications of plasters of such Haridrâs pasted with water to the polypi prove curative in cases of rectal hæmorrhoids. A plaster composed of Haridrâ and Ghoshâ-phalam pasted together proves highly efficacious in removing rectal hæmorrhoids. O thou blissful one, Trikatukam taken wite thrice as much ashes or Alkali treated with clarified butter and dissolved in water speedily leads to the falling off of rectal polypi. Pulps of burnt Vilva fruits prove highly efficacious in cases of bleeding piles. Black sesame taken with butter proves efficacious in the same disease. O thou bull-ensigned deity, a lambative composed of Yavakshâra, Shunthi powders and treacle, taken in equal parts and pasted together, and licked, each morning, improves the digestive capacity. O Rudra, deçoctions of Shunthi, or of Chittrakam, Pippali and Haritaki, taken with rock-salt, proves as a good digestant and stomachic remedy. Powders of the foregoing drugs taken with water, as well as bacon cooked with clarified butter tends to give an acute appetite.

——:o:——

CHAPTER CCX.

O THOU dissipator of woes, take Hastikarna roots, and reduce them to powder. O Thou blissful one, a hundred Palam weight of powdered Hastikarna roots, taken with milk, in the course of a week, will make its user a prodigy of memory and enable him to cope with a lion in prowess and swiftness of motion. Taken with milk, for sixteen days in succession, these powders will impart a ruby-like glow to the complexion of their user and enable him to live for a thousand years. Taken with honey and clarified butter, they tend to increase the duration of life; taken only in combination with honey, these powders make their users extremely endearing to women and enable them to live up for another ten thousand years. Taken with milk curd they impart a thunder-like hardness to the muscles; taken with the expressed juice of Kesharâji, they enable their users to live for a thousand years. By using these powders through the medium of Kânjikam, a man is enabled to live for a century without anywise suffering from the ravages of time. Taken with Triphalâ, they tend to improve the eye-sight; by taking them through the vehicle of clarified butter even blind persons may regain their sight. A plaster of these powders pasted with buffalo milk and applied to the head imparts a sable colour to the hair; O thou bull-ensigned deity, applications of these powders with oil to the head remove baldness and help a luxurious growth of hair. Rubbing of the body with these powders pasted with oil removes wrinkles of the skin and premature greyness of the hair, and grants a sort of immunity from disease. These powders pasted with goat's milk and applied to the eyes, in the manner of a collyrium, for a month, improve the eye-sight. Gather Palâsha seeds in the month of Shrâvana. Reduce these seeds to powder, with their capsules off, and take this powder for six months, living on a rice and milk regimen, and abjuring the use of water. By taking this powder in the way as prescribed, a man is enabled to live for a thousand years, free from disease and decay. Cull Bhringa-râja roots under the auspices of the asterism Pushyâ. Take a Vidálapadam weight of this root with barley-wine for thirty days in succession. Thereby a man will be able to live for five hundred years in the possession of an elephant-like strength of the body and free from disease and premature decay, and as a prodigy of memory.

CHAPTER CCXI.

HARI said:—A cut, or a lacerated wound, filled with melted butter, will heal up at the first instance without producing any pus or inflammation. The juice of Apámârga, squeezed out with finger and poured into the cavity of a cut or wound, will at once arrest the bleeding. O Rudra, a plaster of Hijjala roots and Lángaliká roots pasted together and applied to the mouth of a wound will spontaneously expel any foreign substance, through the passage of its penetration, that might have been lodged therein, no matter how long it might have remained thus imbedded. Applications of plasters composed of Vâna roots and Meshashingi roots pasted together with water will bring about the healing of sinuses. A sinus may be healed by dusting it with powders of Kanku-roots; the patient shall be enjoined to live on curdled buffalo milk and cooked Kodrava grain during the period of treatment. Plasters of Vrahmadandi seeds pasted with water prove remedial to skin diseases due to the vitiated condition of the blood. Take ashes of burnt barley corn, Vidanga, Gandhapâshânam and Shunthi; pound them together, and soak this pulverised compound with Lizard's (Krikalása) blood and dry it in the sun in the manner of a Bhábanâ saturation. Apply this plaster, O Shiva, to abscesses and carbuncles and wonder at the result. Take Shobánjanam roots, burnt linseed, and white mustard seeds; pound them together, O Shankara, and reduce the compound to the consistency of a paste with the addition of whey, which is not acid in its flavour. Plasters of this pasted compound prove curative in Granthikam. For the exorcism of a malignant spirit, an errhine composed of white Aparájita roots pasted with rice-washings should be given to the possessed person. Errhines of the expressed juice of Agastya flowers, saturated with the powders of black pepper, relieve colic pain. O Shiva, plasters of snake-skins, Hingu, Nimva-leaves, Yava, and white Sarshapa pasted together have the virtue of exorcising ghosts. Anjanams composed of Gorochaná, Maricham, Pippali and rock salt, pasted together with honey have the virtue of warding off the influnces of malignant stars and spirit. For relieving quotidian ague and warding off the influences of malignant planets, the patient should be wrapped with a black cloth and fumigated with the vapours of a compound consisting of Guggulu, and owl's feathers pounded together.

—:o:—

CHAPTER CCXII.

HARI said:—The expressed juice of the white Aparájita flowers dropped into the eyes tend to destroy the eye-disease known as Patola-raga. O thou blue and red bodied one, O thou, the destroyer of the demon of darkness, by chewing Gokshura roots, a man may destroy the parasites lodged in his teeth and may get rid of tooth-ache in consequence. By applying a plaster composed of white Arka roots pasted with cow-milk to her private parts, while observing a fast, during her flow, a woman may get rid of the pain of Gulma. O thou bull-ensigned deity, by wearing a white Arka flower consecrated with the aforesaid Mantra round her waist during an act of sexual congress, after the suppression of her monthly flow, a woman is sure to conceive a male child.

O Hara, Palâsha-roots or Apâmârga roots, tied round the wrist of a patient, act as good frebrifuge remedies and tend to ward off the evil influences of malignant ghosts. O thou supreme divinity, Vrishchika roots pasted with water collected over night and given to a fever-patient instantaneously allay the heat, and burning sensation in his body. The same roots tied with the tuft of hair on the crown of a patient proves curative in daily intermittent fever; taken with Kânjikam they prove efficacacious in fever and in the type of Kushthan, due to the vitiated condition of blood. Taken with Vâsyam water they exercise an antitoxic virtue. A bitter animosity is created between him and one, whether male or female, to whom he administers Lajjâluka roots pasted with his own seed. By taking Pâthâ roots pasted with melted cow-butter one is relieved of all effects of a poison. Shirisha roots taken in combination with Vâsyam water act as good antitoxic remedies. The expressed juice of the roots of red Chitrakam poured into the ears (of a patient) proves curative in Ch'o-rosis. The expressed juice of white Kokilâkasha roots taken with goat's milk for three days in succession tends to cure Pthisis. Cocoanut flowers taken in combination (pasted) with goat's milk prove remedial to the three types of Vâta-Raktam. A garland of Sudarshana roots tied round the neck proves curative in tertian ague and tends to ward off the influences of malignant Ghosts and planets. Roots of white Gunjâ plants culled under the auspices of the asterism Pushyâ, and kept in the month, act as a good prophylaxis against a variety of poisons. Tied around the wrist or the neck, the same roots tend to ward off the influences of malignant planets. O thou red and blue bodied one, these roots tied round his waist by a man under the auspices of the fourteenth day of the moon's wane grant an immunity from attacks by lions and other wild beasts. O thou supreme deity, Vishnukrântâ roots tied round the ears by a person act as prophylasis against attacks by crocodiles.

CHAPTER CCXIII.

HARI said :—Pasted Aparâjitâ roots taken with cow's urine cure scrofula. O Rudra, Indra-vâruni roots taken with cold water, as well as errhines of solutions of Eranda, Jingani and Shuka Shimbi pasted together tend to alleviate the pain in the neck and the arms. An application of a plaster composed of Ashvagandhâ or Pippali, or of Vachâ and Kushtam, pasted together with buffalo butter, alleviates pain in the mammæ and the urethral canal. A plaster composed of Kushtham and Nâgavalâ pasted together with butter and applied to the breast acts as a good breast-developer and imparts a graceful contour to the breasts of youthful maidens. The patient, by mentioning whose name an Indravâruni root is thrown from a distance, is sure to be relieved of his splenic enlargement. Roots of white Punarnavâ taken pasted with rice-washings undoubtedly prove curative in abscess. Ashes of burnt plaintain barks administered through drinks relieve all forms of Ascites. Plantain roots cooked in combination with treacle and clarified butter over a gentle fire act as good vermifuge remedies. Daily use of a compound of Nimva leaves and Amlakam pounded together, in the morning, undoubtedly cures Kushtham (cutaneous affection). A plaster composed of Haritaki, Vidanga, Haridrâ, white Sarshapa, Somarâja-seeds (roots according to Benares Edition), Karanja seeds and Sanidhavam, pasted together with cow's urine, proves efficacious in all forms of cutaneous affections. One part of Triphalâ and two parts of Somarâja seeds taken in combination with powdered Pathyâ cure ring-worms. A plaster composed Kharam rubbed in a vessel of Indian bell metal, pasted with cow's urine, cooked in combination with rock-salt and acid whey (Takram), prove curative in all forms of cutaneous affections. A plaster composed of Haridrâ, Haritâlam, Durvâ grass and rock-salt pasted together with cow's urine proves remedial in cases of Pâmâ and ring-worm. Somarâja seeds taken in combination with butter and honey prove curative in all forms of leucoderma. O Rudra, the cure is almost certain through the administration of the foregoing compound, but the patient must live on a whey-rice regimen during the period of treatment. Plasters, composed of white Aparájitâ roots pasted with Sârivâ and applied to the affected region, for a month, tend to cure all forms of leucoderma. O thou bull-ensigned deity, applications of plasters composed of Maricham and Sinduram pasted together with buffalo-butter would certainly cure Pâmâ and dyspnœa. O thou supreme deity, dry Gâmbhâri roots cooked in combination with milk prove antidotal to Shukla-Pittam. Plasters of Mulaka seeds pasted with the expressed juice of Apâmârga and applied to the affected part, prove efficacious in Shilhika. O thou supreme deity, ashes of burnt plantain bark and Apâmârga twigs pasted together with the expressed juice of Eranda and applied to the affected patches prove curative in Siddhma. O thou supreme deity, O thou bull-ensigned one, burn the ashes of a Kushmânda creeper, mixed with the bark of its stem pasted with cow's urine, and Haridrâ pasted with water, in a closed crucible luted and plastered with buffalo-dung. By rubbing his body with this burnt compound, a man is sure to acquire a brilliant complexion. Rubbing of the body with a compound consisting of Haridrâ, Dâru-Haridrâ, and Kushtham pasted together with water tends to impart a brilliant glow to the complexion and a fragrant smell to the skin. Plastering of the body with Durvâ, Kâkajanghâ, leaves of Arjuna and Jambu, and Lodhram pasted together with water tends to remove the bad odours of the skin. Solutions of Lodhram saturated with the powders of Kanakam form the most cooling

84

and agreeable paste for smearing the body in summer. Washing of the body with milk, in the morning, tends to remove the evils of perspiration; rubbing of the body with pasted Kâkajanghâ acts as an agreeable cosmetic plaster. The expressed juice of Vâsaka and Yashtimadhu, taken with honey and sugar, proves curative in Jaundice, Chlorosis, Hæmoptisis, and Hæmorrhage. Even a most acute attack of catarrh may be cut short by taking cold water in the morning. O thou supreme deity, a pulverised compound of Pippali, rock salt and Vibhitakam pounded together and taken with Kânjikam removes hoarsness. Amalakam-powder administered through the vehicle of clarified butter, or a compound consisting of Manahshilâ, Valâ roots, Kola-leaves and Guggulu pasted together, or inhalation of the vapours of a fumigation stick, composed of Jâtipatram, Kola leaves and Manahshilâ pasted together and burnt in a fire of Kola-wood charcoal would undoubtedly relieve congh. Triphalâ and Pippali powders taken with honey, before the midday meal, relieve thirst and fever. The expressed juice of Vilva roots or a decoction of Guduchi taken with honey arrests the three types of vomiting. Durvâ pasted with rice-washings proves antidotal to vomiting.

——:•:——

CHAPTER CCXIV.

HARI said:—Serpents leave the house of him, who takes Punarnavâ roots pasted with water under the auspices of the asterism Pushyâ. O thou bull ensigned deity, he, who carries an image of Garuda, made of bear's teeth, on his person, remains invisible to snakes all through his life. O

Rudra, snakes avoid the presence of one, who takes Shâlmali roots pasted with water under the auspices of the asterism Pushyâ. By tying Lajjâlukâ roots round his hands, or by smearing them with pasted Lajjâluká, a man is enabled to catch hold of Snakes without anywise imperiling his life. Roots of white Arka plants, taken pasted with water, under the auspices of the asterism Pushyâ, prove antidotal to Danshaka (a large kind of mosquito) poison ; Karabira roots similarly taken are found to exercise a similar antitoxic virtue. Plasters of Mahâkâla roots pasted with Kânjikam tend to neutralise the poison of Dundubha or Bodra (Boa) snakes. Tanduliyaka-roots taken pasted with rice-washings through the medium of clarified butter (honey according to others) prove antidotal to all kinds of poison. Either Nily roots, or Lajjâluká roots taken pasted with rice-washings prove remedial to Danshaka-poison. The expressed juice of a Kushmánda creeper taken with the admixture of treacle, sugar and milk tends to neutralise the poison of a Danshaka. Yashtimadhu taken with its own weight of sugar through the medium of milk proves antidotal to mole-poison. Gargles of cold water arrest salivation due to the irritation of the mucous membrane of the mouth through chewing betel leaves. Clarified butter taken with sugar relieves the intoxication of wine. O thou supreme deity, potions of black Ankata roots boiled with water, or errhines of decoctions of black Ankota roots prove remedial, within three days, to any slow poison retained in the system. Warm clarified butter, taken with the admixture of rock salt, relieves, O thou supreme deity, the pain of a scorpion-bite. O thou blissful one, a compound consisting of Kusumbham, Kumkum, Haritâlam, Manah-shilá Karanjam, and Arka roots pasted together, and internally administered, proves antidotal to all kinds of poison. Dregs of oils found in burning oil-lamps, as well as the expressed juice of Kharjuraka undoubtedly neutralise the poison, O Shiva, in cases of centipede (scolopendra) bites. O Rudra, a fumigation of the seat of the bite with the vapours of burning bdellium is sure to neutralise the poison in a case of centipede-bite. Fumigations with the vapours of burning Ankota leaves would prove beneficial in cases of bites by rats. Plasters composed of Nâgeshvaram, Maricham, Shunthi, and Tagarpáduká pasted together with water would prove antidotal to bee-stings, or the seat of the sting should be otherwise plastered with Shatapushpá and rocksalt pasted together with clarified butter. Plasters composed of Shirisha seeds cooked with milk would certainly destroy the poison, O thou supreme deity, in cases of Dundura (poisonous rats) bites. O thou moon-crested one, the expressed juice of Dhusturam administered with the admixture of milk and treacle proves curative in cases of bites by rabid dogs (Hydrophobia). Gargles of a decoction of Vata, Nimva and Shami barks relieve the pain in the mouth due to the efiects of a poison. Plasters of Devadáru and Gairikam pasted together with water, or of Nágeshvaram, Haridrá, Dáru-Haridrá and Manjishtâ pasted together with water prove remidial to spider-poisons. Plasters composed of Karanja seeds, Varuna bark, Tilah and Sarshapa pasted together would undoubtedly destroy all kinds of poison (venom).

—:o:—

CHAPTER CCXV.

HARI SAID :—A single moist, Punarnavá root, or Apámárga root, or the expressed juice of either of these roots, introduced into the vagina, relieves the local plain of young wives or of parturient women. The roots of Bhumi Kushânda taken pasted with rice-washings tend to improve the secretion of milk in parturient women. Plasters of pasted Indravâruni roots, O Shiva, relieve the breast pain in females. O thou supreme deity, ingestions of Pâlikâ cooked with clarified butter relieve an aching pain in the female reproductive organs. Plasters of Káravella roots pasted with water tend to replace a protruded vagina in its natural position. Plasters of Nili, and Patola roots, pasted together with a solultion of Tila and applied with the admixture of clarified butter, prove curative in Jvála-Gardhava. O Rudra, Pâthâ roots taken pasted with rice-washings, as well as Kushtha-roots administered in the same way relieve Pápa-rogam. Solutions of Vásyam taken with honey alleviate the internal burning sensation in cases of Páparogam. O Rudra, clarified butter taken with as much quantity of Lâkshâ through the vehicle of milk cures leucorrhœa. O thou blissful one, powders of Dvijayashti and Trikantakam taken with a decoction of sesame prove curative in Rukta Gulmas of women, and act as a good emanagogue remedy. Bulbs of Raktotpalam, taken with sugar or with cold water, relieve menorrhagia. A decoction of Sharapunkha taken with Kánjikam, Hingu and rock-salt tends to bring about a speedy parturition. A Mátulunga root, if it can be culled out entire, by mentioning the name of an anciente, presages the birth of a male child, if otherwise (pulled out split or served) it predicts the birth of a female one. An Apámárga root inserted into the chignonon of a pregnant woman, O thou blissful one, or Karpura, Madanaphalam and Madhuka pounded together and introduced even into the reproductive organ of an old woman, produces happy results, not to speak of it being used by young maidens. Potions of solutions of Kushtam sweetened with sugar, and impressment of Tilak marks on the foreheads of infants act as a general prophylaxis against the influence of malignant planets, ghosts, and diseases. An infant should be made to wear on its person, O Rudra, Shankánábhi, Vachá,

Kushtham and bits of iron for prophylactic purposes. Powders of Palásha seeds, or powdered Amalakam and Vidanga taken with the admixture of honey and melted cow-butter tend to improve the intellect. Its effect is almost instantaneous; by taking this compound for a month, O thou supreme deity, a person is enabled to conquer death and decay. Powders of Palásha seeds and Tilam, taken for a weak, through the vehicle of honey and clarified butter, would undoubtedly remove, O Rudra, the effects of old age. By taking, for a month, O Rudra, powders of Amalakam in combination with honey and oil, a person would verily become a lord of speech. Water containing powders of Shivâ and A'malakam, sweetened with honey and drunk through the nostrils, each morning, would act as the best strength-giving medicine. By taking Kushtham-powders, each morning, with the admixture of honey and clarified butter, a man would be able to witness a thousand summers in the full possession of all his faculties in a healthy and fragnant-smelling frame. By regularly consuming huskless Mâsha pulse, soaked with clarified butter in the manner of a Bhávaná, or cooked with milk, in conbination with honey and milk, a man would be able to visit a hundred women, each night. Mercury is purified by rubbing it with sulphar and castor oil. A dose of such purified mercury taken with water, thrice a day, acts as a good tonic medicine. By taking milk, that has been cooked with huskless Mâsha pulse and Shimvi seeds, in conbination with Apâmarga oil, one would be able to visit a hundred women, each day.

CHAPTER CCXVI.

HARI said:—To a cow, that shuns, or turns hostile to, her own calf, should be given her milk, duly milched and salted, whereby she would fondly take to her offspring. Bits of dog's bones tied round the neck of a cow or a cow-buffalo lead to the expulsion of vermins from her body. Gunjâ roots internally administered would bring about the castings of horns in horned cattle. External applications of the juice of Varuna-phalas, squeezed out with the hand, would bring about the expulsion of vermins, O Shiva, from the bodies of biped and quadruped animals. O Rudra, pourings of the expressed juice of Jayá would bring about the healing of ulcers in quadrupeds. The urine of a she-elephant internally administered would remove the bodily ailments of honed cattle. Lentil seeds and Shâli rice pasted with whey (Takram) and administered through the medium of cow or buffalo-milk would prove beneficial to bullocks. Sharpunkha leaves given with salt would cure the belbous eruptions (Vâri-sphotam) in horses and bullocks. Ghritakumâri leaves given with salt would relieve itches in horses and bullocks.

—:o:—

CHAPTER CCXVII.

HARI said:—Take eight parts of Chitrakam, sixteen parts of Shurana, four parts of Shunthi, two parts of Maricham, three parts of Pippalimulam, four of Vidanga, eight parts of Mushalíká, four parts of Triphalá, and treacle, double the combined weight of these drugs, and prepare a confection (Modaka) in the usual way. This Modaka covers within the range of its therapeutic application such diseases as indigestion, Jaundice, Chlorosis, dysentery, splenic enlargement, and loss of appetite. Take Vilvam, Agnimantha, Shyonâka, Pâtalâ, Pâribhadrakam, Prasârini, Ashvagandhâ, the two kinds of Vrihati, Kantíkari, Valá, Ativalâ, Râsná, Shvadanshtrâ, Punarnavâ, Eranda, Parni, Guduchi, and Kapikachchhukâ, weighing ten tolas in weight, and make a decoction therewith in the usual way. Take it down from the oven with its quarter part left, and cook the same in a Pâtram full of oil (four seers), add to it cow milk or goat's milk, four times as much as the former, add to it Shatâvari and Saindhavam to the weight of oil. Now hear me enumerate the names of drugs, which are to be added to it in the form of pasted Kalka. *viz.* Shatapushpâ Devadâru, Valá, Prishniparni, Vachá, Aguru, Kushtham, Mánsi, Saindhavam, and Punarnavâ, each weighing a Palam weight. Cook the oil in the usual officinial way. This oil should be employed as errhines or potions for relieving pleurodynia (Pârshva Shulam) and cardiac colic. It includes within the range of its curative efficacy Scrofula, Hysteria, Vâtaraktam, and loss of manhood. By usuing this oil, even a she-mule is sure to conceive, O Hara, what wonder that a woman would be blessed with progeny through its use. It may be likewise employed with advantage in cases of lameness, arched back, and kindred nervous maladies of horses and elephants. Mustard oil cooked in combination with Hingu, Tumvura and Shunthi may be used as ear-drops in relieving otalgia. Ashes of dry Mulakam and Shunthi, Hingula and Nágaram and Shuktam cooked in combination with oil, four times as much, should be employed in curing deafness, otalgia and germination of vermins in the ears, as well as for the purpose of arresting fetid discharges from the ears. A medicinal oil cooked with the admixture of ashes of dry Mulakam and

Shunthi, Hingulam, Nágaram, Shatapushpá, Vacha, Kushtham, Dáru, Shigru, Rasánjanam, Sauvarchalam, Yavakshâra, Sâmudram and Saindhava salt, Granthikam, Vid, Mustam, Madhu, and Shuktam, four times as much, and the expressed juice of Mátulunga and Kadali, should be employed, O Hara, for the purpose of removing diseases of the ears, such as deafness, noise in the ears, otalgia, fetid discharges from the ears. The effect of this oil is almost instantaneous, and O thou moon-crested deity, this is the foremost of all Kshârartailas (alkaline oils) in respect of its efficacy, and instantly cleanses the teeth and the mouth of all impurities. Cook an oil in combination with Chandana, Kumkumam, Mânsi, Karpura, Jâtipatrikâ, Jâtiphalam, Kakkolaphalam. Lavangaphalam, Aguru, Ushira, Turya, Kushtham, Tagarapâduka, Gorochanâ, Priyangu, Valâ, Nakhi, Saralam, Saptaparna, Lâksha, Amaloki, and Padmakam. This oil is highly efficacious in removing bad odour of perspiration from the body and proves curative in itches and other skin diseases. By using this oil, a man becomes a favourite with the fair sex, and is enabled to visit a hundred women, each day. It is possessed of a great spermatopoetic virtue; by using this oil even a sterile woman is blessed with the pleasures of motherhood. Take a Prastha measure of melted cow-butter, cook it, in the usual way, with the admixture of eight Prasthas of water, Yamani, Chitrakam, Dhânyam, Tryushanam, Jirakam, Sauvarchalam, Pippalimulam, Vidanga, and Râjikam. This medicinal Ghritam acts as a good appetiser and may be employed with advantage in Piles, Anasarca and intestinal glands. Take a Prastha measure of mustard oil and cook it in the usual officinial way in an earthen or iron vessel, over a slow fire, with the admixture of eight Prasthas of cow's urine, Maricham, Trivrit, Kushtham, Haritâlam, Manahshilâ, Devadâru, the two kinds of Haridrá Kushtham, Mânsi, Chandana, Vishálá, Karabiram, milky juice of Arka plants and cow-dung-Serum, each weighing a

Karsha, and half a Palam of Vrisham. Used as an external application, this oil cures Pámá, Vicharchikâ, ring worms, malignant sores, and even leucoderma of mature growth or of long origin. Cook a medicinal Ghritam in combination with a decoction of Patola leaves, Kataka, Manjishtha, Shárivá, Nishâ, Jâti, Shami, Nimva leaves, and Madhukam. External applications of this Ghritam alleviate pain and arrest secretions of ulcers. By taking a compound of Agnimantha, Vachá, Vásá, and Pippali with honey and rock-salt, for seven days, a person is enabled to sing as sweetly as a Kinnara. By taking, for three days in succession, a compound of Apámárga, Guduchi, Kushtham, Shatávari, Vachá, Shankhapushpi, Abhayá, and Vidanga, taken in equal parts and pounded together with the admixture of melted cow-butter, one is enabled to learn eight hundred books by heart. Taken with water or clarified butter, Vachá enables a person to learn a thing at the first hearing. One Palam weight of Vachá taken with milk under the auspicies of a solar or lunar eclipse, tends to make its user a profoundly intelligent person. Water boiled with Bhunimva, Nimva, Triphalá, Parpata, Patola, Mustakam, and Vásaka immediately destroys Visphotas (carbuncles). Sticks (Vartis) made of Ketaku fruits, Shankha, Saindhava, Tryushanam, Vachá, Phena, Rasánjanam, Vidanga and Manahshilâ pasted together with honey prove curative in cough, loss of vision and the type of eye-disease known as Patola. Cook two Prastha measures of a decoction of Mâsha pulse with a Drona Measure of water, and take it down with its quarter part left. Cook a Prastha Measure of oil with the admixture of this decoction in the usual way, add to it an A'dakam measure of Kânjikam and a compound of Punarnavá, Gokshura, Saindhavam, Tryushanam, Vachá, salt, Devadaru, Manjishtha, and Kantakarika. Internally administered, or employed as errhines, this oil cures the most acute type of earache; used as an unguent, it removes deafness and proves beneficial in hosts of other bodily distempers. Take two Palam weights of rock-salt. five Palas of each of Shunthi and Chitrakam, five Prasthas of Sauviram, and one Prastha of oil. Cook it in the usual officinial way. This oil proves curative in cases of splenic enlargement, leucorrhœa, and all diseases of the nervous system. A medicinal oil cooked in combination with a decoction of Audumvara, Vata, Plaksha, the two kinds Jamvu, Arjuna, Pippali, Kadamva, Palásha, Lodhram, Tindukam, Madhukam, Amram, Sarja, Vadaram, Padmakesharam, Shirisha seeds, and Ketaka brings on graunlation even in old or long-standing sores, and facilitates their speedy healing.

———:o:———

CHAPTER CCXVIII.

HARI said :—A compound consisting of two kinds of Rajanî, Pâthâ, Kushtham, Ashvagandhá, Ajamodakam, Vachá, Trikatu and common salt pounded together and treated with the expressed juice of Brahmi in the manner of a Bhâbaná saturation, and taken for a week, tends to highly improve the intellect. Errhines, plasters, or pastes of Siddhárthakam, Vachá, Hingu, Karanjam, Devadâru, Manjishthâ, Triphalá, Vishvam, Shirisha, the two kinds of Rajani, Priyangu, Nimva and Trikatu pounded together and mixed with cow's urine prove curative in hysteria, poisoning, insanity, discolouring of the skin, and diseases due to the influences of malignant ghosts. Take Nimva, Kushthâm, the two kinds of Haridrâ, Shigru, Śarshapa, Devadâru, Patolam and Dhanyam ; pound them together and rubb this pulverised compound with whey (Takram). Rubbing of the body with this paste, or with this paste mixed with oil, destroys Pâmâ, itches and allied diseases of the skin. Take Sâmudram salt, Saindhava salt, Kshâra, Râjika, common salt, Vid salt, Katu, iron rust,

Trivrit and Shuranakam in equal parts. Cook them over a gentle fire, with the addition of milk-curd, cow's urine and water. This pulverised compound, which is called Agnivala Churnam, instantaneously relieves all form of colic, whether intestinal, renal, or splenic, or brought about through the enlargement of intestinal glands (gulma.) It should be taken through the vehicle of warm water, and the patient should be advised to take Mâsha pulse with melted butter after the digestion of his ingested food. This is almost a specific for all forms of colic, inclusive of the one known as Parinâma Shula. A compound of Abhayâ, A'malakam, Drâkshâ, Pippali, Kantakârikâ, Shringi, Punarnavâ, and Shunthi boiled together with water, or pounded together, may be given with advantage in all forms of Cough. Abhayâ A'malakam, Drâkshâ, Pâthâ, Vibhitakam, and sugar, taken in equal parts and internally administered, act as a good febrifuge remedy. Triphalâ, Vadaram Drâkshâ and Pippali combinedly exercise a purgative virtue, Abhaya taken with salt and warm water acts as a good purgative. Flesh, blood, excrementitious matter (stool and urine) of female tortoises, fishes, mares, cow buffalos, cows, female monkeys, she jackals, female cats, female crows, female owls, and she bears should be given for relieving fits of fever and insanity. Fumigations with the vapours of burning hairs or feathers) of any of these animals likewise prove beneficial in the foregoing maladies. The god Vishnu, meditateed upon by a person at the time of taking a medicine, undoubtedly relieves him of the trouble.

——:o:——

CHAPTER CCXIX.

HARI said :—O thou self-begotten one, now hear me discourse on the prophylatic formula known as Vaishnavam Kavacham, which grants a certain immunity from attacks of maladies. Having made obeisance unto the birthless, changeless, undecaying and all-powerful reality, having bowed down unto the all-pervading Vishnu, the god of gods, the overlord of the celestials, I shall describe the prophylaxis presently referred to. I make obeisance to the eternal spirit of irresistible prowess, to the dissipator of all woes and misfortunes. May Vishnu protect me in the front, and Krishna, at the back. May Hrishikesha protect my intellect; and Keshava, my tongue. May Vâsudeva protect my eyes, and may Sankarshana guard my ears. May Pradyumna protect my nose; and Aniruddha, my skin. May Vanamâli protect the inside of my throat; and Shrivatsa, the downward portion of my body. May the discus-wielding divinity guard my sides. I consign my left side to the protection of the destroyer of demons and my right side to that of the divine club weapon, that has brought about the annihilation of the Asuras. May the divine Mushala weapon protect my belly, may the divine plough guard my back. May the divine bow protect the upper part of my body, may Nandaka protect my knee-joints. May the divine conch-shell protect my insteps, may the divine lotus flower protect my feet. May the divine Garuda protect me in all concerns of my life. May the boar manifestation of Vishnu protect me in waters, may the dwarf manifestation of the supreme god protect me on undulating and impassable grounds. May Nrisinha guard my person in wilderness; may Keshava shield me everywhere. May Hiranyagarbha give me gold, may the divine Kapila, the author of the Sânkhya system of philosophy, help me to maintain a normal equilibrium among the different vital principles of my organism. May the birthless one that presides over the white isle (Shvetadvipa) lead me to that land; may the destroyer of the demons Madhu and Kaitabha destroy my enemies. May the all-pervading Vishnu always expel sins from my body; may the swan, fish and tortoise manifestations of Vishnu protect me in all the quarters of the heaven. May he, whose prowess brooks no obstruction in the three regions, dissipate all my inequities. May Náráyana protect my intellect, may Shesha grant me that pure knowledge which dispels all ignorance, may the god whose mouth is the submarine, volcanic fire, cleanse my spirit of all sin I have committed in the past with my hands, feet, and mouth. May Dattâtreya grant me increase of friends, progeny and domestic animals. May Ráma destroy with his battle-axe all my adversaries. May the mighty armed Râma, the destroyer of Râkshasas, always guard my body. May Râma, the delight of the race of Yâdavas, kill my enemies with his invincible ploughshare. May juvinility of Krishna, the destroyer of Pralamva, Keshin, Chânura, Putanâ and Kansa, grant me all my heart desires. Dismayed with fear, utterly terror-stricken, I see a noose-holding male figure of a blackish, yellow colour, more sable than the primordial darkness and more dreadful to look at than the god of death, hence do I consign myself to the protection of the lotus-eyed one that suffers no decay. O my soul, I need not fear since the woe-dissipating lord is mine. I am now indeed an adorable Self.

Having meditated upon the divine self of Nârâyana, who guards against all evils and calamities that beset human life, I roam about in this world, bearing this Vaishnava prophylaxis on my person. Since my mind perpetually dwells upon the almighty self of Vishnu, malignant spirits dare not assail me. I am a veritable moving pantheon, full of energies of all the divinities. May success attend me in this life since I have duly recited this (Vaishnabam) Mantram. May

Vishnu strike the eye-sight of those sin-perverted beings, that might chance to behold me with their wicked eyes, or whom I might happen to behold. May the discus of Vâsudeva, as well as the halo (*lit.* spokes) that shines round that weapon, sever my sins and strike those that wish me evil. Happening to fall among monsters, and Pishachas, while crossing a lonely waste or a weird wilderness, in quarrels, in contests, while travelling on the king's high way, in moments of crisis and on apprehension of imminent peril to life, while swiming across a river or to ward off the influences of malignant planets and disease-spirits, at times when attacks by thieves and acts of incendiarism are apprehended, in thunder, in lightning, on the happening of reasonable causes of terror, one should recite this Vâghavatam Mantram, most sacred of all other Mantras. This renowned Bhâgavatam Kavacham, which extinguishes all sin, is the most secret of all secret Mantras. I make obeisance to the lotus-naveled one, the seed of the universe, the self without end or origin that lies inaccessible within the cycles (Kalpas) of evolution, the emanations of his own Mâyâ.

Om, to Time (obeisance) Svâhâ, Om, to the spirit of Time obeisance (Svahâ). Om, to Krishna obeisance (Svâhâ). Om, to the figure of Krishna obeisance. Om, obeisance to Chanda, Om obeisance to Chandarupa, Om, obeisance to Prachanda, Om, obeisance to Prachandrupa. Om, obeisance to Sarva. Om, obeisance to Sarvarupa. These are the texts of disease and poison-incantations. May Vishnu, may Narayana, may Aniruddha, may Samkarshana, may Vasudeva destroy my all kinds of fever.

—o:—

CHAPTER CCXX.

HARI said :—Now hear me enumerate the Mantra, which repeated for seven nights in succession by a person, enables him to witness the realisation of all his wished-for objects. I make obeisance to the Bhagavân, I meditate upon the self of Vâsudeva. I bow down unto Aniruddha, Sankarshana and Pradyumna manifestations of Vishnu. Obeisance to the giver of perfect knowledge, obeisance to the embodied self of pure joy. Obeisance to the one that delighteth in the soul, obeisance to the embodied quiesism, obeisance to the one who observeth no duality in the universe. This universe is thy image, hence do I make obeisance to thee. Obiesance to Hrishikesha, the great spirit reflected in the universe. I make obeisance to Brahma from whom all this has come into being, in whom lies this all and from whom many other eternities will originate. Thou supportest this terrestrial globe, I make obeisance to thee. I make obeisance to Him whom the mind, life and the sense-organs cannot reach and who, like this ethereal expanse, lies extended both in the inside and outside of creatures. Om, obeisance to the Lord, the great Purusha, the Supreme Lord of the Mahabhutas (primordial matter) whose lotus feet are surrouned by the polens of virtues of heirarchies of beings of Sattva qualities. I make obeisance to the final goal of all. By dint of this knowledge, Chitrakatu was lifted to the status of a Vidyádhara.

—:o:—

CHAPTER CCXXI.

Hari said :—O thou, supreme deity, I shall now enumerate the Vishnu-Dharma-Vidyâ, by reciting which, Indra was enabled to kill all his adversaries, and was ultimately installed on the throne of heaven. The Mantras such as Om, etc., should be psychically located by the reciter in his brain, face, heart, belly, thighs, knee-joints and legs respectively. He should then meditate upon these Mantras located as directed in the preceding line. As an alternative, the Mantra running as Namo Nârâyanâya should be located, as above directed, in the limbs in the inverse order of enumeration. Then the rite of Kara-nyâsa should be performed with the twelve-lettered Mantra sacred to the deity (Om Namo Bhagavate Vâsudevâya.) The votary should recite the Mantra running as Om, obeisance to Vishnu, and consider himself as identical with the Shesha manifestation of that divinity, attended with the sixfold energy. May Hari protect me; may the fish manifestation of Vishnu shield my person in water. May Trivrikrama, who exercises absolute power in the three regions, protect me in the skies; may the dwarf manifestation of Vishnu preserve me on land. May the mighty Nrisinha protect me in wilderness; may Râma preserve me on the mountain. May the boar manifestation of Vishnu preserve me on the earth-surface; may Nâráyana preserve me in the air. May Kapila protect the worldly concerns of my life; may Dattátreya preserve my yoga. May Hayagriva, among the celestials, and Makaradhvaja, among the celestial youths, preserve me. May Nárada protect me from worshipping any other god. May the tortoise manifestation of Vishnu preserve me in the south west; may Dhanvantari protect me from the evil effects of unwholesome food. May Nâga protect me from failings of anger and passion. May

Yagna preserve me from the combined energy of diseases, may Vyâsa preserve me from ignorance. May Buddha preserve me from the concourse of heretics (Páshandas), may Kalki preserve me from sin and sinful propensities. May Vishnu protect me at noon; Nârâyana, in the morning; the destroyer of demon Madhu, at after-noon; and Mádhava, in the evening. May Hrishikesha protect me at the dawn of day; may Janârdana protect me at night-fall. May Shridhara protect me at mid-night, may the lotus-naveled deity preserve me during the small hours of the night. May the discus, club (Kaumadaki) and arrows of Vishnu kill my enemies and the Rákshasas. May the lotus and conch shell of Vishnu preserve me from enemies, may the celestial Garuda, and the divine bow and ornaments of Vishnu preserve my life, mind, and intellect. May Shesha and Sarva-rupa preserve me everywhere. May Narasinha preserve me in all angles of the heaven. He, who eyes a person with this Kavacham on his person, is sure to be fascinated, and such a person enjoys a kind of immunity from disease.

——:o:——

CHAPTER CCXXII.

DHANVANTARI said:—Now I shall enumerate to you the Gârudam, as disclosed by Sumitra to Kashyapa. This Gârudi Vidyâ tends to neutralise the effects of all kinds of poison. The five fundamental material principles of earth water, light (heat), air and ether are represented by the different letters of the alphabet as their symbols, which should be regarded as the presiding deities of the occult diagram to be meditated upon at the time of Dhyânam. The deities reside in these five fundamental material principles.

The letters Sa, Ka, and Tha are symbolical of the energy of Shiva (ether). The rite of Ṅyâsa should be duly performed, and the Chaturvaktra Mantram should be psychically located by the votary inside the palms of his hands, in the soles of his feet, as well as in the cavities of his heart and ears. By meditating in this fashion a votary may achieve all kinds of success. First imagine a yellow coloured quadrangle as symbolical of the Earth, of which Indra is the presiding deity. At the centre of this quadrangle should be contemplated the ring of Varuna, at the centre of which is the mystic, translucent lotus upon which the half moon sheds its cool, turquoise-blue beams. Around this should be imagined as transcribed the triangular Mandalam of fire, crossed by a Svastika mark (cross) and burning with the effulgence of primordial fire. Around this should be imagined the circle of Váyu, sable coloured like the inside of a cut bar of black antimony, and impressed with the mark of the occult Vindu. Encircling this ring of Vâyu should be imagined the Vyoma-Mandalam, dreadful in its infinite vastness, lying effulgent and motionless like the ocean of milk (Kshira), or like a sea of molten crystal. The celestial serpents Vásuki and Shankhapâla should be imagined as residing in the quadrangle of the earth; Karkata and Padma-Nâbha, in the ring of Varunâ; Kalika, in the Mandalam of fire; and Takshaka and Mahâvjaka, in the ring of air. The material principles of earth, water, etc., should be imagined by the votary as located in his fingers, starting with the thumb and ending with the small finger, both in the usual and inverse order of enumeration. Likewise, the Jayâ and Vijyayâ Mantras should be located in the bone-joints, the Shiva-Shadanga Mantram in the cavity of the mouth; and the Hrid Mantra in the arms and the tuft of hair on the crown of the head, and the Vyâpakam in the phalangesof fingers. The rite of Bhutanyâsa should be performed with the Shivânga Mantras preceded by "Om" and followed by

"Namas." This rule should be followed in respect of establishing and worshipping all forms of Mantra.

The first letters of the names of these celestial serpents are the Mantras respectively sacred to each of them, which being duly recited by a votary enables him to draw any of them to his side. The Mantras composed of the names of the five fundamental physical principles coupled with "Om" and "Namas" should be then recited, whereby the celestial Garuda would appear unto the votary in all his glory and prowess.

The votary shall again perform the rite of Karanyâsa with the help of the vowel letters, and the rite of Shâriranâysa thereafter. He shall contemplate his vital energy (Prâna) as an unflickering light steadily burning within his heart, and consuming the impurities of his organism, and the Vija Mantra as showering divine ambrosia wherewith his system is being saturated. Thus surcharging his system with the nectarine flow of the Vija Mantra, the votary shall contemplate his self as located in his brain; and the earth teeming with thousands of cities and abodes of men, and guarded by the Lokapâlas (protectors of worlds) and shining with the effulgence of molten gold as located in his lower extremities. The principle of water, clear and smooth, he shall contemplate as occupying the region between his heart and navel. shining with a blue light, and occupying a space, twice as much as that of the earth. The Ravi Mandalam, the seat of heat and light, should be imagined as a triangle occupying the thoracic cavity and resting on an imaginary line across the umbilicus as its base, and extending from the sphere of Bhubanas (worlds) to Brahma. The Vâyu Mandalam, in which is ensconced the image of Self, as permeating the universal space and coloured (deep blue) like broken, black antimony. Over the crown of his head the votary shall contemplate the Divya Mandalam shining with the effulgence of clear, cut crystal, and permeating the boundless expanse of ether, and enshrouding, and enlivening all with divine ambrosia.

First the rite of Bhutanyâsa should be performed, after that, the one in respect of the celestial serpents, by reciting the Vijas commencing with the letters "La" and coupled with the nasal sign of Vindu, to which the Vijas, sacred to Shiva, should be moreover appended. After this, the votary should meditate upon the Mandalam described before. The intelligent one should meditate upon the Mandalas respectively colored as aforesaid at the time of practising this incantation. The feet, pinions, and bills of Garuda should be contemplated as ornamented with rings of black snakes. This figure of Târksha (Garuda) should be invariably meditated upon in cases of poisoning with any animal or vegetable poison. The figures of malignant spirits, planets, Dâkinies, Yakshas, and Rakshas should the votary likewise imagine as located in his limbs, ornamented with black serpents, by an act of Nyâsa. Twofold is the rite of Nyâsa in this incantation; one is in respect of the fundamental material principles and the other is in respect of the serpents. Having thus contemplated the principles of soul etc., in due succession, the votary should commence practising the charm. First the three fundamental principles of Tritattvas should be contemplated, and after that the, principle of bliss should be meditated upon as located above them. The rite of Deha-nyâsa should be performed by the votary, both in the usual and inverse order, in his limbs, as well as in the imaginary figures of the deities meditated upon. The bulb, stem, etc., of the occult lotus, as well as the principles of virtue and wisdom should be worshipped by reciting the Vijas composed of the final letters of the different Vargas appended with the second vowel. The Mantra "Kshaum" should be imagined as located in the polens of the occult lotus. The groups of letters, which are called Aka, Cha, Ta, Tha, Pa, Ya and Sa Vargas, should be imagined as impressed on the eastern petals of this mystic flower, the vowels should be likewise imagined as impressed on the polens of the lotus, two in each, wherein the gods Isha etc., should be worshipped. The goddesses Vâmâ etc., should be considered as the energies of the Rudras worshipped in these polens, after which the votary shall invoke the three fundamental material principles (Tritattvas). The principle of ether he should psychically invoke and locate within his head. He should worship the principle of earth in the western petal of the lotus; the principle of water, in its northern leaf; the principle of fire (Tejas), in its southern leaf and the principle of air, in its eastern one. The Tanmâtras (essential material principles) and Mahâbhutas (gross matter) should be worshipped outside the occult diagram.

This procedure should be adapted in all rites of Nityâ and Naimittika worship. The votary should contemplate his Self as an expanse of beautifully tinted light, pervading all through the universe—its creator, preserver and destroyer—and laving the infinite expanse of ether with its own ambrosial energy. Likewise, he should meditate upon Bhairava in the company of the Siddhas and the celestial Garuda in all acts of incantation—the moon-crested Bhairava, who is possessed of ten arms and four faces and three eyes, burning with a kind of lurid effulgence, with his diabolical teeth exposed in a dreadful grimace and a weird light emanating from his flame-coloured eyes. For the destruction of snakes he should contemplate the image of Garuda, dreadful to look at, the tips of his mighty pinions touching the ends of the welkin, the regions of Patala located in his feet, the seven celestial regions lying ensconced in his bosom, the entire universe nestling round his neck, and all the Rudras, from the first to Isha, who is the last in the list of that class of deities, as located within his head, Garuda, who is but another manifestation of Shiva, is the lord of the universe, the greatest of all the great divinities.

His body is made of the energy of the Mantras (mystic formulas); and the votary shall contemplate him in all acts of incantation as effulgent like the fire of universal dissolution and bent on devouring the poisonous snakes. He, whom the votary may contemplate in his mind after performing the rite of Nyasa as above described, shall come under his control and influence. By performing this Nyâsa, a votary becomes himself a Garuda. Ghosts, demons, monsters, Pishâchas and the different kinds of fever such as, quotodian ague, etc., fly the presence of him who practises this incantation. Dhanvantari said this Gârudi Vidyâ which was first promulgated by Garuda himself to the holy Kashyapa; now hear me discourse on that which was disclosed by Maheshvara to the goddess Gauri.

——:o:——

CHAPTER CCXXIII.

BHAIRAVA said:—Now I shall expound the Tripurâ Vidyâ (Science of Tripurâ) which is known as the Nityaklinná Mantra, which, properly practised, imparts salvation and creature comforts to its votary. Om, Hrim, come O thou, goddess, Om obeisance to Kledeni, the same to the excitress of erotic passions. Am, Hrim, Hrim, obeisance to Nârâyana. Similarly, the deities Vegavati, Maha-pretâsaná, etc., should be worshipped. Om, Hram, Hrim, Kraim, Naim, Kraim, obeisance to Madadravá; Aim, Hrim, obeisance to Tripurâ. Om, Hrim, Krim, obeisance to Pashimavaktra. Om, Aim, Hrim, obeisance to Uttaravaktra; Aim, Hrim, obeisance to Dakshina Vaktra, to Purvavaktra, and to Urdhavaktra. Krim, obeisance to the noose of the deity, obeisance to the mace of the deity, Aim, obeisance to the skull which the god bears in his hand. The rite of Nyâsa should be performed by reciting the Mantra A'dyâm, Bhayâm, Aim, etc.

The deities such as Kámarupa, Asitánga, etc., should be worshipped in the East, the goddess Brahmâni and the deity Vishma-nirma should be worshipped in the South. The deities such as Ruru-Bhairava, Kumâri, Maheshvari and Chanda should be worshipped in the west, the deities such as Ulkâ, Krodha, and Vaishnavi should be worshipped in the north.

The Bhairava, Aghora should be invoked and worshipped in south-east corner of the Mandalam; Unmatta Bhairava in its north-west chamber, the goddesses Mahendri Kulântikâ, and Vilinâ in the south-west chamber The god Jalandhara with his accompanying energies of Bhisanâ and Chamundâ should be worshipped in the north-east chamber of the mystic diagram. In the umbilical region of the imaged goddess should be worshipped the god of death and Chandikâ, as well as the presiding deities of attachment, pleasure and love. The god of love with his five arrows should be likewise worshipped by reciting the Mantra running as Om, Hrim, Hrim, Hram, Shah, obeisance. Hum, obeisance to Gana, Akshas and Kshetrapâlas. Thus meditated upon and propitiated with libations of clarified butter cast in the fire in her honour, the goddess Tripurâ grants the fulfilment of all desires to her votery and bides under his control. The eternal Tripurâ, worshipped in the manner known as Jvâlâmukhi-Krama, dissipates all diseases.

Now hear me discourse on the process of worship known as Jvâlâmukhi-Krama. The goddess Jvâlâmukhi should be worshipped at the centre of the mystic lotus-diagram and her attendent goddesses such as Nityâ, Arunâ, Madanâturâ, Madâ, Mohâ, Prakriti, Kalanâ, Shree, Bhârati, Akarshini Mahendrâni, Brahmâni, Maheshi, Kaumâri, Baishnavi, Vârâhi, Mâhendri, Chamundâ, Aparâjitâ, Vijayâ, Ajitâ, Mohini, and Tvaritâ should be worshipped in the adjacent chambers within the diagram. The goddess Stambhini, Jrimbhani, and Kâlikâ should be worshipped outside the diagram. By worshipping the goddess in this manner, a votary is enabled to neutralise the effects of all kinds of poison.

——:o:——

CHAPTER CCXXIV.

Now I shall discourse on Chudâmani for the ascertainment of auspicious or inauspicious auguries. Having made obeisance to Gana, Soma, and the goddess, the sooth-sayer should obliquely put down three lines on the paper, in the shape of a stream of cow's urine. Then the different symbols of calculation such as the banner, camel, lion, dog, bull and the ass should be put down in the different chambers. The crow should be regarded as the eighth symbol in the diagram. Banner seen in the chamber of the banner presages thoughts about a kingdom or wealth, Dhumra (camel) seen in the chamber of the banner presages thought about metals and gain. Lion seen in the chamber of the banner presages acquisition of wealth and gain. Dog, seen in the chamber of the banner, presages thought about a female slave and the advent of happiness. Bull seen in the chamber of the banner presages thought about, and acquisition of, landed property. Ass seen in the chamber of the banner presages misery and sorrow. Elephant seen in the chamber of the banner presages victory and acquisition of place by the enquirer. Crow seen in the chamber of the banner presages loss of wealth, and thought about pain or misery.

Similarly, banner seen in the chamber of the camel, presages pain followed by pleasure. Camel seen in the chamber of the camel presages misery due to evil propensities of the enquirer. Lion seen in the chamber of the camel foretells an anxiety about, and acquisition of, wealth by the enquirer. Dog seen in the chamber of the camel predicts victory and wealth. Bull seen in the chamber of the camel predicts the acquisition of cattle and wives by the enquirer. Ass seen in the chamber of the camel presages disease and loss of wealth. Elephant seen in the chamber of the camel augurs the acquisition of wealth and kingdom by the enquirer. Crow seen in the chamber of the camel presages loss of wealth and kingdom. Banner seen in the chamber of the lion predicts the gain of wealth and kingdom; camel seen in the chamber of the lion presages the acquisition of a bride and wealth by the enquirer. Lion seen in the chamber of the lion predicts victory and arrival of friends. Dog seen in the chamber of the lion predicts the gain of a village by the enquirer and the fact that he is thinking about a woman. Bull seen in the chamber of the lion foretells the acquisition of a field, house and money by the enquirer. Ass seen in the chamber of the lion augurs the lordship of the enquirer over his own native village. Elephant seen in the chamber of the lion presages good health, joy and longevity to the enquirer. Crow seen in the chamber of the lion predicts the acquisition of a wife, food grain and wealth.

Banner seen in the chamber of the dog indicates the thought about a place and presages the advent of joy and pleasure. Camel seen in the chamber of the dog predicts quarrel and failure in business. Lion seen in the chamber of the dog predicts the success of an undertaking. Dog seen in the chamber of the dog presages loss of wealth. Bull seen in the chamber of the dog predicts the recovery of a patient from a disease. Ass seen in the chamber of the dog predicts quarrel and danger. Elephant seen in the chamber of the dog foretells the meeting of the enquirer with his wife and children. Crow seen in the chamber of the dog augurs disease and loss of bodily strength.

Banner seen in the chamber of the bull predicts the honouring of the enquirer by kings. Camel seen in the chamber of the bull predicts royal favour and pleasure to the enquirer. Lion seen in the chamber of the bull augurs happiness and prosperity to the enquirer. Dog seen in the chamber of the lion predicts beauty, strength and gain of creature-comforts to the enquirer. Bull seen in the chamber of the bull augurs fame, contentment, pleasure. Ass seen in the chamber of the bull predicts great joy and gain for the enquirer. Elephant seen in the chamber of the bull augurs the acquisition of wives and elephants. Crow seen in the chamber of the bull presages the gain of place and honour by the enquirer.

Banner seen in the chamber of the ass augurs sorrow and disease. Camel seen in the chamber of the ass presages terror from thieves and robbers in respect of the enquirer. Lion seen in the chamber of the ass presages honour, prosperity and victory to the enquirer. Dog seen in the chamber of the ass presages loss of wealth and anguish. Bull seen in the chamber of the ass presages happiness and meeting with dear ones. Ass seen in the chamber of the ass predicts pain and disease. Elephant seen in the chamber of the ass predicts joy and birth of sons. Crow seen in the chamber of the ass augurs quarrel and disease.

Banner seen in the chamber of the elephant foretells joy and birth of sons. Camel seen in the chamber of the elephant predicts acquisition of wealth and food grain by the enquirer. Lion seen in the chamber of the elephant augurs success and victory. Dog seen in the chamber of the elephant predicts happiness, prosperity and recovery from disease. Bull seen in the chamber of the elephant presages royal favour and wealth. Ass seen in the chamber of the elephant presages the advent of misery to be followed by days of prosperity. Elephant seen in the chamber of the elephant predicts joy and acquisition of fields and food grain by the enquirer. Crow seen in the chamber of the elephant presages the acquisition of wealth and food grain by the enquirer.

Banner seen in the chamber of the crow augurs the failure of an undertaking. Camel seen in the chamber of the crow presages misery from gratification of wicked inclinations. Lion seen in the chamber of the crow predicts quarrel and mental unrest. Dog seen in the chamber of the crow augurs terror and family dissensions. Bull seen in the chamber of the crow presages terror and loss of place or home. Ass seen in the chamber of the crow presages loss of wealth and defeat. Elephant seen in the chamber of the crow augurs the advent of fortune and fame. Crow seen in the chamber of the crow predicts a sojourn to a foreign country.

—:o:—

CHAPTER CCXXV.

BHAIRAVA said :—Now hear me, O goddess, discourse on the science of the conquest of the vital air, a knowledge whereof enables a person to predict victory or defeat. The four vital airs, which are respectively called Agni, water. Shakra, etc., respectively flow through either of the nostrils. The breath, which courses in an upward direction through the nostril, is called Agni (fire); that, which courses in a downward direction through the nostril, is called Varuna. The breath, that courses in a middling (neither upward nor downward) direction, is called Mahendra. In the light fortnight the breath-wind courses through the left nostril, while during the dark fortnight it courses through the right. For the period of three days, the breath-wind follows the same course after taking a definite direction, changing its course completely on the day of Pratipad (first day of a light or dark fortnight). If the breath-wind rises following the course of the sun, and flows out along the passage of the moon, all good qualities of the breather are supposed to increase; contrary is the result if the breath-wind follows a contrary direction. O thou beautiful-faced one, sixteen are the changing periods of the direction of the breath-wind in the course of an entire day and night. Impairment of health is brought about when this changing period falls at the close of each two hours and a quarter. Pertaking of a meal, and sexual intercourse are good when the breath-wind flows through the right nostril, and victory in battle attends the man, who enters into it, while his breath-wind flows out through the right nostril. A man may safely start on a journey, or undertake any other auspicious act when the breath-wind flows out through his left nostril. No evil strikes a man when his breath-wind flows out in directions called Mâhendra and Varuna. Men breathe through their right nostrils during a season of drought, while breath flows out of their left nostrils during the rains.

—:o:—

CHAPTER CCXXVI.

DHANVANTARI said:—Now I shall expound the Ayurveda which deals with the diseases of horses, and the means of keeping them in sound health. Horses that are crow-lipped, black tongued, bear-faced, as well as those that are hot-palated, or fierce-toothed, or are possessed of a greater or smaller number of teeth than what they naturally possess, or born with only one testicle, or afflicted with scrotal tumours, or possessed of deformed backs or bifurcated hoofs or teats, or footed like cats, or striped like tigers, or coloured like patches of cutaneous affections, or abscesses, as well as those which are extremely diminutive in size, or are eyed like cats or monkeys, should be regarded as inauspicious and unfit for use. The best or first-class horses measure upward of four cubits in length, the second or middling class of horses measure half a cubit less than first class horses in length. The last class of horses measure three cubits and a half in length. Horses, that are long-limbed, short-eared, mouse-coloured and long-lived, are the best. The rite of protection should be done unto horses by worshipping the god, Revanta, and by feeding Brâhmanas. For prophylactic purposes, Saralam, Nimva-leaves, bdellium, mustard seeds, sesame, Vacha, asafætida, saturated with clarified butter, should be tied round the neck of a horse.

Ulcers, which horses are found to be afflicted with, may be divided into two classes as Agantuja (traumatic, or of extraneous origin) and Shâriraja (idiopathic). Ulcers marked by a late suppuration should be regarded as of a Vâtaja origin; suppuration speedily sets in ulcers, due to the action of the deranged Kapham, while those, due to the deranged Pittam, are marked by a burning sensation in their inside. Thick discharges from ulcers should be attributed to the action of the deranged Kaphah; while those, which are of a Sânnipâtika origin, exhibit symptoms peculiar to each of the three aggravated Doshas. A plaster composed of Danti roots, the two kinds of Haridrâ, Chitrakam, Vishvabhesajam, Rasonam, and rock salt pasted together with whey or Kânjikam (a kind of fermented rice or barley gruel) or pastes of sesame, fried barley grain etc, mixed with powdered rock salt and milk curd, or pastes of Nimva-leaves, applied to ulcers in horses, bring about their purification and healing. A medicinal oil cooked in combination with Karabira, Kadali, Arka, Snuhi, Kutaja, Chitraka and Bhallâtaka brings about the healing of sinuses in horses. As an alternative, such a sinus should be washed with a medicinal Ghritam cooked in combination with a paste of the five astringent barks. A compound consisting of the two kinds of Haridrâ, Vidanga, the five kinds of salt, Patolam and Nimva-leaves, Vacha, Chitrakam, Pippali, and Shringavera pounded together and administered through the medinm of water brings about the expulsion of worms from the intestines of horses, and remove their deranged Kapham and somnolence. A decoction of Nimva-leaves, Patolam, Triphalâ, and Khadira should be successively given for three days to a horse, after bleeding it, for the cure of any cutaneous affection. Application of mustard oil proves beneficial in cutaneous affections of horses attended with ulcers. A decoction of garlic should be given to a horse for the alleviation of diseases of the deranged Vâyu. In disorders of digestion, the expressed juice of Mâtulunga, or of Mânsi should be administered as errhines. One Palam weight of this compound should be administered on the first day, and its dose should be daily increased by a Palam weight until it reaches eighteen Palas. The smallest dose of this medicine is eight Palam, and its middling dose is fourteen Palas weight. Errhines should not be given to horses in summer or autumn. In diseases of the deranged and aggravated Vâyu, the medicine should be administered through the medium of oil, or in combination with sugar, clarified butter or water. It should be given through the vehicle of mustard oil saturated with Vyosha (Trikatu) powders in diseases of the deranged Kapham, and through a solution, or decoction of Triphalâ in those of the deranged Pittam. A horse, that lives on milk, Sâli and Shashtika grain, is not to be condemned, as well as the one, that is of the colour of a ripe Jamboline fruit, is not to be rejected. Bdellium should be given to a horse, after it has been in any way hurt or injured, and milk should be administered to it for the purpose of speedily allaying the agitation. In diseases due to the action of the deranged and aggravated Vâyu, milk and boiled rice should be given to a horse as food, while in those of Pittaja (bilious) origin, its diet should consist of a Karsha weight of meat soup mixed with honey, Mudga soup and clarified butter. In diseases of the deranged Kapham, Mudga or-Kulattha-soup mixed with butter or pungent drugs, should be given to a horse, while in cases of deafness, nervous affections, or in diseases of Sânnipâtika origin, bdellium should be freeely given to it. In all diseases a Palam weight of Durvâ should be given to a horse on the first day, and the dose should be increased by a Karsha measure, each day, till five Palam is reached. Eighty Palam is the highest dose. Sixty Palam is the middling and forty Palam is the lowest dose. In ulcers, cutaneous affections, and lameness, the food of a horse should be made saturated with a decoction of Triphalâ) whereas in impaired digestion, and œdema (dropsical swelling) it should be given saturated with cow's urine In diseases due to the actions of the deranged Vâyu and Pittam, as well as in ulcer-cases, the food of a horse should be given mixed with Gokshura and clarified butter, while a goodly quantity of Mâsha pulse should be given to it whenever a general plumpness of its limbs is desired. Five Palam weight of Guduchi should be given to a horse, each morning, in summer and autumn, through the vehicle of rice-paste treated with clarified butter. This food imparts a greater strength and vigour to a horse and acts as a general prophylaxis against disease. Guduchi may be likewise given to a horse with benefit through the medium of milk. For similar purposes, one, three or four Palam weights of powdered Shatâvari and Ashvagandhâ may be given to a horse with Guduchi Paste. A mortal epidemic is presaged when all the horses in a stud are found to assume one colour. The visitation may be warded off by the performance of proper prophylactic rites, and *Homas*, as well as by feeding the pious and learned Bráhmanas. The medicine known as Haritaki-Kalpa may be given with benefit to horses under these circumstances. This medicine (Haritaki-Kalpa) consists in giving five Haritakis, each day, to a horse, pasted together with rock-salt and cow's urine. The dose of the medicine should be increased by five Haritakis, each successive day, until it goes up to a hundred Haritakis. The full dose (of this medicine) is a hundred; and the middling, eighty, the smallest dose being sixty Haritakis.

Now I shall expound that branch of the A'yurvedá, which deals with the medical treatment of the diseases of elephants. Quardruple of a horse's dose is the dose of a medicine for an elephant. Medicines enumerated in connection with diseases of horses may be employed with advantage in those that are found to afflict elephants. The prophylactic, or curative religious rites, in respect of the alleviation of diseases of elephants, consist in making gifts of jewel-decked Kapilâ kine to Brâhmanas, after worshipping the celestials and Brâhmanas. A physician, while observing a fast, shall tie round the tusks of an elephant a consecrated garland of white mustard seeds. The sun-god, Shiva and the goddesses Durgá and Shree, duly worshipped, protect elephants from attacks of diseases. Offerings should be made to the malignant spirits at the close of the worship, and the body of the elephant should be rubbed with ashes and then washed with four pitcher-fuls of water. Food consecrated by reciting the proper Mantras shall be given to an elephant, and the sacred rite of prophylaxis against the influences of malignant spirits serves to grant it an immunity from injury. Decoctions of parchifying drugs, as well as those of Triphalá, Panchakola, Dashamulam, Vidanga, Shatâvari, Guduchi, Nimva, Vâsaka, and Kinshuka, should be given for the cure of diseases of elephants. Thus I have briefly expounded the nature of medical treatment to be employed for the cure of diseases of elephants.

CHAPTER CCXXVII.

SUTA said :—Dhanvantari thus narrated the science of A'yurveda to Sushruta. Now I shall briefly enumerate the different names of the A'yurvedic drugs. Sthirâ, Vidârigandhâ, and Anshumati are the names of Shálaparni (Desmodium Gangeticum). Lángali, Kalasi, and Krashtupuchchha are the names of Guhá (Mucuna Pruriens). Várshábhu is called Punarnavá (Spreading hogneed, Boerhaaria Diffusa). Káravellah is another name of Katillaka (Hairy Mordica-Momardica Charantea). Eranda (castor-oil plant. Riconus Comamnis) Uruvaka, Amanda and Vardhamánaka are synonymous. Nágavalá is called Jhasá (Sida Spinosa). Shivadanstrâ is called Gokshura (Tygophylleæ Tribulus terestris). Shátavari, Vará, Bhiru, Pivari, Vari and Indivari (Asparagus Racemosus) are synonymous. Vyâghri, Vrihati, Krishnâ, Hansapadi, Madhushravâ, Dhámani, Kshudrâ, Simhi and Nidigdhikâ are the names of Kantakâri (Solanum Janthocarpum). Vrischikâli, Amritâ, Kâli, Vishaghni, Sarpadanshtrikâ, Markati, Atmaguptà, and Arsheyi are the names of Kapikachchhuka (Mucuna Pruriens). Kshudra-Sahâ is Mudgaparni (Phaseolus Trilobus), while Mâshaparni is called Mahá-sahá (Teramuns Labialis, Grangea Mádraspatna). Nyagrodha is Vata (Banyan tree); Kapila is the name of Ashvattha (Ficus Religioasa). Parkati Gardhavánda, and Kapitana are the names of Plaksha (Thaspesia Pahulnea). Pârtha, Kukubha, and Dhanvi are the names of Arjuna (Farminalia Arjuna). Prarohi, and Pushtikari are the names of Nandi-Vriksha (a species of figtree). Vanjula is Vetasa (calamus rotong), while Bhallátaka is called Arushkara (Semecarpus Anacardium). Lodhra is called Sáravaka, Dhrishta, or Tirita (Symplocas Racemosa). Vâla-phalâ, and Vrihatphalâ are the names of Mahá-Jamvu (Eugenia Jambolana). Nádiyi and Tritiyá are the names of Jala-Yamvu (wild Jamboline), Kaná, Krishná, Upakulyâ, Shaundi and Mágadhi are the names of Pippali (Piper Longum), while its roots are called Granthikam (Piper officinarum). Ushanam is Maricham (Piper Nigrum), while Vishvam and Mahaushadham are the names of Shunthi (dry gingiber). Vyosham is the name of Trikatu (Shunti, Pippali and Maricham) which is also called Tryushanam. Lángali, Halini and Shreyasi are the names of Gajapippali (Pothes officinalis), Trâyamâna is called Tráyanti (Thalictrum Faliolosum), and Utsá is Vahuvahá. Vanhi, Shiki, and terms signifying fire, are the names of Chitrakam (Plumbgo Zeylanica). Shadgránthà, Ugrá, Shvetá and Heimavatai are the names of Vachá (Sweet Flag). Vrikshaka, Shukra, Vatsaka and Girimallikà are the names of Kutaja (Wrightia Anti-dysenterica), and Arishtam, Indrayava and Kalinga are the names of Kutaja-seeds. Kunti, Hareunká, and terms denoting cloud,. are the names of Mustakah (Mariscus cyprus). Elá (cardemon) is called Vahulâ, the smaller variety is called Truti. Padmâ, Bhárgi, and Kanji are called Brahmana-Yashtiká (clerodendron-Siphonanthus). Tejini, Tikta-balkalá and Madhurasá are the names of Murvâ (Sansevieria Zeylanica). Mahánimva, Vrikshanimva, and Dipyakas are the names of Jamáni (Ptychotis) Vidanga (seeds of Embelia Ribus) and Hingu are called Amatham. Ajáji is the name of Jirákan (cumin seeds), Káravi is Upakanchiká (Nigella Sativa or Indica)., Katuka and Tikta are the names of Katu-rohini (Black Hellibore.) Tagaram, Natam, Chakram, Chocham, and Tvacham are the names of Varângakam, (Cinnamon Bark.) Hriveram (Pavonia Odorata) is synonymous with Udichyam, and Válakam, and terms signifying water, are also used to denote this plant. Hemâva, and terms denoting elephant, are the names of Nâgakeshara (Mesua-ferrea). Asrik, Kâshmira, and Bahlikam are the names of Kumkum (saffron). Compounds signifying Iron denote Ayuguru. Yavishtà, Prâchinâ, Kalikâ, Sushabi, Toshanâshâ and Rambhâ are the names of Kadali (Plantain). Puram,

Kutannat, Mahishâksha and Pâlankash are the names of Kutannat. Kashmari and Shriparni are the names of Katphalâ (Myrica Sapida). Patri, Sarabhi, Shravá and Gajabhakshyâ are the names of Shallaki (Bos Wellia Serrata). Dhâtri is the name of Amalakam (Emblic Myrobalans) Aksha is the name of Vibhitaka (Terminalia Belirica). Pathyâ, Abhayâ and Putanâ are the names of Haritaki (Indian Myrobalans).

The group of drugs, known as Triphalâ or Phalatrikam, consists of Haritaki, Bibhitaka and Amlakam (with their stones removed. Udakiri, and Dirgha-Vrinta, are the names of Karanja (Karanji of the Râja-Nighantam); and Yashti, Yashtàhvayam, and Madhu-Yashti are synonymous with Madhukam (Liquorice-root, Glycyrrhiza glabra). Tâmraparni, Samangâ and Kunjarâ are the names of Dhâtaki (Woodfordia Floribondia). Sitam, Malayajam, Sheetam and Goshirsham, are the terms which signify white sandal wood (Santalam-albam), while the red species is called Rakta Chandanam. Virâ, Vayasyâ, and Arkapushpikâ are the names of Kâkoli, while Shringi is known by the names Karkatâ-Shringi and Mahâghosâ (Rhus Succedanea). Tugâkshiri, Shubhà and Vanshi are the names of Vanshalochanâ (Manna of the Bamboo), and Grapes are called by the epithets of Drâkshâ, Gostanikâ and Mridvikâ (Vitis Vinifera). Lâmajjka are called by the names of Ushirâm and Mrinâlam (Juncus Odoratus), and Sâram, Gopi, and Gopàvalli are the names of Bhadrâ (Hemidesmus Indicus). Danti and Katankeri are the names of Dâru-Haridrâ (Cascinium Fenestratum), and Rajani, Putaká, and terms signifying "Night," are the synonymes of Haridrá (turmeric). Vira-Vriksha is known yb the epithets of Virataru and Varataru, while Rasá, Amritá, Nilavalli and Chchhinna-ruhá are the epithets of Vrikshádani (Tinaspora Cordifolia). Kapota is another name of Suryabhaktá (Cleome Viscosa, Polanisia Icosundra), while Katapam is called Kanthabhallá or Kantha-Shálá, and Kampika, Vashira and Vasukota are all synonymous. Arishta, Ashva-shmit and Katta-bhedaka are the names of Pâshána-bheda (Coleus amboinicus). Ghantaka is known by the epithets of Shushaka, Vacha and Shuchaka. Sagandha, Chchhatrâdi and Chchhatrá are the names of Kusumbha (Safflower Carthamul tenctarius), and Pitashála is known by the epithets of Sarasa and Veejaka (Indian Kino tree, Pentaptera tomentosa). Vajravriksha, Mahávriksha, Sudhá, Gudâ, and Sruk are the names of Snuhi (Uphorbia Neraifolia). Shâla (Shoria Robusta) tree is known by the epithet of Yakshavriksha, while Anisha is called by the name of Tinisha (Indian Jârula tree—Dalbergia Oujeineisis). Upasthá, and Sarasâ are the other names of Tulasi (Holy basil). The second variety of Tulasi is called Sitâ (Ocimum album). Another species of Tulasi is called Arjunaka, Parni, Saugandhaparnikâ and Kutheruká (Assimum Bajilicum). Nilá, Nirgundi, Sugandhikâ, Sugandhaparini, Vâsanti and Kulajá are the names of Sindhuvára (Vitex trifolium). Peeta-Kâstham and Katakâkshya are the names of Kaliyakam (Yellow Sandalwood); Khadira is called Gâyatri (Acacia Catechu), while the white variety is called Kandara (Kadara according to others). Indivaram, Kuvalayam, Saugandhikam, Shatadalam, Kamalam and Avjam are the synonymes of Padma (Nelumbium speciosum), while the blue variety is called Nilotpalam (Nymphæa Stellata). Vâjikarna and Ashvakarna are the names of Sarja (Indian Saltree—Shorla Robusta), while its another variety is known by the epithets of Urja and Ajakarna (Beng:—Jhânji Shál). Shelu and Vahuvâra are the synonymes of Shleshmâtaka (Cordia myxa, narrow leaved Sepistun). Kulânganâ, and Mrigechchhá are the synonymes of Alambusha. Sunandaka, Kukud, Bhadram and Chatraki are the names of Chhatrá (Andropogon citratus). Kavari, Kumbhaka, Karila, Kâmamana, and Dhanakrit are the synonymes of Krishnarjaka. Prâchi, Valâ, Nadi-Krânta and Vàyasi are the names of Kâka-janghâ

(Leea hirta), while Dravanti is known by the epithets of Akhukarnikâ and Mushika-karnâ (croton Polyandrum). Keshamushti and Vishamushti are the names of Drâvanam (Melia Azendarach). Kilihi is called Katukâ black Hellebore) while Amla-vetasa is called Dantaka (country Sorrel-Acido Zeyfolia). Ashvatthá and (Bhu)-A'malaki are the names of Vahupatra (Phyllanthus niruri?). Arashukam, Patrashukam and Kshiri are the names of Râjâdanam (Mimonsops Hexenbra). Dàdimvam is called Mahàpàtram (pomegranate) which is also called Karakam. Vidali, Shashpá Kàlindi Masuri, Kantakàkshyà, Mahà-Shyamà, Vrikshapadi, Vidyà, Kunti, Nikumbhà, Tribhangi, and Triputí are the names of Trivrit (Ipomea tarpethum.) Saptalà is called Sankhini, Sukumàri, Tiktàkshi and Yavatiktà (Kalmegh) and is also used to signify Charma, or Charmaksha (Origaum Vulgaris). Gavàkshi, Amrità, Shvetà, and Girikarni are the names of Gavàdani (Colocynth-Citrullus Colocynthus), while Raktanga, Gunda, and Rochanaka are the synonymes of Kampillaka (Kamila-Melloctus phillipinesis). The yellow species is called Hemakshiri (Gamboge thistle, while the black variety is called Kàladugdhikà. Gàngeruki is another name of Nàgavalá (Sida Spinosa), while Vishali is a synonym of Indra-vàruni (colocynth.) Rasànjanam (extract of Indian Barbary) is known by the epithets of Arjanam and Târksha-Shailam, while the extract of Shálmali (Bombax Malabaricum) is called Mocha-rasa. Pratyakpushpi is another name of Khara, while Mayurka is a synonyme of Apámarga (Achyranthis Aspera). Vàsaka (Adhatoda Vasaca) is also called by the epithets of Simhásya, Vrisha, and Atarushakam. Jivaka, Jivâ Shâkha and Karchura are the names of Shati (Curcoma Gedoaria). Somavriksha (Somavalka?), Agnigandha, and Sugandhika are synonymous with Kat-phalam (Myrica Sapida). Shatapushpà (Dillseed-Aurthum graveyleus) is also known by the epithets of Shatanga, Misi and and Madhurikà. Pushkaram and Pushkarahvayam are but the different names of Pushkaramulam (root of Alpotaxis auriculata). Yàsa, Dhanvayasa and Dushparshà are the synonymes of Duralabhà (Alhagimaurorun Fogonia Arabica) Vàguji and Somavalli are the names of SomarÂji (Serratula Anthelmintica). Mârkara and Kesharaja are the synonymes of Bhringarâja (Wedelia Calendulacea). Edagaja is another name of Chakramarda (cassiatora). Sarangi, Tagara, Vâyasi Vela, Tanduliya and Ghanastana are the names of Mahâkâla. Tiktatumbi and Tiktâlâvu are synonymous with Ikshâku (Bottle gourd, wild variety of Langenaria Vulgaris.) Koshàtaki and Jàminy are but the different names of Dhâmârgava (Laffu Aegyptiaca), Vidyut, which is another species of Dhàmàrgava is also called Kritabhedanam, Jimutaka, Khuddaka, and Devatâdaka. Gridhrâdanâ is another name of Gidhranakhi, which is also called Kâkâdani and Hingu (caparis Sepiaria). Ashvàri and Ashvamâraka are but the different names of Karavira (sweet scented Oleander-Nerrium odorum). Tarasi and Kushaja are the names of Kapithhapatri (Beng Elvaluk). Sindhu, Saindhava, Sindhuttha and Manimuntha are the synonymes of Rocksalt. Ushara, Yavagra and Yavakshâra are the terms which denote a kind of impure carbonate of potash (lit. ashes of burnt barley straw); Sarjikà and Sarjkàkshàra are the names of barilla. Shikhi-kanthâbham, Chitrakam, Tuttham etc., are the terms which denote nitrate of Copper. Kàshisham, Pushpakâshisham and Nétrabhesajam (lit eye-cure) are the terms which signify green Sulphate of iron. Kâshisha and Dhatu-Kàshisha are also the different names of the foregoing substence. Tàpyam and Tàpyutha-sambhabam are synonymous with Makshika (iron pyrites). Naipáli, Kulati and Shilà are the different names of Manah-shilà (red sulphate of arsaniç), while the terms Alam and Manahstalam signify Haritâlam (tri-sulphide of arsenic). Gandha pâshana is but another name of Gandhaka (sulphar) while the term Rasa is used to signify Pàrada (Mercury—lit:—that which bears a person beyond death and disease).

Audumvaram, Shulvam, and Mlechcha-mukham are the different names of Tâmram (copper), and the terms Adrisâram (lit: essence of rock) Ayas, and Tikshnam are used to denote iron (and steel). Kâkshi, Panka-parpati, and Mrittikâksharam are the names of Saurâshtra Mrittikâ. Mâkshikam, Kshaudram and Pushparasam are the synonymes of Madhu (honey). Fermented barley-boilings are called Sauvirakam and Kànjikam. Sità, Sitopalâ, Matsandi are synonymes of Sharkar (sugar). A compound of Cinnamon, Cardemon, and leaves of Lourus Cassia, taken in equal parts, is technically known as Trijâtakam or Trisugandhi. This compound, with one part of Nâga-Kesharam added to it, constitutes what is technically known as Chàturjâtam. A compound consisting of equal parts of Piphali, Pippalimulam, Chavya, Chitrakamulam and Nagar, and combindly weighing a Kolakam (Onetolla) is called Panchakolam. Bhutrilânga, Mahâshâli, and Nivàra are the different species Shâlikâ. Priyangu is another name of Kangukâ (Panicum stalicum), and Kordusha is called Kodra (Paspalum Scrobiculatum). Kalâpa, Lângaka and Putâ are the names of Triputa (Lathyrus Sativus). Satina, Vartula and Vena are the names of Satina (Pisum Sativium). A Suvarmam or Kavalagraham is equal to one Karsha in weight. A Shuktim is equal to a half Palam or eight Máshakas in weight. A Vilvam, or Mushti is equal to a Palam weight. Two Palas make one Prasriti. Four Palas make one Anjali or Kudavam. Eight Palas make one Palam. Four Kudavas make one Prastha; four Prasthas make one Adakam or Kânsapatrah Four Adakas make one Drona. A hundred Palas make one Tula weight. Twenty Palas make one Bhâra. The erudite ones have laid down these measures in respect of dry weight, while in respect of fluid weight these measures should be taken as double.

Valam is another name of Turashkakam, Dâru is another name of Devadáru (Pinus Deodara). Granthi is another name of Sthauneyakam. Vâsakam is also called Bhumikam-trinam. Kushtham is also called Amayam, and Nala-danshanam is but another name of Mánshi. Shukti is also called Shuktinakha and Shankha ; Byaghri is also called Vyaghra-nakha. Puram, Pâlankasham and Mahishákshya are but the different names of Guggalu (bdellium). Rasa and Gandharasa are the different names of Volam (Myrrh), while Sarja is called Sarjarasa (resin). Kundarakam is also called Kundam (Olibanum), and Shunistakam is also called Davam (Gomeopal Sandazack). Priyangu is also known by the epithets of Phalini, Shyámá and Gaurikánti. Artagala is also known by the epithets of Artá, Bhisanâ and Vahukantakâ. Sahachara and Vána are the synonymes of Saireyakah, (Balaria Crastata). Naktamála, Putika, and Chira-Vilvaka are the names of Karanja (Pongamia Glabra). Shobánjana, Jválâ and Mánsa are the different epithets of Shigru (Horse radish tree—Moringaptery Gooperma). Jayá, Jayanti Sharani, Nirgundi are the names of Sindhuvara. Morathá is another name of Pippali-parni, while Tundi is also called Tundikeriká. Gálava, Vodha, Ghota and Ghoti are the different names of Madana tree (Randia Denmetorum). Sampáka is known by the names of Chaturangula and Vyádhighâtaka (Kamila). Know that Aragvadham is also called Rajavriksha and Raivata (Cassia Fistula), Vashtaka is Atitiktâ, Kantaki is also called Vikankata (Flacourtia romontchi). Nimva is also called Arishta (Melio Azadirachta). Vayasthá, Vishvâ, Chchhinná, Chchhinna-ruhá, Vatsádani and Amritâ are the names of Guduchi (Tinaspora Cordifolia). Kiráta-tikta, and Bhunimva are synonymous with Kándatiktaka (plant Agathotes Chirayta.) These are the names, of vegetable drugs that are obtained in the forest. Now I shall deal with Grammar, O Shaunaka, as formerly narrated by Kumára.

CHAPTER CCXXVIII.

KUMARA said:—O Kátyáyana, I shall briefly expound the rules of Grammar which will enable infants to easily comprehend that subject and to understand the formation of words and their derivatives. Terms are either Sup (substantive) or Ting (verb). A Sup has seven cases. The forms of singular dual and plural inflexions of the subjective case are respectively called Su, Au, Jas. The subjective case-endings are added to the subject of a sentence, to the object in the passive voice, and are used in the case of address, in Prátipadikam, and in cases where the subjective sense is implied even in the absence of any verb (Lingártha). A term, that expresses a complete sense even in the absence of a verb or any case-inflexion, is called a Prátipadikam. "Am," "Au," and "Shas" are respectively the singular, dual and plural inflexion-forms of the objective case (Dvitiyá). That which is done by the subject of a sentence is called its object (Karma). Dvitiyâ case-endings are used in the objective case, and are added to terms in association with the terms "Antará" and "Antaréna." "Tá," "Bhyâm," and "Bhis" are respectively the singular, dual and plural inflexion-forms of the Tritiyá (accusative case). Tritiyá inflexions are used in Karanam (accusative.) The instrument or agency through which a subject performs an act is called its Karanam (*lit.* instrument), and he who performs an act is called its Kartá (doer). "Em," "Bhyam," and "Bhyas" are respectively the singular dual and plural inflexional forms of Sampradánam (Dative case.) Dative case-endings are added to persons to which something is intended to be given, or to which something is owed, or to whom something appears likeable or delectable. "Nangsi," "Bhyam" and "Bhyas" are respectively the singular, dual and plural inflexion-forms of Apádânam

(Ablative câse). Ablative case-endings are added to a term from which anything is meant to be fallen or disloged, or from which any fear is apprehended. "Nas," "Us," and "Am" are respectively the singular, dual, and plural inflexion forms of the Shasthi (possessive case). Shasthi implies possession, ownership relationship, or prominence of one among many. "Unga," "Usa," and "Sup" are respectively the singular, dual, and plural inflexion-forms of the Adhikaranam (locative case). Adhikaranam implies the location of a thing in another substance, and its inflexions are added to terms signifying that something is contained in them, or denoting agents under the protection of some body. Ablative case-endings are added to terms which signify objects that are either coveted or disliked, as well as to those used in combination with the prefixes Pari, Apa, and A'm, or in connection with the terms Itara (other) and those which denote the names of the quarters of the heaven. The objective case endings are added to terms used in combination with "Ena," as well as to the objects of a verb. Terms which are used in connection with the terms Saha (with), Hina (without) or are coupled with the prefixes "Anu," "Pari," "Prati" always have the objective case-endings. Likewise adverbs and terms denoting road are always used with the objective inflexions. Terms implying attempt at going or efforts of locomotion may either have the objective or dative case-endings. The object of the verb "Mana," implying an act of light or disrespectful comparison, gets the dative inflexion, if it denotes an inanimate object; denoting an animate object, or a sentient creature, it retains its true objective inflexion. Terms used in combination with Namas (obeisance), "Svasti" (blessing to), "Svadhâ, Svâhâ "Vashat" (obeisance) and Alam (capable) get the dative case endings. Used to denote a sense like "for that reason," or "for that purpose" they are likewise used in the dative case. Accusative case is used in combination with the term Saha (denoting accompaniment), as well as in respect of objects denoting the loss or defect of any bodily organ. Terms denoting the progress or course of time as well as the happening or contingency of an event are used in the locative case. Possessive case endings may be as well used in respect of the foregoing terms. Both possessive and locative case-endings may be added to terms coupled with ;" Svâmi," Adhipali" " Ishvara" (lords or master), " Dayadá " (heirs), and " Sutakas "). Either the locative or possessive case may be used where the predominence of one object amongst many (Nirdhâra), is desired. Possessive case endings are added to terms used with " Hetu" (for that reason). Objects of the root Smri (to remember) always get the possessive inflexion. Similarly, subjects of verbs formed by Krit, as well as substantives used in connection with verbs denoting the import of killing or envying, get the possessive inflexion. Subjects or objects do not get the possessive inflexion in connection with Nishthâ suffixes (such as Ta. etc.),

There are two kinds of Prátipadikam, such as the náma (substantive) and Dhátu (root). A Dhátu or root may be declined in ten tenses or Dasha Lakáras. " Tip, Tas" "Anti" are the inflexions of third person singular, third person dual, and third person plural, in the present tense (Lat). Sip, Thas, Tha are respectively the forms of inflexion of the second person singular, dual and plural in the present tense ; and " Mi" " Vas" and " Mas" are respectively the forms of inflexion of the first person singular, dual and plural in the present tense. These forms are used only in the Parasmai-Padi form. In the Atmanepadi form they are respectively. Te, Ate, Anté ; Sé, Athe, Dhvé ; and A, Vahe, and Mahé. "I" and its plural denote first person, " You" and its plural indicate second person, names other than these are third person. Bhu (to be) etc., are called Dhatus. Lat means the present tense. A verb having the form of present tense signifies the import of a past tense if used in combination with

"Sma." Lang is past perfect tense. The tense Ling is used in conferring blessings or making benediction. In cases of direction, permission, advice, prayer, invitation, request, benediction and asking of well being, Lot is the tense in which a verb is generally used. Lit signifies the past tense, and is used to denote events which have happened in the absence of the speaker (lit, not under the eyes of the speaker, Paroksha). Loong is the name of the tense which is used to denote an event in the past which did not occur at the time of speaking. Lrit indicates simple future. Loot is used to denote a future event which will take place in the presence of the speaker. In cases in which the occurrence of an event or the performance of an act is being completed, the tense Lring is used. Sometimes the past tense (Lit) is used in the place of Lot and *vice versâ*. The Krit affixes may be added to a root in either of the three forms or voices, such as the active, passive and neuter. Trin, Tabya Ghang, Aniya, Shatri, etc., are the affixes which are usually affixed to the roots.

KUMAR said :—Now I shall enumerate the illustrations of Sandhis (unions of words) etc., as are found to occur in the Samhitâs. Vipra and Agram make Viprâgram. "Sa" and A'gatâ make Sâgatâ. "Vi" combined with "Idam" makes Veedam, "Su" and "Uttamam" Süttamam. Pitri and Rishabha make Pitrirshabha, Lângala and I'shâ make Lângaleeshâ, Mana and I'shayâ make "Manishaya" "Gangâ" and "Udakam" make "Gangodakam." To and Likara make Tavalkâra. Rina and Rinam make Rinarnam, Pri and Arnam make Prarnam, Sheeta and Arta make Sheetârta. Tau and likâra make Tavâlkâra. Sâ and Indri make Sanidri, Sa and Okâra make Saukâra. Iti and Api make Atyapi. Vadhu and A'sanam make Vadhvâsanam. Pitri and Artha make Pitrartha, Li and Anabandha make Lanubandha. Nayé and Jayet make Naye Jayet. Lu and Anam make Lavanam. Gau and Ava make Gâva. Te united with Ishvarâ ma Ta

Ishvarâ. Athah and Atra make Atho Atro. Shat united with Iman make Shat Iman. Amih and Ashvah make Ami Ashva. Shat and Ashya make Shadasya, Tat and Navâk make Tannavâk. Tat and Charet make Tachcharet. Tat and Lunâti make Tallunati. Tat and Jalam make Tajjalam. Tat and Shmashânakam make Tat.Shmashânakam. Sugan and Atra make Sugannatra. Pachan and Atra make Pachannatra. Bhavân and Châdayati-Bhavamshchhâdayati. Bhavân and Jhanatkâr make Bhavân Jhanatkâra. Bhavân and Tarati make Bhavâmstarati. Sam and Smritam combinedly make Samsmritam. Bhavân and Likhati unitedly make Bhavâmllikhati. Tân and Shété unitedly make Tamschchhété. Bhavân, Shete Api, Ami and Idrisham combinedly make Bhavang Shetepyameedrisham. Tvam and Karoshi combinedly make Tvamkaroshi. Tvan and Tarasi make Tvantarasi, Sat and Archanam make Sadár Chchanam, Kah and Ihátra make Ka Ihatra.

There are six forms of Samâsas, such as (1) the Karmadhâraya etc., of which the term Shaddvija forms an illustration. The term Trivedi furnishes the example of Dvigu Samâsa. Tatkritascha, Tadarthascha, and Vrikabhiti, etc., are the illustrations of Tatpurusha Samâsa, whereas the terms Tattvajna, Jnâna-dasksha, etc., illustrate the forms of Vahubrihi Samâsa. Examples of the Avyayibhâva Samâsa always commence with the interjectional prefixes of Adhi, etc., while the terms such as Devarshi-Mânava, etc., furnish the instances of the Dvanda Samâsa. The terms such as Pandavás, Shaiva, Vráhma, and Brahmatâ are the illustrations of the applied Taddhita.

The terms Devagni, Sakhi, Pati, Anshu, Krashtu, Svayambhu, Pita (Pitri), Nri (Ná), Prashâstá (Prashastri) Rá, Gau, and Glau, though included within the group of Adajanta words belong to the masculine gender. Similarly, the group of Halanta words consisting of the terms Ashra, Juk, Kshâbhuk, Kravyad, Mrigabedh, Atmân, Râjan, Yuvan,

Pathin, Pushan, and Brahmahan, Shashin, Vedhas, Ushanas, Anudvan, Madhulit and Kâshthatat belongs to the masculine gender. The terms Vanam (wood), Vâri (water), Asthi bone) Vastu (thing), Jagat (universe), Saman (the verses of that Veda), Ahan (day), Karma, (act) Sarpis (clarified butter) Bapus (body) and Tejas (energy) belong to the neuter gender. The terms Jâyâ (wife), Jarâ (old age), Nadi (river), Lakshmi (goddess of fortune), Shree (beauty), Stri (woman), Bhumi (land), Vadhu (bride), Bhru (eye-brows), Punarbhu (a re-married widow), Dhenu (cow), Svasâ (sister), Mâtâ (mother) Nau (boat), Bâk (speech), Srag (garland of flowers), Dik quarter of the heaven), Krudh (anger), Yuvati (maiden) Kukubh, (quarters of the skies), Dyau (effulgence), Dhrite (comprehension), Prâvrish (rainy reason), Ushnik (metre) and Sumanas (flowers) belong to the feminine gender.

Now I shall narrate to you the terms which are respectively included within the masculine, feminine and neuter groups according to the nature of their imports, or the nature of the act they signify. Shukla (white), Kilâla, Shuchi (pure) Grâmani (the master of a village), Sudhi (intelligent one) Vâhu (arms), Kamalabhu (the lotus-sprung deity), Kartâ (master or doer), Vahu (many), Satya (truth), Madhutakshá and Dirgha-pât (belong to the masculine gender. The terms Sarva (all), Vishva (all), Ubha (both), Anya (other), Anyatara (other than that) are terms that are used both in the masculine and feminine genders. Purva, Apara, Uttara, Dakshina, Apara, Antara, Tad, Yad, Idam, Ashmad, and Yushmad are the terms that are used in all the genders.

Here follows declensions of several words and rules of prosody identical with those enumerated in our English translation of the Agni Puranam.

CHAPTER CCXXIX.

SUTA said :—Now I shall relate to you the rules of conduct to be observed by Brahmanas, etc., which Brahmâ first learned from Hari and expounded to the holy Vyâsa, and proper performances whereof grant all things to their performers. A twice-born one, having learnt the Vedas and the scriptural law, shall perform acts (rites) enjoined to be performed in the Vedas; unable to perform the Vedic rites, he shall perform those mentioned in the law codes (Smriti). Even incapable of performing either class of these acts, the intelligent one shall perform acts of good conduct. The S'ruti and the Smriti are the eyes, as it were, of Brâhmanas in respect of detecting the true virtue. Bereft of one of these eyes of S'ruti and Smriti, a Brahmana verily becomes a moral one-eyed; bereft of both he becomes morally blind. Pieties described in the S'ruti and S'astras and the acts of good conduct performed by the pious triply form the eternal virtues (duties eternally obligatory on all). Truthfulness, gift making (charity), absence of greed or avarice, knowledge, performances of religious sacrifices, divine worship, and self-control, are the eight sacred constituents of good conduct. The body and sense-organs of the pious, effulgent with a kind of sanctified light, do not adhere to sin, like water drops to lotus leaves. Of men of all the four orders virtue forms the main stay of existence. Truthfulness, performance of religious sacrifices and austerities (meditation), and charity. are the cardinal duties of house-holders. Non-acceptance of what has not been formally given and made over (to a person), practice of charities and austerities, study, annihilation of all killing or mischief-making propensities, truthfulness, abstention of irascible feelings, and performance of religious sacrifices, are the attributes of virtue. Learning (knowledge), opulence, practice of austerities, valour, noble parentage, and absence of disease (sound health) are the factors that lead to the elevation of a man in this world; all these proceed from the practice of virtue. From virtue proceed happiness and knowledge; knowledge leads to the ultimate emancipation of one's own self. Performances of religious sacrifices, endowments for the public good, study of the Vedas, and practice of charity in conformity with the injunctions of the S'âstras may be described as the eternal duties, commonly obligatory on Brâhmanas, Kshatriyas and Vais'yas. Imparting lessons (teaching) to the pure and the holy, officiating as priests at the religious sacrifices performed by the pure, and acceptance of gifts from persons not in any way impure or unholy are the three means of earning livelihood, open to Brâhmanas, in the opinion of the Munis. Military professions and protection of creatures from hurt or injury are the callings of Kshatriyas. Rearing of cattle, agriculture, and trade are the means by which Vais'yas shall earn their living. Services of the three twice-born classes, to be made preferentially in the order of enumeration, should be the vocations of S'udras. Residence near the preceptor, service of the consecrated fire, study of the Vedas, three ablutions, each day, ritualistic ablutions, wearing of clotted hairs, carrying of staffs, wearing of Mekhalâs, living on alms, residence near the preceptor till death, or a clear-shaving of the head are the duties which are obligatory on Brahmachârins. Perfomances of Agnihotra sacrifices, earning of livelihood by means proper to his order, procreation of sons on his own married wife, and on days not interdicted as Parvas, making offerings to the gods and to his departed manes, as well as feeding of all chance- comers (Atithis) to his house, and perusal of the true imports of S'rutis and Smritis are the duties of a house- holder. Wearing of clotted hairs on the head, performances of Agni Hotra sacrifices, lying down on the bare ground, wearing of deer-skin, residence in the forest, living on roots, bulbs, fruit and Nivâra grains, etc., abstention from all forbidden acts, daily performance of three ablutions, observance of vow, and propitiation of the gods, Atithis and his departed manes are the duties of a forest-dwelling (Vânaprastha hermit). Abstention of all acts or undertakings, living on alms, residence under the trees, non-acceptance of gifts, living in harmony with all and sundry (*lit.* not in conflict with any), practising of equality to all, maintaining equanimity under all painful or pleasurable circumstances, acquisition of mastery over pleasure and pain, purification of both inside and out, practice of silence and meditation, drawing in of all the sense-organs from the external world, practice of constant meditation and attempt at being one with the thought, and purification of ideas are the duties which are obligatory on a Parivrájaka to cultivate. Truthfulness, forbearance, compassion, purity, abstention of all killing propensities and sacred discourse are the bounden duties of all the four social orders. Those, who strictly conform to the aforesaid laws and duly perform their respective duties, come by a better fate.

Now I shall relate to you the duties of a house-holder from the time when he leaves his bed to that when he goes to sleep in the night. Rising at the Bráhma Muhurta (about half an hour before the dawn) a house-holder shall attend to the calls of nature, and then having carefully washed himself, at the close of the night, shall think of his own good both in this world and the next. Then he shall bathe and attend to the rite of his Sandhyâ meditation. He shall perform the rite of his morning Sandhyá after having washed his face and cleansed his teeth. One should void stool and urine, looking towards the north, in the day; and towards the south, in the night. At the two junctions of the day and night, the rule laid down in respect of urination and defecation in the day should be followed. In shade, in darkness, in the day or night, as well as in times of danger to life or of illness, a Bráhmana can void stool or urine, looking towards any quarter of the skies, best convenient. One shall not void urine on cowdung, charcoal, or an ant-hill, nor in clear pure water, or on the furrows of a ploughed field. Similarly, urination near the road side, in an assembly, or over writing materials are forbidden. Earth should not be taken from beneath the water, from a temple, from an ant-hill, from about a mouse-hole, or from a cremation ground. The residue of earth with which one has purified oneself (cleansed one's person) should be avoided. One Mrittiká (half a Prasritiful Earth) should be used in rubbing the external orifice of the urethra, three Mrittikâs should be used in rubbing the anus, three Mrittikas in rubbing the palm of the left hand, and a Half Mrittiiká in rubbing the palms of both the hands, after voiding stool.

Now I shall describe the process of purification, after voiding urine. One Mrittikâ should be applied to the external orifice of the urethra; three, to the anus; ten, to the palm of the left hand; five, to the soles of feet; and seven, to each of the arms. The greatest quantity of Mrittiká (clay) which should be used in cleansing the orifices of the external ducts of the body, under these circumstances, is half of what can be contained in the palm of one's hand, outstretched and hollowed. The second is half of that of the former, and the third is half of that of the second. He, who is incapable of voiding stool or urine in a sitting posture, shall perform half of these purifications, after urination or defecation. Half or a quarter part of the purifying measurs, enjoined to be performed in the day, shall be performed in the night, after voiding stool or urine. Men in health must unfailingly observe these rules of purification; while sick folks shall observe them as far as they are capable of observing. Fat, semen, blood, marrow, saliva, stool and urine, and waxy deposits in the ears, as well as mucous, tears, and perspiration are called the excrements of the human body. A man shall try to purify his person as long as he does not think himself pure; the extent of purification can not be precisely laid down for each individual case. There are two kinds of purification *viz.*, external and internal, the first consists in cleansing the body with clay, water, etc.; the second is the purification of one's thoughts and ideas.

First, thrice sip water in the manner of the rite of Achamanam, then twice rinse the mouth with water, and after that, thrice sip water with the ball of the thumb. Then repeatedly touch your eyes and ears with the tips of the thumb and the index finger joined together. The navel should be touched with the tips of the thumb and the small finger joined together; and the region of the heart, with the palm of the hand. The head should be touched with all the fingers united together, and the back of the arms should be touched with the tips of fingers by rounding the hand. A Brâhmana shall thrice sip water in the manner of Achamanam for propitiating the three Vedas, *viz*, the Rik, the Yajus and the Sáman. Similarly, by twice rubbing the lips he shall propitiate the Arthava Angirasa, as well as the Itihásas, Puranas, and Vedângas in succession. He shall touch the principle of ether in his mouth; the principle of air, in his nostrils; the sun, in his sight; the quarters of the skies, in the chord of vitality in his umbilicus; and the supreme Brahma, at his heart. The god Rudra is pleased by one touching one's head, while the Rishis are propitiated by one touching the tuft of hair on one's crown, at the time of performing an Achamanam. The lord of death, Indra, Varuna, Kuvera, the Earth-goddess and the fire-god are pleased by one touching one's anus, at the aforesaid time. He shall feel the contact of Vishnu and Indra by touching the soles of his feet and that of Vishnu alone by touching his arms. O thou twice born one, the celestial serpents Vásuki etc., are propitiated by the water that one might cast on the ground at the time of performing Achamanam, and the drops of water that he might cast around tend to propitiate the hosts of spirits. The deities, Agni, Váyu, Surya and Indra are situated in the phalanges of one's fingers. The moon-god, with all the sacred pools and sanctuaries, are situated in the palm of one's (right) hand; hence, the (right) hand is always pure. The sacred streams and rivers such as, the Ganges etc., are situated in the lines, that run across the palm of one's (right) hand.

At the approach of dawn, one shall attend to the calls of nature, and cleanse his person; then having cleansed his teeth with a twig, bitten down in the shape of a tooth-brush, he shall take an ablution. A person remains impure, even after cleansing his teeth, after the expiry of the previous night; hence, one shall eat the tooth-twig (twig bitten and smashed in the shape of a tooth-brush), each morning. Twigs of Kadamva, Vilva, Khadira, Karavira, Vata, Arjuna, Yuthi, Vrihati, Játi, Karanja, Arka, Atimukta, Jamvu, Madhuka, Apámárga, Shirisha, Audumvara, Asana, Kshiri, and Kantaki trees and plants are recommended for the purpose of being used as tooth-brushes. Twigs of pungent, bitter, and astringent flavours, used for the purpose of cleansing the teeth, bring health and happiness to the cleanser. Then having washed the tooth-twig and cleansed his teeth, he shall wash his face, while seated in a pure site. Tooth-twigs should not be used on days, marked by the new moon, as well as on the first, sixth or ninth day of the moon's wane or increase. Similarly, the use of tooth-twigs is prohibited on Sundays. In the absence of any tooth-twig, as well as on days in which its use is prohibited, one shall gargle one's mouth with twelve handfuls of water. A morning-ablution, either before or after the appearance of the sun on the horizon, is recommended as wholesome; a pure-souled and pure-bodied morning-bather becomes competent to practise all religious rites of Japa, etc. The human body, extremely filthy within and provided with nine apertures or external ducts, day and night, exudes impure and unclean secretions, and a morning ablution is the means of bringing about its purification, each day. An ablution in the Ganges imparts a cheerfulness to the mind, and health and a beautiful complexion to the body. It dissipates grief and misery. "For the extinction of the ten classes of sin, severally committed by receiving what has not been formally given, by doing forbidden acts, by hurting or killing any creature, by carnally knowing another man's wife, by using abusive language to, or hurting the feelings of any, by speaking falsehood, by practising niggardliness, by improper speaking, by coveting other men's riches, by wishing evil to others, I take this ablution in the Ganges." One shall recite this Mantra, while bathing in the Ganges, on the tenth day of the moon's increase, marked by the asterism Hastâ or Jesthâ, or under the auspices of the astral combination known as Dasha-Pâpa-Harâ. Brief is the ceremony which attends an act of ablution in the morning; while it is elaborate in respect of that which is made at noon. House-holders and forest-dwelling hermits (Vânaprasthas) are only competent to bathe twice a day, *viz.*, at morning and mid-day; while Yatis are privileged to bathe three times, each day. A Brahmachârin shall bathe only once a day. Having performed the rite of A'chamanam, and invoked the sacred pools therein, one shall take a bath in the river. Thirty million is the number of the malignant spirits, called Mandehas, who manifest a desire of devouring the sun at day break. He, who does not attend to his Sandhyâ rite at the meetings of the day and night, verily kills the sun, inasmuch as the libations of consecrated water (offered unto the sun-god in the course of a Sandhyâ) tend to consume these monsters (Mandehas) like streams of liquid fire. The unions or meetings (Sandhyâ) of the day and the night, which are called Sandhyâs, last for the period of two Nâdikas till the sun or the stars appear in the sky. After the performance of his Sandhyâ rite, a person shall personally do the *Homa*. The merit of personally performing the *Homa* is greater than that of getting it done by another. A *Homa* performed by one's Rittvik (priest, son, preceptor, brother, or sister's son is regarded as one done by one's self. The house-holder fire (Gârhapatyâgni) is identical with Brahmâ, Dakshinâgni is same as the three-eyed deity (Siva), Ahavaniya fire is one with the deity Vishnu, while Truth is the god, Kumára. After performing the *Homa*, one shall repeat the Mantra, sacred to S'iva (to the sun according to others.) After that, self-controlled, he shall recite the Pranava and the Sávitri Mantras. He, who daily recites the Sávitri Mantra, coupled with the seven Vyâhritis, as well as the Tripáda Sávitri, has no reason to be afraid of any thing in this world. He, who recites the *Gáyatri*, every morning, on leaving his bed, is not attached to sin, as water lies not attached to a lotus-leaf. The presiding deity of the *Gáyatri* is described as a white-complexioned goddess, clad in silken raiments, seated on a full blown lotus-flower and carrying a rosary of Aksha seeds in her hand. The goddess should be invoked by reciting the Yajus Mantra running as, thou art the light etc. The gods, wishing, of yore, to see the goddess residing in the Brahmaloka in the disc of the sun, invoked her with the selfsame Mántra. The goddess should be bid adieu, after the worship, with acts of obeisance. The deities should be worshipped in the fore-part of the day. There is no higher god than the Supreme Vishnu; hence, he should be constantly worshipped. An intelligent person shall not think Brahma, Vishnu and Shiva as different divinities, but as all one and the same. Bráhmanas, kine, fire, gold, clarified butter, the sun-god, water, king, the eighth in the list, are always auspicious in this world. Hence, one should constantly view, worship and circumambulate these eight holy ones.

The cultivation of Vedic knowledge consists in constantly studying their contents, in constantly committing them to memory, in meditating upon the imports of the Vedic Mantras, and in giving lessons in the Vedas to one's pupils. He, who makes gifts of the Vedas, by getting them transcribed by paid writers, goes to the region of the Vedas. He, who makes similar gifts of works on Itihâsas, Purânas, etc., acquires twice as much merit as that of making Brahmadânam (making gifts of vedic texts). The third part of the day should be devoted to works connected with the maintenance of one's dependants (Poshyas, lit, those who are to be supported) One's own parents, preceptor, brother, poor dependants, Athithis, the sacred fire and guests form the list of one's Poshyas (Poshya-vargas. Support of those, whom it is one's duty to sustain, leads to heaven; hence, one should make his best endeavours to maintain one's Poshyas. He, on whom many depend for their subsistence, truly lives. He, who is concerned only with the pampering of his own belly, is dead in life; even dogs are found to secure their food and appease their appetite. From accumulated wealth and augmented opulence proceed all acts, as rivers spring up from elevated mountains. This earth in whose bowels all gems are interred (land), food grains, animals and women are called money (Artha), because they are invariably connected with the gratifications of desires (Arthas). A means of livehood, which is absolutely inhostile to others, or is slightly hostile to a (microscopic) minority, should be adapted by a Brahmana in times of peace.

There are three kinds of wealth, white, brown, and black, which may be again divided into seven classes. Possessions of all orders of soceity may be grouped under three heads such as, heriditary, obtained as presents of love or affection, and obtained as dowry with a wife. The three specific sources of wealth, in the case of a Brâhmana, are fees obtained for teaching and officiating as a priest at religious sacrifices, as well as gifts received from the pure and the holy. The three specific kinds of wealth (possessions) in respect of a Kshatriya are money obtained in the shape of revenue, fines realised from persons convicted in law courts, and that obtained by conquest. The three specific sources of wealth in respect of a Vais'ya are cattle-rearing, agriculture and trade. Favour obtained by service is the only source of income of a S'udra. In times of danger, a Brâhmana, by pursuing agriculture, trade, or usury, does not commit any sin. The Rishis have described a large concourse of means of livelihood, but usury thrives the best of them all. Unnatural seasons of drought, political disturbances, rats and other pests are the impediments to the successful practice of agriculture, but usury is bereft of them all. The thriving in usury does not cease in day or in night, in dark or light fortnight, nor in summer, winter or rains. The profit, which artisans and traders of different guilds do by sojourneying to foreign climes, the money-lender does by remaining in his native country. Having made a good profit in the business of money lending, one should propitiate the gods, Brâhmanas and one's departed manes with a portion thereof. The gods, etc., thus propitiated, absolve the sin incidental to the practice of usury. Learning, art, service, cattle-rearing, trade, agriculture and alms-taking etc., are the ten means of livelihood. By accepting gifts a Brâhmana shall acquire wealth, a Kshatriya shall acquire wealth by conquest, a Vaishya shall acquire money by plying any lawful trade, whereas a Shudra shall earn money by serving others. A full-bodied river, Sâkas (vegetables), Samids, Kusha-grass, fire, leaves and Omkâra are the best possessions of Brâhmanas. There is no demerit in accepting gifts, offered without asking or seeking, the gods call such articles (gifts) as ambrosia; hence, they should not be rejected. One seeking to propitiate the gods and Atithis may accept gifts from one's servants and preceptor. For these purposes one may accept gifts from any person whomsoever, but one must not appropriate articles of such gifts to one's own use. A Brâhmana, possessed of good qualifications and having very little blemishes in his conduct, is alone competent to receive gifts; a bad or illiterate Brâhmana degrades his Self lowerer by taking any gift. The foremost of Brâhmanas, obliged to earn his livelihood by penmanship, shall subsequently practise a penance by way of expiation.

In the first quarter of the day, a Brâhmana shall collect sesame, flowers, Kusha-grass, and earth for rubbing his body with, while bathing; a bath in a natural stream of water is recommended. Ablutions may be divided into six classes such as, the Nityam (daily obligatory bath, non-performance whereof is sinful), Naimittikam (specific or occasional), Kâmyam (that made for the fruition of any definite object), Kriyângam (which forms the part of, or sequel to, any religious rite), Malâkarshanam (that made for the purpose of cleansing the body) and Kriyâ (bath which in itself forms a religious rite.) Without bathing a man does not become competent to perform his daily rite of Homa, Japa, etc.; hence, he shall bathe early in the morning, each day. An ablution, which is made under specific circumstances such as, the one made for the purpose of purifying one's self, after touching excreta or a Chandâla or a woman in her menses, is called a Naimittika Snânam. Bathing under the influence of any auspicious asterism such as, the Pushyâ etc., and made in accordance with the directions of astrologers, is a called Kâmya Snânam. He, who has not the fruition of any definite object in his heart, must not bathe under such circumstances. An ablution, made with the express object of worshipping any divinity, or of studying any sacred Vedic Mantra, is called a Kriyâ Snânam.

A bath, taken for the purpose of removing the impurities of the body, and for no other object, is called a Malápkarshanam Snánam. An ablution in a sacred pool, or in a natural reservoir of water, when it forms in itself a religious rite, is called a Kriyá Snánam. A mere touch of the water of a sacred pool leads to the purification of the bodily limbs; religious merit is obtained by taking a bath therein. By rubbing the body while reciting the Váruna Mantra, one is immediately absolved of all sin. In the absence of a sacred pool (Tirtha) all ablutions should be made in boiled water. Water, that lies on the surface of the earth, is more purifying than what has been collected and carried away; waters of springs or fountains are more purifying than terrestrial waters. Lake water is more purifying than fountain-water; river-water is more purifying than lake-water; the water of a sacred pool is more purifying than river-water, while the water of the Ganges is the purest of the pure. Ganges-water extinguishes the sin of a man which he might have committed from his birth to death. Of the waters that are to be found in the sanctuaries at Gayá or Kurukshetra, the Ganges-water is the most purifying of them all. The counsels or discourses of the erudite are more purifying in their effect than ablutions in any sacred pool whatsoever; and in conferences of virtue and religion most sanctifying is the Bráhmana, who lives in conformity with the injunctions of the holy Vyása.

Baths on the occasion of the birth of one's own son, or in the event of the sun passing over to another zodiacal sign, or under the auspicies of any blissful astral combination are recommended in the night, if these events take place in the night. Nocturnal baths, under the auspicies of lunar eclipses, are also recommended, otherwise baths in the night are prohibited. A bath in the river, taken in early morning, each day, and just after the appearance of the sun on the horizon, equals a Prâjâpatyam in merit, and tends to extinguish the *Mahápátakas*. By bathing, each morning, for a year, with a devotional spirit, one acquires the same merit which is ordinarily acquired by practising the Prájápatyam penance, for twelve years in succession. He, who desires for the objects of enjoyment, effulgent as the sun and the moon, and wishes to possess an absolutely sound health, shall bathe, each morning, for the two months in the year, *viz.*, Mâgha (January, February) and Phâlguna (February, March). By living on Havisbya food and observing the vow of Shat-Tilam during the month of Mâgha, a morning bather is absolved of all sin. The mother, father, brother, friend or preceptor of a bather, by mentioning whose name he might dive into the water, takes one-twelfth part of the merit of the ablution. The god Vishnu becomes specially fond of A'malakam (Emblic Myrobalans) under the auspices of the eleventh day of the moon's wane or increase; hence, one, wishing personal beauty, shall bathe with Amalakas on his person. Bereavement, infamy, ill-health, etc., reside in the stone of an Amalakam. By anointing one's person a man acquires health, beauty and all things he might set his heart upon. The goddess of fortune remains so long satisfied with a vowist, after he has got his hair clipped by a barber, as he does not touch oil.

Having bathed in the manner above described, one shall propitiate the gods and one's departed manes, as well as perform the rite of Tarpanam unto the canonised men. Standing in navel-deep water, he shall meditate upon the Selves of his deceased ancestors as seated in the air, and invoke their presence by saying, "come, O my departed manes, pleased with the libations of water I have just now offered unto you." By reciting this invocation he shall offer libations of water unto each of them in the southern quarter of the heaven. Then having put on dry clothes and seated on cushions of Kusha blades, the performers of Tarpanas, duly conversant with the rules of offering libations of water unto the gods and their departed manes, shall offer them on blades of Kusha grass, and never in any vessel. "May whatever is impure in this water, may whatever is cruel or unquiet in this water, may that all be removed." By reciting this Mantra and taking a libation of water in his left hand, he shall cast that in the south-west quarter of the sky for the purpose of warding off the advent of malignant spirits, during the performance of the rite.

"May Indra, Varuna and Vrihaspati, Bhaga, Savitâ and the Rishis such as Sanaka, etc., extinguish all the sin, which I might have committed by eating forbidden food, or by accepting gifts from sinful and degraded persons, as well as that which I might have committed by word, thought or deed. May all creatures from the lowest animalculum to the highest Bráhman be propitiated with this libation of water" Saying this, one shall offer three libations of water. Thus I have briefly described the mode of performing Tarpanâm. Bereft of pride and humble in spirit, one shall worship the gods by reciting the Mantras sacred to Brahmá, Vishnu, Rudra, Savitri or Varuna, as the case may be. Each deity should be worshipped by reciting the Mantras sacred to it. Then having made obeisance to it, flowers should be offered to it by appending the term Namas to the name to the deity. The god Vishnu, who is not only full of the energies of all the divinities, but their grand refuge, as well as the sun-god should be worshipped, and offerings of flowers and libations of water should be made to him by reciting the Purusha Sukta. The god Vishnu may be worshipped by reciting the Mantra, which runs as, "By him all this visible universe has been created and arranged in systems," or by reciting any other Tântrik Mantra. First, the Arghya offering should be made to the deity, then scented pastes such as sandal etc., should be offered, after that, offerings of flowers, should be made, and lighted lamps should be waived before the deity.

Brâhmanas, Kshatriyas and Vaishyas should bathe by reciting the Mantras, while S'udras should silently bathe. The performance of a Brahma-yajna consists in teaching the Vedas, that of a Pitri-yajna consists in offering oblations and libations of water to one's departed manes; casting of oblations in the sacred fire (Homa) is called Daiva-yajna; offering of oblations unto the animals is called Bhuta-yajna, and the feeding of Atithis is called Nri-yajna. The rite of Japa (mental recitation of a Mantra), done in the house, bears ordinary merit; made on the banks of a river it gives double merit; made in a cowshed it bears fruit ten times greater; made in a chamber of the consecrated fire it bears fruit, a hundred times greater; made at a sanctuary or in a divine temple it produces a thousand times greater merit; made near the image of Vishnu it bears a hundred millions of times greater merit.

Of the five parts of food prepared in a household, each day, four should be respectively allotted to the use of the Pitris, Devas, men and the insects etc. He, who takes his daily meals, after giving food (boiled rice) to his friends, relations and Brâhmanas, ascends to the region of heaven after death, through the merit of making gifts of food. Articles of sweet flavour should be eaten at the fore part of a meal; things of acid and saline tastes, at it its middle; and those of bitter, pungent and astringent flavours, at its close. Water should be taken after eating a meal. One should never take edibles of a single taste in exclusion of those of all others. Verily the boiled rice of a Brâhmana is like unto ambrosia; that of a Kshatriya is like unto milk; that of a Vaishya is a wholesomefood, and that of a S'udra is like unto blood. Beauty and opulence reside in the person of him, who observes a fast on the day of the new moon. The Gârhapatya fire is located in the belly of a man; the Dakshina fire, in his dorsal region; the Ahavaniya fire, in his mouth; and the Satyâgni in his head—He, who is cognisant of the locations of these five fires in his body, is called an Ahitâgni one. The body, the water, the albumen or the fluid constituents of the body and the various kinds of food-stuff are called Annam, while Prâna, Agni (fire heat) and A'ditya (the sun) are one and the same and enjoy the aforesaid Annam. Food contributes to the invigoration of the principles of earth, water, fire and air contained in my body, and the essence of food, after being properly digested, and assimilated in my organism, brings about a pleasurable condition of my ego. Prepared betel leaves (Tâmvulas) should be smashed with the hands, and then chewed, after eating. After eating one's (midday) meal, one shal hear the narration of histories and Puranas during the sixth and seventh parts of the day. After that, one shall again bathe, and attend to the performance of one's Evening Sandhyâ. O thou twice-born one, thus I have described the daily routine of acts to be followed by house-holders. The erudite one, who hears these rules of conduct narrated, or follows them in earnest spirit, goes to heaven after death. The god Keshava is the narrator of these rules of purity, duty and virtue, and the god Hari is the goal of all expiatory penances, and is the last refuge of the celestials and celestial regions.

Here follow descriptions of the modes of performing ceremonial ablutions and the different forms of Shrâddha, identical with those described in our English translation of the Agnipuranam.

—:o:—

CHAPTER CCXXX.

HARI said :—Now hear me, O Shankara, narrate a catechism of practised pieties, which extinguishes all sin of, and grant enjoyment of worldly pleasures and emancipation of self to, its listner. Grief robs a man of his pleasure, energy, fortitude, strength, virtues and erudition; hence, one should abandon all grief. Acts of a man are the deities that mould his destiny, acts are the factors that determine the nature of his environment as well as the character of the region of his birth, acts are his true friends and relations, and it is his acts that lead him to happiness or misery in this world. Charity is the highest of all virtues; through the merit of practising charity a man may acquire a kingdom or work out his own salvation, and become an emancipâted Self: hence, a man shall practise charity and make gifts to the poor and the worthy. One kind of charity is to make gifts with proper Dákshinâs, another kind of charity consists in succoring the lives of the oppressed and the tyrannised. Those, who obstruct or destroy the piety, which is acquired by practising penances or Brahmacharyayam, or by celebrating religious sacrifices, or [by performing] ceremonial ablutions, go to hell. Those, who are devoted to the performance of Homas, Japas, Pujas and ablutions, and are full of truthfulness, forbearance and compassion, go to heaven. None there is who dispenses happiness or misery to a man; or removes them out of his own sweet will; man suffers misery or enjoys happiness as the effects of what he has done. Those, who live for practising virtues, visit their wives for the procreation of children, and cast offerings to the deities for bringing about their satisfaction, tide over the evils of life. Who is he that cannot live contented on fares of fruits and bulbs? It is through company and entering into relationship that, man dives into troubles. Dreadful is the consequence of greed alone; from greed proceeds wrath or anger; and from wrath, strife; out of greed comes delusion, from delusion proceeds attachment, from attachment proceed pride and egotistic feelings. He, who lives in peace with himself, undisturbed by counter calls of desire, wrath, greed, pride delusion and falsehood, ascends to the region of highest bliss, undefiled by the touch of any sin whatsoever. O Hara, the gods, the celestial sages, the Nâgas, the Gandharvas and Gujhyakas adore the pious and the truthful in this world, and not those who are rich and full of desires. Neither by dint of valour or energy, nor by wisdom or occult power, a mortal can obtain that which he is not fated to obtain hence there is nothing to be deplored in that. As fishes spring upon their prey in water, as wild beasts live upon their prey on land, as birds eat their prey in the sky, so the rich are devoured by designing persons, everywhere. Compassion towards all creatures, control of all the senses, and a knowledge of the transitory nature of all things are the highest bliss. Like the teat-like excrescences on the neck of a she-goat, futile are the lives of those, who do not practise virtues, even with the sight of death ahead. A patricide, a Brahmanicide, a defiler of his preceptor's bed, a cow-killer, or a destroyer of a fœtus in the womb may expiate his sin by making the gift of a plot of land, possessed of all the commendable features. This is my opinion, O thou bull-ensigned deity, that the gift of a cow is the highest of all gifts; the gift of a cow, honestly obtained or purchased, succours the whole family of the giver. No gift can vie with the gift of food (Annam) in point of merit; it is food that sustains the whole world, whether mobile or immobile. The merit, which is acquired by making gifts of horses, elephants, chariots, gems, lands, or of girls, or by performing Japas, or Vrishotsargas (letting loose of a bull on the celebration of a Shrâddha ceremony), does not rank one sixteenth part of that, which is acquired by gifting food to the poor and the needy, in as much as food sustains strength and life, and from food proceed sperm and comprehension.

Excavations of wells, or tanks for public purposes and laying out of fruit-gardens for the use of the public lead to the regeneration of twenty one generations of the donor, who is also glorified for his piety in the region of Vishnu, after death. The sight of the holy is more sanctifying than a pilgrimage to a sanctuary; the merit of a pilgrimage takes time to bear fruit, the company of the holy becomes fruitful on the same day. Truthfulness, self-control, practice of austerities, purity, contentment, forbearance, simplicity, knowledge, compassion and charity—these are the eternal virtues.

CHAPTER CCXXXI.

BRAHMA said :—Now I shall deal with the mode of practising the expiatory penances, which tend to extinguish all sins for which the Self of a man is consigned to the pangs of hell. Flies, ants, drops of water, water that lies accumulated on the surface of the earth, fire, cats, and ichneumons, are always pure. A twice-born one, who, through inadvertence, eats anything, which has been defiled by the touch of the residue of a S'udra's meal, shall fast for an entire day and night and regain his purity by taking Panchagavyam. A Bráhmana, accidentally touched by another Bráhmana, who has not washed his mouth after eating, or happening to touch the residue of the meal of another Bráhmana, shall bathe and recite the Mantras, and take his meal at the close of the day. A Bráhmana, happening to partake of a meal containing a tip of hair or a flee, shall regain his purity by vomiting out the ingested food. He, who takes a meal, held in the hollow of his palm, or on the tips of his fingers, or on his arms, shall regain his purity by fasting for an entire day and night. The residue of water, drunk with left-hand, is as impure as that which is contained in a leather-bag, and hence, that should not be drunk. A Bráhmana, in whose house a Chandâla lies concealed without his knowledge, shall effect his purification by practising a Parâka, or a Chândrâyana penance, whereas a S'udra householder, under the circumstances, shall practise a Prâjâpatyam. He, who takes any cooked food in the house of a low-caste, shall practise a half *Krichchha* penance. He, who eats meals belonging to these harbourers of low-castes in their houses, shall perform a quarter part of *Krichchha Vrata.* A twice-born one having taken the food cooked by a washerman, carpenter, cobbler, or of one who manufactures articles of bamboo, or food belonging to any of these people, shall practise a *Chândrâyanam*. A Brâhmana, having unknowingly drunk water out of a Chandâla's well-cup, shall practise a Sânta-panam. A Kshatriya and a Vais'ya, under the circumstances, shall respectively practise a half and a quarter Sântapanam. A S'udra, under the same circumstances, shall practise a quarter *Chândrâyanam*. Having unknowingly taken any food in the house of one of a vile caste, a Brâhmana shall regain his purity by practising three *Krichchha Vratas*, while a S'udra, under the circumstances, shall practise a Parâkam penance. A Brâhmana having partaken of the residue of the meal of a member of vile caste shall regain his purity by practising a *Chândrâyanam*, while having drunk water in the house of a low caste person a Brâhmana shall fast for six nights (Shad Râtram.) A Kshatriya having unknowingly partaken of the food of a *Chandâla* shall practise a Sântapanam, while a Vais'ya and a S'udra, under the circumstances, shall respectively practise the Shadrâtri and Trirâtri penances. A Brâhmana having unknowingly eaten a fruit, while seated on a branch of the same tree with a *Chandâla*, shall regain his purity by fasting for an entire day and night.

A Brâhmana happening to touch a *Chandâla*, before washing his face, after eating a meal, shall repeat eight thousand times the *Gâyatri*, or a hundred times the Drupada Mantra. Having eaten the food of a *Chandâla* or S'vapacha, or that which has been defiled by the touch of excreta, a Brâhmana shall practise a Trirátram penance, the expiation for the members of other castes, under the circumstances, being the performance of a Parâka Vratam. Having wantonly visited a woman, a man shall practise a Parâka penance by way of expiation. No expiation exists for one, sprung of a vile caste, under these circumstances. A Bráhmana, having drunk water out of a cup which contained wine, shall regain his purity by practising a quarter *Krichchha Vratam*, and by getting himself reinitiated with the holy thread. Bráhmanas, who having renounced the vows of Pravrajyam or Agnihotram wish to reenter the order of house-holders, shall regain their purity by practising three *Krichchha Vratas* and three *Chândrâyanas*, and by again going through the rites of Jata Karma, etc. This is the opinion of the holy Vashishtha. A woman having failed to completely practise a *Prâjâpatyam* shall regain her purity by feeding Bráhmanas. A Bráhmana, with his face unwashed after a meal, happening to be touched by a S'udra, similarly circumstanced as himself, or by a dog, shall regain his purity by fasting for a night, and by taking the compound known as Panchagavyam. Touched by members of other castes, while circumstanced as above, a Bráhmana shall regain his purity by fasting for five nights. Undefiled is a current stream of water; pure are the particles of dust blown about by the wind, women, infants, and old men are above all pollution; constantly pure is the face of a woman, pure are the fruits felled down by birds from their stems, pure is a calf after being delivered of its mother's womb, pure is the mouth of a dog at the time of catching a game. Pure are the aquatic animals in water, pure are the land-animals on the surface of the earth, pure is the person that perform an A'chamanam by resting his feet in water. Articles of Indian bell-metal, undefiled by the touch of wine, are purified by rubbing them with ashes; defiled by the touch of wine or urine, they should be purified by heating. Articles of Indian bell-metal, smelled by kine or defiled by the touch of the residue of a S'udra's meal, or by the contact of a dog or a crow, are purified by being rubbed with the ten kinds of ashes. Having partaken his meal out of the saucer of a S'udra, a Bráhmana shall regain his purity by fasting for a day, and by taking Panchagavyam as well. A Bráhmana having touched a dog, a S'udra, or any other beast, or a woman in her menses, before washing his face after a meal, shall regain his purity by fasting for a day, and by taking Panchagavyam. In a waterless place, or on a road infested by thieves or tigers, a person is not polluted by voiding urine with an article of human use in his hand. He shall place it on the ground, and again take hold of the same, after having cleansed his person. Kânjikam (fermented rice or barley gruel,) milk-curd, milk, whey, meat, honey and Krisharâ, may be accepted, without impunity, even from a S'udra. A Bráhmana, who takes any kind of intoxicating liquor such as Gaudi, Paishti, or Mâdhvikam, shall expiate his sin by taking any flame-coloured wine, or by taking cow-dung and cow's urine. Having carnally known a dancing girl, an actress, a laundress, a carpenter's or Benujivi's wife, or the wife or daughter of one's own mother's brother, or the daughter of one's own spiritual preceptor, or the wife of one's own friend (relation) or uterine brother, one shall practise a *Tapta Krichchham* penance by way of expiation. No expiation exists for the sin of carnally knowing the daughter of one's own mother's sister. Having taken any thing previously eaten by a jackal or a hog, one shall regain one's purity by practising a *Shadrâtram* penance. Having taken dry meat one shall practise a *Tapta Krichchham* penance. Persons, guilty of incendiarism or of administering poison to any body, shall practise a *Tapta Krichchham* by way of expiation. Having partaken of any thing in the house of a S'udra, affected by a birth or death impurity, a Bráhmana shall recite eight hundred times the *Gâyatri* Mantra; having taken a meal in the house of a Vais'ya or a Kshatriya, circumstanced as before, he shall recite five hundred times the *Gâyatri* Mantras. A Bráhmana, who takes his meal in the house of a Bráhmana, impure with a birth or death uncleanness, shall regain his purity by reciting a hundred times the sacred *Gâyatri*.

On the occasion of a birth or death in his family, a Bráhmana remains unclean for ten days; a Kshatriya for twelve days; a Vais'ya, for fifteen days; and a S'udra, for a month.

Uncleanness, incidental to the death of one's relation in battle, in a foreign country, during the celebration of a religious sacrifice, or in execution of a capital sentence passed by the king, as well as that which results from the death of a cognate relation, below six months of age, expires with the very day of the occurrence of the death. Uncleanness incidental to the death of an unmarried girl, of a twice-born son not initiated with the Maunji, of a boy who has cut his teeth, or of a girl of three years of age, lasts for three nights only. Uncleanness, incidental to the abortion or miscarriage of a fœtus, lasts for the same number of days as that of the months of pregnancy in which the said abortion or miscarriage has occurred. Uncleanness in respect of the birth of a child, born before time, lasts for the same number of days as that of the months of gestation in which the birth has taken place. In times of famine or scarcity, during civic disturbances, birth or death-uncleanness does not affect a person, nor does it affect those who are in the habit of practising charities, every day, or those who are being initiated, or are practising vow, or penances, or are residing in any sanctuary. At the time of spiritual initiation, during the celebration of a marriage ceremony, at times when Bráhmanas are feasted in one's house, or while performing an act previously determined, a death or birth uncleanness does not affect. Similarly, a Bráhmana becomes unclean by touching his justly parturient wife. Birth uncleanness does not affect a man in a place where oblations are cast in the sacred fire, or the Vedas are studied, or offerings are constantly offered unto the Vishvedevas. A S'udra, consecrated with the sacred Mantra, regains his personal purity a fortnight after the occurrence of a (birth) uncleanness. Bráhmanas in jeopardised conditions remain unclean for a single day in connection with a birth-uncleanness. A performer of Agni-Hotra sacrifices, a vowist and a reciter of any sacred Mantra are not affected by birth-uncleanness.

A woman in her menses happened to be touched by a dog, or a *Chandála* or a Pukkasa shall fast till the day of her bath of purification, when she shall regain her purity by bathing. Any household work done by her, under the circumstances, should be regarded as an unsanctified act, whereto sin is attached. A twice-born one happening to take his meal in a house under uncleanness shall practise a Trirâtram Vratam by way of expiation. Bráhmanis, Kshatriyâs and Vais'yâs in their menses, happening to touch one another, shall respectively fast for three nights, two nights and one night, while S'udrâs shall be clean again only by taking ablutions. A Drona measure of cooked food or articles of fare, happened to be defiled by the touch of a dog or crow, should not be cast aside as impure; only the superficial stratum of such food should be rejected. The mode of purifying such food consists in sprinkling waters, in which bits of gold have been kept immersed, over its pile and in heating it again on fire. A Bráhmana, a Kshatriya, and a Vais'ya happening to drink the water of a well in which the carcase of a dog, jackal, or monkey has been cast, shall regain their purity by respectively fasting for three nights, two nights and one night. In the event of a well being defiled by the casting of bones, hair, or other excrementitious matter in its water, it shall be purified by dredging its bottom and casting Panchagavyam into it. In the event of a pond or tank being defiled by ashes, sixty pitcherfuls of water should be baled out of its bed, and Panchagavyam should be cast in its water. In the event of a tank being defiled by the washing of catamenial blood of a woman in its water, thirty pitcherfuls of its water should be baled out. Having visited a woman standing in an interdicted relation to him, or used any forbidden article of food and drink such as beef, wine, etc., a Bráhmana, or a Kshatriya is purified by practising a Prájápatyam penance; a Vais'ya, by a Sántapanam; and a S'udra, by a Pancha-rátram penance. After practising an expiatory penance, one shall feed the worthy Bráhmanas and make gifts of kine to them.

The use (wearing) of an indigo-dyed cloth by one in bed or at the time of visiting one's wife is not sinful, otherwise an indigo-dyed cloth should not be touched and an indigo-dyer goes to hell, after death. A Brahmanicide, a wine-drinker, a stealer of gold of more than eighty Ratis weight, he who defiles the bed of his own preceptor, as well as the one who keeps company of these men, are absolved of their sin by paying visit to Setubandha. After return from his pilgrimage, any of these absolved sinners shall feed the pious Bráhmanas and make gifts of kine to them. A Brahmanicide shall live for twelve years in a cottage in the forest; and carrying a human skull on his head he shall stroll out for alms. Thus he shall live on alms for twelve years, whereby he will be absolved of his sin. On the other hand, he shall immolate his self in a blazing fire, or shall renounce his life for the good of a Bráhmana, or shall dedicate all his possessions to use of a Bráhmana. Similarly, a wine-drinker shall immolate his self in a blazing fire. A gold stealer, falling under the category of a Steyin, shall expiate his sin by making gift of all his possessions to a Bráhmana, well-versed in the Vedas. He, who has defiled the bed of his preceptor, shall purchase his absolution by making gifts of a thousand bullocks to Brâhmanas.

If a cow dies, while penned in a shed or an enclosure, her owner shall practise a quarter part of the *Krichchha* penance by way of expiation, in the case where the cow dies with fastenings or halter round her neck, the expiation is the practice of a half *Krichchha* penance, whereas in cases the cow is burnt down to death, or where the death occurs from its being led astray in the wilderness, her owner shall practise a full *Krichchha* Vratam by way of expiation. The practice of a quarter *Krichchha* penance is the expiation in the case where the cow dies from the effects of injudicious fastenings of bells round her neck. Having accidentally broken the horn of a cow, or a bone in her body, or having broken her tail or injured her skin, one shall live, for a fortnight, on Jâvakam. A member of any of the three twice-born orders, having unknowingly taken wine or any excrementitious matter such as, the stool or urine, should be re-initiated with the holy thread. Shaving of the head, carrying of staff, wearing of the grass-girdle (Mekhalá), begging of alms and observance of vows should be omitted in the rites of such second initiation of the twice-born. Raw meat, clarified buttter, honey and seed-oils, kept in the vessel of a man of vile cast, become pure as son as they are taken out of it. The practice of a quarter-Krichchha penance consists in taking a night-meal on the first day, in living on what is obtained without asking on the second day, and in fasting on the third day of its term, while that of a half Krichchha Vratam is double of what is laid down in connection with a quarter-Krichchham. The practice of a Prâjâpatyam penance, which extinguishes all sin, consists in triply doing what is laid down in respect of a quarter-Krichchham. A Krichchham penance, practised by fasting for seven days in succession, is called a Mahâ-Sântapanam Vratam. Take only warm water on the first) three days, only warm milk on the second three days, and only clarified butter on the third three days of the penance. This is called the sin-absolving Tapta-Krichchha-Vratam. The practice of a Parâka Vratam, which extinguishes all sin, consists in fasting for twelve days in succession.

In this penance the penitent shall take one morsel of food (Pinda) on the first day of the light fortnight, and successively increase the number by one, each day, till the day of the full moon, and thereafter go on decreasing it by one, each day, till the day of the new moon. The compound known as the Panchagavyam, the use of which tends to extinguish all sin, shall consist of the milk of a golden-coloured cow, the dung of a white cow, the urine of a copper-coloured cow, the butter made out of the milk of a blue-coloured cow, the curdled milk of a black cow, and the washings of the blades of Kusha-grass, in the following proportions *viz.*, eight Mâshas of cow's urine, four Mâshas of cowdung, twelve Mâshas of cow-milk, ten Mâshas of curdled cow-milk, and five Mâshas of melted cow-butter. O Vyâsa, the holy sages have devoutly practised the pieties I have narrated; those, who propitiate the divine Vishnu, live in comfort and happiness. By performing Japas, Homas, and Sandhyâs, one acquires (is merged in) Vishnu, the granter of virtues, wealth, creature-comforts and emancipation. Vishnu is virtue, Vishnu is vow, Vishnu is worship; Vishnu is Tarpanam. He is Homa, Sandhyâ, meditation and psychic trance.

—:o:—

CHAPTER CCXXXII.

SUTA said:—O Shaunaka, now hear me describe the dissolution of the universe (Pralayam). A thousand of each of the four Yugas make one Kalpa, which, in its turn, constitutes one day of the lotus-sprung deity. Now hear me narrate the rules of conduct and life, etc., which respectively obtained in the said four Yugas. Virtue reigned unimpaired with its four feet of truthfulness, charity, penance and mercy in the cycle of Satyam (truth). The protector of virtue was (S'veta) white-complexioned Hari. Men were contented and erudite in that age, and the duration of human life was four thousand years. At the close of Satya Yuga, Kshatriyas of the twice-born order conquered the Bráhmaṇas, Vais'yas and S'udras; and the valarous Vishnu of mighty prowess killed many Râkshasas. In the Treta Yuga, virtue was robbed of one of its limbs, and was composed of the three factors of truthfulness, charity and compassion. Men were devoted to the performances of religious sacrifices; and the earth was peopled by men of Kshatriya extraction in that cycle of Treta. The red-complexioned Hari was worshipped by the people of that age, and the duration of human life was one thousand years. Bhimaratha of Kshatriya extraction, who was an incarnation of Vishnu, killed many Râkshasas in the Treta Yuga. In the cycle of Dvâpara, when the yellow-complexioned Achyuta was the protector of virtues, the duration of human life was fourteen hundred years, and men born of Bráhmaṇa and Kshatriya parents peopled the earth. The god Vishnu, incarnate in the shape of the holy Vyâsa, considering the smallness of human intellect (comparative dulness of human memory) at the time, divided the Veda into four parts, and taught them to his own disciples in the following order, *viz.*, he taught the Rik Veda to Paila; the Sâma Veda, to Jaimini; the Atharvan, to Sumanta; and the Yajur Veda, to Mahâmuni. To Vaishampâyaṇa he taught the Purânam; and the eighteen Purânas, to Suta, by reading which one is enabled to know the god Hari. A Purânam treats of five topics such as, the creation of the universe (Sarga), dissolution of the universe (Pratisarga), geneologies of kings, specific traits of the different cycles of time as represented by the different Lawgivers, and the annals of royal progeny. The eighteen Mahâ (great) Purânas are the Bráhmam, Pâdmam, Vaishnavam, Shaivam, Bhâgavatam, Bhavishyam, Náradiyam, Skândam, Laingam, Varáhakam, Mârkandeyam, Agneyam, Brahma-Vaivartam, Kaurmam, Mâtsyam, Gárudam, and Brahmándam Purânas. The other minor Purânas, narrated by the holy sages, are the Sanat-kumâram, Nársinham Purânam, Skándam as narrated by the god Kumâra, Shiva-Dharmâksham, directly narrated by Nandisha, the Purânam of wonderful incidents narrated by the holy Durvásá, the one narrated by the holy Nárada, the Kâpilam, the Vâmanam, the one related by the holy Ushanâ, the Brahmândam, the Varunam, the Kâlikâ, the Mâheshvaram, the Shâmbam, the Sarvârtha Sanchayam, the one narrated by Parâshara, the Mâricham, and the Bhârgavam Purânas. The Purânam, the Dharma Sâstras (Codes of Moral Laws), the Vedas with their six kindred branches of study such as, the Nyáya (Logic), Mimânsá (Exegetic philosophy) Ayurveda (Medical Science), Artha Shâstras (Science of Wealth,) Gandharva (Science of Music) and Dhanurveda (Science of War—these are the eighteen branches of knowledge. At the close of the cycle of Dvâparam, the god Hari removed the burden of the world by killing the evil-souled Kshatriyas. In the age of Kali when the god Achyuta will assume a black complexion, the virtue will suffer a great mutilation and eke out a miserable existence, standing on one leg only. Men will be cruel miscreants in that Yuga.

Sattva (principle of illumination or knowledge), Rajas (principle of action) and Tamas (principle of Nescience) are the three qualities that are usually found in men. Even these qualities, O Shaunaka, vary in proportions in the self of a man, augmented by the spirit of the age he lives in. The age in which the quality of Sattva abounds in the mind, intellect, and sense organs of men, and in which they feel an irresistable inclination to practise charity and penances—know that age, O Shaunaka, to be the Satyam Yuga. When men are found to energetically pursue undertakings that lead to fame or bring about the fruitions of desires, and when the mind, intellect and sense-organs of men abound in the quality of Rajas, know then, O Shaunaka, that the Treta Yuga (of triped virtue) has set in. The age in which men are found to energetically follow pursuits of gain or desire, and in which greed, discontent, pride, envy and egotistic feelings assail the minds of men, and in which the qualities of Tamas and Rajas suffer an unhealthy augmentation in the temperaments of beings—know that, O Shaunaka, to be the age of Dváparam (of biped virtue.) The age in which untruthfulness, sleep, drowsiness (laziness), life-killing, grief, delusion, fright, misery, and Tamas rage rampant in the world—know that to be the age of Kali. In the Kali-yuga men will be slaves to lust and low passions, and abusive of one another. Towns and villages will be infested with thieves and robbers, vilifiers of virtue will vilify the Vedas, kings will prey upon their subjects, and Brâhmaṇas will care only for the pampering of their bellies and seek gratifications of their carnal desires. Impure and vowless will be the students and youths, Vikshus will contract various forms of relationship and live with their relations, Tapsvins (ascetics) will live in villages, and Nyâsins will covet riches. Diminutive in size, gluttonous, thievish, and rashly in their conduct, men will walk in the path of iniquity, servants will desert their masters, and Tâpasas (ascetics) will renounce their vows. S'udras, clad in the garbs of ascetics for a living, shall accept alms. The people, dismayed, divested of all ornaments, and filthy as the Pishâchas, shall renounce all ceremonial ablutions and propitiations of the gods and Atithis, and cease to offer oblations and libations of water unto their departed manes. O Shaunaka, men will be S'udras in their lives and habit, and shall be under the thumbs of their wives. Women, mostly unhappy and unlucky, will conceive many children and will grudge the behests of their lords by scratching their heads. Men under the counsel of the unsanctimonious heretics will fall off from the path of virtue and renounce the worship of Vishnu. The only one great redeeming feature in the Brâhmaṇas of Kaliyuga is the fact that they will be able to shake off the fetters of re-birth, by once singing the praise of Krishna. The merit, which is acquired by meditation in the Satyam Yuga, by celebrating religious sacrifices in the Tretâ, by serving the god in the Dwâpara, may be acquired in the Kali Yuga by singing the praise of Vishnu.

Therefore, O Shaunaka, the god Hari should be constantly worshipped and meditated upon.

—:o:—

CHAPTER CCXXXIII.

SUTA said :—After the expiry of a thousand of such four Yugas, occurs the causal or periodical (Naimittika) dissolution of the universe. At the close of each Kalpa, will follow a rainless period of a hundred years, during which the seven suns will rise in the sky, which, by absorbing all water, will burn down the three regions with a dreadful conflagration of fire. Inmates of the regions of Bhu, Bhuba, Sva and Maha will fly to the region of Jana, and the god Vishnu, manifest in the shape of Rudra, shall consume the Nether regions (Pâtâlas. Clouds of all shades of colour will originate from the mouth of this Rudra-form Vishnu, which will incessantly pour down torrents of rain, for a hundred years. From the mouth of Vishnu winds, abnormally augmented and enraged, shall blow in storms for a hundred years. On the annihilation of all creatures, both mobile and immobile, the god Vishnu, assuming the shape of Brahma, shall lie down on the one universal ocean of undivided waters. Thus sleeping for another hundred years, the god Vishnu will again create the universe.

Now hear me, O Shaunaka, describe the Natural dissolation of the universe (Annihilation of Nature.) At the expiry of the full one hundred years of Brahma, the God Hari, absorbed in Yoga, shall get the whole universe, with its progenitor Brahma, merged in his own Self. Those, who might have attained to the region of Brahma at the time, shall reach the final goal of existence. Then will follow a period of drought, with the fierce sun of dissolution consuming every thing with its deadly heat from the heaven of a dissolving universe. After that, primordeal clouds will pour down heavy torrents of rain upon the universe, which, being filled with water in its inside, will finally burst out. Thus at the completion of the life-duration of Brahma, the earth-matter will be resolved into water; the water, into heat; heat, into air; air, into ether; the ether, into essential matter (BhutÂdi), the essential matter, into the principle of intellection; the principle of intellection, into Prakriti (Nature); and Nature, into Purusha (the eternal subjectivity). Thus for a hundred years of his own, the God Hari will repose in sleep, and after that, he will create a fresh universe in the order of evolution, commencing from Nature to the principle of intellection, from the principle of intellection to ether, from ether to air, from air to heat, from heat to water, and from water to earth.

—:o:—

CHAPTER CCXXXIV.

SUTA said:—Knowing fully of the threefold misery such as, the mental, physical, and physiological, the wise one, conversant with the laws of the wheel of existence (SamsÂra Chakra) and possessed of true knowledge and apathy to the concerns of life, seeks his psychic annihilation (A'tyantikam Layam). I shall describe the wheel of existence from the moment a man comes into being, a knowledge whereof leads him to merge his self in its universal and eternal prototype. A man, after quitting his gross material frame, assumes a subtler body in the higher ethereal regions, whence he is carried by the emissaries of death to the mansion of their lord, in the course of a period of twelve days. The offerings, and libations of water containing sesame, which his friends offer unto him, a deceased person takes in the mansion of death. Through piety one goes to heaven, through sin one goes to hell. From hell or from heaven, a man enters into the womb of a woman. At first he becomes manifest in the form of a bifurcated sperm; after that, he assumes a forthy gelationous form, after that, blood is produced in its body, which looks like a lump of muscle of fiesh, from which the limbs, fingers etc., are found to sprout up, and the organs of smell, sight etc., are gradually developed. After the evolution of the sprout-like limbs are developed nails of fingers, and skin; and after that hair. The fœtus lying with its head downward in the womb is delivered in the tenth month of pregnancy. From the moment of his birth the illusion of Vishnu envelopes the soul of a man. Infancy, youth, old age and death—these are the different stages of existence, and human life is repeatedly made to pass through them as a sand glass is repeatedly turned upside down. Liberated from hell, a human soul takes birth in the womb of a low caste woman. O thou intelligent one, for taking gifts from a degraded person, a person is punished with a birth in a low class womb. A twice-born one, who deceives his preceptor, is reborn as a dog. He, who covets the wife or riches of his preceptor, or insults or brings about the humiliation of his friend, is re-born as an ass. He, who oppresses his parents in this life, shall be re-born as a tortoise in his next incarnation. He, who eating the bread of a trustful master, serves another in this life, will be re-born as a monkey in his next. He, who misappropriates any trust property, shall be re-born as a vile worm in his next existence. The self of a envious or malicious person, liberated from hell, shall take birth as a Rákshasa (monster) in this world. He, who commits breach of trust, shall take birth as a fish in his next existence. A stealer of paddy or barley corn shall be reborn as a mouse. A ravisher of other men's wives shall be reborn as a fearful wolf. He, who carnally knows his brother's wife, shall be reborn as a cuckoo. He, who defiles the bed of his preceptor, or knows a woman standing in the interdicted relation to him, shall be re-born as a hog. He, who obstructs the celebration of a nuptial or sacrificial ceremony, or stands as an impediment to one's practising charity, shall be re-born as a vile worm. He, who eats or partakes of anything without first offering it to the gods, departed manes and Atithis, shall be re-born as a crow, after being liberated from hell. He, who insults his elder brother, shall be re-born as a crane. A S'udra, who goes unto a Bráhmaṇa woman, shall be reborn as a earth-worm, whereas having procreated a progeny on her, he shall be re-born as a white ant that eats into the vitals of trees. An ungrateful person shall be successively re-born as an insect, worm, scorpion and a fly. A woman-killer or an infanticide will be re-born as a worm, a pilferer of food will be re-born as a fly. A stealer of cooked rice will be re-born as a cat; a sesame-stealer will be re-born as a rat. A stealer of clarified butter will be re-born as an ichneumon, a stealer of flesh will be re-born as a crow. A stealer of honey will be re-born as a gnat, a stealer of cakes will be re-born as an ant. A stealer of water, or a miscreant will be re-born as a crow. A stealer of Indian bell-metal will be re-born as a Hârita bird or a pigeon. A stealer of a gold-vessel will be re-born as a worm. A stealer of cotton will be re-born as a crane; a fire-stealer will be re-born as a heron. A stealer of pig-ments or vegetables will be re-born as a peacock. A stealer of any red substance will be re-born as a Chakora bird. A stealer of scents will be re-born as a mole. A bamboo-stealer will be re-born as a hare. A stealer of peacock-plumes will be re-born as an eunuch, a wood-stealer will be re-born as an wood-insect. A flower-stealer will be re-born as an indigent man, a stealer of lac-dye shall shall be re-born as a maimed or deformed person. A stealer of edible leaves and plants will be re-born as a Hârita bird;

a water-stealer will be re-born as a Châtaka bird. A stealer of house, after suffering the pangs of many a hell such as the Raurava, etc., will be reborn as an insect, worm, shrub, creeper, or grass. The same fate awaits those who steal gold, or kine. A stealer of knowledge, after suffering the pangs of many hells, shall be re-born as a dumb person. He, who casts oblations in a weak fire, shall be re-born as one suffering from indigestion. Scandalising, ingratitude, hurting other men's feelings, cruelty, shamelessness, adultery, stealing other men's goods, impurity or uncleanness, speaking ill of the gods, cheating and miserliness are the traits in the conduct of those who are just liberated from hell. Compassion towards all, asking good news of all creatures, works for the purpose of acquiring spiritual benefit, truthfulness, good advice to all, judgment in the light of the Vedas and philosophies, performances of good deeds, service of the gods, Rishis and Siddhas, company of the good and friendliness to all are the traits in the conduct of those among men who have come down from the heaven. By practising Yoga with its eight component parts, one is enabled to effect one's A'tyantika Layam (Non-existence of Self.)

——:o:——

CHAPTER CCXXXV.

NOW I shall describe the mode of practising the great Yoga, which absolves a man of all sin and grants him emancipations, and creature-comforts in this life. This (narration), listened to in a devout spirit, serves to extinguish all sin. The sense of "me" and "mine" are the root of all misery. This sense of Egoism does not cease to exist. This is what the holy Dattâtreya narrated to Alarka. This tree, which sprouts up from the feeling of Egoism as its seed, has the sense of "me" and "mine" as its principal trunk, of which one's house and field are the branches, and sons and daughters are the leaves. Riches and paddy (food-grains) are the principal leaves of this tree, virtue and vice are its flowers, and happiness and misery are its fruits. The great tree of non-knowledge exists for the relief and comfort of mortals. Those, who tired with the fatigue of life's journey, repose under the shade of this mighty tree, labour under the delusion of ignorance. By hewing down this tree with the axe of knowledge, mortals become merged in the supreme Brahma. By drinking the sinless and soothing juice of Brahma, men become endued with the perfect knowledge; clamours of contending passions are silenced in their breasts, and perfect happiness results from perfection of knowledge. O king, neither our forms, dimensions, and organs constitute our real Selves. Neither the Tanmâtras (essential matter), nor speech and intellection constitute our true Selves. O thou king of kings, whom do you find to be the principal one in ourselves? Does this self-conscious being, composed of the qualities, take birth again? O thou king, the self-conscious ego and the self, though virtually one, appear, and are thought as two different entities. It is knowledge that dispels this notion of duality or separateness. The Yogins, on the extinction of this sense of separateness, through Yoga, realise their oneness with the supreme Brahma and their difference from the the hosts of qualities or attributes. Realisation of this oneness is called Mukti or Emancipation.

That is house in which one lives, that is food which sustains life, that is knowledge which leads to Mukti (emancipation). Any other kind of knowledge is ignorance or delusion. O king, by enjoying the fruits of virtue and vice in this world, and by discharging all duties which are obligatory on him, a man may exhaust and extinguish his Karma and annihilate his desires in consequence. Cessation of all killing propensities, truthfulness, non-stealing, continence, and non-acceptence of gifts are the five Yamas or Niyamas (rules of self-control). There are two kinds of purity or cleanliness such as, the external or bodily and internal or mental. Contentment, bliss won by practising Tapas, and worship of the god Vâsudeva are called Damas. The different seats or postures in Yoga are called Padmaka, etc., while Prânâyâma consists in checking or controlling the wind (breath). An act of Prânâyâma consists of three parts such as Purakam (taking in of breath), Kumbhakam (arresting the process of breathing) and Rechaka (letting out of the breath). A light (laghu) Prânâyâma consists of ten mâtrâs; one of intermediate form, of twenty and a full Prânâyâma, of thirty Mâtrâs. A pregnant or *Sagarbha* Prânâyâma is that in which the votary meditates upon any definite subject at the time of practising it, while the contrary is called Agarbha. At the first stage of the practice the practiser shall conquer the soporific tendency,* shivering during its second or middle, and the augmented heat during its third stage, which is brought forth through the aggravation of the bodily Vâyu. Hence, these defects should be conquered in the order of their enumeration. With the effulgent image of the Pranava Mantra in his heart, and his mind fully concentrated thereon, a Yogin shall practise Yogam, sitting in a posture so as to press his genitals with his legs. One conversant with the practice of Yoga shall suppress the Tâmasa attributes of his mind with the Râjasika ones, and the latter with the Sâtvika attributes of his mind, finally bringing about a state of mind in which it lies serene, unruffled and devoid of all thoughts and impressions. By withdrawing the mind, consciousness and

---

* A kind of hypnotic sleep which is induced at the first stage of Pranayama, and with which every practiser of the art is too familiar to need any elaborate description.—*Tr.*

sense organs from their respective objects of perception and the external world, and by keeping their functions thus in abeyance, a Yogin shall practise the art of mental abstraction (Pratyâhâra) and control his breath in Prânâyâma to the extent of ten or eight Mâtrâs. These are called the two kinds of Dhâranâ in the parlance of Yoga. A Yogin shall concentrate his whole self either in the region of his umbilicus, or in his mouth, or within his heart, or in the region of his throat, or at the tip of his nose, or in his eyes, or at a point between the eye brows. These are the ten places of Dhâranâ ;or points on which a Yogin shall concentrate his whole Self, by practising which he will suffer no decay. As fire is cast in the fire, so by merging his Self in that of the supreme Brahma, a Yogin shall mentally recite the Omkâra Mantra, which is sacred of the all sacred Mantras and is symbolical of the Self of Brahma. The term Om is composed of three letters, Akâra (A , Okâra (O), and Makâra (M), and is the great exponent of the universal Self (Brahma).

I am Brahma, the supreme light, devoid of a gross, material body. I am Brahma, the supreme light, devoid of death and decay. I am Brahma, the supreme light, divested of the principle of earth-matter. I am Brahma, the supreme light, divested of the principles of air and ether. I am Brahma, the supreme light, devoid of a subtle body. I am Brahma the supreme light which is neither bound by space or non-space (non-extension). I am Brahma, the supreme light, devoid of the Tanmâtra of smell. I am Brahma, the supreme light, devoid of the Tanmâtra of sight. I am Brahma, the supreme light, devoid of the Tanmâtra of sound.* I am Brahma the supreme light, devoid of speech and hands. I am Brahma, the supreme light, devoid of ears and

* Tanmatras are in the world of perception what atoms are in the world of matter.—*Tr.*

skin. I am Brahma, the Supreme light, devoid of tongue and nose. I am Brahma, the supreme light, devoid of the currents of up-coursing and down-coursing vital Vâyus. I Brahma, the supreme light, devoid of the vital Vâyus of Vyâna and Udâna. I am Brahma, the supreme light, void of all Nescience. I am Brahma, the supreme light, the receptacle of supreme bliss; my self is my own wife, and devoid of mind intellect, life, Egoism and cognitive organs. I am Brahma, the supreme light, pure intellect, infinite joy, infinite reality and without a second. I am the supreme Brahma, the embodiment of perfect knowledge, an emancipated self.

Suta said :—O Shaunaka, thus I have described unto you the Science of Yoga with its eight essential appendages, and a knowledge of this Yoga brings about the emancipation of one's Self. Those, who attain to (meet their annihilation in) the Nityam and Naimittikam dissolution, are not liberated from the fetters of Nature (physical laws), and are subjected to the necessity of being born again and again in this world, but not so are those who merge themselves in the Supreme Self. They are emancipated; and thus emancipated, they no longer die, or suffer from disease or affection as they used to do under the influence of Nescience before their liberation. Thus sin affecteth not an emancipated Yogin and ceases to exist for him for all eternity. He is not bound by the chain of necessary re-births, and is not consigned to suffer the pangs of inter-uterine existence. He is one with the unchanging, undecaying Nârâyana. By dint of such an unswerving faith and devotion, one may attain the god Hari, the grantor of emancipation and creature-comforts. The purification of the heart is effected by means of meditation, worship, mental recitations of Mantras, and psalms, and by practising vows of charity and continence, and by celebrating religious sacrifices, and from the purification of heart proceeds knowledge. Twice-born ones, by reciting the Pranava Mantra, have become emancipated selves. Dhruva by devoutly worshipping Vishnu, attained the region of highest bliss, as well as the god Vishnu. Prachetas, the creators of worlds, Kandu and others, by worshipping the lord of lords, became pure in spirit and obtained liberation. In the same way, and by the same means, Uddhava attained the region of highest bliss. Holy sages such as Narada etc., the celestials such as Indra etc., the Gandharvas and the Apsarasas, attained the region of highest bliss by worshipping Vishnu. The gods attained their godhead; the sages, their status of Munis; the Gandharvas, the status of Gandharvas; and the kings, their kingdoms through the merit of worshipping the eternal Vishnu. All these attained the celestial kingdom by worshipping the god Janârdana.

——:o:——

CHAPTER CCXXXVI.

SUTA said:—Now I shall discourse on Vishnu-Bhakti (loving devotion to Vishnu) by means of which a man obtains all that he desires. Nothing is more pleasing to Hari than devotion. Contemplation of the god, Hari is the only palatable fruit of human life, the progenitor of supreme bliss, and the root of the increase of one's animals and progeny. The term Bhakti (devotion) is derived from the root Bhaj to serve; hence the wise shall serve the god, as service strengthens devotion to his Self. The devotees of the lord of the universe weep and shed tears at the time of singing his name and glory, and the hairs of their bodies stand on their roots at the time. Verily they are the real Vaishnavas, the loving servants of God for all eternity, who devote their lives to the daily excution of his divine commands. He, who even without knowing the Pranava, or the commands of God (without any knowledge of religion or theological works), bows down before His all pervading presence, and humbly offers Him the homage of love and and affection, is a true Vaishnava. He, whose love overflows to the servants of god. he who readily approves of His worship, he whose highest joy is in listening to discourses on His love and goodness, he whose voice trembles and eyes look moist at hearing of His all-abiding love; he who has devoted his whole self to the all-pervading divinity and looks upon a Brâhmaṇa as His prototype, is a superb servant of of God (Mahâ Bhâgavata). He, who daily worships Vishnu, and offers him cooked rice, every day, in a spirit of true humility, is a Bhâgavata. There are eight forms of devotion, and even a Mlechcha may be a true devotee of God. A truly god-loving Mlechchha, a true devotee, is the foremost of Brâhmaṇas; he is a Muni (holy sage), a seer, and is an heir to the hghest bliss. To him should be given, from him should be taken (food), he is adorable as the God Himself. O thou foremost of Brâhmaṇas, a true, god-loving, devotional Chandâla, a true servant of god, remembered, spoken to, or adored by a Brâhmaṇa, sanctifies him to any extent he pleases. To say "I am thine" to one who seeks protection, or to one who is oppressed or tyranised, and to say "dread not" to all creatures are the vows sacred to Hari. An expert in the Vedânta is greater than a thousand reciters of Mantras, a devotee of the all-pervading God is greater than a million of such Vedântins. By dint of an unswerving and all-absorbing faith and devotion men attain to the region of highest bliss. It is for this oneness of purpose that god, though impartial and equally kind to all, is lovingly fond of these persons. Hence these devoted servants of God are called Ekântins (single-purposed ones). He, whose devotion remains unflinching even in moments of peril, is the most favourite, among the favoured ones, with the god of gods. May that kind of pleasure which the ignorant find in the things of the world, be mine on divine contemplation, and may a pleasure of similar intensity not leave my heart, when I meditate upon the Self of the all-pervading one (Vishnu). A reader of all the Vedas, a knower of all the philosophies is but the worst of fools, if he is not devoted to Vishnu. He, who has faith in Him and is devoted to His service, has practised all pieties, even without studying the Vedas or celebrating any religious sacrifice.

The foremost of the holy sages do not attain to that elevated status by the study of all the Vedas, or by celebrating the most meritorious of religious sacrifices, as they do through the merit of simple faith in, and unflinching devotion to, Vishnu. Even a man, who is not true to the duties of his social order, or misbehaves himself, if he becomes a Vaishnava, purifies all the regions, like the full-risen, thousand-rayed sun. Even miscreants, who are addicted to vice and wicked acts, come by the highest bliss, if they become devoted to Vishnu. Pleasures of celestial life appear insignificant and inglorious to one, who has a strong and loving faith in Janârdana, inasmuch as such a faith is but the precursor to one's emancipation (Mukti). To persons, who wander about in this dreadful valley of life, where each act spins out a new destiny for man, the only thing, which can be easily caught hold of with the hand, is the faith-appeased Janârdana. He, who does not hear of the glories of the discus-wielding deity, is really deaf and is a spiritual outcast. He, whose bodily hairs do not stand on their roots in ecstacy while engaged in singing the psalms of Janârdana, is indeed a carcase. O thou foremost of the twice-born ones, what wonder that sins of a man will be extinguished by contemplating Vishnu, when by such a contemplation he comes by emancipation. Yama, the lord of death, seeing his emissaries ready to bind the Souls of Vaishnavas with their nooses, says to them: "Leave them alone, O my emissaries, I have power over all men except those who are devoted to Vishnu." Even if the worst of miscreants worships him (Vishnu) alone in exclusion of all other deities, he should be regarded as a holy person. O thou foremost of Brâhmanas, one, who is devoted to Vishnu, soon becomes holy and comes by the highest bliss; a devote of Vishnu never perisheth. What does he care for (fruits of) virtue or (objects of) desire and opulence whose mind is absorbed in the root-cause of the universe (Vishnu)? His Salvation is in his own hands. Verily insurmountable is the Nescience or illusion (Mâyâ) of Vishnu, which is composed of the three qualities (Sattva, Rajas and Tamas); he, who is fondly devoted to him, alone sails across this occean of phenomena. Of what good is the celebration of a religious sacrifice to a man, who performs, every moment, the sacrifice of (contemplates) Hari? It is faith and devotion alone by which a man can attain to Vishnu and by no other means. Neither the various forms of gifts, offered in due form and to worthy recipients, nor the offerings of flowers and scents unto the god, so much lead to his satisfaction, as the homage of heart-felt love and devotion to him. This poison-tree of worldliness bears two ambrosial fruits, one is the service of the Lord and the other is the company of His servants. Inspite of so many easily available offerings to god, such as water, flowers, fruits and vegetable leaves, why should not a man strive for the emancipation of his self by placing absolute confidence in the oldest of Beings, who is attainable through love and faith? Ancestors rebound in joy, and grand-fathers dance in delight (in consideration of the fact that) "a Vaishnava is born in our line and he will succour us all." The ignorant and proud souls, like Shishupâla and Suyodhana, who abused and looked down upon the foremost of the celestials, obtained their emancipation by once thinking of him and were absolved of all sin; what wonder is there that men, who are fondly devoted to him, will be liberated from the trammels of rebirth? Even they, who, devoid of contemplation and communion, are fondly devoted to him, shall overcome death and attain to the blissful region of Vishnu. Control, O Mâdhava, the horse of my mind, who, lashed with the stripes of worldly misery, madly dashes out in the path which is seen through the apertures of my cognitive organs (path of passion), by restraining them with, and fastening them to, thy conch-like white feet. Vishnu is same as the supreme Brahma, this is the conclusion which the Vedânta has arrived at with the help of incontrovertable proofs (argument). This is what the ignorant do not know. He, in whose heart dwells that eternal Purusha, becomes a favourite with the whole universe. His whole heart, filled with the honey of the love of the world, conveys its message of love back to it.

—:o:—

CHAPTER CCXXXVII.

SUTA said:—He, who for his own salvation bows down unto the endless, originless, birthless, changeless, deathless reality, becomes fit to be honoured by all-the regions. Humbly do I make obeisance unto the all-pervading, almighty Vishnu who is pure knowledge and highest joy and who resides in the hearts of beings. I make obeisance to the lord, who, residing in the hearts of beings, bears witness to all their acts, whether good or evil. He, who being capable does not bow down unto Vishnu, is not a man but a consumer of earth's cereals. Even a single act of obeisance unto Krishna, beautifully black as a pregnant rain cloud, the immeasurable reality, the over-lord of all regions, done with true love and humility, instantaneously serves to purify even a Chandâla (lit: eater of dog's flesh). The elevated status, which a person attains to by laying himself prostrate before Krishna, can not be acquired by performing even a hundred horse-sacrifices. Faith in, and devotion and obeisance to Krishna succour those, who wander benighted in the wilderness of the world, or are drifted about by the currents of the ocean of worldliness. Whether standing, seated, or laid down in bed, one should recite the Mantra, Salutation unto Nârâyana. As long as there exists the Mantra "Salutation unto Nârâyana" in this world, and as long as one retains the faculty of speech, pity it is that one should wilfully go to hell. A pure-souled man, if he be a four-mouthed or a hundred mouthed one, will not be able to enumerate a ten thousandth part of the countless attributes of Vishnu. The holy sages such as, Vyasa etc., stopped short in their praise of the destroyer of Madhu on account of their limited comprehension, and not on account of the limited nature of his attributes. By singing his name, a man, even in a moribund condition, is absolved of all sin, and progresses on his journey to Mukti as a liberated spirit, like an elephant liberated from the clutches of a lion. Obeisance to Krishna, to Achyuta (undecaying one), to Ananta (eternal one), or to Vâsudeva; those, who utter any of these Mantras, are never carried to the mansion of Yama. As the sun or fire dissipates darkness, so does the singing of the names of Krishna dissipate the sin of the singer. The term Krishna is an ambrosial antidote to the venom of the serpent of worldliness, those, who are bitten by this serpent, shall do well to recite it. He, on the tip of whose tongue lie the two sounds of Ha and ri (Hari), is sure to sail across the ocean of life and to come by the highest bliss. A man, who is conscious of the guilt of many wilful iniquities, shall not dream of a re birth in this world, if he sincerely seeks his reformation and becomes a devoted hearer of the glories of Náráyana.

——:o:——

CHAPTER CCXXXVIII.

SUTA said :—Only one substantial thing there is amidst the frivolties of life: Every thing here is but a show, a phantom, the only real thing is the contemplation of Hari. He who gives offerings of flowers or libations of water unto Hari by reciting the Purusha Suktam, is supposed to worship and propitiate the universal god. He, who does not worship Vishnu, who protects the universe like a mother, is guilty of the sin of Brâhmanicide. From Vishnu has emanated this universe, by him this universe exists, and in him it will be merged (at the time of dissolution). He, who does not meditate upon the self of such Vishnu, shall be re-born as a worm in the excreta. Yama, the lord of death, addresses a soul, undergoing punishment in hell, as "why have you not meditated upon the destroyer of Keshi (Vishnu) in your life, why have you not worshipped the deity, in your life, that, being propitiated with libations of water in the absence of any other articles of offering, grants to his votary a residence in the region over which he presides himself? One's own parents or brothers do not do what Vishnu, propitiated with true faith, does for him. The only way of propitiating Vishnu by a man who is true to the duties of his own order is to worship him with true faith. The offerings of flowers or perfumes are not more pleasing to Janârdana than true, unsophisticated faith. The god Vishnu should be propitiated with acts of obeisance, or with any other special forms of worship.

—:o:—

CHAPTER CCXL.

SUTA said:—Pondering over the imports of all the Sâstras we have come to the conclusion that, Nârâyana should be constantly meditated upon. Of what worth is the celebration of a sacrifice, gift-making, pilgrimage or penance to one, who, with a steady mind, meditates upon the Self of Nârâyana? The merit of sojourneying to sixty-six thousand holy pools or sanctuaries does not rank a sixteenth part of what is acquired by making an obeisance to Nârâyana. Contemplation of Krishna is the greatest of austerities and most sanctifying of all penitential rites. For him who repents having committed a sin, the contemplation of Hari is the one great atonement. He, who, even for a moment, meditates upon the self of Hari, goes towards the region of Vishnu, not to speak of those who are constantly devoted to him. The state of mind which a Yogin feels in his states of waking, dream and dreamless sleep, is attached to Hari. Whether standing, sitting, talking, entering (a house), eating, sleeping or walking one should contemplate Mâdhava. Discharging their duties or doing their proper works, men should repose their minds in Janârdana. This is the essence of Shâstras. What is the good of saying much? Meditation is the highest of all virtues, meditation is the greatest of all austerities, meditation is the greatest of all purifications, hence a man should always practise meditation. No other worthier object of meditation there exists than Vishnu; no austerity is greater than fasting; greater than these, than all is the contemplation of Vâsudeva. The destroyer of Madhu, meditated upon, grants a status to his votary without solicitation, which is very hard to acquire and which the mind cannot even dream of. Any defect in connection with the celebration of a religious sacrifice is remedied by the contemplation of Vishnu by its celebrator. This is the dictum of the Shruti. Nothing is more sin-absolving in its effect than divine comtemplation, the fire of Yoga burns down the elements which construct the future births of man. The fire of Yoga destroys (*lit.* consumes) the dynamics of the acts of a Yogin, who having brought about his Samâdhi (psychic trance) becomes a liberated Self, even in this life. As a hearth-fire, aided by the wind, consumes a house, so the effulgent Vishnu, located in the heart of a Yogin, burns down all his sin. As gold, under the heat of fire, parts with its dross and becomes pure, so the mind of a man is shorn of all its evil propensities and becomes pure in touch with the universal spirit (Vishnu). The sin which a thousand ablutions in the Ganges, or a million ablutions in the sacred pool at Pushkara fail to wash off, is extinguished by one's recollecting the name of Vishnu. The sin, which requires a thousand Prânáyâmas to be extinguished, is instantly destroyed by a contemplation of Vishnu. If a moment passes without divine contemplation, if one is robbed for a moment of the privilege of meditating upon Vishnu, one should cry aloud, like a rich man, attacked by robbers. Evil advices, counsels of the agnostics and sceptics, and the influences of Kali (evil propensities) cannot assail the mind of him, in whose heart resides the (god) Keshava (the spirit that broods over the universal ocean of uncreated Nature). That day is real day, that night is real night, that phase of the moon is the real phase, that astral combination is the real combination, that moon is the real moon, under the auspices of which a man meditates upon Hari. The moment a man lives without contemplating Vâsudeva is a loss, a dumb moment of idiocy, a gap in the continuity of his existence. A Krita Yuga is a Kali Yuga to one who does not think of Govinda, a Kali Yuga is a Kritâ Yuga (golden age) to one who has Achyutah in his heart. He, who beholds Govinda in his front, and at his back, while moving or in rest, and whose mind tranquilly reposes in Govinda, has indeed achieved the end of his existence. O thou foremost of Bráhmaṇas, he, whose mind never deviates from the contemplation of Govinda at the time of performing a *Japa* or a *Homa*, comes by a nobler possession than the lordship of heaven.

He, who has offered his whole soul to Keshava, becomes able to snap the chord of universal illusion of Vishnu, without the necessity of renouncing his house and world. With Govinda in his heart, a man shows forbearance to the angry, pities the ignorant, and takes delight in the discourses of the virtuous. In all acts of ablution, gift making, or penance, one should meditate upon Náráyana. Their's is the victory, their's is the profit in whose hearts dwelleth the lotus-blue Janârdana; whence shall thy dread discomfiture? Even birds and insects, that have offered their souls unto Hari, shall come by an elevated status (after death), not to speak of wise men. The shadow, which the tree of Vâsudeva casts, is extremely cooling, it subdues heat and obscures the gate to hell,—ah, wherefore should not a man sit under its shadow? O thou foremost of Bráhmaṇás, even the imprecation of Durvása's was not potent enough to destroy the kingdom of Indra, only because he had the destructor of Madhu in his heart. When the mind of a man is permanently attached to God even while he is outwardly busy with the works of life he is said to have realised his Dháraná (comprehension). The God Náráyana of golden body, who is in the disc of the sun, seated on a full-blown lotus-flower, decorated with golden bracelets, ear-rings and necklace and who wields a discus and conch-shell in his arms, should be constantly meditated upon.

I do not wish to say much, enough it is to say that contemplation of Hari tends to absolve one's all sin. There is nothing more purifying than divine contemplation in this world. Sin affecteth not the man who partakes of a Chandala's boiled race, meditating on Hari in his heart. A man constantly thinks of his worldly affairs, if he thus thinks of his God, emancipation would not become rare in this life. Yogins, who by dint of such comprehensions merge themselves in God, are able to annihilate the seeds of their future rebirths, even without renouncing their hearth and home.

——:o:——

CHAPTER CCXL.

SUTA said :—Whom shall one make salutation unto except the man in whose heart is the devotion to Hari? He saves his self from the ocean of misdeeds. A knowledge, that encompasseth Govinda, is the true knowledge; a discourse that is about Govinda is the true discourse, an act, done for his gratification, is the only true act—what is the good of being prolific in its narration? A tongue that hymnises the god Hari is the only true tongue, a heart that dwells in Hari is the only true heart, and those two are the only commendable hands that are engaged in making offerings unto him. The significance of one's head is that it is bowed down unto Hari in an act of obeisance, the significance of the mind is that it is engaged in devising works for his gratification, and the significance of the tongue is that, O Govinda, it sings of, or utters your glories. The accumulated iniquities of a man, even if they have assumed dimensions as great as those of the mount Meru or the Mandâra, are sure to vanish away at the touch of Keshava, like a dreadful disease in the hand of a good physician. By offering whatever acts he does, whether good or evil, to god, a man is not bound by their effects. The whole universe with its inmates of fourfold order of created beings, mobile and immobile, from the smallest grass to the highest Brahmâ, sleeps under the influence of thy Nescience, O lord. He, by reposing mind in whom a man never visits hell, he, to whom offering his Self a man gets rid of all impediments, he, by reposing mind in whom a man does not go to hell; he, in the contemplation of whom lies heaven, he, by locating whom in his heart a man becomes liberated from the fetters of re-birth, when meditated upon by the dull-witted, absolve them of all sin: what wonder is there that a man, by singing the praises of the undecaying one, will be absolved of his sin? He, who has purchased the whole universe with his accumulated pieties, becomes an awakened spirit through the grace of Vishnu. Those, who wish to sail across this ocean of misery, shall perform Agnikâryas (Homas), Japas, and rites of ceremonial ablutions, and worship Vishnu. The king is the refuge of the kingdom, the father is the refuge of his sons, virtue is the refuge of all beings, and the god Hari is the refuge of all. O thou greatest of the holy sages, to those who make obeisance to the eternal Vâsudeva, the parent of the universe, exists not a holier sanctuary (place of pilgrimage) than a contemplation of the god. Without laziness one should meditate upon Govinda; it is immaterial whether he fails to make any offering of gems, or to study any part of the Vedas. A devotee of Vishnu, whether he be a Nishâda or a Chandâla, is equal to a Brâhmana in respect of purity, and the gate of hell is permanently closed against him. If a suppliant is always found to fondly supplicate a rich man for money, what wonder that a man, by supplicating Vishnu, will be liberated from the fetters of re-birth. As a fulll blazed fire consumes even moist fuels, so the contemplation of the effulgent Vishnu consumes all the sin of Yogins. As wilds beasts shun the mountain-summit that is on fire, so all kinds of sin leave the person who is addicted to the practice of Yoga. The success achieved by a man (in matters of psychic knowledge) is proportionate to the extent of his faith in Vishnu. The glory of 'Shree Krishna is so much that even his abusers or vilifiers such as, Shisupâla (who was the son of Damaghosa,) etc., were enabled to come by a better state, not to speak of those who are devoted to him. So long a person labours under the delusion of worshipping separate Godheads such as Brahmâ, Vrihaspati, or such and such holy sages, as long as he is not favoured with the knowledge of worshipping the one and universal Hari.

—:o:—

CHAPIER CCXLI.

SUTA said :—O Shaunaka, now I shall narrate the hymn to Narasinha, as composed by Shiva. The Mâtrikâs of yore addressed the blissful one (Shankara) as follows :—we shall devour, O lord, all the demons and men, if you so permit us. The universe is from thee, O lord.

SHANKARA said :—O you goddesses, I think it is rather incumbent on you to preserve the inmates of the universe: banish, O goddesses, these cruel intentions from your minds.

SUTA said :—Even thus being addressed by Shankara, the ferocious Mâtrikâs paid no heed to his counsels and began to devour the universe with all its inmates, both mobile and immobile. The god Shiva meditated upon the form of Nrishinha while the Mâtrikâs were engaged in devouring the universe. The endless and originless Shiva contemplated a form which inspired terror in the hearts of all creatures. The manes on his neck stood up erect on their ends. His dreadful teeth were illuminated with the lurid light of his lightning-tongue, which fearfully lolled out. His was a voice which resembled the roar of the seven oceans, agitated by the tornado of universal dissolution. He pulled aside the corners of his lips with the tips of his finger-nails, which were hard as 'thunder-bolts. His eyes had a glow, which resembled that of the summits of the mount Meru reflecting back the splendour of the rising sun. His body was like the summit of the Himalayas, illuminated with the reflected blaze of his diabolical teeth. The manes on his neck were burning, like the tongues of fire, with rage. He wore a crown of gold on his head and bracelets of gems round his wrists. Girdles composed of chains of gold decorated his waist, and the whole expanse of universe was illumined with the glow of his complexion, which was like the colour of a blue lotus. Ringlets of hairs grew on his body, and he wore a garland of beautiful and multi-coloured flowers. The god, thus meditated upon by Shankara, instantly appeared before him in this form, and Shankara propitiated this dreadful vision of Nrisinha.

SHANKARA said :—Salutation unto thee, the lord of the universe. Thou hast assumed the form of Narasinha and bearest the entrails of the demon king on thy finger-nails. Obeisance to thee, the lotus-naveled one, whose complexion illumines the whole expanse of the universe. Obeisance to thee, the beautiful one, effulgent as a million suns, and whose voice is like the roar of the universal ocean of dissolution. I make obeisance to thee, who art dreaded by thousands of the lords of death, who bearest the strength of thousand Indras in thy limbs, whose riches exceed those of thousands of Kuveras, who art composed of the essence of thousands of Varunas, who art effulgent with the effulgence of thousands of moons, who art mightier than thousands of planets and thousands of Rudras, art hymnised by thousands of Brahmâs and meditated upon by thousands of Rudras, and looked up to by thousands of Indras, and dost snap the chords of thousands of rebirths and unfetter the chains of thousands of bondage ; dreadful as thousands of winds thou dost compassion to thousands of Indras.

SUTA said :—Having thus hymnised the Nrisinha-shaped Hari, the god Shiva, devoutly bent down, addressed him as follows :—

SHIVA said:—The Mâtrikâs, whom I had created for the purpose of killing the demon, Andhaka, are now devouring the inmates of the universe without paying heed to my admonition. Invincible though I am, yet I do not wish to kill them myself, as it is I who have brought them into being. How can I wish their annihilation, when I am their creator?

SUTA said:—Having been thus addressed by Rudra, the lord (Nrisinha) caused the Mâtrikâs to be merged in his person, and having reestablished peace in this world, vanished in the air. The solf-controlled votary, who reads this hymn to Nrisinha, is enabled, like Rudra, to witness the realisation of his desires. "I meditate upon Nrisinha, whose eyes are like the rising sun, and tongues of blazing fire are emitted from whose lotus-white mouth. I meditate upon the endless, originless Nrisinha, the original subjectivity, the most excellent lord of the universe and its final refuge." Recitation of this hymn by a person dissipates his misery as the sun destroys the dews. The Mâtrikâs fly the presence of such a person, and the god Hara waits upon him to do him a good turn. The destroyer of Tripura (Shiva) first promulgated the worship of Nrisinha, the lord of the gods, in this world, and was enabled to protect its inmates from the depredations of the Mâtrikâs, through his grace.

—:o:—

CHAPTER CCXLII.

SUTA said:—Now I shall narrate to you the hymns of the knowledge of ambrosia as the god Hara, interrogated by Nârada, first disclosed to him.

NARADA said:—He, who is bound by the pairs of opposite, by anger and passion, by good and evil, by objects of the senses, is veritably an evil-minded and tyrannised being. O thou destroyer of Tripura, do I wish to learn from thee, the means of sailing across the sea of existence. Hearing this word of Nârada, Shambhu, the three-eyed deity, with his countenance beaming with joy, replied as follows :—

MAHESHVARA said :—Hear me, O thou foremost of the Rishis, the extremely secret hymn of Jnânâmritam, which dissipates all misery and dispels the fear of chains of re-births. He, through whose illusion all the inmates of the universe, from the humblest animalculum to the four-faced Brahmâ, are enveloped in a delusive sleep of Nescience; if through the grace of such Vishnu one quits his sleep (delusion) and wakes the wakening of perfect knowledge, verily he liberates himself from the chain of necessary re-births, so difficult of achievement even by the gods. Indifferent to cultivation of the knowledge of the Real, an individualised Self (man), introxicated with the wine of power, pride and luxury, sinks down, like a cow, in the oozy mire of worldliness. Fondly attached to their sons, wives and relations, men sink in the ocean of worldliness, as old and worn out wild elephants are drowned in one and the same ocean through an unconquerable instinct of companionship.* I do not find the emancipation of that foolish peoson, even in the course of a hundred millions of re-births, who, like a silk-worm, imprisons his self in a cocoon of delusion. Hence, O Nârada, constantly meditate upon the self of Vishnu, the undecaying god of the gods, the lord of the universe, and worship him with the greatest self-control. He, who contemplates the birthless, originless, endless, omniscient, unmoving, all-pervading spirit, contained within its own self, is liberated from the trammels of life. He, who

* Ekarnave is the word that occurs in the text. It may as well mean the universal ocean of undivided waters at the dissolution of our earthly globe. Perhaps the Rishi had the picture of Pralaya in his mind; worn out elephants, the remnants of a defunct race, being drowned in the waters of that ocean.—*Tr.*

constantly contemplates the eternal Vishnu, the only reality that is unknowable, and which is without any parts (indivisible) and affections, lying beyond the sphere of mortality; the embodiment of sacrifice, the manifest and unmanifest, is liberated from the trammels of life. He, who contemplates the eternal, blissful, occult, all-seeing Vishnu, the infinite reality, devoid of all qualities, beyond all Nescience, is liberated from the trammels of life. He, who constantly meditates upon the disembodied, immoveable, omniscient, all-pervading Vishnu, the ordainer, the enjoyer of thoughts and sentiments, becomes an emancipated self. He, who constantly contemplates the lord Vishnu, who knows without the aid of sensations, who is unmanifest and without any substitute, and lies beyond the sphere of illusion, unaffected by disease or affection, the god Vâsudeva, the preceptor of all, is liberated from the trammels of life. He, who constantly contemplates the birthless Vishnu, the pure and perfect knowledge, which cannot be known by the senses, whom the mind comprehendeth not, and the speech fails to describe, the one unconquerable entity, is liberated from the trammels of life. He, who constantly contemplates Vishnu, who is without any limitation, mind, and sense of egoism, and is not affected by the pairs of opposite, is liberated from the trammels of life. He, who constantly contemplates the eternal, birthless, deathless, decayless, fearless Vishnu, that suffers no change, and has sprung from no seed, is liberated from the trammels of life. He, who constantly contemplates the great Vishnu, the deathless spirit, the infinite joy whom sin touches not and the senses cannot reach, is liberated from the trammels of life. He, who constantly contemplates the great Vishnu, devoid of good and evil, free from the dashings of the six kinds of waves (propulsions of the senses), the only knowable, sinless entity, is liberated from the trammels of life. He, who with undisturbed mind contemplates Vishnu, the embodiment of self, whose determination (cogitation) is truth, and whose seat is purity, is liberated from the trammels of life. He, who constantly contemplates the most excellent Vishnu, the lord of the universe, the knower of past, present, and future, the witness to whatever takes place in the universe, and who is beyond all speech (description), becomes an emancipated self. He, who constantly contemplates Vishnu, that lies beyond the ken of knowledge, the undecaying, eternal subjectivity, is liberated from the trammels of life. He, who constantly contemplates Vishnu, the protector of the universe, the friend, the grantor of all desired objects, the spirit that occupies the three regions and is imaged in the universe, is liberated from the trammels of life. He, who constantly contemplates Vishnu, the dissipator of all misery, the grantor of all bliss, the extinguisher of all sin, is liberated from the trammels of life. He, who constantly contemplates Vishnu, who is always served by the Devas, Gandharvas, Apsarasas, Siddhas, Châranas, Munis, and Yogins, is liberated from the trammels of life. He, who wishing to be liberated from the bond of existence constantly contemplates Vishnu by hymnising him in the abovesaid way, becomes a liberated self. The universe is established in Vishnu, Vishnu is established in the universe; he, who constantly contemplates the birthless Vishnu, the lord of the universe, is liberated from the trammels of life.

Suta said :—The bull-ensigned deity thus addressed the holy Nárada of yore. I have narrated to you (the hymn) exactly as Shiva narrated it to that holy sage. O my child, by thus meditating upon the changeless, indivisible Brahma, you shall attain his eternal Self. The merit of celebrating a thousand horse-sacrifices and a hundred Vâjapeya Yajnas does not rank a sixteenth part of what is acquired by meditating, for a moment, with undivided attention, on the eternal Self of Vishnu. The celestial Rishi (sage) having learnt from Ishvara (Shiva) of the superiority of Vishnu to all the gods devoutly worshipped him and attained to the region of Vishnu. He, who recites this excellent hymn, or hears it recited by others, stands absolved of sin, committed by him in the course of a million re-births. He, who, in a devout spirit, recites this hymn of Vishnu, narrated by Mahâdeva, comes by immortality.

—:o:—

CHAPTER CCXLIII.

SUTA said:—I shall narrate to you that hymn of Vishnu, which was first sung by the holy Mârkandeya. I lie prostrate before the thousand-eyed, lotus-navelled Nârâyana, the original being who is also addressed as Hrishikesha, what shall Death do unto me? I have placed myself under the protection of the birthless, undecaying, lotus-eyed Keshava, who pervades this universe; what shall Death do unto me? I crave the protection of the wielder of discus and conch-shell, the deity manifest in the shape of the visible universe, who may be perceived only with the inner sense; what shall Death do unto me? I have placed myself under the protection of the boar, dwarf, and Nrishinha manifestations of Vishnu, I crave the mercy of Mâdhava and of Janârdana, what shall Death do unto me? I have surrendered myself to the mercy of the lord of the universe, the pure, eternal subject that manifests itself as the Ego in self-conscious individuals; what shall Death do unto me? I crave the protection of the wielder of discus and conch-shell, the deity manifest in the shape of this visible universe, who may be perceived only with the inner sense; what shall Death do unto me? I have placed myself under the protection of the boar, dwarf and Nrisinha manifestations of Vishnu, I crave the mercy of Mâdhava, and of Janârdana, what shall

Death do unto me? I have surrendered myself to the mercy of the lord of the universe, the pure, eternal subject that manifests itself as the Ego in self-conscious individuals, what shall Death do unto me? I have surrendered myself to the protection of the thousand-headed, eternal reality, the great Yoga that is both manifest and unmanifest; what shall Death do unto me? I have resigned myself to the care of the Supreme Self, the soul of all creatures, the one manifest in the shape of the universe, the one, that without taking birth in any womb, is incarnated through the merit of a religious sacrifice; what shall Death do unto me?

The god of Death, hearing this hymn of the Lord recited by Mârkandeya, hastily fled away chased by the emissaries of Vishnu. Thus the holy Mârkandeya conquered Death, nothing is rare to one with whom Nrisinha is pleased, impossibilities may happen even if the Lord wills it so. This death-dissolving hymn was first narrated by Vishnu to the holy Mârkandeya for his benefit. He, who recites this hymn, thrice every day, in a pure and devout spirit, suffers no premature death—a devotee of the undecaying one dies not an early death. Pondering within the lotus of his heart the god Nârâyana, the eternal, infinite, original subjectivity, more effulgent than the midday sun, the Rishi (Mârkandeya) was enabled to conquer death.

—:o:—

CHAPTER CCXLIV.

SUTA said:—O Shaunaka, now hear me narrate the hymn to the decay-less one (Achyuta), which grants to its reciter all that he may wish to obtain, and which Brahmâ being asked by Nârada first related to him.

NA'RADA said:—Be pleased to describe to me, O lord, the undecaying, unchanging Vishnu, the grantor of all bliss, who should be hymnised, every day, at the time of divine worship. Commendable and well-born are they, and they have achieved the end of their existence, who constantly hymnise the undecaying Vishnu. Such men are competent to confer all sorts of happiness on their kindred.

BRAHMA' said:—Hear me narrate, O holy sage, the hymn to Vâsudeva, which grants emancipation to its reciters, and which, being sung at the time of worship by a votary, brings about the gratification of the deity. Om, obeisance to the god, Vâsudeva, the absolver of all sin, obeisance to the pure-bodied one, the embodiment of pure knowledge, obeisance to the lord of all the gods, who wears the ringlets of hair on his breast known as the Shrivatsa. Obeisance to the wielder of sword and buckle, who wears a garland of lotus flowers around his neck. Obeisance to the mainstay of the universe, to the support of the heaven—to the dreadful Nrisinha (Man-lion), to the light that burns in the heart, free from doubt and hesitation (Vaikuntha). Obeisance to the lotus-navelled, thousand-headed one, who lies on the serpent of eternity (Shesha) in the ocean of the milk of ambrosia (Kshiroda). Obeisance to the destroyer of the Kshatriya race, who wields a battle-axe in his hand. Obeisance, over and again, to the adorable and the true-willed one. Obeisance to the lord of the three regions, to the discus-wielding divinity, to the subtlest, original, blissful principle. Obeisance to the dwarf-shaped god, who relieved Vali of the cares of a kingdom—to the spirit of the sacrifice, manifest in the shape of the primordial boar. Om obeisance to Govinda. Obeisance to the highest joy, to the perfect knowledge, to one who is eternal knowledge and original idea and from whom all knowledge proceeds. Obeisance to the supreme, secondless reality, to the foremost subjectivity, to the creator, governor and final cause of the universe, to the fountain source of all knowledge, to the supreme idealist whose idea has taken shape in the form of the universe. Obeisance to the destroyer of Madhu (amativeness), to the killer of RÂvana, and to the god who brought about the ruins of the demons Kansa, Keshi and Kaitabha. Obeisance to the lotus-eyed one, to the Garuda-ensigned divinity, to the destroyer of Kâlanemi, to the one that rides on the pinions of the celestial Garuda. Obeisance to the son of Devaki, to the joy of the race of Vrishni, to the lord of Rukmini, to the son of Aditi. Obeisance to the Gokula-abiding one, to the darling of Gokula, to Krishna, the darling of the milk-maids. Victory to the wielder of the mount Govardhana, to the killer of Vâna, to the destroyer of Chânur and Kâliya; victory to the eternal truth, the eternal witness of the universal phenomena, to the fulfiller of all ends, to the all-giving Mâdhava known only by the Vedântins. Victory to the unmanifest, occult, undecaying reality, that runs through all to perfect knowledge, to the undecaying self of supreme felicity. Victory to the self of eternal peace that is without support (does not depend on any thing), to the adorable Vishnu, the lord of the universe.

Thou art the preceptor, the disciple, the initiation, and the mystic formula. Thou art the Nyâsa (psychic location or projection), the rules, postures and Mudrâs of Yoga; thou art the implements of worship such as flowers, offerings, etc. Thou art the supreme receptivity, the mystic tortoise, the emblem of the pendency of the world; thou art the mystic lotus, the sacrificial platform and the dieties that preside over the mystic diagram (Mandalam) such as, the energies of virtue, knowledge, etc. Thou art Rama, the wielder of the plough-share, the destroyer of Samvara; thou art the Devas and the Brahmarshis, thou art the all-pervading god whose prowess is truth. Thou art the A'dityas, Vasus, Rudras, Ashvis, Maruts, Devas, Dânavas, Nâgas, Yakshas, Râkshasas, and Khagas. Thou art the Gandharvas, Apsarasas, Siddhas,

Pitris, and the immortals. Thou art the universal matter, the senses, the unmanifest one; thou art the mind, intellect, egoism, objects of sense-perception, and the self-conscious ego, the god that resides in the hearts of all creatures. Thou art the sacrifice, the implements of sacrifice, the sacrificial Mantras, the oblations, the priest, the sacrificer, the chanter of the Vedic Mantras, the burnt offering, the priest that casts the sacrifical animal in fire. Thou art the firmament with its suns and starry constellations, the nether regions, the universal expanse of ether, the region of Maha; in short whatever is found to exist among men, beast and Devas, all creation whether mobile or immobile are but the manifestations of thy eternal Self, O Lord. Who can behold thy eternal and universal image, O Lord, which can not be perceived by the senses, which is invisible to the immortals, and which only the Yogins behold in their psychic trance? Who can comprehend thy real, unmanifest, birthless, deathless, changeless, undecaying, all-pervading, perfect, secondless Self, which is infinite reality, perfect purity, pure knowledge, though devoid of qualities and full of supreme felicity? The shape which thou assumest in any particular incarnation, any of them the Devas, in their limited capacity, meditate upon as a substitute for thy real Self. O thou infinite subjectivity, how shall I be able to worship thy real Self, which the mind comprehendeth not and the senses do not perceive. I have been able to worship with offerings of flowers etc., only a few of thy attributes, O lord, manifest in the shape of Sankarsena, etc. Be graciously pleased to pardon me for the defects in my performances of Japas and Homas, as well as for any omission on my part in connection with thy divine worship. I have not been able to worship thee, O lord, as laid down in the Shástras, with due devotion, so be pleased to pardon my inefficiency. Day and night, morning and evening, whether moving or at rest, my devotion is firmly attached to thy feet, O lord. I do not care for my body, I am quite indifferent to the performances of religious rites, my sole delight is in thee, O lord of the universe. What has he not done for the attainment of heaven, or for self-emancipation, who has placed a firm faith in Vishnu, the grantor of all desires? Who is there in the universe, who can worship or hymnise thee to the fullest extent? Be pleased to accept this humble and deficient worship which I have made of thee, to-day.

Thus I have narrated to you, O sage, the hymn to the discus-wielding deity; sing his glories in a devout spirit, if you wish to attain the supreme bliss. He, who recites this hymn at the close of a worship of the universal preceptor, is able to work out his salvation in no time, and becomes freed from the bonds of re-births. Even in the Kali Yuga he, who recites this hymn, thrice, every day, in a pure spirit, obtains all that he wishes to obtain. By reading this hymn to Vishnu, a sonless man obtains a son, a sick person gets rid of disease, an indigent man obtains wealth, a captive obtains his liberty, a seeker after erudition obtains erudition, a seeker after fame obtains renown, even the remembrances of his past births recur to a man who recites this hymn. He, who sings the glories of the absolute subjectivity, is truly wise, is really pure and truthful in his speech. He is omniscient and acquires the merit of performing all the religious rites. Those, who are not propelled to do any thing for the service of Hari (God), or are not fondly moved towards him, are beyond the pale of all religion. No purificatory rite can purify the mind or speech of the miscreant, who has not an unswerving faith in the all-pervading lord (Vishnu). By duly worshiping the god Hari, the grantor of all comforts, a person obtains whatever he wishes to obtain in this life. I make obeisance to the immortal, birthless, all-pervading god, who resides in the hearts of all creatures, and whom the Asuras, Siddhas, and erudite persons can not comprehend in their minds, whom only the holy sages know, and who is the sole witness of the universal phenomena. I make offerings of the flowers of sentiments, of pure, pleasurable faith and love to the eternal, universal lord, the embodiment of self, devoid of all qualities, the absolute purity: may that all-witnessing Self, the perfect knowledge, reside in my heart.

Thus I have narrated to you the hymn to the endless, originless supreme Vishnu. Let a man, whose mind is shorn of all desires, constantly meditate upon his divine self, in as much as he is the god. Where is the Yogin who by contemplating the pure, original, secondless subjectivity, effulgent as the sun, is not merged in his eternal essence? The self-controlled person, who recites this hymn in a devotional spirit, becomes absolved of all sin, and enters the infinite region presided over by Murári. He, who prays for friendship of the god, as well as for liberation of self, and virtue, and object of desire, is freed from all the shackles of life, and attains Vishnu, the adorable refuge of all. He, who abjuring all company takes recourse to Vâsudeva, the absolute purity, the lord, the governor and destroyer of the universe, is freed from the shackles of life, and becomes an emancipated self.

:o:

CHAPTER CCXLV.

BRAHMA said:—Now I shall discourse on the knowledge of Brahma as expounded by the philosophical systems of the Sánkhya and Vedánta. As light, triply divided, resides in the sky (as lightning), in fire, and in the two great luminaries (the sun and the moon) so the supreme light (Atman) runs through three different categories as I, Vishnu, and the supreme Brahma. As butter when it remains within the organisms of kine does not impart any additional strength to them, but being prepared in the usual process and administered to them, it greatly contributes to their bodily strength, so Vishnu, though located in the heart of every body, does not give him any special benefit without being invoked and worshipped in a special way. Karma (action) and Jnâna (knowledge) are the two means open to those who wish to ascend the tree of Yoga. After once having climbed the tree of Yoga, let a Yogin take recourse to knowledge and renunciation. From the desire to know the external objects such as the sound etc., proceed the sense of attachment and repulsion, from these originate greed, delusion, and anger etc., and coupled with these a man commits sin. He, whose hands, genitals, belly and speech are under control, is called a true Brâhmaṇa. The hands, which do not pilfer other men's goods, which do not hurt or kill any creature, nor grapple dice, are said to be well-controlled hands. He, who does not look upon another's wife with lustful eyes, is said to be a man who has controlled his generative organs. He, who ungreedily eats a moderate quantity of food, is said to be a man who has controlled his belly. He, who speaks only what is true, beneficial, and only when necessary, is said to be a man who has controlled his tongue. Of what use is the practice of austerities or celebration of a religious sacrifice to one who has controlled these organs? The concentration of the mind, intellect and the senses (cognition) on the supreme lord of the universe is called Dhyánam (meditation). He, who joins his intellect, focussed in a point between the eye-browss, to thoughts of the external world, even after the cessation of the functions of the cognitive organs and before the mind has assume a state of perfect quisence, dreams many dreams both internal and external. The individualised Self beholds many such dreams even in the wakening state, this is the opinon of the erudite ones. The state called Sushupti (Dreamless sleep) occurs when the Jiva located in the heart and enveloped in the quality of Tamas does not remember 'where,' 'when' and 'wherefrom.' The state called the Turiya (lit, beyond the three states of existence) and in which the self-controlled individual is neither awake nor asleep, neither utterly forgetful nor labouring under delusion, and does not perceive the objects of the senses, occurs when the individualised self, by withdrawing the mind with the cognitive organs from the objects of perception, by merging the sense of egoism in the principle of intellection, by annihilating intellection with the principle of Nature (Prakriti), and by annihilating Prakriti with the energy of the psychic force (Chit Shakti), holds its self within its own self, the self-illuminant, the pure knowledge, the immortal purity, the eternal bliss without action, and running through all. This is what is called to be in the Turiya state. The five Gunas are sound, touch, taste, smell and sight; the Sattva, Rajas, and Tamas forming a group of three qualities. These eight qualities are the leaves of the eight-leaved lotus (the emblem of evolution) of which Prakriti (Nature), representing the state of equilibrium among the three qualities of Sattva, Rajas, and Tamas is the Karnikâ (the seed-capsule). The deity (self), the embodiment of pure knowledge (psychic energy), is located in the Karnikâ of this mystic lotus within the human heart; when the individualised self parts company with this eight-leaved lotus and the Prakriti located therein, it becomes a liberated or emancipated Self. Prânâyâma (control of breath), Japa (repetition of a Mantra), Pratyâhâra (abstraction of the mind from objects of the senses), Dhâranâ (comprehension) and Dhyânam (meditation) are the six principal auxiliaries of Yoga. Control of the senses is sin-absolving in its effect, and brings on the satisfaction of the Devas. A Prânâyâma is called Sagarbha (pregnant with a thought) when the practiser thinks of any definite deity or repeats any particular Mantra at the time of practising it; otherwise it is called Agarbha (unimpregnated.) An act of Prânâyâma consisting of thirty-six Mâtrâs is the best, that consisting of twenty-four Mâtrâs is the intermediate, and that consisting of twelve Mâtrâs is the smallest. All the senses evince a strong attachment to the objects of the external world, Pratyâhâra consists in withholding them from the objects of the senses. He, who withdraws his mind and intellect from the external world and withholds his senses from their respective objects, is said to exist in Pratyâhâra (abstraction). Dhâranâ means the concentration of the mind on the supreme Brahma for the period of time necessary for practising a Pránáyáma, consisting of twelve Mâtrâs. Dhâranâ means the comprehension of the Brahmaṇ in an undistracted state of the mind, in the absence of any other factor, which produces its distraction; Dhyânam (contemplation) means the reposing of the mind in the object meditated upon by one, who is oblivious of the existence of any other object. The great Munis, the foremost of the divine contemplators, call that the great meditation in which the mind is permanently and tranquilly reposed in the object of meditation. The state of mind in which the contemplator sees the whole universe, both inside and out, filled with the presence of the object meditated upon, is called Samádhi. He, whose mind is without any cogitation, and whose cognitive senses have been withdrawn from their respective objects of perception, is said to exist in Samâdhi (psychic trance). The Yogin, whose mind, dwelling upon the supreme Brahma, reposes absolutely therein, is said to exist in the state of Samâdhi. Delusion, hallucination and a distracted state of the mind are the defects which a Yogin must conquer and which are hostile to the successful practice of Yoga.

For the purpose of bringing about the concentration (lit, undistracted state) of the mind, the Yogin shall meditate upon a gross or material object at the outset, and thereafter concentrate his attention on the sun (solar plexus), after the mind is perfectly settled. Nothing really exists in the universe except the supreme Brahma. It is the supreme self that is imaged in this universe; he, who knows this, transcends all delusion. Pranava Mantra (Omkâra) is the symbol of the supreme Self; he, who meditates upon this Mantra, located in the cavity of his heart, by an act of psychic projection, and as an embodiment of the Self, that is without body or self-consciousness, transcends all delusion. First let a man meditate upon the self in his heart, which is enveloped in the principle of Nature (Pradhânam), the latter in its turn being successively encircled by the circles of Sattva, Rajas and Tamas, which are respectively coloured black, red and white, and wherein the Purusha, denominated as the individualised self (Jiva), is located. Over that should be contemplated as located the eight-leaved mystic lotus of qualities and attributes, of which knowledge forms the petals; and science and philosophy, the pollens. Apathy to worldly concerns forms the stem of that mystic lotus, while the religion of Vishnu forms its bulb. Let the votary meditate upon the Omkâra, located in its pollens, with the individualised self as its receptacle, whereby he would be able to work out his liberation. He, who quits this life, meditating upon the mystic lotus in his heart as above described, ascends to the region of the supreme Brahma. A Yogin, by meditating upon the god Hari, ensconced in the cavity of his heart, becomes an emancipated self. Some there are who behold the Self in their persons with the help of the sight of Yoga, others with the help of Sânkhya knowledge, others with the aid of Yoga. Knowledge is that which makes the Brahma visible, and which unfetters the bond of existence; an absolute concentration of the mind in Brahma is called Yoga. The Yogin, who, illuminated with the light of pure knowledge, reposes in the supreme Brahma by conquering his mind and senses, is said to be an emancipated self. The different kinds of seats and postures are not the real auxiliaries of Yoga, the so-called essential paraphernalias are but so many impediments to its successful practice. Even the evil-souled Shishupâla realised his

Self through the constant practice of meditating upon Hari; those, who are addicted to the practice of Yoga, behold their selves within themselves. Compassionate to all creatures, and hostilely disposed to the evil-souled, the Yogins, who have conquered hunger and reproductive functions, become emancipated selves. A Yogin, devoid of all sense-perceptions, reposing in the Supreme Brahma, and existing inert like a log of wood, is said to be an emancipated self. The intelligent one by reducing to ashes all impieties done by him, incarnated as a female, or a member of any caste whatsoever, with the fire of meditation, becomes an emancipated self, and comes by the highest bliss. As fire becomes manifest through churning, so the God Hari shows himself through meditation; the communion which conclusively establishes the oneness of the Supreme and the individualised soul is the best of Yogas. The beholding of the Supreme Brahma, by dint of Sânkhya or Vedânta knowledge, or by practising the rules of Yoga, is is called emancipation. The universe is but a series of appearances, of perceptions of the non-soul as soul, and of the unreal as real.

—:o:—

CHAPTER CCXLVI.

BRAHMA said:—Hear me, O Nârada, now discourse on the knowledge of Self (Atma Jnânam). There are two kinds of Yogas, *viz.*, the Advaita Yoga and the Sânkhya Yoga, the absolute concentration of the mind being the essential factor in both these forms. Practisers of the Advaita Yoga become free from the shackles of existence. Past, present and future acts are destroyed through knowledge. He, who hews down the tree of existence with the axe of right discrimination and takes an ablution in the sacred pool of knowledge and apathy, comes by the bliss of Vishnu. The three states of wakening, dream, and dreamless sleep are the three rods of Ne-science, all are included within this Mâyâ; eternal is the secondless Brahma. Without name, form and action is that supreme Self; He created this infinite universe and established himself therein. I am the knower, the embodiment of reality that transcends all illusion, I am He; it is this knowledge which serves as the only road to Emancipation. Practice of knowledge, meditation, hearing of Shâstras, celebration of sacrifice, practice of charity and penitential austerities, sojourns to places of pilgrimage, and the study of the Vedas are of no avail as far as the working out of one's salvation is concerned. Some acquire knowledge through renunciation; celebrations of religious rites, or performances of Pujas confer no real knowledge. Two kinds of injunctions are found in the Vedas on this subject, one is "do acts" (religious rites), and the other is "renounce acts." Several authorities assert that seekers after Emancipation shall celebrate religious sacrifices for the purpose of purifying their thoughts. They can not confer any other benefit. Those, who meditate upon deities, can not be liberated, even with the aid of right knowledge, in the course of one existence. Uusuccessful Yogins are reborn as Bráhmaṇas in the families of Yogins. It is his acts that bind an animal, liberation lies through knowledge; take recourse to the knowledge of self as otherwise Ne-science will assail thee. Undoubtedly a person comes by immortality the moment the desires in his heart are annihilated. As the self is all-pervading, how can a man go any where else, or where else shall he go, or who is he that goes? As the self is infinite, there is no space for it to move in, as it is disembodied, how can it have any locomotion? As it is without a second, it has no separate existence; as it is pure knowledge, how can it have any Ne-science? How can this all-pervading one, running through all, like ether, can have any locomotion, advent, or location? The state of its wakening, dream and dreamless sleep are apparent only through the working of Nescience (Mâyâ).

—:o:—

CHAPTER CCXLVII.

THE GOD said:—O thou, who art conversant with all the Vedântas, who hast practised Yoga with all its eight essential components, now hear me discourse on the synopsis of the Gitâ as formerly narrated to Arjuna. Realisation of self is the *Summum bonum* of human life; this self is devoid of body, form, egoism, mind and the senses such as, the eyes, etc. Bereft of sensations, this receptacle of life (self) appears to be in a state of dreamless sleep. I am Self, not the combination of misery and phenomena. The self, effulgent as a smokeless fire, like a flash of lightning in the sky, burns itself in the cavity of the heart. The senses such as, the ears etc., do not perceive, it is the omniscient, all-seeing, self-conscious, individualised self (Kshetrajna), that perceives through the means of senses. When through the extinction of sin, the self is reflected on the mind, like a burning flame on a screen, the right knowledge is originated. Like images of objects reflected in a mirror, the self witnesses the objects of sense-perception, the five kinds of gross matter, the mind, the intellect, and the sense of Egoism reflected in itself. When an individualised self sees itself as universal and running through all, it becomes emancipated. O thou son of Pându, by merging all the senses in the mind; the mind, in the sense of Egoism; the sense of Egoism, in the principle of intellection; the principle of intellection, in the Prakriti (Nature); the Nature, in the Purusha (self); and the Purusha, in the Atman (supreme Self) that a man becomes emancipated and perceives his oneness with

Brahma, the supreme light. The intelligent one, who rightly understands the nature of his organism, provided with nine apertures (external ducts of the body), three supports (the fundamental principles of Vâyu, Pittam and Kaphah), five witnesses (the cognitive organs) and lorded over by the self-conscious Ego, is the true seer (Kavi).

—:o:—

CHAPTER CCXLVIII.

THE GOD said:—O Arjuna, O thou the son of Prithâ, rules of self control, rules of penitence, posture, Prânâyâma, abstraction of the mind from the external world, meditation, comprehension and Samâdhi (psychic trance) are the eight essential components of Yoga, which leads to liberation. Cessation of all killing or hurtful inclinations to all creatures and at all times is the highest virtue; compassion spells as the highest bliss. An animal duly killed on the celebration of a religious sacrifice is not killed at all. Speak what is true and pleasant. Cease to communicate an unpleasant truth, nor a pleasant untruth; this is the eternal virtue. Acquisition of a thing by stealth or force is called Steyam, the contrary of this leads to virtue. Renunciation of sexual intercourse at all times and under all circumstances, whether in mind, speech or act, is called Brahmacharyam (continence). Non-acceptance of gifts even in moments of peril and a studious renunciation thereof is called Aparigraha. Purification, which is either external or internal, may be effected either with the help of earth and water, or by purifying the thoughts of one's mind. Contentment is resting happy with whatsoever is easily obtained without solicitation. Tapas consists in concentrating the mind and the senses to any particular object, or in bringing about the emaciation of the body by practising Chândrâyanam and Krichchha

Chândrâyanam penances. The inner purification of a person effected by reciting the Pranava, Shata Rudriya and Vedânta texts is called Svâdhyâyam. An undiviating faith in the god Hari, with performances of rites enumerated in the Shrutis and S'mritis, is called divine contemplation. Svastikas cross) Padmâsanam, etc., are the different postures (Asanas) of Yoga; the Vâyu which courses in the organism of a person is called Prâna (life) and Prânâyama consists in checking the out-flow of breath. O Pândava, Pratyâhâra consists in restraining the mind and the senses from wandering among the unreal objects of the external world. Meditation (Dhyânam) consists in meditating upon the self of Brahma, whether embodied or disembodied. The embodied Self of Brahma should be meditated upon at the outset of Yoga, while the disembodied Brahma should be contemplated in its later stage, with the acquisition of increased psychic power. The knowledge that I am the supreme Brahma represents the state of Samâdhi, the speech, the knowledge, the perception that 'I am Brahma' lead to emancipation.

VYASA said:—The Rishis such as Shaunaka, etc., having drunk these ambrosial words, pertaining to the glory of Vishnu and encompassing the knowledge inculcated in all the Shâstras, became extremely happy. This sacred, purifying, sin-absolving Garuda Puranam should be constantly recited, and by hearing it recited one is enabled to witness the fruition of all desires. The hearer of its narration shall make gifts of beddings, etc., as described before, otherwise he will not acquire the merit of hearing it duly narrated. The text of the Puranam should be first worshipped; after that, the reciter shall be propitiated with presents of land, gold, kine, food and Dakshinâ. Mortals, who recite this sacred Puranam, or hear it recited by others, ascend to the eternal region, absolved of all sin, and freed from the pangs of existence.

THE END.